DMU 0519812 01 3

AF765373

MANAGERIAL ACCOUNTING

METHOD AND MEANING

WITHDRAWN
DE MONTFORT UNIVERSITY
LIBRARY

MANAGERIAL ACCOUNTING

METHOD AND MEANING

•

RICHARD M.S. WILSON

AND

WAI FONG CHUA

SERIES EDITED BY RICHARD M.S. WILSON

Second edition

INTERNATIONAL THOMSON BUSINESS PRESS
I(T)P An International Thomson Publishing Company

London • Bonn • Boston • Johannesburg • Madrid • Melbourne • Mexico City • New York • Paris
Singapore • Tokyo • Toronto • Albany, NY • Belmont, CA • Cincinnati, OH • Detroit, MI

Managerial Accounting - 2nd edition

Copyright © 1988, 1993 R.M.S. Wilson and Wai Fong Chua

I(T)P A division of International Thomson Publishing Inc.
The ITP logo is a trademark under licence

All rights reserved. No part of this work which is copyright may be reproduced or used in any form or by any means – graphic, electronic, or mechanical, including photocopying, recording, taping or information storage and retrieval systems – without the written permission of the Publisher, except in accordance with the provisions of the Copyright Designs and Patents Act 1988.

Whilst the Publisher has taken all reasonable care in the preparation of this book the Publisher makes no representation, express or implied, with regard to the accuracy of the information contained in this book and cannot accept any legal responsibility or liability for any errors or omissions from the book or the consequences thereof.

Products and services that are referred to in this book may be either trademarks and/or registered trademarks of their respective owners. The Publisher/s and Author/s make no claim to these trademarks.

British Library Cataloguing-in-Publication Data
A catalogue record for this book is available from the British Library

First edition 1988, published by Van Nostrand Reinhold (International)Co. Ltd
Reprinted 1989
Second edition published 1993 by Chapman & Hall, Reprinted 1994
Reprinted by International Thomson Business Press 1997 (twice)

Printed in China

ISBN 1-86152-357-2

International Thomson Business Press
Berkshire House
168–173 High Holborn
London WC1V 7AA
UK

International Thomson Business Press
20 Park Plaza
13th Floor
Boston MA 02116
USA

http://www.itbp.com

DE MONTFORT UNIVERSITY LIBRARY:
B/code
Fund: 40F Date: 18/11/99
Sequence:
Class: 658.1511
Suffix: WIL

To Tony Lowe

and all our colleagues who,

over the years,

have helped in developing

the ethos embodied

in this book

Abbreviated Contents

Contents

Series Editor's Preface

The *Method and Meaning* series consists of a text-plus-workbook, along with a Teacher's Guide, for each of the main branches of the accounting and financial management domain:

- Financial Accounting
- Managerial Accounting
- Financial Management

In broad terms this series offers an integrated set of introductory books to be used in courses from which students will emerge with an ability to approach – with a critical awareness – the design of accounting systems and the carrying out of financial analysis *within* an organizational setting, *within* a societal framework.

This approach aims to avoid the presentation of financial techniques in isolation, or as self-evident tools for decision-makers; and it seeks to discourage the uncritical acceptance of current financial practice as being the most appropriate (whether from the viewpoint of individuals, organizations, or society).

To be a little more specific, the series' objectives are:

1) to develop technical skills relating to procedural and computational aspects of accounting and financial management;
2) to develop analytical skills relating to the problem-structuring and systems design aspects of accounting and financial management;
3) to develop evaluative skills in relation to both the theory and practice of accounting and financial management;
4) to develop an understanding of the organizational and societal roles of accounting and financial management;
5) to pursue 1–4 above in a way that highlights the linkages amongst financial accounting, managerial accounting, and financial management.

From these aims you will see the logic underlying the series' title: 'method' relates to the what, when, where and how aspects, whereas 'meaning' focuses on the why, for whom, how else, and consequences aspects of the subject matter.

Within the *texts* there are clear educational objectives for each chapter; a structure that seeks to build a logical and ordered view of the subject matter; a concern with both exposition and evaluation; and annotated suggestions for further reading.

Each chapter in the texts is linked to a chapter in the integral *Workbook* which contains discussion questions (with and without suggested answers);

computational problems (with and without suggested answers); case studies; and reprinted items to illustrate key topics.

Whilst the current institutional affiliations of the authors of the books in this series are diverse – England, Scotland, Australia and Canada – they have considerable experience of working together. Five of the six were colleagues at the same institution until 1982 when two left to take up overseas posts, but the first-named authors of each book continued to be based at that institution (the University of Sheffield) during the writing of the first editions of each of the books, following which two of those left to take up new positions elsewhere. From an editorial point of view it has been a privilege working with such talented colleagues, and I am grateful that they all responded so positively to my invitation to them to get involved with this project.

The writing process led to the production of trial editions of all volumes in 1986, and these were classroom-tested during 1986–7 in a variety of academic institutions (covering college, polytechnic, and university sectors). Substantial revisions have been made on the basis of feedback from students and teachers which should make the series more user-friendly and readable. Further revisions have been made as the books have progressed into subsequent editions.

Apart from the benefits from testing, other major features of the series are:

1) introductory coverage is given across the whole domain of accounting and financial management;
2) all volumes are integrated via the careful initial planning of the contents of each against a common philosophy for the whole, and by means of subsequent cross-referencing at appropriate points;
3) the common philosophy takes a non-technical starting point (the societal role of accounting and finance) which is developed within an organizational setting (but which is *not* myopically restricted to one particular category of organization – such as the commercially-oriented manufacturing company);
4) throughout each volume a major emphasis is placed on developing students' critical awareness and in demonstrating how to establish evaluative criteria for assessing alternative methods;
5) by following the books, students should be able to construct *and* evaluate financial reports, and so forth, but they will also have a broader perspective of the managerial processes that must be considered if accounting methods and financial analysis are to improve organizational – hence social – performance;
6) the inevitable jargon of the subject matter is explained, with terminology being consistent throughout the series;
7) risks of duplication are minimized, but necessary overlaps across the series are used to reinforce the coverage of major issues;
8) the approaches to the subject matter of individual volumes – as well as to the series as a whole – is innovative with a strong interdisciplinary flavour.

What is the role of accounting and financial management against this background? We can propose a role by identifying the main branches of the subject, as in the diagram shown on page xvix. This shows that suppliers of finance (or investors) need to be persuaded to provide finance to enable an organization to get underway, or to grow or diversify once it has become established. Investors put their funds into organizations in exchange for either a share of ownership or a commitment from the owners/managers to repay the investors on specified terms. It is amongst the tasks of *financial management* to balance the sources of finance, and to ensure that the enterprise is able to 'service' its sources of finance (whether via the payment of dividends to shareholders, or of interest to those who have lent funds to the enterprise), and to repay loans on their due date. Appropriate financial analysis will clearly be necessary for these tasks.

However, the above observations relate primarily to the *supply* of funds rather than to the *demand* for funds. Enterprises demand funds to facilitate their on-going activities (e.g. paying suppliers, ensuring wages and salaries can be paid) and to facilitate new (or pending) projects of one kind and another. Determining these needs is another task for financial management – in association with *managerial accounting*. Once projects are under way, the routine handling of financial transactions and the production of annual financial statements is within the province of *financial accounting*, although the role of financial accounting in supplying information to interested parties is more significant than the diagram might suggest.

The three textbooks (and associated teaching material) covered by this series are seen as being usable singly, or in any combination of two, or in their entirety, as the basis for a number of categories of user. In every case the books are seen as being for compulsory student purchase rather than as optional sources of reference.

Intended markets consist of:

1) the primary market, made up of undergraduate students pursuing degree courses in accounting and finance, commerce, or business studies in British institutions of higher education (i.e. 'relevant degrees' in BAEC terms);

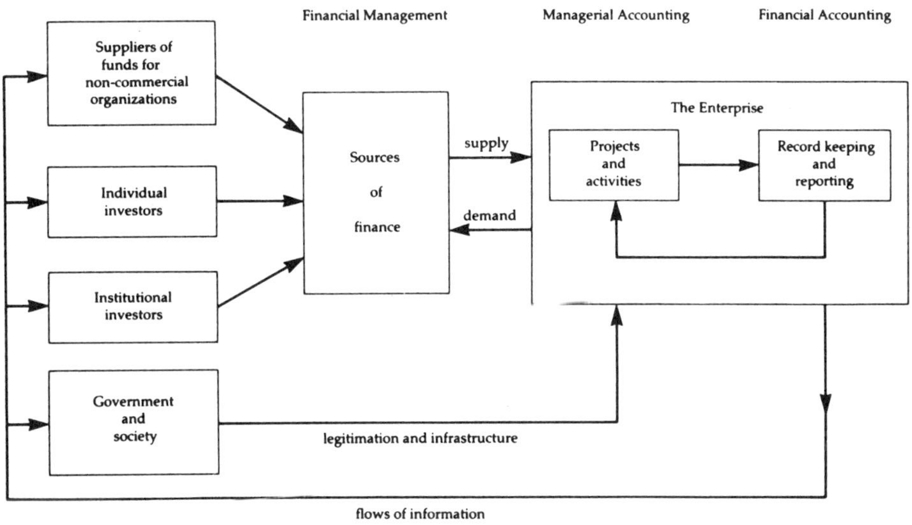

Scope of accounting and financial management.

2) the secondary market, which partly consists of undergraduate students on the increasing range of degrees in, for example, engineering, pure science, and economics that either require, or make available as an option, an introductory, self-contained course in accounting and financial management;
3) the secondary market also includes students on post-graduate programmes in the universities and polytechnics (e.g. for MBA degrees or for the Diploma in Management Studies) which involve an introduction to accounting and finance.

Richard M.S. Wilson
Professor of Management and Accounting,
School of Management and Economics,
Keele University

Authors' Preface

The dominant tendency amongst texts on managerial accounting has been to emphasize technical methods within a manufacturing setting. This has prompted comments such as:

> '. . . [the book under review] would have gained in relevance if less space had been devoted to factory operations and more to the marketing and distribution functions and to service industries generally. These matters are not ignored; but the allocation of space lags badly behind the change in the balance of our economy between goods and services. All books on costing, virtually without exception, continue to suffer from this lag.'
>
> (Solomons, D., in *The Accounting Review* **62**, (4), October 1987, p. 848.)

Moreover, much teaching and research in managerial accounting has failed to keep pace with environmental changes due to academics being:

> '. . . led astray by focusing too narrowly on a simplified model of firm behavior.' (H.T. Johnson and R.S. Kaplan, The Rise & Fall of Management Accounting, *Management Accounting*, **68** (7) January 1987, p. 22).

Amongst the more significant changes of relevance to those who design, operate, and use the output from managerial accounting systems are:

- a substantial increase in the number of service organizations;
- an expansion of the public sector and of other non-commercial sectors with a corresponding need to provide information relevant to the management of organizations within these sectors;
- a greater emphasis on human resource development, especially at managerial levels;
- a deepening awareness of the political and social nature of accounting information;
- an increasing concern with the notions of strategy and competitive position.

Our concern in this book is to deal with some of these changes by:

(i) locating managerial accounting (as a decision-support system) within an organizational context, and focusing on its role in relation to the central notions of organizational effectiveness and organizational control;

(ii) incorporating illustrative examples from service, public sector and other non-commercial organizations as well as from functional areas such as distribution and marketing;

(iii) emphasizing the social processes by which people attach meaning to and make sense of managerial accounting information.

Behavioural issues are discussed from the outset and are woven into every chapter rather than being tacked on later in a separate chapter.

This approach is non-traditional and novel in ensuring that the *meaning* as well as the *method* of managerial accounting is covered.

The book is structured in five parts: Part 1 (Chapters 1–3) establishes a framework for the whole volume; Part 2 (Chapters 4–8) deals with planning and decision-making (both short-term and long-term) from the viewpoint of feed-forward control; Part 3 (Chapters 9–11) covers feedback control; Part 4 (Chapter 12) takes stock of the field by assessing the state of managerial accounting and considering likely directions for its future development; and, finally, Part 5 is a Workbook which exists to support the text. For each chapter in the text there is a corresponding chapter in the Workbook, with the Workbook chapters containing revision questions (with answers), discussion topics, computational problems, and, occasionally, case studies and readings. Students* should work through the relevant Workbook chapter as soon as they have read each chapter in the text in order that the main messages of the latter can be reinforced.

Unlike many other books in which the sequencing of chapters is not especially significant, we have structured this book within a framework that gives a distinct significance to the sequencing of chapters. A progressive logic exists which means that the best results will be achieved by starting at the beginning and working steadily through to the end. We hope you will find it a worthwhile journey.

RMSW
WFC

* Where the pronouns 'he' and 'she' have been used throughout the text in reference to an unspecified person, that person can be taken to be either male or female.

Acknowledgements

The authors are indebted to many people for their help and support in the production of this book.

Since August, 1983, when he first asked Richard Wilson to set up a team to write the 'Method and Meaning' series of which this volume is a part, and right through the many phases prior to publication, John Perrin's encouragement, wise counsel, and constructive criticism have proved to be invaluable. We hope this book – and its companion volumes – fulfil his expectations.

The editorial faith and support of Dominic Recaldin and Alan Nelson at Chapman & Hall, along with the cheerful participation of the editorial and production team in guiding the project through the publishing pipeline, have been greatly appreciated.

Our primary intellectual obligation is to Emeritus Professor E.A. Lowe, to whom this book is dedicated. Other academic colleagues (notably Bill Birkett of the University of New South Wales, Trevor Hopper and Bob Scapens of Manchester University, Peter Miller of the LSE, and David Otley of the University of Lancaster) have also had beneficial impacts on the development of our view of managerial accounting, as reflected in the chapters that follow.

Thanks are due to Gillian Wilson for secretarial support in relation to the second edition, and to Elizabeth Singleton for preparing the index. Paul Saw of the University of Sheffield kindly checked a number of the computational problems for us.

In addition the authors owe a huge debt to their supportive families: to Gillian Wilson for her tolerance; to Eddie, Yeng-Ai and Leng-Ai Chua for their patience and understanding; and to our parents who made our careers possible.

To all these people who have provided inputs into this book we extend our thanks: insofar as the book has faults we absolve them of liability.

Finally, permission has been granted to use the following copyright material, for which we are grateful:

- The Editor of *AA* for the article 'Blow those Clouds Away' by David Allen, which appeared in *AA*, November, 1986, p. 49.
- The American Accounting Association and Professor T.W. Lin (University of Southern California) for the latter's article 'Expert Systems in Management Accounting Research', which appeared in AAA's *Management Accounting: News and Views*, vol. 4, no. 1, Spring, 1986, pp. 11–13.
- The American Marketing Association for Figure 10.17 which appeared in 'A Strategic Framework for Marketing Control' by J.M. Hulbert and N.E. Toy

in *Journal of Marketing*, vol. 41, April, 1977, published by the American Marketing Association.

- Dr J.B. Coates, Messrs. C.P. Rickwood and R.J. Stacey for their proposal relating to 'Investigation into the Causes and Reasons for Differences in the Theory and Practice of Management Accounting'.
- Gower Publishing Co. Ltd for the extract from R.M.S. Wilson's *Cost Control Handbook*, second edition, 1983, published by Gower, appearing here as 'A Note on the Product Life Cycle'.
- Professor Peter Holzer (University of Illinois) for the extract from H.M.W. Schoenfeld's paper 'Management Accounting: Discernable Future Directions' appearing here in Chapter W12, but previously published in H.P. Holzer (ed.): *Management Accounting 1980*, Proceedings of the University of Illinois Management Accounting Symposium, 8–9 November, 1979.
- Richard D. Irwin, Inc., and Professor Gordon Shillinglaw (Columbia University) for two problems (with answers) appearing here as Question 6.1 in section W6.4 of Chapter W6 and Question 6.1 in section W6.5 of Chapter W6, but previously published in Professor Shillinglaw's *Managerial Cost Accounting*, fourth edition, Richard D. Irwin, Inc., Homewood, Illinois, 1977.
- Emeritus Professor E.A. Lowe for Figure 6.1 from his paper 'On the Definition of "System" in Systems Engineering', *Journal of Systems Engineering*, vol. 2, no. 1, Summer, 1971.
- McGraw-Hill Book Company for Figure 11.8 which appeared on p. 158 in G. Shillinglaw's 'Divisional Performance Review' paper in C.P. Bonini, R.K. Jaedicke, and H.M. Wagner (eds.): *Management Controls: New Directions in Basic Research*, McGraw-Hill, New York, 1964.
- Professor David T. Otley (University of Lancaster) for an extract (appearing in Chapter 12) from his paper 'Developments in Management Accounting Research' published in *British Accounting Review*, vol. 17, no. 2, Autumn, 1985.
- Pergamon Journals Ltd for Figure 3.6 from G. Hofstede's article 'Management Control of Public and Not-for-Profit Activities', *Accounting, Organizations and Society*, vol. 6, no. 3, 1981, copyright Pergamon Journals Ltd.
- Prentice-Hall International for Figures 10.28 and 10.29 from Anthony G. Hopwood's *Accounting and Human Behaviour*, Haymarket Publishing, 1974.
- Scott, Foresman and Company for Figure 3.7 from *Managerial Decision-Making* by George P. Huber. Copyright 1980 by Scott, Foresman and Company.
- Simon and Schuster Ltd for Figure 6.3 from *Exploring Corporate Strategy* by G. Johnson and K. Scholes, second edition, 1988, published by Prentice-Hall International.
- South-Western Publishing Co. for Figure 6.2 from p. 202 of John Piper's article 'Classifying Capital Projects for Top Management Decision-Making' which was published in W.J. Thomas (ed.), *Readings in Cost Accounting, Budgeting and Control*, sixth edition, 1983, South-Western, Cincinnati, Ohio.
- Van Nostrand Reinhold (UK) Ltd, and Brian D. Styles (Bristol Polytechnic) for the latter's *Ackroyd plc* case (appearing in Chapter W11) which was initially published in C. Hutchinson (ed.) *Case File in Accountancy*, Van Nostrand Reinhold, Wokingham, 1986.

- Academic Press Ltd. for Figure 4.18 from M. Gietzmann's paper 'Implementation Issues Associated with the Construction of an Activity-based Costing System in an Engineering Components Manufacturer' which appeared in *Management Accounting Research*, vol. 2, no. 3, 1991, p. 193.
- MCB University Press Ltd. for the example in Chapter 6.6(a) derived from Kenneth Simmonds' paper 'The Accounting Assessment of Competitive Position', *European Journal of Marketing*, vol. 20, no. 1, 1986, pp. 16–31.
- Macmillan Publishing Co. for Figures W5.5 and W5.6, plus related discussion adapted and condensed with permission from pp. 410–8, J.L. Heskett, *Marketing*, 1976.
- The Chartered Institute of Management Accountants for Section W1.4 of Workbook Chapter W1, and the extract from M. Bromwich and A. Bhimani's *Management Accounting: Evolution not Revolution* appearing in Workbook Chapter W12.
- The American Accounting Association for the Ajax Manufacturing case in Section W4.6 of Workbook Chapter W4, adapted from J.K. Shank and V. Govindarajan's article 'The Perils of Cost Allocation based on Production Volumes', *Accounting Horizons*, vol. 2, no. 4, 1988, pp. 71–9.
- The Editor of *Management Accounting* for the articles appearing in Section W4.7 of Workbook Chapter W4 by J.A. Piper and P. Whalley and R. Cooper, and in Section W6.6 of Workbook Chapter W6 by R.M.S. Wilson.
- Professor K. Simmonds for Question 6.2 in Section W6.4 of Workbook Chapter W6 based on an example in his paper 'Strategic Management Accounting', published in *Management Accounting*, vol. 59, no. 4, April, 1981, pp. 26–9.
- The Editor of the *Pittsburgh Business Review* for the article by L.R. Pondy appearing in Section W8.6 of Workbook Chapter W8.
- R.D. Irwin Inc. for Question 9.2 in Section W9.4 of Workbook Chapter W9 derived from L.G. Rayburn's *Principles of Cost Accounting: Managerial Applications*, third edition, 1986, pp. 977–8.
- Prentice-Hall, Inc., for the Kinkead Equipment Ltd. case from J.K. Shank's *Contemporary Managerial Accounting: A Casebook*, 1981, pp. 174–6.
- *The Times* for the piece by Michael Dynes ('BR to split national network into local areas') in section W9.7 of Workbook Chapter 9 which was first published in *The Times* on 11 April 1991.

Abbreviations

AAA	American Accounting Association
ABC	Activity-based costing
AICPA	American Institute of Certified Public Accountants
AOS	*Accounting, Organizations & Society*
AH	actual hours (used in variance analysis)
AP	actual price (used in variance analysis)
AQ	actual quality (used in variance analysis)
AR	actual rate (used in variance analysis)
ARR	Average rate of return
BEP	break-even point
CAM-I	Computer Aided Manufacturing-International
CIMA	Chartered Institute of Management Accountants (UK)
CMA	Certificate in Management Accounting (USA)
CPA	Certified Public Accountant (USA)
COGS	cost of goods sold
CRR	cash recovery rate
CVP	cost-volume-profit
DCF	discounted cash flow
DLH	direct labour hours
EDP	electronic data processing
EFTS	electronic funds transfer system
EOQ	economic order quantity
ES	expert system
EV	expected value
FC	fixed cost
FG	finished goods
FIFO	first in, first out
G & A	general and administrative
GAAP	generally accepted accounting principles
GNP	gross national products
IMA	Institute of Management Accountants
IRR	internal rate of return
JBFA	*Journal of Business Finance & Accounting*
JIT	'just-in-time'
LEV	labour efficiency variance
LIFO	last in, first out

LP	linear programming
LRV	labour rate variance
MAS	managerial accounting system
MbO	management by objectives
MIS	management information system
MPV	materials price variance
MUV	materials usage variance
NAA	National Association of Accountants (USA)
NPAT	Net profit after tax
NPD	new product development
NPV	net present value
OE	organizational effectiveness
PB	Payback
PPBS	planning, programming, budgeting system
PLC	product life cycle
P-V	profit-volume
R & D	research and development
RI	residual income
ROI	rate of return on investment
SD	standard deviation
SMV	sales mix variance
SP	selling price
SPV	sales price variance
SQC	Statistical quality control
SQV	sales quantity variance
SR	sales revenue
SVV	sales volume variance
SH	standard hours (used in variance analysis)
SP	standard price (used in variance analysis)
SQ	standard quantity (used in variance analysis)
SR	standard rate (used in variance analysis)
TC	total cost
TP	transfer price
Variances: F	favourable
U	unfavourable
VC	variable cost
WIP	work-in-progress
ZBB	zero-base budgeting

PART 1 Framework

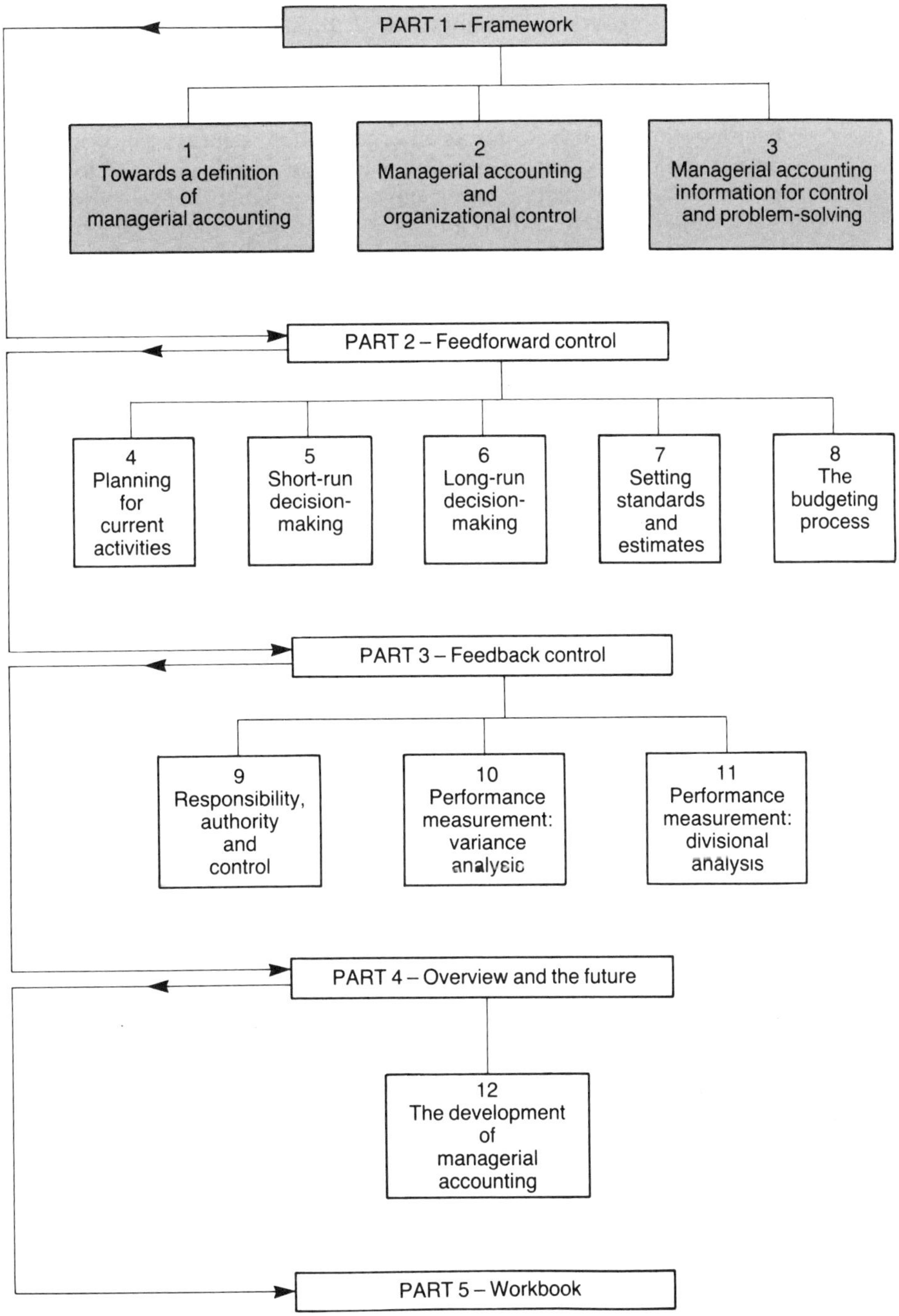

Introduction and overview

Part 1 consists of three chapters which provide a framework for the rest of the book. The logical starting point is to consider what is meant by 'managerial accounting', and this is the initial concern of Chapter 1. It becomes clear very quickly that managerial accounting does not exist for its own sake but rather to help managers in organizations of various kinds to make better decisions in order to control the future of those organizations. We emphasize throughout the book that the organizations with which we are concerned may be commercial or non-commercial, manufacturing or service rendering, large or small. No matter what type of organization you might think of, there is a role for managerial accounting in assisting managers to manage.

Managing presupposes some purpose, which may be making profits (as in the case of ICI plc, for example) or providing health care (as in the case of regional health authorities). In so far as an organization is successful in achieving its purpose it could be said to be effective. However, being successful in achieving some purpose presumes there is some agreement on what that purpose should be, and some understanding of how progress might be made in achieving the purpose. These are problem areas that need to be addressed in order to have a suitable basis for designing appropriate managerial accounting systems.

The question of *design* is important: systems for providing managerial accounting information to help managers solve their problems do not grow on trees! Such systems have to be deliberately designed. This requires careful analysis of the organization within which the system will be located, and of the ways in which people within the organization behave in their decision-making.

Before we start manipulating any numerical data we need to build a framework *within which* we can consider the design of managerial accounting systems *within which* will be numerical data flows. The notion of organization control gives us the basis for erecting a suitable framework, and the context of organizations — as social phenomena — gives meaning to the methods of managerial accounting.

CHAPTER 1

Towards a definition of managerial accounting

Learning objectives

After studying this chapter you should appreciate:

- the historical beginnings of managerial accounting;
- the diversity of the origins of managerial accounting;
- the diversity of managerial accounting as a field of practice;
- the diversity of roles that managerial accounting information might play;
- the inadequacies of existing professional definitions of managerial accounting;
- the definition of managerial accounting used in this book.

1.1 Introduction

The first three chapters in this book are similar to the introductory chapter in the companion volume *Financial Accounting: Method and Meaning*, in that they develop a definition of managerial accounting which is used to organize the remainder of the book. In this chapter it is argued that looking at what managerial accounting has been (its history) and what it is today provides only partial help in arriving at a definition of the subject. As a result, in Chapter 1, we propose a normative definition of managerial accounting as a decision support system that is intended to help achieve organizational control.

The question 'What is managerial accounting today?' may be answered, simplistically, as everything that is not financial accounting or financial management. Or it may be defined as all accounting information that is not reported to outsiders. Both of these easy answers are to some extent correct, in that they describe some aspect of managerial accounting practice, but, as comprehensive definitions, they are unsatisfactory. The first begs definitions of what constitutes financial accounting and financial management, and the second requires the difficult task of deciding very specifically who is 'outside' and 'inside' the organization. Is preparing a product cost report to a government regulatory body reporting to an outsider, and therefore beyond the ambit of managerial accounting? If so, this definition would contradict the 'evidence' of everyday practice, where people labelled managerial accountants often do construct such reports.

Part of the difficulty with answering 'What is managerial accounting today?' lies with the fact that, like any other body of knowledge, it is a changing field. Prior to 1950 the term 'management accounting' was used rarely. By the mid-1960s, however, it was used customarily to refer to a field of practice (of accounting) and to a type of accountant (the management accountant). In addition, a distinctive professional periodical literature and an emerging monograph literature incorporated the label in their titles. Also, the term was used to name a number of professional bodies in different countries, for example, in the United Kingdom and Canada (The Chartered Institute of Management Accountants and the Society of Management Accountants of Canada). By the 1970s, it was also customary to include a field of research and type of education under the rubric. Despite this turn of events, people today do not only use the term to refer to practices that have developed in the last forty years. On the contrary, most people commonly include under the label practices that emerged earlier. This sense of historical change, coupled with a general understanding that managerial accounting information is primarily for internal use, suggests that one could approach the definitional question by historically tracing and listing these 'internal' accounting practices.

Most accounting historians agree that the precursor of modern-day managerial accounting is the cost accounting that was practised by the mechanized, multiprocess, cotton textile factories that appeared in England and the United States around 1800. These factories used cost accounts to ascertain the direct labour and overhead costs of converting raw material into finished yarn and fabric. Generally, these early cost records comprised registers that showed the daily or weekly wages paid to workers, and also log-books recording the pounds of cotton converted each day in processes such as picking, carding, spinning, weaving, dyeing and finishing. By combining data from these two sets of records, it was possible to determine the direct labour cost per unit of output by process at least daily.

Historians argue that it was necessary to construct this cost information because, prior to the establishment of the factory system, such information was obtained via a set of market prices. That is, prior to 1800, a merchant bought raw materials such as cotton in open markets, and consigned these materials to independent household artisans. Using equipment they they owned or rented, these artisans processed the raw materials into finished yarn or fabric. A merchant paid an artisan according to market-determined piece-rates, and he sold the finished goods in open markets. Because the artisan was an independent contractor and not an employee of the factory, there was no need for the merchant to construct accounts that traced the 'labour cost' of production. This information was provided by the market through competitive piece-rates. Throughout much of the 1800s, cost accounts focused on the determination of the cost of direct labour and materials. There was little of what is now called 'cost allocation' of fixed costs to products or to periods. These concerns came much later (and are dealt with in Chapter 4).

By the end of the 1800s, another accounting technology which provided information for internal managerial use – budgeting – had emerged within certain large, vertically integrated firms in the United States. Historians such as Johnson (1983) believe that comprehensive budgets, both for the entire enterprise and for each of its constituent departments, emerged because they enabled the firm's management to coordinate and balance the operating capacities of the separate departments. In addition, by the early 1900s, certain large organizations such as the Du Pont Corporation had begun using information on return on investment to measure the performance of various departments and to allocate resources.

Transfer-pricing systems were also developed in some large organizations, such as General Motors, in the United States. These prices are used by divisions within a single large firm to price products that are sold to one another (see Chapters 9 and 11). The early 1900s also saw a renewed interest in the development of detailed cost information, particularly in the United Kingdom. The work of Loft (1986) suggests that governments played an important part in this renaissance. During the First and Second World Wars, the British government contracted for goods and services on the basis of 'cost-plus' contracts. Accurate cost information was thus required in order to ensure that government agencies were not overpaying their contractors.

By the 1950s, managers within organizations had started to use capital budgeting techniques to allocate scarce resources among several capital projects (see Chapter 6). Finally, in the 1980s and 1990s, certain managerial philosophies, such as a commitment to total quality control and the maintaining of inventories at levels that are absolutely necessary (Just-In-Time inventory systems) are increasingly seen to 'belong' to the field of managerial accounting practice. In addition, managerial accountants are enjoined to think about monitoring changes in the environment pertinent to the firm, and to develop long-term strategies for meeting challenges facing the firm. The term 'strategic management accounting' (described in Chapter 6) is used to refer to these recent developments in practice.

The above brief sketch of historical developments in the field of practice indicates that technologies such as costing, budgeting, transfer pricing and divisional performance evaluation are part of the field of managerial accounting practice. However, a listing of technologies gives but an incomplete understanding of the total field of knowledge. Just as medicine is not a sum of surgical or medical techniques, nor law an amalgamation of different legal forms of redress, so managerial accounting as a field of knowledge that encompasses practice, research and education is but inadequately captured by an enumeration of technologies, both past and present. In the brief description above we have merely listed the major developments in practice; nothing has been said about technologies in research and education. If we continued to define managerial accounting by listing technologies, we could potentially have an endless list.

1.2 The diversity of the origins of managerial accounting

Yet another historical approach to defining managerial accounting might be to develop a classification of the origins of practice. The above historical sketch indicates that different accounting technologies were perceived as being particularly useful at different points in time. Is there some consistent pattern of relationships/events that accounts for the emergence of particular practices at particular times?

One way to read this process of historical change is to impute some evolutionary trend, that is, to assume that managerial accounting, like a living species, is evolving into a more sophisticated and environmentally-adjusted form. Historians and researchers have used such arguments which proceed, with minor alterations, along the following lines: as the environment of the firm changes, the firm evolves and develops new structures to survive, and so does the managerial accounting system. It too evolves in order to ensure long-run survival. Hence, historians argue that as firms moved from being the single-product, single-process firm of the 1800s to the multi-product, multi-process, multi-divisional organization of the 1990s, new managerial accounting technologies have evolved to meet the needs of these new organizational forms.

One of the difficulties with this form of thinking is that it is *environmentally deterministic*. That is, one sees managerial accounting as a passive 'object' that only responds to environmental and organizational change. Accounting is not seen as a proactive social practice. Alternatively, one has to imagine an unseen proactive force – some great invisible mind or hand that 'lies behind' an object called 'managerial accounting' that is guiding its mutation through different environment phases. In effect, what is missing from this evolutionary picture is the 'people element'. It is people, either as individuals or groups, who with their different objectives and interests, actively help shape and determine managerial accounting practice, research and education. But these human interests, which often conflict with one another, are not brought into sharp focus within an evolutionary account of change in managerial accounting. They are dissolved through the use of abstract language that talks about 'environments', 'firms' and 'adaptation'. Consequently, the struggles and contradictions between people that result in uneven and 'curvy' changes in the field of managerial accounting are portrayed as evolutionary developments that move in nice, straight, rational, lines.

More recent research in managerial accounting has pointed out that the reason for the rise to prominence of particular technologies may not be explained by reference to evolutionary adaptation. Mention has already been made of the work of Loft, who in explaining the renaissance in costing in the United Kingdom in the period 1914–32, points to the needs of government during wartime. In addition, she also discusses the influence posed by particular strategies that were employed by professional organizations such as the Chartered Institute of Management Accountants and the Institute of Chartered Accountants in England and Wales to gain control over their respective occupational groups. Neimark and Tinker (1986) also argue that changes in a firm's managerial control system (of which the managerial accounting system is a part) could be explained, not by reference to some evolutionary imperative, but by the need of the owners and controllers of capital assets to continually manipulate and exploit the labouring class, in capitalist countries. Finally, Miller and O'Leary (1987) contend that standard costing took shape in the midst of widespread and pervasive discourses and debates in society about the achievement of national and individual efficiency. The authors essentially argued that the trajectory of managerial accounting 'development' was influenced not by internal demands for effective and efficient environmental adaptation, but by external demands and processes that did not exhibit a singular 'guiding hand'. Collectively, this body of more recent work indicates that there are numerous explanations for the emergence of certain managerial accounting practices. More importantly, they argue that there are diverse origins for the field of managerial accounting. It does not obey some implicit law of natural selection, but is shaped by and helps shape complex interactions among people with quite different objectives. Hence, analysing the origins of managerial accounting provides little help in arriving at an encompassing definition. As Hopwood (1988) argues, managerial accounting as a field of practice, research and (we would add) education has diverse origins. Indeed, not only is it difficult to speak of the *origin* of managerial accounting; casual observation of the field of practice shows it to include diverse skills and tasks.

1.3 The diversity of managerial accounting tasks and settings

Managerial accounting practice, as a set of tasks that people labelled management accountants do, is enormously diverse. Research shows that the job title 'management accountant' is not applied consistently in different organizations. Instead it is used to refer to a diverse range of jobs, types of task, level of seniority and responsibility. This diversity of tasks is partly a reflection of the diversity of organizations that management accountants now work in – small private companies, huge conglomerates, charities, churches, government agencies, quasi-government instrumentalities, etc. In a small family business which employs 50 staff, the management accountant may maintain all the bookkeeping and cost records and prepare the end-of-year financial statements. In an enterprise like BAA plc, there are likely to be several ranks of management accountants, each of which performs specific tasks. For example, an airport management accountant may be involved only with budgets for a single airport, while the chief management accountant may advise top management on budget, cost and pricing decisions covering all airports within BAA's control.

In addition, there are persons called 'treasurers', 'financial managers', 'financial accountants', 'controllers' and 'budget directors' who may be performing tasks thought to be within the province of the management accountant. The Financial Executives Institute in the USA, for instance, states that one of the functions of a controller is to compare performance with previous plans and standards, and to ensure the protection of the assets of a business through internal control. Such a task is often seen in the UK as belonging to the management accountant. Similarly, the American Budget Executives Institute writes that one of the functions of a budget director is to ensure the generation and dissemination of information needed for decision making and planning to each person in the organization having such responsibilities. Again this statement of function does not differ substantially from the definition of managerial accounting given by professional bodies such as the Chartered Institute of Management Accountants in the United Kingdom.

Thus, people who are called 'management accountants' may perform very different tasks, and those who are not called management accountants may in fact perform jobs that are similar to those of the management accountant. This apparent confusion is reflected in Fig. 1.1. Clearly, attempting to know what managerial accounting is by looking at what a person called a 'management accountant' does is insufficient.

Not only is practice diverse, so too is research and, to a lesser extent, education. Managerial accounting research ranges over a wide range of topic areas and styles of research. There are people interested in changing or refining managerial accounting practice so that firms can be more competitive or profitable. There are others who are keen to understand more fully how accounting information is

Figure 1.1

A job description for a management accountant.

	Financial Manager	Controller	Management Accountant
1.	*Provision of Capital* To establish and execute programmes for the provision of capital required by the business.	**Planning for Control* To establish, coordinate and administer an adequate plan for the control of operations.	*Feedforward Control* To develop plans, budgets for control of existing operations and, if necessary, to expand/ discontinue activities.
2.	*Investor Relations* To establish and maintain an adequate market for the company's securities and to maintain adequate liaison with investment bankers, financial analysts and shareholders	**Reporting and Interpreting* To compare performance with operating plans and standards, and to report and interpret the results of operations to all levels of management and to the owners of the business.	*Standard Setting* To develop standards for costs and capacity and to update these as necessary.
3.	**Short-Term Financing* To maintain adequate sources for the company's current borrowing from commercial banks and other lending institutions.	**Evaluating and Consulting* To consult with all segments of management responsible for policy or action concerning any phase of the operation of the business as it relates to the attainment of objectives and the effectiveness of policies, organization structure and procedures.	*Feedback Control* To develop a chain of responsibility reporting and to monitor performance against plans.
4.	**Banking and Custody* To maintain banking arrangements; to receive, have custody of and disburse the company's monies and securities.	*Tax Administration* To establish and administer tax policies and procedures.	*Performance Evaluation* To monitor the performance of staff, departments and divisions.
5.	**Credit and Collections* To direct the granting of credit and the collection of accounts due the company, including the supervision of required special arrangements for financing sales, such as time payment and leasing plans.	**Government Reporting* To supervise or coordinate the preparation of reports to government agencies.	*Satisfaction Assessment* To monitor the level of dissatisfication and people's reaction to and use of accounting information.
6.	**Investments* To invest the company's funds as required, and to establish and coordinate policies for investment in pension and other similar trusts.	**Protection of Assets* To assure protection for the business through internal control, internal auditing and assuring proper insurance coverage.	*To Liaise and Interact with Other Control Systems* To maintain communication links with marketing, sales, research and development, and production.
7.	**Insurance* To provide insurance coverage as required.	**Economic Appraisal* To appraise continuously economic and social forces and government influences, and to interpret their effect upon the business.	

* Activities which are also performed by the management accountant.

actually used by people to change the way people act, think and behave. There are still others who would argue that managerial accounting is an alienating technology that enables superiors to discipline and have power over others. These different research perspectives differ not only in terms of the research questions that they ask, the methods of data collection and analysis used, but also in terms of what counts as 'valid evidence' and 'good theories'. That is, managerial accounting research differs quite fundamentally on a range of philosophical issues (Chua, 1986).

Managerial accounting education is less diverse, to the extent that diverse research perspectives have not as yet yielded textbooks that teach a particular approach to managerial accounting. By and large, students learn managerial accounting as a set of technologies – costing, budgeting, transfer pricing, etc. While it is important for students to learn the mechanics of managerial accounting, this book argues that it is unsatisfactory to study these in an organizational and social vaccum. Accounting, contrary to the image projected by many popular textbooks, is *not asocial*. Instead it is an activity that is intensely human, and therefore social. As the next chapter graphically illustrates, accounting information is manufactured, interpreted, used and structured by people. Managerial accounting practice, like research and education, are social practices. As such, the diversity of practice and research will, it is expected, lead to greater degrees of diversity in the teaching of managerial accounting. Indeed, one of the aims of this book is to encourage students to think more diversely, to think of managerial accounting as being more than a set of technologies.

1.4 The diverse roles of managerial accounting

What does it mean to say that managerial accounting is a diverse social practice? We have already argued that it has diverse origins and is practised quite differently in different settings. In addition, managerial accounting information is put to diverse uses in organizations and societies. First, managerial accounting has a *technical*, instrumental role. That is, managers use an accounting technology to work out what numbers to put in a cash-flow budget, to perform a discounted cash-flow calculation or a break-even analysis, or to attach a cost figure to a product or activity. Accounting information thus can be used technically by managers to set budgets, to decide which capital project to invest in, or which product/activity to promote or drop.

Managerial accounting information, however, is not only put to use technically. Recent research has pointed to the *political* role that managerial accounting information often plays in organizations. If you think about it, budgets are essentially a means of allocating scarce resources: so much to sales and advertising, so much to research and development, so much for investment in new plant and equipment, etc. And where resources are scarce, there will inevitably be struggles among the managers of the respective departments to ensure that their departments receive the largest share of the resources that are being allocated. In practice these departments might submit inflated bids at budget time, or they might always ensure that they use up the present year's allocation in order not to suffer a budget cut in the following year. Part of the reason for the use of accounting information in a political manner will be clarified in the next chapter when we discuss conflicting stakeholder goals. In addition, the use of such political strategies to gain resources will be discussed in more detail in Chapter 8 of this book.

Managerial accounting information also has a *symbolic* role. That is, the managerial accounting system within an organization or society symbolizes or represents key values or beliefs of dominant groups. Spybey (1984) conducted a case study examination of an organization that radically changed its core cultural values and thereby gave differential emphasis to the use of managerial accounting information for control. Early in the life of the organization the owners were two brothers who held 64% of the capital of that company. Their attitude to their managers was autocratic, paternalistic and unchanging over a considerable period of time. This attitude nurtured among their factory managers a strong personal identification with the workforce, and less reliance on the use of indirect forms of control such as accounting performance reports. When the brothers died, control of the firm was won by a group of managers who believed in more 'modern' modes of control that applied management theory and used accounting technologies such as return on investment calculations. As a consequence, managerial accounting information came to assume greater importance within that organization. Berry, *et al.* (1985) also illustrate this symbolic role of managerial accounting systems. They conducted a study within one area of the (then) National Coal Board (now British Coal) in the United Kingdom and found that although cost reports were generated regularly within the organization, people did not pay much attention to them. Instead, at the local colliery level, there was a strong 'physical' culture that focused on 'men down the mines' and the amount of coal that they brought up under highly risky work conditions. This 'physical' culture meant that, in practice, colliery managers paid much more attention to physical counts of inputs and outputs (for example, tonnes of coal obtained per month), as opposed to financial representations of these physical entities (£x of coal obtained per month). The authors further suggested that the cost reports, though little used at colliery level, were duly generated and passed on to head office in London to fulfil the beliefs of head office managers that such reports enabled them to control distant colliery operations.

Both the examples above have focused on *organizational cultures* and how managerial accounting systems represent these particular cultures. There are some indications that managerial accounting systems differ between countries, but the precise connections to national culture are as yet unclear. It is quite probable, however, that some of these differences in the production and use of accounting information are due in part to different cultural beliefs at the national level.

Researchers have pointed out other roles that managerial accounting information might play in organizations and societies – a mythical role (perpetuating corporate myths of unity and solidarity), a disciplining role, a dominating role, etc. We shall not discuss all these roles here, for the objective is not to be comprehensive but to illustrate that managerial accounting might play diverse roles in organizations and societies.

Before concluding this section it should be pointed out that some researchers have distinguished between the intended or potential role of managerial accounting systems and their actual roles. Managers may install managerial accounting systems believing that they will lead to efficiency and effectiveness, but in practice the systems may have quite different effects, some intended but others which are unintended. For instance, hospital A might have installed a product costing system in the hope that it would save the hospital money without adversely influencing the level of care provided to patients. But in practice the focus on costs might prompt physicians to reduce both the quantum and quality of care. For instance, fewer pathological tests might be ordered, or patients might be discharged before full recovery. The point to remember is that the potential of managerial accounting systems to achieve desirable end-states – however defined (efficiency, effectiveness, equity) – can and often does differ substantively from the effects of the systems in practice.

Thus far, this chapter has argued that attempting to define managerial accounting by tracking its past or mapping its present is problematic. Analysing the past to obtain a list of technologies that rose to prominence at different times fails to capture the breadth and depth of managerial accounting as a field of practice, research and education. Further, the present is characterized by great diversity – in terms of the origins of managerial accounting, the tasks that are collected under the label, the people who practise the craft, the uses to which managerial accounting information is put, and the effects which that information has in organizations and societies. Given the fluidity of the past and the diversity of the present, it comes as little surprise that existing definitions of managerial accounting promulgated by professional bodies do not adequately capture the field of managerial accounting.

1.5 A critique of professional definitions

Professional accounting bodies in the United Kingdom and the United States have both sought to define managerial accounting. In 1958, the American Accounting Association (AAA) defined managerial accounting as:

> The application of appropriate concepts and techniques in processing the historical and projected economic data of an entity to assist management in establishing plans for reasonable economic objectives and in the making of rational decisions with a view toward achieving these objectives. (Quoted in AAA, 1972a.)

This definition may be compared with a more recent (1981) statement by the American-based National Association of Accountants (NAA) – recently re-named the Institute of Management Accountants (IMA). This professional body describes managerial accounting as:

> The process of identification, measurement, accumulation, analysis, preparation, interpretation, and communication of financial information used by management to plan, evaluate, and control within an organization.

Let us compare these two definitions. The first indicates that:

(i) managerial accounting deals with both historical and future-oriented information;
(ii) only economic data are processed;
(iii) managerial accounting is intended to assist management in the making of rational decisions; and

(iv) rational decisions are defined with reference to the economic objectives of management.

The second definition indicates that:

(i) managerial accounting identifies, measures, interprets and communicates financial information that is used by management; and
(ii) this financial information is used expressly to achieve control within an organization.

Note that both descriptions emphasize that managerial accounting is intended to be useful:

(i) to management;
(ii) for decision-making.

These emphases are also reflected in the definitions of managerial accounting found in textbooks. For instance, Drury (1988, p. 20) defines managerial accounting as relating to 'the provision of appropriate financial information for people within the organization to help them make better decisions'. Similarly, Arnold and Hope (1990, p. 5) write that managerial accounting is 'concerned with the provision of information to managers who make decisions about the ways in which an organization's resources should be allocated'.

Both professional and textbook definitions reflect the move away from the narrow cost accounting perspective of the early 1900s to an emphasis on decision-making. By the 1970s, the managerial accountant had effectively moved from the factory (where he/she was concerned with determining product costs), to the boardroom. The management (not cost) accountant was now seen to provide an information service to managers within a firm.

However, there remain some aspects of managerial accounting which are left unexplored by existing definitions.

(i) Most of the definitions speak of the provision of *financial* information. Only the AAA definition refers to *economic* as opposed to financial information. This preoccupation with financial information is problematic, as a firm usually has major objectives that cannot be expressed in financial terms. Peters and Waterman (1982), for instance, point out that several successful American companies expressly sought to inculcate a cultural code of behaviour among their personnel. The maintenance and perpetuation of this code was said to help account for the success of these companies. In addition, Kaplan (1984a) points out that firms may seek to maintain good customer relations, high employee morale, or to be leaders in product innovation. Such goals and the measures of their achievement cannot be easily expressed in financial terms. Yet if the management accountant claims to provide information that is of use to management, non-financial information may be as important as financial information.
(ii) Existing definitions of managerial accounting (especially that put forward by the AAA) ignore the social processes that surround and envelop managerial accounting information systems. They assume that accounting information is similar to billiard balls on a snooker table; unambiguous objects that are manipulated and pushed according to generally accepted, well-defined rules. People are assumed to interpret accounting information unambiguously and

to process that information in a passive way and according to well-defined rules. These assumptions are open to three major criticisms.

- *First*, decisions may not be made in a rational manner within organizations, that is, according to generally accepted, well-defined rules that weigh economic costs against benefits. Think: do you feel that the decisions of local councils to cut spending in certain areas (for example, public transport) and to increase it in others (say, funding to the arts) are always rationally made? How often do you think political considerations influence organizational decision-making and the use of accounting information? As pointed out earlier, managerial accounting information may and often does play a political role within organizations because it is a key means of allocating scarce resources.

  Accounting information is produced and used by people and for people. It influences decisions in marketing departments, in production centres, in research and development units. It is read and understood to a greater or lesser extent by accountants and non-accountants. All these various departments and the people within them have particular goals and interests. Given this diversity, accounting information is likely to be used according to rules that are seen to be 'rational' from diverse perspectives. For instance, an embattled sales manager, keen to keep his job, will think it rational to bias his profit forecasts to make him look good (see Lowe and Shaw, 1968). Yet from top management's perspective this gives rise to 'irrational' and inaccurate predictions for the future. Other research studies have shown that accounting information may be used to legitimize decisions which have already been made on political or social grounds, in order that an air of objectivity may be created (Boland and Pondy, 1983; Wildavsky, 1968). That is, managerial accounting information may not play a technical role but rather is used to symbolize or represent desired cultural values such as rationality and objectivity. And this use of accounting information is regarded as 'rational', given the particular circumstances at the time and the interests of people involved.
- *Second*, people may interpret accounting information in diverse ways depending upon their interests, purposes, training, cultural backgrounds, organizational location, personality, even age and sex. A single piece of information for instance, an unfavourable budget variance (e.g. actual sales volume achieved relative to a target) may communicate different messages to different people. One manager may perceive it as a danger signal and react swiftly to find out why the variance occurred. Another manager, who places little trust in accounting information, may choose to ignore that same piece of information. We cannot assume therefore that an accounting number communicates the same information to all receivers of that information.
- *Third*, accounting information may actively shape the problems that people perceive to exist and the alternative courses of action open to them. As the NAA definition indicates but does not fully recognize, accounting information is then not simply a tool to solve a problem, but helps define what the problem is. For instance, workers in a department may be 15–20 minutes late for work. To a social psychologist, the problem may be seen as lateness and job dissatisfaction. To the management accountant, this

problem is translated into hours of idle time, wasted capacity and loss of revenue due to slow production. Like the blind men with the elephant, the accountant helps to define and shape people's perceptions of the reality around them. Accounting information therefore is not passively processed by people, but actively shapes the terms in which organizational problems and solutions are cast.

(iii) Finally, most of the existing definitions of managerial accounting (with the exception of the NAA definition) do not draw the linkages between managerial accounting and organizational control. The primary objective of managerial accounting (as we will argue throughout this book) should be to help achieve organizational control and effectiveness. The concept of achieving overall organizational control, however, is much wider than achieving the economic objectives of management.

Every organization undertakes and participates in a range of economic activities (that is, activities that use scarce resources and have costs and benefits attached to them). It may buy and sell products, sponsor cancer research, operate a closed shop, discriminate against employing women on the shop-floor and take part in youth employment schemes. All these

Figure 1.2

Interest groups.

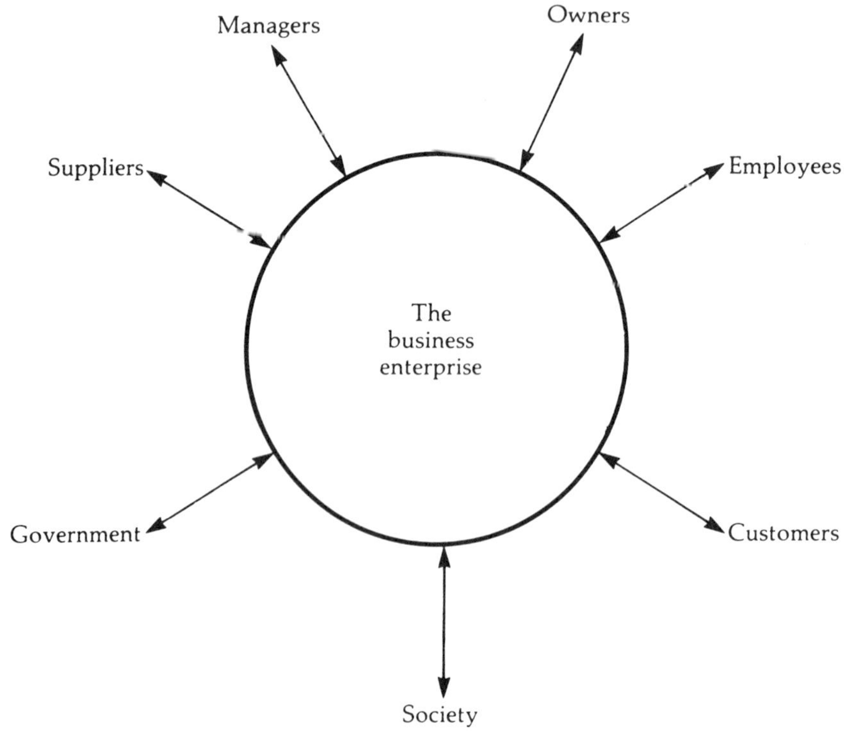

Figure 1.3

Deficiencies in existing definitions of managerial accounting.

(i) Adopt an over-rational view of decision-making in organizations. Ignores the political and symbolic roles of accounting information.
(ii) Neglect to emphasize that accounting information, in the form of budgets and standards, shapes organizational reality.
(iii) Do not adequately discuss the organizational and social context of managerial accounting systems. Relations to other control systems, departments and to diverse people are not analyzed in detail. Profitability assumed to equate with organizational control and effectiveness.

activities are *economic* in the sense that costs and benefits may be attached to them and they use up scarce resources. However, not all of them may be classified as relating to management's objectives. Management may tolerate or allow certain activities, but they may not desire them. In some cases, they may not even be aware of all the activities that are being carried out within the organization. An organization does not consist only of management. There are employees, shareholders, creditors and other parties who have an interest in the activities of the organization, as shown in Fig. 1.2. In order that the organization may survive in the long run, all these parties and their diverse demands have to be satisfied to some extent. Maintaining organizational control means meeting all these demands at a satisfactory level. In the next chapter we shall consider this definition of organizational control in greater detail. For the moment, it is sufficient to point out that a managerial accounting system should cater not only for the needs of management but for the information demands of a coalition of the major decision-makers within a firm.

In summary, accounting information systems do not exist in isolation. They interact, complement and compete with other control and information systems such as personnel selection, marketing research, production scheduling and quality control. They act through people and have effects upon them. An organization is more than its managers; there are other stake-holders who will influence the success or failure of the organization. And organizational control means satisfying a range of parties. Figure 1.3 shows the deficiencies discussed above in current descriptions of the role of managerial accounting information.

1.6 A definition of managerial accounting

The difficulties discussed above do not mean that existing definitions of managerial accounting have no use whatsoever. Neither do they suggest that attempting to define a field of knowledge is a hopeless project that is doomed to failure. What they do indicate is that a definition of managerial accounting as a field of practice needs to incorporate several aspects that are at present neglected. We therefore propose the following definition, which is used throughout this book:

Managerial accounting encompasses techniques and processes that are intended to provide financial and non-financial information to people within an organization to make better decisions and thereby achieve organizational control and enhance organizational effectiveness.

One of the first points to note about this definition is that it is a *normative* definition. That is, it tells us what a managerial accounting system *ought* to achieve, and how it is intended to function. To repeat, the aim of a managerial accounting system is to provide all substantive stake-holders with information that will enable them to make 'better' decisions and so achieve organizational control and improved organizational effectiveness.

This aim may not be achieved. Remember the earlier discussion about the difference between intention and actuality. In practice, a managerial accounting system may be put to purposes that are very different from this stated intention. For instance, information may be manipulated and distorted for political purposes, or to maximize the welfare of particular individuals or groups, as opposed to the collective organization. However, the fact that 'what is' may differ from 'what should be' does not detract from the usefulness of building a normative definition of what managerial accounting should achieve. Otherwise we will have no facility for distinguishing between 'good' and 'bad' practice. If we were pre-occupied with 'what is' we would not be able to change practice and achieve 'better' forms of decision-making. As argued above, observations of the field of managerial accounting suggest that there is great diversity. Unless one moves from a description of what is (which is varied) to a statement of what ought to be, we would not be able to see beyond current diversity to help shape the movement of managerial accounting as a field of human practice.

The second point to note about our definition of managerial accounting is that it focuses crucially on the concept of organizational control. Managerial accounting is intended to help achieve organizational control. But what is meant by organizational control? This question is answered in Chapter 2.

Summary

This chapter has sought to develop a definition of managerial accounting that provides the organizing principle of this book. It was argued that attempting to develop a definition by listing technologies, both past and present, that are generally perceived to be within the ambit of managerial accountants was unsatisfactory. The list was changeable and potentially endless due to the diversity of managerial accounting practice today. Also, this approach did not capture the breadth and depth of managerial accounting. Other ways of seeking a definition were also discussed – by classifying the origins of practices, the tasks performed by people labelled management accountants and by referring to professional and textbook definitions. All these approaches were found to ignore important aspects in the field of managerial accounting. Three main weaknesses were identified: a neglect of the diversity of the origins of managerial accounting practice, inadequate treatment of the linkages between managerial accounting and overall organizational control and effectiveness, and a failure to analyse the social processes that surround and give meaning to managerial accounting systems.

A new definition of managerial accounting was proposed:

Managerial accounting encompasses techniques and processes that are intended to provide financial and non-financial information to people within an organization to make better decisions and thereby achieve organizational control and enhance organizational effectiveness.

Key terms and concepts

Here is a list of key terms and concepts which have featured in this chapter. You should make sure that you understand and can define each one of them. Page references to definitions in the text appear in bold in the index.

- Technical role of managerial accounting
- Political role of managerial accounting
- Symbolic role of managerial accounting

Having now read Chapter 1 of the text, you are encouraged to tackle Workbook Chapter 1 (see pp. 415–23).

Further reading

The idea that accounting has diverse, external origins is also discussed by Hopwood (1987), Miller and O'Leary (1987), Tinker, Merino and Neimark (1982) Lehman and Tinker (1987), Richardson (1988), and Miller (1990).

CHAPTER 2 Managerial accounting and organizational control

Learning objectives

After reading this chapter you should be able to:

- define and understand organizational control and
- the concept of organizational goals;
- understand the role of managerial accounting as a sense-making mechanism.

2.1 The concept of organizational control

The word 'control' is widely used in everyday talk and in scientific language. Herein lies the difficulty. Because it is widely used it means different things to different people in different settings. Indeed, Rathe (1960) showed that there were some '57 varieties' (borrowing the term from Mr Heinz) of the word. The most common meaning is that of dominance, as in A has control over B. But this represents only one possible meaning of the term.

In order to carefully define what we mean by organizational control we shall draw on a body of literature called *cybernetics*. Cybernetics has been defined by one of its founders, Norbert Wiener (1949) as 'the science of control and communication in the animal and the machine'. This definition suggests the disciplines in which cybernetics has had the most impact – physics, biology and engineering. However, as a theory of control, cybernetics is sufficiently general to be of interest to managerial accountants who are interested in managing human organizations.

In cybernetics, control has two distinctive aspects:

(i) control is related to the regulation and monitoring of activities.
(ii) control involves the taking of actions that will ensure that desired ends are attained. Control is therefore related to some notion of goals and of purpose.

We may compare this cybernetic definition of control with an ordinary, everyday use of the term. Ordinary language use connotes the word 'control' in two main ways:

(i) A situation that is 'in control' is seen generally as 'a good thing'. A situation that is 'out of control' is usually considered bad or undesirable. Think of a car, an epidemic, a class or an economy that is out of control. These situations all carry negative connotations.

(ii) To be in control implies a prior notion of proper, desired behaviour. For example, a car or a class of students cannot be said to be 'out of control' unless we have a preconceived idea of how a car ought to function and a class to behave. Therefore, we need a statement of 'what ought to happen', or desired behaviour, in order to know whether uncontrollable behaviour exists.

From an analysis of cybernetic and everyday usage of the term, we note that control:

(i) is related to the regulation and monitoring of activities;
(ii) involves the taking of action that ensures that desired ends are met.

Organizational control may be defined to take account of these important aspects of control. Following Otley and Berry (1980), we shall define organizational control as:

> **The process of ensuring that the organization is pursuing courses of action that will enable it to achieve its purposes.**

This definition of organizational control sounds fine if our organization is a ship, as shown in Figure 2.1. Let us suppose that the ship was set to sail due north, as shown by the dark line. However, high winds, torrential rain and heavy seas are pushing it in a north-westerly direction (shown by the dotted line). This is

Figure 2.1

Ship analogy of organizational control.

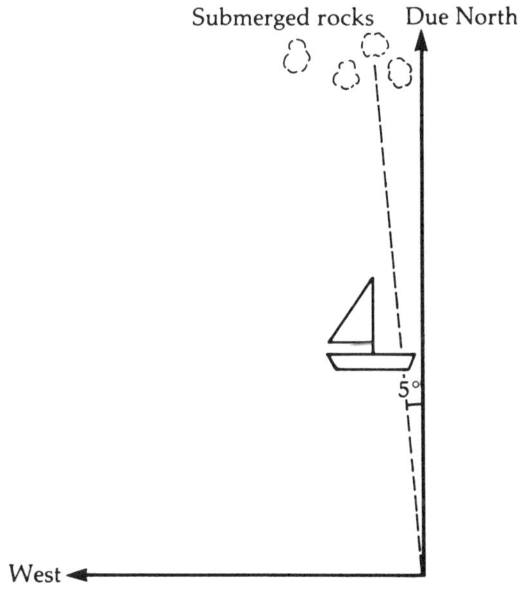

potentially dangerous because there are some submerged rocks in that area which could wreck the ship. Because the ship is not sailing along the desired path (due north) and is being forced onto an undesired path, it may be said to be out of control. In this case, we can easily identify what the goal of our organization (the ship) should be – it is to sail due north. We can also measure how far away from the goal our organization is. We can measure the deviation from true north with a compass – this at present shows a deviation of 5 degrees. We also know what to do to put the ship back on its desired course – increase its speed and power such that it can resist and overcome the external weather conditions that are causing it to sail off-course.

2.2 Difficulties with the concept of organizational goals

Note that in the previous example, we knew the goal of the organization, the extent to which the goal had not been achieved and the corrective measures required to ensure goal attainment. Knowledge of all these factors may be missing, depending on the organization that we are studying.

For an individual, it may be relatively easy to determine goals and purposes. For instance, A's goal may be to arrive at the bus stop at 8.25 am in order to catch the 8.30 am school bus. If A arrives at the bus stop at 8.35 am and misses the bus the goal will not be achieved and, according to our definition of control, the situation may be said to be out of control. Similarly, in *Financial Accounting: Method and Meaning*, Chapter 1, Mr Brain's personal goals could be easily identified, and so could the actions required to help him achieve his goals.

While these statements of goals and purpose are relatively easy to obtain for an individual or a machine, they are much harder to obtain for a formal organization. These are much more complex. In *Financial Accounting: Method and Meaning*, Chapter 2 (section 2.4), the idea was introduced that an organization may be seen as a *system* with several subsystems, for example, a decision and control subsystem, a financial funds subsystem and an operating subsystem. An organization may have other subsystems – a research and development subsystem, a marketing subsystem, etc. As the number of subsystems increases, a system becomes more complex – it is harder to understand and predict the various outcomes of a system.

A human organization is probably one of the most complex systems of all. Von Bertalanffy (1956) and Boulding (1956) both place human organizations as one of the most complex systems to study. Their ranking of systems in terms of increased levels of complexity is as follows:

(i) Static frameworks, for example, a chair or a table;
(ii) Dynamic systems with predetermined motions, for example, the pendulum in a clock;
(iii) Simple cybernetic systems that do not receive information from the environment, for example, a thermostat;
(iv) Systems that are able to regulate some of their functions, for example, biological cells that are able to regulate their temperature;
(v) The living plant;

(vi) Animals;
(vii) Individuals;
(viii) Organizations and all collectivities of people;
(ix) Abstract, extra-terrestrial systems.

As can be seen, in the view of these authors, human organizations are considered one of the most complex systems on earth. Now, in our definition of organizational control, we spoke of 'the' organization and 'its' purpose. It is as though organizations, like ICI, Whitehall and the Trent Regional Health Authority, for example, exist as human beings whose goals we can identify. This manner of talking and thinking about organizations is commonplace. Often, we hear statements like, 'the council will increase its rents by 10%', or 'OPEC will restrict its output of oil to a new minimum'. Such statements appear to make sense to people and they are useful summaries and representations of complex processes. However, they can also be misleading.

Strictly speaking, a complex organization does not exist as an object in the same way that a table or chair exists. We cannot touch, feel or smell an entire organization in the same way we can an inanimate object or machine. The concept of 'an organization' is actually a *social construct*. That is, it is a label that has been created by people (including social scientists) to refer to an abstract entity. In reality, an organization is not a single 'being', but a collective of different people working on certain tasks in certain places with particular machines, etc., for a variety of purposes.

An organization may extend across national boundaries. Price Waterhouse, for example, is an accounting partnership that stretches from North America to Singapore to Australia. Or an organization may be quite small in size, like Mr Smith's motor repair shop that employs two people. In both instances the organization is a collective of more than one person. And it only becomes real to us in terms of the activities and tasks that are conducted by a host of different people who are identified as being 'connected with' the organization. For example, we know that Price Waterhouse exists as an organization because every winter we see recruitment officers who are employed by Price Waterhouse on our campuses, interviewing prospective accounting trainees. Similarly, we know that Mr Smith's organization exists because Mr Smith and his employees regularly repair cars and they charge their customers for the services rendered.

Now, if an organization does not exist as a single human being but as a collectivity of people, how can we talk of organizational control? This question leads us to the next question, which lies at the heart of the problem. How can we talk of *organizational* goals as opposed to *individual* goals? Remember that the concept of organizational control presupposes that we can identify organizational goals that allow us to distinguish between situations that are in or out of control. This problem has vexed social scientists for a long time. In *Financial Management: Method and Meaning*, Chapter 1, for instance, it is pointed out that we cannot assume that an organization has a single goal of profit maximization. In a world of uncertainty people may be neither able nor motivated to maximize profits. There may be other goals that are pursued by diverse groups of people, management, shareholders, bondholders, employees, etc. And the notion of profit maximization becomes an extremely difficult goal to operationalize in practice.

Managerial accounting researchers, however, did not seek to systematically investigate this problem of organizational goals until recently (Otley, 1980). Instead, they operated with an abstract idea, which was borrowed from micro-economics, that the firm's purpose was to maximize 'profit' or 'the return to the shareholders'. Indeed, some textbooks (e.g. Arnold and Hope, 1990) continue to perpetuate the myth that organizations seek to maximize performance on a single goal such as 'the present value of the organization's future cash flows' (Arnold and Hope, 1990, p. 13). But much organizational research has shown that organizations often pursue multiple goals simultaneously, and these goals may fundamentally contradict one another. For instance, an organization at a point in time may simultaneously seek to reduce wage costs, abide by government guidelines on increasing minimum wage levels, and increase bonuses and fringe benefits to senior managers. Research shows that organizational goals are extremely difficult to theoretically define and practically measure (see Steers, 1977; Perrow, 1986).

Yet the concept is fundamental to an understanding of organizations and accounting control systems. The notion of organizational goals provides the rationale for the existence of accounting systems. If we define the aim of an accounting system as the achievement of organizational control and hence organizational goals, we need to resolve the issue of goals as best we can. In the next section, we shall set out our definition of organizational goals.

2.3 A definition of organizational goals

Before proceeding with our definition, it is useful to clarify the distinctions between the concepts of *organizational control*, *efficiency* and *effectiveness*. *Organizational control* was defined as the process of ensuring that the organization's activities will enable it to achieve its purposes. The concept of control has, in fact, been defined in an active, processual sense. That is, organizational control means the pursuit of actions that ensure goal achievement.

Effectiveness, by contrast, measures the extent of goal achievement. It is a statement of a state of affairs. It may be described as a state or outcome variable in the sense that effectiveness measures the results which eventuate after the implementation of organizational plans. There are effective and ineffective organizations; the former are those that achieve their goals, and the latter are those that do not. In between these two extremes, there will be levels or degrees of effectiveness. Thus, we may compare organization A with organization B, and come to the conclusion that organization A is more effective than organization B.

The relationship between organizational control and effectiveness may be summarized as follows:

(i) The concepts of organizational control and organizational effectiveness both relate to organizational goals.
(ii) Organizational control refers to the process of ensuring that goals are achieved.
(iii) Effectiveness measures the extent of goal achievement.

Efficiency is often confused with effectiveness. This is mainly because efficiency itself is often a desired characteristic of organizations and is often venerated in textbooks on economics and management science.

Efficiency refers to the ratio of outputs to inputs (i.e. O/I), so an organization that produces sales revenue of £1,000,000 from a marketing outlay of £250,000 is more efficient (other things being equal) than an organization producing the same sales results from marketing expenditure of £300,000. The respective efficiency measures of the two organizations are:

$$\frac{£1{,}000{,}000}{£250{,}000} = 4 \quad \text{and} \quad \frac{£1{,}000{,}000}{£300{,}000} = 3.33$$

with the higher index being the better of the two.

There are two types of efficiency that are worthy of note:

(i) technical efficiency, in which one seeks to maximize the output from a given volume and mix of inputs;
(ii) economic efficiency, in which one seeks to minimize the input cost for a given level and mix of outputs.

For our present purpose, however, the key points to note are the absence of units of measurement for efficiency, and the concern of both types of efficiency with the cost of generating outputs.

The inputs to an organization may be characterized as a series of Ms – manpower, machines, materials, money, management, messages, markets, motives, etc. (A little poetic licence has been used to express all the inputs in words beginning with the letter 'M'; thus information has been termed 'messages', but the main point is to identify the range of inputs.) These inputs are then transformed and converted by a series of actions into outputs. A simple but useful analogy is to compare the mix of inputs to the list of ingredients in a recipe for a cake. Once assembled, the ingredients need to be baked (i.e. processed or transformed) in order to be converted into output – the finished cake.

Outputs will vary between organizations, and may range from tins of peas to patient care, social welfare to aircraft, advertising services to dental care, education and accounting advice. Figure 2.2 shows an organization as a system with inputs that are converted through a transformation process into outputs. While this model of an organization is a useful summary, it should be noted that we often

Figure 2.2

The organization as an input-transformation process-output system.

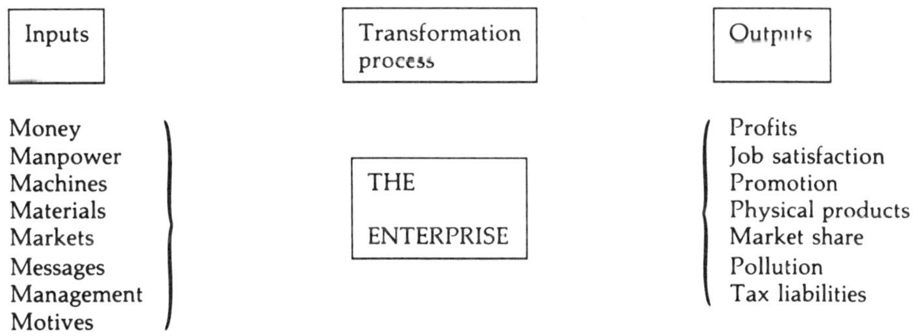

have little precise knowledge about the amount of inputs used, outputs produced and the nature of the transformation process. Thus, it may be very difficult to measure the ratio of outputs to inputs, hence efficiency.

Efficiency is less related to organizational goals, in the sense that irrespective of the actual goals pursued there are efficient and inefficient ways of operating. Efficiency and effectiveness are two related yet independent standards for assessing an organization's performance. Organizations may be:

(i) both efficient and effective;
(ii) neither efficient nor effective;
(iii) effective but not efficient; or
(iv) efficient but not effective.

Figure 2.3

The difference between efficiency and effectiveness.

An Efficient but Ineffective Organization

In 1970, FAS International (formerly Famous Artists Schools) filed for reorganization under the bankruptcy laws. FAS advertised in popular magazines for readers to learn to write or draw under the guidance of famous authors and artists, using a correspondence course. The directors of FAS were well-known artists and authors such as Norman Rockwell. FAS first ran into difficulties when it was reported that FAS always evaluated all its potential students positively. In addition, it was discovered that the guidance provided by mail was not from the famous writers or artists, but from staff personnel hired at relatively low salaries. Under severe public criticism, many of the more famous artists and writers disassociated themselves from the company. When this happened, the company could no longer support its advertising claims.

The company had been efficiently run. It achieved high levels of profits given the number and cost of the inputs (staff, equipment, etc.) used. However, it appears that the company was ineffective if we assume that one of the goals of the company was to survive in the long-run. Of course, if we posit that the goal of FAS was to defraud people and 'to make a fast buck' in an unscrupulous manner, it could be said to have been an effective company! However, the circumstances suggest that the founders and managers of FAS did expect the company to continue in the future and were unprepared for events that undermined the legitimacy of the company's operations.

An Inefficient but Effective Organization

This may be illustrated with the case of the American organization, NASA (National Aeronautics and Space Administration) during the 1960s. The Russians had scored a psychological victory over America when they became the first nation successfully to launch an astronaut, Yuri Gagarin, in space. Partly as a result of this, President John Kennedy promised the American public that Americans would land on the moon within a decade. This promise became the overriding goal for NASA. It was also a goal that was supported by a majority of Congress. As a consequence, huge amounts of resources were devoted to the space programme.

NASA was clearly effective. It achieved its goal when Neil Armstrong and his team landed on the moon in 1969. However, in the relentless attempt to meet deadlines and timetables, duplication was encouraged and waste was widespread. NASA was therefore effective but highly inefficient.

Source: Pfeffer and Salancik (1977).

The difference between effectiveness and efficiency may be illustrated by using the examples given by Pfeffer and Salancik (1977). These are shown in Figure 2.3.

Having classified the distinction between efficiency and effectiveness we can move towards a definition of organizational goals.

Our definition of organizational goals is built on the following ideas about the nature of an organization. These ideas are based on the work of March and Simon (1958) and Tinker (1975):

(i) An organization is made up of diverse individuals and groups of individuals.

(ii) Each individual has his/her own needs and participates in the organizational coalition for a variety of personal reasons.

(iii) It is likely that an individual at any point in time has needs which are similar to those of others, such that a group objective can be identified. Examples of such groups of participants or members may include all female staff, blue-collar workers, white-collar workers, managers, directors, shareholders, creditors.

(iv) An individual may belong to more than one group at a point in time, and move in and out of groups over time. There is therefore great flexibility in the membership of these groups. For instance, Ms A could be an active

Figure 2.4

An organization as a coalition of diverse interest groups.

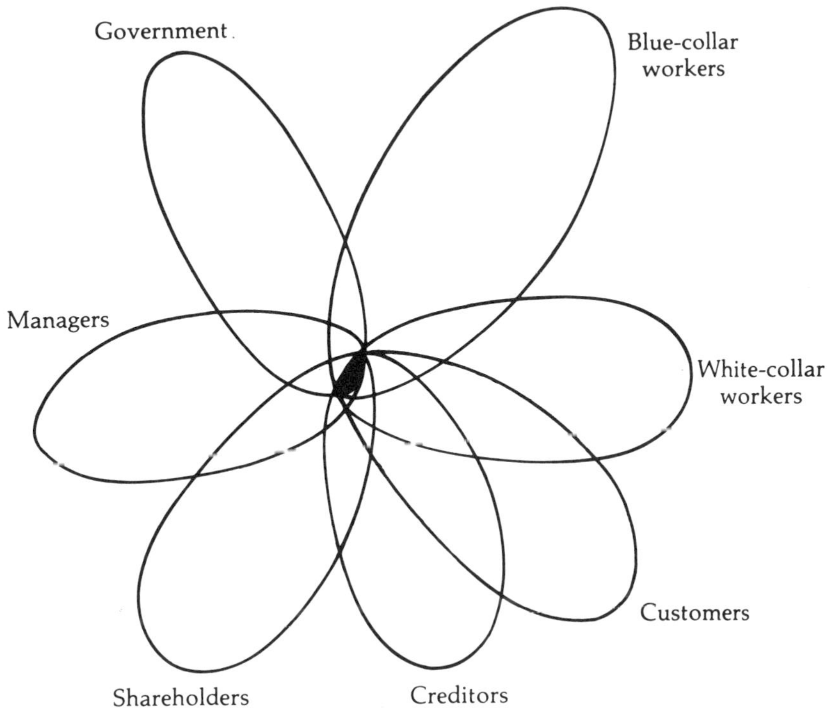

member of the white-collar trade union branch in her company. Her aims are likely to be different from those of Mrs M, who is a director of the company and its major shareholder.

(v) Each group has a set of demands or *inducements* which are necessary to ensure their continued membership in the organization. Figure 2.4 shows a hypothetical organization with seven main groups: blue-collar workers, white-collar workers, shareholders, managers, creditors, the government, and customers.

(vi) The level of demands is determined by the *opportunity costs* of joining the organization, that is, according to the alternative forms of employment available to each group.

For example, if there is a credit squeeze, banks will be able to demand higher interest rates for lending money to the organization. Similarly, if there is a high level of unemployment, workers may not be able to demand and obtain large wage increases. Thus, the kind and level of demands made by each group of members is greatly influenced by the *power* which the group possesses. Powerful groups will be able to demand more than less powerful groups.

Power is related to possession of scarce resources which are required by other people. And scarcity is itself dependent upon social, political, economic and historical factors within the organization and the wider environment of the organization. For instance, in the 1960s, Australian politics at the Commonwealth (that is, central government) level were dominated by discussions of social justice and equity in migration policies. Consequently, one of the more influential ministries within the Whitlam Cabinet was the Department of Immigration and Ethnic Affairs. In the 1990s, when macroeconomic issues became more urgent, the Treasury became the most powerful ministry.

(vii) As well as making demands, each group contributes services or resources which are necessary for the organization to function. Again, the resources contributed will be influenced by environmental factors. For instance, with increasing computerization, accountants need to operate not only manual but also automated systems of financial recording. Hence, we may find more accountants contributing this skill/resource to organizations. Similarly, the role of the government may change; a sympathetic government may contribute substantial subsidies or contracts. With a change of government, such contributions might be curtailed.

Figure 2.5 shows our hypothetical organization, with each group receiving certain inducements and contributing resources to the organization.

(viii) Not all the inducements and contributions of each group can be accommodated, and there is only a small *feasible set* which is acceptable to all participants. This feasible set is shown as the shaded part in Fig. 2.4. In order for an organization to be viable at any point in time there must exist a minimum level of inducement–contribution which is satisfactory to all groups, that is, within the feasible set. If members cannot agree on this minimum level, the organization cannot come into existence with its present number of member groups. For example, if the shareholders refuse to contribute the minimum amount of capital required, the company cannot exist.

Figure 2.5

The organization as a transformer of contributions into inducements.

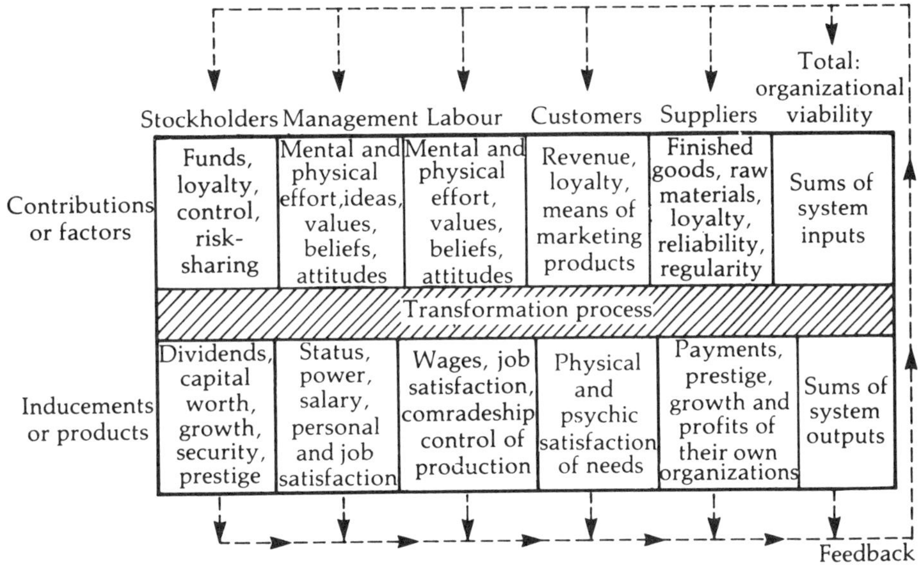

Of course, an organization may choose to operate above this minimum level of inducements and contributions. Shareholders may contribute more than is absolutely required for survival, workers may be paid more than a minimum wage, etc. But whatever the choice now of an inducement–contribution strategy, that choice should be made in a manner which will help ensure that the organization will continue to genuinely satisfy all groups in the future.

In our view the feasible set represents the goal of the organization as a whole. This definition of organizational goals emphasizes that the purpose of an organization should be to genuinely satisfy the needs of members (who are necessary and sufficient for the coalition) in the long run.

Given this definition of purpose, an effective organization is one in which the members choose feasible strategies, which ensure genuine, long-run satisfaction of members' needs. This emphasis on genuine, long-run need satisfaction gives us scope to identify when the organization is out of control. If needs are not being satisfied, if there is suffering or dissatisfaction, we have an indication that something is 'wrong'. The organization is not performing as it should.

For instance, an organization may have been paying a certain category of its workers extremely low wages. While this policy cut labour costs in the short run, most of the workers in the organization (of all grades) are now threatening to take strike action in order to help the low-paid workers obtain higher wages. If the senior management of this organization were to continue to ignore this expression of dissatisfaction, the situation could quickly become 'out of control', and the organization might not survive in the long run.

Similarly, if members are being satisfied now, but in such a way that in the future they will be worse off, the organization is not necessarily in control. An organization, for instance, may pay high wages to all its staff in the belief that all its sales orders will materialize. However, suppose that one of its major customers goes bankrupt and the organization faces a cash flow crisis, and is itself placed into receivership because it cannot pay interest to its main creditor. The organization *did* satisfy all its members, in the short-run. But clearly, short-run need satisfaction may not be carried out, such that long-run need satisfaction is ensured.

Figure 2.6 illustrates how an organization acts as a need-satisficer. The dif-

Figure 2.6

The organization as a need-satisficer.

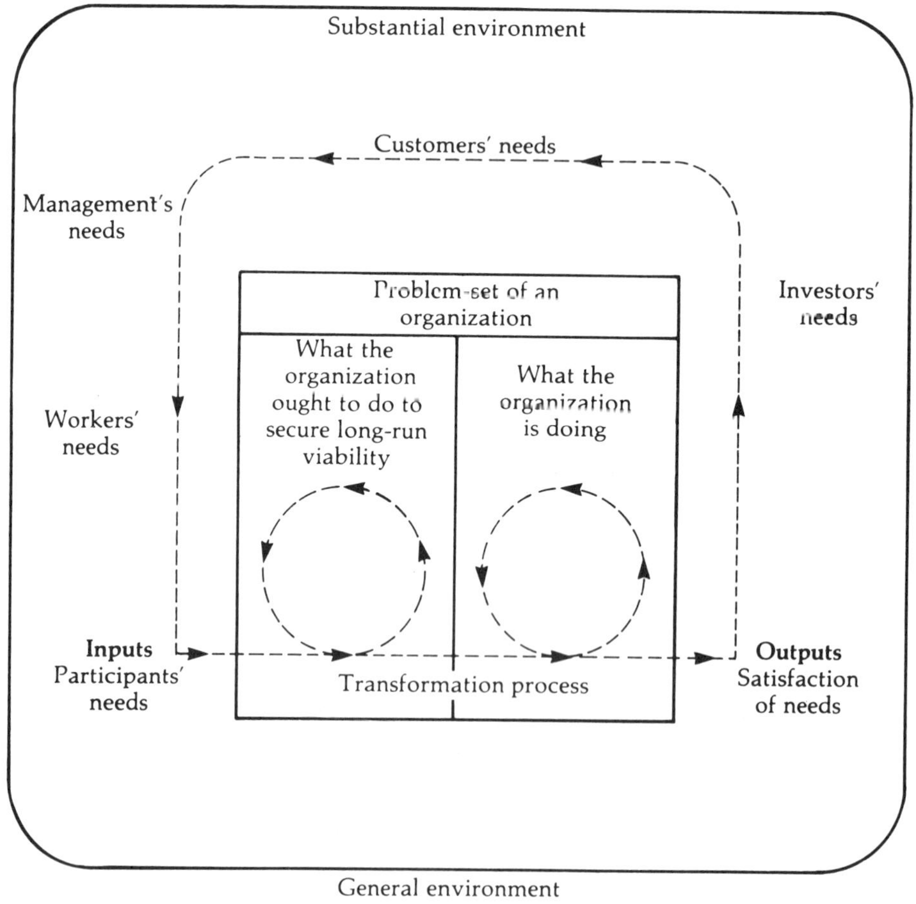

ference between what the organization ought to do and what it is doing gives a measure of the lack of organizational control, and acts as an impetus for change. Note that the inputs into the organization are now represented as the needs of organizational members and the output of the organization is a satisfaction of those needs.

Several characteristics of this model of goals are worthy of note:

(i) It integrates the concept of a system with the agents/people who make up the whole. No longer do we have an abstract idea of 'systems survival'. Instead we substitute the idea of the genuine, long-run satisfaction of human needs. The system is now represented by the complete feasible set of human demands and contributions which requires adequate satisfaction. This human systems model of the organization stresses that an organization expresses itself only in human action, but human action in turn always expresses some organizational/social rule.

For instance, an accounting system does not record financial data, people do. And they record in particular ways which conform to organizational norms. For instance, a system of absorption costing (which is defined in Chapter 4) may have been adopted and hence the accounting staff will keep all records according to this rule. Note also that even the environment is no longer painted in abstract, biological pictures but is seen as being peopled by other companies, social institutions and cultural norms.

(ii) The model is clearly prescriptive. It sets out a normative definition of what an organization ought to do in order to be effective.

(iii) It integrates a consideration of the short-run with the long-run. What we do now makes our future; opportunities may be created or restricted in the future by past and present actions. Hence it is always important to remember the time dimension in our decisions.

(iv) This theory of organizational goals focuses on expressed or overt dissatisfaction as the main indicator of when an organization is lacking in control. What happens if power structures are such that members are not aware of their unhappiness, and demands which are within the feasible set are less than they could/should ask for? At the extreme, what if we have an organization of happy slaves, all genuinely content with their chains, even in the long run? Is that an organization that is in control?

To a large extent this question is rhetorical, as we do not have nor appear to have had such slave organizations which were stable. Invariably, members have formed expectations, however vague, of 'good' or 'better' conditions for participating in and producing for an organization. This dissatisfaction may not be easily identifiable, it may manifest itself in various (perhaps isolated) signs of a vague malaise, a free-floating sense of dissatisfaction. But it is dissatisfaction, nonetheless, and the assessor of effectiveness should seek to explain this dissatisfaction and its causes.

(v) The model stresses the importance of analysing the process by which:
- demands and contributions are deemed feasible and acceptable by all members; and
- a particular inducement-contribution level is chosen.

An analysis of the process by which decisions are made is important because it will help us to understand the power structures of an organization and its environment. This in turn will enable us to know how present choices will affect the future and to identify sources of overt and covert dissatisfaction. If a feasible strategy (for example, a new method of using the budget to evaluate performance) is only grudingly accepted by some members, it may not lead to long-run need satisfaction.

2.4 Making sense of managerial accounting information in the context of conflicting goals

Thus far, we have defined:

(i) *organizational control* as the process of ensuring that an organization is pursuing actions and strategies that enable it to achieve, its goals; and
(ii) the *goal of the organization* which should be to genuinely satisfy the needs of members (who are necessary and sufficient for the maintenance of the organization) in the long run.

In particular, the managerial accounting information system should seek to satisfy the needs of organizational members for certain types of financial and non-financial information. Information is produced, collected and interpreted by people and for people. It is therefore important for a managerial accountant to understand how people react to and interpret or *make sense of* a certain item of information, and why different interpretations of apparently 'the same item' can result.

Words, sentences, numbers and indeed all forms of communication are not 'just' words and numbers. This is because people are not passive processors of information. On the contrary, they are active processors of information who interpret and attribute particular meanings to words and numbers. A person is a *sense-making* individual. He/she makes sense of words and numbers in order to arrive at a certain definition of the situation. Witness the following conversations about an accounting report:

Act I: The Management Accountant and the Managing Director

Accountant: Er . . . As you can see. . . . We . . . er . . . had a gross margin/sales percentage of 10%. This . . . ahmm . . . isn't too bad really, considering that we had severe price competition on our new line of autumn clothing. [*Pause*] Also . . . ahmm . . . we . . . er had a really mild autumn. Really quite unexpected, you know. I mean, if the weather had been like last year's . . . you know, with severe frosts at the back end of September and so on . . . well! I mean, we would really have made it. And we were so prompt in delivering to all our retailers. The boys really did a good job this time. We didn't have a single problem with the distributors–no complaints, nothing. So . . .

Considering the situation overall, it really was quite reasonable. I don't think we have much inefficiency in the system.

Managing Director: All that is very well. But the fact remains, a 10% gross margin on sales is a reduction of 20% from last year's performance. That really is unsatisfactory. It is quite unacceptable.

I want you to undertake a thorough review of our operations and compile a comprehensive report on why – and I mean exactly, why – we did not perform as well as last year.

And all this talk about the weather. That's a lot of codswallop. We've been in the clothing industry now for five years and we should have learnt not to expect last year's weather this year. Who would expect the English weather to be predictable!

Act II–The Management Accountant and the Assistant Accountant

Accountant: Look, this 10% gross margin/sales figure is truly not acceptable. You know, we should have performed much better. I have just had a long discussion with the Managing Director and we both agreed that we need to find out exactly why we did not perform as well as last year.

Now, I want you to analyse all our monthly performance reports carefully and tell me when and in which areas we began to go wrong. Really, you should have picked up the trends much earlier than this. It is your duty to analyse each of these monthly reports and inform me immediately something is amiss.

Assistant Accountant: I er . . . did analyse things . . . But this year, we were always in such a rush . . . you know . . . to get the monthly accounts out . . . And sometimes I just don't have the time . . . Maybe we need more junior staff in the accounting department. With more staff, I could delegate the routine jobs and get on with the analysis . . . What . . ., er . . . what do you think of my idea? *[In a rush]* Don't get me wrong. I know I should have analysed those monthly reports better . . . I'm not dodging the responsibility. But I mean for the future . . . maybe we can do things better in the future?

Notice that the conversations revolve around only one unambiguous number — the gross margin/sales percentage. Yet that number can be interpreted in various ways. It may be seen as 'reasonable', 'unacceptable', 'unsatisfactory', etc. Also, note how issues of power and of blame-shifting occur in the discussions about that number. The management accountant blames the weather in front of the managing director, but puts pressure on his assistant in a later private meeting. This is because of the different interests that are in operation. The management accountant wishes to appear in a favourable light in front of the managing director and wishes to be seen as the boss in control in front of his subordinate.

This short example is used to illustrate the point that accounting information systems do not operate in isolation. Accounting data is produced by and for people. *Individual* attributes such as personality and training will affect the way in which accounting information is accepted and interpreted. Indeed, as Mason and Mitroff (1973, p. 475) point out:

> an information system consists of at least one person of a certain psychological type who faces a problem within some organizational context for which he needs evidence to arrive at a solution . . . and that evidence is made available to him through some mode of presentation.

Depending on the psychological type of the person and the forms of evidence he/she responds to, problems and solutions will be interpreted in particular ways. Even the manner in which accounting information is presented may affect its interpretation. Which of the two reports shown in Figs. 2.7(a) and 2.7(b) enables you to more quickly assimilate the information contained in the reports? Perhaps a fellow student may feel differently.

An individual's values may also influence the manner in which information is processed. The late Sir Geoffrey Vickers (1965) wrote of an 'appreciation system' where judgements of value give meaning to judgements of reality (facts). Judgements of reality are statements of fact about the state of the organization or the managerial accounting system. For instance, a reality judgement would be 'this organization does not have a formal budgeting system' or the 'profit target for 1993 is 10% on the previous year's profit'. Judgements of value involve making

Figure 2.7 (a)

Two types of accounting report.

ABC plc

a. SALES FORECAST

PERIOD	JAN	FEB	MAR	1ST QUARTER
	percentage of first quarter's sales			TOTAL
	%	%	%	UNITS
	36.5	31.9	31.6	352,315

b. PRODUCTION BUDGET

(units)	JANUARY	FEBRUARY	MARCH	QTLY TOTAL
SALES	128,595	112,388	111,332	352,315
+C.I.	22,478	22,266	25,000	25,000
	151,073	134,654	136,332	377,315
LESS O.I.	25,719	22,478	22,266	25,719
PRODUCTION	125,354	112,176	114,066	351,596

b. PRODUCTION BUDGET

	JANUARY	FEBRUARY	MARCH	QTLY TOTAL
MATERIALS	£52,649	£47,114	£47,907	£147,671
LABOUR	£75,212	£67,306	£68,439	£210,958
VAR O'HEAD	£37,606	£33,653	£34,220	£105,479
FIXED O'HEAD	£79,000	£79,000	£79,000	£237,000
TOTAL	£244,467	£227,073	£229,568	£701,108

c. CASH FLOWS

	JANUARY	FEBRUARY	MARCH	QTLY TOTAL
SALES (£)	£255,904	£223,652	£221,551	£701,107
LESS:				
PRODUCN COSTS	£244,467	£227,073	£229,568	£701,108
NET CASH FLOW	£11,437	(£3,421)	(£8,017)	£1

PRODUCT:	MASTER
PRODUCT	
Total Sales	352,315
% Qtly Sales	36.5
	31.9
	31.6
Selling Price	£1.99
closing inv.	20% of next month's sales
April sales	125,000
UNIT COSTS	
materials	£.42
labour	£.60
var o'head	£.30
fixed o'head	£79,000

Figure 2.7 (b)

continued

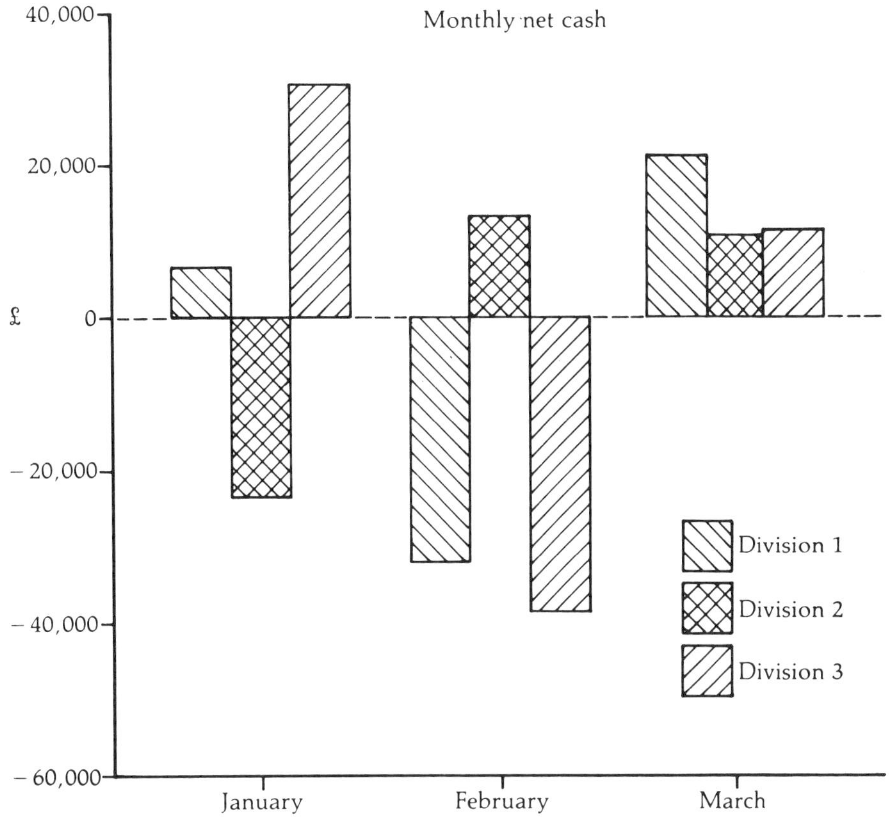

judgements about the significance of these facts. For instance, the non-existence of a budgeting system may be regarded as an indication of disorganization.

Vickers argued that subjective judgements of value give meaning to judgements of reality, as a ship's course gives meaning to a compass card. Information is an incomplete concept because it tells us nothing about the organization of the sender and receiver of a message. It is only when we know something about the people involved that a message or communication becomes informative.

Thus, people make sense of the information given to them. And the exact meanings that evolve will depend on *individual* differences and preferences. They will also depend upon the *social* interactions between people. As the above hypothetical conversations show, an interaction between a person and his/her superior may give one meaning to a piece of information, while an interaction with a subordinate may give rise to a different emphasis. As soon as more than one person is involved in the communication process the participants will 'socially construct' the meaning of the information received.

The significance of the social sense-making processes that people inevitably conduct means we need to place our managerial accounting control systems in context. This is illustrated in Fig. 2.8. It shows that accounting information needs to be interpreted through *interaction* in a particular situation. Interaction takes a variety of forms. It may be direct, i.e. through verbal or written exchange with other people. Interaction may also be indirect, as when we take account of the actions or expectations of other people before we act. Interaction is always rule-bound. Hence, a piece of information needs to be interpreted in the light of these rules of interaction.

Think of some of the rules governing your meeting a person for the first time:

Rule 1 – Shake the person's hand for a few seconds and say 'How do you do?'
Rule 2 – Expect an answer like 'Well, thank you.'
Rule 3 – Do not expect the person to say the following: 'I am not feeling well at all. My boss sacked me yesterday with only one week's pay and my dog died last week. I am really quite miserable and would welcome your advice on what to do next.'

Similar rules govern the production and interpretation of managerial accounting information. These will tend to vary from organization to organization. In some organizations, the following rules may apply in the budgeting process:

Figure 2.8

Managerial accounting information in a sense-making context.

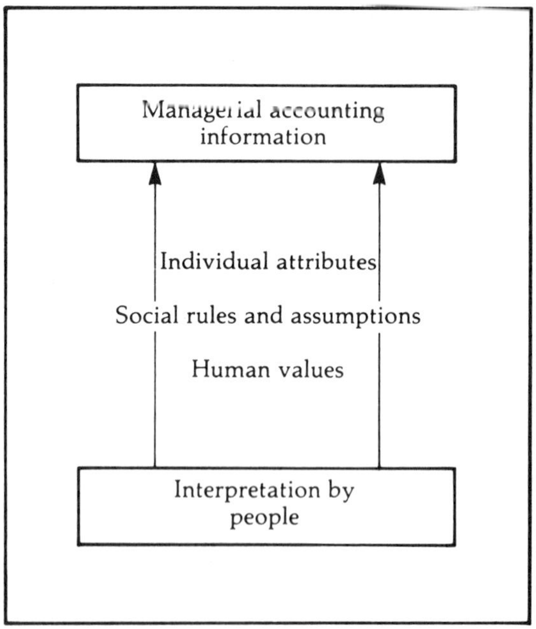

Rule 1 – The department's first estimate of sales and profitability should always be conservative.
Rule 2 – Always ask for more money than is absolutely necessary for the department to function.
Rule 3 – Always spend all the department's budgetary allocations, in case there are cuts in the following year.
Rule 4 – When a superior sets a deadline, add another week to it.
Rule 5 – When the subordinate says 'the budget cannot be achieved', interpret that as 'the budget is moderately hard'; when the subordinate says 'the budget is crazy', interpret that as 'the budget is probably achievable but will involve some really tough decisions'.

In order to understand how managerial accounting information will be produced and interpreted by people within organizations it is important that we know the individual and social processes at work within organizations. By emphasizing the sense-making processes that surround managerial accounting information systems, numerous insights about accounting systems and organizations are obtained:

(i) People in organizations do not always act collectively in a rational manner, that is, with pre-set goals that guide action and decision-making. There are numerous reasons why such means–end rationality may not exist. First, people within an organization may or may not have clear objectives at the individual level. Second, even if clear objectives do exist at the individual level, through interaction the collective end result may not match any of the individual objectives.

For instance, at the start of a divisional budget committee meeting, the members might have the following preferences:

A – seeks to increase the number of staff in her department;
B – wishes to expand the range of subjects offered by his department;
C – no particular preferences but thinks budget meetings are a waste of time;
D – intends to question the process by which funds are allocated to the committee from a central budget committee.

In the course of that meeting all these issues could have been raised. Because the committee was unable to reach an agreement, the final decision was to convene another meeting to consider the entire budgeting process – an issue that was not even on the agenda in the first place!

The important point to note is that through interaction, organizations, viewed as collectivities of people, may not act in totally 'rational' ways. Thus, there will always be an element of uncertainty in predicting the effects of a managerial accounting information system.

(ii) Part of this uncertainty is due to individual differences. Individual attributes such as personality, training and people's values will play a very important role in shaping people's interpretations of information received. As Vickers (1965) pointed out, it is judgements of value that give meaning to judgements of facts. A number may be interpreted differently by different people. To some, a profit shortfall of 5% may be insignificant, to others it may be highly significant.

(iii) Predicting the effects of a managerial accounting information system is also difficult because, in most organizations, there will be unwritten assumptions and social rules about 'how things ought to be done'. For instance, there may be taken-for-granted beliefs that it is important to spend all one's budget allocation in order to avoid a significant reduction in budget allocations for the following year.

(iv) Such tacit assumptions about how managerial accounting behaviour ought to be conducted should regularly be challenged by an effective control system. As Churchman (1971) points out, there is a need not only to provide information which is useful for decision-making, but which also brings critical assumptions into question in order that new understandings may be achieved. Therefore, at times, it may be necessary for the managerial accounting system to act as a devil's advocate, to critically evaluate prevailing beliefs about 'how things ought to be done'. This may be achieved in capital budgeting decisions, for instance, by setting out the financial and non-financial implications of a scenario that is based on a radically different set of prior assumptions about resource availability and the goals of key decision-makers.

(v) Because it is difficult to predict the effects of a managerial accounting information system, it is important for the users of the information system to actively seek to control or manipulate the symbols, signals or messages that are desired. Sense-making processes emphasize that much human behaviour is founded on symbols, rituals, routines and myths. These can greatly influence behaviour. Therefore, a managerial accounting system should seek to manipulate such symbols, etc., to achieve organizational control.

For instance, if a chief accountant suspects that too little information is filtering back to the top of the management hierarchy, she may wish to signal a more open, personal reporting style. Instead of sending a memo round to her subordinates, she leaves her office door open, places her own intercom calls to arrange meetings, and begins a series of regular visits to all the branch accounting offices in the country. In her own words, 'I wanted word to get around our organization that I'm aware of what's going on'.

In our view, the management of symbols should be an integral part of any managerial accounting system.

(vi) A final responsibility of an awareness of sense-making processes is a heightened awareness of the ethical responsibility of the managerial accounting systems designer (Boland, 1979). When the systems designer starts with a notion that people passively accept accounting information, he/she is concerned with issues of how much information to provide and whether the information presents a 'true' picture of the situation. But when the systems designer knows that the information provided can fundamentally shape people's perception of events and situations, he/she has a different responsibility. Accounting does not just provide a model of the organization: it is a model *for* its ongoing social construction by the members of the organization.

Designing a managerial accounting system can affect power positions within an organization. It can influence perceptions of order, of rational planning. Indeed, systems design is an integral part of building a world-view and the systems designer should be aware that, in the final analysis, he/she will become involved in ethical dilemmas about, for instance, the sharing of power and of economic resources. In the next chapter we shall discuss in more detail the concepts of organizational control and what considerations should be borne in mind when designing managerial accounting systems for organizational control.

Summary

Our definition of managerial accounting focuses crucially on the notion of organizational control, which is defined as the process of ensuring that an organization is pursuing courses of action that will enable it to achieve its purpose. And the purpose of an organization should be to genuinely satisfy the needs of organizational members in the long run. It was recognized that organizational stake-holders, such as shareholders, employees and managers, often have conflicting group goals. Only a subset of these goals collectively forms the feasible set of goals that enables an organization to survive in the long run. Thus, put differently, the aim of an organization is to stay within this feasible set.

Given these definitions of organizational control and goals, the aim of a managerial accounting system is normative – it should provide financial and non-financial information to people within an organization, and thereby help them to make decisions that will manage the feasible set successfully in the long run.

In order to achieve this aim, management accountants need to be aware of the individual and social processes that surround and impact upon the functioning of accounting systems in organizations. These human processes add an element of uncertainty to the operation of information systems.

Key terms and concepts

Here is a list of key terms and concepts which have featured in this chapter. You should make sure that you understand and can define each one of them. Page references to definitions in the text appear in bold in the index.

- Cybernetics
- Contributions
- Effectiveness
- Efficiency
- Feasible set
- Inducements
- Organizational goals
- Organizational stake-holders
- Sense-making
  - rationality (reality judgements)
  - value judgements
- Social processes
- Social construct

Having read Chapter 2 of the text you are now encouraged to tackle Workbo pp. 424–28).

Further reading

The idea that accounting is, like other languages, a means by which people make sense of the world is increasingly recognized in accounting research. See Tomkins and Groves (1983) Boland and Pondy (1983; 1986), Preston (1986), Nahapiet (1988), Morgan (1988), and Dent (1991).

The literature on organizational goals is very large. For a brief and useful summary, see Goodman and Pennings (1977), and Cameron and Whetten (1983).

CHAPTER

3 Managerial accounting information for control c problem-solving

Learning objectives

After studying this chapter you should be able to:

- define feedforward and feedback control;
- understand how these forms of control are achieved through a managerial accounting system;
- construct a model of a control system;
- discuss a contingency approach to managerial accounting systems design;
- understand the role of managerial accounting information in problem-solving

3.1 Introduction

In Chapter 1 we defined managerial accounting as playing a major role in ensuring organizational control and enhancing organizational effectiveness. In Chapter 2 we defined organizational control as the process of ensuring that an organization was pursuing actions and strategies that enabled it to achieve its goal. We also defined what we meant by an organizational goal (i.e. to satisfy genuinely the needs of organizational members in the long run).

If the achievement of organizational control is the goal of a managerial accounting system, there are a number of means by which this goal may be achieved, that is, through the exercise of different forms of control. Note that we have specified overall organizational control as an aim, and various forms of control as a means to achieve this end. *Control* (in the singular) is an organizational aim, while *controls* (in the plural) is a generic term that refers to the means of achieving control.

These means to achieve control may be classified according to the form of control being exercised; for example, into open-loop or closed-loop forms of control. Frequently, the term 'control system' is also used. Thus we may hear of an open-loop system or a closed-loop control system. The use of the word 'system' should not worry you. It simply helps us to think of a concrete set of parts that are coordinated to achieve a certain form of control. Think of pop music or classical music as a form of music, and a 'pop music system' or a 'classical music system' as an assemblage of parts that achieves that type of music. As an example, a classical music system might consist of a CD player, a tuner, an amplifier, a set of speakers and a stack of classical compact discs. Similarly, a closed-loop control system will have a particular configuration of relationships between the input, transformation process and output.

In Chapter 2 we pointed out that a managerial accounting system would help achieve organizational control through satisfying people's need for information and thereby help them to make better decisions. In this chapter we shall analyse in detail the process of decision-making (or what amounts to the same thing – problem-solving) and draw the crucial relationship between information, control and problem-solving.

3.2 Basic control concepts

In this section we will distinguish between:

(i) open-loop control; and
(ii) closed-loop control.

We shall also distinguish between two main forms of closed-loop control:

(i) feedforward control; and
(ii) feedback control.

To some extent, therefore, the following discussion will act as a preface to Part 2 of the book (Chapters 4–8) insofar as it deals with feedforward control, and as a preface to Part 3 (Chapters 9–11) insofar as it deals with feedback control.

(a) Open-loop control

This form of control exists when an attempt is made by a system (for example, an organization) to achieve some desired goal, but no adjustments are made to its actions once the sequence of intended acts is under way. A very simple example is that of a golfer hitting a golf ball: his aim is to get the ball into the hole, and with this in mind he will take into account the distance, the hazards, and so forth, prior to hitting the ball. Once the ball is in the air there is nothing that the golfer can do but hope that he did things right.

To take another example, suppose a company wished to sell 100,000 microcomputers over the next 12 months. Its managers would gear the company up to promote, manufacture, and distribute the product at a predetermined price in the light of various assumptions regarding likely patterns of demand, possible competitive actions, and so on. If the company blindly proceeded to carry out its marketing, manufacturing, and distribution plans without any modification to take into account changes in its environment (e.g. competitive reactions in the form of price reductions) this would be an example of open-loop control. Within such a system there is a goal, a plan, but no mechanism to ensure that the plan is accomplished.

Two possible refinements to the basic open-loop model are:

(i) To introduce a monitoring device for the continual scanning of both the environment and the transformation process of the system (that is, the process by which the organization converts inputs into outputs). This will provide a basis for modifying either initial plans or the transformation pro-

Figure 3.1

A feedforward control system.

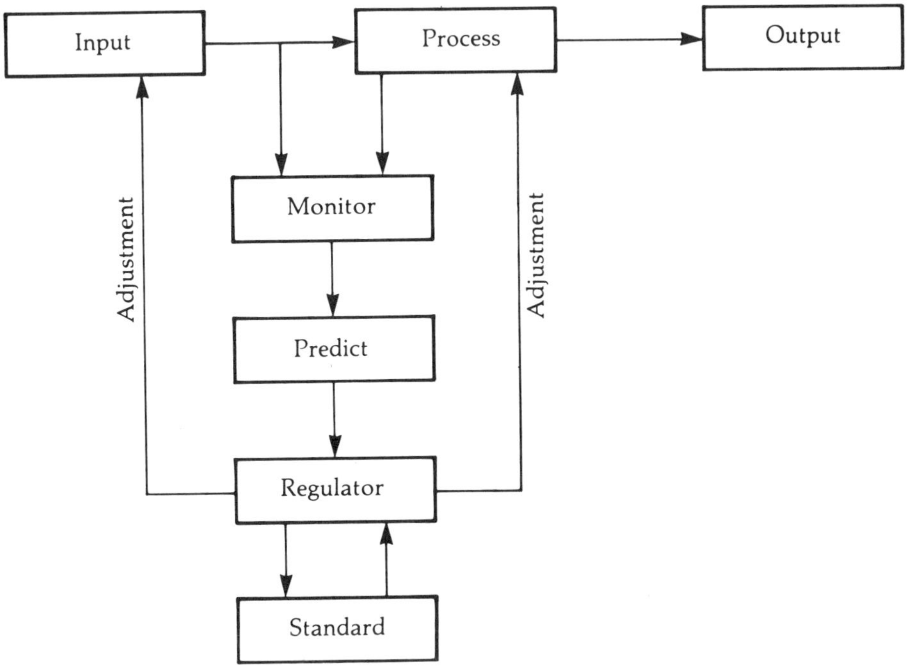

cess itself if it appears that circumstances are likely to change before the plan has run its course and the goal has been realized. This is *feedforward control*, and is illustrated in Fig. 3.1

(ii) To monitor the outputs achieved against desired outputs from time to time, and take whatever corrective action is necessary if a deviation exists. This is *feedback control*, and is illustrated in Fig. 3.2.

Both feedback and feedforward control entail linking outputs with other elements within the system, and this explains why they are termed *closed-loop* control systems.

(b) Closed-loop control

In an open-loop system errors cannot be corrected as the system goes along, whereas likely errors can be anticipated and steps taken to avoid them in a feedforward control system, and actual errors along the way can be identified and subsequent behaviour modified to achieve desired ends in a feedback control system.

The inadequacy of open-loop systems as a basis for organizational control (and hence for the design of managerial accounting systems) largely stems from our

Figure 3.2

A feedback control system.

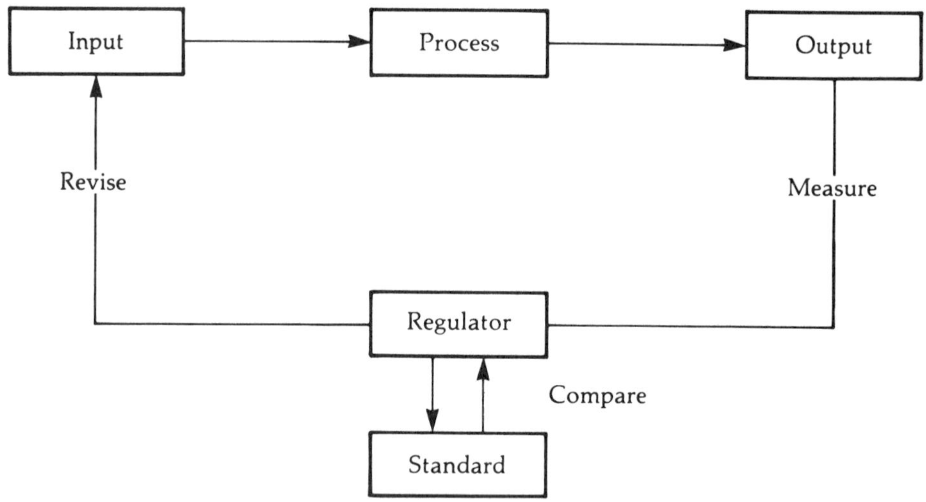

limited knowledge of how organizational systems operate, which in turn reflects the complexity of organizations and their environments, plus the uncertainty that clouds the likely outcomes of future events. If we possessed a full understanding of organizational processes and had a perfect ability to predict the future then we would be able to rely on open-loop systems to achieve the ends we desire since we would be able to plan with the secure knowledge that our plans would be attained due to our perfect awareness of what was going to happen, and how, and when (i.e. control action would be independent of the system's output).

In our current state of awareness we must rely on closed-loop systems, whether feedforward or feedback, in which control action is dependent upon the actual or anticipated state of the system.

It is helpful to think of four types of outcome in connection with the application of closed-loop systems to the problem of organizational control. These are:

S_0 = Initial *ex ante* performance (e.g. a budget based on a set of expectations, which might include, for instance, inflation at 5% p.a.; market growth of 10% p.a.; no labour disputes).

S_1 = Revised *ex ante* performance (e.g. an updated budget that has taken into account the experience of operating the system to date).

S_2 = *Ex post* performance (e.g. a revised budget based on what should have been achieved in the circumstances that prevailed during the period in question, say: inflation at 7% p.a.; market growth of 12% p.a., and a strike lasting three weeks).

A_0 = Observed performance (i.e. that which actually occurred).

An organization's forecasting ability is shown by $A_0 - S_0$ (under feedback control) and, more precisely, by $A_0 - S_1$ (under feedforward control). The extent to which the organization is not using its resources to maximum advantage (its opportunity cost of operating) is given by $A_0 - S_2$.

A feedforward control system will function in a way that keeps revising S_0 as events are proceeding with a view to producing an eventual outcome in which $A_0 = S_1$. On the other hand, a feedback control system will, from time to time, compare A_0 and S_0, and S_0 will only be revised if a discrepancy has been experienced.

It is apparent, therefore, that feedforward control tends to be:

(i) *ex ante*
(ii) proactive
(iii) continuous

and seeks to predict the outcomes of proposed courses of action, while feedback control tends to be:

(i) *ex post*
(ii) reactive
(iii) episodic.

Let us look at each a little more closely.

(c) Feedforward control

A feedforward system can be defined as:

> A measurement and prediction system which assesses the system and predicts the output of the system at some future date.
>
> (Bhaskar and Housden (1985, p. 199.)

This differs from a feedback system in that it seeks to anticipate, and thereby to avoid, deviations between actual and desired outcomes. Its components are:

(i) an operating process (which converts inputs into outputs);
(ii) a characteristic of the process (which is the subject of control);
(iii) a measurement system (which assesses the state of the process and its inputs, and attempts to predict its outputs);
(iv) a set of standards or criteria (by which the predicted state of the process can be evaluated);
(v) a regulator (which compares the predictions of process outputs to the standards, and which takes corrective action where there is likely to be a deviation).

(Cushing (1982), p. 83.)

For a feedforward control system to be effective it must be based on a reasonably predictable relationship between inputs and outputs (i.e. there must be an adequate degree of understanding of the way in which the organization functions).

Some examples of feedforward systems might be useful, and the following are commonly found:

(i) *Cash planning*, whereby an organization's cash balance is maintained at some desired level.

(ii) *Inventory control*, whereby the balance of each item of inventory is regulated at a desired level. The process comprises the procurement, storing and issuing of raw materials, components, finished goods and other supplies. Inventory records contain the necessary measurements, and the regulator may be either a member of the stores personnel or a computer.

The key input variable to an inventory feedforward control system will be either the anticipated level of sales of finished goods (in a marketing operation) or the rate of usage of materials/supplies (in a manufacturing or service operation). Other input variables will include:
- amount of purchases;
- returns (whether of sales or purchases);
- spoilage;
- shrinkage;
- lead times (between ordering goods and receiving deliveries).

While it can be argued that the characteristic to be controlled is the balance of each item held in inventory, it will be apparent that this is a function of stock-holding costs and the target level of service to be offered. (For a fuller discussion, see Koontz and Bradspies (1972).)

(iii) *New product development* (NPD), which aims to introduce successful new products with an efficient use of resources. This requires careful coordination among the R & D, marketing research, engineering, manufacturing, marketing, distribution and finance functions. Feedforward control can help by regulating the timing of related activities and the quality of results. (See Urban and Hauser (1980) for thorough coverage of NPD.)

NPD is a good example of *a project*, and the focus of attention will be on the ultimate success of the project as a whole. Thus the revision of market demand estimates will lead to a prediction of the resulting impact on the new product's likely success and any necessary adjustment of plans for subsequent stages of the project.

(d) Feedback control

Feedback control should ensure self-regulation in the face of changing circumstances once the control system has been designed and installed. The essence of feedback control is to be found in the idea of *homeostasis*, which defines the process whereby key variables are maintained in a state of equilibrium even when there are environmental disturbances.

As a hypothetical illustration, let us consider a company planning to sell 100,000 cassette players during the next 12 months. By the end of the third month it finds that the pattern of demand has fallen to an estimated 80,000 units for the 12 months due to the launch by another company of a competing product. After a further three months the competitor puts up the price of his product whilst the original company holds its own price steady, and this suggests that the annualized level of demand may increase to 150,000 units. Feedback signals would ensure that the company is made aware (e.g. by monthly reports) of the actual versus planned outcomes (in terms of sales levels). The launch of the competitive cassette player would be identified as the reason why sales levels were below expectations in the early months, and the competitor's price increase would be identified as the reason why sales levels subsequently increased. In response to deviations between actual and desired results (i.e. feedback) an explanation needs to be found, and actions taken to correct matters. Amending production plans to manufacture fewer (or more) cassette players, allowing inventory levels to fall (or rise) to meet the new pattern of demand, modifying promotional plans to counter competitive activities, and so forth, could all stem from a feedback control system.

If deviations (or *variances*, to give them their usual accounting name) are minor it is probable that the process could absorb them without any modifications, and inventory control systems, for example, are normally designed to accommodate minor variations between expected and actual levels of demand, with buffer stocks being held for this purpose. But in the case of extreme variations – such as the pattern of demand shifting from 100,000 units to 80,000 and then to 150,000 – it will be necessary to amend the inputs in a very deliberate way once the causes of the variations have been established. Inevitably there are costs associated with variances, and these will tend to be proportional to the length of time it takes to identify and correct them. (Variances are discussed in detail in Chapter 10.)

The most common illustration one finds of a feedback control system – which serves to emphasize its links with mechanical systems – is that of a domestic central heating system (or alternatively, a refrigerator). A thermostat regularly measures the temperature of the air relative to a preset standard (say 65°F). If a variance exists, one of two things will happen:

(i) if the air temperature *exceeds* the standard, the system will cut off (i.e. the boiler will cease working);
(ii) if the air temperature is *less* than the standard, the heating system will either continue (if it is currently in operation) or it will start up.

There are, in general, five basic components in a feedback control system. These are:

(i) an operating process (which converts an input into an output – such as a central heating boiler and its associated pipes, radiators, etc.);
(ii) a characteristic of the process (which is the subject of control – such as maintaining a comfortable degree of warmth);
(iii) a measurement system (which assesses the state of the characteristic – such as a thermometer);
(iv) a set of standards or criteria (by which the measured state of the process is evaluated – such as 65°F as the desired level of warmth);
(v) a regulator (the functions of which are to compare measures of the process characteristics with the standards, and to take action to adjust the process if the comparison reveals that the process is deviating from plan   the thermostat fulfils this role).

Some principles for the proper functioning of a feedback control system can be suggested (e.g. Cushing (1982), p. 80), and might include the following:

(i) The benefits from the system should be at least as great as the cost of developing, installing and operating it. (This is the problem of 'the cost of control' to which we will return). It is often difficult to specify precisely either the benefits (other than in broad terms, e.g. 'better customer service', 'increased efficiency') or the costs relating to different system designs, but it should be possible to make approximate assessments of both.

(ii) Variances, once measured, should be reported quickly to facilitate prompt control action. (This is analogous to the feedback – known as knowledge of results – in psychological learning theory: if one has been tested on what one has learnt it is important to be told quickly whether one is right – to reinforce the earlier learning – or wrong – to facilitate remedial learning.)

(iii) Feedback reports should be simple, easy to understand and highlight the significant factors requiring managerial attention.

(iv) Feedback control systems should be integrated with the organizational structure of which they are a part (which will be the main theme of Chapter 9). The boundaries of each process subject to control should be within a given manager's span of control.

(e) Feedforward versus feedback control

The most significant features of feedforward and feedback control are shown in Fig. 3.3 (adapted from Cushing (1982), p. 97). Feedback systems are typically cheaper and easier to implement than feedforward systems, and they are more effective in restoring a system that has gone out of control. Their main disadvantage, however, is that they can allow variations to persist for as long as it takes to detect and correct them. Feedforward control systems, as we have seen, depend critically for their effectiveness upon the forecasting ability of those who must predict future process outputs. Both feedforward and feedback systems lend themselves to self-regulation.

The most effective approach to control comes from using the two approaches as complements since few (if any) processes could be expected to operate effectively and efficiently for any length of time if only one type of control was in use. (For example, in controlling inventory, feedback data can be used in connection with stockouts, rates of usage, etc., while feedforward data needs to be generated in gauging the raw material requirements for predicted levels of demand and the ability of suppliers to deliver on time.)

Both types of control are fundamentally intertwined with the design of managerial accounting systems. In a feedback control system the functions that managerial accounting will carry out are:

(i) standard setting;

Figure 3.3

Relative strengths of feedforward and feedback controls.

Characteristic	Feedforward	Feedback
Low cost	–	Yes
Ease of implementation	–	Yes
Effectiveness	–	Yes
Minimal time delays	Yes	–
Self-regulation	Yes	Yes

Adapted from Cushing (1982).

(ii) performance measurement;
(iii) reporting of results.

Within a feedforward control system the role of managerial accounting will encompass:

(i) standard setting;
(ii) monitoring process inputs;
(iii) monitoring operations;
(iv) predicting process outputs.

The degree of overlap is modest relative to the degree of complementarity.

3.3 A managerial accounting control system

Thus far we have defined:

(i) organizational control;
(ii) feedforward control; and
(iii) feedback control.

In describing feedforward and feedback control we pointed out that both types of control should be present in order to ensure overall organizational control. These two types of control complement one another.

Using this language of feedforward and feedback control and the notion of a control system allows us to express the idea of organizational control in a more precise way. Until now we have defined organizational control as the process of ensuring that an organization pursues its goal. Let us re-examine this definition and ask: what are some of the processes involved in ensuring that an organization pursues its goal? How do we know when a situation is in control? Or put slightly differently, what are the conditions that must be fulfilled in order that a situation might be said to be in control?

(a) Tocher's approach to control

The answer is implicitly hidden in Figs. 3.1 and 3.2, which describe the conditions necessary for feedforward and feedback control. Here we wish to examine these conditions for control more explicitly. To do so we shall look at Tocher's (1970; 1976) cybernetic model of control. Tocher's model was designed for simple systems, and his ideas are not completely transferable when talking about the control of complex organizations. However, they do provide a useful starting point for a more complete discussion of what organizational control means.

According to Tocher, there are at least four necessary conditions that must be satisfied before a process can be said to be controlled. These *elements of control* are:

(i) an objective for the system being controlled;
(ii) a means of measuring results along the dimensions specified by the objective in (i);
(iii) a predictive model of the system being controlled;
(iv) a choice of relevant alternative actions available to the controller.

A control system containing these elements is shown in Fig. 3.4 (after Otley and Berry, 1980).

We have already discussed the first point, and indeed arrived at a definition of an organizational goal. The second point is important. It shows that organizational control can only exist when we know what the outcome or result of actions taken is. Without feedback information about actual performance, informed suggestions for change and improvement cannot be made.

It is also useful to remember that outcomes should, as far as possible, be measurable. In non-commercial organizations these measures of output (for instance, good patient care) may be extremely difficult to obtain. This has resulted in some organizations paying attention to those outputs which are easy to quantify, but neglecting other important outputs. For example, it is relatively easy for a university to measure and count the number of students who graduate each year.

Figure 3.4

Necessary conditions for a controlled situation or process.

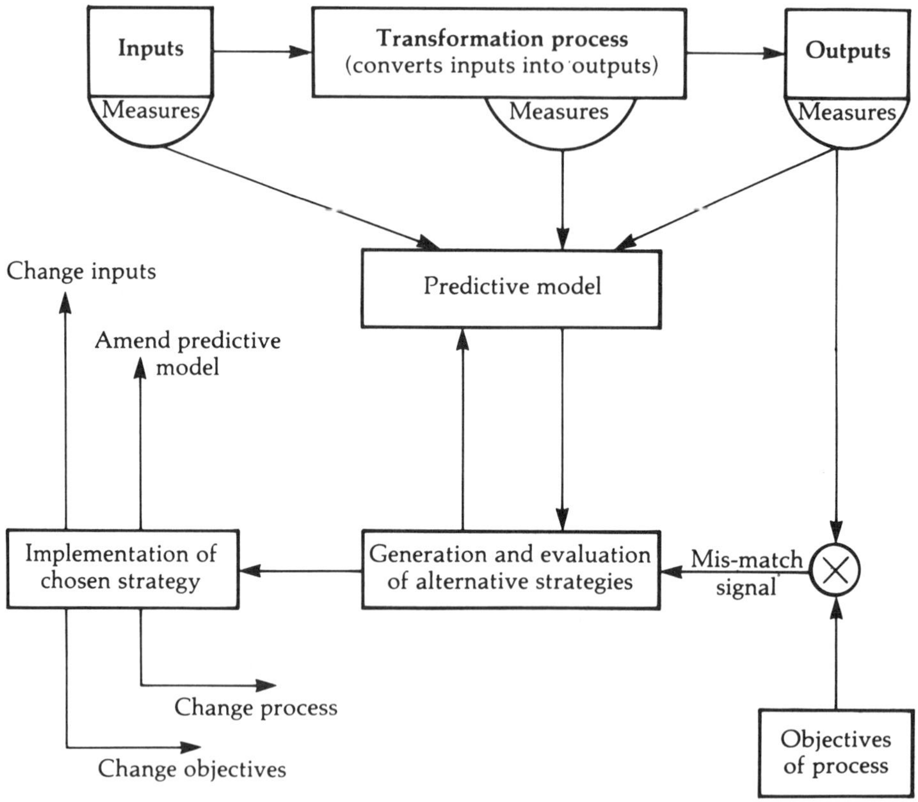

Adapted from Otley and Berry (1980).

However, if the university relies entirely on this measure of output, and does not try to develop measures of 'usefulness to the community', its claim to public sources of funds may eventually be threatened. It is therefore important that organizations develop measures for both the quantitative and qualitative aspects of their diverse outputs.

Having compared actual and desired outcomes, any mismatch should be recorded. This signal should act as a catalyst to people within the organization, to act in such a way that the organization achieves its set goals. In order that corrective action may be possible, the organization needs a predictive model of the process to be controlled. That is, it requires a means of predicting the likely outcomes of various alternative courses of action.

Let us return to our example of the ship (introduced in Chapter 2, p. 19). We know action needs to be taken to enable the ship to return to its original course, but what specific action(s) should we take? In order to answer this question we need information (a predictive model) about the effects of alternative remedies, such as turning the wheel at a certain speed and by a certain amount, increasing/decreasing the speed of the ship by a certain amount, steering into or away from wind, etc. If we lack this predictive information we will be unable to make sound decisions that will return the ship to its desired course.

Finally, the corrective action that is chosen needs to be implemented. There are four main forms of corrective action:

(i) change the inputs to the system;
(ii) change the objective;
(iii) amend the predictive model of the process to be controlled;
(iv) change the nature of the process itself.

Thus, with our ship, we may choose from the following set of alternative courses of action:

(i) change the amount of power that is driving the ship;
(ii) change the set course from due north to (given the present circumstances) some other more desirable course;
(iii) amend our knowledge of how the ship behaves under similar storm conditions;
(iv) install a more sophisticated and powerful steering mechanism which makes sailing in general safer.

Clearly, we may eventually decide to adopt all four strategies. However, some are more pertinent to the present crisis, while others are more long-term considerations. For instance, alternative (i) appears most relevant to regaining immediate control over the ship, while alternative (iv) might well take several years to accomplish.

There are a number of difficulties with applying this model of control to complex organizations. First, measures of the output of an organization may be extremely difficult to obtain. Second, in real life, because people's needs change over time, it may be difficult to obtain knowledge about these needs, and hence about the organizational goal. Despite these difficulties, this cybernetic model of control has gained widespread support among accounting researchers. This is because managerial accounting techniques appear to play a role in each of the elements of control. We shall examine each role in turn.

(b) Organizational objectives

We defined the goal of the organization as the achievement in the long-run of a feasible set of inducements and contributions. That is, each interest group which is necessary for the survival of the organization should be satisfied sufficiently to continue to provide its support and services for the collectivity as a whole.

Accounting systems play a major role in:

(i) identifying alternative feasible sets of inducements and contributions;
(ii) acting as a medium through which bargaining and negotiation among different interest groups takes place such that feasible strategies evolve;
(iii) representing the goals chosen either explicitly or by default;
(iv) stabilizing the goals chosen over time.

A management accountant is often responsible for presenting details of alternative feasible strategies. For instance, a flexible budget for a hospital may set forth feasible activity levels at 10,000, 20,000 and 30,000 patients. It should also detail the amount of inputs required (for example, the number of nursing, medical, auxiliary and administrative staff, number of beds, size of hospital, etc.) to service each of these activity levels.

The budgeting process also acts as a means of bargaining among different interest groups. For instance, the medical staff may argue that they require more sophisticated equipment than is budgeted for, and the nursing department may similarly ask for more staff. Through such negotiation about budget allocations a particular feasible set of inducements and contributions may be chosen. In addition, accounting information may be used to bargain for rewards such as higher pay. Trade unions now often use accounting information on an enterprise's profitability to define its 'ability to pay', and its feasible range of activities.

Budgetary targets and manufacturing standards help to represent the goals and feasible strategies that are operative within an organization. They indicate the expectations of people as regards inputs and outputs.

Finally, managerial accounting information, like budgets, helps to stabilize objectives and goals, especially in organizations which have outputs that are hard to measure (for example, in government departments and agencies). Because detailed knowledge of outputs and of the input–output relationship is difficult to obtain, some organizations only make small incremental changes to the previous year's budget allocations. Altering these budgets in a substantial manner may be too risky, as decision-makers cannot predict the effects of such changes. Thus, for instance, in schools, universities and county councils, budget targets for the present year may only represent 'an across-the-board increase of 10%' over last year's budget. In this manner, accounting information tends to stabilize the goal-formation process. This stabilization effect, however, may lead to an unrealistic conservatism, such that the organization is unable to meet new challenges and changes. The decision-makers and management accountants must carefully monitor the situation, to ensure that rigidity and inflexibility does not result.

(c) Predictive models

The major purpose of the predictive model is to permit answers to questions of the form: if a certain course of action is taken, what consequences will follow; in particular, how will the achievement of the organization's objectives be affected?

As Otley and Berry (1980) point out, two features of predictive models are of particular importance:

(i) The available models are usually imprecise and inaccurate, so that predictions made from them are likely to be inaccurate and to result in unintended consequences.
(ii) Within organizations, there are usually multiple and partly conflicting predictive models. There may be different models of the demand for labour in the marketing and production departments. These diverse models result because:
   – uncertainty leads to the generation of small, partial models; and
   – individuals with particular training and experiences tend to apply their own models and insights.

These features lead to the following implications for managerial accounting control systems:

(i) An accounting model of the organization is only partial, and therefore insufficient to map all the organization's diverse activities. However, it is an important model because it emphasizes the economic and monetary consequences of particular strategies.
(ii) Because it is partial, there may be room for improvement. For instance, management accountants have traditionally been concerned with financial information. It could be that certain forms of non-financial information could be provided by the accountant – for instance, information on product quality, customer service, labour productivity (see Kaplan, 1984).

   In addition, management accountants may provide information to a wider group of users. Traditionally, they have supplied information to management. With the rise of industrial democracy and employee reporting, however, management accountants may need to service the information needs of workers and the government in a more substantial way.

(d) Measures

Two distinctive sets of variables require measurement:

(i) the outcomes of action taken (feedback information); and
(ii) predicted inputs and outputs (feedforward information).

Traditionally, accountants have focused on feedback information on outcomes. Thus, they measure outcome variables such as profitability, sales growth and production/activity level. In addition, although there is a tendency to emphasize the outcomes presumed to be desired by shareholders, management accountants also partly measure the outputs desired by other groups. For instance, there are some attempts to measure price for customers and wages for employees. Further, feedback information is also provided when the managerial accounting system provides information on the difference between actual and expected outcomes.

However, management accountants have not been as successful in the provision of feedforward information on inputs and outputs. This is partly because it is difficult to predict the future and to predict how an organization might interact with its external environment. Despite this, it appears that monitoring the environment will become more necessary as organizations interact to a greater degree with other organizations and government regulatory agencies. Think of the number of external interest groups that could be interested in the activities of British Coal. This would include not only the Prime Minister, Government Ministers, the Monopolies and Mergers Commission, but also the CEGB, BSC, the NUM, BBC, ITN, newspaper corporations and the public generally!

Finally, as pointed out above, organizations should not only measure those outputs that are easy to quantify. Attempts should be made to measure *all* outputs which have a major impact on the organization.

(e) Choice of strategies

As discussed above, there are four major strategies open to an organization to ensure that its goals will be achieved. These are a change of inputs, a change in objectives, an amendment of the predictive model, and a change to the system itself.

These four change strategies may be applied through the managerial accounting system. For instance, a change in inputs and outputs desired could be reflected in changes to the budget and to manufacturing standards. Similarly, the effects of alternative courses of action, such as different activity levels, could be represented through the budget. And, finally, the entire accounting model of the organization (its inputs, outputs and input–output relationship) could be altered.

3.4 A contingency approach to control

There are two broad types of contingency approach to managerial accounting:

(i) organization theory contingency formulations; and
(ii) cybernetic contingency formulations.

Type (i) tends to draw from a base discipline that is loosely defined as organization theory, while type (ii) draws from the field of cybernetics. Because the base disciplines are different, the emphases of the research also vary.

Despite these differences, contingency approaches are built on two fundamental and therefore common premises. These are that:

(i) There is no universally appropriate managerial accounting system that applies equally to all organizations in all circumstances.
(ii) The choice of a particular accounting system will depend on an appropriate match between the features of an accounting system and the circumstances under which it is to operate.

In short, contingency approaches to the design of managerial accounting systems hold that there is no universally 'best' design that is suitable for all circumstances. The 'best' design depends on the situation at hand – it is contingent upon a number of factors (hence the name contingency theory). We shall now focus our attention on the organization theory approach.

(a) Organization theory contingency formulations

These studies form the bulk of contingency research in managerial accounting. As Otley (1980) points out, this research is a recent vogue. Although contingency theory was developed in the organization theory literature in the early to

Figure 3.5

A representation of the contingency argument in managerial accounting.

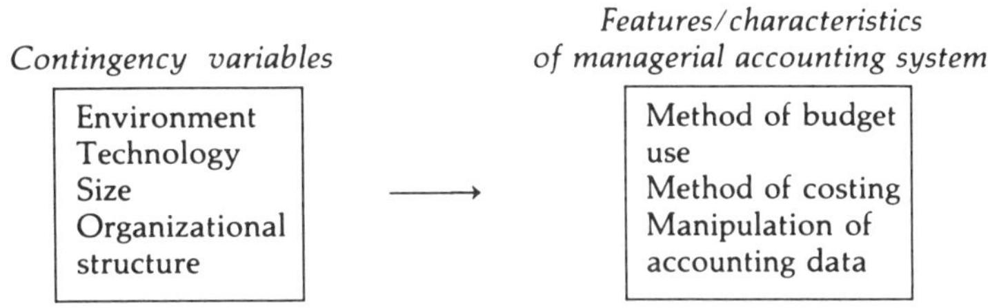

mid-1960s, there was no reference to contingency theory in the accounting literature before the 1970s. However, during the late 1970s and the 1980s, it came to dominate the behavioural and organizational research in managerial accounting (see Hayes, 1977; Spicer and Ballew, 1983; Govindarajan, 1984; Jones, 1985).

Usually, contingency research of this type is set up to analyse the relationship identified in Fig. 3.5. Some factor (or contingency variable) is hypothesized to affect the design of a managerial accounting system. Examples of these factors might be the type of productive technology employed by the organization, the nature of the environment, size, or organizational structure of the organization. These factors are often labelled the *independent variables* in the analysis, while the features of the managerial accounting system are the *dependent variables*. And the research typically seeks to explicate the precise influence which the independent variables have on the dependent variables. We shall look at the research on three of the major independent variables.

(i) The effect of technology on systems design

Technology means the way in which an organization organizes its production process. For instance, we may have mass production, where thousands of units of an identical product are produced on an assembly line, or we may have unit or job production, where a single, unique product is produced. Examples of goods produced on a mass production basis are motor cars, canned vegetables, beer, soap powder, refrigerators and many other household items. Unit production tends to be used in the production of individualized items such as paintings, sculpture, luxury boats, specialized equipment and made-to-order furniture. It is a production process where similar but not identical items may be produced, and much attention is paid to the specifications of the customer. Hence the term 'job lot' is often used to describe a particular unit of production. Batch production lies between the extremes of mass and unit production. It is a process whereby identical items are produced in one batch or production run. Different batches may be processed, each with minor changes. Usually, however, organizations only have a limited number of different batches with standardized variations. For instance, a printing company may print black and white pictures in one batch run, and colour pictures in a different batch run. Alternatively, it may process material that is in block print in one batch and fancy print in another batch.

Technology was argued by Woodward (1965) to have a significant impact on costing practices. It was found that in organizations that had a job order or unit production technology, it was much easier to identify the costs of producing a particular job. There was, therefore, no need to average costs over a large mix of products. However, in mass production technology, it is very difficult to know precisely how much labour time is 'contained' in the can of peas that rolls off the production line. The costs of production, in those circumstances, are usually averaged over many units of the product. As a result of this averaging process, the level of detail and accuracy that is possible in costing unit production cannot be replicated in mass process production.

Thus, production technology is argued to have an important effect on the type of managerial accounting information that can be provided.

(ii) The effect of the environment on systems design

Environmental factors have also been invoked to explain differences in the use made of accounting information. The concept of the environment, however, has not been easy to operationalize and measure in real life. Researchers have sought to distinguish between environments that are complex/simple, dynamic/static, hostile/liberal, competitive/non-competitive, uncertain/certain, heterogeneous/homogeneous, etc. As can be seen, it is not easy to characterize an environment. To add to this difficulty, researchers in different studies tend to use different constructs, and this restricts the degree of comparability among contingency studies.

However, despite this theoretical problem, some empirical results have been obtained. Khandwalla (1972), for instance, examined the effects that the type of competition faced by the organization had on the use of management controls. He concluded that the higher the level of competition faced, the greater was the sophistication of managerial accounting controls used. Moreover, different types of competition (for example, price, marketing or product competition) had very different influences on the use made of accounting controls in manufacturing organizations.

A similar conclusion was arrived at by Otley (1978) who investigated the effect of differences in the environments faced by managers within a single organization. Otley classified environments into tough operating environments, where it was difficult for the departmental manager involved to show accounting profits, and liberal operating environments, where it was relatively easy to achieve profitability. He concluded that senior managers used budgetary information to evaluate managerial performance in very different ways in those two situations.

In general, the research results demonstrate that the type of environment faced by an organization or an individual manager substantially influences the type of managerial accounting system that is most appropriate.

(iii) The effect of organizational structure on systems design

Organizational structure refers to the manner in which tasks and responsibilities are allocated within an organization. A centralized organization, for instance, is one in which all decisions are made by senior management and there is little scope for managers lower down the hierarchy to participate in decision-making. A decentralized organization, by contrast, is one which has been divided into several sections or divisions, and decision-making is delegated down to these divisional managers. An organization may also be classified on a structured–unstructured continuum. A structured organization is one where most of its activities have been formalized into routine, standard operating procedures, whereas an unstructured organization is not so well-regulated. For instance, a structured organization may have a series of operating manuals detailing the duties of staff, the rules governing the taking of sick leave, maternity leave and recreation leave, and the procedures for operating various items of equipment.

In their 1975 study Bruns and Waterhouse argued that a manager's behaviour and use of the budget depends on the organizational structure. They suggest that managers in highly structured organizations tend to perceive themselves as having more influence, they participate more in the budgeting process, and they appear to be satisfied with budget-related activities. However, managers in organizations where authority is centralized are generally held accountable for fewer financial outcomes, they experience stress, and they may feel that budgets are restrictive and unhelpful.

This result appears to be consonant with the results of another study conducted by Hopwood (1972), who distinguished between a budget-constrained and profit-conscious style of using the budget. In a budget-constrained style, meeting the budget was the single most important factor in a superior's evaluation of his/her subordinates. However, in a profit-conscious style, meeting the budget was viewed in terms of its effects on the organization's long-run effectiveness. His study indicated that a rigid, budget-constrained style was associated with high degrees of job-related tension, poor relationships with peers and subordinates, and the manipulation of accounting data. By comparison, the profit-conscious style has no such associations. Hopwood therefore concluded that a more flexible style of budget use was likely to lead to more effective organizational performance. (See Chapter 10 below also, pp. 352–4.)

However, Hopwood's results were not replicated by other researchers. As a consequence, researchers have begun to look for other variables that might play a role in affecting the style of budget use.

(iv) Limitations of the contingency theory of systems design

As can be seen, considerable research has been conducted using a contingency approach to the design of managerial accounting systems. The argument has been: an effective accounting system, that is, one that achieves organizational control, must be designed to match or fit the particular characteristics of the organization and its environment. However, this research needs to be viewed with some caution, for it has a number of weaknesses. These are:

- The nature of contingency variables has not been well researched. Different authors tend to use different constructs, for example, to characterize the environment, and there is little consistency in their use.
- Many of the empirical studies have not been replicated. Where replications have been carried out, they do not support earlier research findings. This indicates that further theoretical and empirical research is required.
- The relationship between the contingency variables, the design of managerial accounting systems, and overall organizational control (effectiveness) is neglected by most contingency researchers. Studies concentrate on notions such as employee satisfaction, motivation, stress levels or attitudes towards superiors as dependent variables. While these outcomes are important, they

need not be coincident with organizational effectiveness and control. For example, a satisfied workforce may in fact be a very ineffective workforce. Employees may be satisfied because they are being paid high wages. However, the organization may not be able to afford these high wages, and it could quickly experience financial difficulties. In that case, a satisfied workforce would not indicate organizational control. By focusing on a dependent variable like job satisfaction, researchers are still unable to predict whether organizational control is being achieved.

– Managerial accounting systems have been studied in isolation. However, in order to achieve organizational control, the activities of the accounting system must be coordinated with the activities of other control systems, such as personnel selection and staff development. These linkages to other control systems have not been studied by contingency researchers.

These weaknesses do not mean that the contingency framework is completely useless to management accountants. On the contrary, contingency theory appeals intuitively and is in accordance with practical wisdom. However, much more research is required before we can conveniently use the research findings to design managerial accounting systems.

(b) Hofstede's approach to control

As we saw in Section 3.3, the cybernetic model of control developed by Tocher does help to illustrate the role played by managerial accounting systems in facilitating organizational control. It has also helped to generate contingency research based on cybernetic ideas of control. A contingency argument basically says that particular situations are more appropriately matched with certain types of control. One valuable contingency approach to control is that of Hofstede.

Hofstede (1981) identified six types of control, ranging from routine control to political control. Hofstede does not use the terms 'feedforward' and 'feedback control' because he has divided up his 'control map' using different dimensions. (His six types of control may be reclassified into feedback and feedforward control. However, it is best not to attempt to do this as this may confuse you. Simply think of Hofstede's six main types of control as additional types of control. That is, there is feedforward control, feedback control and Hofstede's six control types.)

Hofstede begins his argument by stating that organizational control is easiest in situations where:

(i) objectives are unambiguous;
(ii) outputs are measurable;
(iii) the effects of interventions are known; and
(iv) the activity is repetitive.

It is apparent that conditions (i)–(iii) are essentially identical to the first three of Tocher's elements of control discussed above (objectives, measurable outputs and a predictive model of the input-output relationship).

Hofstede then argues that when one or more of the criteria identified is not met, the situation becomes more complicated and different forms of control are needed, depending on which of the four criteria is not met. Figure 3.6 shows how he develops a classification of controls which are deemed most appropriate to a

Figure 3.6

A contingency classification of controls.

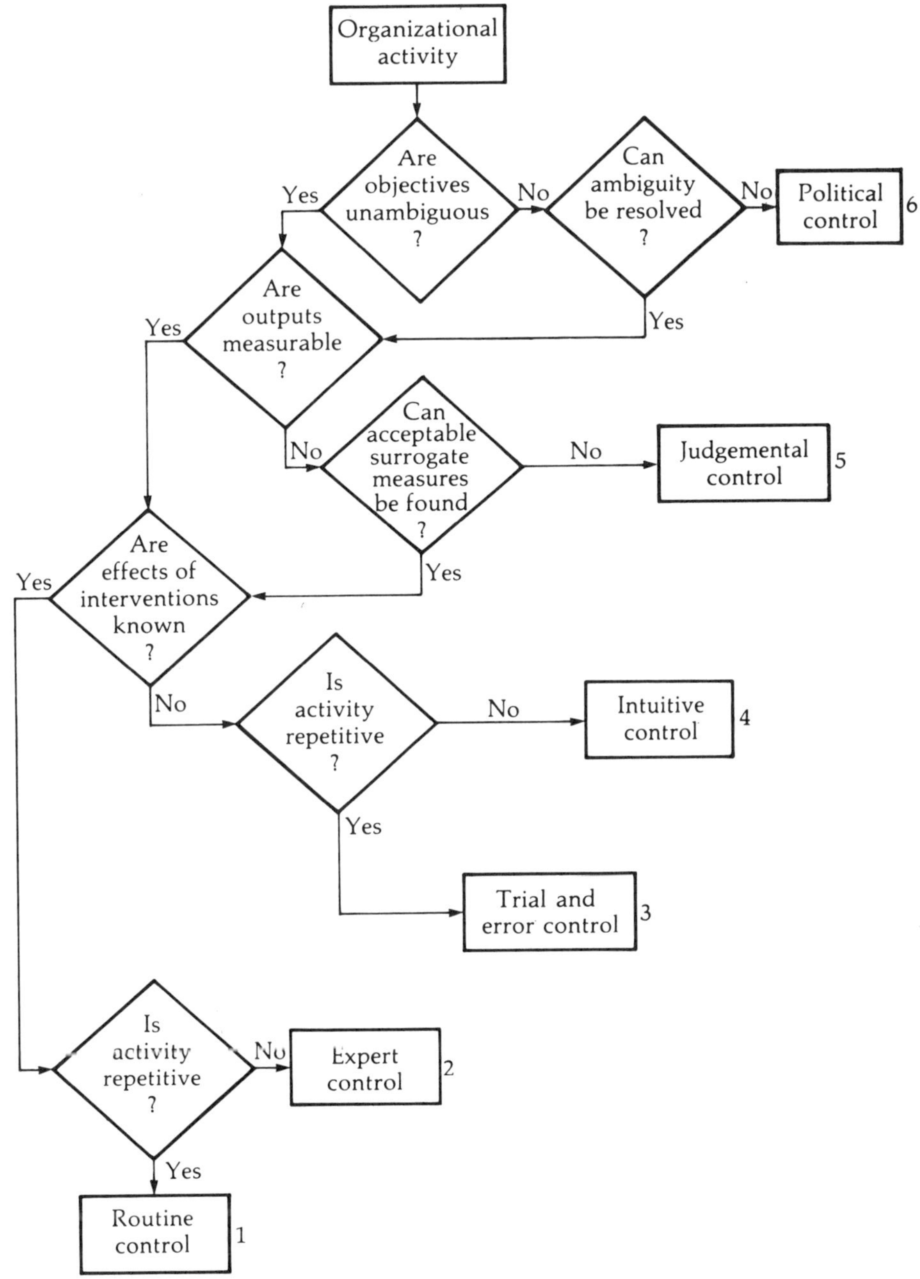

Source: Hofstede (1981), p. 196.

particular situation. Note the difference between 'controls' and 'control'. Controls are the means and processes by which a situation or process is controlled and regulated.

There are six main forms of control, and these are matched' with particular circumstances. The six forms of control are:

(i) *Routine control*. This type of control is only possible when all four conditions set by Hofstede are met. That is, there are clear objectives, measurable outputs, known effects of interventions, and the activity is repetitive. Our example of the ship may be an example of this form of control. Other activities such as filling up one's petrol tank or typing a letter are also amenable to routine control.

(ii) *Expert control*. If objectives are clear, outputs are measurable, the effects of interventions are known but the activity is not repetitive, it makes sense to entrust the control of the situation to an external expert. For instance, a firm of accountants may only deal with audit, tax and accounting work. However, suppose one of its largest audit clients now approaches the firm with a management consultancy problem. Rather than turning the client away, the firm of accountants may find it profitable to hire an external management consultant to advise the client.

(iii) *Trial-and-error control*. This is most appropriate in situations where objectives are clear, outputs are measurable, the activity is repetitive, but the effects of interventions are not known. Effectively, this means the organization lacks a good predictive model of the situation to be controlled. Control in these circumstances can only be through trial and error. Rigid rules and prescriptions for action will not be very helpful to the organization and its decision-makers. However, they must ensure that all successes and failures are thoroughly analysed *ex post* so that more knowledge can be gained about the predictive model. Trial-and-error control is appropriate when organizations are introducing new products and services and this is an activity that will be repeated by the organization.

(iv) *Intuitive control*. When objectives are clear, outputs are measurable but the activity is not repetitive and the effects of interventions are not known, intuitive control is more appropriate. By intuitive control, Hofstede means that the control process is more an art than a science. That is, there are few fixed and definite rules to guide the manager or decision-maker, who has to act and respond intuitively.

Hofstede gives an example of reviving a demoralized football team. The objective of the team is clear – to gain promotion to a higher division. The output is also measurable – in terms of games won, goals scored and the relative position of the team in the division. However, there are few standard operating rules that will teach a football manager precisely how to inject greater enthusiasm and commitment within the team.

(v) *Judgemental control*. This is most applicable when objectives are clear but the outputs are not easily measurable, the activity is not repetitive and the effects of intervention are unknown. When these circumstances prevail, decision-makers within the organization need to make subjective judgements about the effects of interventions and the outputs produced. Vickers (1965) referred to such judgements as 'reality judgements'. As can be seen, judgemental control depends on the knowledge of the decision-makers.

This type of control may be relevant to some activities within non-commercial organizations, like government agencies, schools, universities and hospitals. For instance, an objective of a hospital may be unanimously agreed to be the provision of good quality patient care. However, it is extremely difficult to measure this output. Hence managers in such organizations often have to make judgements about the outputs produced. They may also rely on surrogate measures of outputs, such as the number of patients serviced, the mortality rate compared to other hospitals, the amount of research that is internationally recognized, etc. Unfortunately, these surrogate measures may not capture the essence of 'quality care', and are of limited usefulness at best. Subjective judgements about the inputs required, outputs produced and the effects of interventions will continue to play the major role in such organizations.

It should also be noted that there might be more than one judge within an organization. The power structure of the organization could be one where a powerful coalition of judges exists. Alternatively, power could be so diffused that no single authoritative judge prevails, and control, if it happens at all, is purely by accident.

(vi) *Political control*. This is applicable in situations where objectives are unclear, outputs are difficult to measure, there is a lack of knowledge about interventions, and the activity is not repetitive.

Objectives may be unclear for a number of reasons. (For example, there could be conflicts of interest among different interest groups such that it is not possible to define a common organizational goal, or severe environmental uncertainty may prevent a clear specification of objectives.)

Political control relies on the use of power structures, negotiation processes, the manipulation of scarce resources and organizational symbols and rituals in order to manage conflicts in values and goals. There are a number of political processes that may be used:

- a hierarchy of legitimate authority;
- the formalization of activities through 'impersonal' rules and standard operating procedures;
- the encouragement and/or establishment of negotiation channels among conflicting interest groups;
- the hiring of outside management consultants and experts;
- 'management by crisis', that is, allowing a crisis situation to develop, and then attempting to control the situation.

Hofstede's contingent classification of forms of control is useful because of the following:

(i) It emphasizes that there is a range of control alternatives that are more or less appropriate, depending on the problem situation. This is helpful because traditional managerial accounting systems have operated with only a limited form of control - routine, trial-and-error, and expert control. Budgeting systems, for instance, assume that it is possible to set clear objectives (budget targets), to measure output and compare performance against budget, to take corrective action if deviations occur, and the activity is reasonably repetitive.

However, such assumptions are not often met with in complex organizations. Although a budget target may exist on paper, it is still capable of being manipulated and interpreted in different ways. In addition, even if all four of Hofstede's situational criteria are met and routine control is appropriate, the act of controlling will involve communicating with diverse people. And as soon as people are part of the control process, the effects of interventions are no longer completely known. People may manipulate accounting data and the measurements of inputs and outputs; they may act and intervene for no clear reason; or they may make planned interventions that have unintended consequences.

(ii) It allows greater attention to be paid to the interactions of people in controlling organizations. Unlike contingency formulations that are based on organization theory, it avoids talking about managerial accounting control systems and organizations in abstract categories like 'sophisticated systems' or 'bureaucratic structures'. With the notions of intuitive, judgemental and political control, we are able to delve more deeply into the social processes that surround managerial accounting systems. Remember from Chapter 2 that we illustrated how individual, organizational and societal processes can influence the operation of managerial accounting systems.

3.5 An interim summary

Thus far we have established that:

(i) Managerial accounting systems have a role to play in achieving organizational control by helping to define objectives and feasible regions of activity, measure outputs, and identify the effects of alternative organizational strategies.

(ii) Control through the use of managerial accounting systems is easiest to achieve when objectives are clear, outputs are relatively easy to measure, the effects of interventions are known, and the activity to be controlled is repetitive.

(iii) Traditional managerial accounting systems are less helpful in problem situations which have unclear and conflicting objectives, outputs that are difficult to measure, a poorly-defined predictive model, and the activity to be controlled is non-repetitive. However, these characteristics appear to be commonplace among formal, complex organizations (such as Lansing, Roadline, or the University Funding Council).

(iv) There is a need for management accountants to be aware of other forms of control, such as intuitive, judgemental and political control, three forms of control requiring a deeper understanding of individuals and of people in interaction. This requires a more extensive knowledge of how people make sense of accounting information, a matter which we have already discussed in detail in Chapter 2, and also requires a knowledge of how people make decisions and solve problems in organizations. This leads us into Section 3.6.

3.6 A problem-solving framework

Up till now we have talked about control in rather abstract terms. In everyday practice, control is achieved through making decisions and solving problems. In some writers' eyes, decision-making and management are really the same thing. 'In treating decision-making as synonymous with managing, I shall be referring not merely to the final act of choice among alternatives, but rather to the whole process of decision' (Simon (1960), p. 1). This process is rendered problematic because of the existence of risk and uncertainty, in the face of which some managers postpone making a choice among alternative actions, for fear of that choice being wrong. However, they are actually then making another choice, in that they are deciding *not to decide* (Barnard (1956), p. 193), and this is not a means of eliminating risk, since it seeks to ignore the problem situation rather than resolve it. An example might be found in a company having products that are in decline, and a choice has to be made among several new products in order to improve future prospects. As usual, uncertainty will make the choice difficult, and the significance of the choice may cause management to put off making a decision until it is too late and the sales of existing products have fallen to such a low level that the company is forced out of business.

A central question in management, then, given that at every point someone must make one or more decisions, is how should decisions be made? (See Welsch and Cyert (1971).) This book is particularly concerned with this question, which presents itself to us as a problem requiring a solution in the same way that decision situations are really in the form of problems, each requiring a solution. So let us proceed by considering how we might approach problem-solving in general, and

Figure 3.7

A problem-solving framework.

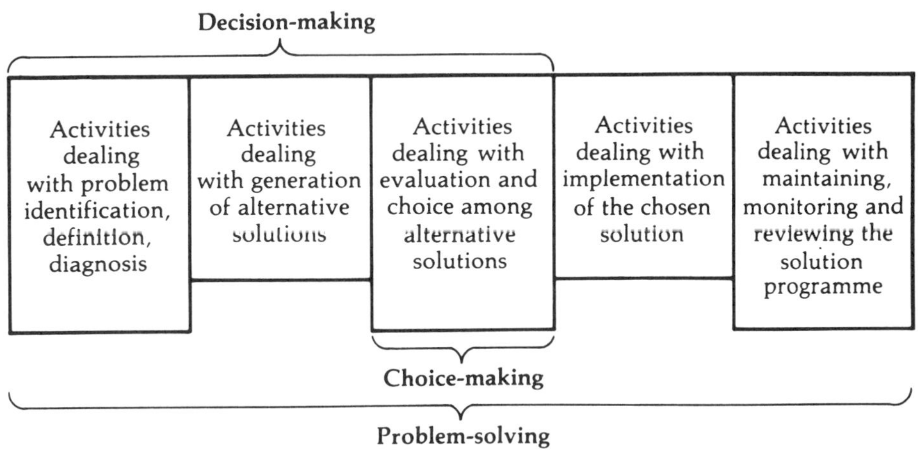

Source: Huber (1980), p. 8.

then narrow this down to cover business decision-making as a particular class of problem.

Figure 3.7 gives a view of the problem-solving framework facing managers. There are three processes contained with this framework: choice-making, decision-making, problem-solving. We can discuss them by means of the following steps, bearing in mind that Step 4 deals with choice-making, Steps 1–4 with decision-making, and Steps 1–6 with problem-solving.

Step 1

The first step is the recognition that a problem exists (in the form of, for instance, a decision that must be taken or an opportunity that may be seized). In articulating the existence of the problem it is necessary to consider the purpose that is to be served by its solution: in other words, what is the objective of the exercise? If more than one objective is present in a particular problem context it may be necessary to make a trade-off (i.e. balance one objective against another by assigning priorities to each, as when a slower rate of market penetration is traded off against higher product quality in order to ensure repeat-buying behaviour patterns for the future on the part of consumers). By specifying clearly at the outset the nature of the problem and the purpose its solution is to serve, the problem-solver is able to concentrate his attention on this matter in an efficient way. It is important to realize, however, that problems need to be perceived: they do not always present themselves in an obvious manner.

Step 2

Having formulated the problem, the next step is to formulate alternative solutions to it. Under conditions of uncertainty (which essentially means in the absence of accurate information) this raises another decision problem: how should a search for alternative courses of action be carried out? We return to this problem later, but at this point we should recognize that the identification of alternatives requires an input of resources as an intermediate step in solving the initial problem.

Step 3

Once enumerated, the competing alternatives have to be evaluated, since it is likely that only one can be adopted. This restriction may be due to the solutions being *mutually exclusive* (in which case they are all attempting to do the same thing, and to adopt more than one would be absurd), or being subject to a rationing mechanism whereby, for example, projects requiring collectively up to £1,000,000 of capital investment in a given period may be adopted, beyond which this amount sets a limit. Evaluation requires a yardstick by which the relative performance of alternatives in relation to the achievement of purpose can be measured, which in turn requires estimates of the probable consequences of each alternative identified in Step 2. Consequences will include the cost, revenue and profit outcomes, both present and future, of the alternatives in the light of anticipated changes either within the organization itself or within its environment. In other words, due allowance must be made for risk and uncertainty in predicting levels of performance.

Step 4

The choice of the best course of action comes next, with 'best' referring to that alternative most likely to lead to the attainment of purpose (i.e. to achieve the objective). If the aim is to select that channel of distribution which leads to the largest contribution to profit, then the channel having the largest expected value for profit (having taken into consideration the volume throughput and the discount structure) will be the preferred alternative. (Expected value is explained in Chapter 5.)

Step 5

After making the choice it is necessary to execute it, so the fifth step is the implementation of the preferred course of action.

Step 6

The story does not end at Step 5, because the problem-solver cannot be sure at that point that his 'solution' will actually solve the problem isolated in Step 1. Thus he must evaluate the outcome of Step 5 and make any revisions that are required in order that a satisfactory solution can be achieved. For this step to be performed the problem-solver requires control information and should approach his task with a non-rigid attitude. Adaptability is vital in situations exhibiting change and

Figure 3.8

Anticipated and unanticipated consequences.

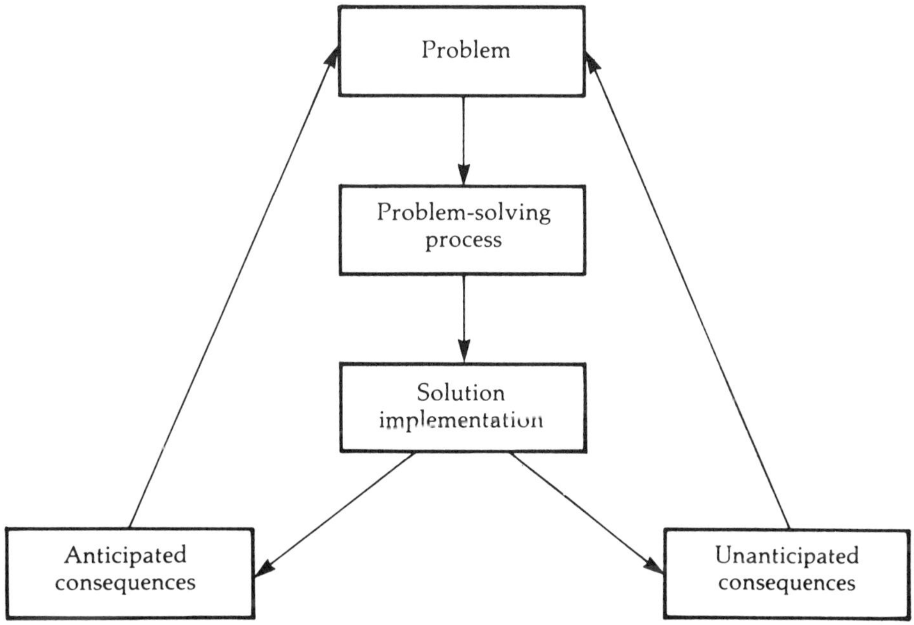

Adapted from Watson (1975).

uncertainty, in order to prevent false assumptions or inaccurate estimates from leading to unsatisfactory outcomes.

It is quite likely that any decision of significance will produce two types of consequences: anticipated and unanticipated. These are shown in Fig. 3.8 (which also seeks to highlight the iterative nature of organizational problem-solving). Unanticipated consequences arise due to:

(i) our imperfect knowledge of cause-and-effect concerning organizational processes;
(ii) our limited ability to predict accurately even the things we understand, which suggests that we cannot (other than by pure chance) generate reliable predictions of factors we do not understand – and even less, of factors we have not taken into account in the first place.

As a result of (i) and (ii) we will find that unanticipated consequences arise from the implementation of most decisions. In addition, of course, we must recognize the possibility that anticipated consequences either do not occur, or occur but at a rate/level other than that expected (which also reflects our limited predictive ability).

Let us now attempt to bring this overview of problem-solving into focus in a managerial context. The essential functions of management can be covered in a simple flow chart, such as Fig. 3.9. The functions of Fig. 3.9 are rather broad, and many writers have elaborated on these elemental parts by the inclusion of organizing, staffing, directing, innovating, representing and communicating. (See, for example, Dale and Michelon (1969), pp. 12–21, which follows a classical organization theory approach.) However, planning subsumes such activities as innovation, and the implementation of plans (i.e. the 'action' phase of Fig. 3.9) leads to

Figure 3.9

Managerial functions

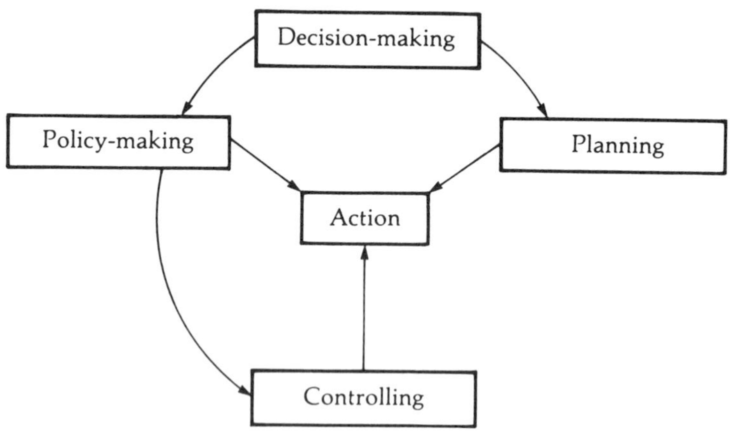

Source: Starr (1971).

a pattern of resource utilization that is represented in the design of the organization, its staffing and its leadership, while control requires effective communication, and so forth. Perhaps the major features of the management process can be more usefully elaborated as in Fig. 3.10.

Initially the objectives of the organization must be determined. These represent not only the *raison d'être* of the organization, but also provide a benchmark against which organizational performance and efficiency can be assessed. The attainment of the objectives is facilitated by means of plans, which are essentially composed of a series of projects. At any point in time some projects will be commencing, some continuing, and some terminating. In fact, a business organization can usefully be viewed as a bundle of projects, which is more helpful in management control terms then viewing it as a mechanistic, functional structure (as portrayed via, say, an organizational chart).

Each project's resource requirements need to be specified, and approval sought to carry out the activities of Stages 2 and 3 through the use of resources determined at Stage 4 (see Fig. 3.10). Stages 1–5 constitute the decision-making phases of planning and policy-making, and these are followed (Stage 6) by implementation of the decisions that have been made.

Hand in hand with implementation go the evaluation and control phases of the cycle. Actual performance, initially measured at the level of each individual project but subsequently consolidated to ascertain progress towards the attainment of plans and hence objectives (Stages 7–9), needs to be monitored and revisions made to the plans and the allocation of resources to reflect any changed circumstances either within the organization or within its environment. This revision is made possible by feedback loops linking the 'planning' and 'control' phases of the cycle, but the cycle itself – on a longer time-scale – is ongoing, and thus gives scope for objectives and their means of attainment to be reviewed and amended on a continuous basis.

Figure 3.10

The cycle of control in problem-solving.

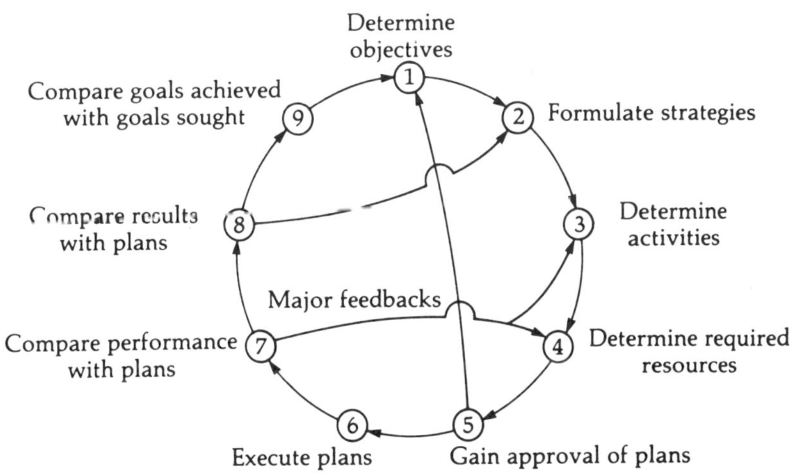

Up to now the impression may have been conveyed that a knowledge of what is to be achieved, along with information derived from a rational decision-making process, are sufficient to produce good decisions. It is certain that these ingredients are necessary to good decisions, yet in themselves they are not sufficient. The missing ingredient is found in the following scheme: judgement.

Fact	=	Event
Data	=	Observed interpreted fact
Information	=	Data + Analysis + Purpose
Decision	=	Information + Judgement
Knowledge	=	Information + Users

The type of judgement that is intended here is not that which stems purely from 'experience', but rather that which reflects value systems (see Vickers, 1968; 1972). Rationality implies objectivity, and thus excludes the subjective reasoning that follows from the values that each decision-maker holds. The nature of personal values (such as one's willingness or otherwise to be involved in marketing cigarettes in full knowledge of the detrimental effect on health of smoking, or the view one has of profit, or of capitalism, or of the use of sexual advertising themes in promoting 'sexless' products) is not well understood, and the choice of personal values is not open to rational analysis. Nevertheless, the values of all organizational members will be inherent in the choice of organizational objectives.

The culture of the society in which we live determines the norms for acceptable behaviour and hence for acceptable objectives. Differences amongst cultures (such as British versus Japanese) will obviously lead to different value systems and different norms of behaviour. However, even within a national culture there are subcultures which result in different value systems developing in government, business, the armed forces and so forth, which can be seen in the very different behaviour patterns of participants in each subculture (see Weinshall, 1977).

Once it is recognized that values play such a prominent — and largely unpredictable — role in managerial behaviour it may discourage some individuals and cause them to dismiss rational analysis as being inadequate in effective decision-making. In the sense that decisions are not made entirely on the basis of rationality, this may seem reasonable, but if we can apply rational analysis to a substantial element in each managerial decision it seems overly pessimistic to assume that this will not be helpful. If alternative courses of action can be analyzed and presented in rational, relatively neutral terms to the decision-maker, it will help him to make his choice even though this itself will be biased in accordance with his personal set of values.

The question of personal values to an individual (or perhaps to a cohesive group) can be extended to the question of ethics (or moral values) to a society. Decision-making behaviour will certainly be influenced to some degree by the ethics of the prevailing social system, although defining ethical objectives becomes fraught with difficulties when society is divided in its views (such as the divergence between the perceived importance in Britain of regenerating economic growth in the private sector, which requires innovative freedom, and the regulation of private enterprise, which discourages such regeneration. Similarly, there is conflict between the 'morality' of the environmentalists and the 'morality' of economic growth). This topic should be kept in mind through the following pages since it constitutes a constraint that may be more restrictive than statutory limitations.

As the discussion above has sought to demonstrate, there is a 'greyness' surrounding problem-solving and decision-making that management accountants must recognize. There can be no perfect answers and no perfect managerial accounting systems: at best the role of managerial accounting is *partial*. This partiality is reflected in the following ways:

(i) *All* accounting is partial in that it typically focuses on issues that can be expressed in financial terms. This excludes such critical elements as managerial competence, employee morale and an enterprise's reputation in the market place.
(ii) Much of the information on which decisions might be based is non-financial (such as that relating to market share, productive capacity expressed in terms of machine-hours, and the speed with which customers' orders can be fulfilled). It follows from this that the accounting system of an enterprise has no monopoly over the information that is available to management.
(iii) Management accountants themselves are partial, in that their training conditions them to view the world in particular ways.

The points listed above suggest that any advocate of managerial accounting must have a degree of humility: financial considerations are not everything. But a lack of financial awareness on the part of the manager can easily lead to undesirable consequences that might threaten the continued existence of the organization, so one cannot ignore financial considerations.

3.7 The time dimension

In considering the role of managerial accounting in relation to problem-solving in order to improve organizational control, which time dimension is most helpful?

The time dimension that is of major relevance in any planning exercise must be the future, rather than the present or the past. There is nothing about an organization that is more important than its future, and the spirit of this was aptly summarized by C.F. Kettering when he said: 'I am interested in the future because that is where I intend to live.'

The past may help us in deciding how to proceed in the future, but there is no way in which we can influence the past, so there is a limit to the amount of effort that should be applied to it as opposed to planning for the future. This is especially relevant when we consider what a constraint to innovation the past might be: in Goethe's terms we see what we know, and if we are obsessed with carrying on along unchanging routes we must expect our viability to become endangered as the environment changes but we fail to adapt to those changes.

Not everyone involved in decision-making seems to appreciate the benefits of anticipating the future, so it should not be taken for granted that it is good to plan. To some people the future may be seen as being unknown, uncertain, vague, treacherous and value-laden, whereas the past may be thought of as being certain, secure, factual and value-free (see Churchman, 1972, pp. 434–43). This would be a simplistic view to hold, because our perceptions and prejudices prevent any view from being value-free, and our understanding of the events of the past will almost certainly never be total. It is worth considering one's own view of the past in relation to one's view of the future, and presumably the conclusion will be that we must be concerned about them both, but to different extents. Taking the future, we can approach it in various ways, such as:

(i) Avoid planning, and wait and see what happens, on the assumption that the future will take care of itself. It has been suggested (Walters, 1972, p. 111) that this is the norm, which is a humbling thought.
(ii) Predict and prepare for whatever we anticipate the future might hold in such a way that we can adapt to ensure objectives are achieved.
(iii) Create change which, in effect, means we are creating the future that we would rather have. This is the most aggressive approach to the future, but those who benefit most from the future will probably be those who have helped to create it (Ackoff, 1970, p. 56; see also Gabor, 1964). The key to creating the future lies in understanding the behaviour of the system involved, since this means that one is able to *explain* its behaviour rather than merely being able to predict outcomes on the basis of past behaviour patterns. The ability to explain necessarily involves the ability to predict. In addition, and of greater importance, understanding provides the basis for redesigning the system in some fundamental way so as either to eliminate problems or significantly improve performance.

The latter two of the above views of the future favour planning, and perhaps it will help to define at this point what is meant by planning. Essentially, planning is the process of deciding in the present what to do in the future, which requires that an organization reconciles its resources with its objectives and the alternative courses of action that are open to it.

However, even in relation to planning, the future is not the only possible time dimension. Clearly time is a continuum, and we habitually divide it into broad bands (past, present, future) and into specific intervals (years, months, weeks). Every manager is accustomed to the annual accounts that the law requires limited companies to produce, and which the Inland Revenue requires other types of enterprise to submit. These accounts reflect, in a partial and stylized manner, the results of a year's activity in the recent past. As *Financial Accounting: Method and Meaning* shows, it is possible to analyse these historical documents in considerable detail in order to help tell a story about organizational performance. But the details relate to water that has passed under the bridge: one cannot change these past events, and actions that were taken to produce the results of earlier time periods cannot retrospectively be changed (unless one is in the fictional business of rewriting history). So what are the benefits of historical accounts? The basic answer to this question is simple: we can seek to learn from the past. If we are able to associate a given action in an earlier period with a particular result, we should be able to use this knowledge – however approximate it may be – to guide our future decision-making.

In order that we might learn effectively from the past we need to keep a reasonably open mind about cause-and-effect relationships, avoiding too many preconceived views. This can be illustrated by the example of business failure: to assume that businesses fail because of financial problems is usually to miss the point of what it was that actually caused those financial problems. An analysis of historical accounts might help in raising further questions – such as why costs may have increased significantly over the last year with no change in the volume of business, or how trading income failed to cover the financing requirements of re-equipping a factory – but it will not supply all the necessary answers. We cannot learn everything from the past, since the world around us is changing so rapidly; nevertheless, we can learn something about the future avoidance of past errors, and the approximate linkages between actions and results. This is important, and managerial accounting has a key role to play in helping managers to gain greater insights into the relationships between inputs and outputs.

We have seen that the range of inputs fed into any organizational system are *resources* of one kind or another (manpower, materials, machines, money, management and so forth). Managers need to focus on three phases in relation to the management of those resources:

(i) In the first instance, resources must be *acquired* – whether to facilitate the initial setting up of a business, or to allow for its continued existence. This is not purely a financial matter, although 'money' is one vital resource and we will need to analyse the extent to which trading activities generate sufficient funds for continued existence. If additional financial resources are needed in order to acquire another resource (such as new equipment), then consideration should be given to the alternative sources and terms. (See Chapters 8 and 9 in *Financial Management: Method and Meaning* for coverage of this theme.) Resource acquisition needs to be planned.

(ii) Once acquired, resources must be *allocated* to purposes that managers have determined. This requires that choices be made among alternative purposes, since resources will invariably be insufficient to allow managers to undertake every available alternative. But how – and by whom – are alternatives to be identified and evaluated? Financial criteria will have a role to play in this decision-making process – even though issues of a non-financial nature will also need to be taken into account.

(iii) Having been allocated to particular purposes, the *utilization* of resources needs to be monitored to ensure that some satisfactory balance is maintained between the actual inputs and the achieved versus desired outputs.

Phase (iii) is primarily concerned with performance measurement as a prelude to phase (ii)'s corrective action, and it is in these phases that it is helpful to know the causal links between inputs and outputs. (If these links are understood for past activities via phase (iii), this knowledge should be useful for phase (ii) which involves predictions of the future.) In assessing the performance of an organization's various activities, two key questions need to be posed:

(i) What are the links between inputs and outputs that help explain the current level of performance?

(ii) How can that performance be improved? (For instance, can more output be generated per unit of input, or can less input be used to produce the same output? Can the actual output be made to conform more closely with the desired output?)

Given the partiality of managerial accounting it is necessary to deal with performance defined in terms of cost incurrence, profit achievement, profitability or productivity levels. In the next chapter we will look at the measurement of *current* performance by looking at a methodology for associating inputs with outputs: absorption costing. This seeks to give us a base-line for raising questions that are of managerial significance for achieving organizational control.

In Chapters 5 and 6 we will deal with ways of producing answers to some of the questions that absorption costing can help in identifying.

Summary

In this chapter we have seen that talking about the role of managerial accounting information in helping people to solve problems or make decisions is similar to discussing how accounting information may be used to achieve organizational control. This is not surprising, since organizational control has to be effected through and by people. It is through people making decisions and solving problems that organizational control is achieved. Through people setting appropriate organizational goals, developing measures of output, knowing the relationship between inputs and outputs and choosing appropriate strategies from a range of possible courses of action, overall organizational control is effected. A managerial accounting information system is intended to help people carry out these activities successfully.

However, as has been pointed out in the text, whether this intention is fulfilled depends upon people's interactions, their judgements, value systems and organizational and societal norms. Accounting information may be interpreted or made sense of in particular ways to suit specific political interests. The part it plays in organizing people's effort may be quite unanticipated. There is, therefore, always an element of uncertainty in predicting the precise outworking of a managerial accounting information system. This is not to deny that organizational control may be achieved through rational forms of problem-solving and decision-making based on managerial accounting information. Rather it is to admit that in certain circumstances control may not be achieved through the rational application of managerial accounting rules.

It is important to see this relationship between problem-solving by individuals and groups and the achievement of organizational control. Problem-solving and decision-making are often divorced from notions of control, whilst discussions of cybernetic control are isolated from considerations of the cognitive process of problem-solving. By highlighting the relationship between the two it is hoped that students will have a more holistic view of how managerial accounting information is intended to achieve organizational control by aiding problem-solving and decision-making.

Key terms and concepts

Here is a list of key terms and concepts which have featured in this chapter. You should make sure that you understand and can define each one of them. Page references to definitions in the text appear in bold in the index.

- Budgeting
- Control
  - feedback
  - feedforward
  - closed-loop
  - open-loop
- Control versus controls
- Control system
- Elements of control
- Measurement
- Partiality
- Planning
- Predictive models
- Problem-solving
- Resources
  - acquisition
  - allocation
  - utilization
- Time dimension
  - past
  - present
  - future

Having now read Chapter 3 of the text you are encouraged to tackle workbook Chapter 3 (see pp. 429–33).

Further reading

For a more detailed discussion of feedback and feedforward control, see Ashby (1956) and Van Gigch (1978).

For a description of rational decision-making and the importance of values and judgement in problem-solving, see Vickers (1968; 1972) and Van Gigch (1978).

For a case-study description of the role of values in using managerial accounting information, see Boland and Pondy (1983). For a discussion of the 'symbolic' and rational use of accounting information see also Boland and Pondy (1986).

The contingency theory of managerial accounting has attracted much research and criticism. Apart from Otley (1980), see Burrell and Morgan (1979), and Clegg and Dunkerley (1980) for critiques of contingency theory.

PART 2 Feedforward control

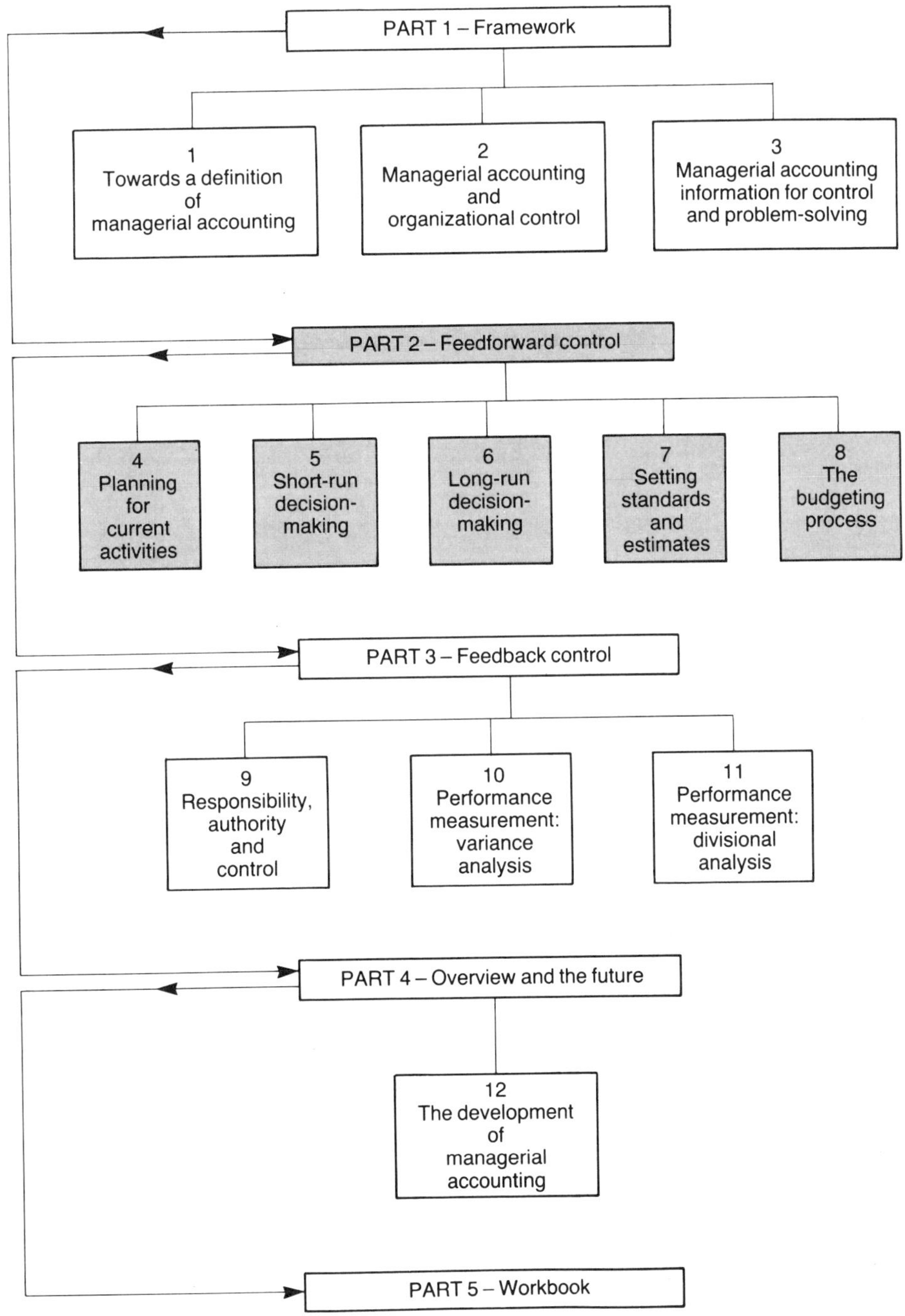

Introduction and overview

Part 2 consists of five chapters, and develops the theme of feedforward control that was introduced in Chapter 3.

The primary time orientation in feedforward control is the future, so our concern in Chapters 4–8 is to explore ways in which managerial accounting systems might be designed to help control the future. As we saw in Part 1, different interest groups will have different aspirations regarding the future (which gives scope for conflict), and our understanding of the relationships between inputs and outputs (hence between the organization and its environment, as well as among the elements within the organization) is far from fully developed. It will be apparent to you, therefore, that seeking to control the future is a tall order!

A logical starting point is to assess where one is now. This is done in Chapter 4 in order to give a base-line. From that starting point one can choose a time horizon that is short or long, and Chapters 5 and 6 respectively deal with the design of suitable managerial accounting systems to help in short-run and long-run decision-making. The shorter the time-scale the more constrained is the decision-maker's freedom: should he do a bit more or a bit less of whatever he is engaged in is the type of decision that might be posed. As the time-span increases so the constraints are relaxed and managerial accounting information becomes less routine in its focus on innovative proposals.

Controlling the future entails having a view of where one should be heading and also a means to that end. Managerial accounting not only offers a means of assessing the consequences (in so far as they can be incorporated into an accounting system) of alternative futures, but also provides a means to the chosen ends via standards, estimates and budgets. Chapters 7 and 8 deal with these matters.

CHAPTER 4 Planning for current activities

Learning objectives

After studying this chapter you should be able to:

- define the term 'cost';
- explain and illustrate the nature and scope of costing (including activity-based costing);
- understand the managerial accounting methodology for determining the control implications of an organization's current activities;
- design appropriate managerial accounting systems for assessing the performance of current activities.

4.1 Introduction

In Part 1 (Chapters 1, 2 and 3) we considered how to define managerial accounting and how to locate this function within an organizational control context. Managerial accounting does not exist for its own sake: it exists to enable managers to make better decisions and thereby improve the effectiveness of their organizations.

We can think of organizations – whether commercial or non-commercial, manufacturing or service rendering, large or small – as consisting of a cluster of projects or activities. Take your college, polytechnic or university as an example: it is made up of degree programmes, recreational activities, committees carrying out assigned briefs, and so on. This mix of projects and activities is ever-changing – thus a new degree scheme combining accounting and organizational analysis might be added, and the students' union's involvement in CND activities terminated. Every project has resource implications, and the shortage of resources invariably means that choices must be made in rationing available resources among competing projects. It may be the case that new projects can only be taken on by an enterprise if old ones are dropped, thereby freeing some resources. (This typically happens in academic libraries in connection with journal subscriptions, to take an everyday example with which you may be familiar: a new journal can often only be subscribed to if an existing journal subscription is terminated.)

In establishing a base-line for assessing the effectiveness with which an enterprise is carrying out its various activities it is helpful to know the cost of those activities. Since we use the term 'cost' in everyday parlance we probably take its meaning for granted. However, in dealing with the resource implications of existing (or prospective) projects and activities we need to consider carefully the nature of 'cost' in its many forms. This is the task of the current chapter, and we will start by defining our terms.

4.2 The nature of cost

Everything that a manager does, as well as many things he or she fails to do, has an associated cost. This is not to suggest that the costs of taking (or not taking) a particular course of action are all identifiable or measurable. However, it does beg the question of what is meant by 'cost'.

In this section we will consider

(a) definitions of 'cost';
(b) the meaning and scope of 'costing';
(c) the nature of 'cost objects'.

(a) Cost defined

In accounting, costs are usually defined as those outlays (or expenses) that cause a reduction in assets – such as the payment of rents and wages – with cash (a current asset) being reduced as payments are made.

Anthony and Reece (1983) define cost in accounting terms as follows:

> Cost is a measurement, in monetary terms, of the amount of resources used for some purpose (p. 549).

Particular points to highlight within this definition are:

(i) it requires *monetary* measurement;
(ii) it involves *resources*;
(iii) it needs a *purpose* to be specified.

It helps in clarifying terminological difficulties within accounting to introduce a time dimension. Cost in accounting is the amount of resource that is given up (or exchanged) at a point in time for a particular purpose, as measured in monetary terms, e.g. the price paid on 30 November to acquire a word processor. (In this sense, cost is a *valuation* concept: under the historic cost convention the value of the word processor can be expressed in terms of the cost of acquiring ownership of it.) At the time the word processor is purchased it has service potential over its future life, and hence is classified as an *asset* (thereby ensuring inclusion in the enterprise's balance sheet). As the service potential is consumed this is shown as an *expense* in the profit and loss account of each period benefiting from the asset's services. In the case of the word processor (as with other fixed assets) this diminution of service potential is represented by the depreciation charges in successive profit and loss accounts. (See Chapter 4 in *Financial Accounting: Method and Meaning*.)

For financial reporting purposes this may be satisfactory, but for decision-making (hence control) purposes it is necessary to define costs in a way that reflects economic reality a little better. Costs are defined by economists in terms of forgone alternatives (or opportunities). Thus the cost of a given input into a system is the maximum value that the input in question could generate in an alternative use. If its use precludes its sale, for example, then its cost is its net realizable value (i.e. what it could have been sold for, less the costs of selling it).

Cost is characterized by the word *sacrifice* and, as such, it is very much in management's interests to control and reduce where possible the sacrifices involved in achieving desired results. In this broad sense cost is equivalent to sacrifices of various types, although they are not all reflected in a company's cash flow. Let us briefly consider some of the concepts of cost that we are certainly all familiar with intuitively, if not more formally.

(i) *Non-financial costs* are those costs that are not directly discernible through a company's cash flow. (While such costs certainly involve sacrifices and they may lead eventually, in complex ways, to a reduced cash flow in the future, they do not represent immediate cash outlays.) 'Psychic' costs are a good example – these are the costs of mental dissatisfaction such as one might find in the lowering of the work-force's morale following a 5% (rather than 10%) pay rise, or on the part of manager B when C is promoted instead on the retirement of A. Another non-financial cost is that associated with a diminution of a company's public image if it is guilty of acts of pollution, unfair trading, etc. (This cost would be reflected in a fall in the value of a company's goodwill – if only we had a satisfactory way of measuring this.)

(ii) *Non-cash costs* are financial sacrifices that do not involve cash outlays at the time when the cost is recognized. Two important examples of this concept are to be found in charges for depreciation and in the idea of opportunity cost.
- Depreciation charges are not associated with any cash flow since they are simply a means of writing-off an asset's value as its service potential is consumed. The cash outflow occurs when the asset itself is acquired.
- Every manager, and consumer, is accustomed to the problem of trying to cope with limited resources, which means that one is invariably unable to do all the things that one would like to do. This is the setting within which opportunity cost is most apparent: if you allocate your scarce resources to one purpose you cannot also allocate the same resources simultaneously to another purpose. One forgoes the potential benefits of strategy X if one applies one's resources to strategy Y, and these *forgone benefits* constitute the *opportunity cost* of strategy Y (i.e. the sacrifice involved in pursuing Y is given by the benefits that one has to forgo by not pursuing X). It will be apparent that there is not a cash outlay corresponding to the opportunity cost of a given situation.

(iii) *Cash costs* are those sacrifices that are reflected in actual cash outflows. Thus when one pays one's fare for an immediate journey by some form of public transport the cost (i.e. that which one gives up) is incurred at the same time as the cash expenditure. In a corporate setting it is a reasonable approximation to equate operating expenses (excluding depreciation) with cash outlays, provided inventory levels are not fluctuating in anything other than a minor way.

Commercial transactions usually involve both reward (or revenue) and sacrifice (or cost), with the difference between the two being gain (or profit). Thus:

Reward − Sacrifice = Gain
Revenue − Cost = Profit

Revenue is relatively easy to deal with but cost is much more difficult.

In measuring the outcome from commercial activity this general concept of sacrifice must be simplified by being expressed in numerical terms in order that it might be manipulated in a company's accounting system. The common denominator in business is money, and it follows that cost is best represented in financial terms, despite the inherent limitations of this.

(iv) *Different costs for different purposes*. It is important to recognize that the term 'cost' only has meaning in a given context and always requires an adjective accompanying it to avoid confusion. There are different cost concepts that are appropriate for different purposes, and no single cost concept is relevant to all situations.

The expression 'different costs for different purposes' has been widely used, and can be traced back to the title of Chapter 9 of J.M. Clark's classic book on *Studies in the Economics of Overhead Costs* (Clark, 1923, p. 175). Clark presented nine different decisions and showed how each needed different cost data. Since then the expression has been rather abused and is often taken to mean that users might need different measures of the cost of a given thing. This is not likely since (as mentioned in the previous paragraph) 'cost' requires an adjective (e.g. full, direct) before it can be operationalized, and the cost object of interest (see subsection (c) below) also needs to be defined. Thus we might wish to know the *full* cost of carrying out a particular research study, or the *direct* cost of using local carriers as opposed to operating our own delivery vehicles.

To be sure, we need to associate appropriate concepts of cost with the *cost objects* (see subsection (c) below) that concern us, and the specification of the purpose to be served will eliminate any major ambiguity. We may want to know how much effort (in the form of resources) is being allocated to the manufacture of product X, and a measure of the full product cost of X will give us this information. However, once we know this it may prompt the question: 'Should we continue manufacturing product X?' In order to answer this we would have to seek a more appropriate measure of cost than full cost. This would be given by the *avoidable* costs (rather than the *full* cost) associated with manufacturing X.

Any controversy should disappear once it is recognized that:

> . . . there are different kinds of problems for which we need information about costs, and the particular information we need differs from one problem to another (Clark, 1923, p. 35.)

If we take an example concerning the *full cost* of a compact disc player this may be (from your point of view) £250 that you would have to pay to buy one (plus, perhaps, the cost of any hi-fi guide you bought to help you choose the best model for your purpose, the cost of a plug, and the transport costs you incur in acquiring the CD player). But from the point of view of either the dealer who sold the CD player to you, or the organization that manufactured it, determining its full cost is much more problematic!

(b) The meaning and scope of costing

Costing is the process whereby the cost of a given activity is measured with a view to providing useful information. This presumes that there are:

(i) users of costing information;
(ii) purposes to be served;
(iii) appropriate cost concepts;
(iv) suitable methods of measurement.

As a general proposition one can argue that cost information should not be compiled unless it is expected that the benefits to be derived from its use will exceed the costs of its compilation. (This is an aspect of the cost of control, i.e. what is the cost of costing? Along with the problematic issue of the value of information, we will consider this question later in the book – see pp. 172–3.) Since managerial accounting information (of which cost information is a part) is not legally required, the question of whether to provide costing data on particular activities will largely be one for management's discretion (influenced, no doubt, by the competence of the organization's management accountant).

In broad terms we can identify the main purposes of costing as being:

(i) to show the cost structure of each activity carried out by the enterprise in order to facilitate planning;
(ii) to facilitate product costing for inventory valuation and income determination purposes;
(iii) to show not only whether a profit has been made on the working of the enterprise as a whole, but whether a profit has been made in each division, job, product, or other segment, thus aiding in the determination of a combination of outputs that improves profit;
(iv) to aid in the pricing decision by distinguishing between fixed and variable costs, with the latter forming the lowest price level that should be set (see Chapter 5);
(v) to prevent wastage by the use of an efficient system of stores and wages control;
(vi) to provide cost data on which to base tenders for government and other contracts;
(vii) to secure more efficient operations, and more effective use of resources, by the comparison of results with predetermined standards (see Chapters 7 and 10);
(viii) to permit the establishing of uniform cost accounting systems for interfirm comparison purposes;
(ix) to achieve control by the assigning of costs to responsibility centres (which will be developed in Chapter 9);
(x) to help in decision-making by giving a basis for identifying the cost implications of alternative courses of action, such as:
   - What would be the effect on the enterprise's net profit of discontinuing product A and re-allocating resources to product B?
   - If an order/contract is accepted at a given price, will that price be sufficient to enable the company to earn a profit on the job?

– What will be the effect of a given wage increase on product costs and hence on profits?
– What effect will replacing specified equipment have on costs?

(c) Cost objects

Costing has been conventionally associated with *product costing*. This is concerned with the determination of the amount of cost to be assigned to each unit of manufactured output as a basis for valuing inventories of goods (as shown in a balance sheet) and as a basis for computing the cost of goods sold (which is deducted from sales revenue to show gross profit – as in a profit and loss account). Apart from aiding in these ways in inventory valuation and income determination, product costing is employed in the cost-plus approach to product pricing (e.g. in the contracting and printing industries).

The approach to product costing is generally to assign to each unit of output a 'fair share' of the total cost of operations. This is quite straightforward in a single product (or single service) enterprise, but complexity tends to increase in proportion to the number of product lines manufactured and/or marketed. In a single product enterprise *all* costs can be seen to be incurred to support that product (e.g. an output of 1,000,000 units at a cost of £5,000,000 gives a unit cost of £5.00). If there are two product lines – or 2,000 product lines – the problem is much more difficult and the cost of any one item from a multiproduct line is impossible to measure accurately.

In addition to product costing, costing is also concerned with deriving costs for other units of activity – or cost objects. The products produced by an enterprise are not the only cost objects; one can be interested in the cost of operating particular departments, in the cost of operating in certain sales territories, in the cost of serving various industries and customer groups, in the cost of using different channels of distribution, in the cost of servicing orders below a given value, in the cost of hiring a new salesman, and so forth.

In fact, the *object of costing* can be anything that one wishes providing it refers to an activity of one kind or another:

(i) How much does it cost to provide 1,000 square feet of executive office space in central Manchester?
(ii) How much does it cost per day for the Royal Hallamshire Hospital to run its intensive care unit?
(iii) How much does it cost MCA to market compact discs in Scotland?
(iv) How much does it cost Swan Hunter to use an hour of a welder's labour?
(v) How much does it cost Alex Lawrie Factors Ltd to have a one page letter typed and mailed to a UK destination?

Cost objects can be as broad or as narrow as the specific purpose that one has in mind. As Staubus says:

> Some objects of costing are tiny, as fabricating a common pin or making an entry on a stores card; others are as large as constructing an aircraft carrier, landing the first man on the Moon, or abolishing poverty. (1971, p. 1.)

The value of costing will clearly depend upon the selection of appropriate cost objects, and a historical fixation on manufacturing processes and their output as cost objects has brought about the widespread prevalence of introspective and retrospective costing systems. This situation has ensured that much of the potential of costing (as an important element within managerial accounting) has been denied due to a restricted perspective. It is essential in control terms to look *outwards and forwards, rather than inwards and back*. This points to decision-usefulness as the primary criterion governing the selection of cost objects.

In contrast to the attention that has been given over the years to the costing of physical products, relatively little has been given to the costing of services (such as those supplied to the final market-place by accounting firms, advertising agencies, management consultants, architects, engineering consultants or solicitors). In part this is due to the difficulty of being able to define and measure that which is to be costed. For example, is it the audit certificate in the case of an accounting firm, or the television commercial in the case of the advertising agency? By far the largest category of expenditure in service firms is on payroll items, but individuals have different rates of pay, work varying numbers of hours, are capable of different qualities of output, etc., so to cost a service on the basis of, say, staff input hours is not a very appropriate approach. The increasing size of the service sector of the British economy, in both its commercial and non-commercial sectors, makes this a problem area of increasing significance, and we should bear it in mind throughout the following discussion. (There are, of course, a number of internal departments within manufacturing and service organizations that provide services as inputs to the final market offer – including personnel, purchasing and training – and the costing of some of these is considered below.)

A word of warning might be useful at this point in connexion with *unit costs*, e.g. the cost of servicing one customer for a haircut, or the cost of producing one unit of output – such as a pair of training shoes.

Unit costs constitute a convenient measure for some purposes, including a comparison of unit costs over time, or against budgets, but the internally-derived unit cost of an output is not the same as the externally-given unit cost of an input. If one more (or one less) unit of the latter is purchased, the total cost will be increased (or reduced) by the unit cost of the item in question. On the other hand, the unit cost of an item of output will usually have been calculated as an average figure, which should not be interpreted as meaning that the total cost will increase (or decrease) by that figure if one unit more (or less) were produced. (This argument applies to the production of lots of similar items, rather than to unique outputs such as the building of the Sydney Opera House, or the construction of an oil tanker.)

In addition, unit costs are produced on a periodic basis. Thus in period 1 the output of a manufacturing process may be 1,000 kilos of liquorice confectionery at a total cost of £1,250, which gives a unit cost of £1.25 per kilo. In period 2 the output may be 1,300 kilos at a total cost of £1,430, which gives a unit cost of £1.10. The reasons for this variability – including differing cost behaviour patterns and economies of scale – will be discussed in Chapter 5.

4.3 Full cost analysis for planning

While plans are primarily concerned with the future, the *process* of planning usually starts from the present or the recent past by examining the pattern of resource allocation and its effectiveness. This can be illustrated by thinking of available resources as *effort*, and then seeking to know how that effort was applied in the recent past, and with what results.

For example, an enterprise might operate in five sales territories which prompts the question: 'How much effort was applied to each sales territory last year, and how much revenue – and profit – did each generate?' Similarly, the enterprise will serve different categories of customers, and the same questions about effort and pay-off can be raised in order to identify the pattern of resource allocation and its effectiveness across customer groups.

Two issues are especially important in this context:

(i) The focus of attention can be on *any* activity (or cost object) that is of managerial interest. The origins of cost accounting – and the subsequent preoccupation of most costing systems as noted above – are to be found in product costing (which seeks to value inventory as a basis for measuring periodic profit), and this explains the traditionally introspective focus of costing on manufacturing processes. However, manufacturing *per se* does not produce profits or generate sales: it is transactions in the market-place that bring in revenue, and this highlights the relevance of sales territories, product lines, customer groups, channels of distribution and size of order as legitimate alternatives to the unit of manufacture when considering relevant cost objects.

(ii) In seeking to establish the pattern of resource allocation it is necessary to make use of simplifying assumptions and techniques that inevitably involve approximations of an unknown (and unknowable) 'full' cost for selected activities. As a result one can only sensibly use full cost data as a basis for asking questions (e.g. 'Which product lines are earning their keep in overseas markets?'; 'How well are salesmen performing relative to one another?'). It is inappropriate to use full cost data as a basis for making decisions (such as adding or dropping product lines, eliminating particular channels of distribution and so on).

Whatever cost object (or activity) is selected as the focus of attention, some costs will be *direct* (in the sense of being traceable to the activity – such as direct labour and direct material inputs into a unit of manufactured output, or a salesman's salary and expenses in relation to his sales territory), whilst others will be *indirect*. By definition, indirect costs cannot be traced directly to cost objects, so any procedure whereby these costs are assigned to cost objects will mean that the resulting full (or 'absorbed') cost is inaccurate to an unknown extent. The assigning of a 'fair share' of indirect costs, along with direct costs, to cost units is at the heart of *absorption costing*.

A particular cost item can only be termed direct or indirect once the cost object has been specified. Thus a salesman's salary will be indirect in relation to the individual product lines he sells (assuming he carries a range of products), but it will be a direct cost of the territory in which he is operating. In the same way the costs of distributing various products to wholesalers may be indirect with regard to the goods themselves but direct if one is interested in costing the channel of distribution of which the wholesalers are part.

The same basic problems arise in attempting to determine the full cost of a cost object in every type of organization, whether a service company, a retailing enterprise, a factory or a non-commercial entity. For example, a garage (as one type of service organization) will treat the servicing of each customer's car as a separate job (or cost object) to which will be assigned the direct cost of the mechanic's time, materials and parts, plus an allowance (usually applied as an hourly rate and associated with the utilization of mechanics' time) for the use of indirect factors (which will include power, equipment, rent, rates, insurances, salaries of reception, supervisory and stores staff, etc.). A similar approach is applied by firms of solicitors or accountants, by consulting engineers, architects and management consultants. Non-commercial organizations typically provide services (such as health care, defence, education and spiritual guidance) and use resources in carrying out their various activities in much the same way as do commercial undertakings. The logic of absorption costing is equally applicable to non-commercial as to commercial enterprises.

We will proceed by looking at:

(i) an example of absorption costing focusing on distribution channels (Section 4.4);
(ii) the application of absorption costing in a manufacturing setting (Section 4.5);
(iii) an approach to segmental productivity analysis based on absorption costing (Section 4.6);
(iv) activity-based costing (Section 4.7).

4.4 Absorption costing: a marketing example

Several reasons can be given for using a marketing example to illustrate full cost analysis, but two are especially significant:

(i) The approach that is invariably adopted in textbooks (and in practice) is to associate full costing with products and production processes. This leads to a kind of tunnel vision whereby direct costs are assumed to be costs directly traceable to production processes or products, whereas direct costs are *those costs that can be specifically associated with whatever cost object happens to be of interest to the analyst or the manager*. In the case of XYZ which we examine below it is channels of distribution that are of interest.
(ii) The costs of marketing activities in recent years have increased drastically and, on average, exceed the costs of production activities. This suggests that a shift of emphasis out of the factory and into the marketing arena is no bad thing, and this is reinforced by the need to relate to environmental issues if one is to be in a position to control the performance of organizations. A marketing focus emphasizes the context in which commercial organizations exist (and avoids the introspective preoccupation that has inhibited the development of managerial accounting systems) in a way that facilitates improved organizational effectiveness.

In Fig. 4.1, which we can take as our starting point, data from the last year's operations of XYZ Ltd is presented in the form of a simplified profit and loss account. XYZ Ltd is a small company engaged in manufacturing and marketing gardening tools. The profit and loss account covers the whole organization, so to

Figure 4.1

XYZ Ltd: basic data.

	£	£
Sales		300,000
Cost of goods sold		195,000
Gross profit		105,000
Expenses:		
Salaries	46,500	
Rent	15,000	
Supplies	17,500	79,000
Net profit		£26,000

gain some insights into how this overall picture is made up we need to analyse the data to discover:

(i) the pattern of resource utilization across its various activities;
(ii) the pay-off (in net profit terms) from those activities.

We can carry out the necessary analysis by following a sequence of logical steps.

Step 1
Specify the marketing activities (or cost object or segment) to be studied. Let us take as our focus of interest the profit performance from operating through different channels of distribution. XYZ Ltd sells its products through three channels:

(i) garden centres,
(ii) hardware shops,
(iii) department stores.

Step 2
Identify the 'functional' expenses by reclassifying the 'natural' expenses that appear in Fig. 4.1. Examples of typical natural and functional expenses are shown in Fig. 4.2.

Within the natural accounts there will be many items that can be directly associated with particular marketing functions:

(i) entertainment will largely relate to personal selling;
(ii) salaries can be readily linked to specific jobs being performed, etc.

However, there will also be many natural expenses that support more than one functional activity, which are therefore indirect to any single activity. Examples include:

(i) rent which is paid for premises accommodating several functions;
(ii) packaging costs that partly relate to each of promotion, warehousing and transportation;

Figure 4.2

Natural and functional expenses.

Typical examples of natural accounts	Typical examples of marketing functions
Rent	*Order-getting*:
Supplies	Advertising
Postage	Sales promotion
Insurance	Personal selling
Heat	Public relations
Utilities	*Order-filling*:
Depreciation	Warehousing
Maintenance	Transportation
Travel	Order-processing
Telephone	*Other*:
Freight	Credits and collections
Entertainment	Marketing research
Advertising	After-sales service
Packaging	Marketing administration

(iii) telephone costs which will be collectively incurred by all functions.

There will be occasions when it will be unnecessary to assign all natural expenses to functions – depending upon the purpose of the exercise. If the aim is to ascertain the cost of operating in a given sales region, for instance, then the expenses incurred by all the personnel operating in that region and the buildings (e.g. warehouses, branch offices) and so forth located within the region are direct costs of the region. These costs can be assigned directly to the segment in question (the region) without being functionalized. It will still be necessary, of course, in carrying out a full cost analysis, to add to the direct costs of the region a portion of the indirect costs in accordance with whatever rules have been established for assigning such costs.

If the aim is the broader one of assessing the productivity of marketing activities more generally then it will be necessary to carry out a full functional cost analysis (see Section 4.6 below).

To return to the example of XYZ Ltd, let us assume that the natural expenses shown in Fig. 4.1 arise from the following four functions:

(i) selling;
(ii) advertising;
(iii) packaging and delivery;
(iv) invoicing and collecting.

We need to establish how much of each natural expense is assignable to each function.

(i) *Salaries* are easy enough to assign to functions when each individual spends all of his/her time carrying out tasks that fall under a single functional heading.

(ii) The allocation of *rent* will usually reflect the amount of space taken up by each functional activity. Packaging is likely to occupy a large area, so if the rent is shared out on a square footage basis it follows that packaging will be assigned a correspondingly large proportion. Since selling takes place in the field no rent expense is assigned to the sales function in the case of XYZ Ltd.

(iii) *Supplies* will include promotional and packaging materials, stationery, fuel oil, and so on. A careful analysis of each item, and its pattern of usage, should facilitate an acceptable functional allocation.

Figure 4.3 shows the allocation of natural expenses to functions.

Step 3

Assign functional expenses to the chosen segments. This is portrayed in Fig. 4.4 as 'phase 2', with 'phase 1' having been carried out via Step 2 above. In order to carry out this phase of the analysis we need to establish some relationship between each category of functional expense and the segments to which we propose assigning those expenses.

As an example let us take selling. The amount of selling effort (or expense) attributable to each segment can be measured via the number of sales calls made. The segments of interest to us are the different channels of distribution, and we should be able to ascertain from records kept by the sales force how many visits were made to each type of outlet. An average cost per call can be calculated (as shown in Fig. 4.5). Similarly for advertising. It should be possible to find out which advertisements were addressed to which audiences, and an average cost per advertisement (as in Fig. 4.5) can be determined – 100 advertisements at a total cost of £15,500 gives a unit cost of £155.

Packaging and delivery and invoicing and collection expenses are assumed to vary in accordance with the number of orders received, so – as we can see from

Figure 4.3

XYZ Ltd: functional allocations.

Natural expense		Functions			
		Selling	Advertising	Packaging and delivery	Invoicing and collecting
	£	£	£	£	£
Salaries	46,500	25,500	6,000	7,000	8,000
Rent	15,000	–	2,000	10,000	3,000
Supplies	17,500	2,000	7,500	7,000	1,000
Total	£79,000	£27,500	£15,500	£24,000	£12,000

Figure 4.4

Determining segmental costs.

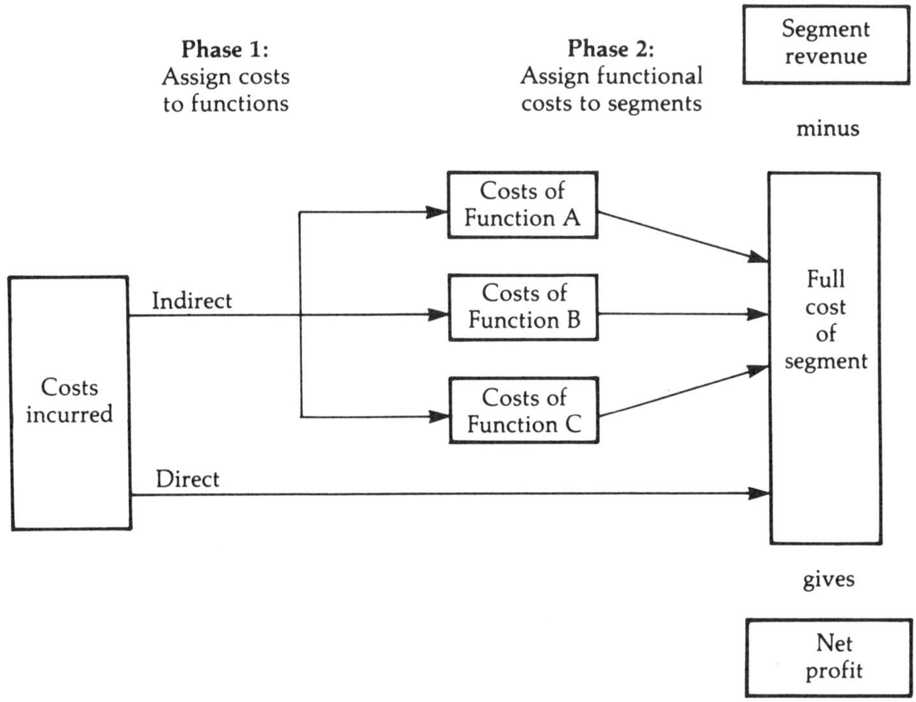

Figure 4.5

XYZ Ltd: Functional cost behaviour.

Channel	Selling	Advertising	Packaging and delivery	Invoicing and collecting
	Number of sales calls in period	Number of advertisements during period	Number of orders processed during period	Number of orders processed during period
Garden centres	200	50	50	50
Hardware shops	65	20	21	21
Department stores	10	30	9	9
Total units	275	100	80	80
Functional expense	£27,500	£15,500	£24,000	£12,000
Number of units	275	100	80	80
Unit cost	£100	£155	£300	£150

Fig. 4.5 – the costs of these functions are divided by the number of orders received during the period to give unit costs of £300 and £150 respectively.

Step 4

We can now compile a net profit statement for each segment (i.e. channel) by deducting the full cost from the sales revenue, as shown in Fig. 4.6.

The allocation of sales revenue to segments is straightforward. It is known what the value of sales is through each channel since orders can be easily classified by source. We have assumed that the cost of goods sold (COGS) is proportional to the volume of sales (thus 50% of sales are via garden centres, so 50% of COGS is charged against those sales). This in turn assumes that both the sales mix and price levels are constant across all three channels, which may not always be the case.

The functional expenses that have been assigned to the three channels are deducted from the gross profit to arrive at the segmental net profit. In the case of hardware shops the total of the functional expenses is made up of:

	£
Selling: £100 × 65 calls	6,500
Advertising: £155 × 20 ads	3,100
Packaging/delivery: £300 × 21 orders	6,300
Invoicing/collection: £150 × 21 orders	3,150
	£19,050

which gives a net loss of £1,550 when deducted from the gross profit of £17,500.

Step 5

Interpret the full cost data. This is the most vital step. It can be seen that sales via garden centres involve only a marginally productive use of resources:

Figure 4.6

XYZ Ltd: net profit statement by segment.

	Garden centres £	Hardware shops £	Department stores £	XYZ Ltd £
Sales	150,000	50,000	100,000	300,000
COGS	97,500	32,500	65,000	195,000
Gross profit	52,500	17,500	35,000	105,000
Expenses:				
Selling (£100 per call)	20,000	6,500	1,000	27,500
Advertising (£155 per ad)	7,750	3,100	4,650	15,500
Packaging/delivery (£300 per order)	15,000	6,300	2,700	24,000
Invoicing/collection (£150 per order)	7,500	3,150	1,350	12,000
Total expenses	50,250	19,050	9,700	79,000
Net profit/(loss)	£ 2,250	£ (1,550)	£ 25,300	£ 26,000

Inputs		£	Outputs	
	COGS	97,500		Sales revenue
	Marketing	50,250		
		£147,750		£150,000

$$\text{Productivity} = \frac{\text{Outputs}}{\text{Inputs}} = \frac{150{,}000}{147{,}750} = 1.02$$

The modest net profit figure of £2,250 relative to the sales revenue figure of £150,000 indicates that the productivity index will only be slightly in excess of unity, which is the case.

For hardware shops the productivity picture is much more worrying:

Inputs		£	Outputs	
	COGS	32,500		Sales revenue
	Marketing	19,050		
		£51,550		£50,000

$$\text{Productivity} = \frac{\text{Outputs}}{\text{Inputs}} = \frac{50{,}000}{51{,}550} = 0.97$$

Since the index is less than unity it follows that a loss is being made, and the loss is £1,550 (i.e. the amount by which the value of the inputs exceeds the value of the outputs).

Turning to sales through department stores the situation is very different:

Inputs		£	Outputs	
	COGS	65,000		Sales revenue
	Marketing	9,700		
		£74,700		£100,000

$$\text{Productivity} = \frac{\text{Outputs}}{\text{Inputs}} = \frac{100{,}000}{74{,}700} = 1.34$$

The index is substantially greater than unity which indicates a highly productive use of resources, as reflected in the net profit figure of £25,300.

Looking at XYZ Ltd as a whole we can see that the outputs exceed the inputs, so it is productive in overall terms:

Inputs		£	Outputs	
	COGS	195,000		Sales revenue
	Marketing	79,000		
		£274,000		£300,000

$$\text{Productivity} = \frac{\text{Outputs}}{\text{Inputs}} = \frac{300{,}000}{274{,}000} = 1.09$$

Figure 4.7

XYZ Ltd: productivity by segment.

	Garden centres	Hardware shops	Department stores	XYZ Ltd as a whole
Outputs (£)	150,000	50,000	100,000	300,000
Inputs (£)	147,750	51,550	74,700	274,000
Productivity index	1.02	0.97	1.34	1.09

A summary is provided in Figure 4.7.

A superficial interpretation may suggest that sales via hardware shops should be terminated immediately to eliminate a loss-making activity. However, full cost analysis of this type can only sensibly be used *as a basis for raising questions*. It is not appropriate to attempt to use full cost data as a basis for providing answers to decisions such as eliminating a segment.

The logic behind this will be covered in detail in Chapter 5, but the key reason can be given here: if sales through hardware shops were to be eliminated the loss of revenue would be (using the given data) £50,000. It does not follow that all the costs assigned to that segment would be eliminated. For example, the rental payment would probably continue at the same level even if XYZ Ltd was packaging and despatching fewer orders. If it was possible to save

	£
COGS	32,500
75% selling costs	4,875
100% advertising costs	3,100
50% packing/delivery costs	3,150
50% invoicing/collection costs	1,575
total savings would be	£45,200

But £45,200 is less than the revenue that would be forgone! This would lead to a less productive use of resources:

Loss *with* hardware shops: £(50,000 − 51,500) = £(1,550)
Loss *without* hardware shops: £(45,200 − 50,000) = £(4,800)

A more creative approach needs to be taken in interpreting full cost data by focusing upon alternative ways in which the inputs might be changed to generate additional output:

(i) Could sales through hardware shops be increased by *additional* advertising?
(ii) Could more advertising be substituted for some of the selling effort?
(iii) Could XYZ eliminate small hardware shops and concentrate on larger outlets?

The answers to these questions will be based as much on expectations concerning the future as on data from the past. Full cost analyses offer a starting point only for evaluating an enterprise's existing allocation of effort as a prelude to planning for the future. In carrying out this type of analysis we need to be particularly conscious of the limitations which stem from the choice of bases for assigning functional costs to segments. If we take the selling expenses from the XYZ Ltd example you will recall that these were assigned on the basis of the number of sales calls made to each type of outlet within a given period. This is a simplification of something that is much more complex: each call will involve a different amount of a salesman's time, and will have entailed journeys of differing length. New customers and large customers may require more attention than long-established smaller customers, and out-of-the-way customers may involve overnight hotel expenses, and so forth. We can see, therefore, that using sales calls to assign selling expenses averages out the complex pattern of cost incurrence. A better single basis might be number of selling man-hours, but even this has limitations:

(i) it is not readily available in the way that the number of sales calls is;
(ii) it is a single measure in a multivariate situation.

At this point you will see the relevance of the issue raised earlier (see p. 79) about the cost of costing. To develop a rigorous model of selling costs in relation to outlets serviced would be exorbitantly expensive, and there is no guarantee that it would be sufficiently valid or reliable to justify its development costs. The expedient alternative is to use bases that have some hint of credibility in that a causal relationship is likely to be present. Thus selling expenses will vary with, *inter alia*, the number of sales calls made, and the latter can be seen to be a reasonable basis for assigning selling expenses to different channels. In contrast, the sales generated would not be a reasonable basis because selling expenses are incurred to generate sales (i.e. the causal relationship is the wrong way round):

Acceptable: Sales calls ⟶ Selling expenses
Unacceptable: Sales revenue ⟶ Selling expenses

Using reasonable or expedient bases is acceptable even if it involves a loss of accuracy *provided* the user of the data understands the limitations.

4.5 Absorption costing in a manufacturing setting

Essentially there are three types of production. These are:

(i) *Job production*. This involves the manufacturing of a single complete unit. The building of bridges and ships are good examples of the one-off nature of job production. 'Jobbing' is a term used to describe work carried out against a customer's order rather than intended to build up inventory.

(ii) *Batch production*. This is employed when the number of units to be manufactured of a given product increases. It involves the work being divided into operations, and each operation will be carried out on the whole batch before the next operation is undertaken. Batch production permits the specialization of labour, although the organization and planning effort required to ensure freedom from idle time is considerable.

In principle, there is little difference between job and batch production.

(iii) *Flow production*. Since the various operations in batch production will inevitably take up different amounts of time, programming the work flow to avoid wasted time is almost impossible. As the scale of operations increases it often becomes possible to establish continuous flow production where there is no wasted time between operations. Such an arrangement requires balancing the times of every operation (including inspection) so that bottlenecks or surplus capacity do not render the production line inefficient. Clearly a fault at any stage will have effects on all other stages of the production line.

In parallel with these types of production organization there are different types of costing system:

(i) *Job/batch costing*. This is adopted when each 'job' is to be regarded as a separate cost object. The job may be one large order or a batch of like items. All costs relating to the job or batch will be charged to a separate account for that job/batch.

(ii) *Process costing*. When units of product are manufactured in large quantities (i.e. flow production) and pass through distinct stages, it is customary to ascertain the cost of each stage. The process, therefore, is the cost object.

Direct inputs to either system will consist of materials, labour and services that are traceable to the job, batch or process. In addition, there will be inputs that

Figure 4.8

Direct and indirect manufacturing inputs.

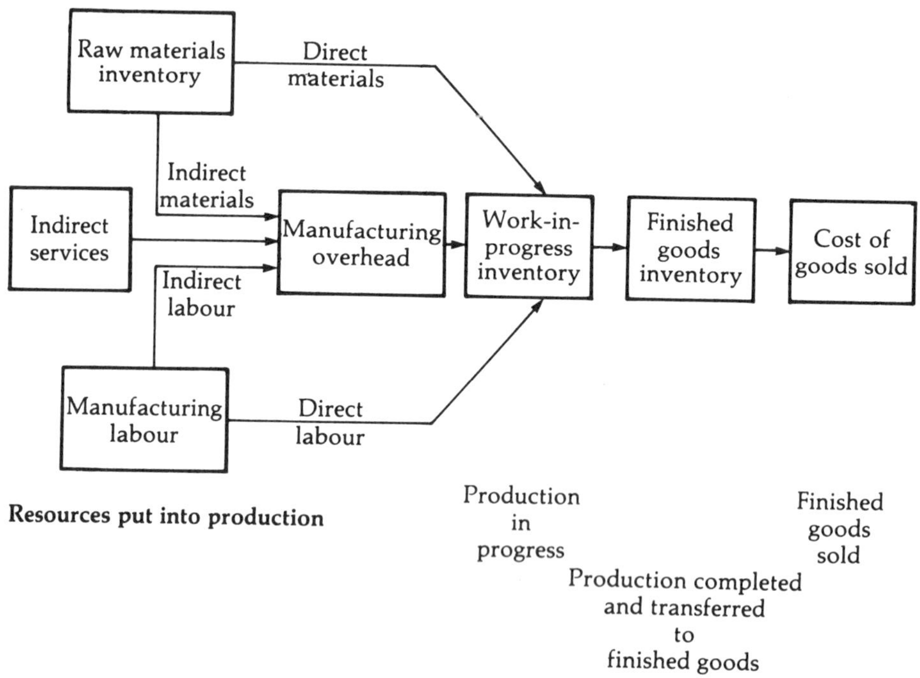

Adapted from Heitger and Matulich (1980), p. 33.

benefit many jobs, batches or processes and which are, therefore, indirect in relation to any specific one. Examples might include lubricating oils used in maintaining equipment, maintenance labour, stores personnel, and so forth. Figure 4.8 shows the way in which materials, labour and services may be either direct or indirect inputs.

This picture is inevitably a simplification of what can be a highly complex situation. Apart from indirect labour, materials and services of the types suggested in the last paragraph there are lots of other indirect costs associated with manufacturing activities, including:

(i) Supervisory and clerical salaries relating to:
- progress
- goods inwards
- time-keeping
- tool room
- production control
- purchasing
- quality control
- maintenance
- drawing office
- personnel administration.

(ii) Premises costs covering:
- depreciation
- heating
- utilities
- rent
  rates
- insurance
- waste disposal
- security
- cleaning
- telephone.

(iii) Other costs including:
- canteen
- training
- laundering
- depreciation of equipment
- hire charges
- fire and safety equipment
- protective clothing.

Some of these costs (such as depreciation of equipment) will be attributable to particular production departments, while others (such as personnel administration) will be incurred by departments that render services to the production departments. In Fig. 4.9 we can see in broad terms how these two categories of indirect

Figure 4.9

Overhead apportionment and absorption.

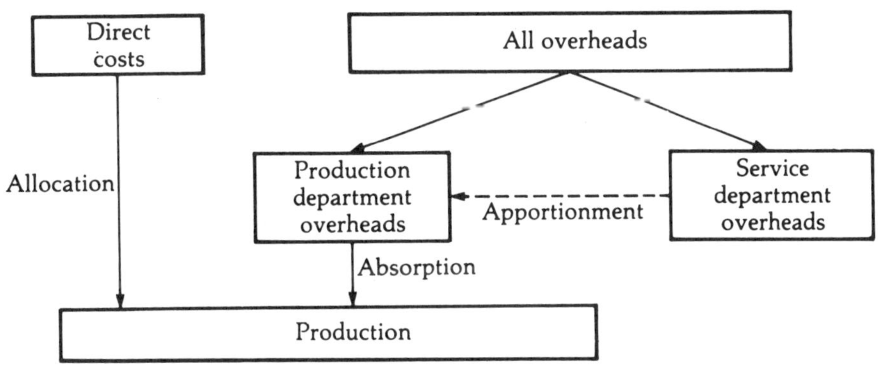

(or 'overhead') costs are treated. However, since the direct costs also must be brought into the analysis it will be most helpful if we go through the steps involved in applying absorption costing in a manufacturing setting. Let us proceed by considering the data inputs to the costing system.

(a) Labour

The initial point to observe in relation to payroll data is that the cost of employing an individual is not just his or her gross wages or salary. In addition to gross earnings the company must pay its contribution for national insurance, superannuation and so on.

In a manufacturing or distribution environment time sheets can be used to record, in summary form, the time that each operative spends on different jobs. The onus will often be on the operative to record the time spent on each job that is worked on during a week. This highlights a major danger: unless there is some incentive towards the accurate booking of time, the validity of labour costings will be highly suspect. An operative may attach little importance to the tedious recording of the time he spends on different tasks if he fails to understand the importance of this function. Further, he may be reluctant to record times accurately because lost time, idle time and waiting time can reflect partly on himself, partly on his supervisor and partly on his colleagues.

An analysis of indirect labour hours – especially where reasons can be clearly given – is of great value in pinpointing areas of weakness. Account codes can be drawn up to facilitate the analysis, and each source of indirect labour expense can be recorded against its particular code as it is incurred. For idle time, for example, we may have the following codes:

X123 Waiting for orders
X124 Waiting for materials from stores
X125 Waiting for materials from previous operation
X126 Waiting for fitter
X127 Waiting for power
X128 Waiting for supervisor
X129 Waiting for drawings
X130 Waiting for maintenance
X131 Waiting for jigs
X132 Waiting for instructions

If idle time booked to X126 (waiting for a fitter) amounted to, say, £15,500 during the course of a year, a good argument could be put forward for hiring another fitter. A weekly report can be compiled to show how lost time is made up and the proportion it bears to direct labour time.

(b) Materials

All issues of materials should be authorized by a requisition, but note should be taken that the requisitioned quantity may not always be available, so either a lesser amount will be withdrawn from stores (in which event the requisition must be amended) or the full amount will be issued when available. A material requisition should bear the cost allocation/job number in every instance.

A difficulty that arises over material issues is the cost to associate with each issue. It might appear simple to charge against production *actual* material cost (i.e. the price paid). However, a problem usually arises because the same type of material has been purchased at a variety of prices. 'Actual cost' then has several different meanings and some systematic method of pricing material issues must be selected. Let us consider three methods by means of an example.

Suppose the following information is available for Material A (given in chronological order);

(a) Opening inventory	100 units	Cost £1.00 per unit	=	£100.00
(1) Issue	75 units			
(b) Purchase	400 units	Cost £1.10 per unit	=	£440.00
(2) Issue	100 units			
(3) Issue	50 units			
(c) Purchase	80 units	Cost £1.20 per unit	=	£96.00
(4) Issue	150 units			
(5) Closing inventory	205 units	(i.e. assuming no wastage)		£636.00

A price per unit is required for issues (1)–(4) and a valuation for closing inventory (5).

(i) First in, first out (FIFO) method

This method assumes that the various units of material are used in the order in which they are received. Closing inventory will consist of the last items purchased. Whenever stores are issued the issue price will be calculated by working forwards from the oldest batch in stock:

		Inventory (a)	Purchase (b)	Purchase (c)	
Issue	(1)	75 × £1.00			= £75.00
Issue	(2)	25 × £1.00 +	75 × £1.10		= £107.50
Issue	(3)		50 × £1.10		= £55.00
Issue	(4)		150 × £1.10		= £165.00
Inventory	(5)		125 × £1.10 +	80 × £1.20	= £233.50
		100 units	400 units	80 units	£636.00

This method is easy to operate unless many small purchases at different prices occur. Inventory balances represent nearly current costs, and costs are recognized in a manner which should correspond to the physical use of the inventory. However, the system is inequitable if a sudden change in price results in similar jobs being charged with different material costs, and where inventory turnover is slow and there are substantial price changes, current material costs will not be apparent in the account.

(ii) Weighted-average cost method

This method assumes that all material of a given kind is so intermingled – such as occurs when liquids are mixed – that an issue cannot be made from a particular lot and the cost should therefore represent an average of the entire supply. A new issue price is calculated every time a purchase is made by dividing: (Cost of material received + Cost of material on hand) by (Number of units received + Number of units on hand):

Issue	(1)	75 × £1.000 =	£75
Issue	(2)	100 × £1.094 =	£109
Issue	(3)	50 × £1.094 =	£55
Issue	(4)	150 × £1.118 =	£168
Inventory	(5)	205 × £1.118 =	£229
			£636

$$\frac{(25 \times £1) + (400 \times £1.10)}{25 + 400} = 1.094$$

$$\frac{(275 \times £1.094) + (80 \times £1.20)}{275 + 80} = 1.118$$

Note that the calculation may be done on a periodic basis instead of on the occasion of every purchase. Issue and inventory pricing would then be recalculated as follows and no entries would be made until the end of the period.

$$\frac{£100 + £440 + £96}{100 + 400 + 80} = £1.093 \text{ per unit}$$

This method is easy to operate, smooths out the sudden jumps likely to occur in pricing under other methods, and gives inventory balances that represent relatively current costs. However, the influence of a large purchase on favourable terms may influence inventory pricing for many periods if usage is slow.

(iii) Last in first out (LIFO) method
This method assumes artificially that the last items purchased are the first used. Closing inventory will be valued at the price of the first goods purchased. Whenever stores are issued the issue price will be calculated by working back from the most recent batch received:

		Inventory (a)	Purchase (b)	Purchase (c)	
Issue	(1)	75 × £1.00			= £75.00
Issue	(2)		100 × £1.10		= £110.00
Issue	(3)		50 × £1.10		= £55.00
Issue	(4)		70 × £1.10 +	80 × £1.20	= £173.00
Inventory	(5)	25 × £1.00 +	180 × £1.10		= £223.50
		100 units	400 units	80 units	£636.00

The only advantage of this method is that it matches recent material cost with current revenue – hence cost of goods manufactured will fluctuate with the market price of material used (unless inventory levels are sharply reduced). However, inventories are valued at prices paid for the earliest purchases (including previous periods) which may deviate considerably from current market values.

(iv) Conclusion

If prices are reasonably stable it matters little which of the above methods is employed. Average cost would probably be best but any of the three applied consistently should be satisfactory.

If prices are not stable the fact that all the above methods (and others) are 'generally acceptable' and therefore are used not only by management internally but for reporting externally is alarming. Some means of isolating the effect of price changes is essential both from a control point of view and an income reporting point of view. One suggestion is to use LIFO for pricing issues and FIFO for pricing inventories, and transfer the ensuing 'difference' to a 'price gains' or 'price losses' account. A far better solution is to employ standard costing whereby all material pricing is based on attainable standards as calculated at the beginning of the period (see Chapter 7). The effect of unforeseen price changes is then automatically segregated and can be both examined for control purposes and reported separately in income statements.

Once purchased, some materials are difficult to control as a result of their physical nature. For example, temperature changes may affect the apparent volume of an issue of a liquid chemical; wastage may arise due to inevitable evaporation or because issues do not correspond with purchases (e.g. galvanized wire may be purchased by the tonne but be issued in coils or lengths). These are all examples of *unavoidable* causes and allowances can (and should) be made for such losses and gains. If experience shows that only 19 issues of 10 lb can be made from a purchase of 200 lb of material X at a cost of £20, it will be necessary to use the following formula to compute the cost per *usable* pound of material X: 20/190 (i.e. £0.105 per lb as opposed to 20/200 or £0.100 per lb).

Avoidable losses are, however, quite a different matter. Such losses may result from causes that include:

(i) pilferage;
(ii) careless handling;
(iii) careless measurement of issues;
(iv) incorrect allowances for variations due to evaporation, absorption of moisture, changes in temperature, etc.;
(v) unsuitable storage.

Care should be taken in deciding which issues to value on an individual basis and which to value on a collective basis. Items of small value (e.g. nails, nuts, etc.) are of the latter type, and although they are strictly in the nature of direct materials (i.e. their cost can be specifically associated with particular products), it will usually be unnecessarily expensive in terms of clerical labour to do this. The usual procedure, therefore, is to issue such items in bulk and classify them in the indirect costs or overheads as consumable materials rather than issue them at a specially computed price to specific jobs.

(c) Indirect cost items

Indirect (or overhead) labour costs will be obtained from work sheets and labour summaries, and indirect material costs (such as the nails referred to above) will be obtained from requisitions. Further indirect cost details covering electricity and other utilities, bought-out services, supervisory and managerial salaries, depreciation and so on will be obtained from expense summaries compiled from either invoices or internal work sheets. The next step is to develop absorption rates by which the indirect costs may be absorbed into the manufactured output. A basic procedure for doing this involves the following steps:

(i) Analyse and classify all costs into their direct and indirect categories. (This can be done as a retrospective exercise using actual costs, or as a predictive exercise using estimated costs.)

(ii) Relate direct costs to the particular jobs, processes, etc., for which they were/are to be specifically incurred.

(iii) Of the indirect costs, some will relate to particular production departments through which products pass in the course of the manufacturing cycle, and others will relate (on a responsibility basis – see Chapter 9) to service or ancillary departments (i.e. non-production departments such as maintenance, production control, stores, costing, etc.). The cost of these service departments is then apportioned to the production departments on some 'fair' basis relating to the different benefits enjoyed by them.

The most important criterion in selecting a base is to relate the indirect cost to its most causal factor: machines require maintenance, space involves paying rates, outputs require inputs. Nevertheless, the whole methodology of apportioning service department costs is plagued by the necessity of having to rely on some arbitrary rules (i.e. relating to 'benefit' or 'fair share') that have been developed in order that service department costs might be rationally spread over production departments. Such apportionments should be carried out solely for product costing purposes: the control of individual indirect costs will not be achieved by cost apportionments, and nor will the method of cost apportionment influence cost control.

(iv) An overhead rate can be established for each production department or *cost centre*, determined by the formula:

$$\frac{\text{Departmental indirect costs} + \text{Apportioned service indirect costs}}{\text{Level of activity}}$$

and applied to each job, process or whatever. This is termed the *recovery of overheads*. (A simpler alternative is to have a single, company-wide absorption rate. However, even in a simple situation, it will often be desirable to know the full cost of each operation (or cost centre) through which the work passes, and also to know the cumulative cost of the product as it passes through the various stages of manufacture.)

Indirect cost or overhead absorption rates in practice are generally determined once a year – and preferably in advance rather than retrospectively, but in changing circumstances it will be advisable to revise them as necessary. The level of activity at which a department is expected to operate during a given period is of crucial importance, and whenever indirect cost absorption rates are determined in advance very careful attention must be paid to estimating this dimension. (Steps (iii) and (iv) are discussed in greater detail in the Workbook, pp. 434–80.)

It is not always necessary to distribute each indirect cost separately. Some fixed costs (such as depreciation, rates, insurance premiums and rent – see Chapter 5) can be spread collectively on the basis of, say, machine hours (since this factor represents the time during which a product 'rents' the machinery and premises).

Other costs, such as maintenance, certain utilities, operating supplies and so forth, may be distributed on the basis of units of output. However, those costs that are proportional to direct labour (such as indirect labour, supervision, holiday accruals, overtime premiums, welfare services, personnel department, etc.), can be distributed on the basis of labour cost, manhours, or the number of people employed – whichever seems most appropriate.

The actual indirect costs of a particular period will only be equal to the applied indirect costs of that period (i.e. Predetermined indirect cost absorption rate × Number of units produced) by chance (unless, of course, the period's costs and activities were all rigidly determined in advance, or the forecaster was in the improbable position of having a perfect view of the future).

If more indirect costs are applied to units of output than are actually incurred, then indirect costs are said to be *over-absorbed* (or over-applied or over-recovered). Conversely, if too little indirect cost is applied to units of output, then indirect costs are said to be *under-absorbed* (under-applied, under-recovered). The degree to which indirect costs are over- or under-absorbed is a useful piece of management information. A record should be kept of the extent to which indirect costs are over- or under-absorbed, and this can be a guide that indicates when indirect cost recovery rates require adjustment. (Because over- and under-absorbed indirect costs are charged directly to the profit-and-loss account, they are not reflected at all in any product cost. Clearly this is unsatisfactory in an absorption costing system that exists purely for product costing reasons.)

An over- or under-absorption of indirect costs may arise because the actual level of indirect costs has varied from the amount anticipated, or because the level of activity actually experienced during a period has differed from the level predicted. Either of these causes – or the two of them acting together – can render the predetermined indirect cost absorption rate inappropriate. (It is also possible for these two causes to act together in such a way that the indirect cost absorption rate remains appropriate. Thus an expected level of activity of 10,000 direct labour hours in conjunction with a predicted level of indirect costs of £20,000 gives an indirect cost absorption rate per direct labour hour of £2.00. If costs actually amount to £25,000 and the level of activity was 12,500 direct labour hours, the effective indirect cost recovery rate remains £2.00 per direct labour hour due to compensating differences).

The explanations behind the major causes of over- and under-recovery are price rises, an expanding level of general economic activity, poor marketing and so on. If plant capacity along with materials are available but sales volume is so low as to create an under-recovery of indirect costs, then this may be considered to be a marketing responsibility. However, if there is a backlog of orders and under-absorbed indirect costs result from the ineffective use of manufacturing facilities, then it becomes a manufacturing responsibility.

(d) Putting the pieces together

Let us now attempt to put all the pieces together in order to show how the full cost of a job/batch/process/activity can be ascertained by combining the direct and indirect cost elements. Figure 4.10 shows a job cost sheet for a job passing through two departments. Direct material costs are obtained from coded requisitions, the

Figure 4.10

Job cost sheet.

JOB COST SHEET

Product__________ Date started__________ Order number__________

Stock__________ Date completed__________ Quantity__________

Customer__________

DEPARTMENT A

Direct material			Direct Labour			Indirect items	
Date	Code	Cost	Date	Code	Cost	Date	Cost

DEPARTMENT B

Direct material			Direct labour			Indirect items	
Date	Code	Cost	Date	Code	Cost	Date	Cost

SUMMARY

Selling price

	Dept A	Dept B	TOTAL
Costs: Direct material			
Direct labour			
Indirect			
Gross profit			

direct labour costs from labour analyses, and the indirect costs on the basis of whichever costing method is employed.

In the job costing example shown in Fig. 4.10 no attempt is made to compute the cost of running a department, but process costing is based on knowing the cost of operating each processing department. Figure 4.11 gives an example of a cost sheet for a process costing exercise in a company having two processes – X and Y. The cost per unit (tonne) can be built up as production progresses from raw materials to the finished product through, initially, process X and then through process Y.

Process costing is associated with flow production in industries such as chemicals, oil, textiles, plastics, paints, glass and so on. All costs of each process (i.e. direct material costs, direct labour costs and indirect costs) are accumulated and related to the units produced.

Figure 4.11

Process cost sheet.

							Month__________		
Details	This month actual		This month budget		Year to date		Budget to date		Remarks
	£	per tonne	£	per tonne	£	per tonne	£	per tonne	
Process X Materials Wages Expenses (detail) Indirect cost allocation Process Y Materials Wages Expenses (detail) Indirect cost allocation									
Office and establishment indirect costs Selling indirect costs									
Cost of sales (A)									
Sales Deduct: outward freight containers									
Net sales (B)									
Profit (B–A)									
Quantity of sales		Tonnes		Tonnes		Tonnes		Tonnes	

4.6 Segmental productivity analysis

It is usually found that enterprises – especially smaller ones – do not know what proportion of their resources are devoted to their various activities or segments, or the profitability of these allocations. Producing useful computations of segmental costs and profit contributions can readily be achieved by adopting analytical methods which, while not difficult in principle, are not widely adopted due largely to the preoccupation with manufacturing cost accounting that exists.

The fact that most companies do not know what proportion of their total marketing outlay is spent on each product, area or customer group may be due to the absence of a sufficiently refined system of cost analysis, or it may be due to vagueness over the nature of certain costs. For instance, is the cost of packaging a promotional, a production or a distribution expense? Some important marketing costs are hidden in manufacturing costs or in general and administrative costs (including finished goods inventory costs in the former and order-processing costs in the latter).

Since few companies are aware of costs and profits by segment in relation to sales levels, and since even fewer are able to predict changes in sales volume and profit contribution (see Chapter 5, pp. 107–8) as a result of changes in marketing effort, the following errors arise:

(i) Marketing budgets for individual products are too large, with the result that diminishing returns become evident and benefits would accrue from a reduction in expenditure.
(ii) Marketing budgets for individual products are too small and increasing returns would result from an increase in expenditure.
(iii) The marketing mix is inefficient, with an incorrect balance and incorrect amounts being spent on the constituent elements – such as too much on advertising and insufficient on direct selling activities.
(iv) Marketing efforts are misallocated among products and changes in these resource allocations (even with a constant level of overall expenditure) could bring improvements.

Similar arguments apply in relation to sales territories or customer groups as well as to products. The need exists, therefore, for control techniques to indicate the level of performance required and achieved as well as the outcome of shifting marketing efforts from one segment to another. As is to be expected, there exists great diversity in the methods by which managers attempt to obtain costs (and profits) for segments of their enterprise, but much of the cost data is inaccurate for such reasons as:

(i) Marketing costs may be allocated to individual products, sales areas, customer groups, etc., on the basis of sales value or sales volume, but this involves circular reasoning. Costs should be allocated in relation to causal factors, and *it is marketing expenditures that cause sales to be made* rather than the other way round: managerial decisions determine marketing costs. Furthermore, despite the fact that success is so often measured in terms of sales value achievements by product line, this basis fails to evaluate the efficiency of the effort (costs) needed to produce the realized sales value (or turnover). Even a seemingly high level of turnover for a specific product may really be a case of misallocated sales effort. (An example should make this clear: if a salesman concentrates on selling product A which contributes £20 per hour of effort instead of selling product B which would contribute £50 per hour of effort, then it 'costs' the company £30 per hour he spends on selling product A. This is the *opportunity cost* of doing one thing rather than another – which we met in Section 4.1 – and is a measure of the sacrifice involved in selecting only one of several alternative courses of action.)

(ii) General overheads and administrative costs are arbitrarily (and erroneously) allocated to segments on the basis of sales volume.

(iii) Many marketing costs are not allocated at all as marketing costs since they are not identified as such but are classified as manufacturing, general or administrative costs instead.

Marketing cost accounting (or analysis) has been developed to help overcome these problems and aims to:

(i) analyse the costs incurred in distributing and promoting products so that when they are combined with production cost data overall profitability can be determined;

(ii) analyse the costs of marketing individual products to determine their profitability;

(iii) analyse the costs involved in serving different classes of customers, different areas, etc., to determine their profitability;

(iv) compute such figures as cost per sales call, cost per order, cost to put a new customer on the books, cost to hold £1's worth of inventory for a year, etc.;

(v) evaluate managers according to their actual controllable cost responsibilities;

(vi) evaluate alternative strategies or plans with full costs.

These analyses and evaluations provide senior management with necessary information to enable them to decide which classes of customer to cultivate, which products to delete, which products to encourage, and so forth. Such analyses also provide a basis from which estimates can be made of the likely increases in product profitability that a specified increase in marketing effort should create. In the normal course of events it is far more difficult to predict the outcome of decisions that involve changes in marketing outlays in comparison with changes in production expenditure. It is easier, for instance, to estimate the effect of a new machine in the factory than it is to predict the impact of higher advertising outlays. Similarly, the effect on productive output of dropping a production worker is easier to estimate than is the effect on the level of sales caused by a reduction in the sales force.

As an example of how productivity analysis can be applied to segments (defined as product lines for this purpose) in a way that combines the approaches of Sections 4.3 and 4.4 above (which covered marketing and manufacturing costs), we might consider Fig. 4.12. This shows, for a hypothetical company, the proportion of each product line's contribution to the net profit of the whole company. Most products make some net profit after their full costs are deducted from the revenues they generate. However, two products (G and H) fail to generate sufficient revenue to cover their full costs.

The segments could equally be sales territory, customer group, etc., and after the basic profit computation has been carried out it can be supplemented (as in

Figure 4.12

Segmental profits statement.

Product	% Contribution to total profits
Total for all products	100.0
Profitable products:	
A	43.7
B	35.5
C	16.4
D	9.6
E	6.8
F	4.2
Sub-total	116.2
Unprofitable products:	
G	−7.5
H	−8.7
Sub-total	−16.2

Fig. 4.13) by linking it to an analysis of the effort required to produce the profit result. (Clearly this is a multivariate situation in which profit depends upon a variety of input factors, but developing valid and reliable multivariate models is both complex and expensive.) As a step in the direction of more rigorous analysis one can derive benefits from linking profit outcomes to individual inputs – such as selling time in the case of Fig. 4.13.

From Fig. 4.13 one can see that product A generates 43.7% of total profits, requiring only 16.9% of available selling time. This is highly productive. By contrast, product E produces only 6.8% of total profits but requires 10.2% of selling effort. Even worse, however, is the 24.8% of selling effort devoted to products G and H which are unprofitable.

A number of obvious questions arise from this type of analysis. Can the productivity of marketing activities be increased by:

(i) increasing net profits proportionately more than the corresponding increase in marketing outlays?
(ii) increasing net profits with no change in marketing outlays?
(iii) increasing net profits with a decrease in marketing costs?
(iv) maintaining net profits at a given level but decreasing marketing costs?
(v) decreasing net profits but with a proportionately greater decrease in marketing costs?

As we have already seen, we cannot answer these questions on the basis of full cost data (and segmental net profit computations).

Figure 4.13

Segmental productivity statement.

Product	% Contribution to total profits	% Total selling time
Total for all products	100.0	100.0
Profitable products:		
A	43.7	16.9
B	35.5	18.3
C	16.4	17.4
D	9.6	5.3
E	6.8	10.2
F	4.2	7.1
Sub-total	116.2	75.2
Unprofitable products:		
G	−7.5	9.5
H	−8.7	15.3
Sub-total	−16.2	24.8

4.7 Activity-based costing

As we have already mentioned (e.g. in Chapter 1), cost systems have their origins in manufacturing industry. However, these origins were a long time ago, and significant changes have taken place in the manufacturing environment over the years. If the design of cost systems fails to take cognisance of these changes then it will be inevitable that their suitability will be suspect. Inappropriate cost systems will generate inappropriate information which will encourage the making of inappropriate decisions. This is unlikely to help bring about organizational control or to enhance organizational effectiveness.

When cost systems were in their early stage of development (about one hundred years ago) the manufacturing environment that prevailed was characterized by:

- cheap labour relative to other costs;
- throughput rates of production that were controlled by direct labour;
- slowly changing technology that resulted in long product life cycles (see pp. 524–7 in Workbook Chapter 6) and infrequent major design changes;
- a managerial focus on labour efficiency;
- resources other than labour (e.g. capital invested in machinery) were used to enhance the direct labour effort.

(See Plossl (1990).)

To suit these circumstances the principal characteristics of traditional cost systems were:

- direct labour costs had a prominent role;
- the bulk of indirect manufacturing costs were closely related to direct labour;
- cost centre activities revolved around direct labour;
- direct manufacturing costs varied largely with throughput, and hence with direct labour;
- capital costs were long-term and fixed.

But the changes that have taken place within manufacturing industry over the last few years – especially in those sectors described as 'high tech' – have been dramatic and have rendered the design of many cost systems obsolete. For examples, changes have occurred as follows:

(i) variations in cost composition (which we will look at in more detail below) with direct labour becoming a less prominent element;
(ii) rapid changes in markets, with sharper competition (characterized by an increasing tendency towards global competitive challenge);
(iii) rapid changes in technology, bringing increased product and process obsolescence in its wake;
(iv) given (iii) above, frequent changes in the design of products and shorter product life cycles;
(v) a proliferation of products and constant changes in processing methods;
(vi) an increasing emphasis on flexibility in manufacturing and short productions runs;
(vii) a focus on material costs and fixed indirect manufacturing costs;
(viii) an emphasis on strategic aspects (which will be dealt with in Chapter 6).

In recent years the notion of *world class manufacturing* has emerged (see Howell (1987), for example). This refers to the ability to compete effectively on an international basis by recognizing global challenges and the need to adapt as change occurs – or to be proactive and *create* change – rather than being overtaken by events. From a managerial accounting perspective, world class manufacturing puts an emphasis on:

- improvements in quality (as part of the increasing concern with *total quality management* – see Oakland (1989) and Mann (1989));
- reductions in inventory (reflecting a just-in-time philosophy);
- faster throughput and greater flexibility;
- increased automation;
- reorganization to accommodate the points made above;
- an increasing use of information technology (IT) to facilitate the above.

As Shillinglaw (1987, p. 9.8) has pointed out, these emphases are reflected in:

(i) an increased need for accurate, up-to-date estimates of product cost;
(ii) a need to measure or estimate the costs of activities that affect the power to compete, such as quality, inventory, and product variety;
(iii) a need to rethink cost classification systems so that more costs can be linked clearly to individual products, not assigned to them by means of broad-based indirect cost rates.

In seeking to link more costs to individual products (point (iii) above), and to do this in a way that is accurate (point (i) above) and relates to the power to compete

Figure 4.14

Full cost.

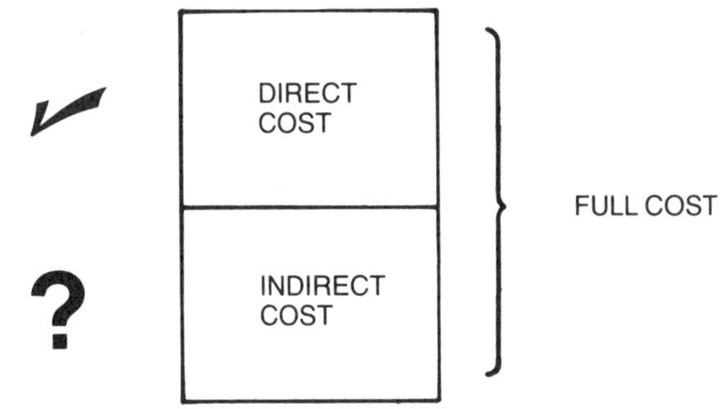

(point (ii) above), a key problem must be overcome. This problem is at the heart of absorption costing: how can one make an acceptable estimate of full cost when there is no way of knowing the real answer? It was observed earlier in this chapter that the real answer is both *unknown* and *unknowable*, given that there is no definitive basis for apportioning or absorbing indirect costs. However, some bases are better than others.

Figure 4.14 shows the impact on full cost of the indirect element.

If an inappropriate approach is used to absorb indirect costs, then the resulting full cost figure is bound to be meaningless and misleading. Such evidence as exists suggests that inappropriate approaches are being used on a wide scale, because cost systems still largely reflect the historical situation that prevailed up to a century ago, rather than the circumstances that prevail today. We can illustrate this phenomenon by drawing on a number of empirical studies. (Whilst none of these studies is as comprehensive as we might like, they all point to a common conclusion.)

Foster and Gupta (1990, p. 314) reported the findings of a survey carried out in the USA in 1985 by the American Electronic Association which was concerned with the manufacturing cost structure for firms in two industries:

	Computers	Instruments
Direct material costs	67.5	54.5
Direct labour costs	6.5	13.1
Indirect costs	26.0	32.4
	100.0%	100.0%

Emore and Ness (1991) undertook a survey of 70 manufacturing companies in the USA in a range of industries and ascertained the following product cost comparisons:

Direct material		Direct labour		Indirect	
% cost	% firms	% cost	% firms	% cost	% firms
≤ 10	5	≤ 10	55	≤ 10	9
11–25	9	11–25	33	11–25	41
> 25	86	> 25	12	> 25	50
	100		100		100

Plossl (1990, p. 63) reported on the changes in cost relationships in manufacturing industry in the USA, as shown in Fig. 4.15.

Figure 4.15

Cost composition — changes over time.

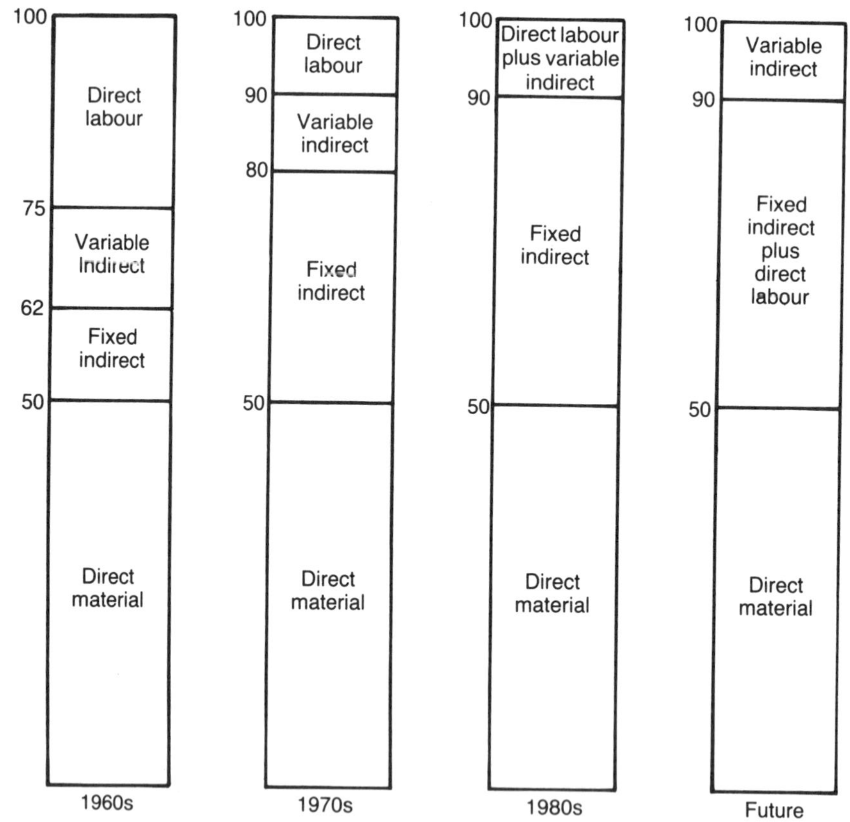

Coopers and Lybrand have shown (in a conference presentation) changes in cost composition also:

	1960	1986	Change
Direct materials costs	56	53	– 5%
Direct labour costs	22	15	–32%
Indirect costs	22	32	+45%
	100%	100%	

It is evident from these empirical studies that direct labour is now much less significant than hitherto; direct material costs have not changed much as a proportion of full cost and remain a significant element; and fixed indirect costs in particular have increased markedly. In some organizations (such as Hewlett Packard) direct labour costs are so small that they are now included with fixed indirect costs – which also highlights changes in the way in which the workforce is viewed. (See Fig. 4.15) But do cost systems reflect the pattern shown in empirical cost studies? The answer, sadly, is that they do not.

Coopers and Lybrand have shown that the allocation of cost control effort is:

Direct material costs	10%
Direct labour costs	75%
Indirect costs	15%
	100%

As shown above, only 10% of control effort is applied to direct material costs which – according to Coopers and Lybrand's figures for 1986 – constituted 53% of total manufacturing cost, yet a massive 75% of control effort is applied to the 15% of manufacturing cost made up of direct labour, and only 15% of control effort is applied to the increasing element of indirect costs.

By the same token the bulk of cost reduction efforts are aimed at producing savings in direct labour costs, because cost systems continue to focus on direct labour costs despite the huge changes that have been taking place in the manufacturing environment. And labour-based indirect cost rates continue to predominate in manufacturing industry, regardless of the evidence which shows that direct labour is an increasingly insignificant element of total cost, and thus an increasingly inappropriate base for recovering indirect costs. Any approximation of full cost that is built up from an indirect cost element based on direct labour is unlikely to be an acceptable approximation (see Fig. 4.14): cost systems need to keep pace with changing circumstances.

As with other aspects of managerial accounting, the evidence of practice in relation to cost systems is rather piecemeal, but such evidence as does exist points very clearly to the dominant role of direct labour as a basis for recovering indirect costs. Emore and Ness (1991), for example, found the following in their USA survey:

Base	% Companies using
Direct labour hours / Direct labour cost	74%
Machine hours	23%
Units produced	21%
Direct material quantity / Direct material cost	20%
Cycle time	7%
Other	4%

A survey by CAM-I (Computer Aided Manufacturing – International) in the UK in 1987 produced the findings shown in Fig. 4.16.

It was evident from this survey that responding companies did not know how to charge indirect costs reliably. Simple methods were typically employed, mainly using a direct labour base of some kind – even in machine-paced manufacturing environments. CAM-I found there to be little recognition that change was needed – although the extensive coverage both in professional media (including articles in periodicals, research reports and conferences/seminars/workshops) and in academic journals of activity-based costing in the years since 1987 is likely to have increased recognition of the need for change. (The work of CAM-I is particularly worthy of comment in this regard: in 1986 it was formed from a coalition of industrial organizations, professional accounting firms, government agencies and business schools to address issues such as this. See, for example, Berliner and Brimson (1988).)

A survey among delegates attending a cost management seminar in London in

Figure 4.16

Bases for allocating indirect costs.

	% Respondents	
	Man-paced environment	Machine-paced environment
Standard labour hours	49%	13%
Actual labour hours	13%	3%
Standard labour cost	10%	13%
Actual labour cost	10%	13%
Standard machine hours	–	41%
Actual machine hours	3%	5%
Units produced	10%	15%
Standard material quantity	15%	5%
Actual material quantity	3%	3%
Standard material cost	13%	13%
Actual material cost	3%	3%
Other	–	5%

1989 showed that the bases in use within the delegates' companies for assigning indirect costs to products were:

(i) Labour hours:	40%
(ii) Machine hours:	15%
(iii) Combination of (i) and (ii):	25%
(iv) Other:	20%
	100%

The consequences of using simple, traditional methods include:

(i) Indiscriminate indirect cost recovery using a single base (e.g. direct labour hours) generates misleading relative product cost data, hence profitability data. (See the Ajax case in Workbook Chapter 4, pp. 456–64.) This in turn is likely to lead to poor tactical and strategic decision-making.
(ii) Failure to understand either the *activities* being carried out by an enterprise or the costs that are created by those activities can lead to an unfocused approach to cost control.

Several authoritative experts have argued that the answer to these problems is to be found in *activity-based costing* (ABC). This is an approach to product costing that recognizes the underlying activities of an enterprise and the costs that *drive* these activities. The basic concept is explained by Innes and Mitchell (1990a) very clearly along the following lines:

Resource consumption incurs costs
Activities consume resources
∴ Activities incur costs
Products consume activities

Figure 4.17

Specimen cost drivers.

Activities	**Specimen cost drivers**
Maintenance	Volume of production
Movement of parts	Number of parts
Stores	Number of issues
Engineering support	Number of engineering changes
Inspection	Number of suppliers
Production	Volume of production
Quality audit	Volume of production
Receiving	Number of receipts
Tool and grinding	Number of factory work orders
Training	Level of people movement
Systems	Number of new systems
General accounting	Number of suppliers
Personnel	Number of employees
Management accounting	Number of variances from plan
Customer services	Number of orders
Boxing and shipping	Volume of production
Security	Number of deliveries

Source: Innes and Mitchell (1991)

The key to understanding ABC is to recognize that cost causality relates to activities rather than, say, to volume throughput (as measured by direct labour hours for instance). This in turn requires an understanding of *cost drivers*: a cost driver is the causal factor in determining the cost of a given activity. Some examples are given in Fig. 4.17.

There will be cases in which an activity's cost may be caused by several cost drivers acting together. (See, for example, Cooper (1989a) (1989b), and Foster and Gupta (1990).) Consider the cost of the activity by which a lorry delivers goods to a number of retail outlets: is the cost of this activity due to the size of the lorry, the number of individuals in the lorry (driver and mate or just driver), the length of the journey, the number of stops/deliveries made, the weight of the goods carried, the average size of a delivery, or the extent to which the items to be delivered are loaded in the correct sequence? (You may be able to think of additional causes of the costs of delivering goods. From this listing you will see that it is too simplistic to think in univariate terms – such as the activity of delivering goods depending solely on miles travelled or the number of units to be delivered. The problem is really of a multivariate nature.)

Gietzmann (1991) has shown (from a case study of an industrial ball bearings company) how cost drivers can link indirect activities to cost objects in order to carry out segmental analyses. He reported the list of cost drivers that were identified in the company in question as follows:

Cost driver	
1	Set-up minutes
2	Total operating minutes
3	Special product inspection time
4	Percentage material value
5	Number of batches
6	Direct costs
7	Number of variable sales order lines
8	Weight of bearings
9	Number of fixed sales order lines
10	Delivery band
11	Number of customers
12	Market support and product support

The indirect activities that need to be costed in any segmental analysis built up on absorption lines are represented in the *indirect cost pools* shown in Fig. 4.18. From this figure it is possible to see how the full costs of different segments can be compiled and, when revenue flows are taken into account, how the profit performance of those segments might be established.

ABC also has a role to play in cost reduction. Conventional cost systems (based on volume throughput measures – such as direct labour hours) will typically misdirect attention and distort the results of actions that are designed to reduce costs. (See Richardson (1988) and Turney (1991).) A comparison is given in Fig. 4.19 between the messages communicated by a conventional cost system on

Figure 4.18

Using cost drivers in segmental analysis.

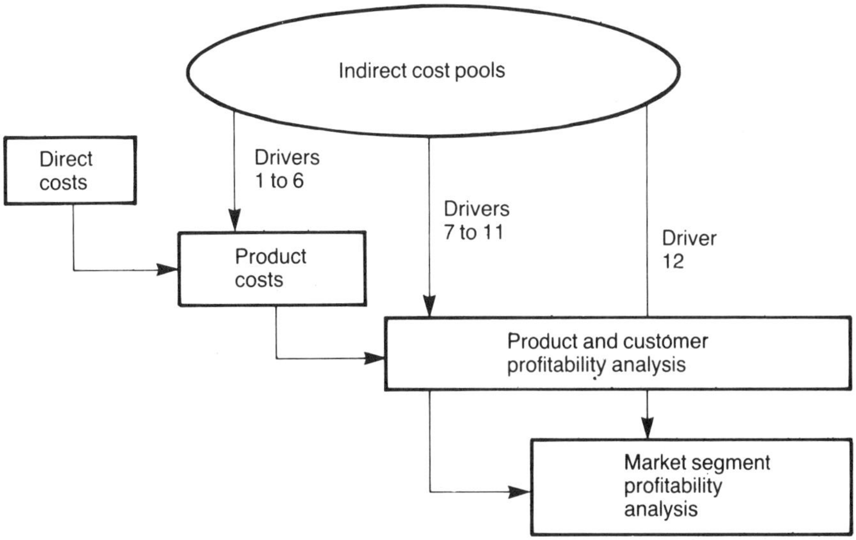

Source: Gietzmann (1991).

Figure 4.19

Examples of messages communicated by conventional and activity-based cost systems.

Examples of ways of achieving cost reduction	Conventional cost system	Activity-based cost system
Reducing set-up time	Ignore or reduce direct labour	Reduce set-up time to achieve low cost diversity
Eliminating material handling activities	Ignore or reduce direct labour	Eliminate activities to reduce the cost of handling
Choosing an insertion process	Pick alternative with lowest unit level activities	Pick lowest cost alternative
Using common components	Using common components achieves no cost savings; using non-common components creates no cost penalty	Use common components wherever possible

Source: Adapted from Turney (1991, p. 32)

the one hand, and those communicated by ABC on the other, with particular reference to ways of achieving cost reduction.

ABC has created a good deal of controversy. There are those who consider its claims to be overstated (see the debate between Piper and Walley, and Cooper in the reprinted articles on pp. 464–80 of Workbook Chapter 4), and those who view the ABC case to be adequately covered by the existing literature which argues for identifying causal factors prior to apportioning/absorbing indirect costs (such as Reider and Saunders (1988)). It seems odd that the work of Staubus (1971, 1991) has not received more attention in this debate.

Perhaps the acid-test of any 'new, improved' technique is to be found in the extent to which it is being used in practice. Subject (again) to the limited knowledge that exists regarding the state of management accounting practice, it does not seem to be the case that ABC has been widely adopted. One report (see NAA (1991a)) has suggested that 11% of companies in the USA have adopted ABC, with more to follow, but the same source (see NAA (1991b)) gives several reasons why the bulk of companies do not intend adopting ABC. Reasons include:

– existing systems considered satisfactory;
– benefits from ABC are uncertain;
– ABC is too costly to develop/install/operate;
– ABC is too complex.

Within the UK, as Newton (1991, p. 30) has observed, few enterprises appear to have fully implemented ABC. Insofar as companies have adopted it successfully and are deriving competitive advantage from ABC, there is no incentive for revealing this to the world at large. For those companies that have tried to develop ABC but have failed to secure any benefits, there is even less incentive for making any public statement.

The Ajax case (see pp. 456–65) should show how an ABC approach gives a basis for securing competitive advantage.

Summary

Within this chapter we have dealt with:

(a) the idea of *cost* and the way in which we might go about calculating the full (or absorbed) cost of activities in which we are interested;
(b) the role of full cost in helping managers to assess the allocation of effort across organizational activities, from which questions can be formulated to guide future decision-making.

Let us review each of these in turn.

(a) Cost and its determination

The essence of cost (in economic terms) is *sacrifice*, which may mean that resources have been given up (which accords with the accounting definition) or that opportunities have not been taken. Any attempt at operationalizing the concept of cost requires the use of an adjective (e.g. we distinguished *direct* cost from *indirect* cost in examining the method by which *full* cost might be determined) and a cost object (which may be any activity of managerial interest).

The designing of managerial accounting systems for ascertaining full cost have usually been introspective and retrospective in that their focus has been on inventory valuation for income measurement (as in the profit and loss account) and balance sheet purposes. We argued that this is merely one use of costing, and not the most significant from a control point of view. It is important to look outwards and forwards, and the selection of cost objects that reflect characteristics of markets, consumers and so forth is to be encouraged.

Whatever the cost objects, the problem of apportioning common costs to functions, and thence to cost objects themselves, is a huge one. Absorption costing really boils down to an attempt to measure that which is both unknown and unknowable. Every attempt – no matter what the logic underlying the selection of bases for assigning costs – can only be arbitrary to a greater or lesser extent. But this does not mean that the results of the exercise are worthless: provided they are used with an awareness of their limitations, and as a guide to raising questions (rather than providing answers), this can help the control effort.

(b) Assessing the allocation of effort

As we saw (with examples from marketing, distribution and manufacturing), absorption costing can indicate the pattern of allocation of effort and its effectiveness (as measured by the ratio of outputs to inputs). In so far as a given segment is performing below par it is possible to formulate possible courses of action to correct this, and so control can be exercised. In this way a link is established between the past and the future.

In any commercial enterprise it is necessary to decide:

(i) what to produce or offer
(ii) where to market one's products or services
(iii) to whom to market
(iv) how to market

and it is helpful in considering such questions to have data available that shows the allocation of effort, and the productivity of that allocation, across segments – including product lines, sales territories, customer groups, etc. (Similar arguments apply in service and non-commercial organizations.)

A number of reasons can be put forward for carrying out full cost analyses that seek to ascertain the net profit of segments of a business:

(i) managers are familiar with net profit data for assessing overall business performance (as reported in published profit and loss accounts) and it seems logical to carry this through to segments;
(ii) the view that each segment should 'stand on its own feet' or 'carry its share of the load' is widely held, and this favours a net profit approach;
(iii) since profit is not realized until *all* operating costs have been covered, it can be argued that costs should be assigned to segmental activities to ensure that they are not overlooked;
(iv) most significantly, it is possible to gain insights into the productivity of segmental activities by means of full cost analyses, and this gives a basis for raising questions about where the organization should allocate its resources in the future to improve its performance.

ABC has emerged (or re-emerged) in recent years as a recommended means by which indirect costs might be more accurately applied to products. There is, as yet, little evidence to suggest that ABC offers all the benefits claimed by its promoters.

In Chapter 5 we will look at ways in which the questions raised by absorption costing might be answered.

Key terms and concepts

Here is a list of the key terms and concepts which have featured in this chapter. You should make sure that you understand and can define each one of them. Page references to definitions in the text appear in bold in the index.

- Cost
  - allocation
  - apportionment
  - absorption
  - direct versus indirect
  - full (or absorbed)
  - opportunity
  - overhead
- Cost driver
- Cost object
- Costing
  - absorption
  - activity-based
  - job/batch
  - process
  - product
- Material issues
  - first in, first out (FIFO)
  - last in, first out (LIFO)
  - weighted average
- Productivity analysis
- Segmental analysis

Further reading

Detailed coverage of the techniques associated with absorption costing can be found in any standard text such as Horngren and Foster (1987), Shillinglaw (1982) or Drury (1992).

Specific coverage of activity costing is offered by Staubus (1971) and (1991). Productivity analysis is covered by Sevin (1965). ABC is dealt with by Kaplan (1988), Cooper and Kaplan (1988), Cooper (1989c), Innes and Mitchell (1990a), Dugdale (1990a, 1990b), and Ward and Patel (1990). See also Williams (1989) and Ames and Hlavacek (1990) on cost management, and the Executive Summary (reprinted in Section W12.6 of Workbook Chapter 12) from Bromwich and Bhimani (1989).

The workbook to accompany this chapter begins on p. 434.

CHAPTER 5 Short-run decision-making

Learning objectives

After studying this chapter you should be able to:

- address the questions raised in Chapter 4 regarding short-run decision-making (where there are no changes of scale);
- identify the costs and revenues that are relevant to short-run decision-making;
- recognize cost behaviour patterns;
- understand the basic ways of accommodating risk and uncertainty in short-run decision-making;
- demonstrate the application of the concepts and techniques discussed in the text to managerial situations.

5.1 Introduction

The essence of management is decision-making – the process of choosing among various courses of action in order to ensure greater organizational effectiveness. Such decisions relate to *future* outcomes and therefore involve considerations relating to risk and uncertainty.

For rational decision-making some form of information is necessary, which presupposes some means of measurement. Preferably, the information will be in quantitative terms, and should relate to the objective to be served. It is easier to make the correct choice when one keeps in mind what one is trying to accomplish. (If there exists more than one objective the decision-maker must balance one against another by making a *trade-off*. For example, the decision-maker may trade off speed for quality in deciding on a particular means of production if this appears to reflect accurately the relative importance of multiple objectives.)

An essential requirement in decision-making is the removal of doubt. Decisions are made in relation to objectives, and are well made if the objectives are attained. However, the uncertainty of the future means that a choice can be wrong. It also means that a single choice has several possible outcomes. (For example, if the decision is made to launch a new product, its sales may be at any one of several levels estimated before the event.) This demands that decisions be reached through systematic analysis.

Making decisions involves focusing on the future. It will be seen later (in Section 5.5) that views of the future are of four types:

(i) ignorance;
(ii) certainty of outcomes (although choices must still be made among various strategies);
(iii) risk – probabilities being assignable to possible outcomes; and
(iv) uncertainty – unable to assign probabilities.

The latter two views are the most usual and, in the case of uncertainty, the decision-maker requires reliable criteria to help in choosing among options, since their consequences cannot be predicted with confidence. This problem can often be solved through the collection of more information, which means that the cost of this information must be balanced with the possible losses due to uncertainty if it is not collected. Further assistance is given by the adoption of a systematic approach to decision-making, such as that contained in Chapter 3.

We will develop this theme of decision-making by looking, in turn, at cost-profit-volume analysis, differential cost analysis and risk analysis. But first it is necessary to deal with some definitions.

5.2 Cost analysis for decision-making

In making decisions managers must pay a great deal of attention to the profit opportunities of alternative courses of action. This requires that, *inter alia*, the cost implications of those alternatives be assessed.

An important distinction in cost analysis for decision-making (but, as we shall see, not the most important one) is often made between fixed and variable costs. A cost can be classified as being either *fixed* or *variable* in relation to changes in the level of activity within a given period of time. (In the long run, of course, *all* costs are variable).

(a) Fixed costs

A cost is fixed if, within a specified time period, it does not change in response to changes in the level of activity. For example, a managing director's salary will not vary with the volume of goods produced during any year, interest payable at 15% p.a. on a loan of £500,000 will not vary with changes in a business's level of activity, and the road tax payable for a motor vehicle will not vary with the vehicle's annual mileage.

Figure 5.1 illustrates a typical fixed cost curve. (If one looks beyond the current time period, however, the managing director's salary may change to £100,000, but not purely in response to changes in output).

If we relate fixed costs to the level of activity (e.g. road tax to miles travelled) we will find that the fixed cost *per unit* of activity is variable: as activity increases, so the fixed cost per unit decreases, and vice versa.

We can categorize an enterprise's fixed costs in the following way:

(i) *Committed costs.* Costs that are primarily associated with maintaining the company's legal and physical existence and over which management has little (if any) discretion. Insurance premiums, rates and rent charges are typical examples.
(ii) *Managed costs.* Such costs include management and staff salaries that are

Figure 5.1

Fixed cost curve.

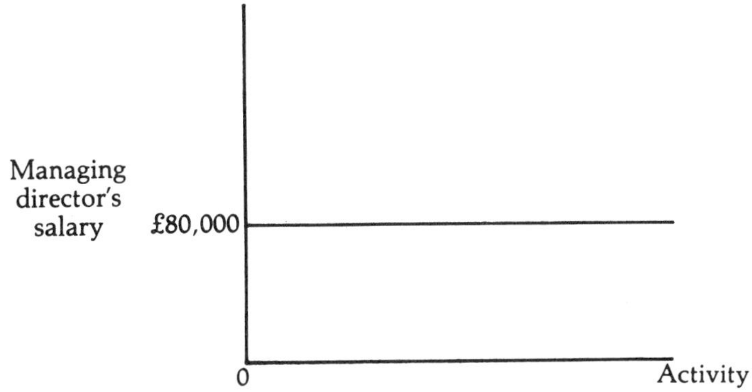

related to current operations but which must continue to be paid to ensure the continued operating existence of the enterprise.

(iii) *Programmed costs.* Costs that are subject both to management discretion and management control, but which are unrelated to current activities. R & D is a good example, and it will be apparent that these costs result from special policy decisions.

(b) Variable costs

A variable cost is one that changes in response to changes in the level of activity. Sales commissions in relation to sales levels, petrol costs in relation to miles travelled, and labour costs in relation to hours worked are obvious examples.

Figure 5.2

Variable cost curve.

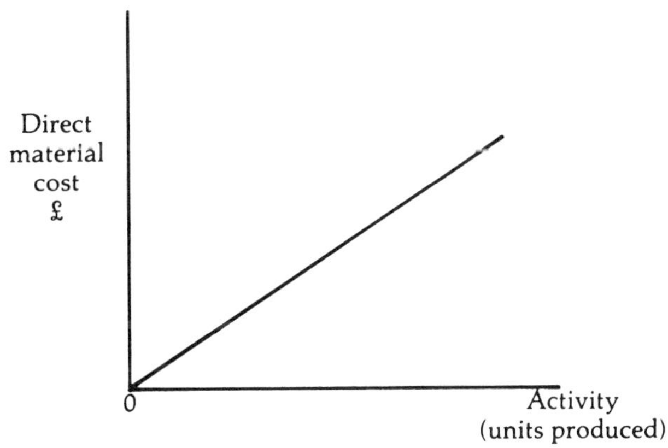

Figure 5.2 shows a variable cost curve for direct materials. It will be apparent that, with certain exceptions, variable costs tend to be fixed per unit of activity but are variable in total in relation to the level of activity. The exceptions result from costs that do not vary in direct proportion to changes in the level of activity. One underlying reason for this – in so far as labour costs are concerned – is the *learning curve*. It is a generally valid element of experience that suggests that our ability to carry out a particular task will be better at the second attempt than it was at the first, and better again, up to a certain optimum point, on each successive attempt. (This gives rise to the adage: 'practice makes perfect'.) This phenomenon applies to groups working together on a common task in the same way that it applies to individuals, and is discussed further in Section 7.4 of Chapter 7.

On the other hand, when a factory is operating at, or near, full capacity it may be necessary for overtime to be worked and this will increase the labour cost per unit of output.

The combination of fixed and variable costs gives us Fig. 5.3.

Figure 5.3

Classified cost pattern for a manufacturing enterprise.

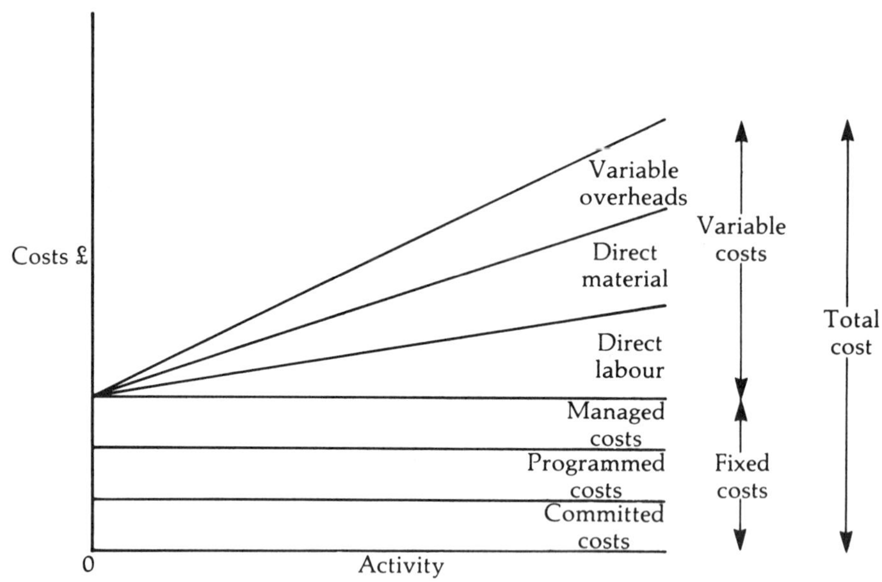

(c) Mixed costs

Certain costs are of a hybrid nature being partly fixed and partly variable. An example is found in telephone charges – the rental element is a fixed cost, whereas charges for calls made are a variable cost. Figure 5.4(a) illustrates this behaviour pattern, and Fig. 5.4(b) shows the semi-variable cost behaviour that

Figure 5.4

Cost behaviour patterns.

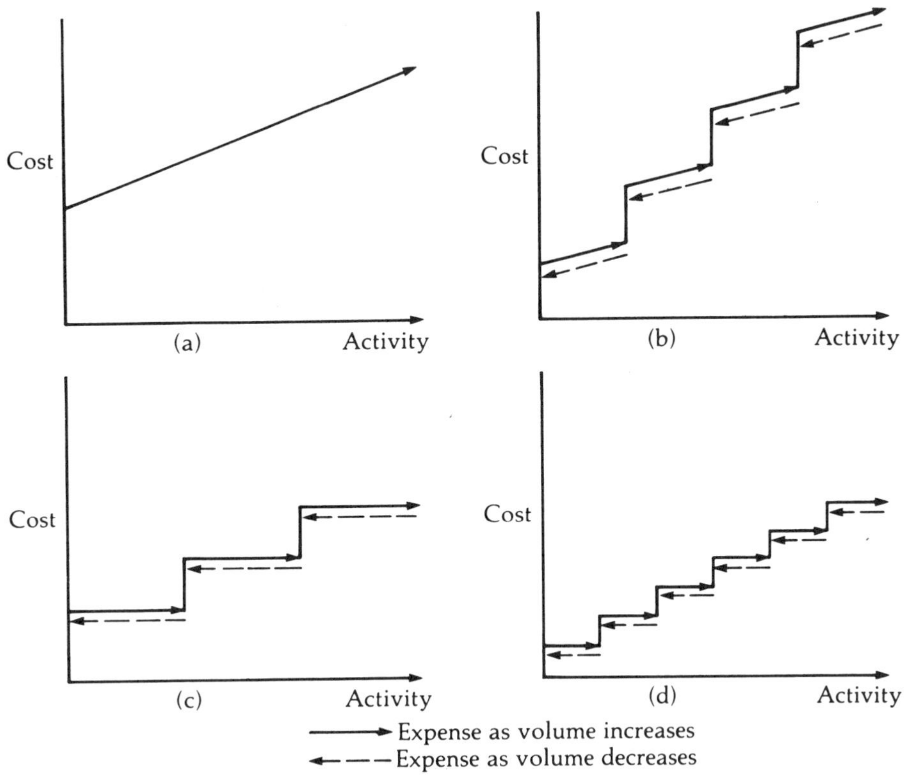

would be found if new telephones are installed as the level of activity changes.

Some mixed costs are characteristically semi-fixed. Up to a given level of output it may only be necessary for a factory to work one shift and it may only need one foreman – a simple instance of a fixed supervisory cost. However, beyond that level of output it may be necessary to start a second shift and recruit a further supervisor, and this gives rise to the stepped cost pattern of Fig. 5.4(c). Maintenance costs payable on a contract basis would tend to follow the pattern of Fig. 5.4(d) if more machines are bought as output increases.

With mixed costs the question arises of whether to treat the cost as partly fixed and partly variable, or as wholly fixed or wholly variable. The answer must depend on the degree of variability of the cost itself and the level of activity.

(d) Usefulness of the fixed-variable split

The importance of separating variable from fixed costs stems from the different behaviour patterns of each, which have a significant bearing on their control.

Variable costs must be controlled in relation to the level of activity, while fixed costs must be controlled in relation to time. From a decision-making point of view, it is also important to know whether or not a particular cost will vary as a result of a given decision.

Because fixed costs must be incurred even when there is no activity, the fixed cost curve (and hence the total cost curve) cuts the vertical axis above the origin, and this results in the total cost curve being proportional – but not *strictly* proportional – to the level of activity.

If a revenue curve is superimposed on the same graph as the cost curves, the result is the *break-even chart* (or profit graph) (see Fig. 5.5) which depicts the profit/loss picture for several possible cost-revenue situations at different levels of activity. Various assumptions underlie break-even analysis – see p. 129. Nevertheless, provided its user appreciates the static nature of this technique he should be able to employ it effectively.

In particular, break-even analysis is useful as a background information device for reviewing overall cost and profit levels, but it can also be used in connection with special decisions such as selecting a channel of distribution or make-or-buy decisions.

Let us consider it in greater detail – and under a better name – in the following section.

5.3 Cost-volume-profit analysis

In making decisions management pays a great deal of attention to the profit opportunities of alternative courses of action. However, in the case of alternatives that involve changes in the level of business, profit does not usually vary in direct proportion to these changes in volume. This is a result of the cost behaviour patterns that were discussed in the last section. Consequently, managers must realize that better evaluations can be made of profit opportunities by studying the relationships among costs, volume and profits, hence the name CVP analysis. Such studies should lead to better decisions.

Profit is clearly a function of sales volume, selling prices and costs. The non-uniform response of certain costs to changes in the volume of business can have a serious impact upon profit. For example, in an enterprise having a high proportion of fixed costs, a seemingly insignificant decline in sales volume from the expected level may be accompanied by a major drop in expected profit. The *break-even chart* or *profit graph* is a simple way of illustrating the interrelationships of costs, profits and levels of business. (This relates to *short-run* relationships only.)

Figure 5.5 shows a simple break-even chart, but this name only emphasizes one aspect of the total analysis – and not the most important aspect in most instances. Thus in Fig. 5.5, point x indicates the units that must be sold in order that total revenue may be equated with total costs at point y.

It is perhaps simpler to show the same relationships by netting total costs and total revenue for each level of activity. This is done in Fig. 5.6 – the profit-volume chart – which highlights the loss area (at levels of activity below the break-even volume) and the profit area (at levels of activity above the break-even volume).

Figure 5.5

Break-even graph or profit chart.

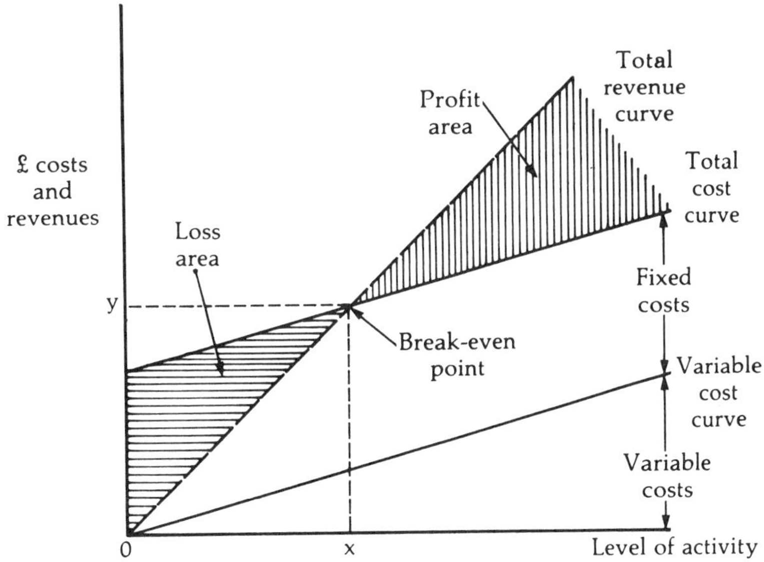

The reason why the total cost curve in Fig. 5.5 does not pass through the origin is the same as the reason why the profit curve of Fig. 5.6 cuts the vertical axis below the point of zero profit: even when there are no sales the fixed costs must be paid and, consequently, the area below the break-even volume represents one of loss (being at its greatest at zero sales).

(a) Relevant range

It has been mentioned that fixed costs are fixed in relation to time, but they are also fixed (or at least deemed to be fixed) through a specific range of activity, termed *the relevant range*. A managing director's salary may be £80,000 in 19X1 as suggested in Fig. 5.1, and this represents a fixed cost of that period. But if the company he directs only operates at 10% of expected activity, or alternatively operates at 200% of expected activity, his level of remuneration or his continued presence at the helm may require further consideration. This could change the level of fixed costs.

Salaries are a good example of a cost that is related closely to responsibility and the size of an undertaking. For this reason top management in large companies earn more than their counterparts in small ones. Costs of an establishment nature are related to the size (hence capacity) of an organization, and this relationship can be expressed in the concept of the relevant range.

A factory may be geared up to producing between 60,000 and 100,000 units of output per period, and its fixed costs will be a major determinant of this potential.

Figure 5.6

Profit-volume chart.

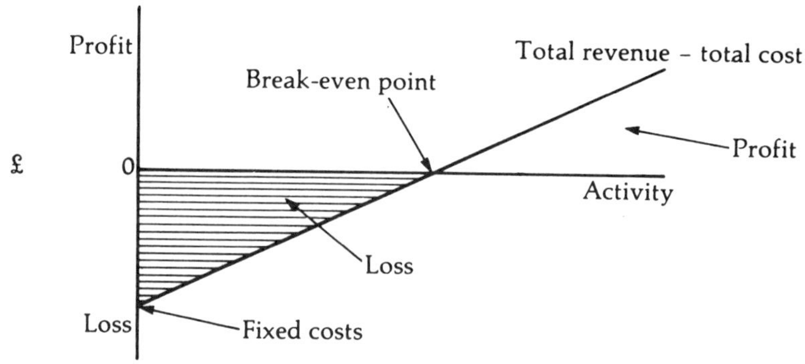

However, if output falls below 60,000 units it may be necessary to close down part of the plant, dismiss executive staff, and cut fixed costs in other ways as well. On the other hand, if output exceeds 100,000 units, the need for further investment in plant and equipment, executive recruitment, and so forth must be considered – i.e. an increase in the level of fixed costs must be contemplated. (Obviously temporary fluctuations in demand will not result in drastic alterations in the capacity base, but prevailing trends over several periods are likely to have this outcome.)

Graphically the situation is shown in Fig. 5.7. Fixed costs will not change when

Figure 5.7

Relevant range — fixed costs.

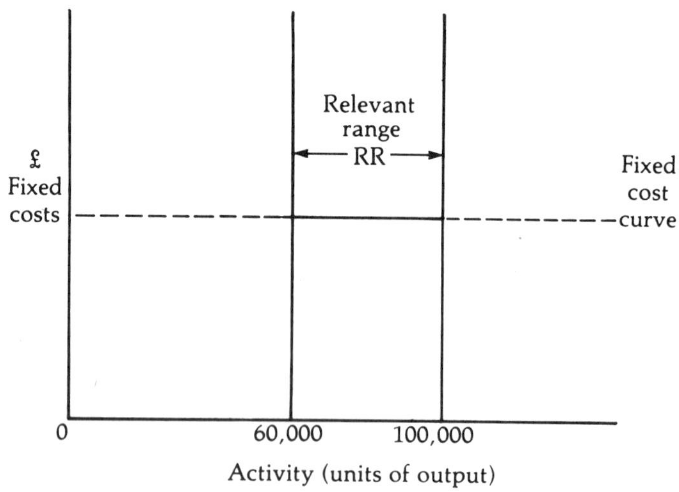

Figure 5.8

Relevant range — variable costs.

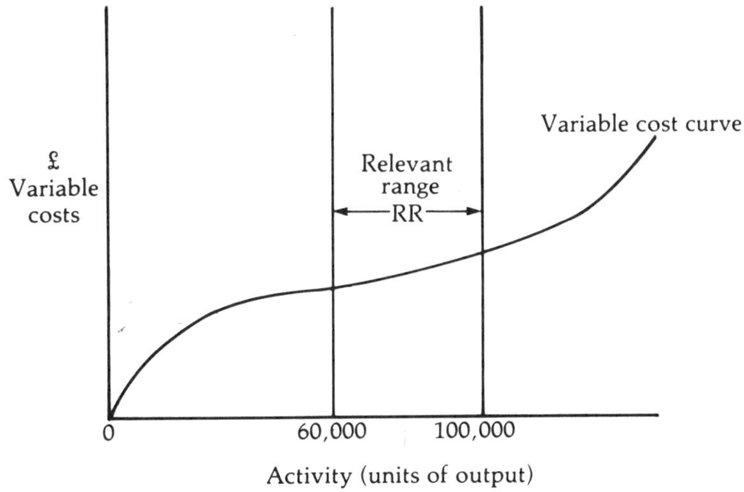

output is within the relevant range of 60,000 to 100,000 units per period. However, at either end of this range a change in the level of fixed costs is quite possible. From this it will be appreciated that discussions of capacity (other than those concerned with further investment in new capacity or, alternatively, divestment of existing capacity) will be in relation to the relevant range.

Within the context of variable costs there is also a relevant range. Figure 5.2 illustrated variable cost behaviour in a very fundamental way. However, the variable cost curve is likely to be curvilinear (as in Fig. 5.8) rather than linear (as in Fig. 5.2). It is conventional practice to treat variable costs as a linear function of output within the relevant range on the basis that a section from a curvilinear function approximates to a straight line. The section on which attention is focused is the relevant range representing the extremes of expected activity: a high of 100,000 units and a low of 60,000 units.

If the curves of Figs 5.7 and 5.8 are superimposed on to a revenue curve (as in Fig. 5.5) we have the relevant range break-even chart of Fig. 5.9. This acknowledges the fact that a wide range of activity is possible, but concentrates on the cost behaviour patterns, revenue function and profit picture within the relevant range. Since the relevant range is related to available capacity and its efficient utilization, Fig. 5.9 is a more realistic device than is Fig. 5.5.

The activity level that is the basis of the measure of capacity in use (e.g. normal activity, practical capacity – see Chapter 7, pp. 222–3) bears no relationship to the break-even volume. If normal activity is the capacity measure used in connection with spreading fixed costs it should be considerably higher than the break-even point – hopefully towards the right-hand side of the relevant range in Fig. 5.9 where a higher level of activity is achieved.

Figure 5.9

Relevant range profitgraph.

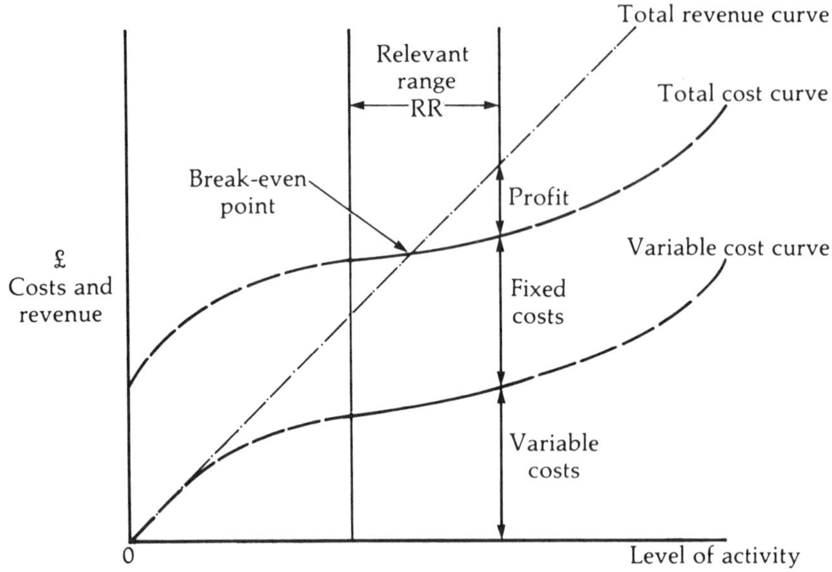

(b) CVP calculations

CVP analysis is not confined to graphical presentations, but extends to the analysis of the relationships underlying the functions shown in the charts. These relationships are amenable to simple mathematical analysis, as will be demonstrated shortly. The basic equation is simple:

Sales revenue = Variable costs + Fixed costs + Profit

It is assumed that any mixed costs have been split into their fixed and variable elements and shown as such.

At the break-even point profit is nil so the equation is even simpler:

Sales revenue = Variable costs + Fixed costs at BE

In physical volume terms the break-even point can be calculated as follows:

$$\text{BE volume} = \frac{\text{Fixed costs}}{\left(\dfrac{\text{Sales revenue} - \text{Variable costs}}{\text{Units sold}}\right)}$$

Thus, if an enterprise had fixed costs of £10,000, variable costs of £15,000 and sold 5,000 units for £30,000, the break-even volume equals:

$$\frac{10{,}000}{\left(\dfrac{30{,}000 - 15{,}000}{5{,}000}\right)} = 33{,}333 \text{ units}$$

In financial terms the break-even volume can be derived by applying the formula:

$$\frac{\text{Fixed costs}}{1 - \left(\dfrac{\text{Variable costs}}{\text{Sales revenue}}\right)} = \frac{\text{Fixed costs}}{\text{Contribution margin ratio}}$$

and, using the data referred to above, is equal to:

$$\frac{10{,}000}{1 - \left(\dfrac{15{,}000}{30{,}000}\right)} = \frac{10{,}000}{0.5} = £20{,}000$$

The proof is simple. The unit price is £30,000/5,000 or £6, and the unit variable cost is £15,000/5,000 or £3. The unit *contribution* is therefore £3 (i.e. £6 – £3) and sufficient units must be sold to cover the fixed costs: £10,000/3 = 3,333 units. At a selling price of £6 each the break-even sales revenue is 3,333 × £6 = £20,000.

The contribution concept is of vital importance in CVP analysis, and represents the difference between the selling price and the variable cost of an item. It is, in fact, the contribution that the sale of a product makes to fixed costs and profits *after* having covered the *avoidable* (i.e. variable) costs of that product. This point indicates the realistic perspective of CVP analysis in not attempting to allocate common costs to units of output since the possibility of volume variations renders a unit total cost, with its associated net profit margin, meaningless.

The *contribution margin ratio* is the percentage of a volume change that is composed of sales revenue minus variable costs. In our example the revenue from an additional sale is £6, and the additional costs, all variable, amount to £3. The contribution margin ratio is, therefore, 1 – 3/6 = 0.5, or 50%. In other words, half the revenue from changes in volume is sufficient to cover the variable costs, and the other half contributes to fixed costs and profits.

The slope of the profit curve in Fig. 5.6 is given by this ratio, indicating that (for this example) a given change in volume will cause the profit to vary accordingly by 50% of the change. The assumption underlying this ratio's application is that other factors must remain constant, and it should be evident that this is a somewhat unrealistic assumption. Nevertheless, if a change in sales (in the above example) of £10,000 takes place, the change in profits will be as shown in Fig. 5.10.

This shows clearly that, with a contribution margin (or profit-volume) ratio of 50%, the profit variation for an upward movement is the same as that for a downward movement, except that it is positive in the former and negative in the latter, and is equal to one half of the change.

A further equation can be devised to measure the *margin of safety*. This is the excess of actual (or budgeted) sales over the break-even volume. The relevant equation is:

$$\frac{\text{Actual sales} - \text{Sales at break-even point}}{\text{Actual sales}}$$

Figure 5.10

Profit-volume variations.

	Original volume £	Increase in volume £	Decrease in volume £
Sales	30,000	+10,000	−10,000
Variable costs	15,000	+ 5,000	− 5,000
Fixed costs	10,000	Unchanged	Unchanged
Total costs	25,000	+ 5,000	− 5,000
Profit	£ 5,000	£+ 5,000	£− 5,000

Again, the data given earlier can be used to demonstrate the application of this equation. In percentage terms, the margin of safety is:

$$£\frac{30{,}000 - 20{,}000}{30{,}000} = \frac{1}{3} \text{ or } 33\tfrac{1}{3}\,\%$$

This ratio means that sales can fall by one-third before a loss will be incurred – assuming that the other relationships are accurately measured and remain constant.

If one considers the case of an enterprise with a high level of fixed costs, a small contribution margin ratio and a low margin of safety, it is apparent that this is not a very healthy situation. Attempts should, perhaps, be made to reduce the fixed costs (i.e. the *programmed* rather than the *committed* costs), and also to increase the level of sales activity, or at least consider an increase in selling prices along with the possibility of a reduction in variable costs.

(c) Managerial purposes of CVP analysis

One of the major purposes of CVP analysis is to enable management to select the most desirable operating plans for achieving the enterprise's profit objective – under the circumstances foreseeable at the time the decision is to be made. Indeed, CVP analysis can be viewed as a way of translating a given objective (e.g. profit level) into a more operational subobjective (e.g. sales volume), and thus aids planning considerably.

More specifically, CVP analysis can aid decision-making in the following typical areas:

(i) the identification of the minimum volume of activity that the enterprise must achieve to avoid incurring a loss;
(ii) the identification of the minimum volume of activity that the enterprise must achieve to attain its profit objective;
(iii) the provision of an estimate of the probable profit or loss at different levels of activity within the range reasonably expected;

(iv) the provision of data on relevant costs for special decisions relating to pricing, keeping or dropping product lines, accepting or rejecting particular orders, make or buy decisions, sales mix planning, altering plant layout, channels of distribution specification, promotional activities, and so on.

The combination of CVP studies and budgets is of value in considering the range of possible outcomes. This is readily done by using preliminary budget figures as the basis for a profit graph. If a particular budget is shown to be unsatisfactory, then the parameters can be recast until a more suitable budget results. In this way the profit graph can conveniently report the overall profit plan to interested parties in a vivid way. One graph is easier to appreciate than a sheet full of numbers, and has the added advantage of portraying the essential relationships in a straightforward manner.

When numerical budget statements are used for short-term planning purposes it is often helpful if they highlight the contribution margins of the various products. This is simply done by distinguishing between the variable costs and the fixed costs, with the latter being shown as a single figure as in Fig. 5.11. Thus the contribution margin statement can explain the cost-volume-profit behaviour in a way that is not possible in the traditional 'full cost' type of statement.

However, the very simplicity of CVP analysis points the way to its weaknesses and limitations. The major weakness is in the underlying assumptions. Profit varies not only with changes in volume, but also with changes in production methods, marketing techniques and other factors. Yet the typical CVP study is unable to allow for these possibilities, and at best indicates the profit that may be expected under a single set of assumed conditions regarding external factors as well as managerial policies. Thus it is a static representation of the situation it purports to illustrate; a different set of circumstances would almost certainly result in a different series of cost-volume-profit relationships.

Any of the assumptions underlying CVP analysis can be modified in order to produce a more realistic model that is better suited to specific circumstances. This can be demonstrated by reference to Fig. 5.12, in which the usual assumption that

Figure 5.11

Contribution and profit statement.

	Total	Product X	Product Y	Product Z
Sales: Units	–	100	250	150
	£	£	£	£
Sales revenue	4,750	1,000	3,000	750
Variable costs	1,950	300	1,400	250
Contribution	£2,800	£ 700	£1,600	£500
Fixed costs	2,000			
Profit	£ 800			

Figure 5.12

CVP analysis with a market demand schedule.

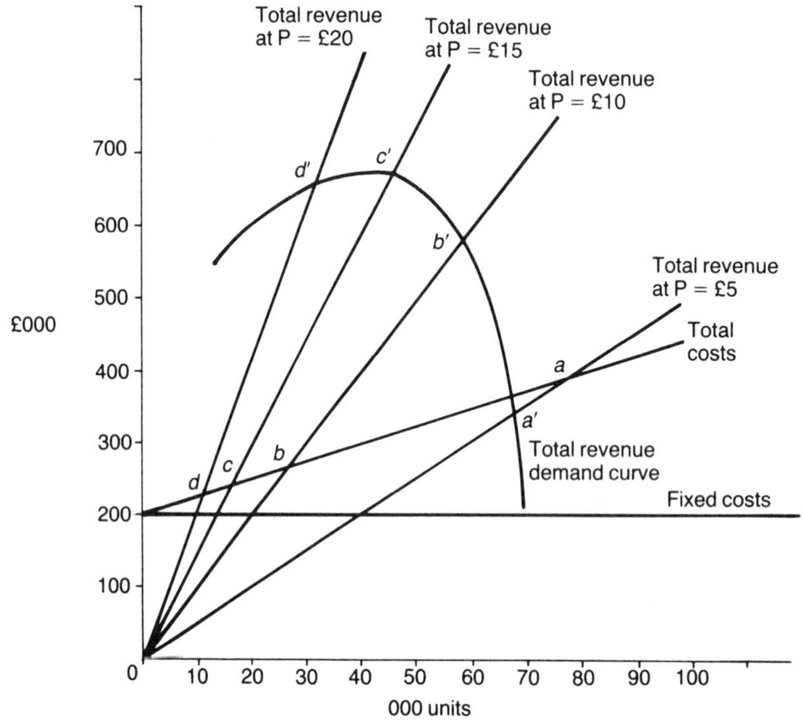

only one selling price applies is relaxed (modified from Cravens and Lamb (1986), p. 31). Fixed costs are given at £200,000, the unit variable cost is £2.50, and demand forecasts are shown for a number of different prices: £5, £10, £15 and £20. The greatest profit is generated by the £15 price, and this can be confirmed by the following calculation:

Sales revenue (45,000 units at £15.00)	£675,000
Variable costs (45,000 units at £2.50)	£112,500
Contribution	£562,500
Fixed costs	£200,000
Profit	£352,500

The break-even volume can be derived from the formula:

$$\frac{\text{Fixed costs}}{\text{Unit contribution}} = \frac{£200{,}000}{£15.00 - £2.50} = 16{,}000 \text{ units}$$

At £15.00 per unit the break-even point expressed in terms of revenue is:

$$16{,}000 \times £15 = £240{,}000$$

This gives a margin of safety of:

$$\frac{£675{,}000 - £240{,}000}{£675{,}000} \times 100 = 64\%$$

In Fig. 5.12 the line connecting the points a', b', c' and d' constitutes the market demand curve for the product in question.

It should not be thought that the limitations outweigh the advantages of CVP analysis. Provided the users of such analyses are aware of the assumptions and limitations this technique is of considerable value in supplying necessary information for planning and guiding managerial decision-making. As with many other modern tools of management, CVP analysis throws some light on a wide range of matters, but needs to be supplemented by other techniques and considerations if balanced decisions are to be arrived at.

(d) Extensions of the contribution approach

Two extensions of the contribution approach warrant our attention: one involves the identification of separable fixed costs for purposes of segmental analysis; and the other involves the valuation of inventory on a variable cost basis, which can have a significant impact on reported profit. Let us take these in turn.

Separation of fixed costs

Figure 5.13 offers a very simple example of segmental analysis using a contribution approach. It will often be the case, however, that some fixed costs are directly

Figure 5.13

Segmental contribution.

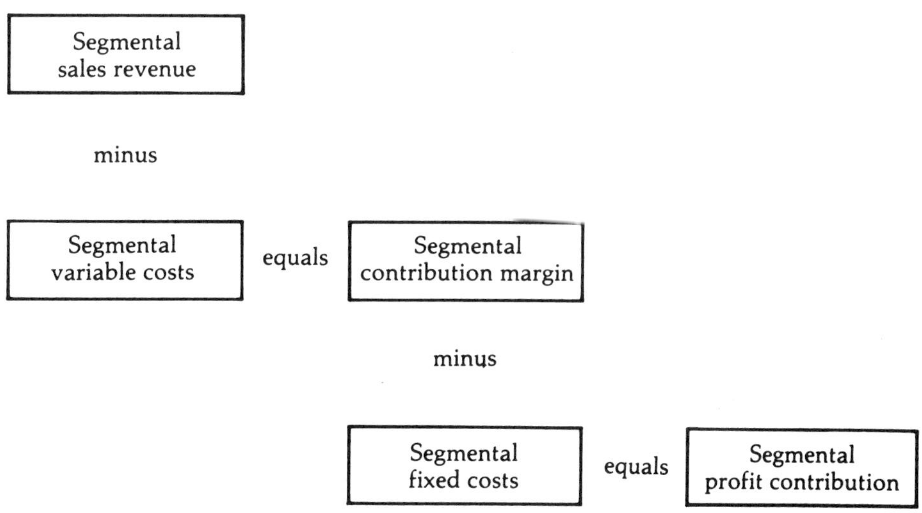

attributable to specific segments: salesmen's salaries in relation to their sales territories; product advertising outlays in relation to product lines; rent, rates, insurance, etc., for regional offices in relation to regional operations. In so far as separable fixed costs can be identified as being specifically incurred for the benefit of a chosen cost object or segment we can define that segment's profit contribution as shown in Fig. 5.13. It is a straightforward matter to translate this approach into a financial statement, and this is done via Fig. 5.14.

In this figure the actual or projected results can be shown for an enterprise's two territories, North and South, as well as for the overall results. The deduction of variable manufacturing cost of sales from net sales revenue (i.e. total sales revenue less discounts and returns) gives us a *manufacturing contribution*. From this we can deduct variable marketing expenses to arrive at a *variable contribution* (which corresponds with the segmental contribution margin in Fig. 5.13. The next step is to assign separable fixed costs to segments. The salaries of salesmen and sales managers – when hired to cover specific territories – are direct fixed costs of their particular territories. Similarly, any advertising or promotional outlays of

Figure 5.14

Segmental contribution statement.

	North territory	South territory	Total
	(£)	(£)	(£)
Net sales	xxx	xxx	xxxx
Variable manufacturing cost of sales	xx	xx	xxx
Manufacturing contribution	xx	xx	xxx
Marketing costs			
Variable:			
Sales commissions	x	x	x
Selling expenses	x	x	x
Variable contribution	xx	xx	xxx
Fixed but separable:			
Salesmen's salaries	x	x	x
Manager's salary	x	x	x
Product advertising	x	x	x
Segment contribution	xx	xx	xx
Non-separable:			
Corporate advertising			x
Marketing contribution			xx
Fixed common costs:			
Manufacturing			x
Administration			x
Net profit			xx

a programmed nature within territories are direct fixed costs of their territories. A *segment contribution* results from the matching of separable segmental fixed costs with the variable contribution.

The segment contribution represents the limit of direct matching. Beyond this it is only possible to apportion costs using bases that are inevitably arbitrary to a greater or lesser extent (as we saw in Chapter 4). In Fig. 5.14, therefore, the non-separable marketing costs (i.e. those that have been incurred for the benefit of the whole enterprise) are not apportioned to territories. In the same way, common fixed costs of manufacturing and administration are treated as corporate – rather than segmental – costs.

From this layout it is immediately apparent how much is being contributed by each segment, and which costs are common. This gives a clear focus for decision-making purposes.

Valuation of inventories

The other extension of the contribution approach – the valuation of inventories using variable costs only – has actually been illustrated in Fig. 5.14 where cost of sales was measured purely on a variable cost basis. Under this variable costing approach (which is also known as direct costing, although this is a slight misnomer since some variable costs are indirect), fixed costs are viewed as being *period costs* and are charged directly to the profit and loss account as costs of the period to which they relate. As a result there is no apportionment of fixed costs to products,

Figure 5.15

Illustration of variable costing to show differences from absorption costing.

Gilligan & Co. Ltd manufactures gazebos and currently operates an absorption costing system for valuing inventory, but the company's financial controller, Leslie Axelby, has suggested that it consider switching to variable costing. To help him understand the impact of the change the managing director of the company has asked Mr Axelby to produce statements that show last month's results using both approaches.

Details relating to last month's operations are:

Opening inventory (units)	Nil
Units produced	500
Closing inventory (units)	100
Manufacturing costs:	
Direct materials	£37,500
Direct labour	£25,000
Indirect	£40,000
Sales revenue	£120,000

Indirect manufacturing costs have not hitherto been split between fixed and variable categories, but it is estimated that a fixed indirect cost rate would approximate to £3.00 per direct labour hour. The direct labour rate paid during the month was £4.00.

Required:

(a) Value the inventory at the month's end using (i) absorption and (ii) variable costing approaches. (Show workings.)

(b) Produce statements that show the trading results for last month under: (i) absorption costing; (ii) variable costing.

and so inventories (and thus cost of sales) are valued wholly on the basis of their variable cost components, namely:

(i) direct material costs;
(ii) direct labour costs;
(iii) variable indirect manufacturing costs.

An example will illustrate both the application of variable costing, and the way in which it differs from absorption costing. This is given in Fig. 5.15.

Solution

Gilligan & Co. Ltd

(a) Since the direct labour rate per hour during the month was £4.00 there must have been £25,000/£4.00 hours worked (i.e. 6,250). The *fixed* indirect manufacturing costs thus amounted to (6,250 × £3.00) = £18,750.

Variable indirect manufacturing costs, in total, must therefore have been £(40,000 − 18,750) = £21,250. This gives a variable indirect cost rate per direct labour hour of £21,250/6,250 = £3.40.

The cost of manufacturing can be calculated as follows:

	Total	Units	Cost per unit
	£	£	£
Direct material costs	37,500	500	75
Direct labour costs	25,000	500	50
Variable indirect costs	21,250	500	42.50
Variable cost	83,750	500	167.50
Fixed indirect costs	18,750	500	37.50
Absorbed cost	102,500	500	£205.00

(i) The closing inventory on an absorption basis is 100 units at £205 = £20,500.
(ii) The closing inventory on a variable costing basis is 100 units at £167.50 = £16,750.

(b) (i) Trading results under absorption costing:

	£	£
Sales revenue (400 at £300)		120,000
Cost of goods sold:		
Opening inventory	0	
Manufacturing costs	102,500	
	102,500	
Closing inventory	20,500	82,000
Gross profit for month		£38,000

(ii) Trading results under variable costing:

	£	£
Sales revenue (400 at £300)		120,000
Cost of goods sold:		
Opening inventory	0	
Maunfacturing costs	83,750	
	83,750	

	£	£
Closing inventory	16,750	67,000
Manufacturing contribution for month		53,000
Less: Fixed manufacturing costs		18,750
Gross margin for month		£34,250

These results can be reconciled as follows:

Absorption cost profit − Variable cost profit =
Change in inventory × Fixed indirect cost per unit

∴ £38,000 − £34,250 = 100 × £37.50
∴ £3,750 = £3,750

In so far as fixed indirect manufacturing costs are not absorbed into cost of goods sold as product costs they will be charged against revenues as period costs.

When inventories of finished goods are rising (i.e. their rate of production exceeds their rate of sale), the absorption-cost-based results will look better than the variable-cost-based results due to fixed indirect manufacturing costs being retained in inventory rather than being charged against revenue. Conversely, when inventories are falling (i.e. their rate of sale exceeds their rate of production), the variable-cost-based results will appear to be better since the period cost of fixed indirect manufacturing costs will be less than the amount contained in absorbed product cost.

Benefits of variable costing

(i) It highlights the contribution that a division or other segment makes to an enterprise's overall profit, avoiding the problems of circular reasoning (volume → cost → volume) that tend to arise in absorption costing.

(ii) It avoids errors that result from managers failing to understand the bases on which indirect costs are apportioned, or the meaning of the resulting full cost/net profit figures, and hence using these figures incorrectly in their decision-making.

(iii) It avoids controversy over the choice of bases on which to apportion or absorb indirect fixed costs.

(iv) It helps focus attention on costs and revenues that will vary between one course of action and another, thereby facilitating differential analysis — and better decision-making.

(v) Contribution figures can often be obtained with less effort than net profit figures due to the elimination of apportionment routines, and this can result in more prompt provision of information to decision-makers.

(vi) In summary, it results in simpler data that is better suited to short-run decision-making.

5.4 Differential cost and revenue analysis

It was stated at the beginning of Section 5.2 (p. 118) that the fixed/variable split was not the most important one for decision-making purposes. That distinction goes to the notion of *differential cost* (and, similarly, to differential revenue) which, in a situation of choice, exhibits the following characteristics:

(i) it is the cost (or revenue) that differs between one course of action and another;
(ii) it is a future cost (or revenue).

We should note that a differential cost may be one that varies with changes in the level of activity, or it may not. Thus it would be wrong to suppose that differential costs are exclusively composed of variable costs in the same way that it would be wrong to suppose that direct costs are necessarily variable. It all depends upon the particular situation and the question at issue.

If a choice is being made between owning as opposed to renting warehouse space as it is needed, the differential cost will include several fixed elements. Among the ownership costs, for example, will be rates, insurance and depreciation, which are all fixed costs in relation to the capacity of the warehouse. In contrast, the cost of renting space varies with the amount of space rented. Differential costs are future costs that differ between one course of action and another – whether fixed or variable.

When the choice is between an existing way of doing something and a new alternative it is helpful to think in terms of *avoidable* versus *unavoidable* costs. Thus the costs of adopting an alternative are avoidable if one persists with the present way of doing things, but not all of the present costs will necessarily be avoidable if one changes to an alternative. (For example, if one manufactures gas appliances, and plans are being made to bring out a new range and cease offering the existing range, it will continue to be necessary – according to British Gas PLC rules – to maintain an inventory of spares for the existing range for 15 years after it ceases to be offered. There are unavoidable costs involved in maintaining stocks of spares.)

A *direct cost* (as we saw in Chapter 4) is one that is traceable to a given cost object. If we are interested in establishing the cost of operating in a particular region the annual rent of the regional office, the salaries of regional personnel, and the depreciation charges on fixed assets located in the region are all examples of direct costs of the region that are of a fixed character.

Once funds have been committed to a particular purpose – especially in the case of capital expenditure (see Chapter 6, Section 6.5) – the chances of recovering them depend upon how much can be obtained from either disposing of the asset, or selling the output from the asset. The funds so committed are termed *sunk costs*, and are irrelevant in deciding whether to abandon or continue operations, or to replace an old asset with a new one. This is so because no present or future action can undo the decision to spend the money. The funds have been spent regardless of what happens next.

We might note at this point the problem over terminology concerning costs for decision-making. Differential costs are also known as relevant costs, incremental costs and marginal costs. Strictly, *marginal* cost refers to the change in total cost resulting from the production of one more (or one less) unit of output. Almost certainly, therefore, marginal cost is a variable cost concept, whereas the other versions may be treated as synonyms and are not restricted to variable costs.

Identifying relevant cost and revenue data for decision-making purposes is not always straightforward. Figures do not automatically emerge with handy labels such as 'differential cost' or 'avoidable cost', but have to be carefully specified and compiled. This task is often made difficult in practice due to the widespread tendency for indirect costs to be apportioned across an enterprise's range of activities. We saw in Chapter 4 that this can be helpful for some purposes, but we also need to recognize that it can hinder others. A cost that is indirect in relation to a given cost object will usually be common to a number of cost objects. If this is so then it is unlikely that it will be avoidable, or relevant, from the point of view of any particular cost objective (but see *attributable cost* – p. 160 below).

(a) Examples of differential analysis

Let us consider first the example of a toy manufacturing enterprise (adapted from Heitger and Matulich (1980), pp. 199–206) which plans to produce a plastic dump truck to sell at £5.00 and which has a choice of two alternative (i.e. mutually exclusive) methods of production.

(i) Method A involves leasing a plastic moulding machine at a cost of £6,000 p.a. and entering into an annual maintenance contract which will cost £2,000 p.a.
(ii) Method B involves the leasing of a more expensive machine at £29,000 p.a. with an annual maintenance contract costing £3,000 p.a. However, this alternative uses less labour than Method A.

The expected costs of the two alternatives are given in Fig. 5.16 (occupancy costs cover the rent, etc., of the premises in which the machine will be located).

All these costs are future costs but not all are differential. Costs that do not vary among alternatives are not relevant to decision-making, so we can ignore occupancy costs (i.e. rent, etc.), and material costs. The truth of this can readily be proven, so let us do so by approaching the choice between Method A and Method B on the basis of all the available data.

If we take a pessimistic estimate of the annual sales volume for the dump truck as being 13,000 units the picture given in Fig. 5.17 emerges.

Figure 5.16

Costs of alternatives.

	Method A £	Method B £	Differential cost
Annual fixed costs:			
Occupancy costs	4,000	4,000	–
Lease cost	6,000	29,000	23,000
Maintenance contract	2,000	3,000	1,000
	£12,000	£36,000	£24,000
Variable cost per unit:			
Material	1.00	1.00	–
Labour	2.50	1.00	1.50
	£3.50	£2.00	£1.50

Figure 5.17

Comparative profits (1).

	Method A		Method B	
	£	£	£	£
Sales: 13,000 at £5.00		65,000		65,000
Fixed costs	12,000		36,000	
Variable costs:				
13,000 at £3.50	45,500			
13,000 at £2.00			26,000	
Total costs		57,500		62,000
Profit		£ 7,500		£ 3,000

In contrast, if a more optimistic sales estimate was 18,000 units p.a. this would produce a different picture as in Fig. 5.18.

At an annual sales volume of 13,000 units Method A is to be preferred, whereas Method B is preferable at a volume of 18,000 units p.a. This approach fails to yield a general solution, but such a solution can be achieved using differential data. In principle what we wish to identify is the *point of cost indifference* at which the lower fixed costs of Method A are exactly offset by the lower unit variable costs of Method B. It is clear that A is preferable up to this point and B is preferable beyond it. Let us call this point X.

At X, the point of cost indifference, the total costs of A will equal those of B:

$$TC(A) = TC(B)$$

Since total costs consist of fixed and variable elements we have:

$$FC(A) + VC(A) = FC(B) + VC(B)$$

(We can show this graphically – as in Fig. 5.19.)

Figure 5.18

Comparative profits (2).

	Method A		Method B	
	£	£	£	£
Sales: 18,000 at £5.00		90,000		90,000
Fixed costs	12,000		36,000	
Variable costs:				
18,000 at £3.50	63,000			
18,000 at £2.00			36,000	
Total costs		75,000		72,000
Profit		£15,000		£18,000

If we substitute the data from Fig. 5.19 into this equation we get:

£12,000 + £3.50X = £36,000 + £2.00X

which reduces to:

£1.50X = £24,000

Therefore X = 16,000 units. At volumes in excess of 16,000 units p.a., then, Method B is the best, but at lower volumes Method A is the best.

Figure 5.19

Comparative costs.

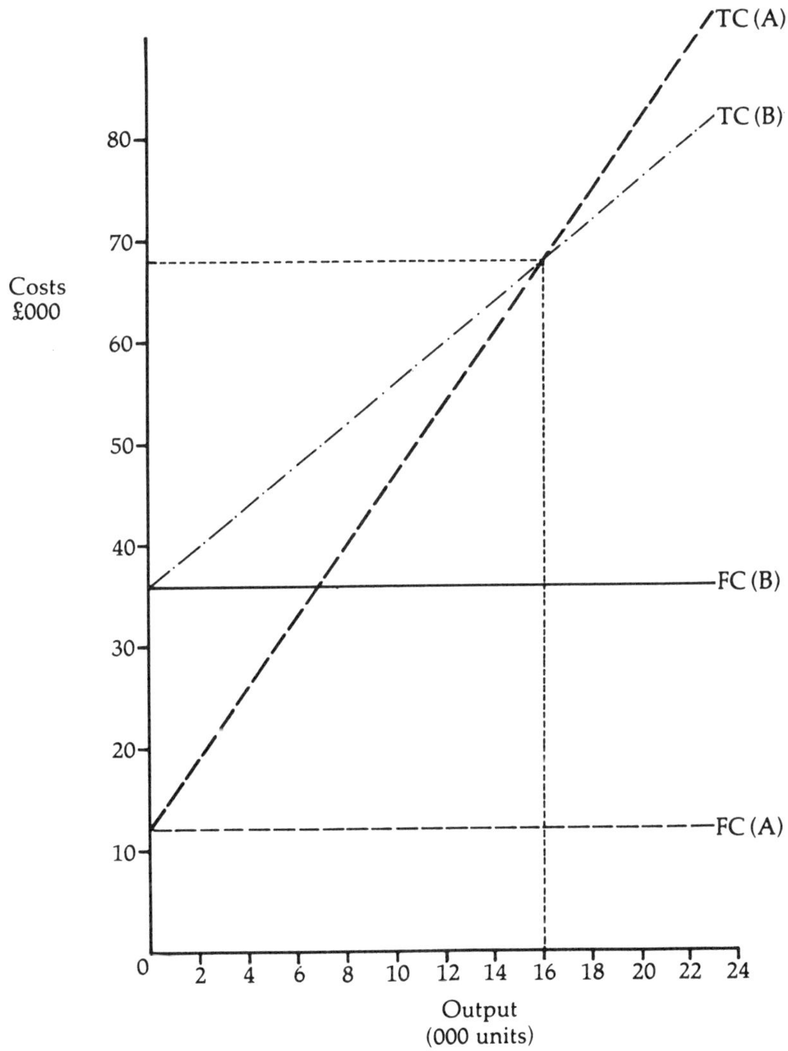

However, we can prove this rather more efficiently by using the differential costs on their own:

$$X = \frac{\text{Differential FC}}{\text{Differential unit VC}} = \frac{£24{,}000}{£1.50}$$
$$= 16{,}000 \text{ units}$$

Figure 5.20 gives a graphical portrayal of this differential cost solution.

As a final aspect of this illustration we can contrast the point of cost indifference with the break-even point. If Method A is chosen the break-even point is given by:

$$\frac{\text{FC}}{\left(\frac{\text{Unit SP} - \text{Unit VC}}{\text{Unit SP}}\right)} = \frac{£12{,}000}{£\left(\frac{5.00 - 3.50}{5.00}\right)}$$

Figure 5.20

Differential costs.

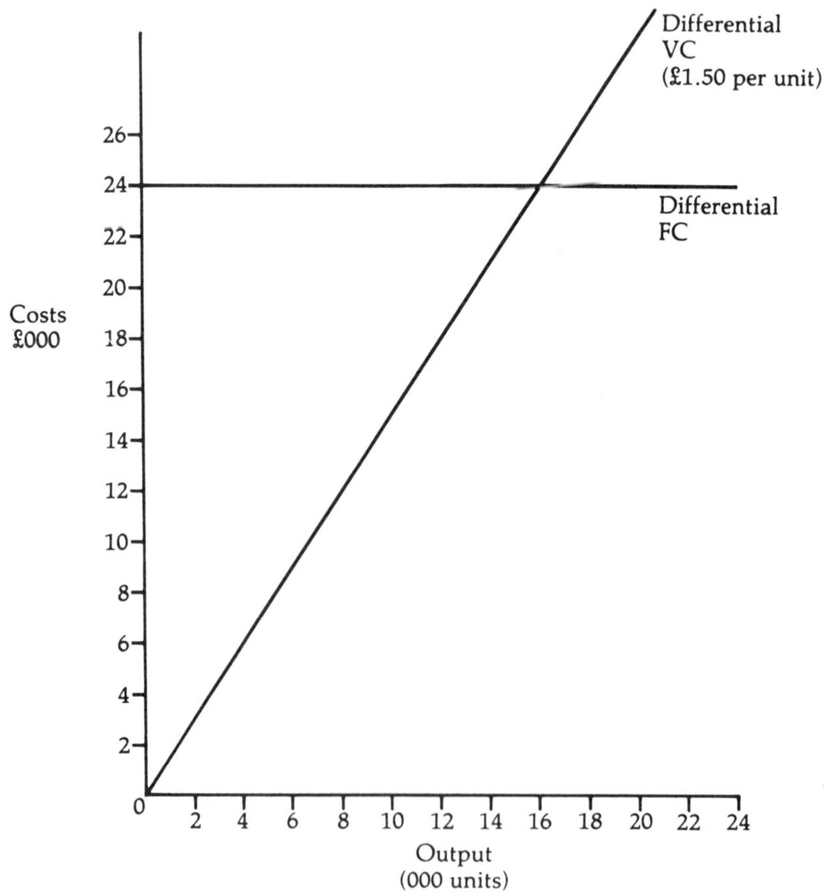

which gives the BEP as £40,000 or 8,000 units.

On the other hand, for Method B the BEP is given by:

$$\frac{£36{,}000}{£\left(\frac{5.00 - 2.00}{5.00}\right)} = £60{,}000 \text{ or } 12{,}000 \text{ units}$$

However, the point of cost indifference corresponds with neither 8,000 nor 12,000 units, being 16,000 units. At an annual sales volume of 16,000 the respective margins of safety are:

$$\text{Method A: } \frac{16{,}000 - 8{,}000}{16{,}000} = 50\%$$

$$\text{Method B: } \frac{16{,}000 - 12{,}000}{16{,}000} = 25\%$$

which seems to favour the former.

Apart from choosing among different ways of doing things another common decision relates to product lines – especially when a particular product line looks to be unprofitable. Let us now consider a situation in which an enterprise has three product lines, X, Y and Z, with the cost/revenue characteristics as in Fig. 5.21.

The overall picture is that total revenue (£206,130) exceeds total costs (£181,560) by £24,570, but when costs are spread across the product lines it appears that product Y is unprofitable. The question, therefore, is whether or not to delete Y from the range in order to improve overall profit performance.

An answer to this question cannot be provided from the data in Fig. 5.21 since that data fails to identify the differential costs and revenues on which sound decisions must be based. A fuller breakdown of costs is needed, and this is offered in Fig. 5.22.

Figure 5.21

Net profit by product line.

	Product X £	Product Y £	Product Z £	Total £
Unit selling price	4.86	3.70	9.87	
Unit cost (fully absorbed)	4.51	3.92	7.43	
Unit net profit	£0.35	£(0.22)	£2.44	
Annual volume (units)	15,000	12,000	9,000	
Total sales revenue	72,900	44,400	88,830	206,130
Total costs	67,650	47,040	66,870	181,560
Net profit	£ 5,250	£(2,640)	£21,960	£24,570

Figure 5.22

Analysis of annual total costs by product line.

	Product X £	Product Y £	Product Z £	Total £
Direct costs:				
Variable:				
Direct material	17,100	8,760	19,620	45,480
Direct labour	16,500	14,880	15,840	47,220
Distribution	6,750	3,000	6,750	16,500
Administration	3,450	2,040	2,790	8,280
Fixed:				
Depreciation	4,950	4,440	4,770	14,160
Total direct costs	£48,750	£33,120	£49,770	£131,640
Indirect costs:				
Variable:				
Manufacturing	8,250	7,440	7,920	23,610
Fixed	10,650	6,480	9,180	26,310
Total indirect costs	£18,900	£13,920	£17,100	£49,920
Total costs	£67,650	£47,040	£66,870	£181,560

What we really need to know is: Which categories of cost are differential? (Or, to put it another way, if product Y is deleted which costs will be avoided?) Taking the categories one by one it is probable that all the direct material costs can be avoided, and if specialist machinery is used for producing Y with a depreciation cost of £4,440 p.a., this can be avoided if the equipment is sold. But direct labour may not be so easy to eliminate: employees may be made redundant – at a cost – or transferred to other duties. If we assume that half these costs are avoidable then the net annual savings on direct labour would amount to £7,440. Similarly, the labour element within distribution and administration may not be wholly avoidable, so let us again assume annual savings of less than the full amount – say 40%.

Of the indirect categories of cost it is likely that some of the variable items (exclusive of labour) will be avoidable – 75%, say, of the sum apportioned to product Y. And of the remaining fixed costs it may not be possible to avoid any in a small enterprise if just one product line is deleted.

On the basis of these assumptions and data we can present the financial evidence in a way that helps lead to a sensible decision. This is given in Fig. 5.23 which reveals that, if product Y is deleted, annual sales revenue of £44,400 will no longer be received whilst costs of only £28,236 will be saved, thereby losing a profit contribution from Y of £16,164.

The impact of this on the overall picture is shown by a comparison of Figs 5.21 and 5.24. The original net profit of £24,570 would fall to £8,406 if product Y were

Figure 5.23

Consequences of deleting Product Y (1).

		£	£
Forgone revenue from Product Y			44,400
Cost savings:			
Direct material	(100%)	8,760	
Direct labour	(50%)	7,440	
Distribution	(40%)	1,200	
Administration	(40%)	816	
Depreciation	(100%)	4,440	
Variable indirects	(75%)	5,580	28,236
Forgone profit contribution			£16,164

Figure 5.24

Consequences of deleting Product Y (2).

	Product X £	Product Z £	Total £
Sales revenue	72,900	88,830	161,730
Costs (as in Fig. 5.21)	67,650	66,870	134,520
Unavoidable costs following deletion of Product Y: £47,040 – £28,236			18,804
Net profit			£ 8,406

deleted. This is quite a vivid illustration of how misleading cost apportionments can be in decision-making. A full cost analysis can draw one's attention (as in Fig. 5.21) to the allocation of effort among an enterprise's activities, but it does not specify the differential (or avoidable) costs and revenues of continuing to offer product Y versus deleting it from the range. It is the latter that we need to have if poor decisions are not to result.

In developing the above discussion we have not considered all the relevant issues – such as the interdependence of sales of X, Y and Z; the ability of the company to increase sales of X or Z if Y is deleted, and so forth. Obviously these matters must be taken into account. We can consider two specific issues that may be relevant in this type of context.

Assuming that the decision was made to delete product Y and that this would leave an inventory of 100 kilos of raw material A (which cost £1.00 per kilo to acquire), there may be two available alternatives:

(i) sell material A back to the supplier at £0.50 per kilo;
(ii) use A in manufacturing Product X in place of material B which is in stock (at a cost of £0.45 per kilo) and which can be purchased at £0.60 per kilo.

On the basis of costs the best solution is clear: use A as a substitute for B. The logic is simple: if A is sold back to the supplier when it could be used for making Product X the company incurs an *opportunity cost* of £0.10 (i.e. £0.60 replacement cost less the sum of £0.50 per kilo that could be obtained by selling A back to the supplier). The cost of £0.45 per kilo that was paid for the inventory of B and the cost of £1.00 per kilo paid for A are good examples of *sunk costs* – they are not relevant to the decision at hand.

The other issue to consider concerns the availability of capacity. If Product Y were deleted then additional capacity would become available to increase the output of X and Z. But if the company was already operating at full capacity and decided not to delete Product Y it will wish to know how best to utilize its capacity. The solution to this type of problem requires us to identify *the limiting factor* and to use this as a basis for maximizing profit per unit of the limiting factor.

Two points need to be emphasized. First, the appropriate profit measure is the *contribution* (i.e. sales revenue minus variable costs) rather than the net profit figures we have seen in Fig. 5.21. Any apportionment of fixed costs will distort the picture. Secondly, consideration needs to be given to the particular factor that provides the constraint which limits the enterprise's output. It could be sales potential (i.e. market capacity), the availability of raw materials, skilled labour, machine hours, funds, and so on. (At different points in time different factors will tend to set the constraint as circumstances change.)

If plant capacity (expressed in terms of machine hours) sets the constraint in our example we need to identify the relative profit contribution of each product line per machine hour. This can be done from the data in Fig. 5.25 and the knowledge that the machine hours required to produce one unit of each product line are:

Product	Machine hours
X	1.21
Y	1.36
Z	1.94

Figure 5.25

Profit contribution by profit line.

	Product X		Product Y		Product Z	
	£	£	£	£	£	£
Selling price per unit		4.86		3.70		9.87
Variable costs per unit:						
Direct material	1.14		0.73		2.18	
Direct labour	1.10		1.24		1.76	
Manufacturing indirects	0.55		0.62		0.88	
Distribution	0.45		0.25		0.75	
Administration	0.23	3.47	0.17	3.01	0.31	5.88
Contribution per unit		£1.39		£0.69		£3.99

The profit contribution per machine hour is:

Product	
X	£1.39 ÷ 1.21 = £1.15
Y	£0.69 ÷ 1.36 = £0.51
Z	£3.99 ÷ 1.94 = £2.06

from which it is evident that the manufacture and sale of Z should be favoured over X and Y because Z generates a much higher rate of profit contribution per machine hour than do the other product lines. Similarly, X would be favoured over Y even though Y itself generates a positive contribution.

(b) Linear programming

The above example of how to make a decision when there is a limiting factor is a simple one, and the technique of linear programming has been developed to deal with situations of greater complexity. This technique can be used to determine the best (i.e. optimal) solution to allocation decisions in the following circumstances:

(i) where there is a clear, stated objective;
(ii) where feasible alternative courses of action are available;
(iii) where some inputs are limited (i.e. where constraints exist);
(iv) where (i) and (iii) can be expressed as a series of linear equations or inequalities.

Let us consider the application of linear programming to a short-run product selection problem in which the decision-maker's objective is to maximize profits. (This illustration is adapted from Dev (1980).) The products in question both offer positive contributions, and market demand is buoyant and likely to be sustained, but there are insufficient resources in prospect to allow for unlimited output. The problem is, therefore, to choose that allocation on available resources which leads to maximized profits.

Boam Brothers produce two products, M and S, and the following data reflects estimated prices, variable manufacturing costs, and contributions for each product for the following financial year:

		Product M			Product S	
		£	£		£	£
Selling price per unit			22.20			14.00
Less Avoidable costs:						
Material A at £1.00 per kilo:	12 kilos	12.00		4 kilos	4.00	
Labour at £3.00 per hour:	1 hour	3.00	15.00	2 hours	6.00	10.00
Contribution per unit			£7.20			£4.00

It is assumed that the material and labour input requirements per unit and the contribution per unit are constant no matter what the level of output. This emphasizes the 'linear' aspect of linear programming.

Available inputs for next year are expected to be subject to possible constraints as suggested below:

Material A	1,200,000	kilos
Labour	400,000	hours

Fixed costs have been budgeted at £560,000. Assume that there are no opening or closing inventories of M, S or A, and that the selling price will stay constant irrespective of the level of sales.

Three possible situations can be envisaged; each is considered below.

(i) No resource constraints

In this case Boam Brothers would produce as much of M and S as they are able (since both make a positive contribution).

(ii) One resource constraint

We might take this as material A being limited to 1,200,000 kilos. The solution is derived as in the limiting factor example given earlier: priority will be given to the product generating the highest contribution per unit of the limiting factor. We can see that this is product S from the following computation:

	Product M	Product S
Contribution per unit	£7.20	£4.00
Kilos of A per unit	12	4
Contribution per kilo of A	£0.60	£1.00

With the available amount of A the maximum output would be:

$$\frac{1,200,000}{12} = 100,000 \text{ units M}$$

$$\frac{1,200,000}{4} = 300,000 \text{ units S}$$

and the maximum contribution would be:

M: 100,000 × £7.20 = £720,000

S: 300,000 × £4.00 = £1,200,000

(or 1,200,000 × £0.60 = £720,000 for M, and 1,200,000 × £1.00 = £1,200,000 for S).

The optimal choice is to produce 300,000 units of S and to give up producing M.

If, on the other hand, the scarce resource was labour hours the analysis would show the following:

	Product M	Product S
Contribution per unit	£7.20	£4.00
Labour hours per unit	1	2
Contribution per labour hour	£7.20	£2.00

The maximum output with 400,000 labour hours available would be:

$$\frac{400,000}{1} = 400,000 \text{ units M}$$

$$\frac{400{,}000}{2} = 200{,}000 \text{ units S}$$

and their respective contributions would be:

M: 400,000 × £7.20 = £2,880,000

S: 200,000 × £4.00 = £800,000

The optimal output is to produce 400,000 units of M and no units of S.

(iii) Two resource constraints

This is a more difficult situation than (ii) above since the material constraint favours production of S and the labour constraint favours the production of M. Four logical alternatives present themselves:

- produce M but no S;
- produce S but no M;
- produce some combination of M and S;
- produce neither M nor S.

The last alternative can be discarded because the contributions of both products are positive. A choice among the remaining alternatives can be made by formulating the problem as follows:

$$\text{Maximize } C = 7.20\ Q_M + 4.00\ Q_S$$

$$\text{Subject to } 12\ Q_M + 4\ Q_S \leqslant 1{,}200{,}000$$
$$Q_M + 2\ Q_S \leqslant 400{,}000$$
$$Q_M \geqslant 0,\ Q_S \geqslant 0$$

where:
C = total contribution
Q_M = units of product M to be produced
Q_S = units of product S to be produced.

The resource constraints are expressed as inequalities (i.e. 'less than or equal to') because it may not be necessary to use all 1,200,000 kilos of A, or all 400,000 labour hours. In addition, a non-negativity constraint is included in the problem formulation to show that negative quantities of either M or S are not desired.

A solution can be derived either by algebraic or graphic methods (and can easily be handled by standard computer programs). Figure 5.26 shows a graphic approach to the solution. Units of M and S are shown on the x and y axes respectively, with line AB showing the maximum output of each under the labour constraint and line CD showing the maximum output of each under the material constraint. AB connects all the possible combinations of M and S within the labour constraint, while CD connects all the combinations that are feasible within the material constraint. However, when we take both constraints into account the combinations of M and S within the triangles ACE and DBE are not feasible because they require more labour and material respectively than is available. This leaves OAED as a *feasible region* within which all the combinations of M and S can be achieved. But which is the best combination (in terms of maximizing profit)?

Figure 5.26

Graphical presentation of solution.

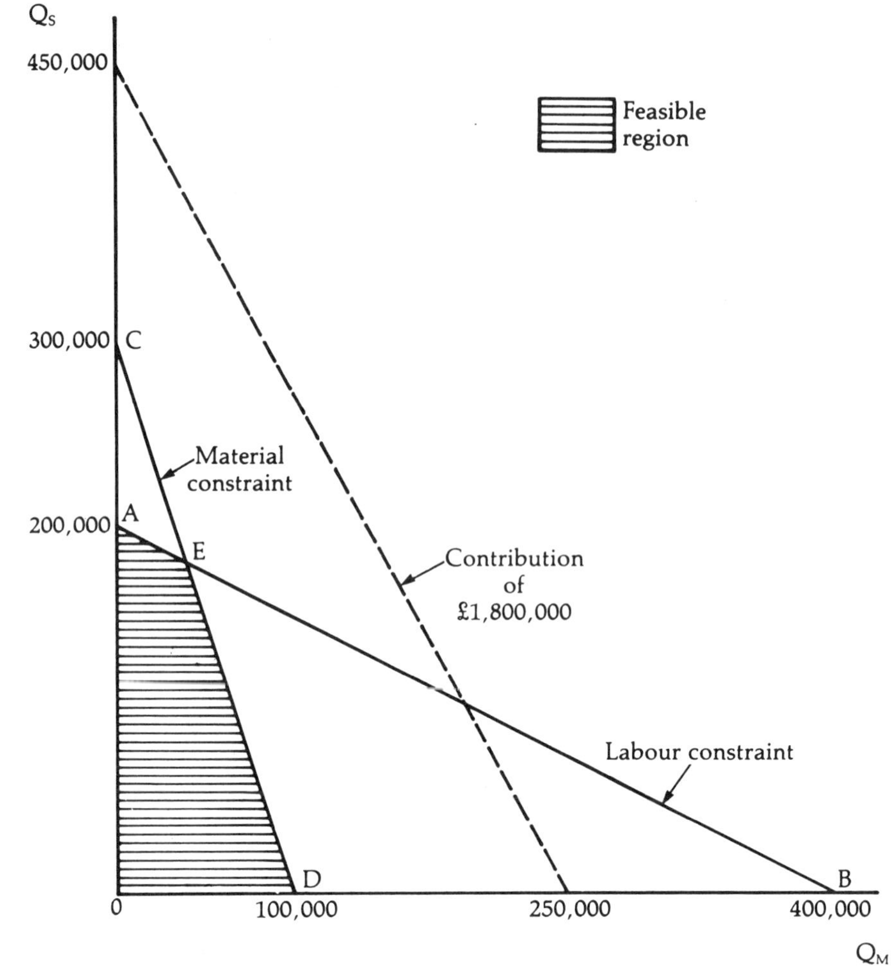

To determine the answer we need to move from quantities to relative contributions. Let us take a contribution figure of, say, £1,800,000. This can be generated by:

$$\frac{1{,}800{,}000}{7.20} = 250{,}000 \text{ units M or } \frac{1{,}800{,}000}{4.00} = 450{,}000 \text{ units S}$$

A curve showing these limits is superimposed on the graph in Fig. 5.26 but none of the possibilities suggested by this line is within the feasible region. By moving back towards the origin with parallel contribution lines we arrive at point E which is within the feasible region, and this gives us the optimal combination of M and S. (The lines will be parallel because the contribution per unit of M and S will be the same regardless of the level of output.) It should be apparent that the closer the contribution line is to the origin the lower will be the total contribution (since the smaller will be the output), so the best point is at a tangent to the feasible region: point E.

The output levels at this point (from the graph) are 40,000 units of M and 180,000 units of S, with the following financial outcome:

	£
Contribution:	
M 40,000 × £7.20	288,000
S 180,000 × £4.00	720,000
Total contribution	1,008,000
Fixed costs	560,000
Net profit	£448,000

You may care to manipulate the combination of M and S represented in this solution to see if any marginal change could improve the profit outcome. (For example, if 5 units less M were produced this would free 60 kilos of A and 5 hours of labour which could be used to produce 2 more units of S – with one hour of labour and 52 kilos of A left over. However, the contribution gained from S would only be £8.00 whereas the contribution lost by M would be £36.00, so it would be a suboptimal change.)

5.5 Allowing for risk and uncertainty

As we mentioned in the introduction to this chapter, decisions must be made in the face of imperfect knowledge about the future. One's view of the future may be characterized in terms of:

(i) *ignorance* – where the future is seen as a blank;
(ii) *assumed certainty* – which is a pretence, for all practical purposes, that the future is known exactly, and estimates become deterministic;
(iii) *risk* – where it is not known exactly what will happen in the future, but the various possibilities are weighted by their assumed probability of occurrence;
(iv) *uncertainty* – where a variety of outcomes are possible, but probabilities cannot be assigned.

There is little that can be done in cases of ignorance other than following a systematic approach and attempting to delay making the decision until further information has been gathered. In cases of certainty, of course, there is no such need for delay. This covers situations in which the decision-maker has full knowledge.

In relation to decision-making under conditions of risk and uncertainty the purpose of expressing an opinion about the likelihood of an event occurring is to facilitate the development of decision-making procedures that are explicit and consistent with the decision-maker's beliefs.

(a) Allowing for risk

In the risk situation *probability theory* is central in rational decision-making. The probability of a particular outcome of an event is simply the proportion of times this outcome would occur if the event were repeated a great number of times. Thus the probability of the outcome 'heads' in tossing a coin is 0.5 since a large number of tosses would result in 50% heads and 50% tails.

By convention, probabilities follow certain rules, such as:

(i) The probability assigned to each possible future event must be a positive number between zero and unity, where zero represents an impossible event and unity represents a certain one.
(ii) If a set of events is mutually exclusive (i.e. only one will come about) and exhaustive (i.e. covers all possible outcomes), then the total of the probabilities of the events must add to one.

The probability of an outcome is a measure of the certainty of that outcome. If, for instance, a sales manager is fairly confident that his division will be able to sell 10,000 units in the forthcoming period, he may accord a probability of 0.8 to this outcome (i.e. he is 80% certain that 10,000 units will be sold). By simple deduction, there is a 20% probability that the outcome will be something other than 10,000 units (i.e. 100 − 80 = 20%).

One development from probability theory is the concept of *expected value*. This results from the multiplication of each possible outcome of an event by the probability of that outcome occurring, and gives a measure of the *pay-off* of each choice. An example should make this situation clear.

Suppose a company has two new marketable products, but only sufficient resources to manufacture and market one of these. Estimates of sales, costs, and profits are as shown in Fig. 5.27.

Figure 5.27

Decision information.

	Sales £	Costs £	Profit £	Probability	Expected value £
Product A:	1,000	500	500	0.1	50
	1,250	600	650	0.4	260
	1,500	700	800	0.3	240
	1,750	800	950	0.2	190
				1.0	£740
Product B:	2,000	800	1,200	0.2	240
	2,300	950	1,350	0.4	540
	2,500	1,050	1,450	0.2	290
	2,700	1,150	1,550	0.1	155
	3,000	1,300	1,700	0.1	170
				1.0	£1,395

The calculations are very simple. If sales of Product A amount to £1,000, the associated costs – as shown above – are £500, and thus the profit is also £500. But there is only a probability of 0.1 that this profit outcome will eventuate, giving an *expected value* of £50 (i.e. £500 × 0.1).

This procedure is followed for the other possible outcomes of Product A sales, costs and profits, and the expected value of each of the profit outcomes is summated to give an expected pay-off of £740. (This is nothing more than a weighted arithmetic average of the data given in Fig. 5.27).

In contrast, Product B has an expected pay-off of £1,395 and this choice is, therefore, the better one of the two – provided that profit is the desired objective, as measured by the pay-off computation.

Apart from the externally given economic and physical conditions surrounding a decision (i.e. the 'states of nature'), the decision-maker's own attitudes towards the alternatives must also be taken into account. His scale of values will determine the *desirability* of each possible course of action, whereas the conventional prediction systems merely assign probabilities.

(b) Applying risk analysis

The application of simple risk analysis is best illustrated by means of an example. Assume that RST Limited has two new products, A and B, but only has the resources to launch one of these. The relevant states of nature relate to competitive activity – no matter which product is launched, it may be assumed that the competition will:

(i) do nothing; or
(ii) introduce a comparable product; or
(iii) introduce a superior product.

On the basis of past experience and current knowledge the management of RST Limited attach probabilities of 0.25, 0.5, and 0.25 respectively to these states of nature. In the light of these alternative conditions the profit of each strategy can be shown in a *pay-off matrix* as in Fig. 5.28.

This matrix shows that if Product B is launched and a comparable competitive product is introduced, a profit of £20,000 will be made, and so forth for the other five possible outcomes. The best decision would *appear* to be to introduce Product B and *hope* that competitive action does not change. But is this so?

Figure 5.28

Pay-offs matrix.

Strategy	State of nature		
	Do nothing	Introduce comparable product	Introduce superior product
Launch A	£40,000	£30,000	£20,000
Launch B	£70,000	£20,000	£0

By using the concept of expected value it is possible to calculate the expected profit (or pay-off) from each strategy by multiplying the probability of each outcome by the profit from that outcome. Thus, for Strategy A (the introduction of Product A), the expected pay-off is given by:

$$(40{,}000 \times 0.25) + (30{,}000 \times 0.5) + (20{,}000 \times 0.25)$$

and is equal to £30,000.

Similarly, for Strategy B the expected pay-off is:

$$(70{,}000 \times 0.25) + (20{,}000 \times 0.5) + (0 \times 0.25)$$

which equals £27,500.

This analysis clearly shows that Strategy A is to be preferred as it has a larger expected profit or pay-off. It is vital, however, that the distinction between the *expected* pay-off and the *most probable* pay-off is understood and attention focused on the former rather than the latter. The most probable pay-off for Strategy A is that involving the competitive introduction of a comparable product, which has a probability of 0.5 and a profit estimated at £30,000. The most probable pay-off for Strategy B has the same state of nature, and a profit of £20,000. But the most probable outcome cannot be used as the basis for decision-making because it ignores the other possible outcomes. It is thought to be 50% certain that a comparable competitive product will be launched, which means it is also 50% *uncertain* that this will occur, and allowance for this eventually should accordingly be made. The use of expected pay-offs allows for this.

(c) Allowing for uncertainty

Uncertainty arises from a lack of previous experience and knowledge. In a new venture, for example, it is possible for uncertainty to be attached to the following factors:

(i) date of completion;
(ii) level of capital outlay required;
(iii) level of selling prices;
(iv) level of sales volume;
(v) level of revenue;
(vi) level of operating costs; and
(vii) taxation rules.

Inevitably, decision-making under conditions of uncertainty is more complicated than is the case under risk conditions. In fact, there is no single *best* criterion (such as expected pay-off) that should be used in selecting a strategy. Of the various available techniques, company policy or the decision-maker's attitude will determine that which is selected. Four possible criteria are given below.

(i) Maximin – criterion of pessimism

The assumption underlying this technique is that the worst outcome will always come about and the decision-maker should therefore select the largest pay-off under this assumption.

In the pay-off table (Fig. 5.28) the worst outcomes are £20,000 for Strategy A and £0 for Strategy B. It follows that Strategy A should be pursued – it is the maximum minimum (i.e. maximin). The philosophy is that the actual outcome can only be an improvement on the profit from this choice.

(ii) Maximax — criterion of optimism

This is the opposite of maximin and is based on the assumption that the best pay-off will result from the selected strategy. Referring again to Fig. 5.28, the highest pay-offs are £40,000 and £70,000 for A and B respectively. Strategy B has the highest maximum pay-off and will be selected under the maximax criterion.

(iii) Criterion of regret

This criterion is based on the fact that, having selected a strategy that does not turn out to be the best one, the decision-maker will regret not having chosen another strategy when he had the opportunity.

Thus, if Strategy B had been adopted (see Fig. 5.29) on the maximax assumption that competition would do nothing, and competition actually did nothing, there would be no regret; but if Strategy A had been selected the company would have lost £70,000 − £40,000 = £30,000. This measures the *regret* and the aim of the regret criterion is to minimize the maximum possible regret. A regret matrix (Fig. 5.29) can be constructed on the above basis.

The maximum regret is, for Strategy A, £30,000, and for Strategy B, £20,000. The choice is therefore B if the maximum regret is to be minimized.

(iv) Criterion of rationality — Laplace criterion

The assumption behind this criterion is that, since the probabilities of the various states of nature are not known, each state of nature is equally likely. The expected pay-off from each strategy is then calculated and the one with the largest expected pay-off selected.

For Strategy A the expected pay-off under this criterion is:

$$(40{,}000 \times 0.33) + (30{,}000 \times 0.33) + (20{,}000 \times 0.33)$$

which equals £30,000; and for Strategy B it is:

$$(70{,}000 \times 0.33) + (20{,}000 \times 0.33) + (0 \times 0.33)$$

which is also equal to £30,000. In this example neither strategy is therefore preferable under the Laplace criterion.

Figure 5.29

Regret matrix.

Strategy	State of nature		
	Do nothing	Introduce comparable product	Introduce superior product
Launch A	£30,000	£0	£0
Launch B	£0	£10,000	£20,000

Although analytical methods can be applied to the evaluation of risk and uncertainty, management may prefer to take other courses of action to reduce risk and uncertainty. Perhaps the best method is to increase the information available to the decision-maker prior to his making a decision. For instance, marketing research can supply further information prior to new product launches via product testing or test marketing.

Alternatively, the scale of operations may be increased, or product diversification pursued. Figure 5.30 illustrates the case of two products, with Product A having a seasonal demand pattern that is the opposite of the pattern of Product B. But in combination Fig. 5.31 shows that the overall result is one of continuous profitability, whereas either product in isolation would result in a loss during part of its annual demand cycle.

Figure 5.30

Diversified products.

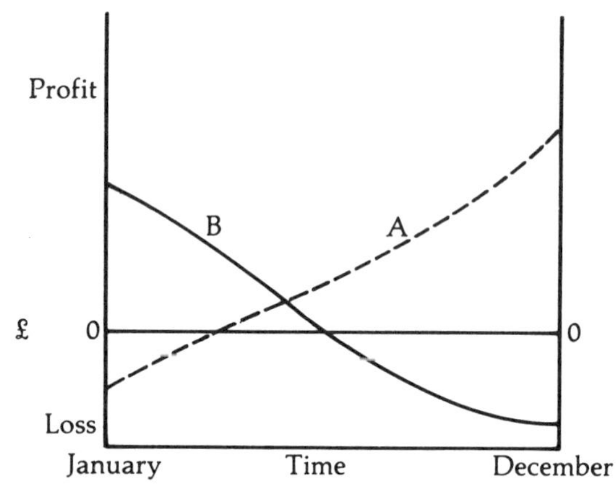

Figure 5.31

Combined profitability.

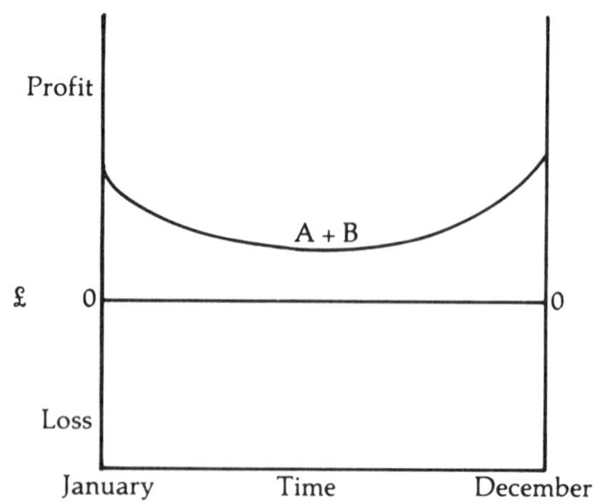

Summary

In this chapter we have looked at ways of presenting managerial accounting information that are intended to be helpful to managers in their short-run decision-making endeavours.

An important role for a managerial accounting system in the context of organizational control is to ensure 'proper' behaviour by guiding and motivating managers to make 'good' decisions. Later chapters (especially Chapters 8–11) will deal in greater detail with the behavioural issues that are entailed in designing and operating managerial accounting systems, but it will be apparent that the argument of this chapter has been developed on the assumption that rational economic behaviour prevails. The focus has been on the generation of quantitative outputs to meet formal quantitative criteria for guiding managers in their decision-making. Amongst these criteria we might have:

(i) increased productivity
(ii) overall cost reduction
(iii) improved segmental profit performance.

However, we should not lose sight of the inhibiting partiality of quantitative data derived in a rational way no matter how appealing the techniques on offer might be.

Section 5.3 of the chapter introduced the distinction between fixed and variable costs, including categories of the former (e.g. discretionary) and the significance of distinguishing between unit and total costs.

The interplay of costs, revenue, profits and the impact of the volume of activity on these variables was discussed under the heading of cost-volume-profit analysis. In addition to having potential value for a range of specific decisions this technique can be used to give an overview of the full range of an enterprise's activities. From it we can derive the contribution, the profit-volume ratio, the break-even point and the margin of safety, but one does need to bear in mind the assumptions on which CVP analysis is based, and hence its limitations.

As Scapens has pointed out (1985, p. 69), the difficulties of applying cost-volume-profit analysis arise both from the simplicity and the complexity of the technique and its data requirements. Looking at these in turn:

(i) the CVP model is a simple one that overlooks many potentially relevant characteristics of real-world problems, including the risk or uncertainty that invariably applies to all the elements in a decision situation;
(ii) estimated future costs, revenues and profits will often be based on inadequate historical data or highly subjective managerial guesses.

It follows that one should proceed with caution in seeking to adopt CVP analysis.

One significant limitation is its emphasis on the fixed–variable split. A more important distinction is that between avoidable and unavoidable costs, and this (along with revenue issues) was dealt with under the heading of differential analysis. Examples were given to show that fixed *and* variable costs can be differential, and that attempting to make decisions on the basis of full cost data is potentially very misleading. Full cost analysis can raise questions, but one needs differential analysis to provide the answers. Through this approach one can see the relevance of opportunity cost and constraining factors and the irrelevance (from the viewpoint of economic rationality) of sunk costs.

Whatever the decision it will have implications for the future, and this requires that we tackle the problems of risk and/or uncertainty. Various approaches to these issues were discussed and illustrated.

Our next step is to look beyond the short run, and this leads us on to Chapter 6.

Key terms and concepts

Here is a list of the key terms and concepts which have featured in this chapter. You should make sure that you understand and can define each one of them. Page references to definitions in the text appear in bold in the index.

- Cost
  - avoidable versus unavoidable
  - differential (or incremental)
  - fixed
  - marginal
  - mixed
  - period
  - relevant
  - sunk
  - variable
- Cost behaviour
  - learning curve
  - level of activity
  - relevant range
- Cost-volume-profit (or break-even) analysis
  - break-even point (BEP)
  - contribution
  - contribution (or P/V) margin
  - margin of safety (MOS)
  - profitgraph (or break-even chart)
- Linear programming
  - limiting factor/constraints
- Risk
  - expected value (EV)
  - pay-off
  - probability
  - states of nature
- Uncertainty

Further reading

You will find that many standard texts deal with the subject matter of this chapter (although not necessarily in the same way). See, for example, Horngren and Foster (1987), Shillinglaw (1982) or Arnold and Hope (1990).

In a series of articles published in 1986, Coulthurst and Piper reviewed some key aspects underlying accounting for decision-making.

Carsberg's 1969 book on linear programming offers as lucid an exposition as you will find, and the 1976 book by Moore and Thomas gives a clear introduction to decision theory.

The workbook to accompany this chapter begins on p. 481.

CHAPTER 6 Long-run decision-making

Learning objectives

After studying this chapter you should be able to:

- appreciate the impacts of time and changes in scale on the design of managerial accounting systems;
- understand the essence of strategy and strategic decision-making by which organizations seek to ensure their long-run effectiveness;
- recognize the main environmental influences that managerial accounting systems must seek to accommodate in providing a service to strategic decision-makers;
- understand the basic ideas behind investment appraisal;
- apply the key features of strategic management accounting.

6.1 Introduction

In Chapter 5 we dealt with the design of managerial accounting systems in relatively constrained circumstances. In focusing on the short-run we were limited to looking at operating decisions that did not involve changes in scale or have the effect of redirecting the enterprise in any major way. In addition, in Section 5.4, we looked at the role of linear programming in guiding decision-making when available capacity was severely constrained.

Within this chapter we will remove some of the constraints of Chapter 5 by lengthening the time horizon and broadening the scope for considering strategic rather than operating decision-making. To some extent this means that the role of judgement on the part of the decision-maker will be more important, and the role of information less so. The reason for this largely stems from the increased complexity of the longer term (in which more variables are at play) and the increase in uncertainty as one relaxes the constraints and faces less perfect information than is available for short-run decisions. Causal relationships are less well understood as one moves into less familiar territory – spatially or temporally.

Many strategic decisions involve investment outlays, and the discussion of strategic decision-making in this chapter will complement that of organizational investment behaviour in the companion volume *Financial Management: Method and Meaning*.

6.2 Long-run versus short-run

(a) Level of resolution

The idea of a *system* has assumed more and more importance in recent years – e.g. economic system, ecological system, social system, transport system, solar system, political system. Systems are pervasive and appear everywhere.

The common link through all of these differing systems is that each is an assembly of interconnected elements that functions as a collective whole. Their extremes of size are worthy of note: at one extreme is the solar system (containing the sun and its planets), beyond which is our galactic system which spreads into the observable universe which contains other galactic systems. At the other extreme are the physicist's atomic systems and the biologist's cell system.

Systems appear in a hierarchy, with large systems encompassing the smaller systems. This gives us the idea of *resolution levels* from which to analyse systems. At different levels of resolution particular systems as such may be observed for the first time. At a given level the way the system in question behaves as a whole may be observed, but it may be necessary to proceed to a higher level of resolution to identify the elements contained within the system and the ways in which these elements interact and behave. Each element thus becomes identifiable as a separate system which can in turn be resolved into its own elements at the next (higher) level of resolution.

By changing the level of resolution we change the time and space dimensions in which systems are observed and analysed. As we proceed to higher levels of resolution we tend to look in greater detail over shorter time spans, and as we lower the level of resolution we tend to observe broader issues over longer time horizons. This gives us the means to focus on different problems. The 'resolution graph' shown in Fig. 6.1 illustrates this point.

At one extreme (level S_1) we have the world economy, and at the other (level S_{11}) we have an assistant scheduling manager as an elemental system within an engineering enterprise. The setting of S_1 is much more constrained than is that of S_1, which means that many more factors must be taken as given, including the applicable time horizon.

How might we distinguish between the short-run and the long-run? The operational answer essentially boils down to the issue of *scale*. The short-run is that time period within which management will be unable to adjust the scale and basic nature of its activities – whether expressed in terms of productive capacity, organizational structure, contractual arrangements, technology employed or services offered. In contrast, the long-run is the time period over which all physical, organizational and other constraints might be relaxed.

The longer the time horizon, therefore:

(i) the fewer are the constraints;
(ii) the greater is the emphasis on non-routine decisions;
(iii) the greater is the need for judgement (as opposed to computation) within the decision-making process.

There is continuous tension between short- and long-term decision-making. Ideally the former should take place within a framework established by the latter. It is more often the case, however, that short-run decisions are taken without

Figure 6.1

Levels of resolution — a resolution graph.

System symbol	Designation	System description at specified level of resolution	Elements of particular systems
S_1	(1) →	World economy →	Economic blocs of states
↓ S_2	(2) →	A particular economic bloc,- e.g. EEC →	Constituent national economies of the common market
↓ S_3	(3) →	British national economy →	British industries (classified according to economic criteria)
↓ S_4	(4) →	British engineering industry →	British engineering groups and independent firms
↓ S_5	(5) →	A particular British engineering group →	Individual firms within that group
↓ S_6	(6) →	Particular firms within that group →	Particular divisions of those firms
↓ S_7	(7) →	Fabrications divisions →	Particular product fabricating departments
↓ S_8	(8) →	Large containers fabricating department →	Section within that department
↓ S_9	(9) →	Production planning and control section (PPC) →	Particular task groups of PPC
↓ S_{10}	(10) →	Scheduling group →	Individual members of that group
↓ S_{11}	(11) →	Assistant scheduling manager (ASM) →	Variables explaining ASM's work behaviour

Source: Lowe (1971), p. 97.

reference to the longer term, or in the absence of a long-term framework. This can result in short-run decisions limiting future courses of action, so we should seek to link the short-run into the longer-run.

Moving beyond the short run brings us face to face with decisions such as:

(i) building more hospitals
(ii) replacing capital equipment
(iii) extending warehouse/factory/office
(iv) introducing new products or services
(v) establishing a new college
(vi) relocating the organization.

The consequences of such decisions can be far-reaching, the financial sums involved may be awesome, the time-span will run well into the future, and risks are present on a large scale.

(b) Attributable cost

Shillinglaw (1963) made a significant distinction between cost concepts that are appropriate to short-run decisions on the one hand and what he termed *quantitative policy decisions* on the other. For the former he specified marginal costs, whilst for the latter he introduced the notion of *attributable cost*.

In considering decisions that are not of a short-run nature Shillinglaw identified two categories:

(i) *Investment decisions* which involve outlays in one period in anticipation of benefits in future periods. For example, building a new motorway, school or department store, each of which is a unique decision involving projections (covering amounts and timing) of the cash flows associated with the investment proposals. (See Section 6.5 and the text *Financial Management: Method and Meaning* which deals in detail with investment decision-making.)
(ii) *Quantitative policy decisions* which deal with the provision of *continuing* answers to *recurring* questions. For example, the establishing of delivery policies, quantity discounts and customer selection. The decisions that determine company policy on such issues are made infrequently and last for relatively long periods of time. However, the *application* of policies occurs on a period-by-period basis, so the focus is short-run in so far as it concerns the matching of inflows and outflows.

The appropriate cost concept for dealing with quantitative policy decisions is *attributable cost* which Shillinglaw defines as:

> The cost per unit that could be avoided, on the average, if a function were discontinued entirely without changing the supporting organization structure.

The key point to note here is that the basic supporting structure (with its fixed cost implications) would not be affected by a change in policy that might affect a given activity (such as delivery of goods to customers). In making policy decisions, therefore, the aim is to find the unit cost figures for the activity in question under alternative configurations while treating the basic organizational arrangements as continuing unchanged. In so doing it will often be the case that some elements within attributable cost will be marginal costs of a fixed nature that are directly attributable to the policy decision (e.g. hiring an additional warehouse manager to facilitate an improved level of delivery). From this it is apparent that attributable cost involves the unitizing of some fixed costs in addition to variable costs.

The logic behind attributable costing is simply that any activity that an organization regularly undertakes should either cover all its costs or be phased out. Attributable costing seeks to measure the amount of cost that would be avoided (perhaps after a little time) if an organizational activity were to be eliminated or modified following a new policy decision.

It is important to stress that *attributable* cost is not the same as *full* cost. The primary distinction lies in the indivisibility of most fixed costs. Fixed costs are included within full cost whether divisible or not, whereas attributable cost only includes divisible fixed costs, and most fixed costs are indivisible from the viewpoint of specific activities.

6.3 Strategic decisions

(a) Categories of decision

There are many different categories of decisions that have consequences that extend beyond the short-term. These include:

(i) expansion, whether into new markets or doing more of the same in existing markets;
(ii) expansion via new product launches;
(iii) expansion via acquisition;
(iv) replacement of (tangible) fixed assets;
(v) investment in (intangible) R & D;
(vi) relocation;
(vii) exploration (e.g. for oil);
(viii) obligatory 'no return' decisions (e.g. to comply with legal requirements);
(ix) optional 'no return' decisions (e.g. to support charitable activities);
(x) other projects designed to reduce costs;
(xi) other projects designed to improve morale;
(xii) other projects designed to improve the quality of the enterprise's output;
(xiii) combinations of (i)–(xii) designed to improve organizational performance.

Piper (1983) has reviewed a number of ways in which projects can be classified as an aid to managerial decision-making. He recommends that a suitable classification scheme can be derived from a consideration of three project-related characteristics:

(i) Does a project produce a traceable financial return? Welfare projects (such as company sports clubs) do not, whereas decisions to introduce cost-saving new equipment do.
(ii) What degree of choice does management have in deciding whether or not to undertake a project? Some projects are truly optional, while others are legally required (e.g. to meet statutory safety requirements).
(iii) What are the risk characteristics of the project? The main types of risk in Piper's scheme stem from cost, market and technical sources: all projects will have cost-related risks, and all commercial projects will have market-related risks, with the incidence of technical risk depending upon the specific nature of the project. (Other categories of risk – such as political risk – will need to be taken into account in some situations.)

Figure 6.2

Project classification scheme.

Return \ Choice	Obligatory	Partial	Full	Risk
Return	*Example* Replacement of boiler which has failed	*Example* Purchase of additional machinery	*Example* Purchase of new business or development of new process	Cost, technical and market risk
No-Return	*Example* Pollution control demanded by HM Inspector of Factories	*Example* Improving canteen facilities	*Example* Educational endowment	Cost and/or technical risk

Source: Piper (1983), p. 202.

Figure 6.2 summarizes Piper's scheme. He argues that the importance of classifying projects is a neglected aspect of strategic decision-making, and that his proposals offer a useful way of structuring this key field. This is a valid viewpoint – especially since an organization will contain a mix of projects and it will always be necessary to balance this mix (or *portfolio*) in a way that reflects the contribution (financial or otherwise) that each project makes to the well-being of the enterprise.

(b) The strategic decision making process

What, then, are the characteristics of strategic decisions?

(i) They are concerned with the scope of an organization's activities, and hence with the definition of the organization's boundaries.

(ii) They relate to the matching of the organization's activities with the opportunities of its substantive environment. Since the environment is continually changing it is necessary for this to be accommodated via adaptive decision-making that anticipates outcomes – as in playing a game of chess.

(iii) They require the matching of an organization's activities with its resources. In order to take advantage of strategic opportunities it will be necessary to have funds, capacity, personnel, etc., available when required.

(iv) They have major resource implications for organizations – such as acquiring additional capacity, disposing of capacity, or reallocating resources in a fundamental way.

(v) They are influenced by the values and expectations of those who determine the organization's strategy. Any repositioning of organizational boundaries will be influenced by managerial preferences and conceptions as much as by environmental possibilities.

(vi) They will affect the organization's long-term direction.
(vii) They are complex in nature since they tend to be non-routine and involve a large number of variables. As a result their implications will typically extend throughout the organization.

As we saw in Chapter 3, decision-making (whether strategic or tactical) is but a part of a broader problem-solving process. In essence this consists of three key aspects: analysis, choice and implementation.

(i) *Strategic analysis* focuses on understanding the strategic position of the organization, which requires that answers be found to such questions as:
   – What changes are taking place in the environment?
   – How will these changes affect the organization and its activities?
   – What resources does the organization have to deal with these changes?
   – What do those groups associated with the organization wish to achieve?
(ii) *Strategic choice* has three aspects:
   – the generation of strategic options, which should go beyond the most obvious courses of action;
   – the evaluation of strategic options, which may be based on exploiting an organization's relative strengths, or on overcoming its weaknesses;
   – the selection of a preferred strategy which will enable the organization to seize opportunities within its environment, or to counter threats from competitors.
(iii) *Strategic implementation* is concerned with translating a decision into action, which presupposes that the decision itself (i.e. the strategic choice) was made with some thought being given to feasibility and acceptability. The allocation of resources to new courses of action will need to be undertaken, and there may be a need for adapting the organization's structure to handle new activities as well as training personnel and devising appropriate systems.

The elements of strategic problem-solving are summarized in Fig. 6.3.

In broadening our perspective into a strategic setting we need to recognize that most managers have a functional role (whether as a personnel specialist or as a transport manager), and thus tend to see the world in terms associated with their function (see Dearborn and Simon, 1958). Accountants are no exception to this, and they usually view matters in financial terms that are associated with existing activities. The risk exists, therefore, of managerial accounting systems being designed as a reflection of past experience, with environmental changes being interpreted in the light of what has gone before. This tendency towards retrospective introspection needs to be changed in a fundamental way if organizational control is to be achieved.

For example, traditional managerial accounting methods might propose that attention be given to:

(i) controlling working capital
(ii) decreasing work-in-progress
(iii) reducing wastage rates
(iv) negotiating modest wage increases

in order to improve an enterprise's performance. But if the enterprise is in a declining industry, or is suffering from intense competitive pressures, or is lagging

Figure 6.3

A summary model of the elements of strategic management.

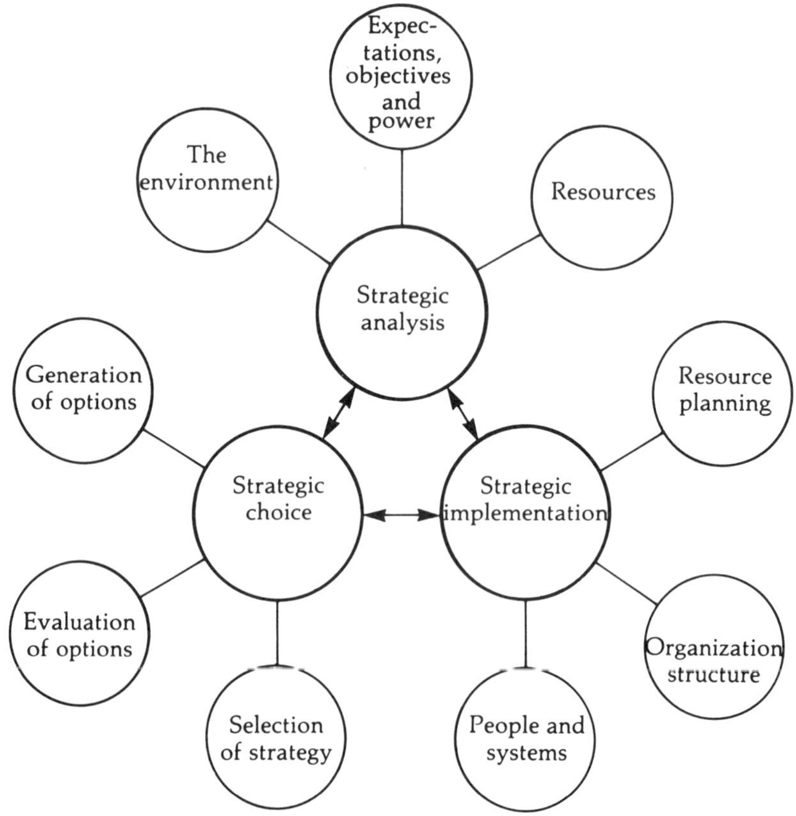

Source: Johnson and Scholes (1988).

behind in the adoption of current technology, no amount of marginal adjustment to insignificant details will improve its fortunes. Of central importance to organizational prosperity is the ability to acquire, allocate and utilize resources in a way that takes advantage of environmental opportunities and avoids environmental threats. The focus for the management accountant is, therefore, outwards and forward.

(c) The nature of strategy

We have given some thought to strategic decisions, but what is strategy? Hofer and Schendel (1978, p. 27) have identified three distinct levels of strategy in a commercial context. These are:

(i) corporate strategy, which deals with the allocation of resources among the various businesses or divisions of an enterprise;

(ii) business strategy, which exists at the level of the individual business or division, dealing primarily with the question of competitive position;
(iii) functional level strategy, which is limited to the actions of specific functions within specific businesses.

Our main concern is with the role of managerial accounting in relation to business strategy (i.e. level (ii) above).

Different authorities have defined strategy in lots of different ways; there is no standard definition. However, a range of elements that most writers seem to subscribe to in discussing strategy have been put forward by Simmonds (1980, pp. 7–9), as follows:

1. Strategy is applicable to business within defined boundaries. While the boundaries may change, the strategy applies at any one time to actions affecting a delimited area of demand and competition.
2. There are specified direct competitors. These are competitors selling essentially the same products or services within the defined demand area. Indirect competitors are those operating outside the defined business and whose products are not direct substitutes. Indirect competition is usually ignored or covered by the concept of price elasticity of demand.
3. There is zero-sum competition between the direct competitors for the market demand, subject to competitive action affecting the quantity demanded.
4. Demand within the defined market varies over time. This variation in demand is largely independent of supplier strategies and is often referred to as the *product life cycle*. At its simplest, it is depicted as a normal curve over time with regularly growing then declining demand. (See pp. 424–7).
5. Strategy unfolds over a sequence of time periods. Competition evolves through a series of skirmishes and battles across the units of time covered by the product life cycle.
6. Single period profit is a function of:
   – The price level ruling for the period.
   – The accumulated volume experience of the enterprise.
   – The enterprise's achieved volume as a proportion of capacity.
7. Market share has intrinsic value. Past sales' levels influence subsequent customer buying, and costs reduce with single period volume and accumulated experience.
8. Competitors differ in market share, accumulated experience, production capacity, and resources. Competitors are unequal, identified and positioned.
9. Objectives differ. Enterprises composed of ownership, management and employee factions and operating a range of different businesses have different objectives. Strategic business thinking, however, will usually express these as different time and risk preferences for performance within an individual business, measured in financial terms.
10. Within a given situation, there will be a core of strategic actions which will be the essential cause of change in competitive position. Non-strategic, or contingent actions, will support strategic actions and should be consistent with them, but will not change competitive position significantly.
11. Identification of an optimal core of strategic actions requires reasoning, or

diagnosis, is not attained through application of a fixed set of procedures and is situational. In short, thinking is required.

Taken together, these elements present a view of business strategy that sees it as a chosen set of actions by means of which a market position relative to other competing enterprises is sought and maintained. This gives us the notion of competitive position. It is apparent from this picture that a period-by-period statement of an organization's profit (whether by a segment or overall), its cash flow, or any other traditional accounting measure of performance is blinkered in at least two respects:

(i) it is an artificial exercise at best to divide time up into arbitrary periods;
(ii) seeking to gauge an enterprise's performance in isolation from changes in its strategic position relative to competing organizations ignores its capacity for generating future cash flows and achieving other aims.

The management accountant can help by carefully considering the segments that form the basis of his systems of reporting. Instead of production processes and products it would improve the flow of relevant information for managers' strategic decision-making if segments having an *external* (rather than *internal*) focus were adopted – such as segments reflecting product/market interactions. It is through segments, projects, programmes or missions that business is carried on, and yet managerial accounting has paid comparatively little attention to this obvious fact of commercial life. Having helped in identifying suitable segments the management accountant can then seek to contribute to the process by which strategic decisions are made – by looking outwards and forward.

It needs to be emphasized that 'strategy' is not synonymous with 'long-term plan', but rather consists of an enterprise's attempts to reach some preferred future state by adapting its competitive position as circumstances change. While a series of strategic moves may be planned, competitors' actions will mean that the actual moves will have to be modified to take account of those actions.

(d) Search

In formulating strategies there is a need to search for alternative directions and means by which those directions might be pursued. As Lowe (1970, p. 4) has pointed out, there is almost an infinite number of ways in which an enterprise can use its resources, but the variety is largely constrained by the imagination of the organization's management and the techniques that are employed for identifying alternative courses of action.

Increasingly refined tools of analysis are being developed, involving advanced mathematics in many cases, but these tools are useless if insufficient attention is paid to the generation of options that they can be used to evaluate. The process of searching for such options is rather neglected in the literature, despite the crucial importance of identifying strategies that will lead to the attainment of improved organizational effectiveness via better strategic decision-making.

Inevitably there are resource implications of searching for alternatives, and at some point the growing cost of searching could exceed the expected value of the strategies identified, or a deadline may be reached at which point a choice has to be made among the alternatives that have been identified.

Evaluating strategies is also a form of searching. The 'best' is being sought, and this requires that evaluative criteria be established to facilitate this part of the search process. Possible criteria might include:

(i) *suitability* in terms of capitalizing on the organization's strengths, for example, or countering environmental threats;
(ii) *feasibility* in terms of how each strategy is to be undertaken, and hence its resource requirements, in relation to the organization's capability;
(iii) *acceptability* in terms of meeting the expectations of different interest groups without undue risk.

It is customary practice to evaluate *ex ante* incremental strategies or projects whilst ongoing ones are routinely continued following their evaluation at earlier points in time. In order to accommodate this issue and the particular needs of non-profit organizations (such as government agencies) as well as providing a focus for more rigorous thinking in relation to programmed or discretionary costs (i.e. those which are determined purely by managerial discretion such as R & D, training, and similar outlays – see Section 5.2 in Chapter 5) *zero-base budgeting* (ZBB) has been developed. This technique was first applied in Texas Instruments in the early 1970s, and aims to help managers allocate resources more effectively.

The origins of ZBB are to be found in the failings of incremental decision-making by which the only projects or strategies that are subject to rigorous evaluation are new ones. This approach tends to be number-oriented, fails to identify priorities, and starts with the existing level of activity or expenditure as an established base, whereas it might be more useful to managers to have a technique that was decision-oriented, helped in determining priorities, and sought to re-assess the current level of expenditures.

It will be appreciated from this last point that in taking as given the current level of expenditure, and the activities that this represents, the incremental approach to decision-making, by looking at desired increases or, occasionally, decreases, is ignoring the majority of the organization's expenditure. This is rather myopic.

The zero-base budgeting alternative is to evaluate *simultaneously* existing and new ways of achieving specified ends in order to establish priorities among them, which could mean that there are trade-offs between existing and new activities. For example, a new project A that is considered to be more desirable than an existing project B may be resourced by terminating project B. In essence the approach is carried out in two stages:

(i) *Decision packages* are identified within each *decision unit*. These decision units are essentially discrete activities that can be described in a way that separates them from other activities of the organization. The decision packages cover both existing and projected incremental activities, and the organizational units responsible for carrying them out are much akin to the responsibility centres that will be discussed in Chapter 9. The object is to define for each decision unit the basic requirements that are needed if it is to perform the function for which it was established. Any costs in excess of this basic level are deemed incremental. (It will be seen, therefore, that the title 'zero-base' is something of a misnomer since the base is certainly greater than zero!) In considering what is needed in order to fulfil a particular purpose, over and above the base level, it is probable that alternative ways of achieving the same end will be identified, and these should be described and evaluated as they arise: these are the decision packages.

(ii) Once the manager of a decision unit has submitted his statement of evaluated decision packages to his superior it is the latter's job to assign priorities to the various submissions from all his subordinates, and to select the highest-ranking decision packages that come within his available resource limits. There are a number of ways in which priorities can be determined, all of which presuppose some explicit criterion of effectiveness in order that competing packages may be ranked.

This approach is logical and has much to commend it in relation to discretionary outlays.

6.4 Environmental impacts

An organization's performance is profoundly influenced by the elements contained within its environment. In turn, of course, the organization also has an impact on its environment: there is a mutual dependency.

It is not far-fetched to argue that the very survival of an organization depends

Figure 6.4

The influence of external factors.

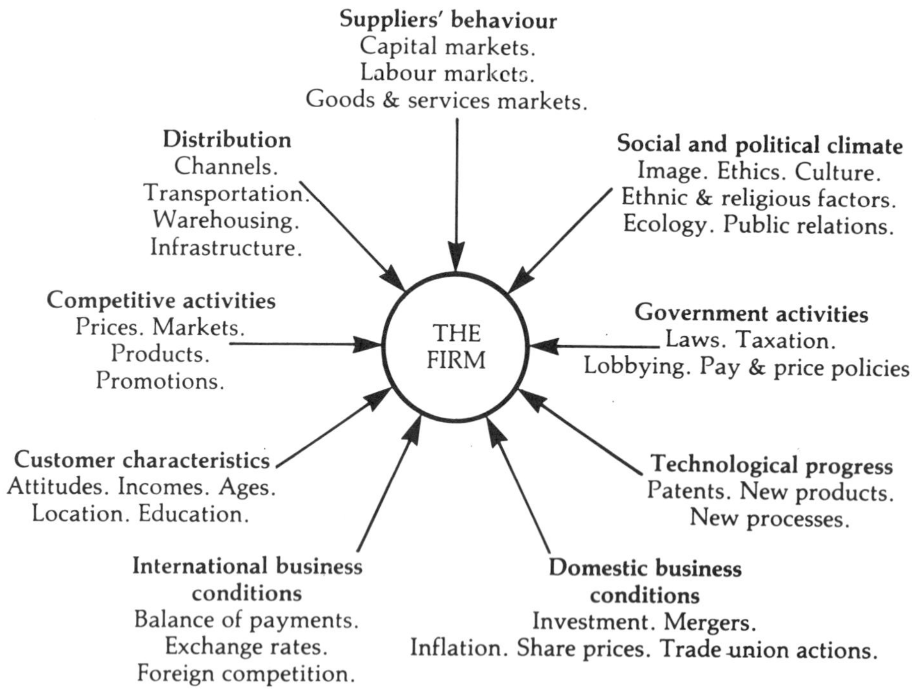

Source: Wilson (1983), p. 109.

critically upon the willingness of its environment to sustain it. The reality of this can be seen if one considers how any organization draws all of its resources from its environment: financiers and other investors must be persuaded to back the organization; 'technocrats' and those with other categories of skill must be encouraged to work for the organization; individuals must be influenced to purchase the market offering; suppliers must be willing to provide goods, services and premises; society (in its various forms, such as government departments, local authorities, communities, the law, pressure groups, etc.) must be willing – at least – to tolerate the organization's activities; and so on. (See Figure 2.4 – p. 25 above). In return the organization must be willing and able to meet the requirements of each of these parties: consumers must be satisfied with their purchases; shareholders must receive dividends; the law must be upheld; society must not be abused; employees must be treated correctly; suppliers must be paid on time; etc. If any key group withdraws its support the future of the organization is bound to be in doubt.

It is the role of a managerial accounting system to predict events that are likely to occur within the environment in order that the enterprise may meet any challenges (or take advantage of any new opportunities). An enterprise's costs are largely made up of payments to the suppliers of various types of factor inputs, and it is a function of a managerial accounting system to anticipate any increase in input prices to enable the enterprise either to renegotiate (possibly with an alternative supplier) or to arrange its finances so that it has the resources to meet higher input prices.

Figure 6.4 illustrates the influence of external factors along the lines of the above discussion. Two environmental factors that warrant particular attention are risk on the one hand and inflation on the other. We will look at these in turn.

(a) Decision trees

How might we attempt to deal with risk in strategic decision-making? Handling risk via pay-off tables was introduced in Section 5.5 of Chapter 5, but the approach used dealt with one level of probability (i.e. what is the probability of specified outcomes occurring?). Both the outcomes and the pay-offs associated with them are probabilistic, however, so we really need to allow for more than one set of states of nature or levels of decision.

One approach that helps in structuring problems in a way that allows risk to be assessed at each stage comes through the use of *decision trees*. A decision tree is a diagrammatic representation of the relationships among decisions, states of nature and pay-offs (or outcomes). An example will show how a decision tree can be used. Imagine a research project that is in progress with a view to developing a new product for commercial launch. There are several aspects to this issue:

(i) the project may be aborted or it may be allowed to continue;
(ii) if it is continued it may or may not result in a potentially marketable new product;
(iii) if it does result in a marketable product the organization may choose to launch it immediately or to postpone the launch;
(iv) competitors may or may not be able to match the organization's endeavours.

Figure 6.5 spells out these aspects, and specifies the two major decisions that

Figure 6.5

A basic decision tree.

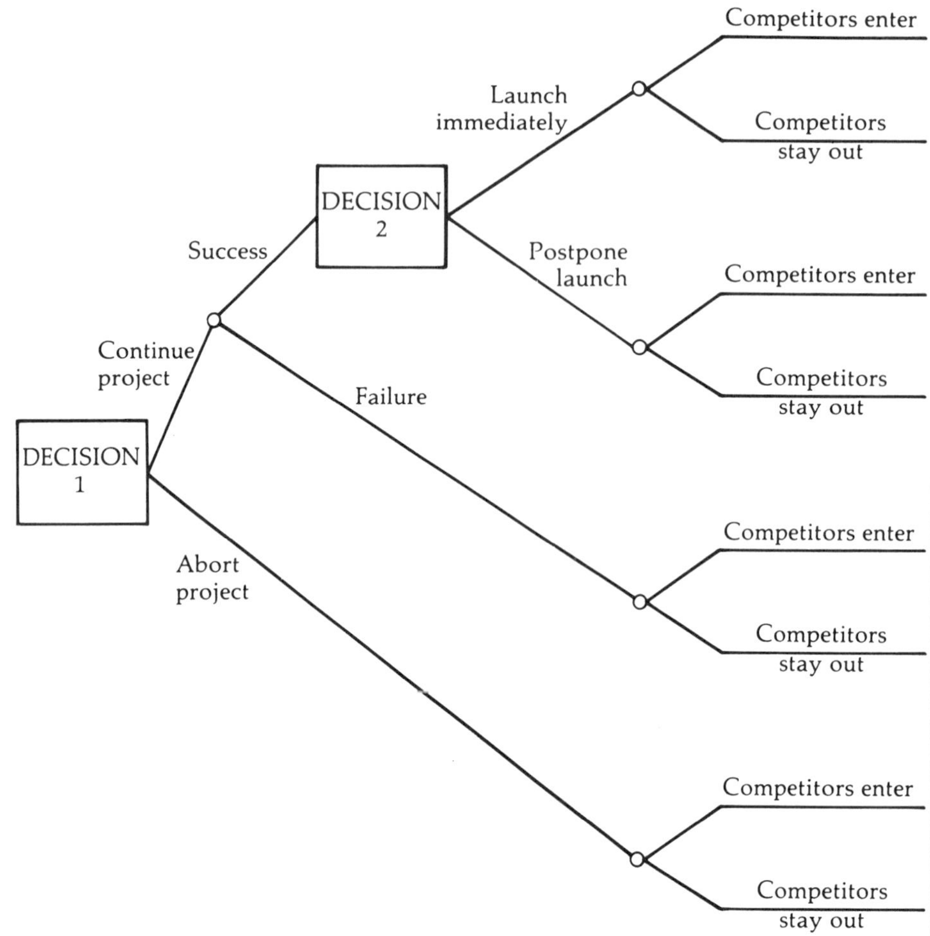

need to be made. (The squares represent points at which decisions need to be made, while the circles represent subsequent events.) It can be seen that each decision, combined with the states of nature that are assumed to prevail, produces distinct outcomes.

The next step is to introduce quantitative data, so let us assume the following:

(i) it will cost an estimated £50,000 to continue the project (which is itself probabilistic);

(ii) if the company decides to postpone the launch of the product (assuming the project is successful) and competitors enter the market there will be a loss of current business amounting to £125,000;

(iii) if the project is successful and an immediate launch is undertaken, the company will generate incremental cash flows of £450,000 if competitors stay out of the market, but only £250,000 if competitors enter the market.

These figures are shown at the end of each branch of the decision tree in Fig. 6.6. We now need to incorporate the probabilities of the events leading to the various possible outcomes, and these are also shown in Fig. 6.6. By working back from the right-hand side of the decision tree it is a simple matter to compute expected values. Taking the branch dealing with the immediate launch of a successful project as an example, the expected value is derived as follows:

£250,000 × 0.7 =	£175,000
£450,000 × 0.3 =	£135,000
Expected value	£310,000

Figure 6.6

Decision tree with quantified outcomes.

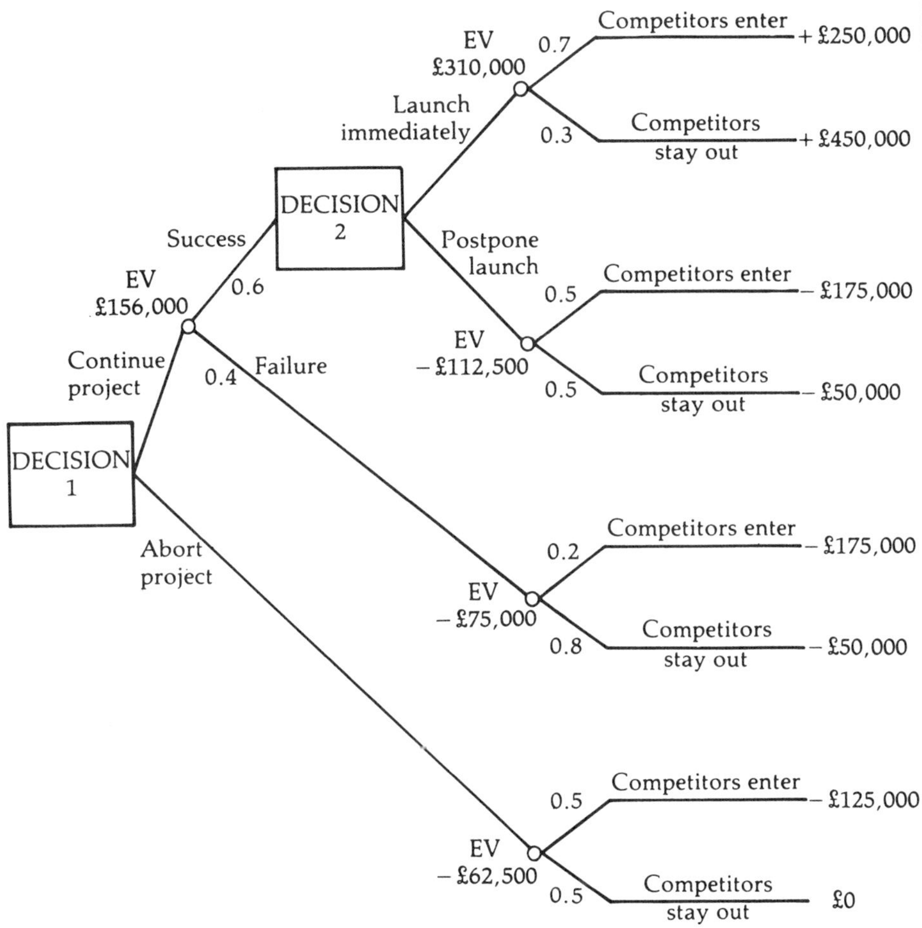

The figures show that an immediate launch is the better alternative if the project is successful than is postponing it (which has an expected value of −£112,500). But this only gives part of the picture, so the expected values need to be worked through to the next event in the tree (moving across from right to left). The logic in doing this is straightforward: if the project is successful and the launch is immediate there will be a larger pay-off than if the launch is postponed, so the latter branch can now be ignored. This gives an expected value for continuing the project of £156,000 calculated thus:

£310,000 × 0.6 =	£186,000
−£75,000 × 0.4 =	−£30,000
Expected value	£156,000

A comparison of this pay-off with the expected value of aborting the project (−£62,500) shows the desirability of continuing with the project.

(b) Sensitivity analysis

There are several alternatives to the basic decision-tree approach to allowing for risk which can be employed. It is not possible within the limits of this volume to cover them, but there is space to refer to *sensitivity analysis*. In its applied organizational setting this may be broadly defined as:

> . . . a study to determine the responsiveness of the conclusions of an analysis to changes or errors in parameter values used in the analysis.
>
> Rappaport (1967), p. 441.

Sensitivity analysis seeks to test the responsiveness of outcomes from decision models to different input values and constraints as a basis for appraising the relative risk of alternative courses of action. It is also possible to use sensitivity analysis for helping to determine the value of information in addition to its role in strategic decision-making.

In effect what sensitivity analysis allows the management accountant to do is to experiment in the abstract without the time, cost or risk associated with experimenting with the organization itself. This can be seen symbolically in the following expression:

$$V = f(X, Y)$$

where:

V = a measure of the value of the decision that is to be made;
X = the set of variables that can be directly regulated by the decision-maker (i.e. the decision variables);
Y = the set of factors (variable or constant) that affects outcomes but which is not subject to direct regulation by the decision-maker (i.e. the states of nature);
f = the functional relationship amongst V, X and Y.

One can manipulate any element within X or Y and see the consequent impact on V.

Reference has been made in earlier chapters of this book to balancing the cost

Figure 6.7

Cost and value of information.

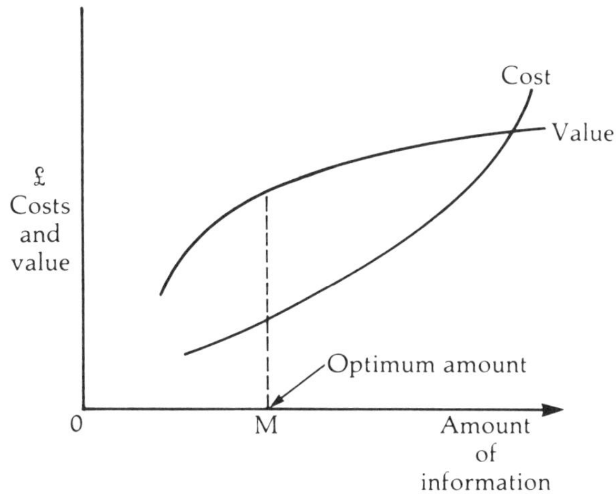

and value of information. The broad picture is given in Fig. 6.7 from which you will see that the optimum amount of information in a given situation (OM) is to be found when the difference between the value and cost curves is greatest. For a number of reasons (including overload) the value of information starts to decline as more is made available, whereas the cost of providing information increases at an accelerating rate as more is made available (due to increasing accuracy, faster transmission, etc.).

In operational terms how can we assess the value of information? We can readily grasp the principle that by evaluating the consequences of a particular decision based on a given amount of information on the one hand, and then evaluating the consequences of the same decision made with additional information on the other, the difference (in consequences) reflects the value of the extra information. This value gives the maximum sum that should be spent on generating the extra information. To apply this principle requires that we:

(i) enumerate the possible outcomes of future information collection efforts;
(ii) compute the probabilities of these outcomes;
(iii) indicate how the information will change the decision-maker's view of his choice

These are demanding requirements!

(c) The impact of inflation

During periods of inflation the purchasing power of money falls, and the longer the time period that is being considered when making decisions the more significant will be the impact of inflation on the outcomes of those decisions. When inflation rates are quite low (such as the 3% rate achieved in Britain in May,

1986, which was the lowest annualized rate for eighteen years) it is tempting for managers to ignore inflation. However, even with a rate as low as 5%, the value of money falls by about half over only fourteen years, and when inflation is running at 10% it only takes seven years or so for the purchasing power of money to fall by 50%. This is too significant to be ignored.

If price-level changes are in prospect – which will invariably be the case for strategic decisions – there are two basic ways of allowing for them in compiling managerial accounting reports:

(i) make predictions of costs and revenues in terms of constant purchasing power (i.e. using the value of today's money);
(ii) make predictions that are based on nominal values that reflect expected changes (i.e. using expected cash inflows and outflows).

Method (i) has the effect of eliminating inflation from the predicted figures, which should make it easier for managers to evaluate alternatives strategies. In contrast, method (ii) builds inflationary increases into the figures which is helpful for predicting cash flow but not necessarily very helpful for comparing competing projects.

Alternatives to (i) and (ii) include making predictions in physical terms (e.g. units of output, machine hours of input), but this is severely limiting for complex decisions that involve projects with long lives even though it can remove the distortion of inflation itself.

An interesting problem is that concerning the allowance for inflation in long-term contracts. Some contracts are negotiated on a fixed-price basis, and these require that an allowance for price changes be built in (along the lines of method (ii) above). If the contractor makes an error in his estimates he may make additional profits (when inflation is at a lower rate than he anticipated) or he may be forced out of business (when inflation is higher than anticipated).

An increasingly popular alternative to fixed-price contracts is the use of cost escalation clauses. This makes it possible for a contract price to be agreed between the parties involved that relates to the level of current costs (i.e. method (i) above), with inflation to be allowed for by the application of a cost index to the initial costs. There is no need for the contractor to attempt to predict inflation with any precision since he will be able to recover from the customer whatever inflationary increases may arise over the life of the contract. As Gee has noted (1979, p. 339), this allows for fair prices to be negotiated, and it seeks to remove the risk of a contractor having to skimp in order to meet a tight budget which can arise in fixed-price contracts. However, care must be taken to distinguish between cost increases that are due to inflation (which can be passed on to the customer under escalation clauses) and increases that stem from excess usage of inputs (which are the contractor's responsibility). Reference must be made to the inputs as originally specified in the contract when applying the relevant cost index.

6.5 Investment appraisal

Any investment involves the outlay of resources at one point in time in anticipation of receiving a larger return at some time in the future. This return must repay the original outlay, as well as providing a minimum annual rate of return (or interest) on that outlay. If an individual invests £100 in a building society, he will expect to receive that £100 back at some future time, along with compound interest. This is a typical investment situation.

The aim usually will be to secure the maximum net cash flow (after tax) from the investment, and this will be achieved only from investments having the highest rate of interest of those available. (This rate will be that on the *outstanding*, as opposed to the initial, balance over the life of the investment – as determined by the discounting methods of appraisal outlined later in this section.)

Characteristically, an investment decision involves a largely irreversible commitment of resources that is generally subject to a significant degree of risk. Such decisions have far-reaching effects on an enterprise's profitability and flexibility over the long term, thus requiring that they be part of a carefully developed strategy that is based on reliable forecasting procedures.

Typical examples of investment projects are:

(i) expansion projects;
(ii) replacement projects;
(iii) selection among alternatives; and
(iv) buy or lease decisions.

Projects for analysis and appraisal do not just appear – a continuing stream of good investment opportunities results from hard thinking, careful planning, and often from large outlays on R & D. Replacement decisions are ordinarily the simplest to make, as the enterprise will have a very good idea of the cost savings to be obtained by replacing an old asset, along with the consequences of non-replacement. (A central problem is that of accurately predicting the revenues and costs associated with particular projects for many years into the future.)

Over-investment in capital assets will result in heavy fixed costs, whereas under-investment may mean:

(i) an enterprise's equipment is not sufficiently modern to enable it to produce competitively; or
(ii) it has inadequate capacity to maintain its share of a growing market.

Investment is one of the main sources of economic growth since it is required not only to increase the total capital stock, but also to employ labour in increasingly productive jobs as old plant is replaced by new. The application of reliable means of appraising investment proposals brings out more systematically and reliably the advantages of investing where it will increase efficiency, and thus helps to secure faster growth.

Various criticisms have been put forward in relation to the methods of appraisal that many companies employ. Among the most important are the following:

(i) Although most companies only make investment decisions after careful consideration of the likely costs and benefits as they see them, these decisions are often reached in ways that are unlikely to produce the pattern or level of investment that is most favourable to economic growth – or even most profitable to the company.
(ii) Many companies apply criteria for assessing investment projects that have little relevance to the measurement of the expected *rate of return on investment* (ROI). (See Chapter 11 for a review of ROI.)

(iii) Even though a calculation of the ROI of each project may be made, the methods used vary widely and are sometimes so arbitrary as to give almost meaningless results. (For instance, a failure to assess returns *after* tax is a frequent weakness of many widely used methods, since alternative opportunities can only be effectively compared and appraised on an after-tax basis.)

This faulty use of (or use of faulty) means of investment appraisal may result in over-cautious investment decisions in which too high a rate of return is demanded before a proposal is accepted. This will cause delay in economic growth. Alternatively, faulty methods may mean that investment decisions are made that result in the selection of projects that yield an unduly low ROI. This causes a waste of scarce capital resources, which is also unfavourable to economic growth.

From an information flow point of view, the use of inadequate means of investment appraisal results in a damaging restriction in the flow of information to top management since these methods are incapable of fully exploiting relevant data. Because a company's future is inextricably linked to its investments, poor methods that give poor information that leads to poor decisions are likely to result in many mistakes.

Realistic investment appraisal requires the financial evaluation of many factors, such as the choice of size, type, location and timing of investments, giving due consideration to the effects of taxation and alternate forms of financing the outlays. This shows that project decisions are difficult on account of their complexity and their strategic significance.

No matter which technique is adopted for investment appraisal, the same steps will need to be followed. These steps are:

(i) determine the profitability of each proposal;
(ii) rank the proposals in accordance with their profitability;
(iii) determine the cut-off rate (e.g. minimum acceptable ROI);
(iv) determine which projects are acceptable and which unacceptable in relation to the cut-off rate; and
(v) select the most profitable proposals in accordance with the constraints of the company's available funds.

(a) Cash flows

In considering investment decisions it does not matter whether outlays are termed 'capital' or 'operating', nor whether inflows are termed 'profit', 'tax allowance', or whatever. All outlays and inflows must be taken into account.

Cash flow in this context is not the same as the cash flow through a bank account, nor is it identical to accounting profit, since changes in the latter can occur without any change taking place in the cash flow. For purposes of investment appraisal, the cash flow is the incremental cash receipts less the incremental cash expenditures solely attributable to the investment in question. The future costs and revenues associated with each investment alternative are as follows:

(i) *Capital costs*. These cover the long-term capital outlays necessary to finance a project, and working capital. (Since residual working capital is recoverable at the termination of a project's life, this leads to the investment having a net terminal value that should be taken into account.) Typically, additional working capital will be required to cover a higher inventory, or a larger number of debtors, and to be worthwhile the project must earn a return on this capital as well as on the long-term capital.

(ii) *Operating costs.*

(iii) *Revenue.*

(iv) *Depreciation.* In the case of the discounting methods of appraisal (discussed below) the recovery of capital (i.e. depreciation) is automatically allowed for from the net cash flow, so depreciation need not be included as an accounting provision. This has the important advantage that the discounted profitability assessment is not affected by the pattern of accounting depreciation chosen.

(v) *Residual value.* As with working capital, the residual assets of the project may have a value (as either scrap or in an alternative use or location). This residual value (net of handling costs and tax allowances or charges) should be included within the net cash flow.

An investment decision implies the choice of an objective, a technique of appraisal, and a length of service – the project's life. The objective and technique must be related to a definite period of time. In a static world, that period would quite naturally be taken as being equal to the physical life of the asset that is the purpose of the investment, which would be known with a good deal of certainty on the basis of past experience. However, in a dynamic world the life of the project may be determined by:

(i) technological obsolescence; or

(ii) physical deterioration; or

(iii) a decline in demand for the output of the project – such as a change in taste away from the product manufactured.

No matter how good a company's maintenance policy, its technological forecasting ability or its demand forecasting ability, uncertainty will always be present because of the difficulty of predicting the length of a project's life.

(b) Time value of money

To permit realistic appraisal, the value of a cash payment or receipt must be related to the time when the transfer takes place. In particular, it must be recognized that £1 received today is worth more than £1 receivable at some future date because £1 received today could be earning interest in the intervening period. This is the concept of the *time value of money.*

To illustrate this, if £100 was invested today at 5% per annum compound interest, it would accumulate to 105 at the end of the one year (i.e. £100 × 1.05), to £110.25 at the end of two years (i.e. £100 × 1.05 × 1.05, or £105 × 1.05), and so on. In other words, £110.25 receivable in two years' time is only worth £100 today if 5% per annum can be earned in the meantime (i.e. 110.25/(1.05 × 1.05) = 100).

The process of converting future sums into their present equivalents is known as *discounting*, which is simply the opposite of *compounding* (see Fig. 6.8). Compounding is used to determine the *future value of present* cash flows, whereas discounting is used to determine the *present value of future* cash flows.

Another example will clarify this further. An investor who can normally obtain

Figure 6.8

Discounting and compounding.

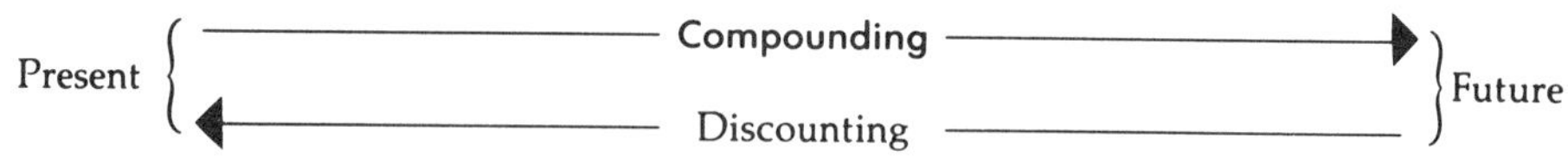

8% on his investments is considering whether or not to invest in a project that gives rise to £388 at the end of each of the next three years. The present value of these sums is:

$$\frac{£388}{1.08} + \frac{£388}{1.08 \times 1.08} + \frac{£388}{1.08 \times 1.08 \times 1.08} = £1{,}000$$

If the investment's capital cost is less that the present value of its returns (say £800) then it should be accepted, since the present value of the return of this outlay is a larger amount (i.e. £1,000 − £800 = £200 gain from the investment). The gain is the *net present value* (NPV) of the investment.

The interest rate does not always relate to an outlay of cash as the concept of interest applies equally to the use of internal funds. The reason why interest must be considered on *all* funds in use, regardless of their source, is that the selection of one alternative necessarily commits funds that could otherwise be invested in some other alternative. The measure of interest in such cases is the return forgone by rejecting the alternative use (i.e. the opportunity cost).

(c) Financial evaluation

The techniques of evaluation fall into two categories.

(i) Traditional methods of evaluation

The **payback period** is the most widely used technique, and can be defined as the number of years required to recover the cost of the investment. By definition, the payback period ignores cash generation beyond this period, and it can thus be seen to be more a measure of liquidity than of profitability. In addition, it fails to take account of the time value of money, and these limitations make it seriously defective in the aim of reflecting the relative financial attractiveness of projects.

Projects with long payback periods are characteristically those involved in long-term planning, and which determine an enterprise's future. However, they may not yield their highest returns for a number of years and the result is that the payback method is biased against the very investments that are most important to long-term success.

Average rate of return (ARR) (alternatively known as 'rate of return', 'accountant's method', or 'return on capital') is defined as the profit from the project (after allowing for accounting depreciation but before tax) as a percentage of the required investment. (This investment base is sometimes the initial investment, and sometimes the average investment over the project's life.)

This method is superior in some respects to the payback period, but is still fundamentally unsound. While it does take account of the earnings over the entire economic life of a project, it fails to take account of the time value of money. This weakness is made worse by the failure to specify adequately the relative attractiveness of alternative proposals. It is biased against short-term projects in the same way that payback is biased against longer term ones.

These traditional methods of investment appraisal are misleading to a dangerous extent. A means of measuring *cash* against *cash* that allows for the importance of time is needed. This is provided by the discounting methods of appraisal, of which there are basically two, both of which meet the objections to the payback period and average rate of return methods.

(ii) Discounting methods of evaluation

Both discounting methods relate the estimates of the annual cash outlays on the investment to the annual net-of-tax cash receipts generated by the investment. As a general rule, the net-of-tax cash flow will be composed of revenue less taxes (when paid), plus depreciation. Since discounting techniques automatically allow for the recoupment of the capital outlay (i.e. depreciation) in computing time-adjusted rates of return, it follows that depreciation provisions implicitly form part of the cash inflow.

The internal rate of return (IRR) (or discounted cash flow) method consists of finding that rate of discount that reduces the cash flows (both inflows and outflows) attributable to an investment project to zero – this being, in principle, the true rate of return. (In other words this 'true' rate is that which exactly equalizes the net cash proceeds over a project's life with the initial investment outlay.) If the IRR exceeds the minimum required rate then the project is *prima facie* acceptable.

Instead of being computed on the basis of the average or initial investment, the IRR is based on the funds in use from period to period. The actual calculation of the rate is a hit-and-miss exercise because the rate is unknown at the outset, but tables of present values are available to aid the analyst. These tables show the present value of future sums at various rates of discount, and are prepared for both single sums and recurring annual payments. (See Appendix, pp. 650–1).

The net present value (NPV) method discounts the net cash flows from the investment by the minimum required rate of return, and deducts the initial investment to give the yield from the funds invested. If this yield is positive, then the project is *prima facie* worthwhile, but if it is negative the project is unable to pay for itself and is thus unacceptable. An index can be developed for comparative purposes by relating the yield to the investment to give the yield per £1 invested. This is the *excess present value index* and facilitates the ranking of competing proposals in order of acceptability. (It is not important in their evaluation in terms of profitability that competing proposals require widely different outlays as the index reduces alternatives to a common base.)

(iii) Comparison of discounting methods

In ordinary circumstances the two discounting approaches will result in identical investment decisions. However, there are differences between them that can result in conflicting answers in terms of ranking projects according to their profitability.

In formal accept/reject decisions both methods lead to the same division since all projects having a yield in excess of the minimum required rate will also have

Figure 6.9

Ranking comparison (1).

Projects A and B both require an outlay of £1,000 now to obtain a return of £1,150 at the end of year 1 in the case of A, and £1,405 at the end of year 3 in the case of B. The minimum required rate of return is 8%.

Internal rate of return:	A = 15%	
	B = 12%	
Net present value:	A = (1,150 × 0.926) − 1,000 =	£65*
	B = (1,405 × 0.794) − 1,000 =	£115*

* *Note*: 0.926 is the factor that reduces a sum receivable one year hence, at a discount rate of 8%, to its present value; and 0.794 is the discount factor that reduces a sum due three years hence to its present value. These discount factors are derived easily from published tables: see Appendix, pp. 650–1.

a positive net present value. Figure 6.9 provides an example to show that this is so. Both projects have rates of return in excess of 8% *and* positive net present values; but on the basis of the IRR method, project A is superior, while on the basis of the NPV method, project B is superior.

Confusion arises because the projects have different lengths of life, and if only one of the projects is to be undertaken (i.e. they are mutually exclusive) the IRR can be seen to be unable to discriminate satisfactorily between them. This is because, as with any rate of return, there is no indication of either the *amount* of capital involved or the *duration* of the investment. The choice must be made either on the basis of net present values, or on the return on the *incremental investment* between projects. (In the above example, of course, the same amount of investment is required for each, thus project B is to be preferred on the strength of its higher net present value.)

The two methods make different implicit assumptions about the reinvesting of funds received from projects – particularly during the 'gaps' between the end of one and the end of another.

Considering the example further, if it is explicitly assumed that the funds received from project A can be reinvested at 10% per annum between the end of years 1 and 3, the situation will be as shown in Fig. 6.10. All three formulations

Figure 6.10

Ranking comparison (2).

IRR:	A = (15 + 10 + 10) ÷ 3	= 11.667%
	B (as Fig. 6.9)	= 12%
NPV:	A = [(150 × 0.926) + (115 × 0.857) + (1,126 × 0.794)] − 1,000	= £32
	B (as Fig. 6.9)	= £115
Terminal value:	A = (1,150 × 110% × 110%)	= £1,391
	B (as given)	= £1,405

clearly show project B to be superior, illustrating the importance of project characteristics when only one can be undertaken.

The NPV approach assumes that cash receipts can be reinvested at the company's minimum acceptable rate of return, thereby giving a bias in favour of long-lived projects. In contrast, the IRR approach assumes that cash receipts are reinvested at the same rate (i.e. a constant renewal of the project), giving a bias in favour of short-lived projects.

It follows that the comparison of alternatives by either method must be made over a common time period, with explicit assumptions being made about what happens to funds between their receipt and the common terminal date.

(d) Aspects of application

(i) Alternative proposals

The selection of a particular proposal should follow a careful appraisal both of alternative uses for funds and of alternative means of undertaking a particular project. For instance, a company may wish to double the capacity of its production line and determines three means of accomplishing this, namely:

- introducing double-shift working;
- installing a second production line; or
- scrapping the existing production line and building a new line with double the initial capacity.

The choice of a particular alternative will depend on how it accords with the enterprise's established investment objectives, and the choice of projects will depend on both corporate objectives and the availability of funds. But the fact remains that if the most advantageous alternative has been overlooked, no amount of technical evaluation and appraisal can overcome this basic omission.

(ii) Capital rationing

In terms of financing investment projects three essential questions must be asked:

- What funds are needed for capital expenditure in the forthcoming planning period?
- What funds are available for investment?
- How are funds to be assigned when the acceptable proposals require more than are available?

The first and third questions are resolved by reference to the discounted return on the various proposals, since it will be known which are acceptable, and in which order of preference.

The second question is answered by a reference to *the capital budget* (see Chapter 8). The level of this budget will tend to depend on the quality of the investment proposals submitted to top management. In addition, it will also tend to depend on:

- top management's philosophy towards capital spending (e.g. is it growth-minded or cautious?);
- the outlook for future investment opportunities that may be unavailable if extensive current commitments are undertaken;
- the funds provided by current operations; and

- the feasibility of acquiring additional capital through borrowing or share issues.

It is not always necessary, of course, to limit the spending on projects to internally-generated funds. Theoretically, projects should be undertaken to the point where the return is just equal to the cost of financing these projects. If safety and the maintaining of, say, family control are considered to be more important than additional profits, there may be a marked unwillingness to engage in external financing, and hence a limit will be placed on the amounts available for investment.

Even though the enterprise may wish to raise external finance for its investment programme, there are many reasons why it may be unable to do this. Examples include:

- The enterprise's past record and its present capital structure may make it impossible – or extremely costly – to raise additional debt capital.
- Its record may make it impossible to raise new equity capital because of low yields – or even no yield.
- Covenants in existing loan agreements may restrict future borrowing.

Furthermore, in the typical company, one would expect capital rationing to be largely self-imposed.

Figure 6.11

Cash flow projections.

Proposal: Add a new line of toys.

Cash investment (£'000):

Production equipment	1,000
Recruiting and training salesmen	100
Promotional material	10
Inventory and debtors	190
	1,300

Projected sales volume (£'000):

Year 1	600
Year 2	1,000
Year 3	1,200
Year 4	1,000
Year 5 (final year)	800

Cost of sales

30% of sales value

Direct operating costs

£100,000 per annum

Depreciation of equipment

£200,000 per annum. No salvage value.

Figure 6.12

Cash flow analysis and evaluation.

(£000)	YEAR 0	1	2	3	4	5
1. Cash investment	(1,300)					
2. Sales revenue		600	1,000	1,200	1,000	800
3. Cost of sales		(180)	(300)	(360)	(300)	(240)
4. Operating costs		(100)	(100)	(100)	(100)	(100)
5. Recovery of investment in inventory and debtors						190
6. Cash flows	(1,300)	320	600	740	600	650
7. Discount factor at 18%	1.00	0.847	0.718	0.609	0.516	0.437
8. Discounted cash flow	(1,300)	271	431	451	310	284
9. NPV	447					

(iii) Post-audit

Each major project should be followed up to ensure that it conforms to the conditions on which it was accepted, as well as being subject to cost control procedures. (See, for example, Neale (1989) and Gordon and Myers (1991).)

(e) An example

The following example illustrates the importance of accurate forecasts of cash flows (representing sales value, cost of sales, operating costs, and initial investment). Taxation is deliberately ignored. (The example is adapted from Winer (1966).)

A proposal has been put forward in the form of a marketing plan to launch a new line of toys. Cash flow forecasts are shown in Fig. 6.11. Note that depreciation is not, in fact, a cash cost. It is shown here simply as a footnote to indicate that there will be no cash inflow at the end of year 5 from the sale of the equipment, since that equipment is not expected to have any residual value at that point in time.

The evaluation of the plan is shown in Fig. 6.12, which is largely self-explanatory. Cost of capital is shown as being 18%. This can be taken to be the minimum required rate of return from the plan (thus reflecting equivalent returns from alternative plans of comparable risk). The plan's net present value is £447,000 which results when the discounted inflows and outflows are summed and the initial investment deducted from the total.

Total discounted value of inflows and outflows from Year 1 to Year 5	£1,747,000
Initial investment	£1,300,000
Net present value	£447,000

From these figures it is also possible to calculate the PV index:

$$\frac{£1,747,000}{£1,300,000} = 1.34$$

In other words, the plan promises to generate £1.34 for every £1.00 invested in it, expressed in terms of current £s. Since the PV index exceeds unity, the NPV is positive and the plan appears to be economically viable. However, various additional questions need to be raised, such as:

- Is there sufficient funding available to meet the initial investment requirement of £1,300,000?
- Can the plan be modified to earn even more than £1.34 per £1.00 of investment?
- Are there alternatives available that may be more attractive?
- How sensitive is the plan's NPV to changes in flow estimates, including their timing?

From the data given in Fig. 6.11 it is possible to calculate the payback period of the plan and the accounting rate of return, as follows:

Payback period is the length of time it takes to recover the initial investment.

		£000
	Year 1	320
	Year 2	600
380/740	Year 3	380
		1,300

It will be 2 years 187 days (assuming an even pattern of inflows). The investment is exposed, therefore, over half of the anticipated life of the plan.

The accounting rate of return is an accounting (rather than cash flow) measure of the average profitability of the plan.

- Average profits will be (in £000):

$$\frac{£(320 + 600 + 740 + 600 + 460)}{5} - £200$$

$$\frac{£2,720}{5} - £200 = £344$$

It is necessary to deduct depreciation as an expense in calculating the average accounting profit.

- Average investment will be (in £000):

$$\frac{£1,300 - £190}{2} = £555$$

- The ARR will be:

$$\frac{£344}{£555} \times 100 = 62\%$$

6.6 Strategic management accounting

(a) Introduction

How can managerial accounting help managers make better strategic decisions? Perhaps the first response to this question is to discourage any approach to the design of managerial accounting systems that increases bureaucracy with results such as:

(i) the time taken to process proposals is increased, along with the cost;
(ii) the guidance given to managers for assessing the real merits of proposals is diminished.

Underlying assumptions may be incorrect, among which we can identify the following:

(i) finance is the primary scarce resource that must be allocated judiciously;
(ii) analysing proposals is costless;
(iii) accurate economic analysis is critical to success.

Care must be taken in allocating *all* organizational resources, and the analysis necessary for this to be done in a controlled manner is inevitably costly. However, it is better for management to have accounting information that is *approximately* right rather than *precisely* wrong. The success of strategic actions is just as much a function of judgement as it is of information.

In a commercial setting it is strategic decisions that determine an enterprise's competitive market position, and for this reason they are the most important decisions. It follows that the value of information is potentially higher in relation to strategic decision-making since the cost of mistakes is so much greater. An important role of managerial accounting can be seen in terms of providing relevant and timely information to facilitate strategy formulation and implementation.

Simmonds (1981) has defined strategic management accounting as:

> The provision and analysis of management accounting data about a business and its competitors for use in developing and monitoring the business strategy.

He emphasizes the particular importance of relative levels and trends in:

(i) real costs and prices;
(ii) volume;
(iii) market share;
(iv) cash flow;
(v) the proportion demanded of an enterprise's total resources.

The key notion here is that of an enterprise's position *relative to* competitors' positions. In so far as strategy is concerned with competitive position it has been largely ignored by management accountants, but in a number of papers Simmonds (1972; 1980; 1981; 1982; 1985; 1986) has proposed how this failing might be overcome.

A basic plank in his argument is the preoccupation that accountants have with the recording, analysing and presentation of cost data relating to existing activities. This 'data orientation' begs some fundamental questions – such as why the data is being collected in the first place. An alternative, and preferable, approach is one of 'information orientation' which starts with the diagnosis of problems, leading to the structuring of decisions, and thence to the specification of information that will help in making appropriate decisions. The focus shifts from the analysis of costs *per se* to the value of information.

Change – whether environmental or internal – is so pervasive that a perspective which asks: 'What should be done in this situation?' and then: 'What information will help in making appropriate decisions?' is much more likely to contribute to organizational control than a perspective that concerns itself solely with determining the costs of current activities. The broader, outward-looking perspective moves away from a concern purely with financial data to encompass notions of volume and market share, for example, which represent both the cause and consequence of financial outcomes. (Marketing activities generate revenue and marketing costs are incurred to build market share, so costs determine volume which in turn determines revenue. On the other hand, volume determines production and distribution costs. This is not to say, of course, that all cost flows are strictly variable with volume, but non-variable costs will typically be determined by an anticipated scale of activity which is a volume-related measure.)

It will help to consider the application of strategic management accounting in a little more detail, following the lines of Simmonds (1980; 1981). Consider the manager wishing to make decisions that will safeguard his organization's strategic position. He must know by whom, by how much and why he is gaining or being beaten. In other words, strategic indicators of performance are required. Conventional measures, such as profit, will not suffice. (It is quite possible that *improvements* in strategic position will accompany *reductions* in periodic profit due to the cost of achieving that position.) The strategic management accounting approach requires an emphasis on the enterprise's costs, sales volume, prices, market share and profit relative to those of competitors.

Let us take comparative costs as a starting point. It is intuitively the case that organizations having a cost advantage (i.e. lower unit cost for a product of comparable specification) are strong and those having a cost disadvantage are weak. If we relate this to the idea of the learning curve (which was introduced in Chapter 5 and will be expanded upon in Chapter 7) it will be appreciated that, if costs can be made to decline predictably with cumulative output, that enterprise which has produced most should have the lowest unit cost and, therefore, the highest profits.

In his 1981 article Simmonds shows the relative position of three enterprises within a given industry, and from this he demonstrates that the firm that is able to increase its sales level at a greater rate than its competitors will improve its market position and either reduce its cost disadvantage or increase its cost advantage. The link between cost levels and market share is significant, and this points to the strategies of:

(i) being first into the market with a new product and building up a relative cost advantage that competitors will be unable to catch;
(ii) in rapidly growing markets seeking to increase market share by taking advantage of the growth element rather than by cutting directly into competitors' sales volumes.

Apart from cost an enterprise may seek to gain strategic advantage via its pricing policy. In this setting the management accountant can attempt to assess each major competitor's cost structure and relate this to their prices – taking care to eliminate the effects of inflation from the figures being used. Applying cost-volume-profit analysis to one's competitors is likely to be more fruitful than simply applying it internally.

> Clearly, competitor reactions can substantially influence the outcome of a price move. Moreover, likely reactions may not be self-evident when each competitor faces a different cost-volume-profit situation. Competitors may not follow a price lead nor even march in perfect step as they each act to defend or build their own positions. For an adequate assessment of the likelihood of competitor price reactions, then, some calculation is needed of the impact of possible price moves on the performance of individual competitors. Such an assessment in turn requires an accounting approach that can depict both competitor cost-volume-profit situations and their financial resources.
>
> Simmonds (1982), p. 207.

After dealing with costs and prices the next important (and related) variable to consider is volume – especially market share. By monitoring movements in market share an enterprise can see whether it is gaining or losing position, and an examination of relative market shares will indicate the strengths of different competitors.

Reporting market share details along with financial details can help in making managerial accounting reports more strategically relevant. For example, a report showing improved profits for the most recent operating period may also show that:

(i) this has been due to prices being higher than before, and above the competitive level;
(ii) market share has fallen.

How might this be interpreted? By placing periodic results in a strategic framework it appears to be the case that the enterprise's competitive position has weakened *despite* the current profit figures since future profits will be harder to earn unless action is taken to regain lost market share. (Conversely, a fall in current profits may be due to actions undertaken to build market share and secure relative cost advantage, which will help ensure future improvements in profit performance.)

(b) Assessing competitive position

The significance of competitive position has been highlighted by Simmonds (1986) as being the basic determinant of future profits and of a business's value. Moreover, since competitive position can change over time, so can profits and value, but it should not be assumed that an improvement in competitive position will be associated with an improvement in short-run profits. In fact, the opposite is likely to be the case due to the need to incur costs in building up a competitive position, which has the effect of depressing current profits in favour of future profits. This raises the question as to whether competitive position can be measured in accounting terms – not just for a given business, but also for its main competitors; and not just at a point in time, but also over time. Simmonds has attempted to do this by applying strategic management accounting. He makes it clear, however, that it is not possible to express competitive position as a single figure. Instead it is possible to offer an array of indicators relating to the competitive situation. From these indicators managers can gain insights into a business' competitive position which will help them in judging whether or not things are moving in their favour.

Simmonds recommends that competitive data is built up for the market leader, close competitors, and laggards rather than for all competitors. The following data* might most usefully be developed:

(i) Sales and market share

Sales revenue of each firm relative to the total market is a cornerstone, and changes in market share should be closely monitored. A decrease in market share suggests a loss of competitive position, with unfortunate implications for future profits.

Conversely, an increase in market share suggests an improved competitive position, with the prospect of improved future profits. By adding market share details to management accounting reports, managers are able to make much more sense of what is happening.

Figure 6.13 gives sales and market share data for Firm A and the total market for product X.

We can see from Fig. 6.13 that, despite an increase in sales revenue of 20% for Firm A, the market share has slipped from 19% to 16%. This is explained by the growth in the total market of 44%. It seems probable that the firm's failure to keep pace with the overall market growth will be reflected in a poorer competitive position: not only might competitors have gained market share at the firm's expense, but this is likely to be accompanied by cost advantages – hence improved profits. Some details are given in Fig. 6.14.

Relative market share is calculated by dividing each competitor's market share by that of one's own firm, and it indicates any gains or losses. As Fig. 6.14 makes clear, Firm A has slipped relative to both the market leader and its closest competitor. The leader's market share has increased to three times that of Firm A, and this will almost certainly have lowered its unit costs.

Figure 6.13

Sales and market share data, product X.

	Firm A	*Total market*
Sales (£000)		
Last year	1,000	5,200
This year	1,200	7,500
% change	+20	+44
Market share (%)		
Last year	19	100
This year	16	100

*The above example is derived from that given in Simmonds (1986) and is used with permission.

Figure 6.14

Relative market shares.

	Sales (£000)	Market share (%)	Relative market share
Total market:			
Last year	5,200		
This year	7,500		
Firm A			
Last year	1,000	19	
This year	1,200	16	
Leading competitor			
Last year	2,200	42	2.20
This year	3,600	48	3.00
Close competitor			
Last year	1,200	23	1.20
This year	2,000	27	1.67

(ii) Profits and return on sales

If a competitor has a higher return on sales than Firm A, it may well reduce price, or improve quality, or increase its marketing efforts in order to improve its competitive position further.

The data in Fig. 6.15 shows sales, market share, relative market share, and profit (before tax but after interest) over the last three years for all firms supplying product X. Over that period the market leader's profit has grown by 400%, the closest competitor's by over 200%, and Firm A's by only 90%. In absolute terms the market leader's profit in year 3 is almost five times that of Firm A, giving a huge source of funds for expansion, R & D, etc., whilst in relative terms the leader's return on sales of 22.2% in year 3 is well ahead of any other competitor.

Firm A's task seems to be to reinforce its competitive position relative to both laggard firms on the one hand, and to develop a defence against the strong competitors on the other.

(iii) Volume and unit cost

Details of volume and costs are given in Fig. 6.16. Changes in unit costs reveal each firm's relative efficiency: the further a competitor's relative cost falls below unity the more of a threat this becomes, and vice versa. (Costs are calculated by substracting profit from sales revenue, and unit costs are obtained by dividing the costs by volume, year by year).

The market leader has a cost advantage in year 3 of 69p per unit relative to Firm A, whereas Laggard 2 has a cost disadvantage relative to Firm A of 73p per unit. Perhaps more significant than these figures are those that compare volume and cost changes. Thus, for example, Firm A's two main competitors both increased volume between years 2 and 3 by more than 70%, yet the close competitor's cost per unit fell by only 3% or so, whilst the market leader's cost per unit fell by more than 9%. Is the explanation to be found in the close competitor's investment

Figure 6.15

Sales, market shares, and profits for all suppliers of product X.

	Sales (£000)	Market share (%)	Relative market share	Profit (£000)	(%)
Firm A:					
Year 1	700	17.5		90	12.8
Year 2	1,000	19.2		130	13.0
Year 3	1,200	16.0		170	14.2
Leading competitor:					
Year 1	1,400	35.0	2.0	200	14.3
Year 2	2,200	42.3	2.2	400	18.2
Year 3	3,600	48.0	3.0	800	22.2
Close competitor:					
Year 1	1,000	25.0	1.4	120	12.0
Year 2	1,200	23.1	1.2	170	14.2
Year 3	2,000	26.6	1.7	260	13.0
Laggard 1:					
Year 1	500	12.5	0.71	55	11.0
Year 2	500	9.6	0.50	60	12.0
Year 3	500	6.7	0.42	50	10.0
Laggard 2:					
Year 1	400	10.0	0.57	40	10.0
Year 2	300	5.8	0.30	20	6.7
Year 3	200	2.7	0.17	5	2.5
Total market:					
Year 1	4,000	100.0		505	12.6
Year 2	5,200	100.0		780	15.0
Year 3	7,500	100.0		1,285	17.1

in competitive position – such as in R & D, marketing programmes, or new plant?

(iv) Unit prices

In Fig. 6.17 are shown the unit prices charged for product X by each competitor over the last three years, along with costs and the profits and market shares that have resulted. (Unit prices are simply calculated by dividing sales revenue by units sold.)

The pattern of price changes reflects the use of price as a competitive variable, and this can be related to cost and market share data to see how competitive positions are changing. For example, the market leader has reduced the price by more than any other firm, but its price reductions have not been as great as its cost reductions, hence profit per unit has increased each year – as has the number of units. This places that firm in a very strong competitive position.

Patterns of price, cost, profit and volume change for Firm A and its closest competitor are less clear, but for the laggards the picture of a downward spiral is clear enough.

Figure 6.16

Volume, costs and unit costs.

	Volume in units (000)	Increase (%)	Cost (£000)	Cost per unit (£)	Relative cost per unit
Firm A:					
Year 1	100		610	6.10	
Year 2	156	56	870	5.58	
Year 3	192	23	1,030	5.36	
Leading competitor:					
Year 1	200		1,200	6.00	0.98
Year 2	350	75	1,800	5.14	0.92
Year 3	600	71	2,800	4.67	0.87
Close competitor:					
Year 1	140		880	6.29	1.03
Year 2	190	36	1,030	5.42	0.97
Year 3	330	74	1,740	5.27	0.98
Laggard 1:					
Year 1	70		445	6.36	1.04
Year 2	75	7	440	5.86	1.05
Year 3	80	7	450	5.62	1.05
Laggard 2:					
Year 1	56		360	6.42	1.05
Year 2	45	(20)	280	6.22	1.16
Year 3	32	(29)	195	6.09	1.14
Total:					
Year 1	566				
Year 2	816	44			
Year 3	1,234	51			

(v) Cash flow, liquidity and resource availability

Competitive gains and losses will arise over longer periods than the financial year, and the capacity of a competitor to continue in the fray is a function of more than simply profit or market share at a particular point in time. A firm's ability to continue to compete will also depend upon its liquidity position and the availability of other resources over time. For example, a firm with poor cash flow, a high level of debt, and out-of-date production facilities is not likely to be able to compete for long.

(vi) The future

Having analysed the relative positions of each firm supplying product X over the past three years, the real crunch comes in attempting to make the next move.

The management of Firm A will be able to see that the market leader is controlling the competitive situation with the highest volume and profits, plus the lowest unit costs and price. If that firm reduced its price by, say, 10% it would force the laggards out of the market and limit the close competitor's profit (assuming it followed suit and reduced its own price). Firm A needs to reduce its costs and

Figure 6.17

Unit prices, profits and market shares.

	Average price per unit (£)	Average cost per unit (£)	Profit per unit (£)	Market share (%)
Firm A:				
Year 1	7.00	6.10	0.90	17.5
Year 2	6.41	5.58	0.83	19.2
Year 3	6.25	5.36	0.89	16.0
Leading competitor:				
Year 1	7.00	6.00	1.00	35.0
Year 2	6.29	5.14	1.15	42.3
Year 3	6.00	4.67	1.33	48.0
Close competitor:				
Year 1	7.14	6.29	0.85	25.0
Year 2	6.31	5.42	0.89	23.1
Year 3	6.06	5.27	0.79	26.6
Laggard 1:				
Year 1	7.14	6.36	0.78	12.5
Year 2	6.66	5.86	0.80	9.6
Year 3	6.25	5.62	0.63	6.7
Laggard 2:				
Year 1	7.14	6.42	0.72	10.0
Year 2	6.66	6.22	0.44	5.8
Year 3	6.25	6.09	0.16	2.7

strengthen its position against its two main competitors whilst there is scope for growth in the overall market for product X.

Using Figs. 6.13–6.17 as a basis, various possibilities can be projected for the future, each building on explicit assumptions regarding:

- future market demand;
- likely competitive actions;
- likely competitive reactions;
- competitors' liquidity and solvency.

This takes us a long way from conventional single entity, single period management accounting, yet the adaptations that need to be made are not so difficult to comprehend – but the benefits from gaining a clearer picture of one's competitive position and how this is changing should be enormous. Strategic management accounting can help realize these benefits.

A further detailed example will illustrate more fully how strategic management accounting might be developed and applied. This relates to a hypothetical company, Midas plc, and its main competitor, Alpha plc.

(c) The Midas case

Midas plc is in the business of high-security printing. Between them, Midas plc and their main competitor Alpha plc, have consistently held an 80% share of

Figure 6.18

Market size.

Year	Total market volume (million items)
1985	340
1986	380
1987	420
1988	395
1989	430
1990	440
1991	485
1992	525

the market for years (see Fig. 6.18); the rest of the market is held by smaller firms.

In preparation for a Midas plc board meeting in December 1992, figures have been prepared which show Midas's market share and average price per item for the last eight years, all inflation-adjusted. Alpha's figures are included for comparison (Fig. 6.19). Figures for revenue and operating profit for both companies are also available (Fig. 6.20).

There are two schools of thought among the directors. One is that prices should be increased, as they often have been in the past. This would put up the average price to something like 39p at current prices. 'After all, we project the total market in 1993 to be something like 600 million items – why don't we just keep on doing what we have been doing, successfully!'

The other is that the price should be held for another year. 'We've got room to move, and Alpha haven't, if we maintain price parity. It would give us the chance to expand as fast as we're investing in new technology.'

The problem, then, is to calculate the probable effect of the two pricing strategies on the 1993 profits of Midas plc and Alpha plc, on the basis of the data provided above, in order that an appropriate decision might be made.

Figure 6.19

Price and share data.

Year	Average price (£)		Market share	
	Midas	Alpha	Midas	Alpha
1985	0.21	0.21	50%	30%
1986	0.23	0.22	47%	33%
1987	0.23	0.23	49%	31%
1988	0.30	0.23	42%	38%
1989	0.34	0.26	36%	44%
1990	0.28	0.28	38%	42%
1991	0.35	0.33	34%	46%
1992	0.35	0.35	36%	44%

Figure 6.20

Revenue and profit data.

Year	Midas plc Revenue (£m)	Midas plc Profit (£m)	Alpha plc Revenue (£m)	Alpha plc Profit (£m)
1985	35.7	3.6	21.4	(13.3)
1986	41.2	4.1	27.6	(11.2)
1987	47.4	5.2	29.9	(3.9)
1988	49.8	6.4	34.5	(1.5)
1989	52.7	7.5	49.2	11.4
1990	46.8	6.5	51.7	12.8
1991	57.8	8.7	73.6	29.0
1992	66.2	19.0	80.9	37.0

One way in which this problem might be addressed can be developed from the following analysis of the given data.

We can start by producing an analysis of the physical volumes involved, as shown in Fig. 6.21.

The next step is to generate average revenue per unit for Midas and Alpha, along with relative price indices, followed by average cost per unit for each company plus relative cost indices, and then profit summaries, as in Figs. 6.22–6.24.

From Fig. 6.21 it is evident that there has been a change in relative position over the period 1985–92. In the earlier years Midas had a larger share of the market than Alpha – as revealed by the relative market share index: when this is less than unity it means that Midas has a larger share than Alpha, but when it exceeds unity it means the opposite. The index is calculated as:

$$\frac{\text{Alpha's market share}}{\text{Midas's market share}}$$

Relative market share is a primary indicator of competitive position. In a growing market, with an increase of 54% (from 340 million items in 1985 to 525 million items in 1992), it is apparent that Midas has failed to achieve the same growth rate

Figure 6.21

Market share analysis.

Year	Total market (m. items)	%	Midas m. items	%	Alpha m. items	%	Other m. items	Relative market share
1985	340	50	170	30	102	20	68	0.60
1986	380	47	179	33	125	20	76	0.70
1987	420	49	206	31	130	20	84	0.63
1988	395	42	166	38	150	20	79	0.90
1989	430	36	155	44	189	20	86	1.22
1990	440	38	167	42	185	20	88	1.11
1991	485	34	165	46	223	20	97	1.35
1992	525	36	189	44	231	20	105	1.22

Figure 6.22

Revenue and price analysis.

	Midas			Alpha			
Year	Items (m.)	Revenue (£m.)	Average price (£)	Items (m.)	Revenue (£m.)	Average price (£)	Relative price
1985	170	35.7	0.21	102	21.4	0.21	1.00
1986	179	41.2	0.23	125	27.6	0.22	0.96
1987	206	47.4	0.23	130	29.9	0.23	1.00
1988	166	49.8	0.30	150	34.5	0.23	0.77
1989	155	52.7	0.34	189	49.2	0.26	0.76
1990	167	46.8	0.28	185	51.7	0.28	1.00
1991	165	57.8	0.35	223	73.6	0.33	0.94
1992	189	66.2	0.35	231	80.9	0.35	1.00

Figure 6.23

Cost analysis.

	Midas			Alpha			
Year	Items (m.)	Cost (£m.)	Average cost (£)	Items (m.)	Cost (£m.)	Average cost (£)	Relative price
1985	170	32.1	0.19	102	34.7	0.34	1.79
1986	179	37.1	0.21	125	38.8	0.31	1.48
1987	206	42.2	0.20	130	33.8	0.26	1.30
1988	166	43.4	0.26	150	36.0	0.24	0.92
1989	155	45.2	0.29	189	37.8	0.20	0.69
1990	167	40.3	0.24	185	38.9	0.21	0.88
1991	165	49.1	0.30	223	44.6	0.20	0.67
1992	189	47.2	0.25	231	43.9	0.19	0.76

Figure 6.24

Profit summaries.

	Midas				Alpha				
Year	Revenue (£m.)	Cost (£m.)	Profit (£m.)	Average profit (£)	Revenue (£m.)	Cost (£m.)	Profit (£m.)	Average profit (£)	Relative profit
1985	35.7	32.1	3.6	0.02	21.4	34.7	(13.3)	(0.13)	–
1986	41.2	37.1	4.1	0.02	27.6	38.8	(11.2)	(0.09)	–
1987	47.4	42.2	5.2	0.03	29.9	33.8	(3.9)	(0.03)	–
1988	49.8	43.4	6.4	0.04	34.5	36.0	(1.5)	(0.01)	–
1989	52.7	45.2	7.5	0.05	49.2	37.8	11.4	0.06	1.20
1990	46.8	40.3	6.5	0.04	51.7	38.9	12.8	0.07	1.75
1991	57.8	49.1	8.7	0.05	73.6	44.6	29.0	0.13	2.60
1992	66.2	47.2	19.0	0.10	80.9	43.9	37.0	0.16	1.60

(170 million to 189 million represents an increase of only 11%). In contrast, Alpha's growth rate has been much higher (102 million to 231 million, an increase of 126%). Midas has achieved a smaller share of a growing market and has clearly been losing competitive position relative to Alpha.

From Fig. 6.22 we can see the average unit prices charged by both companies. The relative price index is calculated as:

$$\frac{\text{Alpha's average price}}{\text{Midas's average price}}$$

When this is less than unity it means that Alpha has a price advantage (i.e. is charging a lower price); when it exceeds unity it means that Midas has a price advantage. In no year did this index exceed unity, suggesting that Alpha always had a price advantage – and this was especially evident in 1988 and 1989. It was during these two years (see Fig. 6.21) that Alpha's relative market share overtook that of Midas.

Over the span of eight years the increase in price of both companies was 67% (from £0.21 to £0.35), but at no time was Alpha's price greater than that of Midas. In fact, by increasing its price by larger amounts in the middle years, Midas lost out in terms of its competitive position.

Turning from revenue to costs, we can see from Fig. 6.23 that the relative cost position of the two competitors changes significantly over the years in question. This index is measured by:

$$\frac{\text{Alpha's average cost}}{\text{Midas's average cost}}$$

The *total* cost figure is computed by deducting profits from revenue (or adding losses to revenue) year by year. An average figure is arrived at by dividing costs by the number of items.

In relative cost terms Midas had a clear advantage in the period 1985–7, when the index was greater than unity. However, Alpha established an advantage from 1988 when the index dropped below unity. This coincided with the marked improvements in Alpha's relative price and relative market share position. Over the entire span of eight years Alpha's average unit cost has fallen by 44% (from £0.34 to £0.19) whereas Midas's average unit cost has increased by 32% (from £0.19 to £0.25).

The profit picture is portrayed in Fig. 6.24. It can be seen that Midas had an advantage in the period 1985–8, but that Alpha secured the advantage in the years from 1989 onwards. The relative profit figure is given by:

$$\frac{\text{Alpha's average profit}}{\text{Midas's average profit}}$$

When this exceeds unity it means that Alpha has the advantage.

Midas improved its average profit per unit from £0.02 in 1985 to £0.10 in 1992 – an increase of 500%. But Alpha's improvement was from a loss of £0.13 to a profit of £0.16 – an improvement of £0.29 per unit.

In terms of relative price, relative cost, relative profit, and relative market share we can conclude that, prior to the decision that needs to be made, Midas has been losing out to Alpha in its competitive position. The graphs that follow show the

Figure 6.25

Unit costs and volume — Midas.

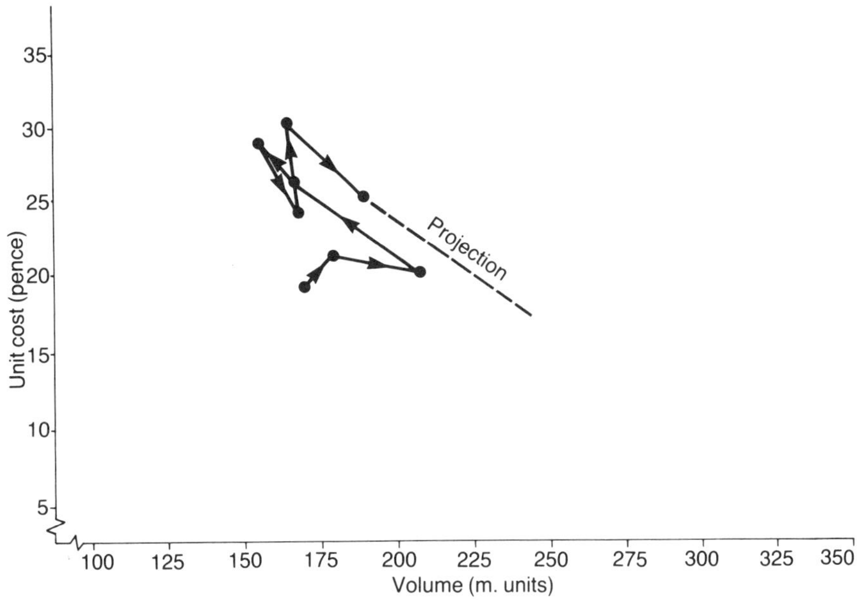

patterns in a slightly different format for costs (see Fig. 6.25 for Midas, and Fig. 6.26 for Alpha), and market share at different prices for both companies (Fig. 6.27).

What we need to do is establish some relationship between volume and costs that can be projected into the future, and some relationship between market share and price that can also be projected into the future. (All cost and revenue flows are deemed to be inflation free.)

Taking cost–volume relationships first, as Figs. 6.25 and 6.26 show, the higher the volume the lower is the unit cost. This is much clearer in the case of Alpha, but it is still broadly the case for Midas. We would expect this to be applicable in the future too, so we might use Figs. 6.25 and 6.26 as a basis for projecting cost data in the light of anticipated volumes.

The volume dimension will depend not only on the price (hence market share) that Midas sets, but also on the competitive reaction of Alpha. Figure 6.27 reveals that Alpha has been achieving higher market share as its price has increased, whereas Midas's market share has fallen as its price has increased. The explanation for this seemingly odd pattern is to be found in the relative prices of the competing companies: as noted above (and see Fig. 6.22), Alpha's price has never exceeded that of Midas during the time-span we are considering. It is evident, therefore, that Alpha has been gaining market share because its price has either been lower than Midas's, or because its price has been no higher. We can infer that the market for high-security printing is price-sensitive.

Figure 6.26

Unit costs and volume — Alpha.

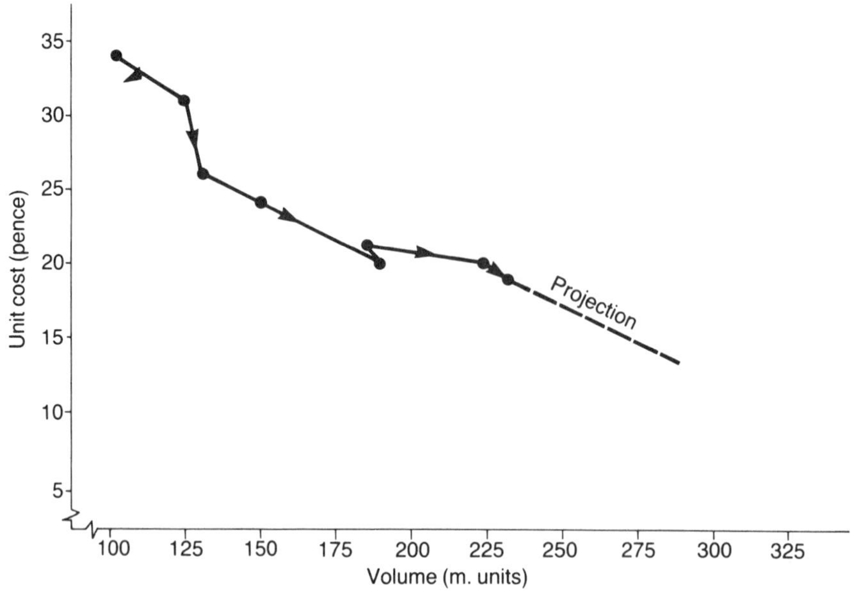

In 1985 Midas was the market leader (50% share), whereas Alpha had become the leader by 1992 (44% share). When price parity prevails Midas tends to gain share at Alpha's expense, but when there is no price parity (i.e. Alpha's prices are lower than those of Midas) Alpha gains share at Midas's expense. See Fig. 6.28.

In quantitative terms we can say that Midas gains 2% p.a. in market share when price parity exists, and that Alpha gains (on average) 1% p.a. in market share for each lp difference in price.

If Midas increases its price (option 1) from 35p to 39p it is likely that one of the outcomes shown in Fig. 6.29 will occur.

Taking the total volume for 1993 as 600 million items (as given in the case) the projections in Fig. 6.29 can readily be turned into physical quantities (relating to market share) and revenue possibilities.

Probabilities could be attached to the likelihood of Alpha reacting in any of the ways suggested in Fig. 6.29. Using the historical data as a basis for this we can see that in four years out of eight Alpha matches Midas's price; the difference was lp in one year; 2p in one year; and more than 2p in two years. Let us adopt the probabilities shown in Fig. 6.30.

Since there is no historical evidence to show that Alpha has either increased its price above that of Midas or reduced it below the level of Midas, it seems safe to assume that, if Midas chooses to hold its price at 35p through 1993 (option 2), Alpha will also hold its price at 35p.

We can now compute the probable effects on the profits of Midas and Alpha

Figure 6.27

Market share and price data.

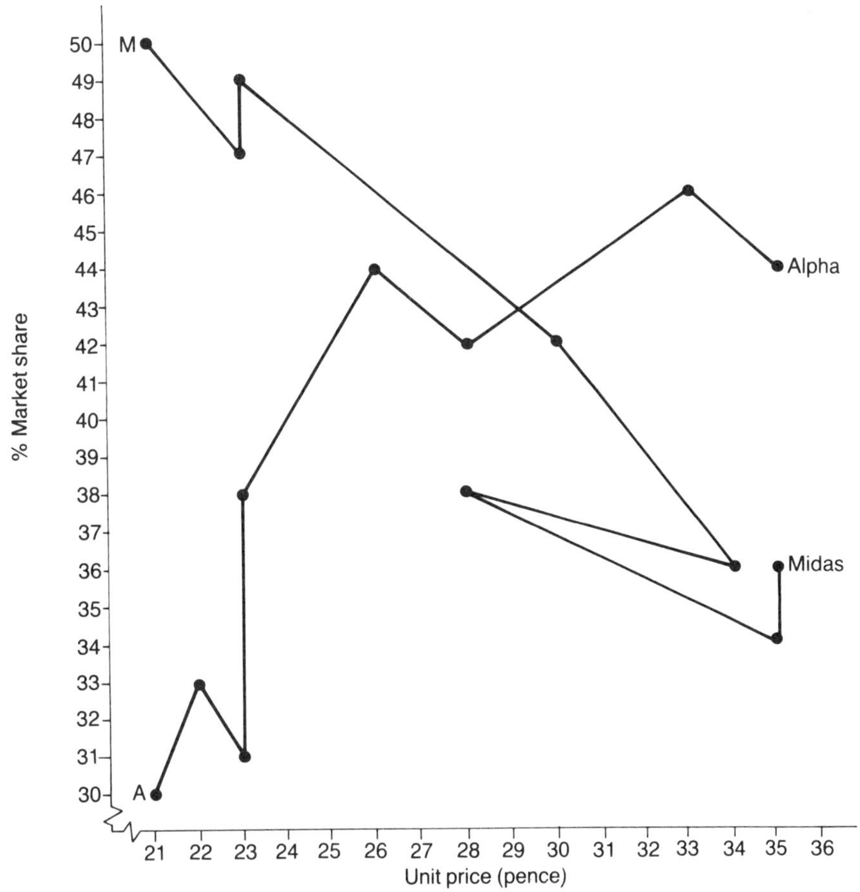

of the two pricing options. This is shown in Fig. 6.31 and reveals that Midas will be better off if option 1 is adopted, since this gives it a higher expected value for profit than option 2.

On the other hand, under option 1 the expected value of the market shares are:

Midas	35.75%
Alpha	44.25%

which is a weaker situation for Midas than is the market share picture under option 2. Moreover, under option 1 it is clear that the expected profit outcome for Alpha is much better than it would be under option 2. In other words, given that market share is the main source of profit, and that the greater the relative profit performance of competitors the greater is their scope for investing in improving

Figure 6.28

Brand-switching patterns.

	Change in Midas's market share (% points)	Price difference (pence)	Change in Alpha's market share (% points)
1985	–	0	–
1986	−3	1	+3
1987	+2	0	−2
1988	−7	7	+7
1989	−6	8	+6
1990	+2	0	−2
1991	−4	2	+4
1992	+2	0	−2

Figure 6.29

1993 price and share projections.

Price		Market share	
Midas	Alpha	Midas	Alpha
39p	35p	−4%	+4%
39p	36p	−3%	+3%
39p	37p	−2%	+2%
39p	38p	−1%	+1%
39p	39p	+2%	−2%

Figure 6.30

Probabilities.

Price		Probability
Midas	Alpha	
39p	35p	0.125
39p	36p	0.125
39p	37p	0.125
39p	38p	0.125
39p	39p	0.500
		1.000

their competitive position, there could be some logic in Midas selecting option 2. Midas's relative cost position is expected to be much better under option 2 than under option 1. This would give a basis – coupled with the larger market share under option 2 – for fighting back against Alpha's superior position.

Figure 6.31

Overall analysis.

	Midas price (p)	Alpha reaction (p)	Brand switch M (%)	Brand switch A (%)	Market share M (%)	Market share A (%)	Volume M (m.)	Volume A (m.)	Revenue M (£m.)	Revenue A (£m.)	Unit cost M (p)	Unit cost A (p)	Cost M (£m.)	Cost A (£m.)	Profit M (£m.)	Profit A (£m.)	Probability	Expected value M (£m.)	Expected value A (£m.)
Option 1	39	35	−4	+4	32	48	192	288	74.9	100.8	24.5	13.5	47.0	38.9	27.9	61.9	0.125	4.0	7.7
		36	−3	+3	33	47	198	282	77.2	101.5	23.5	14.0	46.5	39.5	30.7	62.0	0.125	3.8	7.8
		37	−2	+2	34	46	204	276	79.6	102.1	22.5	14.5	45.9	40.0	33.7	62.1	0.125	4.2	7.8
		38	−1	+1	35	45	210	270	81.9	102.6	22.0	15.0	46.2	40.5	35.7	62.1	0.125	4.5	7.8
		39	+2	−2	38	42	228	252	88.9	98.3	21.0	17.0	47.9	42.8	41.0	55.5	0.5	20.5	27.8
																		37.0	58.9
Option 2	35	35	+2	−2	38	42	228	252	79.8	88.2	21.0	17.0	47.9	42.8	31.9	45.4	1.0	31.9	45.4

After all this analysis it is still a matter of judgement – preferably *informed* judgement – that should underpin Midas's choice between the two options. The analysis is relevant, if not wholly precise. For example, using the cost curves in Figs. 6.25 and 6.26 instead of experience curves is a rather crude proxy, and the anticipated level of sales in 1993 (600 million items) is taken at face value as a reliable point estimate. Nevertheless, the analysis generates insights into the competitive position of Midas relative to Alpha, and these insights should lead to better decisions, hence enhanced organizational effectiveness.

Summary

Within this chapter we have lowered the level of resolution from that adopted in Chapter 5. This has allowed us to consider the longer term during which scale changes are permissible due to the relaxation of many of the constraints that organizations face in the short-run.

The types of decisions that are strategic in nature were outlined and categorized according to whether they aim to produce a financial return or not, whether they are optional or not, and the nature of their risk characteristics. Classification is important in providing a suitable framework within which decision-relevant managerial accounting information might be generated.

Strategic decisions were located within the strategic decision-making process which involves analysis, choice and implementation. Strategy itself was defined in terms of a set of chosen actions that lead to a competitive market position. This perspective requires that management accountants look outwards in order to focus on their organization's position relative to competitors.

Growth is not necessarily the obvious object of strategy. Careful thought needs to be given to both the desired direction and the appropriate methods to adopt in formulating strategic decisions. In a commercial setting useful frameworks have been provided via Ansoff's growth matrix (see Ansoff (1965)) and BCG's product portfolio matrix (see Boston Consulting Group (1970)), which both highlight the central role of product–market interactions.

The criteria by which strategic choices might be made cannot be purely financial since organizational effectiveness is a much broader notion, and strategy must lead to improved organizational effectiveness (however defined). Suitability, feasibility and acceptability need to be among the criteria. Moreover, it may be beneficial when making strategic choices to do this from a zero base rather than taking the continued value of ongoing projects for granted.

In considering the environment we saw the wide range of impacts that can affect orgaizational effectiveness. Many of these cannot be accommodated within the design of managerial accounting systems due to the partiality of these systems. However, it is possible to deal with some environmental factors in so far as they lend themselves to quantification and have a measurable relationship with organizational activities. The probabilistic nature of these relationships and their outcomes can be accommodated to some extent through the use of decision trees and sensitivity analysis. Inflation is an especially significant environmental factor that must be allowed for in making strategic decisions.

Managerial accounting systems need to be oriented towards external events in order *inter alia* to emphasize an enterprise's position relative to its competitors' positions, and to offer an information (rather than data) orientation for the benefit of those who have to make strategic decisions. We looked in some detail at the way in which strategic management accounting might be developed and applied in order to meet these requirements.

Key terms and concepts

Here is a list of the key terms and concepts which have featured in this chapter. You should make sure that you understand and can define each one of them. Page references to definitions in the text appear in bold in the index.

- Investment appraisal
  - cash flow
  - discounting versus compounding
  - internal rate of return (IRR)
  - net present value (NPV)
  - payback
  - rate of return on investment (ROI) or average rate of return (ARR)
  - time value of money
- Level of resolution
  - long-run versus short-run
  - scale
- Risk
  - decision trees
  - sensitivity analysis
- Search
- Strategy
- Strategic
  - analysis
  - choice
  - implementation
  - management accounting
- Zero-base budgeting

Further reading

You might usefully look at Ansoff (1965) or Johnson and Scholes (1988) on corporate planning; at Piper (1983) on project classification; and Simmonds (1982;

1985; 1986), Wilson (1991) and Shank (1989) on aspects of strategic management accounting.

Beyond these items the following are of potential interest: Gordon, *et al.* (1978); Goold (1986); Goold and Quinn (1990); Schreyögg and Steinmann (1987); Dent (1990); Berry (1984); Barwise, *et al.* (1986); Marsh, *et al.* (1988); and Lumijärvi (1991).

The workbook to accompany this chapter begins on p. 511.

CHAPTER

7 Setting standards and estimates

Learning objectives

After studying this chapter you should be able to:

- understand the role of estimates, standards and budgets as elements of feed-forward control;
- calculate estimates using the main techniques of estimation;
- recognize the main types of standards set for manufacturing and non-manufacturing organizations; and
- understand the motivational and learning aspects of setting standards.

7.1 Introduction

Following the definition of Bhaskar and Housden (1985) given in Chapter 3, a feed-forward control mechanism is a measurement and prediction device that is able to assess and predict the performance of a system at some future date. The system that we are trying to predict may be the entire enterprise itself, a division of an organization, a particular activity, market segment or product line. The feed-forward control mechanism that we are interested in is the managerial accounting system.

In order that the accounting system may act as a feedforward regulator, it needs to supply information that is:

(i) future-oriented;
(ii) predictive;
(iii) performance-centred; and
(iv) a basis for control.

Let us look at these characteristics in more detail.

(a) Future-oriented, predictive information about performance

Feedforward information has to be future-oriented, predictive and performance-centred because it is intended to enable the organization to know, and therefore to predict, its future performance. As was pointed out in Chapter 3, to do this the accounting information system must have a good model (image or representation) of the input–output relationship of the organization. That is, it should be able to predict what output (performance) levels are associated with different configurations of inputs. Hence, given a certain set of inputs, the managerial accounting system should know what performance level might be expected. Or alternatively, given a performance level, what configuration of inputs would be the most efficient.

We shall illustrate how this notion of feedforward control may be applied in a service organization like a restaurant that has decided to add two new dishes to its menu: a melon cocktail and an apple strudel. The restaurant wishes to serve 'one normal helping' of a melon cocktail in port. That is the output desired. What are the inputs required and how much are the expected costs of these inputs? These questions should be capable of being answered by the management accountant (working in conjunction with the chef, of course!) Figure 7.1 presents the accountant's answer.

Note that these estimated costs are only as useful as the assumptions about the future that the accountant has used in arriving at the estimates. Some of these assumptions might be that inflation will remain at 5%, fruit and vegetable supplies will not be interrupted, spoilage of these perishable items will not exceed 2%, the mint bush at the back of the restaurant will continue to produce sufficient mint leaves, etc. The point to remember is this – estimates of any activity are intended to help control the future by making it more certain. We estimate the costs of our melon cocktails and apple strudels in order to help us know (with confidence) whether it will be profitable for us to serve these new dishes. But in making these estimates to control the future, we have to make assumptions about that future. And our estimates will only be as good as these predictive assumptions. Therefore, to control the future, we need to predict it accurately – hence the need for feedforward information that correctly maps the input–output relationship.

However, a predictive feedforward control system should not only provide static but also dynamic input–output information. That is, it should also know how changes affecting the activity could affect output. For example, let us imagine that demand for our melon cocktails far exceeded initial expectations and we now

Figure 7.1

Analysis of a restaurant menu as feedforward control.

Estimated cost of 1 normal helping

Melon Cocktail in Port	£	Apple Strudel	£
Water melon	0.08	Apples	0.17
Rock melon	0.19	Puff pastry	0.20
Honeydew melon	0.21	Raisins	0.16
Egg white	0.10	Castor sugar	0.05
Castor sugar	0.02	Butter	0.08
Port	1.28	Icing sugar	0.02
Mint leaves	–	Cream	0.21
Icing sugar	0.01		
Orange wedge	0.03		
Total cost	£1.92		£0.89

need to purchase a special device that shapes all the melon pieces into neat little balls (this task had been done manually before). This device is expected to cost £100 and will take up a small corner of the limited amount of kitchen worktop space. In addition, the price of rock melon from Australia has increased by a massive 100%, the cost of transporting these melons from the docks in Southampton to the restaurant has also increased (by 10%) and we now have to buy our mint leaves as the mint bush (at the back of the restaurant) was killed by severe frost last May.

How will all these changes affect the estimated costs of our melon cocktails? Will it still be worth our while to serve the dish or is there some other dish that could be substituted without loss of custom? These are questions which the management accountant should be able to help answer with an efficient feedforward control system.

(b) Feedforward information as a basis for control

We have said that in order to control the future we need to predict accurately future events and happenings. What does controlling the future mean? It means being able to manipulate present organizational structures and strategies efficiently and effectively given our predictions of the future. For instance, if we estimate that the demand for our apple strudels would peak in winter, we could place orders now for cheaper quality apples in summer (when no bulk discount would be available due to the small quantities bought) and better quality apples in winter. In addition, we may arrange to hire an extra kitchen hand only in winter in order to help make the pastry required for the dish. By placing these contracts for raw materials and for labour now, the restaurant may be able to negotiate better prices and quality of supply than when purchasing emergency supplies. As can be seen, if our predictions of the future turn out to be correct, we will have made a number of decisions now that will help the organization to increase its efficiency.

In addition, feedforward information should act as a basis for feedback control. By comparing predicted outcomes with actual outcomes, decision-makers would know to what extent the initial predictions were achieved. If there was a significant difference between predicted and actual outcomes, this should act as a trigger for further investigation. For instance, in the example above, it was estimated that the cost of a serving of apple strudel would be £0.89. If, after a month in operation, the restaurant found that its apple strudels in fact cost £2.00 (over 100% increase above its original estimate), some form of investigation should be carried out since the apple strudels could have been priced too low to recover their costs. As Chapter 3 pointed out, a comparison of expected and actual levels of performance (feedback control) helps an organization to keep 'in control'. This will be developed more fully in Chapter 10.

In summary, feedforward control has the following purposes:

(i) to predict and control the future by making appropriate decisions in the present;
(ii) to provide decision-makers with a means of comparing actual with expected performance;
(iii) to highlight processes that are or may be 'out of control'.

In order that such feedforward control is achieved, the managerial accounting system has to provide information that is:

(i) future-oriented;
(ii) predictive; and
(iii) performance-centred.

To do this, the information system needs to have a good model of the current and expected input–output relationships of the organization.

What kinds of feedforward information is provided by a managerial accounting information system? The most valuable form of feedforward information provided takes the form of estimates of future input-output relationships.

(c) Types of estimates

Theoretically, estimates of the future activities of an organization may be developed from a number of aspects. In general, we could have three main types of estimates:

(i) input estimates;
(ii) output estimates;
(iii) input–output estimates.

These three main types can be further classified into physical or financial estimates. For instance, input estimates may be expressed in physical units or in financial terms. Thus, we may estimate that one helping of apple strudel will require half an apple or 17p worth of apple. Similarly, for output estimates, we may speak of an expected output level of 100 helpings of apple strudel or express those 100 helpings as the cost of producing them (i.e. £89). Alternatively, we could express the same 100 helpings in terms of the sales revenue generated or the profit earned. In the same way, input–output estimates can also be expressed in physical or financial units. Thus, we might expect that to serve 100 helpings of apple strudel, part of the inputs required would be 50 apples, 5 kg of castor sugar, 4 kg of butter, 40 hours of labour and 2 hours of machine time. Alternatively, we can express these physical quantities in terms of costs.

In addition, like costs, estimates may be set for any object or activity that needs to be predicted. For instance, we may be interested only in estimating the direct costs of producing/manufacturing the apple strudels. On the other hand, we may be interested in estimating the total costs, both direct and indirect, of production. For yet another purpose, we may wish to project all the revenue and total costs which the restaurant will face in the next five years. Note that in the first two instances we were interested in estimating costs of apple strudels (object of estimation) while in the third instance our object of estimation consisted of the expected revenues and costs of the restaurant for the next five years.

Given the diversity of input and output estimates that could be obtained, we shall limit ourselves to looking at three main types of estimates for feedforward control that are provided by the managerial accounting system. These are:

(i) cost estimates (financial estimates of the cost of inputs required);
(ii) standards (physical/financial estimates of the inputs/outputs required);
(iii) budget targets (estimates of both inputs and outputs expected for a certain period of the future).

All three types of information are predictions of the future. They express that which is expected to occur; hence the word estimates is used correctly to describe all three types of information. In addition, they all relate to some aspect of the input–output relationship of the organization. However, because each type of accounting information refers to a particular aspect of the input–output relationship, and through usage has come to take on a specific meaning, each of these three types of information will be discussed separately. But remember, all three types of information have much in common:

(i) they all present predictive information;
(ii) each models (or gives a representation of) some aspect of the current and expected input–output relationship.

7.2 Cost estimates as elements of feedforward control

Feedforward control is, thus, essentially concerned with:

(i) identifying and predicting future input–output relationships;
(ii) providing information that acts as a basis for feedback control;
(iii) alerting decision-makers to situations that could be out of control.

In order to achieve this predictive capacity, an organization needs to set cost estimates which help control the future. Cost estimates are essentially financial estimates of the inputs required by an organization. For instance, in the example given in Section 7.1 above, the cost estimates represent what the restaurant expects to incur for purchasing each item of input and for serving the product as a whole.

Cost estimates are as necessary in public sector organizations as in private enterprises, in manufacturing as well as in service industries. Organizations from hospitals, accounting firms, charities and churches to British Petroleum, British Steel and British Coal need to develop cost estimates. At times, it may be difficult to estimate costs for public sector activities. What is the estimated cost to the community of increased noise pollution, of longer traffic delays, of unsightly motorways? However, even in these instances, some attempts have been made to develop financial costs for non-commercial service activities.

(a) Cost estimation

Cost estimation is linked to feedforward and feedback control. Because of its importance, a variety of methods of cost estimation are available at present. Some are more sophisticated and complicated than others. The choice of a particular method will depend on the size of the enterprise, the nature of the production process, management's belief in the usefulness of particular methods and the cost of implementation relative to the benefits expected.

The basic aim in cost estimation is to arrive at desired or targeted costs which act as bench-marks for the activity in question, thereby facilitating control. It aims to answer the question: how much is an activity expected to cost? Let us assume that our purpose here is to estimate the total cost function of the organization. If this is the case, then we are seeking to complete the following CVP equation:

Total cost = Fixed cost + Variable cost

To do this, we need to answer three questions.

(i) Fixed, variable or mixed costs?

Which of our costs are fixed, variable or mixed? In the short run, costs such as rent and council and water rates are likely to be fixed. That is, they do not vary with the level of activity. Other costs will be variable. For instance, the cost of medical supplies and nursing staff time will tend to vary with the number of patients admitted to a hospital, while the cost of providing staff meals in the hospital canteen will tend to vary with the number of staff employed by the hospital. Still other hospital costs such as telephone, electricity and lease payments are likely to have both fixed and variable components. For example, to lease a photocopier the hospital may have to pay a fixed sum per month and a variable amount that depends on the number of copies made.

(ii) What is the variable?

We also have to know with what variable a cost varies. Is it the number of cars sold, hamburgers produced or patients discharged? The management accountant tries to select a variable that is likely to have the most influence on the cost under investigation. In ABC jargon, the interest is in *cost drivers* (i.e. the determinants of cost). For example, a cost like the repair and maintenance of surgical equipment is most likely to be influenced by the number of operations performed. Hence repair and maintenance is said to be a *function* of (that is, depends on) the level of activity. In other words, the number of operations *drives* the repair and maintenance costs. Mathematically, this cost relationship or cost function is written as:

$$Y = bX$$

where Y represents repair and maintenance costs, X the number of operations performed and b the average repair cost per operation. Y is said to be the *dependent variable* because it depends on or varies with X, and X is called the *independent variable*. In the above equation b is a *parameter* that specifies the precise relationship between Y and X. Because Y is a strictly variable cost it varies directly or proportionately with variations in X and there are no fixed amounts involved. Thus, if b equals £5 and X is 2,000 units the repair cost incurred would be £5 × 2,000 which equals £10,000. Similarly, if the level of activity is 1,000 operations, the repair cost would be £5 × 1,000 which equals £5,000. A graphical example is shown in Fig. 5.2 see p. 120 above.

For a fixed cost function, the mathematical equation will be different. It will take the form:

$$Y = a$$

where a is a constant sum (say £100,000). In this case, the parameter a is a fixed amount that does not vary with another variable. A graphical representation is shown in Fig. 5.1 (see p. 119).

Finally, where Y represents a mixed cost, such as lease payments which have a fixed rent component and a variable component that depends on the level of activity, the equation is:

$$Y = a + bX$$

where Y = lease payments
X = level of activity
a = fixed rent
b = average cost per unit of activity.

Note that the cost function has two parameters, a and b, because it has both a fixed and a variable component. (See Fig. 5.4(a) for a graphical representation). If a is £500, $b = 0.1$ and the level of activity is 1,000 units, the lease payment for the period would be:

$$Y = 500 + 0.1(1{,}000) = £600$$

You should be able to draw the graphs for these three cost functions as you have already encountered fixed, variable and mixed costs in Chapter 5. Remember that it is important to define the relevant range for the values of Y and X which have been taken to form the cost estimate. This is because cost patterns may not behave in an identical manner at values outside this range.

The examples given above were simple. It was assumed that the variable and mixed costs in question varied only with one other variable. Clearly this may not be the case. A cost may depend on a number of factors. For instance, the cost of maintaining a legal department within an organization could depend on the number of specialist legal staff employed, the amount of administrative and secretarial resources used and the amount of heating and lighting used.

A mathematical function which could represent this relationship might be:

$$Y = a + bX1 + cX2 + dX3$$

where Y = cost of legal department
X_1 = number of legal personnel employed
X_2 = amount of administrative and secretarial resources used
X_3 = heating and lighting used
a = constant number.

Note that b, c, and d are called the *coefficients* of X_1, X_2 and X_3 respectively. They are the numbers by which X_1, X_2 and X_3 must be multiplied in order to specify precisely the relationship between the dependent and independent variables.

As you might expect, once several variables are involved in the cost relationship the analysis becomes quite complicated. For present purposes we shall assume that we have only one independent variable.

(iii) What is the relationship between the variables?

When we have answered the first two questions, we should know whether we are dealing with fixed, variable or mixed costs, and which cost varies with which variable. Our third question concerns the specific *functional form* of the relationship between the independent and dependent variable. In our simple mathematical examples above we have assumed a linear functional form. Yet, as indicated in Fig. 5.8, we could have non-linear relationships between the dependent and independent variables. The mathematical equations necessary to represent these relationships could be very complicated. For the sake of simplicity, we shall assume in the rest of the chapter that all our relationships are linear (that is straight-line graphs) where the dependent variable varies directly with the independent variable.

Given that we know what cost information is desired, where do we find such information? There are two main sources of information:

(i) that gathered by industrial engineers; and
(ii) that contained in an organization's historical cost accounting records.

Each source of information has its weaknesses and strengths. We shall discuss each of these in turn.

(b) The industrial engineering approach

This approach is used to collect cost information that is not available in an organization's records and is particularly relevant when an organization is just beginning a new activity. It first involves an estimation of the physical quantities of inputs required to achieve a certain level of output, such as the expected amount of raw materials required, the number of labour hours to be used, or the number of machine hours that are necessary. Estimates of raw materials may be based on the specifications of a prototype, and time and motion studies may be used to estimate the labour required. The task of producing these estimates is usually done by industrial engineers, hence the name of the method.

After the physical quantities of the materials, labour, etc., requirements have been estimated, expected prices for each input factor will have to be obtained in order to determine the expected direct cost of the activity. Next, the engineer may have to estimate the indirect costs (for example, the amount of maintenance, repairs and supervisory labour) required in order to achieve the given level of output. These indirect costs are usually more difficult to predict. This is because estimates have to be made of the useful, 'productive' life of machines and of the amount of joint costs that should be allocated to a particular activity. However, the engineer may be able to obtain some information from trade journals or from trade associations, the Centre for Interfirm Comparison or other organizations that engage in similar lines of activity.

The engineering method is useful when input–output relationships are relatively simple, stable and can be clearly defined. For instance, time and motion studies can be used to estimate the average time taken to type a certain number of words without error, to check out items at a supermarket outlet, or to punch a given line of data onto a computer card. In all these activities it is possible to specify clearly the input (labour time) and the output desired. However, it would be difficult to use the engineering method to estimate costs for activities in which the input–output relationships are not clear, for instance when we wish to estimate the time taken to create a work of art, to develop a safe space shuttle or to create a popular television advertisement.

The engineering method is also appropriate when direct costs form a significant proportion of total costs. As already pointed out, estimating indirect costs is usually a more difficult task and liable to lead to errors. By definition, indirect costs enter indirectly into the activity being estimated and the input-output relationship is therefore weaker. For instance, how much of the supervisory management costs and costs associated with quality control should be classified as costs that are indirectly linked to the production of a unit of output?

Although the engineering method is useful in certain circumstances, its largest drawback is the cost. Conducting time and motion studies and carefully setting out activity estimates is extremely time-consuming and requires considerable expertise if the activity to be estimated is complex. In addition, the use of time and motion studies may be resented by certain segments of the work-force. Trade unions may actively oppose the introduction of these studies, fearing that the information may be used to place greater demands on their members. Hence, the use of the approach requires careful planning and the relevant expertise.

(c) Cost estimation methods using historical cost information

Most organizations have production processes of one kind or another (organizations may process peas, patients, students, semiconductors) which have been in operation for some time. If these production processes have been relatively stable and are expected to remain so, then historical cost information may be used to estimate future cost relationships. There are several methods which use past data to predict the future.

(i) The account inspection method

This requires that the management accountant inspect each item of expenditure within the ledgers at a given level of output to determine whether a cost is fixed, variable or mixed. For instance, the following information may be obtained for an activity level reflecting the processing of 10,000 social security claims:

	£
Case officers' payroll cost	40,000
Secretarial payroll cost	20,000
Depreciation of office furniture and equipment	9,000
Repair and maintenance of office equipment	1,500
Office stationery and postage	5,000
Total	£75,500

The accountant, upon inspection of these accounts, may decide that the case officers' and secretarial payroll costs are variable costs and thus compute a variable cost per claim processed. Depreciation and office stationery and postage may be regarded as period or fixed costs that are expensed at the end of the appropriate financial period. Finally, repair and maintenance costs may be classified as mixed costs that have a fixed component of £500 and a variable component of 10p per claim processed. If this were the case, the cost information above would be analysed as follows:

	Variable costs per claim processed £
Case officers' payroll	4.00
Secretarial payroll	2.00
Variable repair and maintenance	0.10
Total variable cost	£6.10

	Variable costs per claim processed £
Fixed costs of processing 10,000 claims £(9,000 + 5,000 + 500)	£14,500

The total cost of processing the 10,000 claims would be:

	£
Variable costs (6.10 × 10,000)	61,000
Fixed costs	14,500
Total	£75,500

This approach to cost estimation appears simple. However, in practice it is extremely difficult to know which costs are period expenses, and therefore fixed, and which variable. In the case of mixed costs, it may be even harder to decide what proportions are fixed. Thus, this method of cost estimation may be highly subjective and prone to human error.

For cost information to be useful it has to be accurate, be unaffected by costs outside the control of the department, and be reasonably representative of the cost behaviour of the activity in question. These desirable characteristics may not be achieved through account classification. Also, note that in the above example, the cost information relates only to one level of processing activity – 10,000 claims. Is this pattern of cost behaviour representative of processing activity at other levels? If it is not, the information cannot be used to derive valid estimates of the general cost behaviour of the activity.

(ii) The visual method of fit

One cost estimation method which does seek to incorporate more information than the account inspection method is called the visual method of fit. To use this method, the accountant first plots all the output and cost information for the relevant range on a chart, called a *scattergram*. This plotting of information is vital and it is recommended that, irrespective of which method of cost estimation is being considered, the accountant should first obtain a scattergram of the relevant output and cost information.

Figure 7.2 shows such a scattergram. An inspection of the scatter of data points will indicate, in a rough and ready manner, the relationship between costs and level of activity. It reveals whether the relationship can be approximated by a linear mathematical function. In this example the answer is yes – a line is drawn through the data points such that it best captures the information provided by all the data points. Ideally, all the points should either sit on the line or be close to it.

This method of visual fit is relatively simple to apply and it does attempt to use all the information in the relevant range of production to arrive at the estimated cost function. However, it remains rather crude and does not adequately handle data points which are far away from the main body of points (called outliers). Figure 7.2 shows that in fitting a line to a set of data points, there could be several outliers which cannot be incorporated. Ignoring these may cause the estimated cost function to be inaccurate. In addition, a visual fit is quite subjective and there

Figure 7.2

A scattergram.

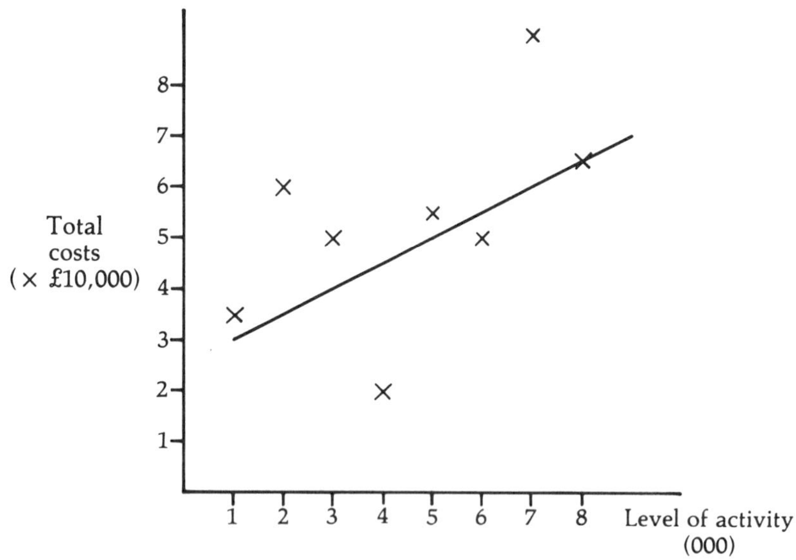

is no clear method of testing whether the line is the best fit (that is, the most representative of the underlying cost function). Despite these shortcomings, the method may be sufficient for the small company that does not possess the expertise to use complicated statistical techniques for cost estimation.

(iii) The high–low method

Like the visual fit method, this method does try to use cost and output information at more than one level of activity. It consists of taking the cost information at the highest and the lowest levels of activity. For instance:

	Claims processed	Fixed costs £	Variable costs £	Total costs £
Highest level of activity	80,000	30,000	190,000	220,000
Lowest level of activity	30,000	30,000	30,000	60,000

We need first to calculate the estimated variable cost per claim processed. This is:

Difference in cost = £220,000 – £60,000 = £160,000
Highest volume – Lowest volume = 80,000 – 30,000 = 50,000 claims

Expressing these two numbers as a ratio gives us a variable cost per claim of:

$$\frac{£160{,}000}{50{,}000} = £3.20$$

Using this estimated variable cost per claim processed, the estimated cost for pro-

Figure 7.3

High-low method of cost estimation.

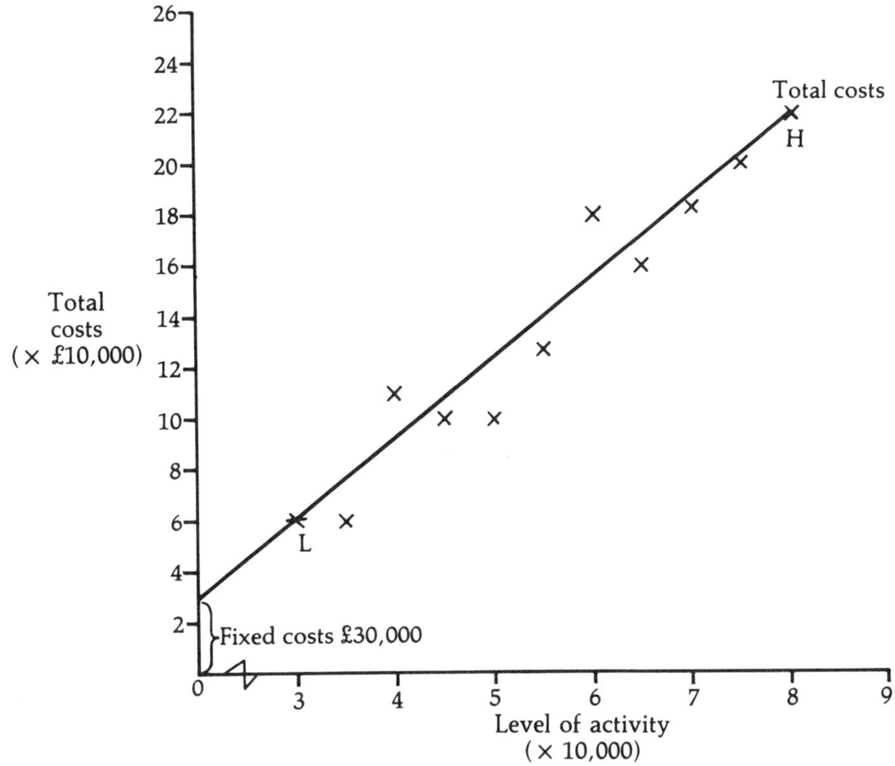

cessing, say, 50,000 claims becomes £30,000 (fixed costs) + £(50,000 × 3.2) = £30,000 + £160,000 = £190,000.

Figure 7.3 shows a scattergram based on the cost information given above. It also shows other levels of activity and their associated costs of processing. By using the high-low method, we are assuming that the cost function is best represented by the straight line HL. However, as the diagram illustrates, this may not be true. For the relevant range of activity, the scattergram shows that most of the data points lie underneath the straight line HL. If we were to use all the activity and cost information given to us, instead of just using the highest and lowest figures, we are likely to obtain a more representative picture of the cost relationship. The difficulty with the high-low method is that it uses only two pieces of information. All other information is ignored. Such an approach can be quite misleading.

(iv) Simple linear regression analysis

This method is often regarded as providing more rigorous information than the other methods. In this chapter we shall look at regression analysis when there is only one independent variable. It is known as simple linear regression.

A regression equation seeks to estimate a relationship between a dependent variable (usually cost) and one or more independent variables (such as level of activity, for example, claims processed or machine hours used) by using past observations. Linear regression assumes a linear relationship between the independent and dependent variables. Basically, the technique allows us to do two things.

- It enables a straight line to be fitted to the observed relationships between the dependent and independent variables. This is known as the *line of best fit*.
- It enables the management accountant to assess the *goodness of fit* of the regression line.

Neither of these two features is available with the other methods of cost estimation. In addition, they are performed using statistical and mathematical formulae which provide rigorous answers. Hence, judgement is largely eliminated with the use of a formula. There is therefore less chance of a subjective, human error. Finally, the information provided by all the data points is used in the analysis. No loss of information occurs as with the other methods. Sub-section (v) below illustrates the approach that is recommended.

(v) The least squares method of fitting a line

We shall first discuss how to fit a line through a series of observations of the dependent (Y) and independent (X) variables. To begin, we need to be clear about the task at hand and the terminology required.

Because there is only one independent variable we say Y is a function of X:

$$Y = f(X)$$

The precise mathematical expression of the relationship that we are trying to estimate is written as:

$$Y = a + bX$$

Let us assume that:

X = level of activity
Y = total cost for a period
a = total fixed costs for the period
b = average variable cost per unit processed.

Note that if $a = 0$, we have no intercept on the Y-axis. Effectively, this means that there are no fixed costs, only variable costs which vary proportionately with the level of activity.

In Figure 7.4 we give a table and a scattergram of the data used. The data represents the number of specialized furniture units manufactured by a small company.

There are several mathematical techniques for performing a simple, linear regression analysis. The method we shall use is called the *least squares method*. This method minimizes the sum of the squares of the vertical distances from the regression line to the data points. This means that the sum of the squares of these distances is less than the sum of the squared distances from any other line.

Figure 7.4

Scattergram and table of levels of activity and total cost.

Month	x	y
January	3	4,000
February	5	7,000
March	6	8,000
April	7	9,000
May	9	12,000

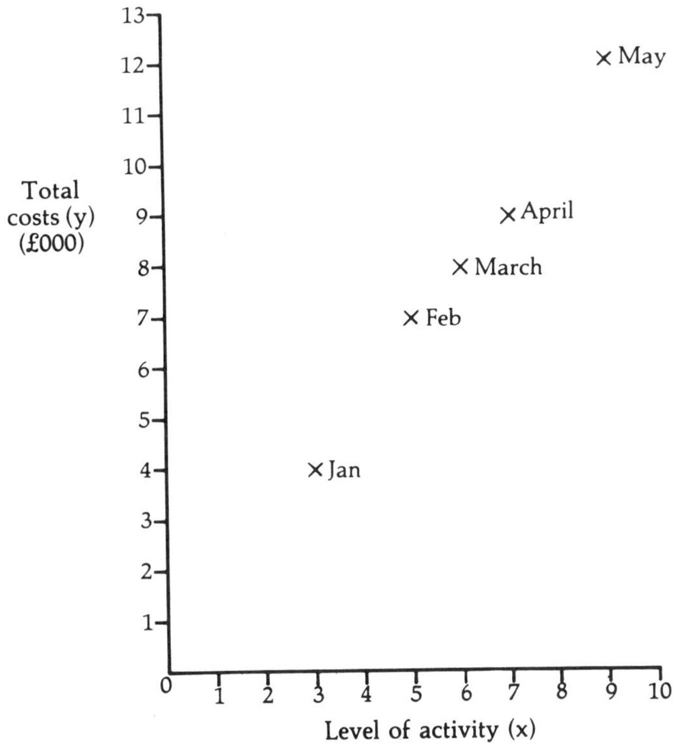

The least squares method uses two simultaneous equations called *normal equations* for solving the problem. These equations are:

Equation 1: $\Sigma Y = na + b\Sigma X$
Equation 2: $\Sigma XY = a\Sigma X + b\Sigma X^2$.

where: n = number of paired observations
X = the observed values of X
Y = the observed values of Y
X^2 = the squares of the observed values of X
XY = the product of each pair of the observed values of X and Y.
Σ = 'the sum of'

Using these two equations, we can solve for a and b. The equations for doing that are:

$$b = \frac{n(\Sigma XY) - (\Sigma X)(\Sigma Y)}{n(\Sigma X^2) - (\Sigma X)^2}$$

$$a = \frac{\Sigma Y}{n} - b\frac{\Sigma X}{n} \quad \text{or} \quad \bar{Y} - b\bar{X}$$

$\bar{Y}$ = mean value of Y

$\bar{X}$ = value of X

The table below shows all the data required for solving for a and b:

	X	Y (000s)	X^2	XY (000s)	Y^2 (000s)
	3	4	9	12	16
	5	7	25	35	49
	6	8	36	48	64
	7	9	49	63	81
	9	12	81	108	144
Totals	30	40	200	266	354

Using the data given:

$$b = \frac{n(\Sigma XY) - (\Sigma X)(\Sigma Y)}{n(\Sigma X^2) - (\Sigma X)^2} \qquad a = \bar{Y} - b\bar{X}$$

$$= \frac{5(266) - (30)(40)}{5(200) - (30)^2} \qquad = \frac{40}{5} - 1.3\left(\frac{30}{5}\right)$$

$$= \frac{1{,}330 - 1{,}200}{1{,}000 - 900} \qquad = 8 - 7.8$$

$$= \frac{133}{100} \qquad = 0.2$$

$$= 1.3$$

The estimated regression line can now be described by the following equation:

$Y^p = 0.2 + 1.3X$ (in £000s) $\qquad Y^p$ = predicted values of Y

or:

$Y^p = £(200 + 1{,}300X)$

Using this least squares regression equation, the points on the straight line that has been estimated can be determined by substituting various values for X into the equation:

X	Y (000s)	
3	4.1	$Y = 0.2 + 1.3(3) = 0.2 + 3.9$
4	5.4	$Y = 0.2 + 1.3(4) = 0.2 + 5.2$
5	6.7	$Y = 0.2 + 1.3(5) = 0.2 + 6.5$
6	8.0	$Y = 0.2 + 1.3(6) = 0.2 + 7.8$
7	9.3	$Y = 0.2 + 1.3(7) = 0.2 + 9.1$

Figure 7.5 shows the regression line plotted on the scattergram of the observed values of X and Y. As you can see, there will usually be a difference between the actual cost incurred for a certain volume of production and the estimated cost. For instance, when 3 units were produced, the estimated cost was £4,100 while the actual cost was £4,000. Similarly, when 7 units were produced, the actual and estimated costs were respectively £9,000 and £9,300.

Such differences can be expected because the estimated costs represent average costs. Nevertheless, it is important that the management accountant knows how good the estimated regression line is. Does it provide a close approximation to actual past observations? How reliable is the regression line when compared with

Figure 7.5

Regression line plotted on scattergram.

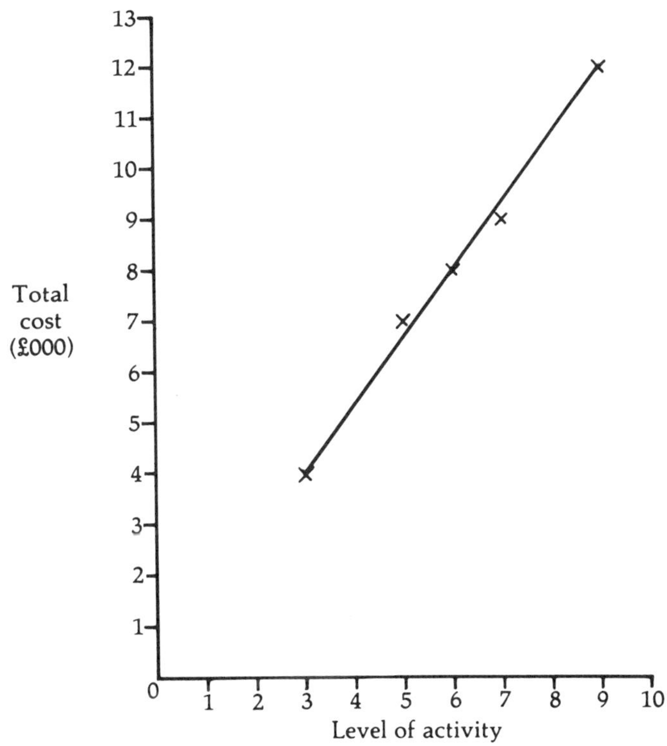

past observations? These questions can be answered through the use of certain mathematical techniques which lie beyond the scope of this volume. (See for example, Arnold and Hope (1990), pp. 138–40, for lucid coverage.)

As can be seen, the management accountant has a number of cost estimation techniques that enable predictions of the future to be made. The choice of a particular method will depend on the size of the organization, type of production process used and the level of skill of the accounting department. We shall now look at standards as elements of feedforward control.

7.3 Standards as elements of feedforward control

In the previous section we illustrated how an organization seeks to achieve feedforward control by estimating the cost of inputs. We also looked at different cost estimation methods. In this section we shall look at standards and their role in feedforward control.

(a) What are standards?

Standards are predetermined or current estimates of inputs or outputs. They may be expressed either in financial or physical units. In principle, standards may be set for any of an organization's inputs or outputs and for any of its activities. For instance, standards may be set for the expected amount of usage of typewriters in a general administration department or of the computer facility in an operations research department. However, the major area in which standards have been established is in the manufacturing sector. In addition, within the manufacturing sector, standards have generally been set for inputs per unit of output. Thus, we speak of standards for the inputs expected to be used in manufacturing one unit of output of a product.

We shall begin with a discussion of input standards for manufacturing activities and in Section 7.5 discuss briefly standards for non-manufacturing activities.

Before leaving this section, note that standards are:

(i) predetermined estimates
(ii) established for inputs and outputs
(iii) applicable to all routine aspects of an organization's operations.

In manufacturing, they have been established mainly for inputs per unit of output.

(b) Why set standards?

Standards have the following purposes:

(i) to act as a form of feedforward control that allows an organization to plan the manufacturing inputs required for different levels of output;
(ii) to act as a form of feedback control by highlighting performance that did not achieve the standard predicted, thus alerting decision-makers to situations that may be 'out of control' and in need of corrective action;
(iii) to motivate workers by acting as challenging, specific goals that are intended to guide behaviour in the desired directions;
(iv) to trace/allocate manufacturing costs to each individual unit produced.

The first two purposes for setting standards are similar to those for the forecasting of cost estimates. The third purpose is based on the idea that people work harder and attain higher levels of performance if they are set specific, difficult goals.

The fourth purpose arises because decision-makers wish to know the expected 'full' or total cost of producing a unit of output. These manufacturing costs include direct material costs, direct labour costs and indirect or overhead costs. Indirect costs are the most difficult to estimate because, by their very nature, indirect manufacturing costs cannot be specifically associated with individual physical units. Yet, the making of goods cannot take place without incurring indirect costs such as factory rent, heating, lighting, insurance, taxes, janitorial services and rates. All these factors cost the company valuable resources. By estimating these indirect costs, management is able to estimate how much it will cost the organization (both in terms of direct and indirect manufacturing inputs) to produce at a level of activity. This full (absorbed) cost information may subsequently be used to price the final product, to forecast income or to value inventory. Full and variable costing has already been discussed in Chapters 4 and 5.

(c) Manufacturing standards

What kinds of input standards are set for manufacturing activities? Consider a company, TT plc, that produces a particular type of wooden toy train. Imagine that the only material used in the production process is the wood and that two tradesmen are required to perform the cutting and glueing operations necessary to produce the toy trains. Through experience (or careful study) the company will be able to specify the amount of wood that should be used to produce one train and the price the company should pay to purchase a length of wood. In addition, the company should be able to determine the amount of time it should take the two tradesmen to produce one train and the hourly wage rate that should be paid to the tradesmen. Using this knowledge, the company will be able to establish standards for direct material and direct labour inputs. These are illustrated below.

The *direct material standard* for one unit of output:

1 metre of wood (100 mm × 50 mm) at £2 per metre

The *direct labour standard* for one unit of output:

2 hours of direct labour at £10 per hour

In addition to setting standards for the direct materials and labour used in producing these toy trains the company will need to set standards for both fixed and variable indirect manufacturing costs. For instance, the costs of renting the factory premises, the cost of insurance, rates, etc., should be included in the full cost of a product since they are directly related to the productive activity.

The *standard indirect manufacturing cost* might be:

£4 per hour of direct labour (along the lines suggested in Section 4.5(c) of Chapter 4)

Once these standards are set and predetermined, it is then possible to predict what the full standard cost for each toy train should be.

In general, standards should be set such that they are realistic and attainable. It is pointless setting standards that do not allow for normal levels of breakage, spoilage, wastage and rest time. For instance, employees may not be able physically to cut and glue bits of wood together for 4 consecutive hours. Similarly, keyboard operators are seldom able to work accurately for longer than 3 hours at a time. Some rest period should therefore be built into a direct labour standard such that it reflects the average length of time taken to complete a task.

Standards for direct materials should also be set to reflect the average amount of material used. In the above example, 1 metre of wood was set as the standard. This may not be appropriate if, for example, on average 1.5 metres of wood is used per toy train produced. Setting the standard at 1 metre would result in:

(i) a standard direct material cost that is too low;
(ii) unfavourable differences (or variances) from the standard being consistently reported;
(iii) predictions about costs and profits for the organization as a whole which would be inaccurate.

It is therefore important that achievable standards be set. If standards are set too tightly or at too high a level, employees may be frustrated because they feel the standard is unrealistic and too demanding. When they are demotivated, employees will not accept the standard and cease to strive to meet the level set. On the other hand, if standards are set too low or too loose, they may lead to inefficiencies and high costs within an organization. A standard should therefore be set such that it is tight enough to challenge and motivate an employee and lead to efficient production. However, it should not be too tight such that employees 'give up'. In the next chapter, we shall discuss other important motivational and social aspects of standards and budget targets.

Measurement of activity levels

You will find that in setting most indirect manufacturing cost standards the underlying activity level is expressed either in terms of direct labour hours (dlh) or machine hours (mh). But, as stated earlier, one may still find levels of activity expressed in units produced for the purpose of setting indirect manufacturing cost standards. (Refer back to section 4.7 in Chapter 4, pp. 105–14).

Even having decided on a suitable index for the level of activity, our problems are not over. This is because there are a number of alternative measures of activity level. For instance, let us imagine that the maximum capacity of a given factory is an annual production level of 10,000 units. Each unit uses 10 direct labour hours. The maximum activity level for the factory is then 100,000 dlh. However, for the coming year, in view of environmental and trade union demands, management has decided that a realistic production level is 8,000 units. The expected activity level for the year is therefore 80,000 dlh. Which of these is the appropriate activity level to use in calculating an indirect manufacturing cost standard?

In general, there are three alternative measures of activity level:

(i) *Practical capacity*. This is the maximum production level of the existing physical facilities given normal efficient conditions. It is usually estimated over a long period of time – perhaps several years. However, because this production level reflects the maximum efficient use of facilities it is seldom achieved in any year. Note that in using this activity level we are relating activity to the physical production capacities of the factory.

(ii) *Normal capacity*. This is the annual level of activity required to meet the estimated average level of sales for several years (3–5 years). It represents average sales, and hence output level, over a period that is long enough to smooth out seasonal variations and to allow for significant trends to be identified. Because the measure reflects *average* demand, an organization's *actual* annual volume of production commonly differs from the normal volume.

(iii) *Expected or budgeted capacity*. This is the expected or planned activity level for the coming accounting or operating period. As such it is likely to be the level closest to the actual activity level.

The most commonly used activity level is the budgeted activity level. It is the easiest to forecast, is related to current activities and is the measure most likely to minimize differences between applied and actual fixed indirect manufacturing costs. However, the other two measures of activity are also useful. The use of practical capacity may highlight instances of under-utilization of factory capacity, while the use of normal activity means that cyclical changes in demand will not

Figure 7.6

Calculation of fixed and variable indirect manufacturing cost rates.

Estimated variable indirect manufacturing costs:	£
Factory electricity	50,000
Lubricants	5,000
Materials handling	10,000
Overtime premium	40,000
Idle time	5,000
Total estimated variable indirect manufacturing costs	£110,000
Estimated fixed indirect manufacturing costs:	
Rates	60,000
Depreciation	30,000
Insurance	20,000
Supervisory salaries	50,000
Land taxes	5,000
Total estimated fixed indirect manufacturing costs	£165,000

Budgeted annual activity level:

(i) Direct labour hours = 55,000

(ii) Predetermined variable indirect manufacturing cost application rate $= \dfrac{£110,000}{55,000}$ = £2.00 per dlh

(iii) Predetermined fixed indirect manufacturing cost application rate $= \dfrac{£165,000}{55,000}$ = £3.00 per dlh

(iv) Predetermined total indirect manufacturing cost application rate $= \dfrac{£275,000}{55,000}$ = £5.00 per dlh

influence the indirect manufacturing cost standard.

Once the index and the appropriate capacity level for the budgeted annual activity level has been determined, calculation of the indirect manufacturing cost standard should be relatively straightforward. An organization may also wish to set a standard for variable indirect manufacturing cost as distinct from fixed indirect manufacturing cost. In Figure 7.6 it is estimated that, at an expected activity level of 55,000 dlh, the variable indirect manufacturing costs should amount to £110,000. This leads to a variable indirect manufacturing cost rate of £2.00 per dlh. Note that in this calculation both the numerator and denominator are variable quantities (that is, they vary with the level of production).

In calculating the variable indirect manufacturing cost rate it is possible for an organization to specify a certain level of variable indirect manufacturing costs as the standard for the expected annual level of production. However, with fixed expenses this cannot be done because fixed indirect manufacturing costs do not vary with the level of production. Thus, the organization can only relate whatever level of activity is expected to the fixed indirect manufacturing costs. In Figure 7.6 it is estimated that, irrespective of the budgeted annual level for the coming year, the fixed indirect manufacturing costs will amount to £165,000. At the budgeted annual activity level of 55,000 dlh, this leads to a fixed indirect manufacturing cost rate of £3.00 per dlh.

Standard cost cards

Once we have obtained all the relevant information, we can summarize it on a standard cost card. Figure 7.7 illustrates a standard cost card for one toy train produced by TT plc.

Note that the quantity of variable and fixed indirect manufacturing costs depends on the number of dlh used per unit of output produced. Since 2 dlh are needed, the quantities for variable and fixed indirect manufacturing costs are also 2 dlh.

Revision of standards

In the example of the cost card given in Fig. 7.7 above, we had a date on it. This is important because standards may need to be changed to accommodate changes in the organization or its environment. Standards that are out of date will not

Figure 7.7

Standard cost card.

Date of standard: 1 January 1993

	Quantity	Standard unit cost (£)	Standard cost per unit produced (£)
Direct materials:	1 m	2	2
Direct labour:	2 dlh	10	20
Variable indirect:	2 dlh	2	4
Fixed indirect:	2 dlh	3	6
Total standard manufacturing cost per unit produced			£32

act as effective feedforward or feedback control tools. They will not help us predict the inputs required nor help us evaluate the efficiency of a particular department.

If standards are continually not being achieved and large deviations (or variances) from the standard are reported, they should be carefully reviewed. Also, changes in the physical productive capacity of the organization, or in material prices, wage rates, etc., may indicate that standards need to be revised. Chapter 10 deals in detail with these matters.

7.4 Standard-setting and the learning curve

We have already referred to the need to set standards that are neither too slack nor too difficult. Slack standards lead to inefficient operations while unattainable standards cause employee frustration, demotivation and non-acceptability of the standards set. Research from the budgeting literature (discussed in detail in Chapter 8) also indicates that standards may be more effective motivators if both superiors and subordinates participate in their determination. However, participation in standard-setting has also been shown to lead to improvements in job satisfaction but not in overall job performance (Harrell, 1977). In addition, for a deviation from standard to act as an effective feedback control mechanism, that information must be made available to decision-makers as soon as possible. Long delays in the provision of feedback information lessens the impact and value of such information.

There are other important individual, social and organizational influences on standard-setting and on the operation of standards in different organizations. Since the research findings on these factors are equally applicable to the setting of budget targets and the operation of budgets, a detailed discussion of the social context of standards will be postponed until the next chapter. There, the discussion will be integrated with a consideration of budgets and their social significance.

Finally, we shall look at the effect of learning on the setting of manufacturing standards. In certain tasks (as was pointed out in Section 5.2(a) of Chapter 5) the labour required to perform that particular task diminishes as the employee becomes more experienced and familiar with the task. For instance, typing, knitting, weaving, driving and simple physical tasks (such as putting letters into allotted boxes) all take less time as the employee becomes more dextrous and agile in the performance of that task. Eventually, however, a plateau level of performance is reached and no additional learning takes place.

In setting standards such as a direct labour standard, the management accountant should consider the effect of learning. The relationship between learning and output per labour-hour or machine-hour is usually shown in a graph called a learning curve. With the help of a learning curve the decision-maker is able to predict how, for instance, labour costs would change as the employees become more experienced in the performance of the task concerned.

In the manufacturing context, a learning curve is a cost function that shows how average labour costs per unit of output declines as cumulative production rises. For instance, it may take 10 hours for you to knit your first scarf but only 15 hours to knit your first and second scarves. With the first scarf the average time taken

Figure 7.8

80% learning curve.

Cumulative production			
Number of job lots	Number of units	Cumulative average time per unit (min)	Cumulative time (min)
1	10	10	100
2	20	10 × 0.8 = 8	160
4	40	8 × 0.8 = 6.4	256
8	80	6.4 × 0.8 = 5.12	409.6
16	160	5.12 × 0.8 = 4.096	655.36

was 10 hours but with the two scarves the average time taken was only 7.5 hours (15 hours/2). On average, you only took 75% of the previous time to complete your first and second scarves.

Research has shown that the time taken per unit of output should be progressively less at some constant percentage rate as learning takes place. For instance, we may improve the time taken to produce one unit of output to 80% of the previous time as cumulative production doubles. This 80% learning curve is illustrated in Fig. 7.8.

This information may be graphed to illustrate how the learning effect gradually levels off. As Fig. 7.9 shows, the reduction in average labour time per unit gradually diminishes. When total production is large enough the time per unit would become quite stable. The learning effect thus tapers off and gradually ceases to influence the time taken to perform the task.

Because the effect of learning gradually declines the learning curve is most applicable for setting labour standards during the start-up phase of a productive activity. Once an organization has been conducting a repetitive activity for a sufficient length of time the activity reaches a steady-state phase. That is, there would no longer be any reduction in average labour costs per unit and hence no further increases in efficiency.

Organizations often fail to consider the learning effect in setting standards. At times steady-state standards used by one department may be used by another department that has just started an identical productive activity. This can lead to low employee morale as the standards could be too difficult to achieve. In addition, production scheduling would be affected as insufficient time has been allowed for inexperienced employees.

The reverse also happens. A standard that is applicable to the start-up phase of a productive activity may be used to predict and evaluate steady-state activity levels. In effect, these standards would be too slack and inefficiencies will result.

Therefore, not only must the management accountant be aware of the learning effect; he/she must also consider which type of standard should be used in each particular phase of the productive activity.

An important distinction needs to be drawn between the learning curve and the

Figure 7.9

80% learning curve shown as a graph.

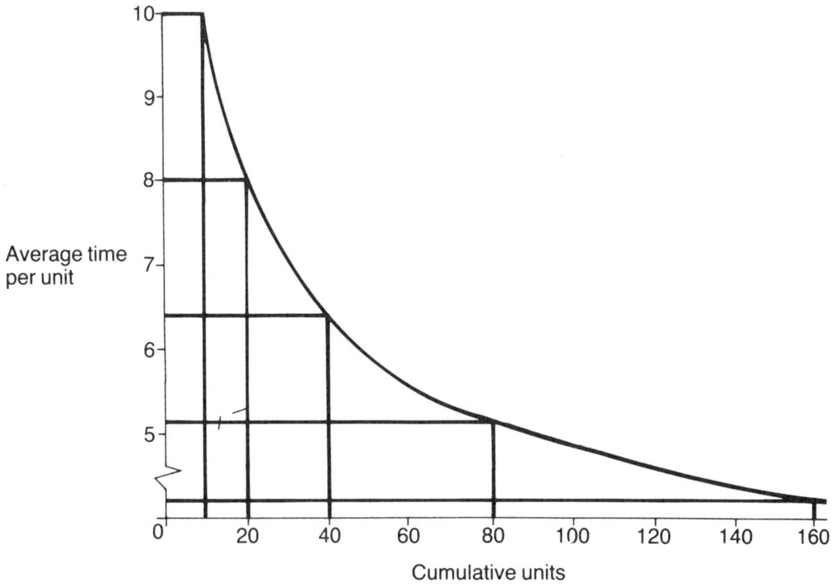

experience curve. The former was initially observed during the 1920s, and it was a significant feature of calculations of the labour hours required for building aircraft during the Second World War – but it only relates to labour hours (hence labour cost). As a consequence the reduction in costs due to the learning curve effect is much lower than that due to the broader-based experience curve. *All* costs and cost effects are reflected by the experience curve.

Several causes of cost reduction act together within the experience curve, such as:

- the learning experience;
- the effect of labour specialization;
- scale effects due to increased volume.

The experience curve is derived not from accounting costs but by dividing the cumulative cash inputs by the cumulative output of end products, and the cost decline is shown by the rate of change in this ratio over time. From this rate of change managers can see how – and why – their competitive costs are shifting. If estimates can be made of competitors' experience curve effects this should reveal which are the low-cost competitors and which are not, hence which are at risk and from whom.

The main strategic message from the experience curve is that, if costs per unit in real terms decrease predictably with cumulative output, then the market leader has the potential to achieve the lowest costs and the highest profits. This is illustrated in Fig. 7.10.

Figure 7.10

Advantages of experience.

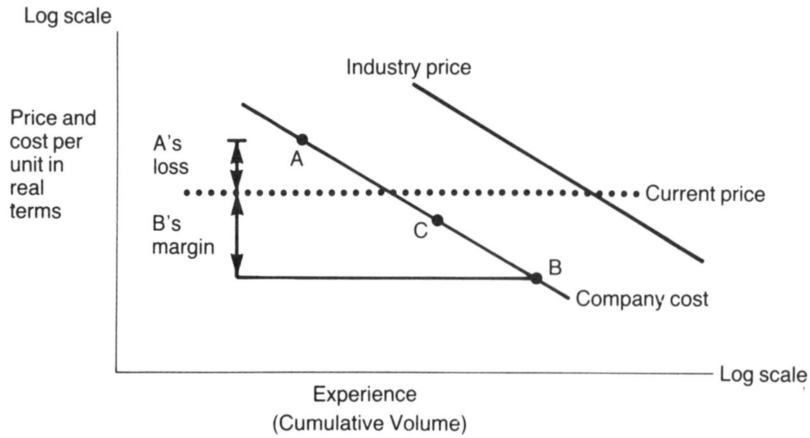

Firm A has less experience than Firm B, hence the latter has a significant cost advantage. In this rather extreme (but not implausible) example, A's unit cost is higher than the current market price, so it sustains a loss on each unit sold. By contrast, B's unit cost is well below the prevailing price, so it achieves a substantial margin on each unit sold. Firm C is operating profitably, but Firm B could take advantage of its leadership position in the following way: since the industry price falls with cumulative volume Firm B can cut prices as its costs also fall due to its greater experience. Firm A has virtually been driven out, and the same fate could befall Firm C.

7.5 Non-manufacturing standards

So far the discussion has been on setting standards or predictions for manufacturing activities. This is because many manufacturing activities are repetitive and routine using technologies that are stable and easy to predict. Once set, standards may not need to be changed for a number of years. In addition, it is easy to identify the input–output relationship in these circumstances. For instance, even the task of assembling a complex product, such as a car, may be broken down into distinct, repetitive sub-tasks.

It is also possible to set standards for repetitive, routine tasks in non-manufacturing organizations. However, for standards to succeed, the relationship between inputs and outputs must be easily identified. For instance, in a typing pool we can set a standard for the number of words typed per minute. In the mail sorting room we can determine the number of letters that one expects to be franked within an hour. Standards can be set for these non-manufacturing activities because the inputs (labour or machine time) and outputs (typed words, franked letters) can be easily matched.

However, imagine trying to set a standard for the number of patients who recover on a hospital ward (during a specified period) and the quality of nursing care. Can we predict that given quality A, 10 patients will recover, while given quality B, only 8 patients will recover? There are several problems with developing such standards for service activities that do not have a clear input–output relationship, including:

(i) Many factors influence the productive activity. In the above instance, nursing care is but one of a number of inputs into the productive activity called 'helping patients to recover'. Clearly, patient recovery will depend on the quality of medical care, the technological resources of the hospital, the sanitation conditions of the ward and the personal beliefs and will-power of the patient. It is difficult as a consequence to set clear standards when the relationship between input (quality of nursing care) and output (healthy patients) is ambiguous.

(ii) It is also difficult to measure qualitative inputs and outputs. How can one measure 'quality of care'? Even healthy patients may not be easy to assess in these terms. There are levels of healthiness. In times of scarce resources when there is a great pressure for hospital beds, patients may be defined as healthy and discharged sooner than when there is no pressure for beds. Health and quality of care are qualitative outputs that often defy accurate measurement.

Hence, standards are often developed only for those aspects of non-manufacturing activities that have a clear input–output relationship. The standards set in a non-manufacturing context will vary depending on the activity in question. The table below shows examples of some standards used.

Non-manufacturing activity	*Standard set*
Typing	Number of words per minute
Mail sorting	Number of letters sorted
Computer card punching	Number of correctly punched cards
Packing	Number of items packed per hour
Questionnaire decoding	Number of questionnaires decoded

(a) Setting non-manufacturing standards

Such standards are usually set through the use of time and motion studies and of work analysis. That is, the task performed has to be analysed and timed. This involves observing people performing the task and consulting supervisors and workers as to the average amount of time that should be allocated to the task. The use of time and motion studies has to be carefully planned so as to obtain maximum cooperation from all employees concerned.

Again, standards set should be realistic and attainable. Slack and high standards should be avoided as these produce inaccurate information for decision-making and lead to motivational problems among employees.

Part of the difficulty with setting non-manufacturing standards is that the task is non-homogeneous. For instance, some questionnaires may only contain 10% of the answers required while others may contain 90%. Similarly, the items to be packed may vary in size. Some may be more difficult to pack than others. In these circumstances, it would be difficult to derive a standard that could be applied to all employees performing the given task. Where standards cannot be determined with a reasonable degree of accuracy it may not be appropriate to use standards for feedforward and feedback control. However, in many non-manufacturing activities the tasks are sufficiently homogeneous to justify the setting of standards for prediction and control.

7.6 Budgets as elements of feedforward control

Budgets and the budgeting process will be discussed in greater detail in the next chapter. Here, we include a brief description of budgets to show their relationship to cost estimates and standards in ensuring feedforward control.

A budget, like a cost estimate or a standard, is an estimate of the organization's future input.output relationship. It differs from a standard or estimated cost in that it is more comprehensive in its coverage. A budget looks at the organization as a whole, though segment budgets may also be prepared. It is not restricted to forecasting costs (which is the case with cost estimates) nor to predicting productive inputs per unit of output (which is the role of standards). By contrast, a budget may take the form of a projected profit and loss statement, balance sheet, cash-flow statement or statement of sources and applications of funds. There are also production, sales, marketing and capital investment budgets.

Like cost estimates and standards, budgets have as their main roles:

(i) feedforward control;
(ii) feedback control;
(iii) motivation of employees;
(iv) performance evaluation.

Each of these will be discussed in detail in the next chapter.

Summary

In this chapter we have discussed:

(a) the role of estimates, standards and budget targets in:
    (i) ensuring feedforward control;
    (ii) ensuring feedback control;
    (iii) motivating employees;
    (iv) helping to provide a basis for performance evaluation;
(b) the main types of estimates, standards and budgets set;
(c) different techniques of estimation;
(d) the motivational and learning factors to be considered in standard-setting.

We have sought to highlight the role of these managerial accounting tools in maintaining organizational control. In order to control the present and the future, we need to be able to predict and control the future. Estimates and standards are essential means to this end.

In the next chapter we shall look in detail at the role of budgets in organizational control and at the social and organizational context of budgeting.

Key terms and concepts

Here is a list of the key terms and concepts which have featured in this chapter. You should make sure that you understand and can define each one of them. Page references to definitions in the text appear in bold in the index.

- Capacity
  - practical
  - normal
  - expected (budgeted)
- Coefficient
- Estimate
- Experience curve
- Functional relationship
- High-low method
- Industrial engineering
- Learning curve
- Linear regression
  - sum of least squares
- Parameter
- Scattergram
- Standards
  - manufacturing
  - non-manufacturing

Further reading

On statistical analyses and costing, see Johnston (1972), Benston (1966) and Nurnberg (1986).

On the learning curve, see Hirschmann (1964) and Abernathy and Wayne (1974).

The workbook to accompany this chapter begins on p. 533.

CHAPTER 8 The budgeting process: technical and social aspects

Learning objectives

After studying this chapter you should be able to:

- understand budgets as means of feedforward and feedback control;
- construct comprehensive master budget schedules;
- compile flexible budgets;
- recognize the distinctive nature of budgeting for non-manufacturing organizations;
- appreciate the need for capital budgeting processes;
- analyse the motivational, social, political and symbolic aspects of organizational budgeting.

8.1 Introduction

As can be seen from the previous chapter, standards or estimates may be set for the inputs to or the outputs from any repetitive productive activity. In a conventional manufacturing company the inputs may be manpower, materials and machines, while in a consulting firm the key input may be the creative ideas of particular individuals. Similarly, the outputs could range from consumer products to health care to opera management. Standards may also be set for certain input–output relationships (transformation processes). For instance, such a standard may stipulate that each secretary should type 100 words per minute or that only 0.6 metres of wood be used in the manufacture of a single toy train.

Budgets are *similar* to standards in several ways:

(i) they are estimates of the future performance of an organization;
(ii) they help people within an organization to plan the future (feedforward control); and
(iii) they enable people to know how well they and the rest of the organization have performed (feedback control).

However, budgets are *different* from standards in that they model the activities of the organization as a whole. In this way a budget presents a more comprehensive picture of the organization and its range of activities.

The budget for an organization is essentially a model (representation) of the expected physical, financial and (to a limited extent) non-financial consequences of all its activities for a certain period in the future. The contrast between standards (as the term is conventionally understood) and budgets may be illustrated by comparing Figs 8.1 and 8.2.

As can be seen from the examples, standards tend to be applied to a narrower segment of the activities of an organization while budgets are used to predict the performance of an organization as a whole.

The major activities of an organization are sometimes referred to as *programmes*. A programme is usually a long-term commitment to a product or an

Figure 8.1

Examples of standards.

		£
Direct materials:	5 lb of flour @ 30p per lb	1.5
Direct labour:	0.5 hr @ £10 per h	5.0
Variable indirect costs:	£8 per direct labour hour	4.0
Fixed indirect costs:	£5 per unit	5.0*
Total standard cost per unit		15.5

* Based on an expected activity level of 12,000 units per month and £60,000 of fixed indirect costs per month.

Figure 8.2

Examples of budgets set in December 1992 for 1993.

Cash receipts budget:

	January £	February £
Collection of current month's sales	50,000	60,000
Collection from prior months' sales	100,000	120,000
Total budgeted receipts	£150,000	£180,000

Cash expenses budget:

	January £	February £
Material purchases	20,000	25,000
Salaries	150,000	160,000
Sales commissions	15,000	12,000
Fixed selling expenses	30,000	30,000
Taxes		45,000
Total budgeted expenses	£215,000	£272,000

Sales budget:

	January £	February £
Budgeted sales	300,000	365,000

industry, which may consume human and capital resources over a sustained period of time. Even a conglomerate like the Hanson Trust will have a restricted group of these key strategic operations (for instance, the manufacture of certain brands of cigarettes). A budget is usually prepared for each of these key programmes, which may be an existing or an entirely new programme. Budgeting for existing programmes is easier as usually only small, incremental changes are made to existing operations. (But see Section 6.3(d) in Chapter 6 on zero-based budgets.) Budgeting for a new programme is more difficult as estimates of output, revenue, expenses, capital requirements and labour inputs are more uncertain.

As the above examples of budgets illustrate, a comprehensive budget for an organization or for a particular programme may be subdivided into 'mini-budgets' for particular accounting items such as sales, cash receipts, production and sales administration expenses. Different organizations will prepare different individual budgets for particular accounting items, but the following list is representative:

Figure 8.3

A sequence for budget development.

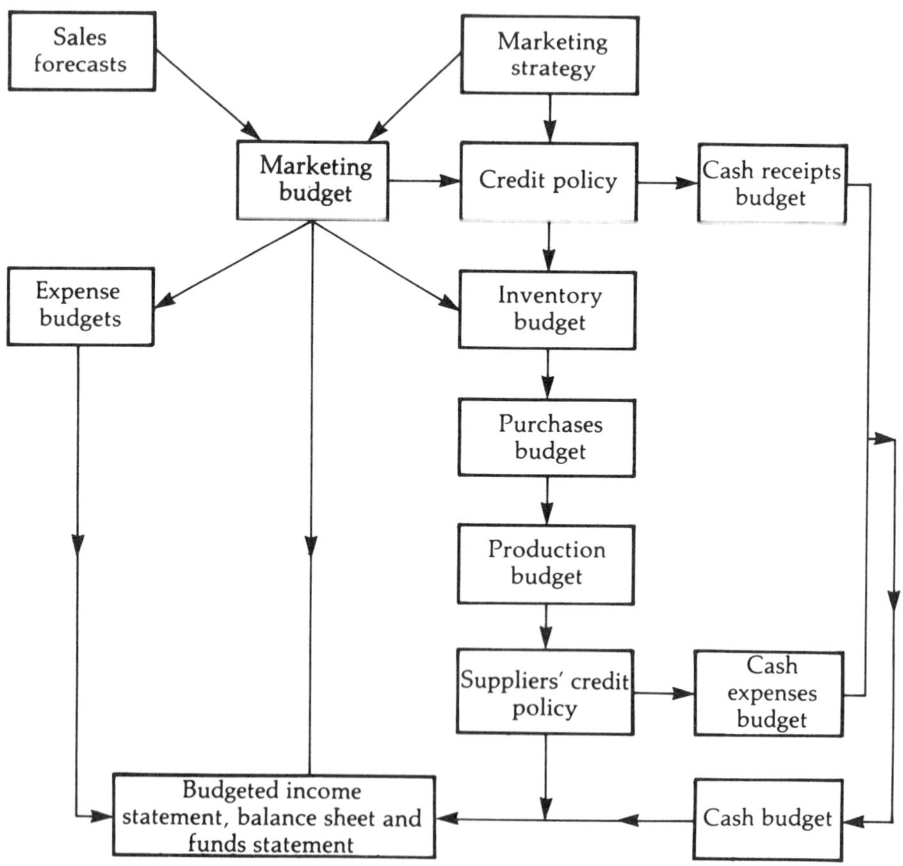

(i) *Marketing budget*, perhaps by product, area, class of customer, or other segments of interest;
(ii) *Production budget*, by product or plant;
(iii) *Purchases budget*, for instance, for materials;
(iv) *Labour budget*, by type of worker, or labour hours required;
(v) *Production cost budget*, by product or plant;
(vi) *Cash receipts budget;*
(vii) *Cash disbursements budget;*
(viii) *Cash budget*, that summarizes the receipts and disbursements;
(ix) *Budgeted income statement;*
(x) *Budgeted balance sheet;*
(xi) *Budgeted source and applications of funds statements.*

Typically, these budgets are prepared in a particular order every year, starting with the sales or revenue budget. From this budget will flow other budgets such as the production budget and the sales expense budget. Figure 8.3 illustrates a typical procedure for the development of budgets.

Top management will need to decide which budgets should be provided and by whom. In addition, one of the earliest budgeting decisions would relate to the time horizon of the budget. Usually, budgets are prepared for a financial year. However, in some cases where the future is very uncertain, a shorter period might be preferable. Hence, budgets may be prepared on a six-monthly, monthly, fortnightly or weekly basis. In other instances, where it is possible and essential to develop long-term plans, budgets may be prepared for two to five years into the future. The appropriateness of the time frame for a particular budget depends on the nature of the organization's operations and its environment. If there is a high level of complexity, uncertainty and external competition, it may be necessary to budget on a more frequent basis.

8.2 Why budget?

The budget is one of the most important communication devices within an organization and is intimately related to the process of organizational control. We shall illustrate some of the roles which budgets play in organizations through Tocher's control model (see Chapter 3). To refresh your memory, Tocher (1970; 1976) argued that for an activity to be controlled there must exist:

(i) an objective for the activity being controlled;
(ii) a means of measuring the inputs and outputs along the dimensions specified by the objective;
(iii) a predictive model of the activity being controlled; and
(iv) a choice of relevant alternative actions available to the decision-maker(s).

(a) Budgets and objectives

Objectives and budgets are related in two main ways. First, a decision-maker or group of decision-makers may have reasonably clear corporate objectives such as:

(i) increase the market share of the organization by 20%;

(ii) expand into the retail/wholesale market;
(iii) take over certain related businesses which have an asset base of £2–4 million.

These general objectives will need to be further specified into detailed operating goals for key decision areas. For instance, the objective of increasing market share by 20% may be translated into a sales target of £10 m for Division A and £15 m for Division B. In this manner, a budget helps to represent and communicate the broad objectives of top management to middle management and operating personnel.

This function of budgets is feasible only when senior management has a reasonably clear set of objectives. At times, however, such clarity of purpose may be lacking and key decision-makers may in fact be unsure what the objectives of the organization should be and how they might be achieved. This state of affairs may be due to changes in the environment or to succession problems within the organization. When decision-makers face new and unfamiliar threats, either from external interest groups or from key internal individuals, the budget may cease simply to represent the objectives of senior management. Instead, it may be a means whereby goals are negotiated, renegotiated and situations defined. That is, in times of uncertainty, the budget no longer acts as a passive communication device for the goals of top management because these are now not available. Instead, it serves actively to shape definitions of 'the problem', 'the situation', the 'appropriate objective' and 'the way forward'.

Boland and Pondy (1983) describe how the University of Illinois experienced such a period of uncertainty in the early 1980s. During that period contracting student numbers and a decline in state funding meant that the university faced a more hostile environment than before. Although it did not actually experience budget cuts, the university had suffered reduced annual increments and certain items such as staff pensions had been consistently underfunded. Against this changed environmental backdrop the university's budgeting system became a means whereby definitions of the new situation were shaped and a reconsideration of the values and priorities of the university was undertaken. For instance, departments such as the College of Commerce and Business Administration continued to submit new programmes for budget approval although funds were not available to fund these programmes. Through a discussion of these (unfundable) projects in the budgeting process, departments and personnel were able to define, explore, articulate and negotiate the central values and beliefs of the university. They were also able to canvass potential solutions to the threat of reduced funding and student numbers. Thus, in this manner, the budgeting process became a means not of *representing*, but of *defining* organizational objectives.

(b) Budgets and the choice of inputs, outputs and strategies

Budgets also help give form to alternative courses of action by measuring in financial terms the inputs and outputs of a particular strategy. A project or an activity may begin as someone's 'dream' or idea. That idea cannot be implemented unless there are clear measurements of the inputs required to implement the idea and the outputs that may be expected to eventuate.

For instance, the chief executive of a company may decide that it should become more involved in 'investment'. This vague idea may eventually be refined into a specific decision to buy a certain portfolio of shares, government bonds and unit trusts, to set up an investment and consulting department, to merge or take over a number of small hotel investment companies. Each of these strategies competes with others for scarce resources. How can a choice be made among them? Conventional market forces require that a strategy be more than just a good idea – it must meet certain requirements on cash flow, rate of return, and risk characteristics. And until each of the alternatives has been arrayed in terms of its effects on the organization and compared, a choice cannot be made. In order to know whether to set up an investment department or to buy an investment company we need to know the relative costs and benefits of each strategy. A budget is a means whereby the inputs and outputs associated with a future course of action may be expressed in financial terms.

(c) Budgets and predictive models

A budget also enables an organization to express estimated input–output relationships. For instance, sales budgets may be constructed using three sales estimates: £2 m, £2.5 m or £3 m. Each of these estimates will give rise to a set of production, cash and income budgets. Having generated these three sets of budgets which in effect represent three different scenarios for the organization, decision-makers can determine which scenario is feasible and acceptable. Note, however, that the quality of the budget (that is, the accuracy of the budget estimates) depends on the knowledge available about the relationship between inputs and outputs. If the predictive model of the input–output relationships is erroneous the sets of budgets produced will only be of limited value.

In analysing the relationships between different levels of inputs and outputs, the management accountant may also be able to identify the *critical success factors* of an organization. That is, what are the most important ingredients in the success of a particular programme or product? For instance, in some consumer product industries (especially personal care products such as soap and toothpaste) market share is vitally important because the products bear heavy selling and advertising expenses and require very high volumes if they are to be profitable. By contrast, for many manufacturing companies, the critical success factors are product quality, research and development and tight cost control. (See Section 10.2 in Chapter 10 for a fuller discussion.)

Finally, budgets enable an organization to study the sensitivity of the operations to certain changes. For instance, if sales revenue changed from £2 m to £3 m, what is the corresponding change in the expected net income? By constructing a series of budgets with different starting assumptions it may be possible for decision-makers to predict how the organization would perform and adapt under changing circumstances.

In the aspects discussed above budgets are shown to play an important part in achieving *feedforward* control. They help managers in an organization to control and plan the future by developing estimates for important segments of the organization's operations. Budgets also play a role in achieving *feedback* control. If you remember, Tocher's control model showed that comparisons need to be made between planned and actual performance. Deviations and differences between the two should then be transmitted as signals for possible corrective action. We shall now look at the role of budgets in feedback control.

(d) Budgets and feedback control

A budget target, like a standard, expresses a desired and expected level of performance. For instance, a sales budget of £2 m means the organization expects and desires to achieve £2 m worth of sales revenue. Once this sales target has been specified and accepted by people within an organization it may be assigned to a particular person, for example, the chief sales executive. This executive bears overall responsibility for the achievement or non-achievement of this target. Thus, at the end of the budget period, if the sales target is not achieved, the chief sales executive will need to account to the marketing director (or possibly to the managing director) for the failure to achieve the budgeted sales level. In this manner, budgeting enables specific responsibilities to be assigned to particular individuals who are then held accountable for the achievement of the budget target. This assignment of responsibilities for specific performance is called *responsibility accounting* and is widely used by many organizations.

Responsibility accounting, when used in conjunction with budgets, enables an organization to 'track' how well it is performing on a regular basis. This feedback control also enables corrective action to be taken if it is deemed necessary. For instance, Organization A sets a sales target of £2 m. Sales are expected to occur evenly throughout the year (that is, there are no significant seasonal variations in the amounts sold). Halfway through the budget period the managing director is notified that sales revenue to date amounted to only £500,000. This is 50% below the expected sales figure of £1 m for the six-month period. Given the significant deviation, it would be wise for the organization to consider strategies that could improve its sales performance (for example, price discounts, a heavier investment in advertising and promotion, etc.) The managing director could also analyse the expected effects of these new strategies by revising the organization's budgets to reflect new expected costs and benefits.

Thus, budgets enable an organization to achieve both feedforward and feedback control. In addition, budgets become involved in the social and organizational processes of organizations. We shall discuss some of these in greater detail later in this chapter. For the moment we shall concentrate on analysing the sense-making roles that have been attributed to budgets. Earlier we discussed how budgets help people in uncertain situations to make sense of changed circumstances and help define objectives. Budgets are, in fact, important sense-making and sense-giving (they give a sense of) devices which are indispensable in the exercise of intuitive, judgemental and political control within an organization.

(e) Budgets in sense-making and sense-giving roles

What does it mean to say that budgets play sense-making and sense-giving roles? What exactly do we mean when we say budgets help us to make sense of or reflect organizational life? There are numerous ways in which this sense-making role is served.

(i) Making sense of 'facts'

First, budgets help us to make sense of a situation by placing a particular interpretation on events, happenings, problems and situations. For instance, as management accountants, we may report that Organization A achieved a sales level of £500,000 in the period January–June 1993. This is a description of a state of affairs.

However, we can use the budget to make another interpretation of this 'fact'. We may, for example, point out that this level of sales was 50% below budget. This immediately colours our view of the prevailing state of affairs. Initially, when we were informed that the sales level was £500,000, no positive or negative meaning was attached to the number. But in using the budget as a bench-mark against which to assess the level of sales performance, we now attach a new significance to the number of £500,000 – it was 50% below our expectations. Such a deviation usually has a negative connotation (it is a 'bad' thing) and decision-makers may judge that it amounts to a 'serious' deviation and take corrective action.

(ii) Making sense of objectives

Second, as pointed out above, budgets are used to represent the goals of primary decision-makers within an organization and denote input–output combinations that are 'feasible' and 'possible'. Through such representation budgets give a sense of the values, goals and beliefs that are held by powerful individuals and groups within an organization. In addition, changes in these goals and beliefs will usually be reflected in budgets.

For instance, in the 1970s, Remploy's organizational goal was to provide employment for as many people as possible and special emphasis was placed on the employment of disabled people. If the organization ran into financial difficulties and experienced large budget overruns and deficits these were always funded by the government via the Manpower Services Commission (which is now the Training, Education and Enterprise Directorate of the Department of Employment). However, in the 1980s, this goal was replaced with a concern for 'efficiency' and 'value for money' in creating job opportunities. As a consequence of this change in policy Remploy's budgeting system was changed such that only part of a budget deficit (that which related to the employment of disabled people) was funded by the government.

Because budgets help to signify factors that are considered 'important', 'desirable', 'feasible' or 'necessary' within an organization, they are an important means of communication. Hence, if key decision-makers wish to signal that objectives and goals have changed, this signalling may be achieved primarily through the budgeting process.

(iii) Making sense of power and authority

Third, budgets give a sense of the authority and power networks within an organization. Budgets are usually constructed in two main ways. In the *top-down* approach senior managers state what they expect from their subordinate managers with respect to performance on revenue, profitability, cost savings and other dimensions. The subordinate managers may then try to negotiate with senior managers the budget targets which they consider to be unreasonable or unrealistic. For example, if a senior manager in British Rail sends down a budgeted freight target of £500,000 to an area manager, he/she may try to lower the target on the basis that it is not achievable.

In the *bottom-up* approach to budgeting, budgets are developed first by lower level managers. These managers will submit budgets to their superiors based on their perception of achievable goals and the resources needed to achieve those goals. Senior managers may (and usually do) review and revise these budgets through a process of negotiation with lower level managers. For example, a district nursing officer may ask for five additional administrative positions and an increase in the total nursing budget for his/her particular district. These requests will usually be accompanied by an explanation of why these increases in resources are necessary and how they will be deployed within the district. In addition, the district nursing officer may argue that should the request be refused, the management of nursing within the district cannot be carried out efficiently. Given this budget request, it is the task of the area and regional nursing officers to analyse carefully the case for and against granting the request. Inevitably, there will be much negotiation before a final budget target is agreed to by both parties.

Budgets thus give a sense of who should report to whom, who has authority over whom and over which resource area. Often, budgets reflect and mirror the formal lines of authority within an organization. Thus, budgets are typically either developed in a 'top-down' or 'bottom-up' manner. In both cases the roles of the participants to the budgeting process are dependent on their relative positions in the organization's managerial hierarchy. In the top-down approach it is the task of top management to decide on budget targets and 'send them down' to lower level managers. In the bottom-up approach lower level managers play a more active role in the setting of initial budget targets.

Budgets also highlight and make people aware of the extent of their legitimate or formal authority and responsibility. For instance, a district manager may only be able to budget for and authorize expenditure on projects up to a limit of £150,000. Expenditure above this limit may have to be submitted to the area or regional manager for approval. Similarly, one manager may only be responsible for setting a cost budget while another may be responsible for both cost and revenue budgets. Further, budgets are used to evaluate managerial performance and are a means whereby rewards and sanctions are effected within an organization. Thus, Manager A who has exceeded her budgeted revenues by 10% may receive a 10% rise in budget allocation for the following year while Manager B who has not met his budget target may be held back on the promotion ladder and suffer a decline in the budget allocation for the future. (Performance appraisal is discussed further in Chapters 10 and 11.)

Lastly, the budgeting process can reveal both informal and formal power networks. *Formal* power is usually referred to as authority and is defined as power which is sanctioned by the organization. For instance, a district manager will have certain powers which are generally accepted by all other members in the organization. These may include the power to hire and fire staff at the district level, to construct a district-level budget and to participate in certain senior management meetings. *Informal* power is power that is not legitimately sanctioned by an organization. For instance, a divisional management accountant may only have limited formal authority but because he/she has expert knowledge in the development of computerized accounting systems, may have more informal power than a more senior management accountant. Similarly, a charismatic shop steward may have little formal decision-making authority but may, nevertheless, have the ability to influence union decisions in a substantial way.

As pointed out above, budgeting, whether in a top-down or bottom-up approach, is essentially a *bargaining* process which acts as a medium for the negotiation of different interests and goals. Managers and interest groups often have different priorities – the district manager may wish to improve the performance of his/her district while the chief accountant may desire more equipment and greater prestige for his/her department. In seeking to achieve these diverse goals, managers and interest groups bargain for scarce resources. Through a careful analysis of this bargaining process it is possible to locate key individuals and groups within an organization who possess formal and/or informal power.

For instance, we may discover that the final budget in Organization X usually represents the wishes of senior managers and be led to the conclusion that budgeting in that organization closely represents the formal power network. Or we may discover the contrary. Crozier (1964) gives an account of maintenance personnel in a cigarette factory who, through their skill, acquired substantial informal power. This was because whenever machines broke down and production was halted they were the only people who could repair the machines. Through the possession of this informal power the maintenance men were able to further their own interests better than other classes of workers. Informal power thus enables participants to bargain more successfully for scarce resources within an organization. And the negotiation and bargaining processes surrounding a budget highlight the operation of informal and formal power networks.

Budgets are thus important means by which an organization's power and authority network is reinforced, revealed and even changed.

(iv) Making sense of organizational culture

Budgets are also important means of reflecting the 'culture' or 'climate' of an organization. These concepts refer to the principal values, beliefs and social norms concerning human interaction within an organization. The culture of an organization, like the culture of a race, is often reflected and embedded in symbols, rituals, ceremonies and distinctive forms of talk, language and dress which permeate and traverse organizational life. Just as the tea ceremony has particular meanings for the Japanese and the shadow play particular significance for a Balinese, so an annual general meeting, a Christmas party, an open door to the managing director's office and a budget meeting have particular meanings for organizational members.

The concept of organizational culture is relatively easy to illustrate when comparing Anglo-Saxon and Japanese organizations. Japanese and Western managers have quite distinct beliefs about human beings and the ways in which they should be managed. Japanese managers, like their Western counterparts, see each individual as having economic, social, psychological and spiritual needs. But, unlike Western managers, they assume that it is their task to attend to the whole person and not leave so much to other institutions (such as the government, family or church). Hence, some Japanese organizations offer employment for life and employees are encouraged to see the organization as part of an extended family. Employees may stay in housing that is subsidized by the company, send their children to company-run schools and buy most of their household goods through the company.

Most British organizations do not adopt such a view of management and most employees do not have life-long employment. Neither do they salute the company flag, sing the corporate anthem, send their children to company-sponsored schools or live for extended periods in company-subsidized housing. These differences in beliefs about people and how they should be managed are clearly reflective of wider differences between the two societies. But they emphasize that different organizations can have radically different organizational cultures. Think of the culture of a colliery, a university department, a firm of accountants, a rock band. Each of these organizations will have distinctive, often taken-for-granted values and beliefs which govern interaction among people.

Budgets are part of this organizational culture. They help to constitute and reinforce prevailing values and beliefs. Let us compare two organizations with very different corporate cultures. In Organization A, senior managers believe that people are intrinsically lazy, work principally for money and do not derive any sustained satisfaction from work. The task of management is therefore to supervise closely and control employees such that they perform their work efficiently. The budget in this organization is used as a tool to provide information that helps managers to control their subordinates by highlighting inadequate performance. As soon as performance falls short of budget, the employee is expected to account fully for the deviation and to bear the responsibility for performing below budget.

Compare this situation with that in Organization B where senior managers believe that people can be motivated to work hard and to be high-achievers. These managers perceive that their role is to motivate employees in the appropriate manner and to provide them with satisfactory conditions of work. In this organization, the budget is produced through extensive consultations between superiors and subordinates and is used as a means of communicating information throughout the organization. In addition, deviations from budget targets are viewed with long-run profitability and performance in mind.

Budgets, therefore, not only reflect the objectives of key decision-makers, they also reflect and constitute the culture of the organization. Indeed, the process of budgeting, like the Japanese tea ceremony, is an important organizational ritual or ceremony. It indicates central beliefs in people, how they work, how they should be managed and how resources should be and are allocated among them.

(v) Making organizations objective and orderly

Budget numbers and categories often exude an air of objectivity. However, this objectivity may be only skin-deep for both budget numbers and categories may be manipulated to give certain impressions. Boland and Pondy (1983) provide examples in their research on the budgeting process at the University of Illinois of the relative political acceptability of certain budget categories. Budget titles like 'academic development fund' and 'graduate research board' were favoured because they gave an impression of excellence in teaching and scholarship. Similarly, although funds were to be used for the payment of salaries and research, they were requested under the categories 'repair and maintenance' and 'equipment'. It was felt that government legislators would understand these categories better and therefore be more willing to grant funds under them.

Budgets also help to give a sense of order and of rational planning. The very fact that an organization engages in budgeting indicates that some member of the organization sees the need for systematic future planning. This sense of rational order may or may not be deceptive. For instance, if budgets are prepared regularly and are genuinely used as an aid in decision-making, the impression of rational order may be correct. However, some organizations prepare budgets which do not appear to have a significant impact on decision-making. Other organizations construct budgets that are constantly inaccurate and therefore ignored by organizational members. In these situations, the impression of rational, future planning may be more mythical than real.

These sense-making roles indicate that budgets are often closely connected to the political and symbolic activities of an organization. As pointed out, budgets help to highlight the formal and informal power networks within an organization. In addition, rewards and sanctions are based on a comparison between budgeted and actual performance. Further, budgets are concerned with the allocation of scarce resources. And scarcity means that interest groups may seek to manipulate the budget to give particular impressions, to motivate employees in a particular way and to convey certain images and meanings. Indeed, the budgeting process is an important means whereby conflicting interests and goals are highlighted, reflected, resolved and compromised. Budgeting is therefore both a technical and a political activity within organizations.

We shall now discuss the technical aspects of budgeting and then conclude by analysing in detail some of the widespread social and organizational effects of budgets on human behaviour.

8.3 The technical process of budgeting

Budgets may be developed over a range of time horizons. There may be monthly, yearly or five-yearly budgets depending on the content and purpose of the budget. For the purpose of this section we shall concentrate on the preparation of the annual budget as this is one of the most common budgets found in organizations. Usually an annual *master* or *fixed* budget is first prepared. A master budget is a budget that is based on a particular, fixed level of activity or output. For instance, let us assume that the expected level of activity for the coming year will be 500,000 units. That is, we expect to produce or service 500,000 units. Using this level of activity as our base, we then construct revenue, expense and cash budgets as well as budgeted income statements and balance sheets.

The method by which the annual budget is prepared will clearly differ from organization to organization. In some organizations budgeting may be a well organized, well documented procedure, while in others the budget may be prepared in a rather *ad hoc* and disorganized manner. Thus, not all organizations will follow the budgeting procedure set out below. This procedure is representative and illustrative of the method usually followed by organizations but there can be many variations depending on the circumstances facing each organization.

The stages in budgeting usually include:

(a) communication of objectives or general budgeting guidelines to the people responsible for preparing the budget;
(b) determination of the key success factors of the organization;
(c) preparation of the sales or revenue/fund budget;
(d) initial preparation of budgets for all major operating activities;
(e) negotiation of budget targets;
(f) final coordination and review of budgets;

(g) acceptance and communication of all budgets;
(h) continous monitoring of actual performance against budget targets.

(a) Communication of objectives

We have argued that budgets may be developed in the presence or absence of clear-cut objectives. Where objectives have already been agreed among organizational members the annual budget is used as a tool for implementing these objectives. Where objectives are unclear, the budgeting process becomes a means whereby goals and objectives emerge through interaction and negotiation among different parties. In either case, the budget should reflect and encapsulate important policy assumptions and objectives. For instance, the preparers of the budget may need to make assumptions about the anticipated rate of inflation, expected movements in the exchange rate, expected tax changes and national wage increases. Also, they will need to know of changes to the sales or production mix, any intended expansion or contraction of specific operating activities and planned acquisitions of or mergers with other organizations.

(b) Determination of key success factors

The performance of every organization will be particularly influenced by certain critical success factors (discussed in greater detail in Chapter 10). In organizations which are already operating at maximum capacity, the most critical success factor is likely to be productive capacity. This is the factor that will most significantly influence the performance of the organization. However, in the majority of organizations the most critical success factor is likely to be consumer demand or the expected level of revenues or funds. Because of this, the sales or funds budget is usually the first budget to be prepared. It will determine the content of other related budgets.

(c) Preparation of the sales or funds budget

The sales or funds budget is the starting point of most master budgets. In manufacturing organizations sales budgeting begins with the forecasting of the sales of individual products. These forecasts may be by geographical area, by class of customer or by some other segment.

Forecasting sales is a difficult task as many assumptions need to be made about consumer demands and environmental conditions. For instance, assumptions have to be made about likely customer demand at different prices, the probable prices for similar products sold by competitors, the economic activity in the regions where the product is sold, the number of sales personnel required to service the estimated demand, the appropriate level of advertising and promotional expenditures, the impact of anticipated changes in exchange rates and changes in taxes such as value added tax or customs and excise duties.

Because of the range of assumptions that need to be made it is highly likely that different managers will arrive at different sales forecasts for each product or product line. In addition, different forecasting techniques will lead to different forecasts, so a sales forecast is not a sales budget. Management will have to exercise judgement and decide which assumptions are most probable and use these to construct the sales budget. A sales budget, therefore, reflects either explicitly or implicitly a particular set of forecasting assumptions. It is one particular scenario for the future.

In developing sales forecasts or a sales budget, the management accountant plays an important role. Some sales managers are conscious of only particular critical success factors, such as total volume and market share. They may not be able to analyse the costs and benefits of alternative strategies. The management accountant may then aid by determining whether, for instance, an increase in sales volume obtained by reducing prices and increasing advertising expenditures would be more profitable than some other strategy. In addition, the management accountant may be actively involved in developing sales forecasts. This is because management accountants are among the principal providers of much of the information used in forecasting and are trained in forecasting techniques – but it would be wise for management accountants to collaborate with experts in market research.

In Chapter 7 we discussed some of these forecasting or estimation techniques – the use of scattergrams, regression analysis, the high-low method and the visual fit method. These methods are all available to the management accountant in helping to construct a sales forecast. Another method often used is *time series analysis*. This literally means analysing the historical patterns of sales that have occurred in the past as a means of predicting future sales. This method can be useful when no major environmental changes are expected and it does highlight seasonal variations in sales and consumer demand. However, time series analysis is limited when organizations face volatile environments. In addition, the method fails to explain why sales in the past have been at particular levels or to consider whether management action in the past has been good, bad, efficient or effective. For instance, through time series analysis we may discover that the organization's sales rose by 5% over a two-year period. This information tells us little about the effectiveness of managerial action. They may, in fact, have been very ineffective if the market for the product rose by 10% in that period. Time series analysis is, however, extremely useful in the forecasting of industry sales, and if the organization has been able (or expects to be able) to capture a specific percentage of the market, a good forecast of the organization's sales may be obtained.

Yet another method used for forecasting is the Delphi technique. This relies on the judgement of a number of skilled 'judges' (such as experienced marketing managers, management accountants, production managers and managing directors). The Delphi technique works like this:

(i) estimates of sales are obtained from each judge independently;
(ii) these independent estimates are circulated in aggregated form for information and reflection to all other judges;
(iii) this leads to new estimates being made by all judges;
(iv) the entire process is repeated until consensus is reached on an acceptable sales forecast.

The Delphi technique is based on the assumption that the judgement and skill of experienced managers is the most valuable forecasting tool. However, the technique remains subjective and inexact. It can also be time-consuming – especially if initial estimates differ significantly from one another.

Different organizations will use different forecasting techniques. Each technique has its drawbacks and it is up to decision-makers within an organization to choose a suitable forecasting method.

(d) Preparation of other budgets

Once the sales budget has been determined from a range of sales forecasts it is possible to construct the other budgets. In some organizations this task is performed by senior managers (the top-down approach) and in others by lower level managers (the bottom-up approach). There are no hard-and-fast rules concerning the precise budget targets that should be set. The previous year's budget may be used as a starting point with only small incremental changes being made to produce the current year's budget. For example, the advertising budget for this year may simply be 110% of last year's amount. However, budget preparers need to take into account likely changes in future conditions when setting budget targets. As may be inferred, effective budgeting in the face of change requires a great deal of skill and judgement.

In today's computerized world the actual mechanics of budgeting are usually performed by a computer, whether by a program written specifically for the organization or by a commercial electronic spreadsheet such as Lotus 1-2-3, Multiplan, Symphony or Visicalc. Computerized software helps to eliminate arithmetical errors and tedious arithmetical calculation. However, it does not help to overcome relationships that are wrongly specified. For example, if 50% of customers pay 30 days after a sale and 50% pay 60 days after a sale, this relationship must be correctly modelled within the computer system. Thus assuming that 100% of all sales will be paid for within 30 days will lead to an inaccurate budget. Also, a computerized budgeting system should be logically correct. It should not, for example, calculate that 50% of all sales will be paid for in 30 days and 60% will be paid in 60. There cannot be a sales total of 110%!

Irrespective of whether budgets are actually calculated manually or by computer, attention should be paid to the specification of the relationships within the budget. Adding and subtracting numbers is easy enough but it is deciding which numbers should be added and subtracted that lies at the heart of an accurate budget.

(e) Negotiation of budgets

As discussed earlier, budgets may be prepared in a top-down or bottom-up manner. In either process, the budget will need to be negotiated by superiors, subordinates and by different departments competing for the same 'basket' of scarce resources. This process of negotiation allows the exercise of both formal and informal power. It may also be accompanied by diverse attempts to manipulate budget categories and targets. For instance, targets may be deliberately biased or fictitious numbers instituted to the benefit of particular parties. (The question of bias will be further discussed later in this chapter.)

Another issue that will be discussed is the desired amount of participation by lower level managers in the budgeting process. Considerable research has been conducted into the effect of participation in budgeting. (Later in this chapter, we shall look at this research in detail.) Broadly speaking, participation in budgeting appears to lead to more positive attitudes towards the budget and greater acceptance of it. However, it does not appear to be positively linked to job performance and several factors appear to influence the success of participative budgeting. It is therefore important for management to consider these factors before deciding on a particular budgeting style.

(f) Coordination and review of budgets

As the different budgets – e.g. sales, production and cash – are constructed, they need to be coordinated with each other so that they are compatible. Incompatibility and inconsistency may arise because the budgeting process usually involves a number of different departments – e.g. sales, production, marketing – and numerous senior and lower level managers. It is the task of the management accountant to ensure that separate parts of the total master budget are internally consistent. In order to ensure that such consistency is achieved, the management accountant usually prepares a budgeted income statement, balance sheet, cash flow statement and funds statement.

(g) Acceptance and communication of budgets

After the master budget has been agreed upon by both senior and lower level managers it is approved and passed back down the managerial hierarchy for implementation. It is essential that each manager responsible for implementing budget policy be informed as to his/her responsibility. Budget targets are of little use if they are not well communicated and understood by the people responsible for meeting these targets.

(h) Budget monitoring

It is important that the actual performance of each manager should be regularly and frequently compared against budget targets. Like the helmsman of a ship, the management accountant must constantly monitor the course of the organization in order to prevent it from getting 'out of control'. Hence, regular performance reports should be made, for example on a monthly basis, and sent to the appropriate budgetees (i.e. managers responsible for achieving particular budget targets). In this way a budgetee can pinpoint when and in what areas the budget is not being achieved and take appropriate action. Remember, according to Tocher's control model, such action may involve a change in an input–output relationship, an alteration to the quantity of inputs used or a revision of the budget target.

8.4 An illustration of a master budget

Let us look at an illustration of the budgeting procedure for a manufacturing organization using the information below.

ABC plc manufactures a single product known as Poppy from three basic raw materials – steel, wood and plastic. The standards set for the production of one unit of Poppy are:

Direct materials:
Steel: 4 m at £0.50 per m = £2.00
Wood: 1 m^2 at £1.00 per m^2 = £1.00
Plastic: 2 m^2 at £1.50 per m^2 = £3.00

Direct labour:
Cutting: 0.1 hour at £10.00 per hour = £1.00
Assembly: 0.3 hour at £10.00 per hour = £3.00

Fixed indirect manufacturing costs:
Based on 12,000 units per quarter: £9,000/12,000 = £0.75

However, in the second, third and fourth quarters of the budget period, the fixed indirect costs are expected to rise to £15,000. As we shall see later, this is because production in those quarters is above the normal level of 12,000 units per quarter. The fixed indirect cost application rate thus changes to £15,000/12,000 = £1.25

Variable indirect manufacturing costs:
0.4 dlh at £7.5 per direct labour hour = £3.00
This variable indirect cost rate is based on a relevant range of 9,000 to 19,000 units.

Other relevant data are as follows:

Sales forecast
It is expected that units of Poppy can be sold in two separate markets in the UK – the northern and southern markets. The markets are sufficiently separate to enable price differentiation. A price of £30 will be charged in the northern market and a price of £32 will be charged in the southern market. The pattern of sales is expected to vary between quarters in the following manner (in units):

	Quarter 1	Quarter 2	Quarter 3	Quarter 4
Northern market	5,000	10,000	6,000	6,000
Southern market	4,000	8,000	8,000	10,000
	9,000	18,000	14,000	16,000

Inventory policy
The company has a definite inventory policy that seeks to maintain adequate stocks of raw materials and of finished goods. The following policy is intended to apply throughout the budget period and into the first quarter of the following year:

	Quarter 1	Quarter 2	Quarter 3	Quarter 4	Next year Quarter 1
Steel (m)	2,000	4,000	3,000	3,000	3,000
Wood (m^2)	2,000	3,000	2,000	2,000	1,000
Plastic (m^2)	2,000	4,000	2,000	2,000	1,000
Finished goods (units)	500	1,000	500	500	500

Raw materials are purchased on credit terms which require the company to pay for 80% of its purchases during a given quarter by the end of that quarter and the final 20% in the following quarter. Sales are also expected to be on credit. Customers are expected to pay for 80% of the sales in the quarter when the sale is made, 18% in the following quarter, and 2% is likely to be written off as bad debts. Direct labour and indirect manufacturing costs are also paid in cash each quarter except for the depreciation component of indirect costs. The latter is a fixed cost of £16,000 per year.

With this information, we are now able to construct a comprehensive master budget for ABC plc. Note that this master budget is based on a specific sales forecast and particular assumptions about selling price and inventory policies.

(a) The production budget

In order to construct the production budget we need to know the level of sales expected in each quarter and the desired change in inventory. This is because:

Production (in units) = Desired change in inventory (in units) + Sales (in units)

To understand this formula, remember that (in units):

Opening stock + Production − Sales = Closing stock

Therefore:

Production = Closing stock − Opening stock + Sales

The item 'Closing stock − Opening stock' may be conveniently referred to as 'Desired change in inventory'.

Also, bear in mind that the closing stock in one quarter becomes the opening stock in the next quarter.

The Production Budget for ABC plc is:

	Quarter 1	Quarter 2	Quarter 3	Quarter 4
Finished goods:				
Desired change in inventory (units)	500	(500)	0	0
Sales (units)	9,000	18,000	14,000	16,000
Production (units)	9,500	17,500	14,000	16,000

(b) The direct materials purchases budget

Given that we now know the direct materials standards, the numbers of Poppy that need to be produced in each quarter and the required inventories of direct materials, we can construct a budget for the purchases of direct materials. Again we need to rely on the following formula to calculate the required purchases of direct materials:

Purchases = Desired change in inventory + Usage

Remember:

Opening stock + Purchases − Usage = Closing stock

Using this formula, we obtain the following Purchases Budget:

	Quarter 1	Quarter 2	Quarter 3	Quarter 4
Steel:				
Desired change in inventory	2,000	(1,000)	0	0
Usage (m)	38,000	70,000	56,000	64,000
Purchases (m)	40,000	69,000	56,000	64,000
Cost (£)	20,000	34,500	28,000	32,000
Wood:				
Desired change	1,000	(1,000)	0	(1,000)
Usage (m^2)	9,500	17,500	14,000	16,000
Purchases (m^2)	10,500	16,500	14,000	15,000
Cost (£)	10,500	16,500	14,000	15,000
Plastic:				
Desired change	2,000	(2,000)	0	(1,000)
Usage (m^2)	19,000	35,000	28,000	32,000
Purchases (m)	21,000	33,000	28,000	31,000
Cost (£)	31,500	49,500	42,000	46,500
Total cost of all purchases of direct materials	£62,000	£100,500	£84,000	£93,500

Let us illustrate how we obtained the usage figure of 38,000 m of steel in Quarter 1 and the cost of £20,000. In order to calculate these figures, we need to refer back to the direct materials standards given earlier.

In Quarter 1 we need to produce 9,500 units

Therefore, we need 9,500 × 4 m = 38,000 m of steel

We also need to build up the inventory of steel from 2,000 m to 4,000 m.

Thus, we need a total of 38,000 + (4,000–2,000) = 40,000 m of steel.

As the standard cost of 1 m of steel is £0.50, the standard cost of purchasing 40,000 m of steel is 40,000 × £0.50 = £20,000.

Similar calculations are performed for all the other direct materials requirements.

(c) The direct labour budget

The direct labour budget may be constructed given that we know that 0.4 dlh are required per unit of Poppy produced and each direct labour hour costs £10.00. This is shown below:

	Quarter 1	Quarter 2	Quarter 3	Quarter 4
Direct labour (hours)	3,800	7,000	5,600	6,400
(£)	38,000	70,000	56,000	64,000

(d) The indirect manufacturing cost budget

Indirect expenses are shown below. Note that fixed expenses in fact change in the second quarter of the budget period due to an increase in the amount of indirect labour. This is not uncommon as costs are usually fixed only for a certain range of relevant activity levels. When that range has been exceeded certain fixed costs may show a sudden increase or 'jump'. Indirect labour has both a fixed and a variable component. It is obvious from the figures given that the fixed component of indirect labour has increased to a new 'fixed' amount in the second quarter of the budget period.

	Quarter 1	Quarter 2	Quarter 3	Quarter 4
	£	£	£	£
Indirect manufacturing costs:				
Fixed portion:				
Supplies	1,000	2,000	2,000	2,000
Insurance	1,000	3,000	3,000	3,000
Indirect labour	2,000	5,000	5,000	5,000
Maintenance	1,000	1,000	1,000	1,000
Depreciation	4,000	4,000	4,000	4,000
	£9,000	£15,000	£15,000	£15,000
Variable portion:				
Indirect labour (£7.50 per dlh × 0.4 = £3 per unit)	28,500	52,500	42,000	48,000
Total indirect manufacturing costs	£37,500	£67,500	£57,000	£63,000

Note that the fixed indirect cost application rate for quarter 1 is no longer applicable in quarters 2 to 4. This is because fixed indirect costs have increased to £15,000 since production is above the expected level of 12,000 units per quarter. As a result, the total fixed indirect costs must be taken into consideration without attempting to use the fixed indirect cost application rate per unit from quarter 1. By contrast, we can obtain the total variable indirect costs by using the variable indirect cost application rate of £3 per unit and multiplying that by the number of units required to be produced in each quarter. For the calculation of variable indirect costs, we can either use the variable indirect cost application rate or the number of direct labour hours required for production multiplied by the dlh rate of £7.50.

(e) The selling and administrative expenses budget

All these expenses are paid in cash in the quarter in which they are incurred. Note that some elements of these expenses do not vary with the level of activity (for instance, interest payments and travel) while other items appear to bear some relationship to production levels (for example, advertising).

	Quarter 1	Quarter 2	Quarter 3	Quarter 4
	£	£	£	£
Selling expenses:				
Advertising	20,000	30,000	20,000	25,000
Travel	1,000	1,000	1,000	1,000
Clerical wages	10,000	10,000	15,000	15,000
	£31,000	£41,000	£36,000	£41,000

	Quarter 1 £	Quarter 2 £	Quarter 3 £	Quarter 4 £
Administrative expenses:				
Office expenses	50,000	50,000	50,000	52,000
Interest	23,000	23,000	23,000	23,000
	£73,000	£73,000	£73,000	£75,000

(f) The cost of goods manufactured and sold budget

Having constructed budgets (a)–(e) we are now able to construct a cost of goods manufactured and sold budget. ABC plc adopts a definite policy with respect to the valuation of finished goods. It has decided to value them at standard cost. Because there is a change in budgeted fixed indirect costs through the budget year, this standard cost also changes. It is £13.75 per unit in Quarter 1 and £14.25 per unit in Quarters 2, 3 and 4.

COST OF GOODS MANUFACTURED STATEMENT

	Quarter 1 £	Quarter 2 £	Quarter 3 £	Quarter 4 £	Total £
Opening stocks:					
Steel	1,000	2,000	1,500	1,500	1,000
Wood	2,000	3,000	2,000	2,000	2,000
Plastic	3,000	6,000	3,000	3,000	3,000
	£6,000	£11,000	£6,500	£6,500	£6,000
Add: Purchases of direct materials:					
Steel	20,000	34,500	28,000	32,000	114,500
Wood	10,500	16,500	14,000	15,000	56,000
Plastic	31,500	49,500	42,000	46,500	169,500
	£62,000	£100,500	£84,000	£93,500	£340,000
Less: Closing stocks:					
Steel	2,000	1,500	1,500	1,500	1,500
Wood	3,000	2,000	2,000	1,000	1,000
Plastic	6,000	3,000	3,000	1,500	1,500
	£11,000	£6,500	£6,500	£4,000	£4,000
Cost of direct materials used in manufacture	57,000	105,000	84,000	96,000	342,000
Add: Direct labour	38,000	70,000	56,000	64,000	228,000
Indirect costs	37,500	67,500	57,000	63,000	225,000
Total manufacturing costs	£132,500	£242,500	£197,000	£223,000	£795,000
Add: Opening stock of finished goods	6,875	14,250	7,125	7,125	6,875
Less: Closing stock of finished goods	14,250	7,125	7,125	7,125	7,125
Cost of Poppys sold	£125,125	£249,625	£197,000	£223,000	£794,750

(g) The budgeted income statement

The information from these preceding budgets may now be summarized in a budgeted income statement. In addition, it is assumed that the corporate tax rate is 50% on accounting income and that a dividend of 25% (£125,000) is paid on the paid-up capital of £500,000. Note that bad debts in a quarter were estimated to be 2% of sales for that quarter.

BUDGETED INCOME STATEMENT
ABC PLC
YEAR ENDING 30 APRIL 1994

	Quarter 1	Quarter 2	Quarter 3	Quarter 4	Total
	£	£	£	£	£
Sales revenue	278,000	556,000	436,000	500,000	1,770,000
Less: Cost of sales	125,125	249,625	197,000	223,000	794,750
Gross margin	152,875	306,375	239,000	277,000	975,250
Less: Bad debts written off	5,560	11,120	8,720	10,000	35,400
Selling expenses	31,000	41,000	36,000	41,000	149,000
Office expenses	50,000	50,000	50,000	52,000	202,000
Interest	23,000	23,000	23,000	23,000	92,000
Net income before tax	43,315	181,255	121,280	151,000	496,850
Less: Corporation tax 50%					248,425
After tax profit					248,425
Less: Dividends 25% × paid capital of £500,000					125,000
Additions to retained earnings					£123,425

As can be seen, ABC plc appears to be in a satisfactory financial position at the end of the budget period. However, a budgeted income statement may not give us the full financial picture of the organizations's state of affairs. This is because profit is not equal to cash and there are profitable companies which do not have sufficient cash to meet demands. In order to evaluate an organization's cash position in the future it is necessary to construct a cash flow budget or a cash flow statement.

(h) The cash flow budget

In recent years, given high interest rates (which makes borrowing more expensive), organizations have begun to place more weight on monitoring their cash flow positions. It is important that an organization be able to predict whether and when it may not have sufficient cash to meet its demands, for creditors may apply to the courts to have the organization placed into receivership should it be unable to meet its debt commitments.

The concept of a cash flow budget is relatively straightforward. We begin with a stock of cash to which we add cash inflows and deduct cash outflows to arrive at a cash balance. Cash inflows are usually derived from items such as sales receipts, debt collection, rent, interest, dividends, etc. Cash outflows normally result from payments for purchases, salaries, heating, lighting, rates and other expenses. Note that depreciation is a non-cash item and should never be included in a cash flow budget.

In order to construct a cash flow budget for ABC plc we require more information. Let us assume that in Quarter 1 the organization had a cash stock of £20,000, outstanding debtors of £85,000 and creditors of £20,000. Remember that the credit terms for both suppliers and customers have been given above. In addition, the organization wishes to pay a dividend of £125,000 in the budget year. This is to be paid in two lots – an interim payment of £25,000 in Quarter 1 and a final payment of £100,000 in Quarter 4. Finally, in Quarter 3, the organization plans to spend £150,000 on the purchase of new capital assets. The cash flow budget for the organization is shown below:

BUDGETED CASH FLOW STATEMENT
ABC PLC
YEAR ENDING 30 APRIL 1994

	Quarter 1	Quarter 2	Quarter 3	Quarter 4
	£	£	£	£
Cash at start	20,000	57,300	211,840	105,420
Collection of debtors:				
Current quarter	222,400	444,800	348,800	400,000
Previous quarter	85,000	50,040	100,080	78,480
Cash holdings plus cash receipts	327,400	552,140	660,720	583,900
Cash payments:				
Purchases:				
Current quarter	49,600	80,400	67,200	74,800
Previous quarter	20,000	12,400	20,100	16,800
Direct labour	38,000	70,000	56,000	64,000
Indirect costs:				
Supplies	1,000	2,000	2,000	2,000
Insurance	1,000	3,000	3,000	3,000
Indirect labour	30,500	57,500	47,000	53,000
Maintenance	1,000	1,000	1,000	1,000
Selling expenses	31,000	41,000	36,000	41,000
Administrative expenses	73,000	73,000	73,000	75,000
Dividend	25,000	–	–	100,000
Capital expenditure	–	–	250,000	–
Total cash payments	270,100	340,300	555,300	430,600
Cash at end of quarter	£57,300	£211,840	£105,420	£153,300

As can be seen from the cash flow position, the company appears to be in a satisfactory cash position throughout the budget period. There is a positive cash balance at the end of each quarter. However, it should be remembered that this cash flow budget is based on certain assumptions about the level of sales, selling prices and input quantities and prices. Should there be an unexpected decline in the sales of the product or abnormal rises in the prices of factor inputs, the organization may find itself in a tighter cash position than anticipated. It is important therefore that the organization carefully monitors its cash position on a regular basis. For instance, weekly checks on the current and future cash flow position of the organization may be prudent.

(i) Conclusion

From this illustration of a comprehensive master or fixed budget it can be appreciated that budgets can be constructed for any activity in an organization, whether it be production or advertising. In addition, budgets that represent and summarize these activities for the organization as a whole (in the form of budgeted income statement, cash flow budget and budgeted balance sheet) are important planning and control tools. They enable an organization to predict its future resource requirements.

Clearly, annual budgets are easier to construct than long-term budgets for five or ten years. And predicting far into the future will always require a great deal of judgement, experience and intuition on the part of the management accountant. However, long-term budgets do enable decision-makers to clarify their strategic plans and priorities for the organization.

But the use of a master or fixed budget is not without its difficulties. We shall discuss some of these in the following section, and how they may be remedied through the use of flexible budgets.

8.5 Flexible budgeting

In the example given in the previous section we constructed a master budget based on certain assumptions about the level of sales at particular prices, inventory policies, the costs of inputs and the quantity of inputs. However, these expectations may not be met and it is essential for management accountants to know the financial consequences of a range of alternative scenarios. For instance, we may have budgeted for an activity level of 1,000 units and predicted that selling and administrative expenses would amount to £300,000. The actual amount spent on selling and administration may have amounted to £450,000 and the activity level may also have been higher than budgeted – 1,200 units. How shall we evaluate the organization's performance? Was it badly managed and inefficient? Did the organization actually overspend its selling and administrative budget by £150,000?

Clearly, it is incorrect to compare the actual costs of £450,000 for an activity level of 1,200 units with budgeted costs of £300,000 for a budgeted activity level of 1,000 units. This is because not all costs are fixed, irrespective of the level of activity. Because some costs are variable or semi-variable (and thus vary with the level of activity) we need to determine actual and budgeted costs and revenues for *the same level of activity*. In our example above we would need to compare actual and budgeted selling and administrative costs at the activity level of 1,200 units. When the budgeted expense is 'flexed' to 1,200 units we may discover that we would have budgeted for an expense of £480,000 at an activity level of 1,200 units. If we compare this budget target with actual costs we would obtain a *favourable* deviation (or variance) of £30,000 instead of an erroneous unfavourable deviation of £150,000.

Flexible budgets are budgets which are constructed for varying levels of sales and productive activity. They may be relatively straightforward budgets – as when only the sales forecast is allowed to vary and all other items and relationships are held constant. Provided the alteration to the sales forecast does not change the unit selling price or cause the unit variable cost of production to change, and that fixed costs remain the same within the relevant range, a change in sales forecast will lead budgeted net income to change by the number of units multiplied by the contribution margin of the product. However, the construction of flexible budgets may become quite complicated if a change in one variable causes a range of other variables in the accounts to alter.

Flexible budgets are important aids to decision-making. They serve a number of functions. *First*, they enable an organization to predict its performance and income levels given a range of sales levels and activity levels. Thus, in order to construct a flexible budget, we require an adequate predictive model of the input–output relationships. That is, we need to know how inputs change in response to changes in sales levels and activity/output. In Figure 8.4 we show an example of a flexible budget for ABC plc at different sales levels. As can be seen, a flexible budget shows the impact of changes in sales and production levels on revenue, expenses and, ultimately, income.

Secondly, flexible budgets enable more accurate assessments of managerial and organizational performance. Suppose ABC plc decided to operate with a sales budget of 9,000 units and a production budget of 9,500 units. Then suppose it actually sold 8,000 units and only 8,500 units were produced. How may we assess the performance of the company with the help of a flexible budget? In order to assess accurately the company's performance we need to compare its actual performance with a budget flexed to a sales level of 8,000 units and an activity level of 8,500 units. This is done in Fig. 8.5.

The variances in the last column are obtained by comparing actual performance with budgeted performance at a sales level of 8,000 units and an activity level of 8,500 units. This comparison shows that on the whole the organization performed better than budget in both the sales and production area. However, on some expense items (such as direct materials) the organization performed worse than budget. Note that a comparison with a master budget figure for sales of 9,000 units and production of 9,500 units would have led to an over-optimistic review of the performance of the organization.

Figure 8.4

Flexible budget (1).

Accounting item	Formula	Sales level		
Sales (units)		7,000	8,000	9,000
Sales (£)	£20 per unit	£140,000	£160,000	£180,000
Required output (units)		7,500	8,500	9,500
Costs of production:		£	£	£
Direct materials	£6 per unit	45,000	51,000	57,000
Direct labour	£4 per unit	30,000	34,000	38,000
Fixed indirect		10,000	10,000	10,000
Variable indirect	£2 per unit	15,000	17,000	19,000
Total costs of production	£12 per unit + fixed indirect costs	£100,000	£112,000	£124,000

Figure 8.5

Flexible budget (2).

A Performance Report for ABC plc

	Master budget (9,000 units)	Actual	Flexible budget (8,000 units)	Variance
Sales (units)	9,000	8,000	8,000	
Sales (£)	180,000	162,000	160,000	2,000 Fav
Required output (units)	9,500	8,500	8,500	–
Costs of production:				
	£	£	£	£
Direct materials	57,000	52,000	51,000	1,000 Unf
Direct labour	38,000	32,000	34,000	2,000 Fav
Fixed indirect	10,000	10,500	10,000	500 Unf
Variable indirect	19,000	16,500	17,000	500 Fav
Total costs of production	£124,000	£111,000	£112,000	£1,000 Fav

The notion of the flexible budget should be used as the basis for all variance analysis, which is discussed in detail in Chapter 10. Meanwhile, we should bear in mind the distinction between fixed and variable costs and the need to predict accurately the behaviour of individual input and output items and their input-output relationships.

8.6 Budgeting for non-manufacturing organizations

The method of budgeting for newly established non-manufacturing and non-commercial organizations is essentially similar to that discussed above. In each case, the desired output or level of activity is first predicted and this determines the relevant costs and revenues. For instance, when budgeting for a hospital or dental service, the management accountant would first need to estimate the number of patients to be treated, the type of service required and the duration of treatment. From these estimates predictions could then be made as to expected hospital charges and the cost of the nursing, medical or dental resources required to cope with the workload.

However, for established non-manufacturing and service organizations, the budgeting process normally begins with the decision-makers calculating the expected costs of maintaining current ongoing activities and then making incremental changes to accommodate changes in the level of services provided. The various cost budgets will then need to be compared with the expected revenues. If insufficient resources are available, the organization may need to consider new means of fund-raising or revise their initial level of activity so that it can be financed from available funds. For instance, a local authority council may use its cost structure in 1992 as a basis for its 1993 budget. The council may decide to increase all input items by 10% and in addition increase the budget for childcare facilities and roadworks by a further 20% and 15% respectively. Having calculated the expected costs of providing the desired level of services the council will need to compare its expected costs with its expected revenues (which come mainly from rates and government grants). If there is a shortfall, the council may decide to levy a higher level of rates. However, the political consequences of a substantial rate increase will clearly need to be considered by councillors and their treasurers. If an acceptable rate increase still does not generate sufficient revenues the council may need to revise its initial expenditure budgets.

In Fig. 8.6 we show an example of a typical budget for a city council.

Similar budgets are produced by various ministerial departments. Usually these budgets are submitted for review by government officials a few months before the end of the previous financial year. They are then presented to Parliament some months into the financial year to which they relate. This means that by the time of presentation to Parliament many financial decisions have already been taken and funds committed to particular strategies. In any event, much government expenditure is usually already committed by custom or statute. There is thus little room for making discretionary cuts or increases. We give an example of a budget for the Australian Department of Trade in Fig. 8.7.

This budget shows that the 1993 estimates of expenditure for the Department

Figure 8.6

City council budget.

Mayfield Council
Budget Summary for 1993

	Gross revenue £	Gross expenditure £	Net expenditure £
Public works	50,000	800,000	(750,000)
Childcare facilities	150,000	450,000	(300,000)
Community welfare	600,000	1,000,000	(400,000)
Public services	300,000	1,700,000	(1,400,000)
Council properties	10,000	410,000	(400,000)
Parks and gardens	5,000	100,000	(95,000)
Miscellaneous purposes	150,000	850,000	(700,000)
Total	1,265,000	5,310,000	
Net expenditure			(4,045,000)
Other expenses:			
Loan repayments		350,000	
Purchases of capital assets		300,000	
Financial charges		500	
Transfers to reserves		1,000,000	
Contingency fund		100,000	(1,850,500)
Other revenues:			
Rates	4,084,000		
Sale of properties	45,500		
Sale of land	500,000		
Bequests	1,000		
	£5,895,500		£5,895,500

Figure 8.7

1993 budget for the Australian Department of Trade.

A/C code	Functional items	1993 Estimates	1992 Appropriation	1992 Expenses
		$	$	$
Salaries and payments in the nature of salary:				
A1	Salaries, wages, allowances	5,590,000	5,450,000	5,400,000
A2	Leave payments	72,300	55,000	46,550
A3	Overtime	93,000	86,000	85,550
		$5,755,300	$5,591,000	$5,532,100
Maintenance and working expenses:				
B1	Subsidiary staff charges	42,650	66,500	40,500
B2	Building charges	1,500,000	1,450,000	1,650,000
B3	Transport allowances	132,000	140,000	130,000
B4	General expenses	900,000	856,000	600,000
		$2,574,650	$2,512,500	$2,420,500
Other services:				
C1	Grants to regional boards	500,000	480,000	480,000
C2	Publications	65,000	50,000	55,000
C3	Purchase of motor vehicles	15,500	....	....
C4	Legal expenses	20,000	16,000	15,000
		$600,500	$546,000	$550,000
Total – Department of Trade		$8,930,450	$8,649,500	$8,502,600

of Trade total $8,930,450. These expenses are broken down into sub-expenses that are coded using A, B and C codes. Comparison figures are available for the previous financial year. These show that the amounts appropriated (set aside) in the 1991–1992 budget totalled $8,649,500 and the sum actually spent in that budget period was $8,502,600.

There is yet another reason why only small changes are made in the budgets of non-commercial organizations from year to year and why budgeting in such organizations usually starts with maintaining the existing level of activities. This is because in non-commercial organizations it is extremely difficult to measure outputs in fianancial terms. Because outputs are hard to measure, input–output relationships are difficult to predict. For instance, if a council decides to spend £100,000 improving its parks and gardens, by how much is community satisfaction increased? Will it significantly improve the council's chances at the next local election? Similarly, if the council does not set up a new kindergarten, by how much is the community disadvantaged? On account of these difficulties, budgeting in non-commercial and non-manufacturing organizations tends to be relatively conservative. Only small, incremental changes are made to inputs as the effects on outputs are hard to predict.

Another feature of the budgeting process is its emphasis on inputs (that is, on the control of expenditure). The budgeting process tends to compare actual cash inputs with budgeted cash inputs. For example, a local authority may compare actual expenditure on roadworks with budgeted expenditure. There is little emphasis on measures of output such as community welfare, an 'improved health and safety standard', 'a better quality of patient care', a more 'broad-based educational system'. Equally, there is little emphasis on managerial performance in output terms. Instead, budget managers are usually evaluated in terms of their ability to control input costs. Thus, a manager may be subjected to an *efficiency review* which essentially evaluates his/her ability to use resources efficiently. Measures of effectiveness, particularly in terms of the satisfaction of the needs of organizational members, are by comparison much neglected in non-commercial organizations. In recent years, however, increased efforts have been made to measure the effectiveness of non-commercial organizations. One of these newer budgeting tools is planning, programming, budgeting systems (PPBS).

(a) Planning, programming, budgeting systems

Planning, programming, budgeting systems (PPBS) have been introduced into non-commercial organizations to enable them to make more informed decisions about resource allocation. Budgets constructed within a PPBS differ from traditional non-manufacturing and non-commercial budgets in that they are constructed on the basis of *programmes* (that is, planned activities that have specified objectives). A local authority council may have the following programmes: the computerization of all rate accounts, the upgrading and extension of childcare facilities, an improvement of health facilities for mentally handicapped geriatrics, or the fluoridation of all the council's drinking water supplies. Each of these programmes will involve coordinating the work of several departments. For instance, the childcare programme may include:

(i) the construction of 3 new kindergartens;
(ii) the repair and extension of 5 existing kindergartens;
(iii) the employment of 10 new nursery school teachers;
(iv) the establishment of a childminding scheme that is based in the homes of mothers with young children of their own;
(v) the setting up of an occasional childcare centre;
(vi) the introduction of an hourly baby-sitting service.

The provision of all these services may involve the personnel, public works, community welfare, educational, health and social services departments. However, the budget for the programme calculates the estimated costs of the programme as a whole and does not relate costs solely to particular departments. Hence, a programme budget for childcare expenditure may look like Fig. 8.8.

The traditional budget for a non-commercial organization had been organized around items for a department or for an organization as a whole. Figure 8.9 is an example of such a traditional line item budget.

Compare this with a welfare budget that details how much is being spent on particular programmes, as in Fig. 8.10.

In the welfare programme budget, line/functional items for the whole department are not presented. Instead, the expenses associated with specific programmes

Figure 8.8

1993 Childcare Programme Expenditure Budget.

Mayfield Council

	£	£
Capital expenditure:		
Purchase of land	1,000,000	
Buildings	1,500,000	
Sub-total		2,500,000
Recurrent expenditure:		
Repairs	800,000	
Salaries and wages	900,000	
Supplies	80,000	
Rent	60,000	
Transport	50,000	
Sub-total		1,890,000
		£4,390,000

Figure 8.9

1993 Expense Budget for the Public Works Department.

Mayfield Council

	£
Salaries and wages	1,300,000
Depreciation	500,000
Supplies	600,000
Transport charges	25,000
Financing charges	1,000
Advertising charges	2,000
Other expenses	2,000
Total	£2,430,000

are detailed. This form of presentation has several advantages compared to traditional departmental/functional budgets:

(i) Programme budgets cut across departmental barriers and provide decision-makers with information that is specific to the activities carried out by the organization. Scarce resources and skilled personnel are usually located within specific departments. PPBS enable these diverse resources to be coordinated on a particular project or programme. In this way, they help to achieve an efficient use of resources.

(ii) PPBS also encourage decision-makers to identify explicitly and evaluate the activities which are carried out in terms of their efficiency and effectiveness.

(iii) PPBS enable decision-makers to recognize the long-term commitments made

Figure 8.10

1993 Welfare Budget.

	Mayfield Council Assistance to the handicapped	Assistance to the aged	Assistance to veterans
	£	£	£
Pensions and allowances	6,500,000	12,000,000	8,600,000
Home care services	3,000,000	5,000,000	2,500,000
Rehabilitation services	500,000	150,000	250,000
Equipment grants	1,450,000	90,000	10,000
Miscellaneous	8,000	2,000	1,500
Total	£11,458,000	£17,242,000	£11,361,500

in certain programmes. For instance, a childcare programme may involve capital expenditure over a five-year or ten-year period. In constructing the annual programme budget, a decision-maker will need to take into consideration resource projections and future demands and commitments. PPBS thus help to place the annual budget into a long-term context.

PPBS are built on a rational model of decision-making and usually consist of the following stages:

(i) Identify programme objectives and select performance measures. It is important that the objectives of a programme be clearly specified and output measures developed to assess the effectiveness of the programme. However, as discussed earlier, it is often difficult to develop these measures and this feature of PPBS is at once its strongest and weakest aspect. If a PPBS fails, it is usually due to a poor and inadequate specification of objectives.
(ii) Identify alternative methods of achieving the objectives set out in stage (i). For each alternative, the costs and benefits of implementation should be clearly set out.
(iii) Present proposals for acceptance. All budget proposals by non-commercial organizations such as government agencies will require bureaucratic and legislative approval. It is in the process of securing such approval that the budget will be subjected to a range of interpretations and political negotiation among different interest groups.
(iv) Implement the selected alternative and monitor performance. Once a programme budget has been approved, its implementation needs to be carefully monitored to ensure that the situation does not become 'out of control'. Comparisons between actual and budgeted performance, therefore, need to be continually made and corrective action taken in order to ensure that the programmes' objectives are achieved given the resources allocated to those programmes.

How useful are PPBS? These programme budgets were first used in the United States in the 1960s and appeared to be generally effective in the US Department of Defense. However, the department performed badly in the 1970s and it has been argued that PPBS contributed to this poor performance. In particular, it was suggested that setting objectives and output measures was simply too difficult for some government departments and that it led to a rigidity in outlook. At times objective-setting became a ritualistic exercise in which little real attention was paid to the objectives that were documented. Nevertheless, despite these reservations and criticisms, PPBS continue to be widely used in Western government agencies. In some countries the systems have been modified to avoid some of the problems experienced in the USA and PPBS do appear to serve some useful planning function. (See also the discussion in Chapter 6, pp. 167–8, dealing with ZBB).

8.7 Capital budgeting

So far, we have been discussing annual budgets. There are also capital budgets – these are used to plan an organization's long-run flow of funds. Capital decisions (as we saw in Chapter 6) usually involve large sums of money, have long time-spans and carry some degree of risk and uncertainty. For instance, an organization may need to decide whether to purchase another organization, acquire new plant and equipment or invest in new production technologies. Should it build new warehouses, roads, staff accommodation, schools, canteens or hospitals?

A capital budgeting decision, if made in a rational mode, follows the same series of steps as that we discussed in Chapter 3:

(i) identify objectives;
(ii) search for alternative investment opportunities;
(iii) list possible outcomes;
(iv) develop measures of these outcomes;
(v) evaluate opportunities in terms of these measures;
(vi) select investment opportunities;
(vii) implement investment projects;
(viii) monitor and review investment decisions.

Let us suppose that Organization X, which is an accounting practice, wishes to expand by taking over another similar accounting practice. Organization X should first consider what it wishes to achieve by such a take-over – is it to buy new expertise, for instance, in the computing audit or insolvency areas? Is it to acquire a chain of offices in locations that it does not presently service? Or is it simply to add on identical services on a larger scale? Having decided upon its main objective, Organization X should draw up a list of prospective practices to take over. It should then attempt to elucidate the possible outcomes associated with taking over each of these practices and measure these outcomes as best it can in order to select the 'best'. Having selected a practice, negotiations can then begin with the owners on a suitable purchase price.

Note that this description of a decision-making process is based on an assumption that people act in particular ways. As pointed out in Chapters 1–3, this image of decision-making may only represent an ideal that may not be achieved in practice. You should always bear this in mind in any discussion of decision-making.

While a management accountant may be involved in all aspects of making such a capital decision, his/her input is especially required in making decisions such as:

(i) Which investment projects should be selected?
(ii) What are the financial and non-financial outcomes associated with a particular investment strategy?
(iii) How are the projects to be financed?

You will already be familiar with the kinds of information that may be provided to help answer these questions. The subject area is covered in the companion volume *Financial Management: Method and Meaning*, Chapters 4–6. Given this, and our earlier coverage in Chapter 6, we shall not discuss capital budgeting in any more detail in this book.

8.8 Budgeting and human processes

As a technical process, budgeting often becomes a relatively straightforward and routine process in organizations. The more problematic issues, however, arise when budgets are used by various organizational participants to interpret, organize, manage and make sense of the world around them and their intentions and goals. We shall discuss the 'human side of budgets', under two broad headings: the individual and organizational aspects of budgeting.

(a) Budgets and individuals

There has been considerable research in this area which has focused on two main questions: what is the impact of budgets on work attitudes and performance and how should budgets be designed to minimize undesired effects? The first question may be labelled descriptive or positive as it seeks to find out 'what is'; the second may be referred to as normative as it seeks to discover an optimum budgeting system (i.e. 'what should be').

(i) Budgets and motivation
One of the earliest 'what is' questions that researchers asked was: how do budgets influence the motivation of people at work? By motivation, we mean the 'force' or the energy which prompts people to act in particular ways. Hence, the question above may be rephrased as: how do budgets influence people's desire to act in a certain manner?

One of the earlier studies on budgeting is closely related to a body of psychological research called *goal setting theory* (see Locke, *et al.* 1981; Mento, *et al.* 1980). Essentially goal setting theory states that people will perform better if they are given specific targets (goals) that are relatively difficult. Specific, difficult goals were invariably found to lead to higher performance levels than general or 'do your best' goals. The goal, however, must not be so difficult that it is rejected by the individual concerned; it must be accepted by him/her.

A budget target represents a specific goal that is usually assigned to a budgetee (the person responsible for meeting the budget). The question which arose was: did the existence of a budget target lead to or motivate higher levels of performance? A well-known study by Stedry (1960) investigated this issue and demonstrated that, in a simulated budgetary situation, the formulation of a specific target did improve performance. However, the precise effect of the budget target was influenced by the individual's own personal goal or *aspiration level*.

Individuals who were given a high (that is, difficult) budget target achieved high levels of performance only if they stated their personal aspiration level after they had received their budget target. Those who stated their aspirations, which were lower than the budget target, before receiving the difficult budget performed very poorly. That is, A stated an aspiration level of 100 wins but was given a budget target of 150 wins. A performed poorly. B was given a budget target of 150 wins and then stated an aspiration level of 160 wins. B performed well. This result was cited as an example of individuals with low aspirations rejecting difficult budget targets as 'too difficult' and 'unrealistic'. The implication of this research is that budget targets should be set on an individual basis and should take into consideration the aspiration levels of particular individuals.

However, this study should be read with caution because the research was conducted as an experiment which used as respondents students who were given a monetary reward based on performance. A simulation of an organizational setting always remains a simulation, with constraints on its applicability to a real-life organizational setting. Nevertheless, despite these caveats, the study did demonstrate some points that are consonant with goal setting theory. These are:

- Budgets have no motivation effect unless they are accepted by a budgetee. That is, the budget target must be in line with an individual's own aspiration level.
- As long as budget targets are accepted, the more difficult the target, the higher the level of performance that will be achieved.
- Difficult but specific budget targets are also perceived as being more relevant to organizational decision-making than budgets that are easily achievable (that is, 'loose' budgets). However, if a budget target is seen as being 'unrealistic' performance may decline dramatically.
- Budgets are likely to be accepted where good upward (from subordinates to superiors) communication exists. The use of departmental meetings was found to be helpful in communicating budget targets to budgetees and in facilitating their acceptance by the people involved.
- Cultural, organizational and personality factors all affect an individual manager's reaction to a budget target.

(ii) Budgets and participation

As can be seen, whether a budget target is accepted by an individual is crucial to the success or failure of a budgeting system. If targets are not accepted work performance could be much worse than when a budget target had not been set. This has prompted some research into how a budgetee may be persuaded to 'accept' a budget target. Again, much of this budgeting research owes its origins to ideas that have been debated in the psychological literature, particularly in the area of human relations/resource management. We shall review briefly some of the work in this area before proceeding to discuss how this research has influenced studies of the budgetary process.

In the 1960s a number of psychologists (like Maslow, Herzberg, McGregor and McClelland) were advocating that managers should place a greater emphasis on the *higher-order needs* of individuals. This concept stems from the work of Maslow (1954) who presented a hierarchy of needs such as that shown below in Fig. 8.11.

Maslow's theory of needs consists of the following main points:

Figure 8.11

Maslow's hierarchy of human needs.

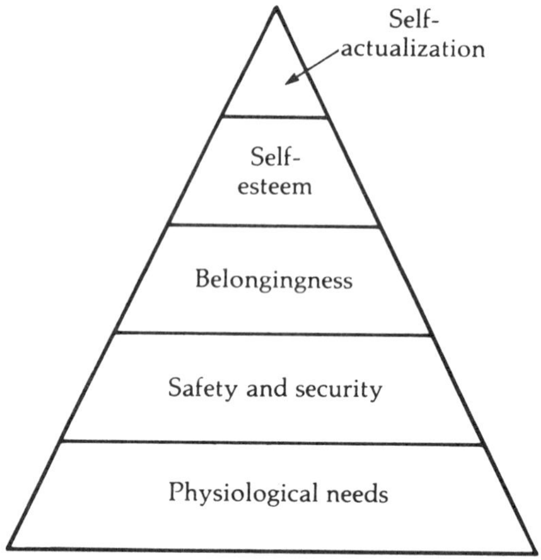

(i) Human beings have only a limited number of needs. These are arranged in a hierarchy, progressing from physiological to self-actualization, as follows:
   - *physiological*: the need for food, drink, relief from pain;
   - *safety and security*: the need for freedom from threat;
   - *belongingness*: the need for friendship, affiliation, love;
   - *esteem*: the need for self-esteem and esteem from others;
   - *self-actualization*: the need to fulfil oneself by using one's innate potential to the fullest.

(ii) People will seek to satisfy their lower-order needs first before seeking to satisfy higher-order needs.

(iii) Once a need has been satisfied it no longer acts as a motivator. Thus, when a person decides that he or she is earning enough money for the level of contributions required by the organization, money loses its power to motivate higher levels of performance.

(iv) Most people have already satisfied their basic needs but have unfulfilled higher-order needs. Maslow proposed that the typical adult has satisfied 85% of the physiological need, 70% of the safety and security need, 50% of the belongingness need, 40% of the esteem need but only 10% of the self-actualization need. Therefore, in order to motivate people, it is important to concentrate on meeting their unfulfilled self-actualization needs. In short, people have an inbuilt need to grow, develop and maximize their potential and this need is often unsatisfied.

Maslow's ideas have been the subject of much criticism but they appear intuitively appealing and have been influential. In addition, Maslow's ideas appear to be supported by the work of Herzberg and McGregor. Herzberg, *et al.* (1959) argued that factors such as salary, job security and other working conditions did not motivate employees. Instead, employees were *energized* by motivators such as a sense of achievement, advancement, responsibility, the possibility of growth and of recognition within the workplace. Similarly, McGregor (1960) advocated that managers should seek to operate with a Theory Y version of people. Theory Y assumes that people are usually committed to self-actualization goals, and seek job responsibility, autonomy and creativity at work. This is in contrast to Theory X which assumes that, on average, people lack ambition, dislike job responsibilities, prefer close supervision, intrinsically dislike work and will try and avoid it as much as possible. McGregor argues that managers, by operating with Theory Y, will seek to involve employees in all phases of the management process and thereby increase their (the employees') commitment to the organization's goals and their level of work performance.

The theories of motivation offered by these three authors are sometimes referred to as *content theories of motivation*. This is because they focus on the factors within the person that energize, direct and sustain behaviour. They attempt to specify the needs which motivate people. Essentially, content theories argue that for the average person, his/her lower-order needs have been satisfied and hence these do not motivate employees. This distinction between non-motivating lower-order needs (or *hygiene factors*, to use Herzberg's term) and motivating higher-order needs is further developed by *process theories of motivation*.

Process theories of motivation seek to study how individual behaviour is energized and directed. One of the more influential process theories is called *expectancy theory* (see Vroom, 1964). Expectancy theory has three main concepts:

- *expectancy* – the probability that a given level of effort will result in high performance;
- *valence* – the utility or desirability of an outcome or reward such as salary increase, promotion, low-cost housing loans, etc.;
- *instrumentality* – the probability that high performance will lead to outcomes such as promotion, salary increase.

The expectancy theory of motivation is illustrated in Fig. 8.12.

As shown, an individual's effort is directed towards achieving a level of performance. Performance is sometimes labelled a *first-order outcome*. This outcome (that is, performance) has a certain valence (utility) for the individual. This valence depends on the individual's probability estimate that performance will lead to a series of *second-order outcomes* (for example, promotion, salary increase) and the valences associated with these outcomes.

Second-order outcomes are divided into two main types: extrinsic and intrinsic outcomes. Extrinsic outcomes are those controlled by others such as salary increase, career advancement, fringe benefits. Intrinsic outcomes are those that adhere to the performance of the work itself, for instance, a sense of satisfaction with the work done, enjoyment, pride, self-esteem. As can be seen, this distinction between extrinsic and intrinsic second-order outcomes is very similar to the content theories' notions of higher-order and lower-order needs. However, in contrast to the content theories, expectancy theory does not predict that the average employee has sufficient extrinsic rewards and will not be motivated by them. Instead, expectancy theory argues that the motivating strength of these extrinsic

Figure 8.12

The expectancy theory of motivation.

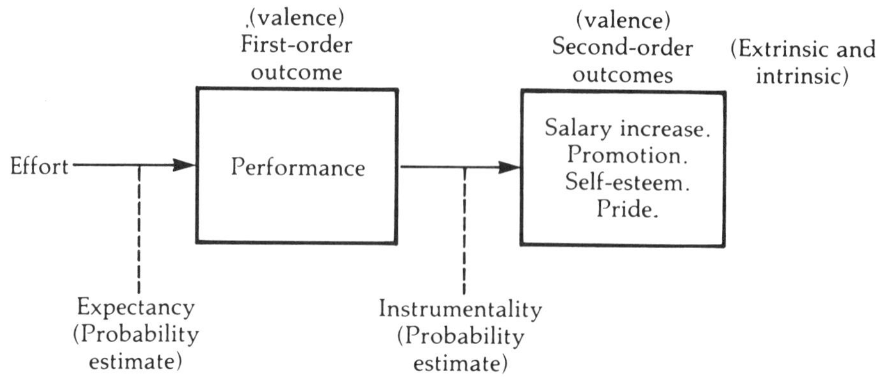

rewards will depend on the valence of these rewards and the associated expectancies and instrumentalities.

The probability estimate that effort will lead to performance is called expectancy or the E-P probability. The probability estimate that performance will lead to second-order outcomes is called instrumentality or the P-O probability.

According to this theory of motivation, what an individual does may be represented through a three-stage mental process. This process may be consciously or subconsciously performed. The individual will ask three questions:

- How much do I value the various second-level outcomes that are offered? (Valence)
- Will the first-level outcome (high performance) lead to the second-level outcomes? (Instrumentality)
- Will the exertion of effort actually lead to high performance? (Expectancy)

And the manager in seeking to motivate employees should do the following (see Nadler and Lawler, 1977):

- Determine what outcomes are important to each employee.
- Clearly identify what behaviour and performance levels are desired. The subordinate should fully understand the manager's expectations in this respect.
- Establish levels of performance that are challenging yet attainable.
- Link important and desired second-order outcomes to desired performance levels.
- Ensure that changes in second-order outcomes are large enough. Small changes often result in very small increases in effort.

Like the content theories of motivation, expectancy theory has a number of difficulties. One of the major problems is adequate testing of the entire expectancy model using representative work groups. However, despite difficulties, expectancy theory, like the content theories of motivation, appears to offer some advice to practising managers and accountants. It indicates that managers need to determine what outcomes are valued by employees. In addition, content theories of motivation suggest that at the workplace most people have already satisfied their lower-order needs and hence can be motivated only by activities that help satisfy their higher-order needs (for instance, through participating in decision-making).

Such participation should enable an employee to have greater influence over the activities of the organization and enable him/her to exercise innovation and autonomy at the workplace. Theoretically, by appealing to the higher-order need of an employee for self-actualization, participation should lead to greater levels of organizational commitment and work performance. This emphasis on participation in decision-making at the workplace has given rise to notions such as worker directors and participative management. It has also led to an implementation of participative budgeting. Participative budgeting usually means that the budgetee helps to set the budget target. That is, budgeting is not a strict top-down or bottom-up approach but both subordinates and superiors are involved from the beginning of the budget process.

It is argued that by allowing employees to participate in budgeting the following benefits would accrue:

- Budgetees who participate in setting budget targets will be more likely to accept them than if targets were imposed by senior managers.
- Through participation, a budgetee's job is enriched and he/she takes on added responsibilities. This increased job content may be interpreted by an employee as formal recognition of his/her abilities and lead to greater job satisfaction and higher levels of self-esteem.
- Budgetees who participate are likely to have more positive attitudes towards the organization as a whole, which should lead to higher levels of performance and morale.
- Participation should ensure that employees who have the greatest knowledge of local conditions and difficulties will take part in budget formulation. This should lead to more accurate budgeting and predictions of the future.
- Participation should decrease the likelihood of information distortion and manipulation.

These arguments may be supported by reference to both content and expectancy theories of motivation. From the viewpoint of Maslow's need hierarchy, participation allows employees to achieve higher-order needs such as self-esteem and self-actualization. From the standpoint of expectancy theory, participation allows an individual to predict clearly the probability estimates associated with obtaining the final rewards (expectancy and instrumentality). This should lead to a higher level of motivation. In addition, the process of involvement in decision-making may enhance the intrinsic rewards connected with work performance. (Remember that there may be both intrinsic and extrinsic rewards.)

(iii) Does participation work?

The short answer is that it does and it does not! The connections between participation, work attitudes and performance are highly complex and we do not have all the necessary answers to predict the effect that participation has on people. There appear to be a number of variables involved and we shall look at each of these relationships in turn.

First, what effect does participation have on work attitudes? Research consistently shows that participation has a positive effect on attitudes towards the budget, the job and even the organization (Milani, 1975; Collins, 1978; Cherrington and Cherrington, 1973; French *et al*. 1960). Employees who do participate in budgeting usually report higher levels of satisfaction at work. In addition, Hopwood (1972) suggests that where employees did participate, they felt less job-related tension and had better relations with their superiors and colleagues.

Second, what effect does participation have on performance? Here the answers are extremely mixed. Some studies (Argyris, 1952; Bass and Leavitt, 1963; Kenis, 1979) have found that budgetary performance was better when budgetees participated in the budgetary process. However, work by Milani (1975), Morse and Reimer (1956) and Bryan and Locke (1967) found that the association between participation and performance was weak and even negative. That is, participation appeared to lead to lower levels of performance.

These mixed responses have prompted other work to be undertaken that sought to discover what factors influenced the relationship between participation and performance. Brownell (1981), for instance, argued that budgetary participation has a positive effect on performance when budgetees have certain personality traits. In particular, if they were people who felt that they had a large degree of control over their own destiny. Other personality traits studied include that of authoritarianism. It was argued that participation is most effective for people who are low authoritarians (Vroom, 1960). Recently, Chenhall (1986) has indicated that participative budgeting leads to higher levels of job satisfaction when both subordinates and superiors display the same levels of authoritarianism, be that high or low. Unfortunately he did not study the effect on performance. (See also Harrison (1991).)

To conclude, participation has been found to be positively related to increased morale, better acceptance of the budget, and favourable attitudes toward the organization and the job. However, it does not always lead to higher levels of performance. There appear to be personality and possibly organizational and cultural factors that influence the relationship between participation and performance.

(iv) Budgets and feedback

Budgets (and especially budget variances) also play another important informational role in organizations. They provide feedback control, that is they enable decision-makers to evaluate their performance against expectations and to take appropriate corrective action. Feedback about the effectiveness of an individual's actions has long been recognized in the psychological literature as essential for learning, for improving motivation and performance (Sassenrath, 1975; Ilgen *et al*. 1979). In general, feedback is postively associated with performance (Cook, 1968). However, there are numerous 'ifs and buts' to this general statement. As may be expected, the relationship between feedback and performance is a complex one. In addition, this psychological research on feedback has not been applied explicitly in a budgetary setting. As a result, much of the research on feedback provides only suggestive evidence on the role which budgets play in providing feedback information.

What inferences may be drawn about the relationship between budgetary feedback and performance? Psychological research indicates the following:

- The longer the delay in the receipt of feedback the less the effect of feedback on performance. Budget reports should therefore be provided fairly soon after a certain activity has occurred in order to provide prompt feedback on any differences between actual and expected performance.
- Positive feedback (that is, good news) is perceived and recalled more accurately than negative feedback (bad news). This suggests that budgetary performance that is below expectations, which may be perceived as 'bad news', may need to be carefully relayed and discussed in order that it is clearly understood by both superiors and subordinates. It is usually recommended that specific feedback should be provided so as to leave less room for distortion.
- In general, the more frequent the feedback the better is performance. This suggests that budgetary reports should be prepared fairly frequently. However, care must be taken not to report too frequently as budgetees may feel a loss of personal control and fail to rely on their own skill in judging their own performance.
- The source of the feedback (that is, the person giving the feedback) is of the utmost importance. To be accepted, feedback must come from a person who is regarded as credible and who is trusted by the receiver of feedback. Thus, a budgetee must trust his superior and the accounting information which he receives. If a budgetee feels that the budgetary information has been manipulated or is based on suspect assumptions, he/she may not accept that feedback.
- Feedback on a task should relate mainly to those aspects of the task which are within the control and responsibility of the individual concerned, not that of the technology, the outside environment or the work of others. This suggests that budgetary information should highlight the areas of performance which are within the control and responsibility of the budgetee.
- Individual personality traits influence the perception and acceptance of feedback. For instance, people who believe that they are in control of their destiny performed better when feedback was supplied by another person. By contrast, people who believe that others are in control of their fate preferred feedback through 'self-discovery' (see Baron *et al.* 1974). Even the age of recipients of feedback appears to influence the degree to which feedback is accepted (Meyer and Walker, 1961). Older persons used feedback less than younger ones.

  These research results suggest that, to be effective, budgetary feedback must be given in a manner which takes account of individual differences in reactions to feedback. There is a need to modify the nature of feedback to fit the individuals for whom it is intended. For instance, high performers and low performers should have budgetary feedback of varying frequency, detail and regularity.

As discussed, we have little research evidence on the role of budgets as a form of feedback. There is therefore much research to be done in this area. Indeed, one of the first questions we have to ask is whether budgetary feedback as it stands is an effective (that is, leads to appropriate corrective action) form of feedback. Budgetary feedback usually consists of a deviation figure – the difference between expected and actual performance. This may be seen as a form of 'outcome feedback' and some psychological research has shown that this is one of the most ineffective forms of feedback. Other more effective forms of feedback might include feedback on the nature of the task and on the environment which resulted in the difference.

(b) Budgets and groups

Moving from an analysis of the effects of budgets on individual behaviour we shall now take a brief look at the operation of budgets in groups. One of the major studies in this area was conducted by Becker and Green (1962) who looked at the relationship between participative budgeting and performance, with group cohesiveness as an intervening (a 'middle') variable. A group is a cohesive group when group members value their group membership highly and accept the norms of the group in order to continue to enjoy acceptance by other members of the group.

Participation increases interaction among employees. If this increased interaction leads to greater group cohesiveness, and if the group norm is to perform at a high level, then participative budgeting will tend to be positively associated with high levels of performance. However, if the group norm is to perform at a low level, participation, in encouraging acceptance of this group norm, may in fact lead to lower levels of performance. In other words, the following circumstances must hold in order that, say, group A will achieve high levels of performance:

(i) A's norm is to improve its previous year's budgetary performance by 25%;
(ii) A is a cohesive group in which all members believe in achieving the norm of the group;
(iii) group A participates in setting budget targets.

However, if A's norm is to achieve a performance level that is 5% lower than the previous year's level, then participative budgeting is likely to lead to low levels of performance.

In summary, group norms may play an important role in influencing the effect which budgets have on work performance and attitudes.

(i) Budgets and political and symbolic processes in organizations

Budgets become involved in the political and symbolic processes in organizations for two main reasons:

- budgets are concerned with the allocation of scarce resources; and
- budget performance is often used as a means whereby superiors evaluate subordinates' performance and competence.

Because of these two reasons budgets often become both the basis and the means through which employees seek to achieve their particular goals, such as to make themselves look good to superiors or to assert and increase their power position within the organization. These political and symbolic effects of budgets should not necessarily be seen as being dysfunctional or atypical. Indeed, they are inevitable given that budgets touch on two central issues in social life: the distribution of scarce resources and of wealth (that is, of rewards and sanctions). We should expect that budgets (like other social phenomena) would become entangled in the political and sense-making web of organizational experience. We shall analyse these processes under more specific headings.

(ii) Budgets, slack and misinformation

Because budgets are used to measure employee performance, managers and workers may seek to protect themselves by creating *budgetary slack* (that is, by obtaining some spare resources which act as a buffer against unexpected demands). Slack effectively acts as a cushion that enables a budgetee to avoid the likely penalties of failing to meet budget targets and may be created by underestimating sales revenue or overestimating costs in budget requests (Schiff and Lewin, 1970). There is some evidence that slack building is cyclical with budgetees satisfying their personal goals through the use of slack in 'good' years and reconverting this slack into profits in 'bad' years (Williamson, 1964).

In order to create slack, budgetees often bias their budget estimates. One of the major studies on budget bias was conducted by Lowe and Shaw (1968). They defined bias as the extent to which a forecaster adjusts his forecast due to his own personal interests and independently of factors which might influence the actual result. They found that there were three main reasons why bias occurred:

- managers were evaluated on the basis of performance measured against budget expectations;
- managers were expected to follow an implicit organizational norm of continued growth and expansion; and
- some managers felt psychologically insecure because their recent performance had been poor. This caused them to give over-optimistic budget forecasts. These managers felt that by promising improved future performance they might continue to obtain the approval of their superiors.

Given these circumstances, managers biased their budget estimates because it was economically rational for them to do so. Through biasing they sought to improve their chances of obtaining organizational rewards and of avoiding penalities.

Besides the Lowe and Shaw study, other studies have shown that subordinate managers consistently bias and distort the information provided to senior managers in order that they might not be informed of unfavourable performance (Read, 1962). Because bias appears pervasive it is not surprising that research has shown that superiors often consciously counter-bias budget estimates supplied by subordinates (Lowe and Shaw, 1968). However, the study also indicated that counter-bias does not always remove all elements of bias in budget targets.

Besides these conscious attempts at bias, budget estimates may be subject to errors in estimation. For example, it has been shown that the level of sales budgeted tended to be an underestimate when sales were rising and an overestimate when sales were falling (Lowe and Shaw, 1968). These estimation errors are also likely to increase in times of uncertainty. The more uncertain and complex a forecasting situation, the greater the likelihood that forecasting errors will arise. Hence, constant supervision of budget relevance is necessary and the use of flexible budgets is especially needed in times of change. Dealing with these problems is discussed on pp. 42–3 above and pp. 335–42 below.

(iii) Budgets and legitimated authority

Budgets typically follow the formal hierarchy of authority in an organization. That is, budgets proposed by subordinates are reviewed by superiors and budgetary performance is used by superiors to assess the performance of subordinates. This association between budgets and formal or legitimated authority means that, at times, managerial styles may significantly influence the operation of budgets.

Hopwood (1974a), for instance, found that a *budget-constrained* style of leadership, in which the supervisor evaluated subordinates primarily on whether they achieved short-term budget targets, led to high levels of job-related tension, poor relationships between superiors and subordinates and among peers, and accounting data manipulation. In addition, there were low levels of innovation and service to customers was of a poor quality. By contrast, a *profit-conscious* style did not lead to such effects. This is a style in which budgetary information is used in conjunction with other information in a flexible approach to performance evaluation. (We pick this up again in more detail in Section 10.5 of Chapter 10.) It has been noted that Hopwood's results have not been replicated in subsequent studies (Otley, 1978), and it is likely that there are other factors at work. Hirst (1981) and Brownell and Hirst (1986) suggest that task uncertainty may be one such factor. Specifically, in tasks which are highly ambiguous and uncertain, a rigid adherence to budgetary information as a means of performance evaluation would not be helpful. On the other hand, in tasks which are low in uncertainty, a budget-constrained style may be more appropriate.

(iv) Budgets and organizational politics and symbolism

Budgets are not only implicated in the authority relationship between superiors and subordinates; they also give us powerful insights into the political struggles that characterize all organizations. As pointed out in Chapter 1, organizations are coalitions of people with diverse aims and who compete for scarce resources. In the process of obtaining these resources alliances are formed, friends persuaded and enemies created through battles over budget allocations. And budget allocations often represent political compromises. As such, they are often the outcomes of political contests rather than the result of the application of 'rational', neutral decision rules (Wildavsky, 1979; Hills and Mahoney, 1978). As Wildavsky puts it:

> If organizations are viewed as political coalitions, budgets are mechanisms through which subunits bargain over conflicting goals, make side-payments, and try to motivate one another to accomplish their objectives.
>
> Wildavsky, 1968, p. 193.

This view of budgets as the outcome of political struggles rather than 'rational' rules has been supported by several studies on university budgeting (Pfeffer and Salancik, 1974; Pfeffer and Moore, 1980; Hills and Mahoney, 1978). These studies showed that budget allocations were directly related to the power possessed by each department. Indeed, this research indicated that budget allocations were not only independent of changes in the workload of departments but were actually negatively related to changes in teaching demands over the period (Pfeffer and Salancik, 1974).

Similar research by Boland and Pondy (1983) also suggests that budgets are open to all kinds of political manipulation. They provide an example of how the Governor of Illinois, having made a pre-election promise of a 10% increase in academic salaries, 'fiddled' the numbers such that the 10% increase was actually achieved through a *real* (that is, inflation-adjusted) decrease in academic salaries. In addition, it has been argued that one of the most important functions of budgets is to reinforce existing power relations in organizations. Budgets, through mirroring the authority structure, help reinforce the power of superiors (Burchell, *et al.* 1980). However, other research argues that this reinforcement may be less than initially thought because budgets are also used by subordinates to counter-control their superiors (Covaleski and Dirsmith, 1983).

Such research has prompted some researchers to talk about two 'theories of budgeting' (Covaleski, *et al.* 1985). The first theory of budgeting corresponds to the ideas presented earlier in this chapter. That is, budgeting is a device that can be used as a rational means of allocating resources and of achieving feedforward and feedback control. This is, if you like, the public, front-stage image of budgeting. However, there is a private, back-stage image of budgeting. This second theory views budgets not as rational allocation and control devices but as forms and sources of power and political processes. In this second view a budget is primarily a political tool for resolving conflict and a means for negotiation in organizations.

Some researchers feel that the second view of budgeting provides a more realistic picture of the role which budgets actually play in organizations (Cooper, *et al.* 1981; Burchell, *et al.* 1980; Hayes, 1983). To them the public, rational image of budgeting is but an empty symbol, a myth that hides the 'real' role of budgeting in organizational politics. Budgeting, then, is not usually based on neutral, economically rational rules, such as 'allocate the most resources to those areas that generate the most income'. Instead, budget allocations are determined mainly on the basis of which departments have the greatest power and influence within the organization.

Our position on this matter is similar to that of Covaleski, *et al.* (1985). Both the public, rational face of budgeting and its private, political face are valid, 'real' faces. Both are equally relevant in helping us to understand the roles which budgets play in organizational life. Budgets, then, are Janus-like. They have two faces; at times one may dominate and at other times the other may come into play. Covaleski *et al.* describe how, in a health-care delivery service, some organizational members genuinely used and applied the theory that budgets were rational resource allocation devices. Other members, however, saw and used budgets primarily as political tools.

In a similar dual role, budgets may be used as plans for the future or the budgetary process may be used as a means of making sense of the present (Boland and Pondy, 1983). Boland and Pondy argue that when an organization does not face substantive change the budgeting process serves as a planning tool for the future. However, when there are unexpected threats it may be used both to make sense of the present and to plan for the future. They give an example of a university that was threatened with large cuts in government funding and reduced student numbers. In the face of such uncertainty the university found that it could not adequately budget for the future because it did not even know what it was currently trying to do given the reductions in funding. The budgetary process then did not function as a planning tool. Instead, it enabled organizational members to reclarify their central values and beliefs about the role of the university. The budgetary process then became a means of making sense of the present.

In conclusion, we may make the following points about the relationship between budgets and human processes in organizations:

- Budgets affect individuals' work attitudes and their level of performance.
- These individual effects are moderated or influenced by group norms, organizational and societal norms and beliefs.
- Budgets are a Janus-faced social phenomenon. There is a public, rational face and a private, political face. Both are equally real and operative in organizational life.

Summary

In this chapter we have discussed the following:

(a) the role of budgets in helping to achieve feedforward and feedback control;
(b) the technical process of budgeting, especially for manufacturing organizations;
(c) the roles which budgets play within the human and social processes of an organization.

Essentially, it was argued that budgets have multiple roles. Some of these accord with a traditional view of budgets as rational devices to achieve feedforward and feedback control, while other roles focus on the politics and symbolism of organizational interactions. Budgets are therefore Janus-faced, being both rational and non-rational, and forming both the source of power and the medium through which power is exercised within organizations.

Budgeting is one of the primary means of resource allocation within an organization. Not only is it important to understand the techniques associated with budgeting in commercial and non-commercial organization; it is equally relevant that we are aware of the human processes associated with budgeting processes. In this chapter, we have attempted to introduce budgets as a formal, rational means of feedforward and feedback control. At the same time, we have tried to illustrate how budgets may not always be used in this rational mode. People, as individuals and groups, have particular interests and goals. The precise role played by a budget will depend on how these interests work themselves out in complex organizational processes and events.

Key terms and concepts

Here is a list of the key terms and concepts which have featured in this chapter. You should make sure that you understand and can define each one of them. Page references to definitions in the text appear in bold in the index.

- Budget
  - capital
  - flexible
  - master
  - negotiation
  - slack
- Budgeting
  - top down
  - bottom up
- Key success factors
- Motivation
  - level of aspiration
  - hierarchy of needs
  - content theories
  - process theories
- Organizational culture/climate
- Participation
- Power
  - bargaining
  - formal vs. informal
- Planning Programming Budgeting System (PPBS)
- Responsibility accounting
- Variance

Further reading

On motivation theory, see Maslow (1954), McGregor (1960), Locke, *et al.* (1981) and Lawler and Rhode (1976).

On human processes in budgeting, see Hopwood (1972), Lowe and Shaw (1968), Stedry (1960), Schiff and Lewin (1970), Argyris (1952), Wildavsky (1968), Hofstede (1967), Cyert and March (1963), Brownell (1981), Chenhall (1986), Brownell and Hirst (1986), Covaleski and Dirsmith (1986), Boland and Pondy (1983), Collins, *et al.* (1987); Harwood, *et al.* (1991), and Brownell and Dunk (1991).

On budgeting in non-commercial organizations, see Novick (1973).

The workbook to accompany this chapter begins on p. 546.

PART 3 Feedback control

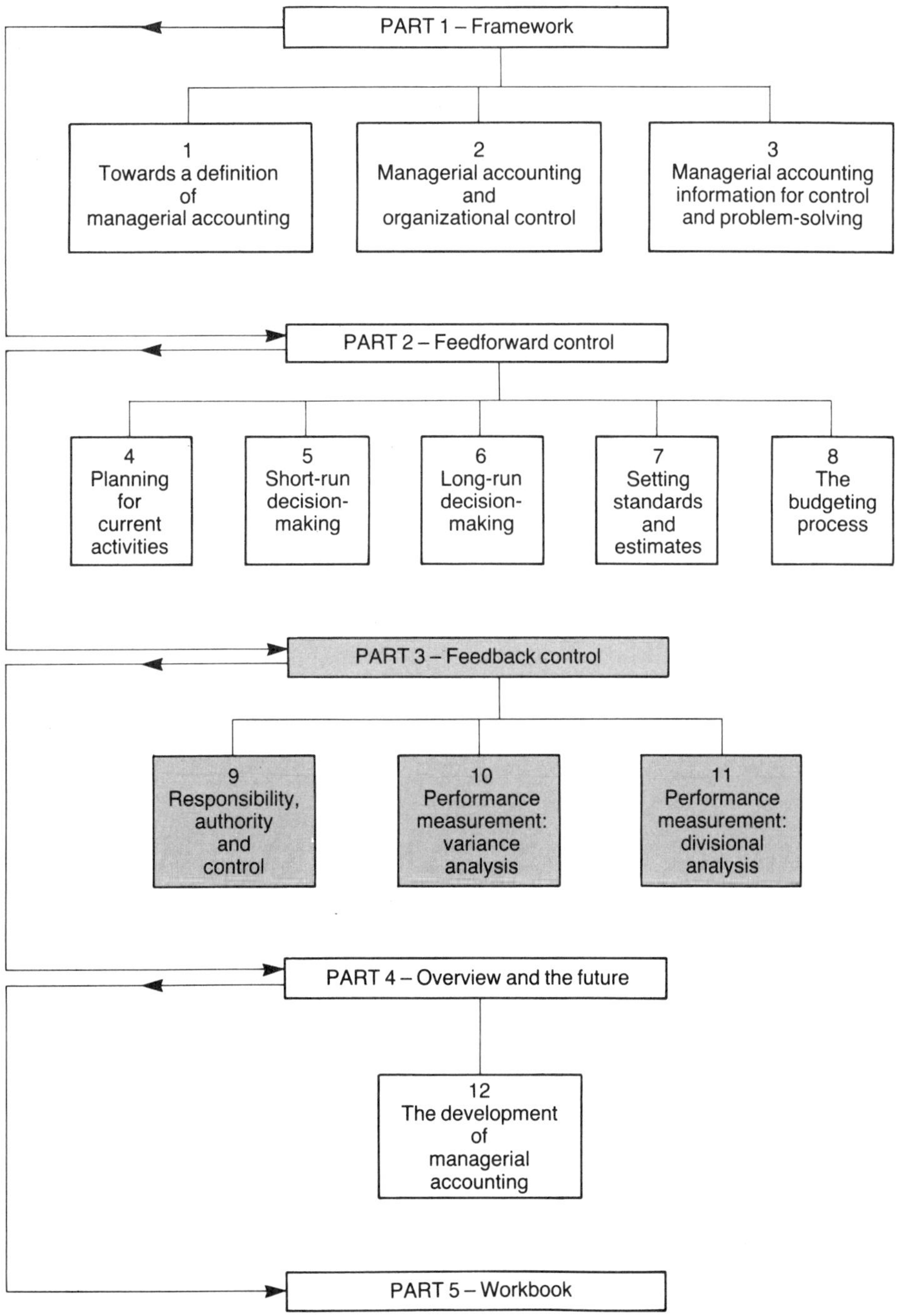

Introduction and overview

Part 3 consists of Chapters 9 to 11 and develops the theme of feedback control that was initially introduced in Chapter 3.

There is an inevitable lag in feedback systems between outcomes and responses: while feedforward systems require *proactive* behaviour, feedback systems rely on *reactive* behaviour. In other words, feedforward systems *anticipate* the need for change whereas feedback systems *adapt* to change.

To be effective a feedback control system must be integrated with the organization's structure: we can only control through people. This theme has been present since Chapter 1, but Chapter 9 takes it further. In its coverage of responsibility accounting it pays particular attention to setting prices for transfers of goods and services among the divisions of a decentralized organization, and to the behavioural consequences of the prices set.

Chapters 10 and 11 take up the theme of performance measurement. In essence this topic revolves around the comparison of actual outcomes with desired (e.g. standard or budgeted) outcomes, and the significance of any discrepancies. This significance is partly of a statistical kind (i.e. whether the discrepancy was due to chance as opposed to an assignable cause) and partly behavioural: people react in ways that are often unpredictable as well as undesirable when their performance is being assessed.

As one approach to regulating the behaviour of individuals within organizations there are often procedures that are prescribed and these facilitate *internal control* (e.g. over matters such as the handling of cash receipts). This is associated with, but distinct from, *internal audit* (which, in turn, has links to the external — or statutory — audit, but which is also distinct). We do not deal with these in this book but we do need to ask *quis custodiet ipsos custodes* (who is to guard the guardians themselves)?

CHAPTER 9 Responsibility, authority and control

Learning objectives

After studying this chapter you should be able to:

- understand the principles of responsibility accounting;
- explain the role of responsibility accounting in decentralized organizations;
- calculate transfer prices;
- discuss the motivational and organizational aspects of transfer pricing.

9.1 Introduction

Thus far we have concentrated on certain managerial accounting techniques such as cost–volume–profit analysis, budgeting and standard costing, and focused on their feedforward control function. In the next three chapters we shall focus on feedback control and the role played by accounting and organizational control techniques such as responsibility accounting and decentralization.

But first let us refresh our memory of what feedback control means. From Chapter 3 we know that feedback control is control which is effected by comparing actual performance with expected performance. Based on this comparison, a mismatch signal may be generated and organizational members may choose from the following alternative courses of corrective action:

(i) change the inputs to the process being controlled;
(ii) change the objective of the process;
(iii) amend the predictive model of the process being controlled;
(iv) change the nature of the process itself.

Feedback control has been illustrated (see Fig. 3.2) as a form of closed-control loop. Note that, as pointed out in Chapter 3, feedback control is *ex post*. That is, it occurs only after action has been taken and an output has been produced. It is also *reactive* in the sense that control is initiated only if a mismatch signal is generated and decision-makers decide to act on that signal.

Feedback control is also a form of *regulation by error* (Ashby, 1956). Regulation by error occurs when an organization cannot effectively prevent an action from having an effect on the performance of that organization. The organization can only react and respond to that action after it has had an effect on the organization. For instance, let us suppose the following:

(i) D represents a particular disturbance that threatens the performance of the organization, for example restrictive government legislation, withdrawal of government funds or subsidies, the entry of foreign competitors, a shortage of skilled personnel;
(ii) E represents the environment of the organization;
(iii) P represents the collective set of factors or variables that define organizational performance. P, for instance, may include profitability, growth, support from the community, employee loyalty, employee satisfaction;
(iv) R represents the regulator. It is the mechanism that helps to ensure that particular desired levels of P are achieved.

The relationships between D, E, P and R can be illustrated as in Fig. 9.1. D, the disturbance, acts through the environment and influences the level of performance of an organization, P. Note that in Fig. 9.1 the regulator, R, does not know what the precise effect of D on performance is. R does not monitor levels of P. Instead, it only monitors the environment of the organization and is only able to record threats emerging from that environment and environmental change. An example of such a regulator might be a market survey department that is only able to identify the existence of competitive products in the environment but is unable to know the precise impact of these competitors on the organization's performance.

For feedback control to occur, the control relationships need to take the form shown in Fig. 9.2. In this example the disturbance that acts through the environment has had an impact on the performance of the organization before R is able to take preventive action. Indeed, in Fig. 9.2 R is affected only by the actual effect on P. Feedback control, in fact, represents error-controlled regulation. That is corrective action cannot be taken (and therefore, regulation implemented) until the disturbance has actually had an effect on P.

In everyday life, error-controlled regulators are extremely common. A well-known example is the thermostat-controlled room heater (R). This regulator is unable to say 'I can see a cold wind (D) blowing through the open windows, which is going to lower the temperature of the room. I must act now to prevent this

Figure 9.1

Model of disturbance and regulation.

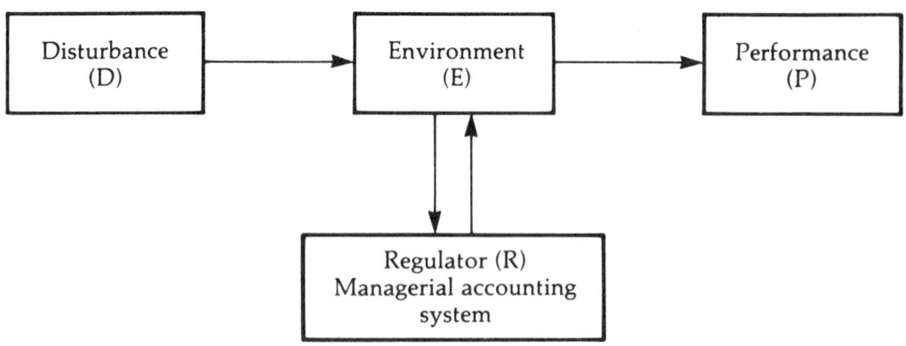

Figure 9.2

Error-controlled regulator.

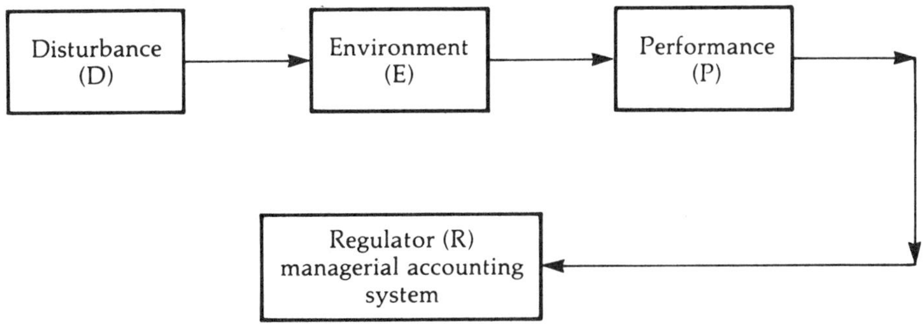

undesirable consequence.' On the contrary, the regulator (that is, the thermostat) gets no information about the disturbance (the cold draught) until the temperature of the room (P) starts to fall.

In the same way, the managerial accounting system of an organization may act as an error-controlled regulator. The disturbance, D, could be the emergence of new competitors selling similar products (for example, private hospitals and clinics which compete with hospitals under the National Health Service, private universities – such as at Buckingham – which compete with state-financed universities, a new boat manufacturer that makes winged keels that give more speed than traditionally designed keels, etc.). D is transmitted through the environment of an organization and substantially influences the performance of the organization under analysis, P. The managerial accounting system is seen as R, the regulator.

Usually, the managerial accounting system is unable to know precisely what the effect of increased competition is until that competition has influenced the level of performance of the organization. For example, the effect may be that the organization's actual performance is 15% below the level which was initially budgeted. This information is 'picked up' and relayed to decision-makers by R, the managerial accounting system. Note, however, that R was unable to know *ex ante* what the impact of competition was. It was only *after* performance had been affected that the effect of the disturbance, D, was known. Hence, feedback control is essentially error-controlled regulation. It is control 'after the fact', after certain actions or events have already had an effect on the performance of the organization. In this way, feedback control is different from feedforward control which exhibits predictive and *ex-ante* characteristics.

As Ashby (1956, p. 223) pointed out, a fundamental feature of error-controlled regulation is that it can never be perfect. This means an error-controlled regulator cannot help an organization actively to control, predict and manage its environment. It can only respond passively after disturbances have already had an impact on the performance of the organization. An error-controlled regulator means that the organization's performance is to a large extent determined by environmental disturbances.

Nevertheless, for most organizations, feedback control (error-controlled regulation) remains a useful form of control. This is because performance levels have some degree of flexibility. Organizations, like human beings, do not have only two states – either existence or non-existence. Instead, there are varying degrees of 'ill-health'. Thus, a human being can pass through numerous degrees of dehydration before dying of thirst. Similarly, an organization may exhibit many signs of ill-health through member dissatisfaction before it is disbanded or goes into liquidation. And appropriate remedial action part-way through this process of ill-health may enable the organization to overcome its problems and prosper. Hence, the presence of a band of survival levels ranging from prosperity to destitution makes feedback control of the greatest practical importance. Small disturbances or errors are allowed to occur, these provide information to R, the managerial accounting system, and they provide a form of control against greater errors.

In addition, the managerial accounting system does not act just as an error-controlled regulator. As shown in Chapters 5 to 8, it also seeks to provide feedforward control. However, in this chapter we shall concentrate on certain accounting techniques which have feedback control as their prime focus.

9.2 Responsibility accounting

As shown in Section 9.1 above, feedback control involves:

(i) the identification of 'errors' (that is of deviations between expected and actual performance); and
(ii) the taking of appropriate corrective or remedial actions to steer the organization and its members on a more desirable path.

Now, it is easy to commit the error of reification referred to in Section 2.2 of Chapter 2 and talk of the organization taking corrective action. An organization is an abstract, theoretical construct that is used to refer to a complex collectivity of people. Exactly who within that collectivity should take the appropriate corrective action? An organization does not act in a literal sense, only people do. Who then ought to act? Responsibility accounting is a technique that seeks to answer this question.

(a) The essence of responsibility accounting

The concept of responsibility accounting is simple. It seeks:

> To identify those financial elements in a certain area of activity which form a controllable set and to appoint a person to be responsible for managing this set of financial elements.

For instance, upon examination of the activities of several functional departments, key decision-makers may decide that the costs of the accounting department are controllable and that the management accountant should be responsible for managing and controlling them. Similarly, the senior managers of IBM may decide that the production and sale of its personal computers gives rise to costs and revenues which are controllable and appoint a manager who is responsible for managing these costs and revenues. Responsibility accounting thus requires the identification of particular costs and/or revenues as the responsibility of certain individuals or groups in an organization. That is, managerial accounting information is classified and reported by area of responsibility.

Closely allied to the concept of responsibility is the notion of *controllability*. A traditional rule for responsibility accounting is that people should only be made responsible for financial elements which they can control (that is, have some influence over). People should not be made responsible for items of cost which they cannot control; neither should they be rewarded for revenues which are not a result of their efforts.

Controllability and responsibility often closely mirror the authority hierarchy of an organization. For instance, a foreman may only be responsible for controlling direct labour and direct materials costs. By contrast, a divisional manager may be held accountable for all the direct and indirect production costs of his/her division and any capital expenditure up to, say, £500,000. In general, decision-makers who are placed higher up the authority hierarchy will be held responsible for a greater number of financial elements. In addition, it should be remembered that in the long-run all costs are controllable by someone in the organization. For instance, while the level of external competition may not be controllable by anyone within the organization in the short-run, over a long period of time it may be controlled by top management – at least to some extent – by means of a takeover of one of its competitors.

A *responsibility centre* may be defined as an area of responsibility which is controlled by an individual. There are three main types of responsibility centres:

(i) a *cost centre* where managers are accountable only for the expenses which are incurred in generating specific physical outputs;
(ii) a *profit centre* where managers are accountable for revenues or funds and expenses;
(iii) an *investment centre* where managers are accountable for revenues or funds, expenses and capital investment decisions.

Cost centres are generally regarded as centres with the least amount of autonomy as only costs are controlled in relation to specified physical outputs. They are common in manufacturing organizations where the required inputs and the outputs produced are both easily measured. For instance, cost centres are common in fast-food franchises where the costs of producing a certain quantity of hamburgers, fried chicken, pizzas and milkshakes can be easily measured.

In general, managers of cost centres are not held responsible for variations in activity levels in their centres. That is, they are given a certain activity level, say, 1,000 units a week. The task of the cost centre manager is to ensure that this activity level is achieved with the most efficient combination of resources. Efficiency is measured as the amount of inputs used in order to produce the required level of output. Finally, managers of cost centres are not responsible for setting the prices of their products. Hence they are not accountable for the level of revenues generated by their centre.

A manager of a *profit centre* is responsible for both revenues and costs in seeking to achieve agreed profit targets where $P = R - C$. See section 11.4(a) in Chapter 11 below. In a manufacturing context he/she would be accountable for marketing and production. That is, the manager can make decisions on the product mix, the quality of production, the selling price of the output and the sales mix.

When the manager of a profit centre has the additional responsibility for capital investment decisions, the responsibility centre becomes an *investment centre*. In general, an investment centre manager has a larger amount of discretion than either a profit centre manager or a cost centre manager. This discretion comes from having to achieve an agreed rate of return on investment. In seeking to achieve this the manager can manipulate revenue costs and investment: see section 11.4(b) in Chapter 11 below.

As pointed out above, responsibility accounting provides a practical method of implementing feedback control. In order that corrective action may actually be taken by somebody, an individual has to be held responsible for that action. Responsibility accounting also has implications for feedforward control. Thus a responsibility centre manager would need to try and predict the environment in order that the centre could grasp opportunities for growth and expansion. If the manager only responded to environmental challenges that had already affected the organization's performance, he/she would not be able to effectively control the environment.

Responsibility accounting is also often said to lead to positive motivational effects as it appears to accord well with prevailing theories of motivation. As discussed in Chapter 8, content motivation theorists such as Maslow, Herzberg and McGregor imply that the average employee has already satisfied his/her basic, lower-order needs. Responsibility accounting, by providing opportunities for the exercise of discretion, autonomy and innovation in decision-making, appears to help satisfy higher-order needs. However, these positive effects of assigning responsibility may be reduced due to inappropriate management styles. Later on in this chapter we shall discuss some of the issues and problems associated with managing a responsibility accounting system.

(b) The design of a responsibility accounting system

The design of a responsibility accounting system involves a number of stages:

(i) Identify the relevent areas of responsibility. This may be a difficult task requiring judgement and experience. Usually, the areas of responsibility bear some relationship to the authority hierarchy in the organization. For instance, responsibility areas may parallel authority levels such that the foreman is accountable for certain costs, the department manager for more costs and the divisional manager is responsible for both costs and revenues. Responsibility areas may also be related to the products being produced, the segmentation of the markets serviced by the organization and the functional specialization of departments (for example, production, sales, services, etc.).

(ii) Design suitable performance reports that are relevant with respect to:
- the content;
- the frequency of reporting; and
- the level of detail required.

To be relevant with respect to content, only those items that can be controlled by the particular responsibility centre manager should be reported.

Determining the appropriate frequency of reporting and the degree of detail is again a matter that requires judgement. Reports may be issued at weekly, monthly, quarterly or six-monthly intervals. In general, in manufacturing organizations, detailed production data with respect to direct and indirect costs are collected and reported to section foremen on a frequent basis. However, this same data is reported to more senior management in a summarized form and at less frequent intervals. This is because such information is usually within the direct responsibility of foremen, while senior managers are responsible for more long-term, strategic decisions.

In addition, when an organization faces rapidly changing environments, reporting may need to be on a more frequent basis. However, if the environ-

Figure 9.3

Examples of Organization X performance reports (a) Foreman A — Paint Section; (b) Production manager; (c) General Manager.

(a) Foreman A-Paint Section

Item	Actual cost	Budgeted cost	Difference
	£	£	£
Direct labour	15,500	17,000	1,500 (−)
Direct materials	25,000	24,200	800 (+)
Indirect labour	6,000	6,000	–
Supplies	500	800	300 (−)
	£47,000	£48,000	1,000 (−)

(b) Production Manager

Item	Actual cost	Budgeted cost	Difference
	£	£	£
Paint section	47,000	48,000	1,000 (−)
Cleaning section	60,000	60,500	500 (−)
Assembly section	80,500	79,000	1,500 (+)
	£187,500	£187,500	0

(c) General Manager

Item	Actual cost	Budgeted cost	Difference
	£	£	£
Production department	187,500	187,500	–
Sales department	187,000	190,000	3,000 (−)
Office administration	55,000	56,000	1,000 (−)
Interest on loans	15,000	15,000	–
	£444,500	£448,500	£4,000 (−)

ment is fairly predictable and stable, reporting for those segments of the organization facing such an environment could be on a less frequent basis.

In Fig. 9.3 we provide an example of performance reports for three possible levels of an authority hierarchy in Organization X. All the data presented is for the month of August, 1992.

Points to note from these three performance reports include:

(i) Each performance report focuses on those items that are within the responsibility of the manager concerned. For instance, in the foreman's performance report, only the relevant production cost information is included.
(ii) The information provided becomes increasingly aggregated as one moves up the hierarchy. The production manager is responsible only for sections within the production department while the general manager is responsible for a range of departments.
(iii) Attention is directed to the mismatch signals (that is, to variances from the expected level of performance). In the next chapter we shall discuss this form of reporting in greater detail.

(c) Management by objectives

A responsibility accounting system may be used as part of a total management by objectives (MbO) programme. MbO is a management technique that emerged in the early 1950s. Two of its most influential proponents were Drucker (1954) and Odiorne (1965). The original work by Drucker and others provide the following main guidelines for implementing MbO:

(i) Superiors and subordinates meet and discuss objectives which, if met, would contribute to overall organizational goals (remember how we defined these in Chapter 2 as the minimum set of inducements and contributions that would keep all participants satisfied).
(ii) Superiors and subordinates jointly establish attainable objectives for the subordinates. These goals should also be challenging, clear and comprehensive.
(iii) The criteria for measuring and evaluating goal performance are agreed upon.
(iv) The superiors and subordinates establish some intermediate review dates when the goals will be re-examined.
(v) Superiors and subordinates meet at these predetermined dates and evaluate the subordinates' progress towards the objectives. The superior should play more of a coaching, counselling and supportive role and less the role of a judge and jury. The entire evaluative process is intended to focus upon results accomplished, the counselling of subordinates (rather than upon their mistakes), and organizational requirements.

As can be seen, MbO in a managerial accounting context is similar to the use of participative budgeting together with a responsibility accounting system. The exact procedures employed in implementing MbO will vary from organization to organization. However, the basic elements of objective setting, the participation of subordinates in objective setting, and feedback and evaluation are essential parts of any MbO programme. An MbO programme is intended to lead to greater motivation and satisfaction among employees by providing them with feedback about performance, specific targets and opportunities for higher-order need satisfaction. It also enables evaluation decisions to be based on results instead of on personality traits, and helps to improve supervisory skills in such areas as listening, counselling and evaluation.

Does it work? MbO-type programmes have been used in organizations throughout the world. In 1975, in the United States, 40% of *Fortune*'s 500 largest industrial enterprises reported using MbO-type programmes. However, MbO programmes and responsibility accounting have also been criticized. The major criticisms are:

(i) A narrow focus on short-term budgeting results can only lead to low morale and dissatisfaction within an organization. As the study by Hopwood (1972) showed, a *budget-constrained* style of evaluation led to poor relationships between superiors and subordinates, among peers, and to higher levels of job-related tension.

In addition, a focus on results only may distract attention away from how the assigned goals may be achieved in a more efficient manner. A subordinate receiving feedback about what has been achieved may still not be certain about how to make performance corrections. For instance, a superior may inform a subordinate that the sales target was missed by 5%, but this type of feedback is incomplete. The subordinate who did not achieve his/her target needs further guidance and feedback on how he/she might accomplish the sales goal in the future.

(ii) Through a rigid division of responsibility areas, responsibility accounting may lead to the development of *tunnel vision* where each department and its members are only concerned with the interests of the department *per se* and not with overall organizational objectives. Later on in this chapter we shall see how the setting of transfer prices is especially open to distortion because of a concern with departmental objectives.

A concern with departmental matters may in turn lead to frequent interdepartmental conflict, thus contributing to a reduction in innovative and adaptive behaviour. Such a process could seriously affect the ability of an organization to respond to changes in its environment.

(iii) A clear division of responsibility is also not always possible. In many instances, decisions are influenced by joint effects and it may be counterproductive to attempt to delineate clear lines of responsibility. For instance, the success or failure of the introduction of a new product depends partly on the characteristics of the product itself, on effective sales, marketing and distribution, on the maintenance of product quality and on the provision of support services. While responsibilities may be assigned to each of these aspects (for example, for product quality, customer services, etc.), the responsibility for the success or failure of the entire product is more difficult to allocate. This is because it depends on a number of joint activities and also on environmental factors which may not be within the control of a single individual.

(iv) Responsibility accounting frequently mirrors the legitimated authority structure of an organization. Thus, it reinforces existing patterns of power, authority and domination. When these patterns do not cause undue dissatisfaction among organizational members the responsibility accounting system may function effectively. However, where there is severe discontent the responsibility system will reinforce and even amplify this dissatisfaction. For instance, if the chief executive of a company is widely regarded as incompetent, conservative and stubborn, if the responsibility accounting system requires that, on financial matters, all second-line managers report directly to him, the perception of incompetence and dissatisfaction may be strengthened through this enforced interaction.

In additon to these difficulties, MbO programmes and responsibility accounting systems have suffered from a lack of senior management involvement, too much paper work and inadequate training preparation for employees who are asked to establish goals. Finally, in MbO programmes, it may be difficult to compare different employees with different goal sets. In traditional performance evaluation programmes all subordinates are rated on common dimensions. In MbO each individual usually has a different set of goals and these are difficult to compare across a group of subordinates.

Hence, although responsibility accounting systems and MbO programmes have been instrumental in promoting performance in some organizations, these techniques have also created a number of problems. It is therefore important that management accountants should be aware of these potential difficulties.

9.3 Decentralization

So far, in discussing responsibility accounting, we have implicitly assumed that it is possible to 'divide up' an organization into areas of responsibility. We may, for instance, designate certain departments as cost, profit or investment centres. In 'dividing up' the organization we are, in effect, *decentralizing* the organization. That is, the responsibility for making decisions is no longer made by one person, the chief executive, or by one department. By decentralizing we mean the delegation of decision-making authority away from the centre or headquarters of the organization to employees who are situated lower down the authority hierarchy. For instance, as shown in the example of performance reports (see Fig. 9.3 on p. 287) the responsibility for minimizing production costs no longer lies directly with the general manager but with the production manager and the foremen of the various production sections. In Fig. 9.4 we show an example of a decentralized organization. Note that each product line is organized into a profit centre and each geographical market is organized into a cost centre.

By dividing up the organization into specific responsibility areas we facilitate the flow of feedback information and help to achieve feedback control. Are there other reasons for decentralization? Why do senior decision-makers delegate their decision-making authority to employees lower down in the authority structure? There are a number of reasons. Some are discussed below, but see also Section 11.3 in Chapter 11.

(a) Bounded rationality

As organizations grow in size and complexity it is simply impossible for a single decision-maker or a small group of decision-makers to possess all the information necessary to manage the organization. For instance, Company X may deal in gold

Figure 9.4

A decentralized organization.

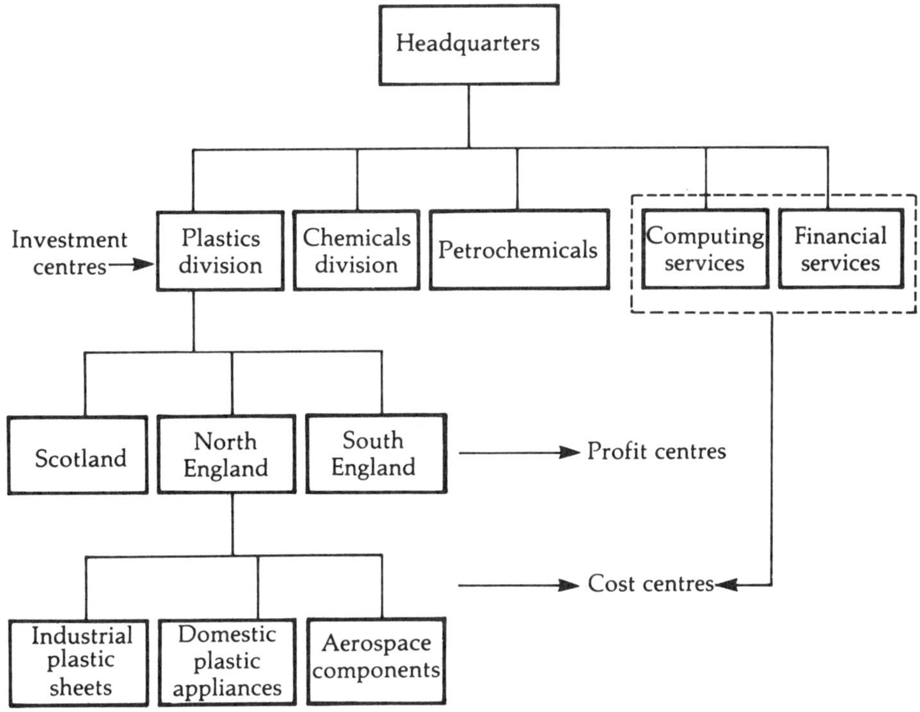

mining, hotel investment, real estate, the manufacture of soap powder and telephones, the provision of management consulting services, and a range of other diversified activities. It may operate in 10 countries spread across four continents with highly diversified product markets. It would be extremely difficult for a central management team to manage such a diversified organization without delegating decision-making authority to local managers who will possess more information about circumstances affecting the production and marketing of any particular product or service on offer.

Bounded rationality is a term coined by Herbert Simon to refer to the limited cognitive abilities of human beings. Because human beings are intrinsically bounded in their ability to process information it is necessary to decentralize decision-making. At some point organizational activity will become too difficult and complex for the managerial capacities of one individual or small group of individuals located in one place.

(b) Economics of labour specialization

By decentralizing, senior management becomes able to concentrate on longer-term strategic decision-making while delegating operational decision-making to local managers. For instance, by delegating the management of IBM Australia (Pty) to a local manager, the senior decision-makers of IBM are able to concentrate on developing a long-term (15 year) world-wide strategy for the enterprise as a whole.

In addition, delegation ensures that localized decisions are made by local managers who have gained a specialized stock of knowledge about local conditions. For instance, British American Tobacco operates cigarette making factories in countries such as Malaysia and Singapore. In order to operate successfully in overseas countries with different cultures, values and beliefs, it is important that decision-making be delegated to local managers who have more up-to-date information and who have built up networks of local contacts.

(c) Motivational implications

Finally, as indicated above, delegating decision-making authority to local managers is intended to lead to higher levels of motivation. Good managers are usually people with a high need for achievement. If they are only allowed to act on instructions from senior managers they may be demotivated and feel frustrated at not being able to exercise any authority. Thus, allowing decision-making at a local level will encourage managers to be more entrepreneurial in their actions.

Decentralization also provides a training ground for local managers. If all decision-making is centralized, local managers will only be skilled at the carrying out of orders rather than the giving of orders. Management and leadership are skills that cannot be developed if a manager only follows orders. Hence, by decentralizing decision-making, local managers receive on-the-job managerial training.

There are, therefore, numerous factors which make decentralization an attractive management alternative to centralized control. However, it also creates problems. One of the major difficulties relates to the calculation of transfer prices. In the next section, we shall look at this issue in detail, and we will look further at decentralization and divisional performance measurement in Chapter 11.

9.4 Transfer pricing

In a centralized organization the procurement of inputs for the production process (for example, raw materials, and labour) is usually conducted in an external market that is usually competitive. Similarly, the output produced is typically sold to external buyers who are not part of the organization. In a decentralized organization, however, some buying and selling of goods and services among divisions is quite common. For instance, Division A might make components which are needed by Division B in the manufacture of air-conditioners. Or Division X might be a specialist Research and Development unit that charges Division Y for the research that it performs on Division Y's behalf. If divisions are organized as profit centres a charge will need to be made for goods and services that are transferred between divisions in order that each division's profit may be accurately assessed (and similarly for profitability in the case of investment centres).

A *transfer price* is, as its name suggests, the price at which goods and services are transferred between divisions in a decentralized organization. They are normally set for *intermediate products*. These are goods and services that are supplied by the selling division to the buying division. The goods that are produced by the buying division and sold to the outside world are known as *final products*. Usually, the buying division purchases the intermediate product and subjects it to further processing before the final product is sold to external buyers.

What transfer price ought to be charged? Clearly, both selling and buying divisions will be keenly interested in this price. This is because the price charged constitutes a revenue to the selling division and a cost to the buying division. Therefore the price charged will affect the profit of both divisions in a way that means any benefit to one division can only be made at the expense of the other division. For instance, the selling division can benefit by charging a high price for the goods/services sold. However, this means that the buying division will incur higher costs. Because transfer prices affect the profit of divisions they need to be carefully set. Often they are a source of considerable interdivisional conflict and dissatisfaction.

What rules might we use in setting transfer prices? Anthony and Dearden (1980) suggest the following:

(i) Transfer prices should motivate the division manager to make decisions that are organizationally effective. These are actions that will improve the reported profit of the division as well as of the organization as a whole.

(ii) Transfer prices should help to provide a reliable and accurate measure of divisional performance.

(iii) Transfer prices should ensure that divisional autonomy and authority is preserved. This is important, for one of the purposes of decentralization is to enable local managers to exercise greater autonomy. It is pointless for top management to give local managers authority by placing them in charge of decentralized operations and then to remove that authority by dictating transfer prices that affect the performance of the division.

As can be seen, these rules are a potential source of conflict. On the other hand, transfer prices may seek to encourage divisional managers to make maximum profits or to minimize costs. Yet, by so doing, divisional managers may make decisions that are suboptimal for the organization as a whole. For instance, let us assume that Division A makes components that have a marginal or incremental cost per unit of £150. Division A decides to sell its components to Division B at £200 per unit because it regards a 33.3% mark-up on marginal cost as the minimum mark-up necessary to maintain its previous year's profit position. Division A is not operating at full capacity and there are no other buyers for its product.

Division B buys this component and further processes it at a marginal cost per unit of £100. This means, Division B incurs a total marginal cost of £200 (for the component) + £100 (further processing) = £300. Let us also assume that the market price for the final product produced by Division B is £280. Given this final product price, Division B will most likely decide to discontinue further processing of the component purchased from Division A. This is because, for every unit processed, the division loses £20. Yet from the point of view of the organization as a whole the correct decision is for Division A to forgo some of its profits and charge a lower mark-up and for Division B to continue to process the component.

This is because the total marginal cost of producing the final product is £150 (marginal cost of Division A) + £100 (marginal cost of Division B) = £250. The organization as a whole will gain £30 for each unit of the final product that is sold (£280 − £250 = £30).

Later on in this chapter we shall discuss this classic transfer pricing problem in greater depth. For the moment, let us accept that the correct decision for the organization as a whole is for Division A to sell its components to Division B which further processes them and sells the final product for £280. How can we persuade Division A to change its mark-up to ensure that this optimal decision is made? After all, the manager of Division A has been informed that his/her performance evaluation is closely related to the profitability of the division. In addition, the manager has also been instructed to use his/her discretion to improve profits and reduce costs. As may be appreciated, transfer prices that are designed to maximize the profitability of a division may not be optimal from the point of view of the organization as a whole. The conflict between autonomy in decision-making and of ensuring overall organizational control lies at the centre of the transfer pricing problem.

Leaving aside the organizational issues for the moment, let us look at how transfer prices may be determined. There are a number of methods by which such prices may be set.

(a) Market prices

In general, if a highly competitive market exists for the intermediate product, the current market price is recommended as the correct transfer price. A competitive market is one in which the selling division can sell as much of the product as it wishes to external customers and the buying division can buy as much as it wishes from external suppliers without the price of the intermediate product being affected. When these conditions prevail, transfers that are made at market prices result in reported profits that are more representative of the economic contribution of the division to total organizational performance. This is because, under competitive conditions, a market price is the opportunity cost of the goods. It represents the incremental cost to the buying division of buying the goods and further processing them. And incremental or marginal cost information is the most useful type of information in assessing the contribution of an activity.

In addition, using market prices as transfer prices also makes it possible to evaluate the buying and selling divisions as though they were independent organizations. A division that cannot make long-run profit by selling its intermediate products at market prices to other divisions presumably could not succeed as an independent organization and – arguably – should cease producing that intermediate product. Similarly, a division that cannot make long-run profit by buying products from another division and further processing them could not succeed as an independent organization.

A final advantage of using market prices is that they help to preserve the autonomy of divisional managers. A manager has the option of transacting either with another division or through an external party at the same market price. There is therefore no need for a transfer price that is imposed by senior management. The example below shows that, at market prices, the profits of the organization and division as a whole are unaffected by whether the transactions are conducted internally or externally. Let us assume that 100 units of the intermediate product are produced and 100 units of the final product are sold. The selling price of the intermediate product is £15 and of the final product £20. The incremental cost of producing the intermediate product is £12.

(i) *Buy and sell the intermediate product externally; sell the final product externally:*

	£	£
Revenues to selling division		
100 × £15		1,500
Incremental costs of selling division		
100 × £12		1,200
Contribution of selling division		£300
Revenues to buying division		
100 × £20		2,000
Costs of buying division:		
Incremental processing costs	300	
Purchase costs of intermediate products	1,500	1,800
Contribution of buying division		£200

(ii) *Buy and sell the intermediate product internally; sell the final product externally:*

	£	£
Revenues to selling division		
100 × £15 (transfer price)		1,500
Incremental costs of selling division		
100 × £12		1,200
Contribution of selling division		£300
Revenues of buying division		
100 × £20		2,000
Costs of buying division:		
Incremental processing costs	300	
Transfer cost of intermediate products	1,500	1,800
Contribution of buying division		£200

Note that, in this example, when transfer prices are set at market prices it makes no difference to divisional and organizational profits whether the transactions are conducted internally or externally. This is because both the buying and the selling divisions are operating with market prices or transfer prices that accurately reflect the opportunity costs facing the organization as a whole.

In practice an organization will usually encourage internal rather than external transactions. This is because there is usually a saving on selling, marketing and distribution expenses when the transaction is conducted internally. To encourage internal transfers it is normal for organizations to offer an internal discount off the market price when intra-organizational transfers are conducted. Divisional managers also need to be careful that the market prices quoted by external suppliers are not *distress prices* that are exceptionally low. At times an external supplier may quote a very low price that will only operate in the short-term in an attempt to attract business. A division should not switch its source of supply from an internal division to an external supplier unless it is sure that distress prices are not being quoted.

(b) Limitations of market prices

One of the major limitations of using the market price rule is that markets are not perfectly competitive. Indeed, a market for the product transacted may not even exist. For instance, the selling division may produce a product that is specifically tailored to meet the specialist requirements of the buying division. In addition, there are often products or components that an organization will neither buy nor sell outside for a variety of strategic reasons such as quality control, the protection of trade secrets, the encouragement of specialist research and development, or the facilitation of a steady, reliable supply. Where markets do not exist it becomes extremely difficult to establish reliable market prices.

An attempt can be made to establish market prices by calling for quotations from external suppliers for identical or similar products. However, outside suppliers may not quote realistic market prices. If the external supplier does not expect to get any business it will not spend much time determining an accurate market price. At times, distress prices may be quoted in an attempt to obtain business. If these prices cannot be maintained in the long-run it would be extremely misleading for divisional managers to change sources of supply based on short-term price information.

Given these difficulties, it is usual for the market price rule to be adapted. Remember that the market price rule is applicable only under restrictive conditions, i.e. when there is perfect competition in the intermediate product market. This means that the selling division is operating at capacity and can sell as much as it wishes to external customers and the buying division can buy as much as it wishes from external suppliers without either division affecting the price of the good being transacted.

(c) Transfer pricing in imperfect markets

To illustrate one of the difficulties with the market price rule let us look at an example of an organization where Division A sells an intermediate product, a highly specialized radar system, only to Division B. There is no external market for this product and Division A is in effect a captive seller to Division B. Ignoring transfer prices for the moment, the following financial data is provided for the two divisions:

	Incremental cost		
Quantity	Division A	Division B	Organization
	£	£	£
1,000	500,000	300,000	800,000
1,200	600,000	400,000	1,000,000

Assume that the sale price of the final product is £1,500. The following revenue and profit outcomes for the organization are:

Quantity	Revenue (Organization) £	Profit (Organization) £
1,000	1,500,000	700,000
1,200	1,800,000	800,000

Note that if we consider only the incremental or marginal costs of each division, the profit for the organization as a whole is greater at 1,200 units than at 1,000 units. By introducing transfer prices into the picture, we are allocating this organizational profit between the two divisions. Let us see what happens when the transfer price for the intermediate product is set at £500 and £800.

(*i*) *Transfer price of £500*

Revenues

Quantity	Division A £	Division B £	Organization £
1,000	500,000	1,500,000	2,000,000
1,200	600,000	1,800,000	2,400,000

Costs

Quantity	Division A £	Division B £	Organization £
1,000	500,000	800,000*	1,300,000
1,200	600,000	1,000,000**	1,600,000

Profit

Quantity	Division A £	Division B £	Organization £
1,000	—	700,000	700,000
1,200	—	800,000	800,000

* £800,000 = £500,000 (cost of intermediate product from Division A) + £300,000 (additional processing costs incurred by Division B).

** £1,000,000 = £600,000 (cost of intermediate product from Division A) + £400,000 (additional processing costs incurred by Division B).

As can be seen, the organizational profit with or without transfer prices remains the same. This is because, from the point of view of the organization, the important question is, should the transfer of intermediate products occur, given the costs of production and the final product price of £1,500? Transfer prices are merely internal bookkeeping allocations of the organizational profit between divisions in order to help assess the individual contribution of each division to the sale of the intermediate and final products.

(*ii*) *Transfer price of £800*

Revenues

Quantity	Division A £	Division B £	Organization £
1,000	800,000	1,500,000	2,300,000
1,200	960,000	1,800,000	2,760,000

Costs

Quantity	Division A £	Division B £	Organization £
1,000	500,000	1,100,000	1,600,000
1,200	600,000	1,360,000	1,960,000

Profit

Quantity	Division A £	Division B £	Organization £
1,000	300,000	400,000	700,000
1,200	360,000	440,000	800,000

At a transfer price of £800 Division B earns less profit at the production levels of 1,000 and 1,200 units of the intermediate product. Instead of earning £700,000 and £800,000 at the respective levels of production, it now earns only £400,000 and £440,000. The other part of the profit is earned by Division A. As can be seen, the total organizational profit remains at £700,000 (1,000 units) and £800,000 (1,200 units). The transfer price of £800 does not affect this total organizational profit, merely the share of the profit attributed to each of the two divisions. At a transfer price of £500 Division A does not record any profit; at a transfer price of £800 it records profits in the range of £300,000–360,000.

Division B will clearly prefer to transfer at £500. If this occurs it means that the intermediate product is being transferred at the marginal (incremental) cost of Division A. The marginal cost of the product is obtained as follows:

$$1{,}200 - 1{,}000 = 200 \text{ units}$$
$$£600{,}000 - £500{,}000 = £100{,}000$$
$$100{,}000/200 = £500$$

However, Division A is not likely to agree to a transfer price of £500. This is because at that price the division is only recovering its incremental or marginal costs. No contributions are being made to the recovery of fixed costs. In addition, the manager of Division A knows that, at a transfer price of £800, Division A can make profits in the order of £300,000. What then is an appropriate transfer price? Given that no external market exists for the intermediate product (and, even if it did, the market would not be perfectly competitive), how can we apply the market price rule? In the following section we will show alternatives to the market price rule.

The case of the captive division indicates that when one division exists primarily to serve the needs of another there is considerable doubt as to whether the captive division should be treated as a profit centre. The reason is that, from the point of view of the organization, the ideal transfer price is an approximation of the marginal cost of the captive division. However, the manager of the division is unlikely to be satisfied with this price. And if he/she is forced by senior managers to transact at that price, the notions of divisional autonomy and performance evaluation may be seen as farcical concepts within the organization.

(d) The general rule

The preceding section illustrates that the market price rule cannot be applied in most organizations. The conditions of perfect competition generally do not exist in intermediate product markets. How then can we set transfer prices? Is there a general rule that provides the correct answer? The short answer is no. In order to achieve the multiple goals of divisional autonomy, divisional performance evaluation and goal congruence between divisions and the organization viewed as a whole, there is no single, comprehensive rule for transfer pricing. However, the following general rule may be used as a first step in setting transfer prices. The general rule for setting transfer prices such that the buying division makes the economic decisions that are optimal from the viewpoint of the total company is to transfer at:

$$\begin{pmatrix}\text{Marginal/incremental} \\ \text{cost to the selling} \\ \text{division}\end{pmatrix} + \begin{pmatrix}\text{Implicit opportunity} \\ \text{cost to the organization if} \\ \text{goods are transferred} \\ \text{internally}\end{pmatrix}$$

This is the price that would usually make the selling division indifferent as to whether the output is sold internally or externally. The selling division's profit should be the same under either alternative.

The marginal or incremental cost of the selling division includes all the cash outflows that are directly associated with the production and transfer of the goods or services. (Sometimes these costs are referred to as marginal costs, variable costs, differential costs, out-of-pocket costs or outlay costs.) The opportunity cost of the organization represents the maximum contribution to the profits of the organization that are forgone because the goods are transferred internally. For instance, if the selling division has to offer a discount on the transfer price and this reduces the total organizational profit, then it should be included as an opportunity cost to the organization. Similarly, if the selling divisions had to operate above capacity to meet internal demand and thus incur additional production costs, these again need to be considered. Thus, if no idle capacity exists, the general transfer pricing rule is:

$$\begin{pmatrix}\text{Marginal cost of} \\ \text{intermediate} \\ \text{product}\end{pmatrix} + \left[\begin{pmatrix}\text{Market price of} \\ \text{intermediate} \\ \text{product}\end{pmatrix} - \begin{pmatrix}\text{Marginal cost} \\ \text{of intermediate} \\ \text{product}\end{pmatrix}\right]$$

However, if the selling division is operating below capacity and there are no alternative uses for the idle capacity, the implicit opportunity cost to the organization is zero. The general transfer pricing rule then becomes:

Marginal cost of intermediate product + 0

9.5 Alternative approaches to the transfer pricing problem

Because of the difficulties associated with the use of transfer prices a variety of alternative approaches to setting transfer prices have been developed. In practice an organization may use a combination of these approaches.

(a) Cost-based transfer prices

When the selling division is operating below capacity and no adequate market prices are available the marginal cost rule as stated in Section 9.4 above provides the theoretically ideal transfer price. When the division is operating at capacity and competitive market prices are available, market prices are ideal transfer prices. However, the problem with marginal costs is that they do not provide an accurate basis for divisional performance evaluation (which will be discussed in detail in Chapter 11). In addition, if transfer prices are imposed by senior management, it militates against the principle of divisional autonomy. Finally, in situations where selling divisions are captive sellers, or where internal transfer is the preferred option given certain strategic corporate considerations (for example, the need to keep trade secrets or maintain steady supplies), it appears unrealistic and unreasonable to treat a sister division as though it was just another external buyer or supplier. In these circumstances some form of cost-based transfer price may be used.

In effect, cost-based transfer prices are allocations; they help to allocate the organizational profit between divisions such that the selling division records a revenue item and the buying division is charged an amount for the consumption or use of an intermediate product. Thus, the problem is not *whether* allocations are to be made, but *how* they should be made to the satisfaction of both buying and selling divisions.

(i) Actual costs

Using actual costs (whether variable or full costs) or actual costs plus a mark-up as a transfer price is probably the worst basis for setting transfer prices. This is because the method allows the selling division to pass on completely all costs to the buying division. The selling division may be operating very inefficiently and incurring unnecessary production costs. However, because it is able to charge all these production costs to the buying division, the manager of the selling division will not be encouraged to control costs.

Let us consider the following example. Assume that the manager of Division B buys 100 units of an intermediate product from Division A. The transfer price is to be actual full cost plus 5% profit. In addition, both variable and fixed indirect costs are applied on the basis of the number of direct labour hours. The standard cost information for each unit of the intermediate product is:

		£
Direct materials	2 m × £5	10.00
Direct labour	1 dlh × £8	8.00
Variable indirect	1 dlh × £0.5	0.50
Fixed indirect	1 dlh × £1.5	1.50
Total standard cost		20.00
Allowance for 5% profit		1.00
Total standard price		£21.00

Assume that, due to inefficient production scheduling, the direct labour hours used per unit increased to 1.5 dlh. This increases the direct labour cost per unit to 1.5 × 8 = £12, variable indirect costs to 1.5 × 0.5 = £0.75 and fixed indirect costs to £2.25. This results in an actual cost per unit of £25. Adding the 5% mark-up leads to a transfer price of 1.05 × £25 = £26.25. Because transfers are priced at actual costs, Division A will be able to pass on all this inefficiency to Division B.

The transfer price could be even higher if *actual* fixed costs are used rather than *applied* fixed costs. This is because any adverse fixed indirect cost budget variances would be included in the transfer price. In addition, the level of activity achieved would affect the actual fixed indirect cost per direct labour hour, which in turn would affect the fixed indirect costs allocated to each unit of output. In order to avoid this problem actual variable costs could be used instead of actual absorbed or full costs. If actual variable costs are used, variations in the level of activity during the period would not affect the transfer price. However, using actual variable costs still does not avoid the problem of one division being able to pass on inefficiencies to another division.

(ii) Standard or budgeted costs

Because of the difficulties associated with the use of actual costs as a basis for transfer pricing standard or budgeted costs may be seen as a viable alternative. In some organizations variable costs are a close approximation to marginal or incremental costs. In those circumstances it may be suitable to use standard variable costs as a transfer price. By using standard costs it would be more difficult for one division to pass on inefficiencies to other divisions.

However, standard variable costs again meet up with the problem of motivating divisional managers to maximize profit performance. When standard variable or marginal costs are used as transfer prices the selling division does not record a profit. This is because no allowance is made for the recovery of fixed costs and for a contribution to be made to profit. Clearly, the managers of selling divisions will not be satisfied with such transfer prices if they are to be evaluated on the basis of the performance of their divisions.

Why not use standard absorbed cost, either with or without a profit mark-up? This would overcome the motivational problems associated with standard variable costs and the inefficiency issue caused by the use of actual costs. But because absorbed costs do not follow the general marginal cost rule decisions may be made which are optimal for the division but not for the organization as a whole. Consider the following example. Assume that we have the same Divisions A and B as discussed in (i) above. The same intermediate product is transferred and the transfer price is set at £21 with a 5% profit mark-up.

Assume that Division B now knows of an external supplier who is willing to supply the intermediate product at the same quality as the internal product at a price of £20.30 per unit. If the manager of Division B is a profit-maximizer he or she will seek to buy solely from the external supplier at £20.30 instead of buying from Division A at £21. Division B will only buy from Division A if that division is willing to charge a price lower than its standard absorbed cost. Note that from the point of view of the organization as a whole, Division B should buy internally because the total standard variable (marginal) cost of supplying the intermediate product is only £18.50, compared with an external price of £20.30. The manager of Division A should be prepared to meet this price of £20.30 because it provides a contribution of £1.80 per unit transacted towards the recovery of fixed costs and profit. However, if the manager of Division A continues to apply a transfer pricing rule based on the use of standard absorbed costs suboptimal decisions will be made.

(iii) Standard costs plus lump sums

In order to overcome the above difficulties with the use of standard variable and standard absorbed costs it is often recommended that standard variable costs be used together with a predetermined amount that is allocated to the selling division. Hence, goods are transferred at standard variable costs. In addition, a predetermined lump-sum charge is made for fixed costs plus a lump-sum profit. This charge is then added back to the revenues of the selling division either on a monthly or annual basis. This lump-sum amount is calculated based on expected long-run transactions between the two divisions.

For instance, in our example, Division A might charge a standard variable cost of £18.50 for each unit of the intermediate product transferred. In addition, the division might charge an annual lump-sum of £50,000. This lump-sum could be determined in a number of ways. It could represent an estimated 'use' of fixed resources, thus being an approximation of fixed costs. Or it could simply represent a negotiated amount that is considered 'fair and reasonable' by both divisional managers.

There are some advantages to this method. First, transfers are priced at variable costs which usually are good approximations of marginal cost. This should help ensure that divisional managers make decisions that are optimal from the point of view of the organization as a whole. Second, the buyer's decisions on how many units to buy each period will not be influenced by the selling division's fixed costs or profit. The lump-sum is a sunk cost that is irrelevant in this decision. As a consequence of these advantages this method is often recommended for use in organizations. However, it should be noted that both divisions must be satisfied with the lump-sum charges in order to avoid interdivisional conflict.

(iv) Prorating the overall contribution

Recall that in an earlier example in Section 9.4 of this chapter we showed that transfer prices effectively allocated organizational profit between the buying and selling divisions. In that example we showed the results with transfer prices of £500 and £800. We can explicitly recognize this allocation effect by providing for it. Assume that the following data is available for two divisions, Division X (selling division) and Division Y (buying division):

	£	£
Revenue from sale of final product:		300,000
Standard variable costs:		
Division X	150,000	
Division Y	100,000	250,000
Contribution to organizational profit		£50,000

Further, assume that these costs were incurred for an activity level of 1,000 units of the intermediate product. This means that the standard variable cost at which the transfer should be priced is £150,000/1,000 = £150.

In addition, Division X is to be credited with a certain proportion of the organizational profit of £50,000. The exact proportions would be negotiated between the two divisional managers. One method might be to proportion the £50,000 according to the proportions of standard variable costs incurred by the two departments. Applying this rule, the proportions would be Division X: Division Y, 60%: 40% (i.e. 150,000/250,000 = 60%; 100,000/250,000 = 40%). This would result in Division X being credited with £30,000 and Division Y being credited with £20,000.

This method is essentially similar to a standard variable costing system with a mark-up. In this case, the mark-up depends on the overall contribution to organizational profit.

(v) Dual pricing

A method that appears to offer an optimal solution is based on the idea that there is no necessity to have a single transfer price. One transfer price may be used because it promotes divisions to make decisions that are optimal from the point of view of the organization as a whole. Another could be more suitable for divisional performance evaluation. For instance, we could charge the buying division with the standard variable costs of the units transferred. Thus, for 1,000 units of the intermediate product, Division Y, the buying division, may be charged with the standard variable costs of £150,000. Note that these are the standard variable costs incurred by Division X in producing that level of output. Division X, however, will record a revenue figure of £150,000 plus, say, a mark-up of 20%. This mark-up results in a total revenue figure of £150,000 + £30,000 = £180,000. You will see that with this method of using two transfer prices the charge to the buying division is always lower than the revenue recorded by the selling division.

This method of using two transfer prices is called *dual pricing*. It is not widely used in practice because the differing transfer prices cause some confusion and are often seen by managers as contrived, artifical and 'playing with numbers'. With this method the combined income of the divisions will exceed the income of the organization as a whole. This artificial difference is usually written off in the organization's books at the corporate headquarters' level of responsibility.

Besides its lack of acceptance by managers the method has additional disadvantages. Unless the standards for the variable costs of the selling division are constantly monitored and kept reasonably efficient the manager of the selling division may become complacent in cost control. This is because he/she is always assured of a good price for the product sold. In addition, the buying division is almost a captive buyer because it is unlikely that the buying division will be able to find an external supplier able to sell at a price that is equal to or less than the internal standard variable cost. It is therefore important that cost standards in the selling division are kept up to date to ensure that cost inefficiencies are not passed on to the buying division.

(vi) Cost-based transfer prices and human processes

Throughout this discussion of cost-based transfer prices we have implied the importance of maintaining adequately tight cost standards. Because transfer prices affect the bottom-line profit figure of divisions, and therefore their performance, managers have been known to bias or misestimate cost standards.

For instance, assume that Division A is the selling division and its manager knows that senior managers have adopted a policy of transferring at standard variable costs. The manager of Division A is reasonably satisfied with this policy. However, he/she feels that there is still room to build some slack (remember budgetary slack-see pp. 273–4 above) into the system. The manager of Division A may then decide to overstate standard variable costs. It is rarely possible to estimate variable costs with certainty, and it is unusual for other divisions to question the estimates provided by the manager of a division. After all, divisional managers are supposed to be the people with the most experience and expertise in the management of their division! It would therefore be difficult for, say, the manager of Division B to demonstrate conclusively that the manager of Division A was overstating the standard variable costs for the product. Theoretically, if standards were too loose, relatively large cost variances would be generated and these might alert senior managers. However, as far as the transfer pricing issue is concerned, the manager of Division B is unlikely to know whether large variances were in fact being recorded. Hence, it remains the task of senior managers to monitor closely all aspects of divisional managerial performance.

(b) Negotiated transfer prices

In the everyday world perfectly competitive markets for intermediate products typically do not exist. In addition, a theoretically ideal transfer price will rarely be obtained such that the multiple objectives of goal congruence (between divisions and the organization as a whole) and divisional autonomy are achieved simultaneously. Thus, a common practice is to allow divisional managers to negotiate transfer prices that are satisfactory to both parties. Senior management should only intervene in this negotiating process if a deadlock occurs.

This method may help to encourage interdivisional understanding, interaction and cooperation. Through frequent contact, divisional managers may appreciate better the difficulties and problems faced by other divisions. However, this method of setting transfer prices means that the price set depends on the relative power and negotiating skills of the individual divisional manager. For instance, a divisional manager may have greater negotiating power because he/she has the personal support of a senior manager. In those circumstances the negotiated transfer price would be subject to political influences as well as efficiency considerations. But this criticism may be countered by arguing that negotiating skills are an important part of a manager's expertise and an effective manager should seek to develop those skills. In addition, senior management should carefully (but discreetly) monitor the situation and act in the role of final arbitrator if necessary.

(c) Transfer prices and linear programming

Remember that the general rule for setting transfer prices is to use a transfer price that is the sum of the incremental or marginal cost of producing the intermediate product and the opportunity cost to the organization as a whole of having the transaction conducted internally. The application of this general rule suggests that when the selling division is operating at capacity it should transfer goods at the external market price because this represents the opportunity cost of selling the goods. However, when imperfect markets exist, capacity constraints are in operation and a number of departments are involved in internal transfers of goods and services, it may be extremely difficult to use market prices or some of the alternative methods already discussed. In those circumstances it may be feasible to rely on mathematically derived transfer prices.

One of the most powerful mathematical techniques available for handling situations with a number of constraints is called *linear programming*. Linear programming enables an organization to calculate the opportunity costs of using scarce resources. (This technique was introduced in Chapter 5 — see pp. 145–9.)

Let us look at a simple example of using linear programming to obtain opportunity cost information that will help us to set a transfer price. Division M produces a petrochemical compound called MX5 which can be sold on the external market at £50 per tonne after incurring variable processing costs of £30 per tonne. This means that the contribution margin of Division M amounts to £20 per tonne.

Alternatively, MX5 can be further processed in Division M at an additional £10 per tonne, transferred to Division M where it is further processed and sold on the external market as a final product at £110 per tonne. The incremental variable processing costs of Division N are £30 per tonne. This means that the total processing costs (per tonne of final product) incurred by Division N are £30 (basic variable processing costs incurred in Division M) + £10 (additional processing costs incurred by Division M) + £30 (incremental processing costs incurred by Division N) = £70. The processing costs incurred by Division M are in effect transferred to Division N. With this total cost structure, the contribution margin of Division N is £(110 − 70) = £40 per tonne of final product.

Assume that both Divisions M and N operate under capacity constraints. Division M has a capacity constraint of 1,000 tonnes and Division N has a capacity constraint of 600 tonnes. In order to obtain a transfer price we need to solve a linear programming problem which we can characterize in the following way:

Let M be the output from Division M to the external market

Let N be the output from Division N to the external market

Without keeping inventories of outputs the amount transferred to Division N will be equal to the amount sold by that division during the period. And for the organization as a whole the optimal strategy is given by the following linear programming problem:

Objective function: maximize 20M and 40N
Subject to the following constraints:

$$\begin{aligned} M + N &\leqslant 1{,}000 \quad \text{(M's capacity constraint)} \\ N &\leqslant 600 \quad \text{(N's capacity constraint)} \\ M, N &\geqslant 0 \end{aligned}$$

In any linear programming problem we need to be able to specify an objective function or organizational objective. In this case the objective function is to maximize the contribution margins from Divisions M and N. In addition, this objective is subject to certain capacity constraints as stated earlier. Finally, there is the constraint that both the output levels of Division M and N must be greater than or equal to 0. In other words, they cannot be negative numbers.

There are a number of ways of solving this problem as we saw in Chapter 5.

Graphical methods, for instance, may be applied. In this case, however, the problem is sufficiently simple to solve with the use of simultaneous equations. These equations are:

$$M+N = 1{,}000 \qquad (1)$$
$$N \quad = \quad 600 \qquad (2)$$

Substituting eqn 2 into eqn 1 we obtain the following results:

$$M = 1{,}000 - 600 = 400$$
$$\therefore \; N = \quad 600$$

This means that the optimal production strategy is for Division M to produce 400 tonnes of MX5 for the external market and for Division N to produce 600 tonnes of the final product.

This production strategy gives rise to a total organizational contribution of £32,000 (i.e. (400 × £20) + (600 × £40)). From the information given above it is clear that, from the point of view of the organization as a whole, Division M should be encouraged to transfer the goods to Division N as the contribution margin of this alternative course of action is £40 per tonne. On the other hand, if Division M did not transfer but sold the intermediate product on the open market the organization as a whole would only earn a contribution margin of £20 per tonne.

What is an appropriate transfer price for the intermediate product? Let us look at the picture from Division M's point of view. Division M would need a price that recovered its processing costs (which amount to £30 + £10 per tonne) plus the amount of contribution that is forgone by not selling to the external market. This forgone contribution amounts to £20 per tonne. Hence, Division M would require a transfer price that was at least equal to £60 per tonne of intermediate product.

From Division N's point of view, the division can afford a transfer price of a maximum of £(110 − 30) = £80 per tonne. This is the amount at which Division N breaks even. A transfer price that is higher than £80 per tonne would lead Division N to make a loss.

Given these two points of view it can be seen that an ideal transfer price would lie in the range £60 < P < £80. Irrespective of what transfer price is actually chosen within this range the optimal output mix would be 400 tonnes of M and 600 tonnes of N with total organizational profit amounting to £32,000.

More complicated transfer pricing problems will involve a greater number of simultaneous equations and more complicated methods of solving these equations exist. However, we shall not proceed to look at these in detail.

There are a number of difficulties with using linear programming methods to obtain transfer prices. This is why the practice is not widespread. These difficulties, as pointed out by Bailey and Boe (1976), are:

(i) The linear programming model assumes that the central headquarters of organizations possess detailed knowledge of the divisions under their control. Vital information such as the supply and demand curves facing each division may not be known to central management. Indeed, even divisional managers may only possess incomplete knowledge as to the demand and supply functions applicable to the divisions. In addition, even if such knowledge is known in detail, divisional managers may not be motivated to disclose this information to senior managers.

(ii) The model also assumes that it is possible to arrive at a unanimous objective function. In organizations with conflicting interest groups it is extremely difficult to agree on an objective function – as discussed in Chapter 2.

(iii) No time lags are involved in the implementation of output and pricing decisions. If such time lags occur, a set of transfer prices that were calculated given certain assumptions and constraints may no longer apply when these constraints change. Many organizations today face fast-changing environments; should such change impact upon production constraints,linear programming may not be a useful planning and control tool.

9.6 Social and individual controls

Control has tended to be viewed by some as a set of administrative and feedback controls that are instituted to prevent inefficient and inappropriate use of an organization's resources. Interpreted this way, internal control in particular is seen as consisting of a set of technical, preventive procedures. This traditional view of control has a number of disadvantages:

(i) it does not highlight the social and individual aspects of control; and
(ii) it is negative in orientation in that it does not focus on *how* members of an organization might be positively encouraged to develop creativity, adaptability and learning in the management of the organization's problems.

Through this book we have argued that an organization is first and foremost a collectivity of people with diverse needs and personalities. In addition, people do not function as atomistic beings. They engage in sense-making and political processes in interaction with one another. Given this, it is important to conclude this chapter with a review of social and individual controls.

(a) Social controls

Technical, procedural controls (including transfer pricing) constitute one approach to exerting control. Equally important are social and political controls. Assume we have two groups of students who are similarly troublesome and uncooperative in the classroom. Teacher A is responsible for one group and Teacher B for another group. Both teachers have available to them a set of administrative rules for the discipline and motivation of students. Teacher A is able to maintain order and improve performance without the use of the administrative rules available. Teacher B, unfortunately, attempts to do precisely the same but is reduced to frustration, anger and tears. The class becomes even more uncontrollable than before the arrival of Teacher B.

Similar situations occur every day in organizations where an identical set of technical, administrative rules are in operation but the results of managing within those rules may differ markedly between managers. *Leadership style* was mentioned in Chapter 8 (but see also Chapter 10, pp. 852–4) as an important instrument of social control. Remember that we argued that budgets could be used according to a number of different leadership styles. We could, for example, operate with a budget-constrained or profit-conscious style. In addition, we might encourage genuine subordinate involvement in setting budget targets or set them in a top-down approach.

These different management styles are related to different basic assumptions about human nature. Thus, an authoritarian management style may be associated with a Theory X version of human beings as basically lazy, work-avoiding people. Alternatively, we may manage with a Theory Y version of people as individuals who are capable of initiative and hard work given the appropriate environment. Douglas McGregor, the proponent of Theory Y, argued that a Theory Y perspective on human beings was more likely to lead to both effective organizational performance and the personal satisfaction and development of the managers and employees involved.

Similar arguments have been made by Rensis Likert who conducted extensive empirical research to support his theory. Likert evolved a four-fold classification of managerial attitudes, beliefs and behaviours:

System 1: An exploitive and authoritative style of management;
System 2: A benevolent but authoritative style of management;
System 3: A consultative style of management; and
System 4: A participative and group oriented style of management.

Likert argued that, based on his evidence, System 4 was the preferred approach to managing people and to achieving both high levels of performance and of satisfaction. As can be seen, his recommendations are similar to those of McGregor in stressing individual development, equality and participation in the workplace. These emphases have received a mixed reaction.

Cynics have argued that these theories lead to pseudo-concern for the welfare of individual employees and are merely ploys for a disguised emphasis on productivity and cost reduction. It should also be pointed out that these views on social control all emerged in Anglo-Saxon countries in the 1960s and early 1970s, a period which has been termed the 'Age of Aquarius' and of 'flower people and flower power'. That is, in certain countries, this period saw a widespread humanist concern for the individual's personal well-being and peace. Thus McGregor's and Likert's managerial theories appealed to emerging social values and popular political philosophies. Since then a period of economic recession has hit those same Western countries; governments have become increasingly conservative; and financial stringency has focused on issues of cost control and organizational efficiency. There is now a suggestion that these humanistic modes of control are not appropriate in a hostile and competitive environment.

It is difficult therefore to summarize whether the kinds of social control advocated in the 1960s and 1970s are appropriate for managing in the 1990s. Certainly some managements have used the managerial theories discussed above in a non-genuine manner to introduce coercive work practices. In addition, pseudo-participation in budgeting may have been experienced. However, Likert's arguments are based on extensive and systematic research. He assembled an impressive set of evidence. In addition, he and his colleagues point out that the precise impact of any managerial style will depend upon many other factors which influence and constrain human behaviour in an organization. If managers and workers perceive that there is a genuine effort to provide for both the interests of 'the organization' and for the individual employee it is likely that a humanistic manager will bring about higher levels of performance and job satisfaction.

In addition, the importance of social controls is well-exhibited in the research on work group performance. Work is usually performed by *groups* in organizations. There are, in general, two main types of groups in organizations – formal work groups and informal groups. An example of a formal group is a project group (that is a group of people gathered round a specific project such as a marketing exercise or a research and development project). Another example of a formal group is a task group – a team of nurses on a ward, a departmental team of accounting personnel, or a bevy of tea-ladies. Informal groups include friendship groups. These are people who may not belong to the same formal task group but share common interests (for instance, in sport, politics, ethnic cultures, music or even forms of gambling!).

There are two aspects of formal work groups that are of particular concern to management accountants. First is the existence of *group norms*. Norms are the standards that are shared and accepted by members of a group. They operate effectively as a form of social control upon the behaviour of group members. According to Gibson, *et al.* (1979), norms have certain characteristics that are worthy of note:

(i) Norms are only formed with respect to things that have significance for the group. If production is important, then a norm will evolve; if not providing information to other groups is vital, such a norm will also form.
(ii) Norms are accepted to various degrees by groups members. Some norms are accepted by all members, while others are only partly accepted.
(iii) Norms may apply to every member, or they may apply to only some group members. For example, every member may be expected to comply with a production norm, while only group leaders are expected to set the agenda at group meetings.

The type of group norms that are operative in formal work groups may substantively influence the level of a group's performance; its ability to work with other individuals and groups; and its acceptance of the goals of other groups. For instance, a formal group may decide to set a production norm of 150 articles per shift when it is possible for the group to produce 180 articles, and operate a policy of non-cooperation with other work groups. Should these be the group norms, the performance of the group would be much lower than the performance level which is feasible. Alternatively, a group may set high production standards and operate a policy of maximum cooperation with other work groups.

Group norms can be seen to be an important means of internal group control. However, as Hopwood (1974) points out, their form and strength, and the direction which they take can vary from organization to organization. Research studies indicate that the following factors will influence the operation and type of group norms formed:

- the technology and administrative hierarchy of the organization;
- the product and labour markets facing the organization; and
- personal characteristics, values and beliefs of group members.

In an electrical engineering workshop, for example, Lupton (1963) found that there was a well-developed system of social sanctions which was instituted to regulate earnings and work among the men employed on the assembly work. By contrast, in a garment workshop which employed women on assembly work, he found that although the work groups were close-knit, as a result of both personal and external factors, the social pressures had not been directed towards setting norms for either input or output.

Apart from the type of group norms that are operative, the second aspect of groups that is of importance to management accountants is the level of *group cohesiveness*. A cohesive group is one in which all the members possess a 'closeness or commonness of attitude, behavior, and performance' (Gibson, *et al.*, 1979, p. 148). A group that is low in cohesiveness does not possess interpersonal attractiveness for the members.

In general, as the cohesiveness of a work group increases, the level of conformity to group norms also increases. In a cohesive group members are highly committed to group norms. This may or may not be beneficial to the aims of other groups such as senior management. If group norms contradict managerial goals a cohesive group will be seen as 'dysfunctional' and 'troublesome' by management. However, if group norms closely mirror managerial goals a cohesive group may be seen as a valuable asset to the organization. Thus, group cohesiveness is a double-edged sword, which may or may not serve the aims of the management group.

Its role as a form of social control, however, should not be underestimated. In a now-famous study conducted by the Tavistock Institute in the United Kingdom in the 1940s and 1950s, group cohesiveness was found to substantially affect people's acceptance of a new form of technology. After the Second World War a number of changes in mining equipment and procedures were introduced into the coal-mining industry in England. In the 'old' days miners worked together as teams. The teams dug out the coal, loaded it into cars, and moved it to a station where it was taken from the mine. The tasks involved, physical proximity, dangers of mining, cultures of the mining villages and the intergenerational nature of mining families resulted in the development of highly cohesive work groups. People worked well with team members who tended to remain in the same teams for many years.

The new technology, called the 'longwall mining method', disrupted these groups. Machines took over some of the tasks previously performed by the miners. Groups became separated and there was also an increase in the physical distance between miners. As a result, miners began to show stress and there was a higher incidence of sick leave and absenteeism. Production was reduced significantly. Although other groups formed, these were not as attractive to the miners as the traditional teams.

Thus, a cohesive group may or may not be seen as beneficial. Much depends on the group norms established and the extent to which these accord with the goals of other groups.

(b) Individual controls

Individuals who are personally motivated to achieve particular organizational goals and targets may be said to exhibit *self control*. They require fewer formal administrative controls to ensure that organizational objectives are achieved. However, cynics may argue that such self-controlled individuals may in fact be the most controlled of all employees, in that they have been 'brainwashed' into internalizing (that is, fully accepting) organizational objectives. Despite this scepticism, it is observed that some individuals are self-motivated to achieve organizational objectives. Their personal objectives become fused with organizational targets.

In Chapter 8 we discussed both content and process theories of motivation. Essentially, the work of Maslow and Herzberg indicated that people are really interested in opportunities for recognition, achievement, responsibility and intrinsic interest. They suggested that if large organizations could provide for these through job enrichment and job enlargement programmes, instead of employing people on minor repetitive tasks, many of the problems of internal control would be alleviated.

As Hopwood (1974) points out, these views contain many important grains of truth. Many managers are successfully putting these theories into practice. However, these motivation theories on self-control have also been found to be over-simplistic. They do not cater for the possibility that different people, and groups of people, might be motivated by different things. For instance, the research by Goldthorpe and his colleagues (1970) found that car workers on an assembly line were keen to stay on the assembly lines because of the high wages earned. These workers had given up jobs which offered more interest, status, responsibility and opportunities to use their skills and abilities, in order to work on a repetitive, dehumanized task. They sought high earnings from their jobs and they defined their place of work as simply a source of income. Accordingly, they were prepared to endure the hardships and the deskilled nature of the work. Indeed, they reported a high degree of satisfaction with their job because it provided what they wanted – money.

Contrast this finding with the work of Maslow and Herzberg who indicated that money would not act as a motivator because the average worker had enough and had satisfied his lower-order needs. The social experiences and conditions of the car workers were such that they saw work as a means to an end – money. They were not interested in participating in decision-making or in being praised by their superiors. They were quite content to earn a 'fair day's pay for a fair day's work' and go home to their families and friends. Indeed, they were not even interested in mixing with their workmates after work!

Such conflicting research results may be reconciled by simplistic modifications to Maslow's hierarchy of needs. However, recent research suggests that such an approach is based on dubious assumptions about the structure of human needs. In summary, we know that self-control and motivation play a very important part in ensuring that individuals behave in ways that are considered desirable from the point of view of the organization as a whole (not just management). However, any understanding of the control which individuals themselves exert over their own behaviour must be based on a detailed knowledge of the needs which are activated in specific situations by both the individuals themselves and the other factors influencing them.

Summary

In this chapter we have discussed how feedback control may be effected through a system of responsibility accounting. It was also pointed out that a responsibility accounting system, while being of primary use in the provision of feedback information, could also help to pinpoint responsibility for exercising feedforward control.

A responsibility accounting system is based on the principle that a manager should not be held accountable for items which he/she cannot effectively control. However, it should also be remembered that, in the long-run, all financial factors are controllable by somebody within the organization. The ultimate decision, of course, is to decide to disband the organization and cease to exist.

A responsibility accounting system usually allocates responsibilities in such a way as to parallel the formal authority system within an organization. Typically, employees further down the authority hierarchy are made responsible for the day-to-day operations of the organization while the most senior managers are responsible for the strategic management of the organization as a whole. Performance reports must be tailored to the specific responsibilities of each manager. Usually, reports to lower-level employees provide greater detail on the day-to-day operations while senior managerial reports show aggregated operational information but provide more information for strategic feedforward control.

Responsibilities may also be allocated such that certain managers are responsible only for costs, or for costs and revenues, or for costs, revenues and investment. This in effect amounts to a decentralization of decision-making authority to the managers of responsibility centres. Such decentralization is said to give rise to benefits such as:

(i) a greater specialization of expertise;
(ii) the provision of managerial training for divisional managers; and
(iii) the provision of incentives to divisional managers to act in a creative and entrepreneurial manner.

Decentralization, however, creates problems – especially when goods and services are transferred between divisions. If these divisions are set up as profit centres, prices will have to be charged for the transfer of goods and services. These prices, called transfer prices, are effectively a means of allocating organizational profit among divisions. Transfer prices are difficult to set because they need to serve several (often conflicting) roles. Transfer prices should:

(i) encourage divisional managers to exercise autonomy and an entrepreneurial spirit;
(ii) motivate divisional managers to maximize divisional profit, subject to the overriding objectives of the organization as a whole.

However, a transfer price that meets the first objective may not meet the second objective. Hence, although a variety of transfer pricing methods may be used, each of these has its own disadvantages and advantages. For instance, the use of market prices is justified only if perfectly competitive markets exist for the intermediate product being transferred. Should this condition not be met, the use of market prices will not lead to optimal solutions for the division and for the organization as a whole.

If an organization does encounter substantial difficulties in setting transfer prices the question must be raised as to whether it has designed an appropriate responsibility accounting system. Allocating responsibilities to decentralized divisions may not be the most suitable alternative. This is so if divisions do conduct a great deal of interdivisional trading in goods and services for which no external markets exist. In these circumstances either the selling or buying division might be a captive seller/buyer of the other division. Some centralization might in fact be the more suitable alternative. Such situations demonstrate that the allocation of responsibilities and of decentralized decision-making authority needs to be carefully considered. The costs and benefits of alternative responsibility systems should be explicitly considered and 'appreciated' (in Vickers' sense of the word) by senior managers.

Control is often thought of only in terms of certain accounting and administrative forms of control. In today's computerized age, the traditional notion of control has been extended to include monitoring procedures surrounding computerized accounting information systems. A more powerful form of control is exerted through the cultural norms that circumscribe individual and group behaviour within organizations. Yet we find few discussions of this form of control within managerial accounting texts.

Key terms and concepts

Here is a list of the key terms and concepts which have featured in this chapter. You should make sure that you understand and can define each one of them. Page references to definitions in the text appear in bold in the index.

- Controllability
- Decentralization
- Management by exception
- Management by objectives (MbO)
- Regulation by error
- Responsibility accounting
- Responsibility centres
  - cost centres
  - profit centres
  - investment centres
- Transfer prices
  - cost-based
  - market-based
  - negotiated
  - via linear programming
- Transfer pricing
  - final products
  - intermediate products

Further reading

On transfer pricing see Watson and Baumler (1975), Abdel-Khalik and Lusk (1974) and Benke and Edwards (1980). On divisional performance measurement and accounting practices in divisionalized organizations see Solomons (1965), and Scapens and Sale (1981). On controllability in responsibility accounting see Choudhury (1986) and Antle and Demski (1988).

The workbook to accompany this chapter begins on p. 560.

CHAPTER 10 Performance measurement: variance analysis

Learning objectives

After studying this chapter you should be able to:

- appreciate the theme of performance measurement within organizations – with particular reference to variance analysis;
- demonstrate how to measure and interpret variances in a range of settings;
- understand the variance investigation decision and its statistical extensions;
- locate variance analysis in the context of organizational control.

10.1 Introduction

The preparation of budgets and the setting of standards have been covered in Chapters 7 and 8 and these represent, *inter alia*, desired outcomes. Chapter 9 has emphasized the need to personalize responsibility for the attainment of desired outcomes if control is to be achieved. Moreover, to facilitate the attainment of control it is necessary to know from time to time how actual performance compares with desired performance, and this chapter focuses on this issue.

This comparison answers the question about *what* is happening, and responsibility accounting ensures that managers know *who* is to be accountable. Establishing *why* divergences occur is problematic, as is the question of deciding *how* to apply corrective action in order that control may be effective.

Our initial perspective is a broad overview of performance measurement which goes beyond a simple preoccupation with, say, profit as a single criterion. Whatever bench-marks are used for assessment purposes – whether budgets, standards, ratios or other criteria – the key issues are:

(i) what to measure;
(ii) how to measure; and
(iii) how to interpret measurements as a prelude to action.

A comprehensive range of variances will be presented, and approaches to measuring them will be illustrated and explained. Coverage will include single (e.g. price) and two-factor (e.g. price and quantity) analysis as the building blocks for manufacturing, marketing and distribution examples (see Workbook, Sections W10.4 and W10.5).

Deciding whether or not to investigate a reported variance will be influenced both by its likely cause and by its significance. Ways of determining the significance of variances (including the percentage approach, but paying particular attention to the statistical approach) will be outlined and illustrated. Notions such as management by exception and tolerance limits will be explained, along with their implications for the design of managerial accounting systems.

How should variances be interpreted? What impacts will this have on managers' motivation and subsequent behaviour? Questions such as these will be addressed in a way that contrasts the apparent technical interpretations with the possible behavioural consequences of variances.

10.2 Performance measurement

A central notion in considering control is the evaluation of performance – whether *ex ante* (as in feedforward control) or *ex post* (as in feedback control). This can be undertaken at several levels: at the societal level, at the level of the enterprise as a whole, at the level of a division or other segment – as activities, or at the levels of the group or individual. In essence what is required is a comparison of desired outcomes with expected or actual outcomes, an assessment of any divergences, and proposals for future courses of action. Putting this another way, three questions need to be posed:

(i) What has happened?
(ii) Why has it happened?
(iii) What is to be done about it?

The need to view performance evaluation within a control context is highlighted by our posing all three questions, rather than just the first two.

At the broadest level there are social goals and performance indicators, as reported by Terleckyj (1970), AAA (1972c) and in a tribute to Raymond Bauer (see *AOS*, **6** (3) 1981, pp. 217–270). But there are major measurement problems at this level:

> The need for progress in measuring social change is evident. Without measurement it is improbable that desirable goals can be reached. Yet, in contrast to a few exceptionally advanced fields, most areas of social concern and public policy suffer from lack of even the most elementary information, leaving the field wide open for guessing, emotion, low-grade politics, and waste, while the problems remain.
>
> Terleckyj (1970), p. 765.

Narrowing the focus a little, several studies by IMTA/CIPFA (1972, 1974) and the American Accounting Association (1971a, 1971b, 1974) have looked at performance measurement in non-commercial organizations, as have Sorensen and Grove (1977), Mayston (1985) and Ramanathan (1985) – the latter two being in the first issue of a journal devoted to public sector and non-commercial organizations.

In looking specifically at performance assessment in institutions of higher education, Sizer (1981, p. 231) states:

> Given the complexities and difficulties surrounding . . . non-profit performance evaluation . . . it is not surprising that there is a tendency to recognize those parts of the system that can be measured and monitored with a high degree of precision. . . . However, do those who develop and employ such partial performance indicators always remember that optimizing the parts does not necessarily optimize the whole?

One particular feature that applies in all service-oriented non-commercial organizations is the problem of specifying outputs (see Wilson (1978)). A consequence of this is the practice of using resource inputs as surrogates for the unspecified outputs, which is a clear reflection of the modest state of the art in this domain. The absence of adequate output specifications limits the extent to which the following control questions can be resolved:

Quantity: How much was accomplished?
How much should have been accomplished?
Quality: How good was that which was accomplished?
How good should it have been?
Cost: How much did the accomplishment cost?
How much should it have cost?

The concept of performance measurement is a simple one to comprehend, but it can only be put into practice if plans are carefully prepared before decisions are made. In the absence of a plan (expressed in terms of standards and budgeted levels of performance) there is no bench-mark for evaluating the performance of segments of an enterprise, individuals in responsible positions, or the organization as a whole, and attempting to improve it. The existence of standards of performance eliminates many of the opportunities and excuses for poor performance, and provides a reference point for improvements.

Measuring the performance of the various types of responsibility centre (i.e. cost, profit and investment – as discussed in Chapter 9) will usually focus on financial aspects of organizational activity. This will not always be appropriate, although it tends to be the general case that managers are held accountable in terms of quantifiable performance rather than performance that is qualitative (such as employee morale or public relations). However, let us look in rather more detail at the role of profit in relation to performance measurement.

The amount of profit an enterprise earns is a measure of its effectiveness if that enterprise has a profit objective. (In this sense we can define effectiveness in terms of achieving that which one sought to achieve.) Since Profit = Revenue (Output) – Cost (Input) it can be seen to be a measure of efficiency also in that it relates outputs to inputs. Thus an organization having revenues of £100 m and costs of £60 m is more efficient than one in the same industry having revenues of £100 m and costs of £70 m since the former uses less input to produce a given output.

Despite its ability to act as a measure both of effectiveness and efficiency, profit is a less than perfect measure because:

(i) it is a monetary measure, and monetary measures do not measure all aspects of either input or output;
(ii) the standards against which profits are judged may themselves be less than perfect; and

(iii) at best, profits are a measure of what has happened in the short-run whereas we must also be interested in the long-run consequences of management actions.

Nevertheless, profit measures can still play a distinctly valuable role in the control effort. For example:

(i) A profit measure can provide a simple criterion for evaluating alternatives. (Although it will be necessary to take into account many factors other than profit in making a choice among alternative courses of action, on the face of it option A is more attractive than option B if A will produce more profit than B.)
(ii) A profit measure will permit a quantitative analysis of alternatives to be made in which benefits can be directly compared with costs. (Assuming a market exists for an enterprise's output, these benefits will be measured by the revenue flow from its sale.)
(iii) A profit measure can provide a single, broad measure of performance in that it is arrived at after all financial costs and revenues have been taken into account, and it thus subsumes many other aspects of performance.
(iv) Profit measures permit the comparison of performance to be made over time for one organization, or comparisons at a point in time to be made for a group of organizational units (e.g. divisions or competing enterprises within an industry), even if they are performing dissimilar functions. This is not possible with other measures, although it may be necessary to standardize accounting practices in measuring profits for this purpose and to ensure that the valuations of assets are made on the same bases.

This all sounds very promising, but we need to bear in mind the limitations of the profit measure. Among these are:

(i) Organizations have multiple objectives and will often forgo profit opportunities in order to avoid conflict over some other objective (or constraint) such as the desired image for the company or some ethical standard.
(ii) Social costs and benefits are excluded from corporate profit figures. At best profit is a measure of an enterprise's success as an economic entity, but this does not measure that enterprise's net contribution (or cost) to society such as the arts sponsorship it might offer, or the pollution it might cause.
(iii) As already mentioned, profit measures typically focus on current rather than long-run performance: actions can be taken to improve the former at the expense of the latter (e.g. by cutting advertising, R & D, training and maintenance budgets).
(iv) Profit is an inadequate basis for comparing organizations' relative performance or for monitoring one organization's performance over time. The real test is actual versus target profit, but we are really unable to specify this latter figure in any sensible way because it should be based on *profit potential* and a company's profit opportunities are not all identified. It follows that an apparently high profit figure, even when this corresponds with the target figure, may in reality be poor when related to missed opportunities.
(v) Accounting rules are also inadequate since they often do not permit the recording of economic reality. (Costs should reflect the use of resources, but accounting practice does not allow this to be measured when it values assets

on the basis of historical cost rather than their opportunity cost, i.e. current value in an alternative use, which has an impact on the depreciation charge, etc.).

(vi) Profit measures are not applicable in certain segments of a business, notably those that incur costs but do not generate revenue (unless a transfer pricing system is introduced to impute revenue flows). Examples of these types of segment are R & D, the legal department, the personnel department and the accounting department.

Let us broaden our perspective on effectiveness (as discussed in Chapter 2) and consider measures that go beyond profit and profitability (to which we return in Chapter 11). Can we define for any type of organization what is effective and what is not? Early organizational analysts talked of such criteria as:

(i) profit maximization:
(ii) high productivity;
(iii) good employee morale; and
(iv) provision of an efficient service,

as sufficient to indicate effectiveness. But these criteria are inadequate because:

(i) organizations behave ineffectively from some points of view if a single criterion is used; and
(ii) organizations fulfil multiple functions and have multiple goals, some of which may be in conflict. It would be inappropriate to assess an organization's performance on the basis of any one criterion.

The difficulty, as will be apparent, lies in identifying those multiple criteria that are necessary and sufficient to ensure corporate well-being and survival. One way is via the application of *Pareto's Law*.

Pareto's Law (or the 80/20 rule) is widely thought to apply to a range of situations in which most of the behaviour or value of one factor is deemed to depend on only a little of another factor. For example, it is often asserted that 80% of inventory movements within an organization are attributable to 20% of items stocked, 80% of sales volume comes from 20% of customers, or 80% of profits are derived from 20% of product lines. The main point here, of course, is that one can effectively control an inventory if one can focus attention on the critical 20% of active items, or one can control the level of sales if the key customers are properly serviced. This can be greatly beneficial both in terms of cost savings (through eliminating unnecessary control effort on the 'insignificant' 80% of items that only make up 20% of stock issues) and in terms of improved organizational effectiveness (due to better control of the key elements).

The application of Pareto's Law is known by a number of different names. Perhaps the most frequently encountered are: key variables, critical success factors, and key result areas.

To illustrate the idea further we can consider a generalized example, and then a number of specific industry examples (see Rockart (1979)). Figure 10.1 identifies for each main sphere of activity the factors that are likely to be of some major significance to corporate performance. Each factor has financial implications,

Figure 10.1

A general example of key variables.

Sphere of activity	Critical factors
Environment	Economic – interest rates inflation rates concentration Political stability
Marketing	Sales volume Market share Gross margins
Production	Capacity utilization Quality standards
Logistics	Capacity utilization Level of service
Asset management	Return on investment Accounts receivable balance

and if they can be controlled it is probable that the overall company can be controlled.

Within specific industries there is likely to be considerable variation in key variables, as Fig. 10.2 illustrates. Johnson (1967), for example, looks in more detail at this key issue question.

Figure 10.2

Specific industry examples of key variables.

Food processing:
- New product development
- Good distribution
- Effective advertising

Motor vehicles:
- Styling
- Efficient dealer networks
- Tight control over manufacturing costs

Life assurance:
- Development of agency managerial personnel
- Effective control of clerical staff
- Innovation in creating new types of policies

Oil:
- Decentralization
- Liquidity
- Government-business relationship
- Societal image
- New ventures (to broaden its base)

As a slight variation on the theme the (US) General Electric Company gives a classic illustration of one organization's attempt to identify the major variables that management needs to monitor if total company performance is to be controlled. Eight key result areas were determined in accordance with the following criterion: 'Will continued failure in this area prevent the attainment of management's responsibility for advancing General Electric as a leader in a strong, competitive economy, even though results in all other key areas are good?' (See Greenwood (1974) .) The eight variables that met this requirement are shown in Fig. 10.3.

While these eight factors might seem to be generally applicable, it is their precise definition within the context of a particular company's activities that determines how critical they are. This highlights a fundamental aspect of designing any control system: it must be highly 'situational' if it is to be effective. In other words, it must be tailored to the specific characteristics of the situation, which means *this* company's objectives, *this* company's operations, *this* company's managers, and *this* company's environment (remember contingency theory from Chapter 3).

The General Electric approach seeks to balance two conflicting tendencies: on the one hand, the diffusion of effort over multiple goals and the failure to perform as well as might be expected in any one area; and on the other hand, the tendency to emphasize one particular goal with the result that other goals are not attained.

The most common tendency in commercial enterprises is often said to be to focus on the short-run maximization of net profit (or sales) without considering the damage that this might do to the long-run position (e.g. by postponing repairs or maintenance work; by cutting back on advertising, or on research, training or quality control expenditure; by deferring capital investment outlays; or through exhortations to employees to increase productivity). Short-term 'gains' achieved in this way tend to be illusory because the subsequent need to make up lost ground, e.g. via heavier advertising or training in later periods, more than outweighs short-term gains.

To the extent that effectiveness is a multiple criterion we must avoid the trap of focusing too sharply on one contributing factor. It would be a mistake to assume that effectiveness would be assured simply through selecting and training the right people. Given our definition of effectiveness in Chapter 2, effectiveness may be assessed in terms of a system's capacity:

Figure 10.3

General Electric's key result areas.

1. Profitability
2. Market position
3. Productivity
4. Product leadership
5. Personnel development
6. Employee attitudes
7. Public responsibility
8. Balance between short-run and long-run goals

(i) to survive, adapt, maintain itself, and grow – regardless of the functions it fulfils; and
(ii) to achieve (i) through its bargaining position with its environment in relation to the acquisition of resources.

Turning from these broad questions to the more technical ones concerning the measurement of variances leads us to the next section. In working through this section you should assume that:

(i) the organization has a budgeting system in operation, which embodies standards for selling prices, costs, etc. (as discussed in Chapters 7 and 8);
(ii) the budgets have been developed by those who are to be held accountable for their attainment (as outlined in Chapters 8 and 9), and represent the levels of performance that are expected;
(iii) performance reports are produced each month (or other regular frequency) to compare actual with desired outcomes;
(iv) each responsible manager's superior will require to know why significant variances occurred, and what remedial – or reinforcing – actions are proposed for the future.

Our interest is both in the methods of measurement involved in performance evaluation and in the meaning of measures in control terms.

10.3 Variance analysis

The computation and classification of variances (as starting points for analysis and corrective follow-up) represent a vital feature of standard costing and cost control.

What causes variances? There are many causes, some of which are indicated below:

(i) Bought-out materials and components can vary in price.
(ii) Changes in product design will alter the cost of inputs.
(iii) Policy decisions of various kinds relating to, for example, organization structure may affect cost levels.
(iv) The value of money is constantly changing.
(v) Longer or shorter hours may be worked.
(vi) The amount of (for example) idle time may vary due to production hold-ups, strikes, power failures, etc.
(vii) Labour rates/salary levels may change due to union negotiations, policy decisions, merit increases, progression along a scale, or the changing composition of the work-force with regard to length of service.
(viii) Selling prices may change.
(ix) In a multiproduct company, the product sales mix may vary, and if (as is likely) different product lines have different margins, the overall profit contribution will vary.
(x) Improving systems can bring about reductions in costs.
(xi) Changes in productivity (i.e. the level of effort) on the part of operatives, supervisors, management and clerical staff can help or hinder cost levels.
(xii) Investment in new capital equipment, and scrapping of old equipment/

processes/methods, can have immediate effects on direct operating cost levels (direct labour and direct material inputs) as well as on indirect cost items (such as depreciation charges and insurance premiums).

If a variance is significant it signals the need for managerial investigation. It is essential to appreciate fully that the identification of a variance is of no value in itself – the value lies in ascertaining the cause of the variance and acting to correct it. The cause of variances can be personalized, so variance analysis operates in accordance with the principles of responsibility accounting: production foremen will be responsible for direct labour time variances, marketing management for sales price and sales mix variances, the purchasing department for material price variances, and so on.

Even though specific variances may be seen to be the responsibility of specific individuals, the existence of any variance is only a *prima facie* indication of good or poor performance. The truth of the situation may be a standard that was set at the wrong level in the first place.

Let us proceed initially by dealing with manufacturing variances relating to direct materials, direct labour and indirect costs, and then move on to look at variances in a marketing setting.

(a) Direct material variances

Four direct material variances will be considered: price variance, usage variance, mix variance and yield variance.

The first of these, the *direct material price variance*, can be illustrated by means of a material X that has a standard cost of 50 p per kilo, and 100 kilos are bought for £53.00. This gives an unfavourable material price variance of £3.00 in total or £0.03 per kilo, and it is a straightforward matter to isolate this total variance immediately the material is invoiced, with the result that material X is booked into stock at its standard cost per kilo of 50 p, and so the company's stock records can be kept in either monetary units or kilos in the knowledge that they are interchangeable.

In formula terms, material price variance (MPV) is given by:

$$\text{MPV} = (\text{AP} - \text{SP}) \times \text{AQ}$$

where SP = standard price per unit
AP = actual price per unit
AQ = actual quantity bought

therefore:

$$\text{MPV} = £(0.53 - 0.50) \times 100 = +£3.00$$

Let us now suppose that the standard direct material input of material X into product A is 4 kilos per unit, so that the standard direct material cost per unit is:

$$4 \times £0.50 = £2.00$$

If the purchase of 100 kilos of material X is fully used up in producing 24 units of product A then a *direct material usage* (or quantity) *variance* (MUV) can be calculated by applying the formula:

$$MUV = (AQ \times SQ) = SP$$

where SQ = standard quantity
AQ = actual quantity used
SP = standard price per unit

therefore:

$$MUV = (100 - 96) \times £0.50 = +£2.00$$

This unfavourable variance has arisen because 4 kilos too much have been used, but usage variances may arise due to other causes such as:

(i) materials may deteriorate in poor storage conditions;
(ii) purchases may be of a substandard quality;
(iii) the wrong materials may be issued;
(iv) machinery may not be properly set or poorly maintained;
(v) tools/jigs may be faulty;
(vi) an inadequately trained operative may cause a high rate of scrap to result from poor work, etc.

Both the direct material price variance and the direct material usage variance can be derived from Fig. 10.4. Alternatively the picture can be shown as in Fig. 10.5 which analyses the total variance in a graphical manner.

Management can analyse the direct material price and usage variances and then investigate them by asking:

(i) Why has excess material been used (MUV = + £2.00)?

Figure 10.4

Marketing variances (1).

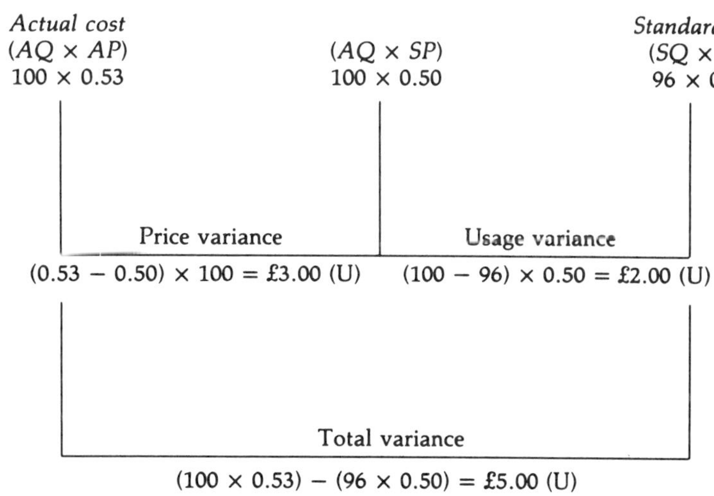

U = Unfavourable

Figure 10.5

Direct material variances (2).

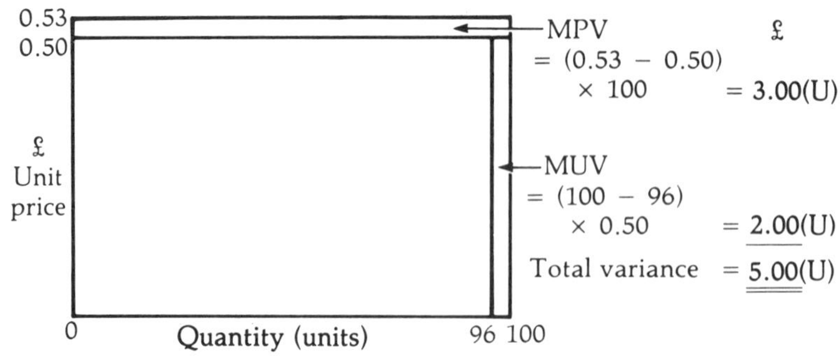

U = Unfavourable

(ii) What is the difference between actual and standard costs for the material (MPV = + £3.00)?

In certain processing industries where raw materials are mixed together in standard proportions it is sometimes found that there is a temporary shortage of one type of material and so a substitute must be used, involving varying the standard mix of materials. This can also happen if the standard materials are blended in non-standard proportions. Since different materials have different costs, the cost of an actual (i.e. non-standard) mix will vary from the standard cost of the standard mix and thus give rise to a *direct materials mix variance.*

To take an example, if the production of 100 litres of product Z requires a standard mix of:

			£
Material A	30	litres at standard cost £0.50 =	15.00
Material B	50	litres at standard cost £1.00 =	50.00
Material C	20	litres at standard cost £0.25 =	5.00
	100		£70.00

The standard cost of 100 litres of this materials mix is therefore £70.00.

However, material C may be in short supply, so the mix may be varied in the following way:

			£
Material A	40	litres at £0.50 =	20.00
Material B	50	litres at £1.00 =	50.00
Material C	10	litres at £0.25 =	2.50
	100		£72.50

Varying the mix in this manner gives rise to an unfavourable direct materials mix variance of £(72.50 − 70.00) = +£2.50.

It could have happened that, as a result of some chemical reaction, the non-standard materials mix shown above may only have produced 95 litres of product Z. Such an outcome – the output is less than the input – is common in chemical processing and, in so far as it is 'normal', can be allowed for in a control system. But unexpected outcomes produce *direct material yield variances*.

Continuing with the above example in which it is assumed that the non-standard mix of materials A, B and C produced 95 litres of product Z, the yield variance (YV) is given by:

$$YV = (AY - SY) \times SC$$

where SY = standard yield
AY = actual yield
SC = standard cost of standard mix per unit of output

therefore:

$$YV = (95 - 100) \times £0.70 = +£3.50$$

The actual cost per litre under these circumstances is £(72.50/95) = £0.76 as opposed to a standard cost per litre of £(70.00/100) = £0.70. The total unfavourable variance of (76 – 70)p – 6p per litre is made up of:

Material mix variance per litre	2.5p(U)
Material yield variance per litre	3.5p(U)
Total variance per litre	6.00p(U)

Mix and yield variances should not be confused with material usage variances because their causes are quite different: a materials *mix* variance may be due to a lack of availability of the correct materials; a materials *yield* variance may be due to the processing of a standard mix of standard materials at the wrong temperature; and a material *usage* variance may be due to an excessive number of rejected units of output.

(b) Direct labour variances

The variances stemming from differences between actual labour costs and standard labour costs that will be discussed are direct labour rate variance, efficiency variance, mix variance, idle time variance and calendar variance.

The *direct labour rate variance* is equivalent to the direct material price variance (in the same way that the direct labour efficiency variance is analogous to the direct material usage variance).

While the factor of time does not generally affect any direct material variances, it can have an impact on direct labour variances. As a result of payments to labour being related to the length of time spent on various processes, etc., any variations in amounts paid can be seen to be related to the degree of efficiency exhibited as well as to the rates of pay in force.

When devising a standard labour time for a job, if a worker of a higher grade than was initially intended is used for the job, then a *direct labour rate variance* will arise. For example, a job may have a standard time of 10 hours and may be intended to be performed by a particular grade of operative at a standard hourly direct labour rate of £0.65, giving a standard direct labour cost for the job of £6.50. However, an operative from a more highly skilled grade earning £0.75 per hour may actually do the work, with a resultant cost (assuming he took 10 hours) of £7.50 and an unfavourable direct labour rate variance (LRV) of £1.00. The formula for computing this variance is:

$$\text{LRV} = (\text{AR} - \text{SR}) \times \text{AH}$$

where SR = standard direct labour rate per hour
AR = actual direct labour rate per hour
AH = actual direct labour hours

therefore:

$$\text{LRV} = £(0.75 - 0.65) \times 10 = +£1.00$$

Taking this example further, if the skilled operative had done the job in 8 hours rather than 10, a *direct labour efficiency variance* (LEV) would have arisen, as shown by applying the formula:

$$\text{LEV} = (\text{AH} - \text{SH}) \times \text{SR}$$

where SH = standard hours allowed
AH = actual hours taken
SR = standard direct labour rate per hour

therefore:

$$\text{LEV} = (8 - 10) \times £0.65 = -£1.30$$

This is a favourable variance, and the combined effect of a job for which SR = £0.65 and SH = 10 being done with AR = £0.75 and AH = 8 is shown in Fig. 10.6.

Figure 10.6

Direct labour variances (1).

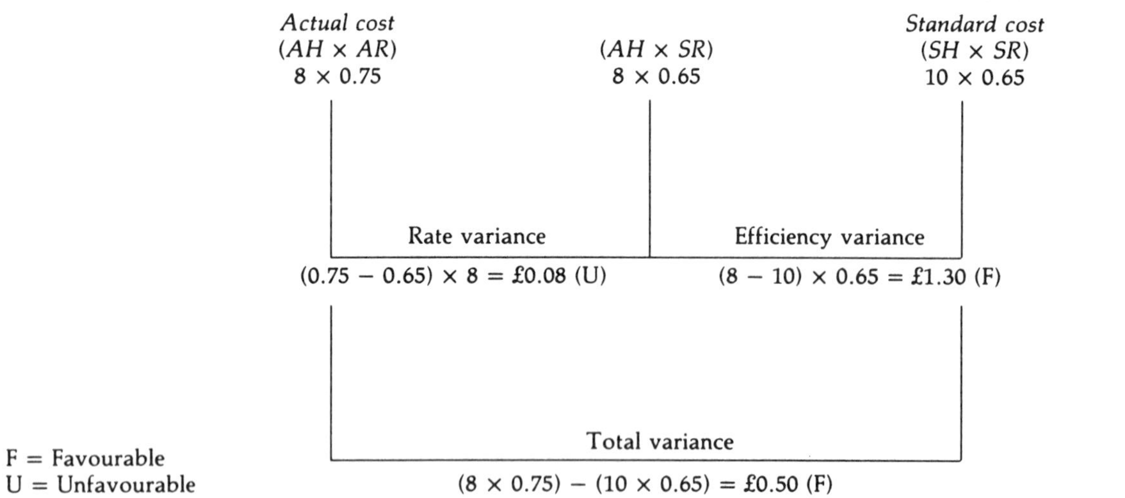

Figure 10.7

Direct labour variances (2).

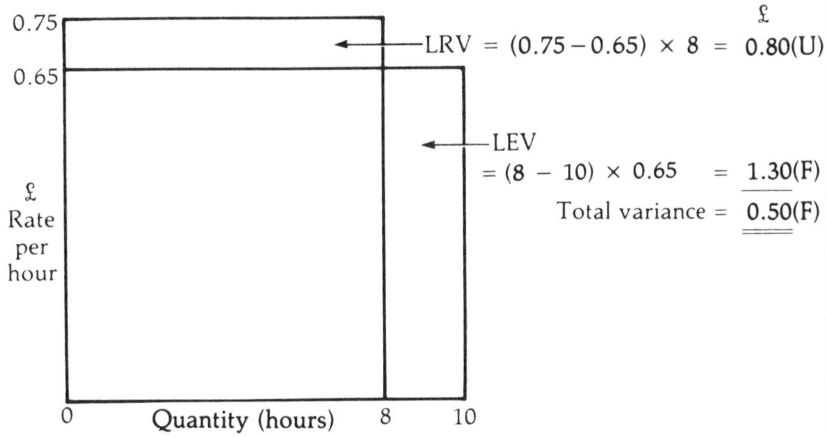

F = Favourable
U = Unfavourable

As with direct material price and usage variances, a graphical analysis of direct labour rate and efficiency variances can be made (see Fig. 10.7). The net outcome of the favourable LEV and the unfavourable LRV is a favourable total direct labour variance of £0.50.

Labour efficiency variances are not simply due to the amount of effort that a worker puts into his job but can be caused by many other factors, among which are the organization of the flow of work, the adequacy of materials, jigs, etc., the efficiency of support services (e.g. set-up time may be excessive, maintenance may be needed, training/inspection/instruction may be needed), and so on.

As with the example given in the previous section for materials mix, so the standard mix of different grades of direct labour may not be achieved and so a *direct labour mix variance* will arise. Take an example. If the production of 100 litres of product Z requires a standard labour input as follows:

			£
2 hours (apprentice rate)	at £0.25	=	0.50
4 hours (unskilled rates)	at £0.40	=	1.60
6 hours (skilled rates)	at £0.60	=	3.60
			£5.70

and if the actual labour input is:

			£
4 hours (apprentice rate)	at £0.25	=	1.00
2 hours (unskilled rates)	at £0.40	=	0.80
6 hours (skilled rates)	at £0.60	=	3.60
			£5.40

then it can be seen that there is a favourable direct labour mix variance of £(5.40 − 5.70) = £0.30.

A mix variance is due to a lack of availability at a particular point in time of a particular type of labour, but *idle time variances* are due to a lack of work. When direct production workers are prevented from being productive for known reasons, these reasons should be noted, the cost of the enforced idleness they cause recorded, and remedial action taken. There is a close relationship between idle time and labour efficiency since the causes of idle time lead to inefficiency, but idle time should be isolated and treated as an indirect cost whereas direct labour efficiency variances are not indirect costs. If the lack of availability of raw materials causes the loss of 200 direct labour hours at a standard rate of £0.65 this gives an unfavorable idle time variance of £130.00.

When a budget is compiled on the basis of an assumed number of working days – hence hours – per month, the occurrence of a public holiday will alter the calculations and this can lead to a *calendar variance*. The formula for working this out is simply the total number of hours lost due to the holiday multiplied by the standard hourly rate.

Direct cost variances – labour and materials – are summarized in Fig. 10.8.

Figure 10.8

Direct cost variances.

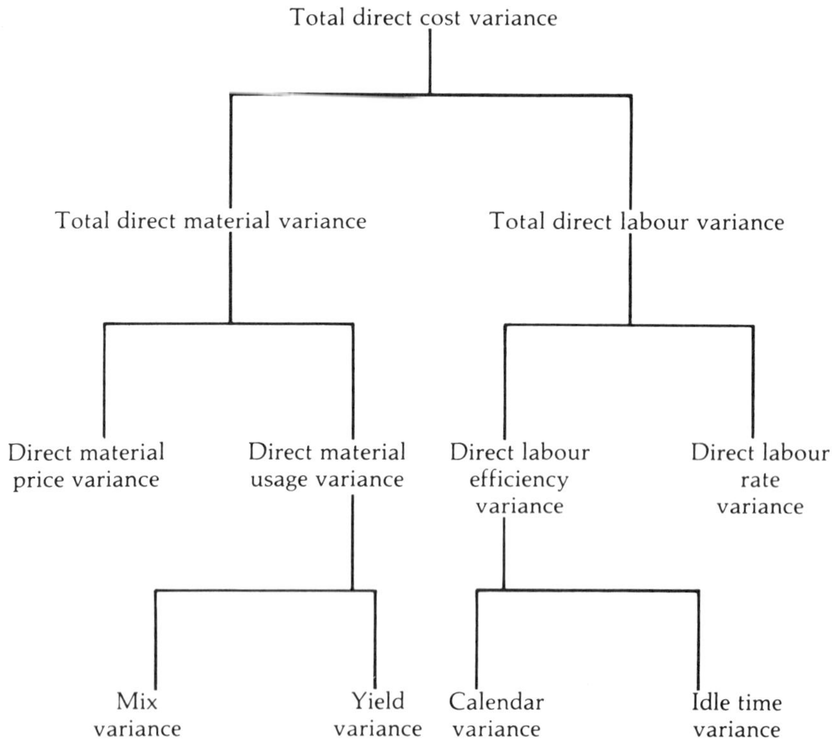

The use of standard costing variance analysis (and variance analysis related to budgeted versus actual costs) should enable the accountant to report the following matters to management in connection with direct material costs and direct labour costs:

(i) Which variances have arisen?
(ii) Who is responsible?
(iii) Why have the variances arisen?

Remedial action is, of course, a managerial prerogative.

(c) Indirect manufacturing cost variances

Indirect cost variances arise in any company employing an absorption costing system when there is a difference between:

(i) standard (or budgeted) costs of indirect items and actual costs;
(ii) standard (or budgeted) usage of indirect items and actual usage;
(iii) normal capacity and the actual level of capacity utilization experienced during a given period.

These three sets of differences give rise to budget (or cost) variances, efficiency variances and capacity variances respectively.

The analysis of indirect cost variances can be performed by dealing initially with variable indirect cost variances, and then with fixed indirect cost variances. Since variable indirect costs are directly proportional (at least within the relevant range) to output the only variance that can normally arise is a *budget variance* caused by a difference in prices (i.e. actual prices $\neq$ budgeted prices). In certain circumstances, however, a variable indirect cost efficiency variance may be found because a larger or smaller amount of an indirect cost item has been consumed for a given level of output than the quantity budgeted. Similarly, when direct labour hours are used to absorb variable indirect costs, a difference between actual direct labour hours and standard direct labour hours will result in a variable indirect cost efficiency variance given by the formula:

$$(AH - SH) \times VR$$

where SH = standard direct labour hours
AH = actual direct labour hours
VR = variable overhead recovery rate per direct labour hour.

On the assumption that AH = SH (hence no variable indirect cost efficiency variance), Fig. 10.9 shows a simplified analysis of variable indirect cost variances.

In connection with fixed indirect costs, the variances that can be identified are the *budget variance* (where the actual expenditure on fixed indirect items differs from the standard or budgeted expenditure) and the *capacity variance*. This latter variance is only associated with fixed indirect costs and it occurs when the level of activity used to spread fixed indirect costs over production (i.e. normal capacity or whatever other method may be chosen) differs from the level actually experienced. The fixed indirect cost capacity variance is a measure of the benefit of working above (or the cost of working below) normal capacity and it is given by:

Figure 10.9

Variable indirect cost variance report.

Department: ________ *Month ending:* ________

Variable indirect cost items	Actual	Budget for 8000 standard hours	Variance		Explanation
	£	£	£		
Materials handling	8,325	8,000	325	U	Wrong grade of worker
Idle time	850	800	50	U	Machine breakdown
Rework	825	800	25	U	Apprentice used
Overtime premium	250	400	150	F	Closed two Saturdays
Supplies	4,000	3,600	400	U	Substitute cutting materials
	£14,250	£13,600	£650	U	

Budgeted rate: £1.70 per standard hour
Standard hours allowed: 8,000

U = Unfavourable
F = Favourable

(Normal activity (in hours) – AH) × Fixed indirect cost absorption rate

It is inevitable, given the nature of fixed cost behaviour and the problem of absorbing fixed costs into production, that capacity variances will frequently occur because it is unlikely that management will be able to operate continually at normal capacity, which is the only way to avoid capacity variances (other than revising the fixed indirect cost recovery rate so that fixed costs are fully absorbed by the level of output achieved). The causes of a fixed indirect cost capacity variance (i.e. the reasons why actual activity is not equal to normal activity) may be poor production scheduling that leads to bottlenecks and low output, unexpected machine breakdowns, strikes, a shortage of skilled operatives or materials, acts of God (such as floods), and so forth. Fig. 10.10 summarizes a fixed indirect cost variance report.

From Fig. 10.10 it can be calculated that the total fixed indirect cost variance is £2,200 made up as follows:

	£
Actual fixed indirect costs incurred	10,200
Fixed indirect costs applied (AH × SR = 8,000 × £1.00)	8,000
Total variance	£2,200 (U)

Of this total, the budget variance is £10,200 – £10,000 = +£200, and the capacity variance is (10,000 – 8,000) × £1.00 = +£2,000, both of which are adverse variances and which together account for the total fixed indirect cost variance of £2,200 (U).

Indirect cost variances – both fixed and variable – are summarized in

Figure 10.10

Fixed indirect cost variance report.

*Department:*________ *Month ending:* ____

Fixed indirect cost items	Actual £	Budget £	Variance £	Explanation
Supervision	1,700	1,700	–	
Depreciation – plant	2,000	2,000	–	
Depreciation – equipment	5,000	5,000	–	
Rates	1,150	1,000	150 U	Increased assessment
Insurance	350	300	50 U	Increased cover
	£10,200	£10,000	£200 U	

Normal capacity: 10,000 standard hours
Budgeted rate: £1.00 per SH
Actual level: 8,000 standard hours

U = Unfavourable

Fig. 10.11. (Together with Fig. 10.8, Fig. 10.11 summarizes the major direct and indirect cost variances.)

The analysis contained in Figs 10.9 and 10.10 can be combined as shown in Fig. 10.12 in a most valuable manner for appreciating the overall situation with

Figure 10.11

Indirect cost variances.

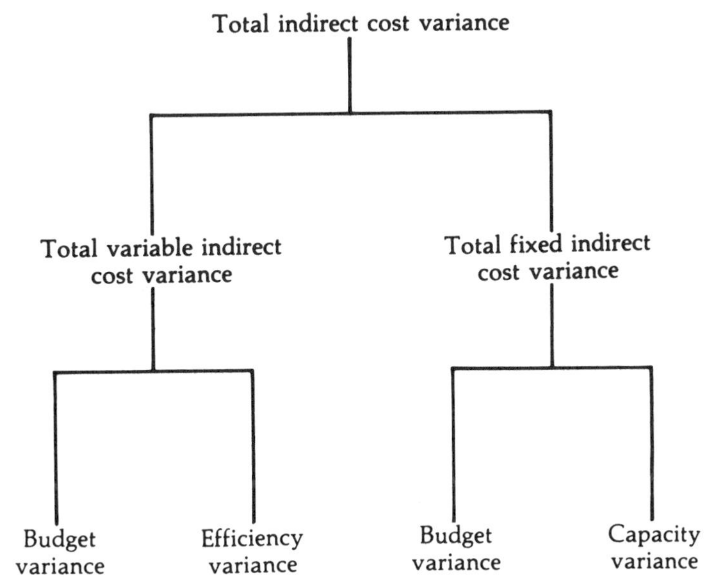

Figure 10.12

Fixed-variable indirect cost analysis.

Department: ________ *Month:* ________

	Actual	Budget (Based on standard hours) SH = 8,000 VC = £1.70 per SH FC = £10,000 per month		Applied (Rate × Standard hours) FC rate = £1.00 per SH VC rate = £1.70 per SH	
	£		£		£
VC	14,250	£1.70 × 8,000	13,600	£1.70 × 8,000	13,600
FC	10,200	£10,000 for month	10,000	£1.00 × 8,000	8,000
Total	£24,450		£23,600	£2.70 × 8,000	£21,600

Total budget variance

	£
V	650 U
F	200 U
Total	£850 U

Total capacity variance

	£
V	Not applicable
F	2,000 U
Total	£2,000 U

Total indirect cost variance

	£
V	650 U
F	2,200 U
Total	£2,850 U

U = Unfavourable

regard to indirect costs. Figure 10.12 shows exactly where indirect cost variances arose and the explanation for fixed and variable variances are shown in Figs 10.9 and 10.10.

An overall summary of direct and indirect cost variances is shown in Fig. 10.13. Included in this summary are three further variances relating to fixed indirect costs (efficiency, idle time and calendar variances) that are analogous to their direct labour equivalents. Also an additional direct material variance for scrap is shown, but it is straightforward to calculate provided you appreciate that it emphasizes spoilt *output* rather than excess *input*.

(d) Marketing variances

In the same way that standards can be set for non-production items so can variance analysis be carried out for non-production items.

When actual selling prices differ from standard selling prices a *sales price variance* can be computed. Standard selling prices will be used in compiling budgets, but it may be necessary to adapt to changing market conditions by raising or lowering prices, so it becomes desirable to segregate variances due to price changes from variances due to changes in quantity and product mix.

Figure 10.13

Direct and indirect cost variance summary.

Type of variance	Cause of cost variation	Primary responsible individual
1. *Direct material*		
(a) Price variance	Increase/decrease in actual cost	Chief buyer
(b) Usage variance	Increase/decrease in actual usage	Production manager
(c) Yield variance	Increase/decrease in actual output	Production manager
(d) Mix variance	Increase/decrease due to material mix differing from standard mix	Production manager or chief chemist
(e) Scrap variance	Increase/decrease in actual scrap	Production manager
2. *Direct labour*		
(a) Rate variance	Increase/decrease in actual rates	Production manager
(b) Efficiency variance	Increase/decrease in rate of output	Production manager
(c) Mix variance	Increase/decrease due to labour mix differing from standard mix	Production manager
(d) Idle time variance	Standard labour cost of abnormal idle time	Production manager
(e) Calendar variance	Standard labour cost of lost time due to paid holidays	Uncontrollable
3. *Variable indirect*		
(a) Budget variance	Increase/decrease due to price changes	Chief buyer
(b) Efficiency variance	Change in consumption per unit of output	Production manager
4. *Fixed indirect*		
(a) Budget variance	Increase/decrease in actual costs	Analysis of specific causes needed to determine responsibility
(b) Capacity variance	Increase/decrease in budgeted output	
(c) Efficiency variance	Increase/decrease in budgeted rate of output for hours worked	
(d) Idle time variance	Standard fixed indirect cost lost due to abnormal idle time	
(e) Calendar variance	Standard fixed indirect cost lost due to paid holidays	

Quantity and mix are the two components of *sales volume variances*, and variations in profit can be explained to some extent by analyzing sales quantity and sales mix. (Some writers – such as Malcom (1978), Bastable and Bao (1988), and Gibson (1990) – have argued that sales mix variances are potentially misleading, other than in specific situations.)

The formulae for computing sales variances are:

Sales price variance = Actual units sold × (Actual price − Standard price)

Sales volume variance = Sales quantity variance + Sales mix variance

Sales quantity variance = Budgeted profit on budgeted sales − Expected profit on actual sales

Sales mix variance = Expected profit on actual sales − Standard profit on actual sales.

'Expected profit on actual sales' is calculated as though profit increases or decreases proportionately with changes in the level of sales. 'Standard profit on actual sales' is the sum of the standard profit per unit for all units sold. (For a single product enterprise, or in one where the profit per unit of sales is constant over the product range, the standard profit on actual sales is equal to the expected profit on actual sales, and the sales mix variance will necessarily be nil.)

Let us clarify the method with an example. Assume budgeted sales of a company's two products for a forthcoming period were as follows:

Product A 500 units at £2.00 per unit
Product B 700 units at £1.50 per unit

and their costs were:

Product A £1.75 per unit
Product B £1.30 per unit

Actual sales for the period were:

Product A 560 units at £1.95 per unit
Product B 710 units at £1.40 per unit

Budgeted sales revenue	= £[(500 × 2.00) + (700 × 1.50)] = £2,050		
Actual sales revenue	= £[(560 × 1.95) + (710 × 1.40)] = £2,086		
Budgeted profit	= £[(500 × 0.25) + (700 × 0.20)] =	£265	
Actual profit	= £[(560 × 0.20) + (710 × 0.10)] =	£183	
Total sales variance			−£82
Sales price variance	= £[560 × (1.95 − 2.00)] + [710 × (1.40 − 1.50)] =		−£99
Sales volume variance:			
Quantity variance	= £265 − [2,086/2,050 × 265] =	+£4	
Mix variance	= £269 − [(560 × 0.25) + (710 × 0.20)] =	+£13	
Sales volume variance			+£17
Total sales variance			−£82

Standards can be developed for repetitive activities, and it is possible to determine standards in a marketing context for the following illustrative activities:

(i) cost per unit of sales
(ii) cost per sales transaction
(iii) cost per order received

(iv) cost per customer account
(v) cost per mile travelled
(vi) cost per sales call made.

The degree of detail can be varied to suit the particular requirements. Thus 'cost per unit of sales' may be 'advertising cost per £ of sales revenue for product X' and so on.

It is clearly more difficult to establish precise standards for most marketing activities than is the case in the manufacturing or distribution functions. Physical and mechanical factors are less influential; psychological factors are more prominent; objective measurement is less conspicuous; tolerance limits must be broader; and the range of segments for which marketing standards can be developed is much greater. But the discipline of seeking to establish standards can generate insights into relationships between effort and results that are likely to outweigh any lack of precision. (See Wilson (1981), (1984), (1988), (1993).)

It is possible for an organization to develop marketing standards by participating in an interfirm comparison scheme (such as the one run by the Centre for Interfirm Comparison). As Westwick (1987) has shown, integrated sets of ratios and standards can be devised to allow for detailed monitoring of performance. (See also Wilson (1973), (1979) and Wilson, *et al.* (1992)).

When budget levels and standards are being developed it is vitally important to note the assumptions on which they have been based since it is inevitable that circumstances will change and a variety of unanticipated events will occur once the budget is implemented. Bearing this in mind let us work through an example. Figure 10.14 illustrates an extract from a marketing plan for product X (column 2), with actual results (column 3) and variances (column 4) being shown for a particular operating period.

Figure 10.14

Operating results for Product X.

Item (1)	Plan (2)	Actual (3)	Variance (4)
Revenues:			
Sales (units)	10,000,000	11,000,000	1,000,000
Price per unit (£)	1.00	0.95	0.05
Total revenue (£)	10,000,000	10,450,000	450,000
Market:			
Total market size (units)	25,000,000	30,000,000	5,000,000
Share of market (%)	40.0	36.7	(3.3)
Costs:			
Variable cost per unit (£)	0.60	0.60	–
Contribution:			
Per unit (£)	0.40	0.35	0.05
Total contribution (£)	4,000,000	3,850,000	(150,000)

The unfavourable contribution variance of £150,000 shown at the foot of column 4 is due to two principal causes:

(i) a variance relating to contribution per unit; and
(ii) a variance relating to sales volume.

In turn, a variance relating to sales volume can be attributed to differences between:

(iii) actual and anticipated total market size; and
(iv) actual and anticipated market share.

Therefore a variation between planned and actual contribution may be due to variations in price per unit, variable cost per unit, total market size and market penetration.

In the case of product X we have:

(i) *Profit variance*:

$$\begin{aligned}(C_a - C_p) \times Q_a &= £(0.35 - 0.40) \times 11{,}000{,}000 \\ &= (£550{,}000)\end{aligned}$$

(ii) *Volume variance*:

$$\begin{aligned}(Q_a - Q_p) \times C_p &= (11{,}000{,}000 - 10{,}000{,}000) \times £0.40 \\ &= £400{,}000\end{aligned}$$

(iii) *Net variance*:

	£
Profit variance	(550,000)
Volume variance	400,000
	£(150,000)

where: C_a = actual contribution per unit
C_p = planned contribution per unit
Q_a = actual quantity sold in units
Q_p = planned quantity of sales in units.

Figure 10.15

Marketing variances (1).

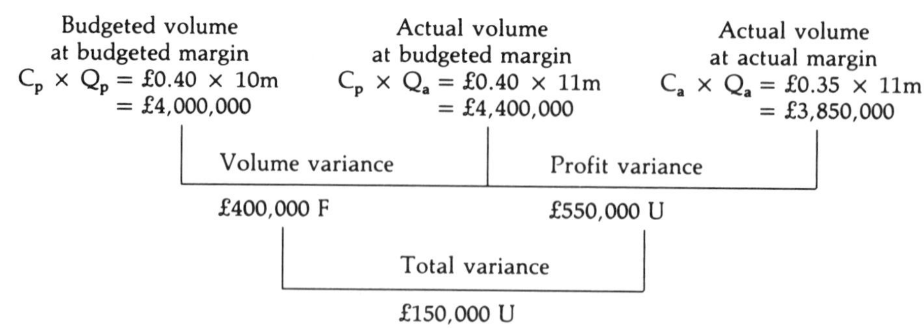

Figure 10.15 illustrates the relations.

However, (ii) can be analysed further to take into account the impact of market size and penetration variations.

(iv) *Market size variance*:

$$(M_a - M_p) \times S_p \times C_p = (30{,}000{,}000 - 25{,}000{,}000) \times 0.4 \times 0.4 = £800{,}000$$

(v) *Market share variance*:

$$(S_a - S_p) \times M_a \times C_p = (0.367 - 0.40) \times 30{,}000{,}000 \times 0.4 = £(400{,}000)$$

(vi) *Volume variance*:

	£
Market size variance	800,000
Market share variance	(400,000)
	£ 400,000

where: M_a = actual total market in units
M_p = planned total market in units
S_a = actual market share
S_p = planned market share.

See Fig. 10.16 which illustrates these relationships.
In summary, the position now appears thus:

	£	£
Planned profit contribution		4,000,000
Volume variance:		
Market size variance	800,000	
Market share variance	(400,000)	400,000
Profit variance		(550,000)
Actual profit contribution		£3,850,000

But this is not the end of the analysis! Variances arise because of unsatisfactory performance and unsatisfactory plans. It is desirable, therefore, to distinguish variances due to the poor *execution* of plans from those due to the poor *establishing* of plans. In the latter category are likely to be found forecasting errors reflecting faulty assumptions, and the estimates of total market size may constitute poor bench-marks for gauging subsequent managerial performance.

It is difficult to determine categorically whether market share variances are primarily the responsibility of forecasters or of those who execute the plans based on forecasts. On the face of it the primary responsibility is likely to be attached to the latter group.

In interpreting the variances for product X it can be seen that the favourable volume variance of £400,000 resulted from two variances relating to market size and market share. Both of these are undesirable since they led to a lower contribution than intended. Had the forecasting group correctly anticipated the larger

Figure 10.16

Marketing variances (2).

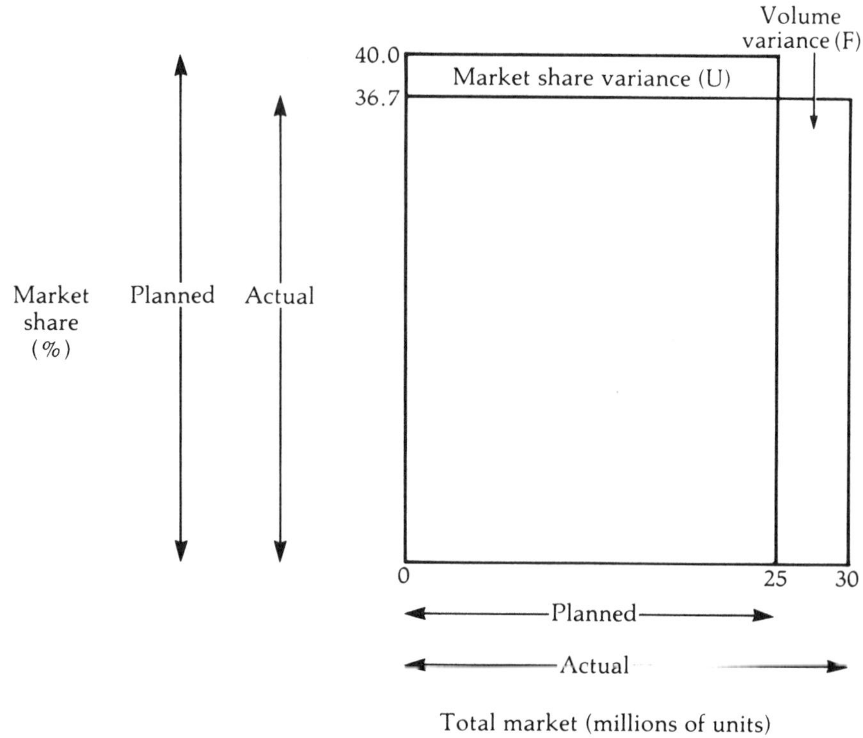

total market it should have been possible to devise a better plan to achieve the desired share and profit contribution. The actual outcome suggests that competitive position has been lost due to a loss of market share in a rapidly growing market. This is a serious pointer.

Lower prices resulted in a lower level of contribution per unit, and hence a lower overall profit contribution. The reasons for this need to be established and future plans modified as necessary.

As an approach to improved learning about the links between effort and results – especially in the face of active competitive behaviour – it is helpful to take the above analysis further and to evaluate performance by considering what *should have happened* in the circumstances (which is akin to flexible budgeting in a manufacturing setting). (See also p. 42 above.)

At the end of the operating period to which Fig. 10.14 refers it may become known that a large company with substantial resources made an aggressive entry into the market-place using lots of promotions and low prices. Furthermore, an unforeseen export demand for product X may have arisen due to a prolonged strike in the USA's main manufacturer. On the basis of these details it becomes possible to carry out an *ex-post* performance analysis in which the original plans are revised to take account of what has since become known.

A clearer distinction can be made via *ex-post* performance analysis along these lines since a distinction can be made between:

(i) *planning variances* due to environmental events that were:
  – foreseeable,
  – unforeseeable;

(ii) *performance variances* that are due to problems in executing the plans.

The situation is summarized in Fig. 10.17.

This example has focused on a single product line (product X), but multiproduct companies will typically have product lines with differing cost structures, prices and hence profit characteristics. It will be apparent, therefore, that the *mix* of products sold will have an impact on the overall profit outcome. For example, an enterprise may offer three product lines with budgeted characteristics relating to the next operating period as given in Fig. 10.18.

Figure 10.17

Ex-post *performance analysis.*

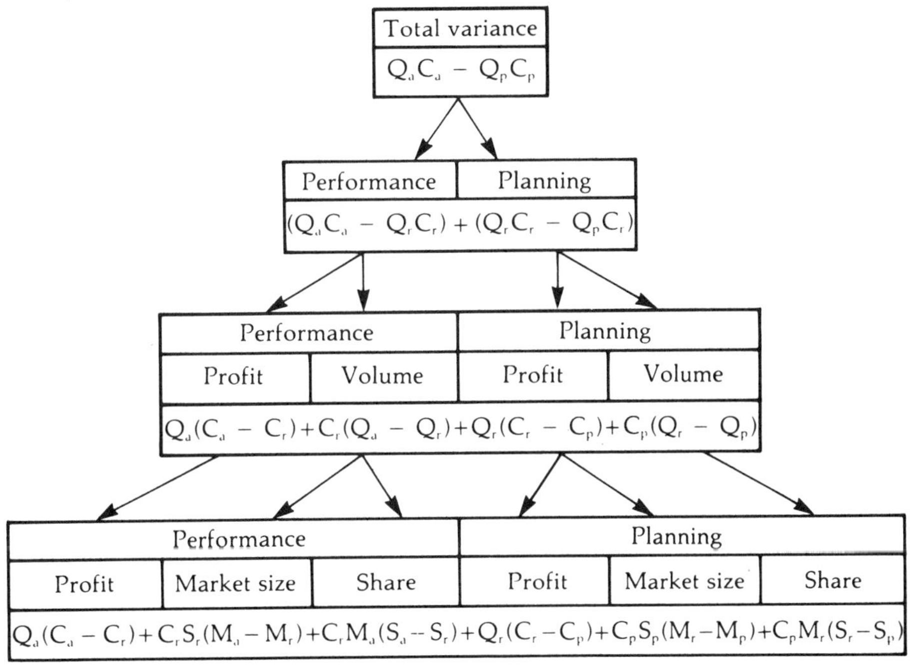

Legend

Subscripts	Variables
a = actual	Q = Quantity
p = planned	C = Contribution margins
r = revised	S = Share
	M = Market

Figure 10.18

Budgeted operating results by product line.

	Product A	Product B	Product C	Total
Budget sales (units)	100,000	200,000	50,000	
Budgeted unit selling price	£12.00	£10.00	£20.00	
Budgeted unit variable cost	£6.00	£4.50	£8.00	
Budgeted unit contribution	£6.00	£5.50	£12.00	
Budgeted unit contribution	50%	55%	60%	
Budgeted contribution	£600,000	£1,100,000	£600,000	£2,300,000

Figure 10.19

Actual operating results by product line.

	Product A	Product B	Product C	Total
Actual sales (units)	90,000	220,000	45,000	
Actual unit selling price	£12.00	£9.00	£20.00	
Actual unit variable cost	£6.00	£4.50	£9.00	
Actual unit contribution	£6.00	£4.50	£11.00	
Actual contribution	50%	50%	55%	
Actual contribution	£540,000	£990,000	£495,000	£2,025,000

Each product line has a different contribution per unit, so the total contribution from all lines is dependent upon the particular mix of sales across all product lines. If the actual outcomes for the period in question were as shown in Fig. 10.19 we can explain the total variance of £275,000 U (i.e. actual profit contribution £2,025,000 minus budgeted profit contribution £2,300,000) as in Fig. 10.20.

In summary we have:

	£
Volume variance	32,863 F
Mix variance	42,863 U
Profit variance	265,000 U
Total variance	£275,000 U

In other words, the total variance was partly due to overall volume being higher than budgeted (355,000 units rather than 350,000 as budgeted), which gives a favourable variance of £32,863 made up of favourable volume variances for each individual product line; the actual mix of sales differed from budget in a way that produced an unfavourable variance of £42,863 made up of unfavourable variances

Figure 10.20

Marketing variance (3).

Product	Budgeted volume at budgeted margin for budgeted mix		Volume variance	Actual volume at budgeted margin for budgeted mix*		Mix variance	Actual volume at budgeted margin for actual mix		Profit variance	Actual volume at actual margin for actual mix	
		£	£		£	£		£			£
A	100,000 × £6.00 =	600,000	8,580 F	101,430 × £6.00 =	608,580	68,580 U	90,000 × £6.00 =	540,000	0	90,000 × £6.00 =	540,000
B	200,000 × £5.50 =	1,100,000	15,703 F	202,855 × £5.50 =	1,115,703	94,297 F	220,000 × £5.50 =	1,210,000	220,000 U	220,000 × £4.50 =	990,000
C	50,000 × £12.00 =	600,000	8,580 F	50,715 × £12.00 =	608,580	68,580 U	45,000 × £12.00 =	540,000	45,000 U	45,000 × £11.00 =	495,000
Total		£2,300,000	£32,863 F		£2,332,863	£42,863 U		£2,290,000	£265,000 U		£2,025,000

* The budgeted mix was 100,000/(100,000 + 200,000 + 50,000) = 100,000/350,000 = 28.57% for product A, and so on. Applying this proportion to actual sales units gives 0.2857 (90,000 + 220,000 + 45,000) = 101,430 for product A, and so on for B and C.

for products A and C which were partly offset by a favourable variance for product line B; and the actual margins were less than budgeted for product lines B and C, giving an unfavourable profit variance of £265,000.

The volume variance can be analysed further along the lines suggested in the previous example, but the main point to note from this example is the impact that variations in the mix of products sold can have on the profit outcome. If all product lines had the same percentage margin there would be no mix variance, but this situation is not normal, so we need to be aware of the impact of mix changes.

10.4 The variance investigation decision

A major inhibiting factor in seeking to control via feedforward systems (see Chapter 3) is our limited ability to make reliable estimates of the outcomes of future events. (This reflects our modest understanding of causal relationships both within the subsystems of the enterprise and between the enterprise and its environment.) All planning is based on estimates (e.g. of prices, costs, volumes) and actual outcomes will rarely be precisely in line with these estimates: some variation is inevitable. Should we expect a manager to investigate *every* variance that might be reported to him when we know that some deviation between actual outcomes and budgeted outcomes is bound to occur? On the other hand, if no variances are investigated the control potential of this form of managerial accounting system is being ignored. An appropriate course of action lies somewhere between these two extremes.

Causes of variances (or 'deviations') can be categorized in the following broad way (after Demski (1980)) with particular variances being due to one or more deviations:

(i) *Implementation deviation* results from a human or mechanical failure to achieve an attainable outcome, e.g. if the mileage rate payable to employees using their own vehicles for business trips is 35 p per mile, but due to clerical error this is being paid at only 25 p per mile, the required corrective action is easy to specify. The cost of correction will be exceeded by the benefits.

(ii) *Prediction deviation* results from errors in specifying the parameter values in a decision model, e.g. in determining indirect cost absorption rates *ex-ante* predictions must be made of, *inter alia*, the future level of activity. If the predictions are wrong then the indirect cost absorption rate will be wrong and variances will result.

(iii) *Measurement deviation* arises as a result of error in measuring the actual outcome – such as incorrectly adding up the number of hours worked in department X, or the number of units sold of product P.

(iv) *Model deviation* arises as a result of an erroneous formulation in a decision model. For example, in formulating a linear programme (as discussed in Chapters 5 and 9) the constraints relating to the availability of input factors may be incorrectly specified.

(v) *Random deviations* due to chance fluctuations of a parameter for which no cause can be assigned. These deviations do not call for corrective action, but in order to identify the causes of variances it is helpful to separate random deviations from deviations (i)–(iv) above in order that the significance of the latter might be established.

While these five categories of deviation appear to be mutually exclusive their interdependences should not be underestimated. The traditional accounting view is to assume that variances are due to implementation deviations but this is patently simplistic. It is also potentially inequitable since it may deem individual managers to be responsible for variances that arose from reasons beyond their control (such as (iii) and (v) above).

In setting up bench-marks (e.g. budget targets or standard costs) it is important to recognize that a range of possible outcomes in the vicinity of the bench-mark will usually be acceptable. In other words, random variations around the bench-mark are to be expected, and searching for causes of variances within an acceptable range of outcomes will incur costs without generating benefits. Only when variances fall outside an acceptable range will further investigation be desirable.

This prompts the operational question of how one actually determines whether a variance should be investigated. As Fig. 10.21 suggests, if it was known in advance that a variance arose on a random basis it would not be necessary to investigate it since there will be no assignable cause. On the other hand, if a variance is of a non-random nature it would not pay to ignore it if it was significant.

How can significance be determined? This boils down to a statistical question, and the technique that is of proven help is that developed for use in quality control situations to which we will turn very shortly.

A more conventional approach to evaluating the significance of variances is either to:

(i) look at the absolute size of the variance (i.e. Actual − Standard) such that all variances greater than, say, £1,000 are investigated; or

Figure 10.21

The variance investigation decision.

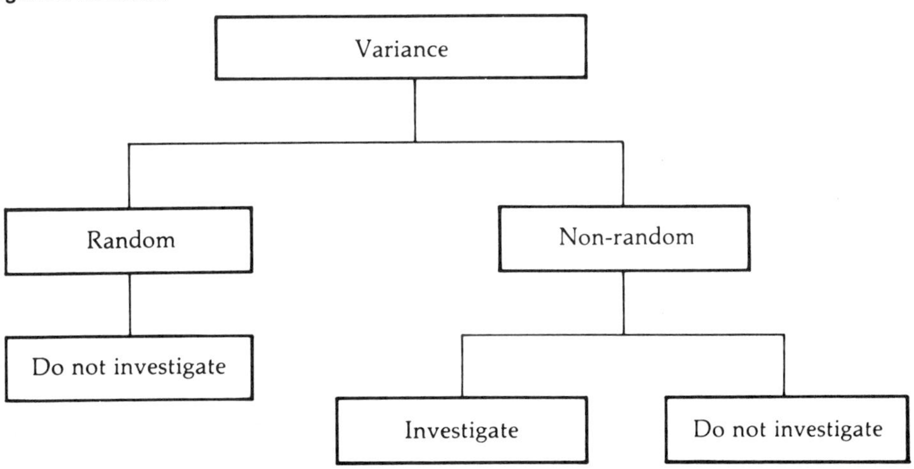

(ii) compute the proportionate size of the variance (i.e. Variance/Standard) and investigate all those exceeding, say, 10%.

Both (i) and (ii) must depend upon the manager's intuition or some arbitrary decision rule when it comes to deciding whether or not to investigate a given variance.

The advantages of (i) and (ii) are their simplicity and ease of implementation, but both fail to deal adequately with the issues of significance (in statistical terms) and balancing the costs and benefits of investigation. We can resolve these issues with the help of the approach adopted in *statistical quality control.*

Statistical quality control (SQC) is based upon the established fact that the observed quality of an item is always subject to chance variability. Some variability in the observed quality of an item will be due to assignable causes which exist beyond the boundaries due to chance causes. (Assignable causes are, by definition, identifiable and steps can be taken to remove them. Examples include faulty raw materials, mechanical faults, etc., that are characteristics of the productive processes themselves. In contrast, chance causes are uncontrollable and cannot be removed. Examples are the occasional blemish in a piece of cloth due to a broken thread, an irregular bore hole through a piece of metal due to the operative's failure to clear shavings away before drilling, and so forth). The major task of SQC is to distinguish between assignable and chance causes of error in order that the assignable causes may be identified, their causes discovered and eliminated, and acceptable quality standards maintained.

Even with automatic machine-produced items there will be chance variations around, for example, the required thickness of a component. This can be illu-

Figure 10.22

Frequency distribution.

Thickness (cm)	Number of observations (frequency)
0.993	1
0.994	1
0.995	2
0.996	3
0.997	5
0.998	7
0.999	8
1.000	9
1.001	8
1.002	7
1.003	5
1.004	3
1.005	2
1.006	1
1.007	1
	63

strated by thinking of a component that has a specified thickness of 1 cm with a tolerance of 0.005 cm, so this means that the acceptance levels are those within the range of 0.995–1.005 cm. If the process is under total control (i.e. no assignable variations exist) the pattern given in Fig. 10.22 may emerge after 63 units have been examined and measured and expressed in the form of a *frequency distribution*.

This data can be plotted in the form of a *histogram* as in Fig. 10.23. (This diagram can easily be converted into a bell-shaped curve that is known as the *normal distribution* and which has special properties.) Given that the machine is producing normally (i.e. it is under control) the average thickness of each component will be 1 cm with the majority of variations falling within the range 0.995–1.005 cm. When the process is under control in this manner the variability of product quality can only be affected if the production process itself is altered in some way. Let us suppose that components produced by the machine are inspected at regular intervals and that the average value increases to 1.002 cm with a range of 0.996–1.008 cm. In this event the machining operation would be said to be out of control and the process should be stopped until the cause (which may be a worn cutting tool) is found and corrective action taken.

The quality of units of output can, of course, be measured in various ways, but when we are concerned with mass-produced items it is usually expedient to measure quality by a fairly simple characteristic of the item under consideration. The width of a screw, the hardness of a bearing or the strength of a material are representative examples.

Once the characteristic of quality is specified, SQC proceeds by checking

Figure 10.23

Histogram.

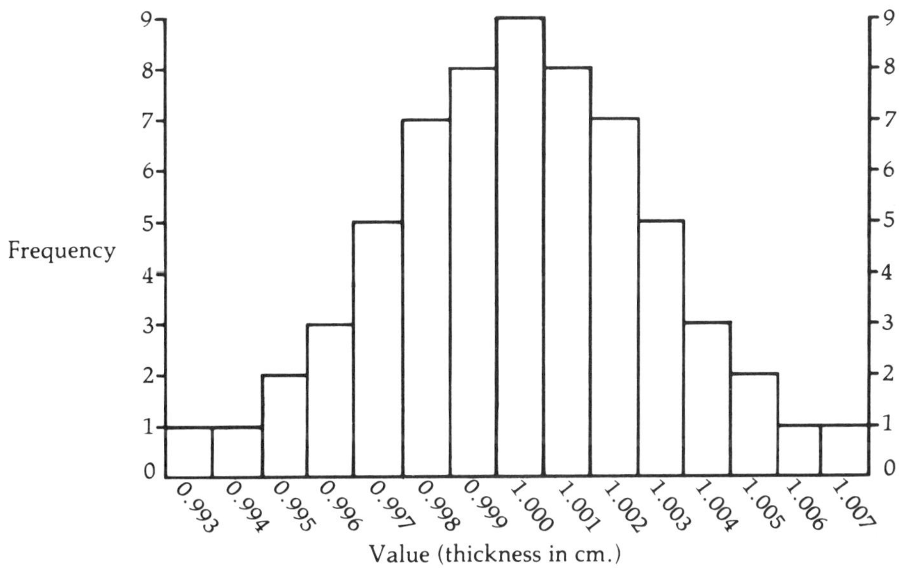

samples of a specified (and statistically predetermined) size at regular intervals of time. The whole procedure is mathematically based and provides a check within predetermined limits of accuracy.

As pointed out above (in connection with Fig. 10.23), the histogram can be converted into a continuous curve of the type shown in Fig. 10.24. The highest number of observations will tend to cluster around the specified value which represents the highest point of the curve. There will be a reducing number of observations both above and below this specified value. This spread of observations is termed the *dispersion*.

In the case of a 1 cm thick component it has already been noted that, while the process is under control, the average thickness of all observations will be 1 cm, despite variations around this value. The average (or central) value is represented in statistical terminology by $\bar{x}$ (known as 'bar x'), and the spread or dispersion can be measured by computing the *standard deviation* (represented by the lower case Greek letter sigma σ) which is given by the formula:

$$\sigma = \sqrt{\sum \frac{(x - \bar{x})^2}{n - 1}}$$

where: x is the value of each observation
n is the number of observations
Σ (capital sigma) means 'the sum of . . . .

It is found that the proportion of observations falling within various limits (as given by a specified number of standard deviations on either side of $\bar{x}$) is constant for processes under control *whatever the process*.

Between one standard deviation below the mean ($\bar{x}$) and one standard deviation

Figure 10.24

Normal distribution.

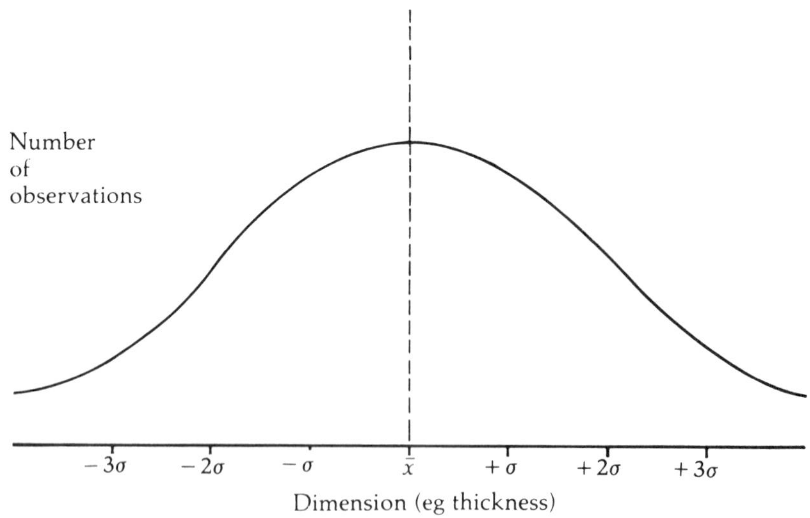

above it (i.e. within the range $+\sigma$ to $-\sigma$) there will always be 68.27% of observations; between $+2\sigma$ and -2σ there will always be 95.45% of observations; and between $+3\sigma$ and -3σ there will always be 99.8% of observations.

If a tolerance limit of $\pm 3\sigma$ is taken as being acceptable, then in a process that is under control 998 out of every 1,000 observations will fall within this range. This situation exists when pure chance alone causes variation in 2 units out of every 1,000 and such variations cannot be assigned or removed. However, should more than 2 units in a sample batch of 1,000 be found to be defective, then the process is almost certainly out of control and an assignable cause should be found and corrective action taken.

The size of the sample that should regularly be taken will depend upon the required degree of accuracy, with a larger sample for a given value of σ being required the higher the desired degree of accuracy.

Actually applying SQC to a production process can be divided into two stages. The first stage requires $\bar{x}$ and σ to be determined. The process average, $\bar{x}$, is the specified dimension (e.g. thickness of 1 cm), and the process standard deviation, σ, can be computed from a series of observations (when no variations due to assignable causes can be detected) by using the formula given on p. 346. From a knowledge of the values of $\bar{x}$ and σ it is possible to specify *control limits*. In practice, the limits given by:

$$\bar{x} \pm 3 \frac{\sigma}{\sqrt{N}}$$

where N is the size of samples to be taken, have been found satisfactory in the sense that it has usually been economically justifiable to check the production process when an observation lies outside these limits.

The second stage in applying SQC involves plotting the data drawn from samples to see whether or not their means lie within the control limits. (A sample

Figure 10.25

Statistical control chart.

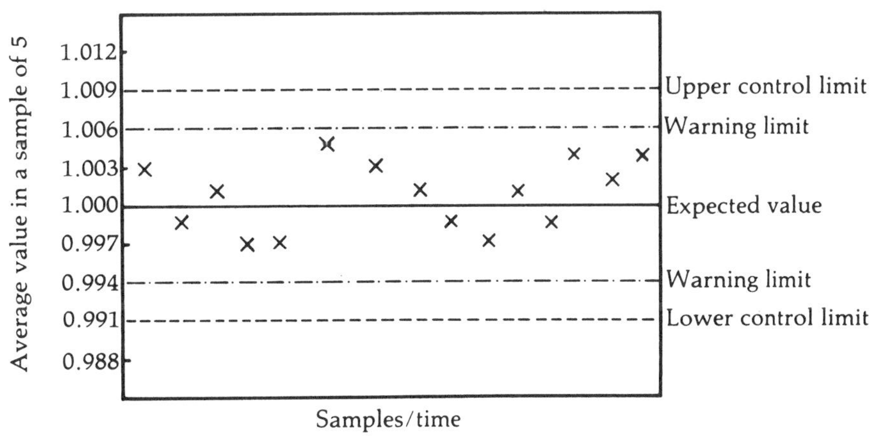

size of 15 is very often used with satisfactory results.) A *control chart* of the type depicted in Fig. 10.25 is extremely helpful in this task.

Figure 10.25 illustrates various points that have already been mentioned. It relates to several samples, taken at regular intervals over time, of 5 items per sample, with the mean (or average) of each sample being plotted on the chart. The predetermined central value is 1 cm in thickness and the predetermined control limits are 1 ± 0.009 cm. An extra control device is a *warning limit* at 1 ± 0.006 cm: any observation between 1 ± 0.006 cm and 1 ± 0.009 cm gives a warning, but any observation beyond 1 ± 0.009 cm leads to investigative action as the process is then considered to be out of control (i.e. variations are assumed to be due to an assignable cause rather than to chance, with a very high degree of certainty). Investigation may also arise if a trend appears, if an unusually large number of observations are above or below the central value, or if several observations are near a control limit. Figure 10.25 does not suggest the need for any investigation as the process appears to be under control with all observations lying well within the control limits and all within the warning limits. It should be emphasized, of course, that tolerance limits should not be less than the control limits otherwise corrective action would not result if observations exceeded the allowable tolerance but were within the control limits. Suitable tolerance limits for the situation shown in Fig. 10.25 might be 1 ± 0.01 cm.

These basic principles of SQC can be applied in areas other than production. An example is given of a control chart for monitoring advertising expenditure as a percentage of sales in Fig. 10.26. The standard of performance that is expected is that advertising expense will be 8% of sales revenue, but random causes (i.e. chance) can make this figure vary from 6% to 10% of sales revenue. If the range of 6–10% represents 3 standard deviations on either side of a mean of 8% (i.e. $\bar{x} = 8$ with confidence limits of $\pm 3\sigma$), then observations would be

Figure 10.26

Advertising control chart.

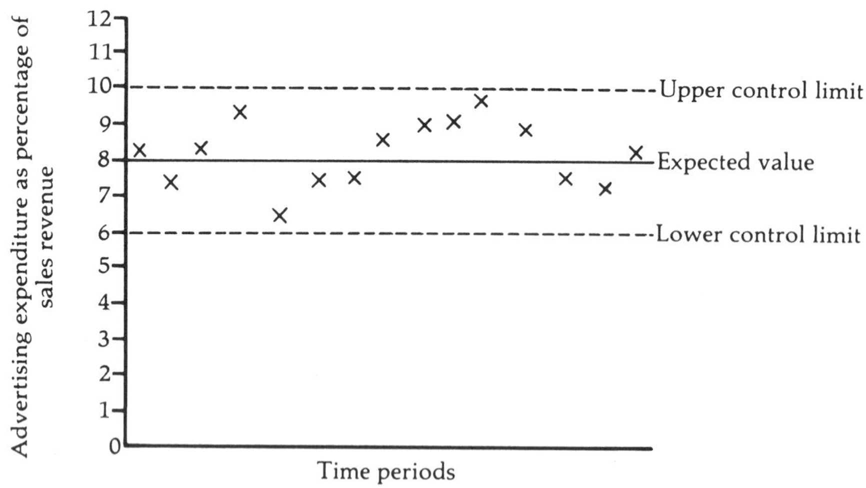

expected to fall within this range in 998 out of 1,000 cases.

However, when an observation falls outside these limits two opposing hypotheses can be put forward to explain the situation:

(i) The observation is the freak 1 out of 1,000 that exceeds the control limits by pure chance, and the company still has the situation under control.
(ii) The company has lost control over the situation due to some assignable cause such as a new competitor entering the market.

If hypothesis (i) is accepted it is unnecessary to investigate – with the risk that something has actually happened to cause the situation to fall out of control. On the other hand, if hypothesis (ii) is accepted and investigations are begun into assignable causes there is always the risk – albeit very small – of the first hypothesis being correct and hence investigation being unnecessary.

Investigations to identify the causes of variances – even when the latter are deemed to be significant – involve costs, so we must again reflect on the cost-benefit issue: if the likely penalty from *not* identifying and correcting the cause of the variance is less than the likely cost of the investigation it hardly seems worth the trouble.

Consider a hypothetical case in which the cost of investigating a reported variance is estimated at £200 whilst the penalty for not identifying a correctable cause is likely to be £600 (which could be the value of cost savings – or extra profit – that will arise once the cause of the variance is removed). If an investigation is undertaken and no cause is discovered, the enterprise will be £200 worse off, whereas it will be £400 better off (i.e. £600 – £200) if a cause is ascertained and corrected.

Brown (1985) reports on an empirical study in which subjects were asked to estimate the likelihoods of four potential causes of a department's weekly labour efficiency variance within a division of a manufacturing enterprise. The main focus of Brown's research was to ascertain the ways in which information (e.g. variance reports) affects managers' diagnoses of the causes of operational performance. It is well established, for example, that a manager's understanding of a production variance will depend upon his inferred theory of the process that generated the variance. Moreover, his behavioural response will vary depending upon his belief regarding the cause of a given variance.

In rather simplified terms, Brown was able to conclude that managers were able to assign likelihoods to the causes of variances *provided* appropriate evidence was available to allow them to test their personal hypotheses concerning potential causes during the period in which the variance arose. This requires prior experience of the workings of the organization on the part of the manager in order that he might have a relevant framework within which hypotheses might be developed and tested. In other words, there must be learning.

Individuals learn through assessing their experience, and organizations learn through their members. However, the extent to which individuals – and thus organizations – can learn is constrained by the rules of the organization (governing decision-making, delegation, membership and other restrictions). Dery (1982) has pursued this question by focusing on the links between erring (e.g. when variances arise) and learning. His argument is as follows:

(i) the recognition of errors is a function of interpretation rather than simply

an observation of events – it requires that desired and actual outcomes be compared and interpreted before one can assert that an error exists;
(ii) the interpretation of events is influenced by organizational rules, etc., which also serve to constrain the extent to which learning can take place;
(iii) it is insufficient to assume that better learning at the organizational level can stem from the learning ability of individual members since the latter is constrained by the rules of the former, hence an additional factor is required that will change the organization's rules.

10.5 Variance analysis and organizational control

Control via variance analysis has traditionally emphasized a technical focus relating to systems design rather than a concern with the human implications of variance analysis. Equally, those who have criticized traditional control systems have usually done so by listing their behavioural limitations rather than by prescribing alternative designs or procedures. Little effort has been devoted to investigating whether or not seeking to control via traditional variance analysis is likely to inhibit or encourage positive human response.

Perhaps the main fault in the technical orientation of variance analysis is the assumption that control is exercised *downwards* within the organization (i.e. variances allow the superior to monitor subordinates' behaviour on the basis of reports that flow *upwards* through the organizational hierarchy and to prescribe corrective actions when necessary). However, one can argue that it is the individual who actually exercises control by:

(i) accepting or rejecting standards;
(ii) exercising care – or not – in the performance of his duties;
(iii) accepting or resisting efforts to change his behaviour to achieve some organizationally determined end.

There is considerable evidence to show that individuals can be very active in resisting the imposition of standards which they do not understand or consider to be legitimate. Similarly, a good deal of energy can be devoted to 'beating the system' by circumventing standards or procedures with which individuals disagree. Conversely, when organization members have accepted and understood standards they will characteristically act in a creative and constructive manner in order to meet them, and voluntarily adjust their behaviour in order to correct any deviations.

Ansari and Tsuji (1981, p. 573) have argued – as have Miles and Vergin (1966) – that most approaches to variance analysis are engineering-oriented and that their assumptions regarding human behaviour are untenable. (See also Thomas (1989).) As a reference point Ansari and Tsuji illustrate the engineering view of control by means of Ashby's model (see Ashby (1956), Chapter 11). This is illustrated in Fig. 10.27 which is a modest variation on Figs 9.1 and 9.2.

The problem (in the light of Fig. 10.27) is to prevent the disturbance D from causing the values of the key variable E to exceed the acceptable range S. R and T are linked in a way that forms a regulatory mechanism designed to prevent disturbances D from reaching E. Thus information from D can only reach E after passing through T, and if the values of E go beyond acceptable limits the regulator

Figure 10.27

The error-controlled regulator.

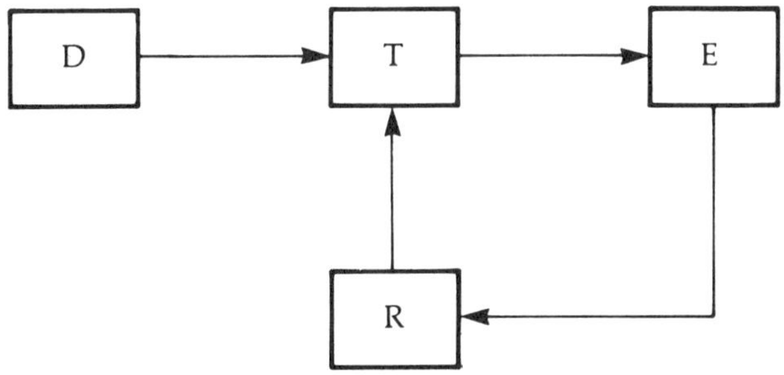

D = a set of environmental disturbances
T = those parts of the system in contact with the environment and buffering the system against it
E = the essential (or controlled) variable
R = the regulator
S = the acceptable subset of the values of E

R, in conjunction with T, will take corrective measures.

This can be most readily illustrated by a statistical quality control (SQC) model applied to the control of manufactured output. Desired product quality, defined in Fig. 10.27 as E, will have specified tolerance limits (i.e. S) reflecting upper and lower bounds to E. The machine operation producing the output is given by R, and T represents the controls within the machine. Corrective action will be needed whenever S is exceeded, and is brought about by R. While values of E lie within S the system is deemed to be in control since variations are considered to be random. But once values of E go beyond the control limits given by S the system is deemed to be out of control and corrective effort will be required. This will entail an investigation to identify the cause of the variation.

Within the managerial accounting domain the investigation of variances has usually been seen as analogous to the SQC model, and it is in this assumed equivalence that the limitations of the engineering approach can be seen. That which is appropriate to a production process cannot be treated as being applicable to a financial setting. The reason for this can be clearly stated: the central assumption with SQC is that there is independence between the control policy (i.e. the specification of desired values for E and S) and the subsequent behaviour of the control system, but in organizational settings it is *not* the case that people fail to react to control policies. Evidence suggests that the control limits used in variance analysis within a budgeting system influence participants' behaviour for two reasons:

(i) these limits indicate the range of performance that a given individual's superior considers to be acceptable, which influences the ease (or difficulty) of attaining acceptable performance. The higher the perceived difficulty, the greater is the likelihood that actual performance will be lower on account of a fear of failure;

(ii) in providing feedback information on performance control, limits are able to engender feelings of success or failure. Negative feedback (i.e. that which indicates that actual performance is moving away from the desired range) has been held to lower aspiration levels, which in turn lowers effort and performance levels, and vice-versa (see Stedry, 1960).

From a behavioural point of view the impact on a manager's motivation is likely to be adverse when variance investigations are in prospect due to the empirical tendency for investigations to be associated with failure. Machines may be unaffected by the presence of control mechanisms, but human behaviour is inevitably influenced by the prospect of investigation.

Organizational rewards – which include remuneration, promotions, etc. – are the principal means by which top management seeks to motivate subordinates towards effective performance. Via their involvement in measuring performance accountants are associated with the reward process – and this almost certainly plays a role in influencing attitudes towards accountants and their function. (See Emmanuel, Otley and Merchant (1990).)

Figure 10.28 offers a simple representation of the measurement-reward process (see Hopwood, 1974a, p. 97). A set of organizational goals is specified, but this is unlikely to correspond with the set of personal goals of managers within the organization unless some deliberate steps are taken to establish a system of rewards to encourage behaviour that is consistent with the fulfilment of organizational purposes. Even with such a system the match between A and B is unlikely to be perfect so some conflict is invariably found as a feature of organizational life. To some extent this manifests itself in variances, but it also results in behaviour colloquially termed 'playing the system'. This arises because managers focus their attention on that which is being measured and by which their performance will be judged – irrespective of its organizational relevance. Examples include bias in setting budgets (see Lowe and Shaw, 1968; Schiff and Lewin, 1970) and the reluctance of managers to invest in new plant – when this is in the organization's best interests – due to a concern that writing off existing plant would have a detrimental impact on current profit performance by which managers are assessed (see Dearden, 1960; 1961).

Irrespective of its technical design, the effectiveness of any managerial accounting system will be influenced by the way in which the information it produces is used. This is particularly important in the context of evaluating individual managers' performance, as in the case of variance reporting.

Hopwood (1972; 1973; 1974a,b) identified three distinct ways in which individuals use accounting information in evaluating the performance of their subordinates:

(i) *Budget-constrained style of evaluation*. Despite the many problems of using budgetary information as a comprehensive measure of managerial performance those assessors who behaved in a budget-constrained manner evaluated their subordinates' behaviour primarily upon their ability to meet continually the budget on a short-term basis. In his empirical work on this topic (in the USA) Hopwood found that this criterion was stressed at the

Figure 10.28

The measurement-reward process.

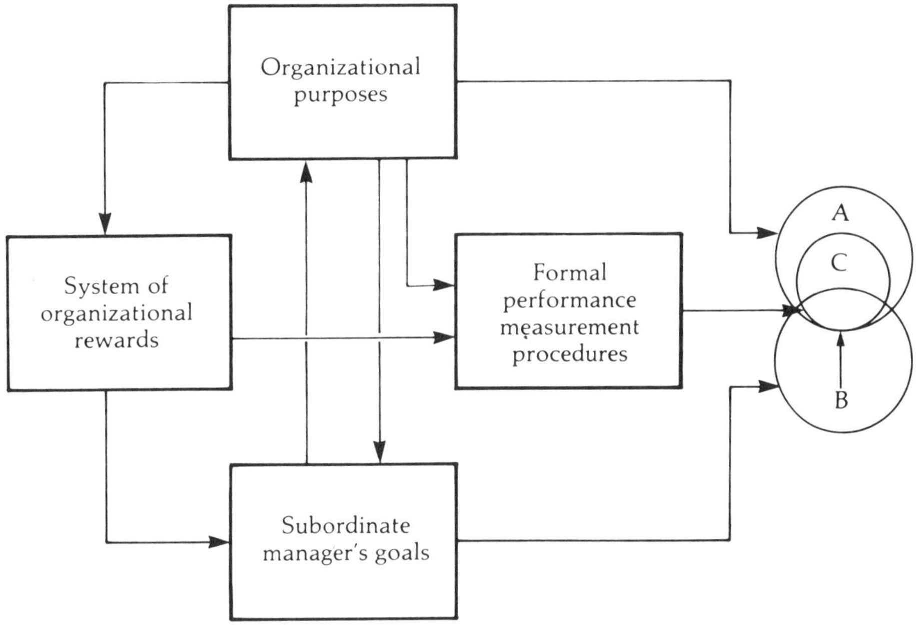

A: Aspects of behaviour which are necessary for achieving wider organizational purposes

B: Aspects of behaviour on which subordinates are likely to concentrate in fulfilment of their personal goals

C: Measured behaviours

Source: Hopwood (1974), p. 97.

expense of others, and that managers would receive unfavourable feedback from their superiors whenever their actual costs exceeded budget – irrespective of other considerations.

(ii) *Profit-conscious style of evaluation.* Assessors adopting this approach evaluated their subordinates' performance on the basis of their ability to increase the general effectiveness of their respective responsibility centres' operations in relation to the long-term purposes of the organization. One example of this would be the encouragement that a cost centre supervisor might get for endeavouring to reduce long-run costs.

(iii) *Non-accounting style of evaluation.* Under this approach the reports emerging from the managerial accounting system play a minor role in the evaluation of subordinates' performance.

The profit-conscious style was the only one that succeeded in attaining a high concern for costs without causing either emotional costs for subordinates or defensive behaviour on their part (i.e. 'playing the system'). This was largely due to a concern on the part of assessors adopting this style to see budgets as *means* to ends (rather than as ends in themselves), and hence to concern themselves with a wider perspective than those who adopted a budget-constrained approach. The latter approach resulted in subordinates believing that their evaluations were unjustly carried out, which produced widespread tensions. Some of the characteristics of the different styles are shown in Fig. 10.29, from which the dangers of the budget-constrained style are evident. In Hopwood's words it engenders '. . . fiddling, short term horizons, distrust, rivalry and parochial attitudes . . .' (1974a, p. 113).

In a more recent paper Otley (1985a) has suggested that budget estimates are rarely precisely attained for two primary reasons:

(i) the forecasting models that managers use are imperfect and give rise to errors;
(ii) the reward systems under which managers operate may prompt them to bias both the level at which budget estimates are set and the actual performance that is reported.

The second of these reasons accords with points made above about 'playing the system': managers '. . . deliberately influence the budget-setting process so as to obtain budgets which differ from their best estimates of actual outcomes and they may then adjust their actual behaviour so that some desired relationship between actual and budgeted performance is obtained' (Otley, 1985a, p. 415). This illustrates the notion of *organizational slack* which is allocated to different parts of an organization via the budgetary process through the tendency of managers to *understate* expected revenues and to *overstate* expected costs. The underlying logic is that performance will appear favourable if the under/overstated budget is accepted and actual outcomes are in line with unbiased expected outcomes, or that attainment of the budget will still be feasible even if the manager's superiors tighten up the initial biased estimates. (See also p. 273, above.)

It should be apparent to you that the use of creative talent to ensure that the message conveyed by budgetary information (i.e. the elimination of variances

Figure 10.29

Summary of the effects of styles of evaluation.

	Style of evaluation		
	Budgeted-constrained	Profit-conscious	Non-accounting
Involvement with costs	High	High	Low
Job-related tension	High	Medium	Medium
Manipulation of the accounting reports	Extensive	Little	Little
Relations with superiors	Poor	Good	Good
Relations with colleagues	Poor	Good	Good

Source: Hopwood (1974), p. 113.

due to manipulation of the initial estimates or actual performance) serves the manager's own interests rather than those of the organization, is a waste, and fails to bring about control actions that are conducive to organizational effectiveness.

Finally in this section let us consider the frequency of reporting of variances (or other performance data). As a general proposition there are distinct benefits to be derived from minimizing the time lag between the occurrence of an event and the reporting of the outcome of that event. The validity of this assertion is derived from psychological learning theory from which it is evident that prompt feedback (or *knowledge of results*) serves to reinforce correct behaviour and to facilitate learning when outcomes are other than correct. Our everyday experience provides evidence of both of these aspects: when we do something right – and are informed that we have done it right – it boosts our confidence and demonstrates that we are capable of behaving in the desired manner. Conversely, when we have failed to produce the right outcome we need to be advised of this quickly in order that we might seek the correct answer and thereby learn to associate causes with effects (or actions with outcomes) more effectively in the future. (We have already discussed this in Chapters 8 and 9.)

An exception to this general rule (as pointed out by Jaques (1966) and Dearden (1968b)) applies in connection with information designed to help evaluate performance: in some circumstances this could be *less* useful as the time lag is reduced, and these circumstances are represented in the notion of the *time-span of discretion*. Jaques (op. cit., p. 17) has defined this as 'the longest period which can elapse in a role before the manager can be sure that his subordinate has not been exercising substandard discretion continuously in balancing the pace and quality of work.'

In other words, it is the length of time during which an employee can use his own discretion before his performance is reviewed and evaluated by his superior. The higher the employee is within the organizational hierarchy the longer will be his time-span of discretion. This has two immediate implications for designing and operating managerial accounting systems:

(i) not all managerial accounting reports should relate to the same time period;
(ii) the time-span of a given manager's job should be an explicit factor in developing appropriate managerial accounting reports.

As examples, consider how long it might take before the launch of a new product might be evaluated, or the introduction of a new bonus system for manual workers, or the installation of a computerized inventory system. The answers may be years, weeks, and months respectively, so we can see that inherent in any job is a time-span that reflects the tasks making up the job in question. It follows that any attempt to assess performance too quickly will be inappropriate, so feedback cycle time should cater for the period that must transpire until there is sufficient evidence to allow a given manager's performance to be evaluated. At lower managerial levels this may be congruent with minimizing the time lag between the occurrence of an event and the reporting of the outcome of that event, but we must not assume that this is always the case.

Summary

The measurement of variances is a mechanical task that has no importance in itself. The value of variances comes from an analysis of significant variances, the identification of their causes, and the correction of these causes.

Management by exception is an approach that is recommended throughout this book, and this hinges upon the identification and analysis of significant variances. But what is a 'significant' variance?

Answering this question requires a consideration of random deviations or variances (i.e. those that arise purely due to chance) on the one hand, and statistically significant deviations (i.e. those that are unlikely to have arisen due to chance) on the other. Random deviations are uncontrollable whereas statistically significant deviations have assignable causes; once these causes have been discovered it is possible to eliminate them and thereby bring operations back into control.

Given that the magnitude of a deviation is important in determining whether it is worthy of investigation, how can 'small' be distinguished from 'large'? To some extent this will depend on the amount from which a given deviation deviates, thus a deviation of of £10,000 from a standard of £1,000,000 is not as large (in percentage terms) as is a deviation of £10,000 from a standard of £20,000. Conventional accounting procedures are only able to produce (i.e. measure) deviations, but control must be based on some measure of the importance of these deviations. Statistical method provides means by which a range for a particular cost item can be established in such a way that deviations falling within this range are considered to be acceptable whereas deviations beyond the range (i.e. outside the tolerance limits) are deemed worthy of investigation. The basis of one of the most widely-used statistical techniques for cost control is to determine the probability distribution for each cost item at different levels of activity and to establish tolerance limits from this.

A large number of reasons are at play in causing variances – indeed, any agent of change is a potential source of a variation between an actual outcome and a desired (standard or budgeted) outcome.

In addition to standard costing variances it is also possible to analyse variances in other areas of organizational activity. A variance is merely a difference between two observations so variance analysis can be performed whenever an actual result can be compared with a planned result and it is sought to explain their difference. An obvious extension of the analysis of production variances is the analysis of marketing and distribution variances, and variance analysis is an essential feature of budgetary control which stretches to every part of an organization's operations.

There is a strong tendency for attention to centre on unfavourable variances which arise when:

$$\text{actual cost} > \text{budgeted cost}$$
$$\text{actual revenue} < \text{budgeted revenue}$$
$$\text{actual profit} < \text{budgeted profit}$$

The cultural norm is for favourable variances to be applauded – but not investigated – while unfavourable variances are deplored. On control grounds this perspective is both illogical and undesirable. If a bench-mark (e.g. budget figure) is sensible – which may be problematic in itself – then any variance that is significant, whether favourable or otherwise, warrants investigation. If the organization is doing something better than expected it is desirable to know why in order to do it at least as well next time. Similarly, of course, if something is being done badly it needs correcting. Knowing why events turn out as they do, and how to respond, is central to the control process; it is vital to be able to improve one's understanding of organizational processes in order that organizational problems might be solved in the future. This is the essence of learning.

We can conclude with the following considered opinion:

> . . . There is a need to move towards designing accounting systems which are less evaluative in approach. At the present time, so much of the ethos which is reflected in the design of accounting systems stresses personal responsibility, accountability, and past achievement, often at the expense of providing the information which is necessary for learning and improvement. Where this is the case, the procedures themselves do little to encourage problem-solving rather than evaluative uses of the information.

Hopwood (1974a), p. 117.

Key terms and concepts

Here is a list of the key terms and concepts which have featured in this chapter. You should make sure that you understand and can define each one of them. Page references to definitions in the text appear in bold in the index.

- Critical success factors
  - key variables
  - key result areas
  - Pareto's Law
- Management by exception
  - control charts
  - significance of variances
  - statistical quality control (SQC)
  - tolerance (or control) limits
- Performance measurement
- Styles of evaluation
  - budget-constrained
  - profit-conscious
  - non-accounting
- Variance
  - budget
  - calendar
  - capacity
  - efficiency/usage
  - mix
  - performance
  - planning
  - price/rate
  - profit
  - selling price
  - volume
  - yield
- Variance analysis
- Variance investigation

Further reading

On critical success factors see Johnson (1967) and Rockart (1979) who offer a broad perspective for performance measurement.

Technical aspects of variance analysis are dealt with in many standard texts such as Horngren and Foster (1987) or Drury (1992). Behavioural extensions are covered by Ansari and Tsuji (1981), Hopwood (1972; 1973; 1974a; 1974b), Armstrong (1989), and Luckett and Eggleton (1991).

The workbook to accompany this chapter begins on p. 575.

CHAPTER 11 Performance measurement: divisional analysis

Learning objectives

After studying this chapter you should be able to:

- appreciate more fully the theme of performance measurement (introduced in Chapter 10) – with particular reference to divisionalized organizations;
- understand the logic behind the development of decentralization and the emergence of divisions;
- identify, illustrate and evaluate the main accounting measures of divisional performance;
- relate divisional performance measurement to the transfer pricing problem;
- draw out the behavioural implications of divisional performance measurement and assess their impact on the design of managerial accounting systems.

11.1 Introduction

The process of performance measurement can focus on individuals or activities – or both. Individuals are responsible for initiating activities, or for continuing activities that were initiated by someone else, so the performance of the activity will – to some extent – be reflected in the performance of the responsible individual.

As activities become aggregated into organizational units, however, it becomes less easy to make a direct linkage between the performance of the manager of a unit and the performance of each specific activity carried out via that unit. Broader measures become necessary as activities become aggregated. This inevitably brings problems: for instance, the *economic* performance of an organizational unit – such as a division – is not equivalent to the *managerial* performance of the individual who runs the division. The distinction is vitally important since one needs to be absolutely clear at the outset what it is that one is seeking to assess if an appropriate measure of performance is to be selected. Similarly, one must know what purposes a managerial accounting system is to serve before one can begin to design it.

Performance may be thought of in lots of ways – as Chapter 10 indicated. Some ways favour financial measures while others do not; some measures are qualitative while others are not. Single measures are unlikely to grasp the richness of the activities encompassed within a division, but it is difficult attempting to handle batteries of measures which do not fit together in an additive manner.

Within this chapter we will look at the aims of performance measurement in a divisional context, and the usefulness of alternative measures for securing organizational control. Profit and profitability will figure prominently in our discussion, but not in isolation of the behavioural implications both of performance measures and of the evaluation process itself for the managers involved. Contrary to some popular beliefs, there is nothing neutral about managerial accounting systems when it comes to performance evaluation.

The main accounting measures we will examine are variations of 'profit', return on investment (ROI), residual income (RI) and the cash recovery rate (CRR). Among the problem issues we will cover are those concerning definitions, those associated with the interdependencies of divisions (and especially the transfer pricing problem), those stemming from our imperfect predictive capability, and those associated with individual bias.

11.2 Performance evaluation

Feedback reports based on the comparison of actual and desired performance on the part of divisional managers serve to facilitate both monitoring and motivation. These two aspects of feedback – as Scapens (1979, p. 282) has pointed out – are interrelated in the following way: top management can review (i.e. monitor) the performance of their divisional subordinates and encourage good performance (or discourage poor performance). Poor managers may face the prospect of losing their jobs and good managers may receive bonuses, promotions, etc., which have motivational impacts, but it will not always be clear what is bad or good performance since some divisions may generate high profits regardless of poor management while other divisions may hardly generate any profits – even under the best available management.

Rewards given to divisional managers will usually be in the form of financial as well as non-financial incentives, to induce them to perform effectively. Motivation can be seen to be partially dependent upon:

(i) financial rewards – such as bonus payments, salary increments, profit participation, share incentive schemes, commissions;
(ii) non-financial rewards – such as promotion, recognition by peers and superiors; and
(iii) feedback and performance reviews to enable managers to know how well (or badly) they are performing.

However, motivation is only part of the picture. The monitoring to which Scapens refers facilitates learning:

> In sum, the evaluation system is desirable to the extent that (1) in conjunction with the rewards based thereon, it provides a vehicle for motivating good decision making by subordinates and (2) it provides a basis for learning and for improving decision making in future period.
>
> Dopuch, *et al.* (1982), p. 180.

The learning can take place at different levels, so senior management can learn from the performance evaluation reports relating to their subordinates' activities in the same way that subordinates can learn from having their activities evaluated.

It is suggested in Chapter 10 that performance reports should facilitate three separate but interrelated forms of appraisal. These are:

(i) to help division managers improve the performance of their division's operations (i.e. *operations evaluation*);
(ii) to help top management assess the desirability of continuing the division's activities (i.e. *economic evaluation*);
(iii) to help top management evaluate the performance of profit-responsible division managers (i.e. *managerial evaluation*).

Taking (iii) a little further, top management must have some way of assessing how well the authority delegated to divisional subordinates has been used. This requires that bench-marks be established by which performance can be judged. In setting bench-marks (in the form of targets, budgets, or standards) it will be necessary for the following two criteria to be met if divisional managers are to accept the bench-marks as being valid (and hence to assume responsibility for attempting to achieve them). These criteria are:

(i) current attainability in the light of the situation facing each division (such as anticipated market demand, available productive capacity, competitive position, etc.);
(ii) controllability at the divisional level so that it is – within limits – possible for the division manager to influence the profit outcomes from his actions.

We will return to this theme in Sections 11.3 and 11.4(d) below. At this point, assuming that appropriate bench-marks have been established, it is important to be aware that any performance measurement system will draw the attention of both superiors and subordinates to specific facets of the latter's activities. In most situations within hierarchic organizations any enquiries that superiors might make concerning the causes of variances are bound to be seen as being potentially threatening by subordinates: the latter's positions, welfare and careers are at stake and this makes for a situation of potential conflict between superiors and subordinates. One valuable way of alleviating this situation is for the system to encourage self-control by the subordinate. Instead of the subordinate having to explain variances period by period he may be able to respond more positively to less frequent interviews with his superior in which he explains his plans for the future, noting any problems that have arisen and the ways in which they were resolved since the last interview.

Two significant behavioural points are worthy of comment in the context of the operation of divisional performance measurement systems.

(i) The prospect of being assessed can affect the behaviour of individuals and this can have dysfunctional consequences. Consider, for example, a division manager who has agreed a particular profit target with his superior. The fact that this target has been agreed and will be used for gauging the division manager's performance gives it a prominence. As a result the manager is likely to work hard at meeting the target even though this may mean ignoring other issues that he previously deemed to be important. This is dysfunctional to the extent that it causes undesirable changes in behaviour. The target – intended as a means to an end – can become an end in itself.

(ii) While generalizations can be made about the behaviour of *groups* of people it is virtually impossible to predict how given *individuals* within given organizations might respond to different control systems. Some people, for instance, work well in unstructured situations whereas others require a very full specification to work to.

Point (i) above interacts with point (ii) in that it is not possible (at least with any high degree of confidence) to anticipate reliably the impact of any evaluation system on a specific individual's behaviour. A traditionally held view has been that managerial accounting reports play a neutral role, thus having no impact on recipients' behaviour (other than to provide information to aid in decision-making etc.). But a great deal of evidence now exists to show that this is far from the truth (e.g. Stedry (1960), Hopwood (1972)).

This point can be illustrated by means of a phenomenon of recent interest to organizational behaviour researchers: 'entrapment'. This occurs when a responsible individual increases his or her commitment to an ineffective course of action in order to justify the previous allocation of resources to that task. In colloquial terms this involves throwing good money after bad, but it will entail resources such as time, energy, skill and self-identity as well as funds.

Entrapment is seen as being one example of a broader psychological process that focuses on commitment. The commitment of an individual to a particular course of action is likely to depend upon, *inter alia*:

(i) responsibility for the action (e.g. individuals tend to feel greater commitment to decisions in which they participated);
(ii) responsibility for the consequences of the action (e.g. an individual's commitment is likely to be greater when he will be held accountable for the outcomes of his actions);
(iii) the salience of the action (e.g. individuals typically feel more committed to actions performed in public rather than in private);
(iv) the consequences of the action (e.g. the more irrevocable the consequences are seen to be, the greater will be the individual's commitment). (See Brockner *et al.* (1986), p. 110.)

Investment projects – and especially giant projects – give rise to particularly difficult problems of control and it is in this context that entrapment is most likely to emerge. For instance, the Trans-Alaskan Pipeline Project was one of the largest and most complex privately-financed construction projects ever undertaken. The project's manager, Frank P. Moolin, Jr, summed up the characteristics of such projects in the following terms:

> A giant project is compressed change. Change is what project management is all about. Starting with nothing, other than a concept in someone's mind, a giant project eventually becomes something that affects the lives, economics and the entire fabric of our society. Because of the velocity of projects, because of the tremendous physical impact these projects have, because of the fact that we start with nothing and end with something very significant, it is necessary to frequently change the strategy of the organization and

> management approach to a project. Frequent organizational changes, including different styles of management, are required. Giant projects experience as many organization and management changes in a period of three to five years as corporations see in ten to fifteen years.
>
> 'Giant Projects Require New Management Approaches — What We Learned from the Trans-Alaskan Pipeline', speech at University of Wisconsin at Milwaukee, 23 April, 1979.

Whilst entrapment is not easily explained in terms of economic rationality, there are various plausible explanations reflecting psychological rationality. For example:

(i) there is a need for the decision-maker to assert himself and reaffirm the wisdom of his initial decision;
(ii) the initial commitment was made as a result of the decision-maker's belief in the correctness of the course of action, hence self-justification, justification to others, and the norms of consistency are served by continuing;
(iii) continuing avoids the waste of the investment already made (which is known as the sunk cost fallacy);
(iv) further investment gives further opportunities for the project to come good;
(v) negative feedback is treated as a learning experience (i.e. a cue to revise the inputs rather than cancel the project);
(vi) negative feedback, alternatively, may be seen as a chance variation;
(vii) a state of inertia has been created by which a project's financial past cannot be divorced from its future: prior investment then motivates the decision to continue;
(viii) decisions are not made in a social vacuuum, hence social costs and benefits must be considered relating to self-image, organizational image, reputation and face-saving: continue so long as the social and psychological benefits are greater than the economic costs;
(ix) information processing has behavioural underpinnings – such as selective perception in which we see what we want to see;
(x) an organization's reward system may work to encourage the decision-maker to overlook short-term setbacks and continue with the original project through bad times.

Prospect theory (Kahneman and Tversky, 1984) has been used to explain the phenomenon of entrapment, and Fig. 11.1 illustrates this. A value function (i.e. the curve in Fig. 11.1) shows the relationship between objectively defined gains and losses and the subjective value placed on these by the decision-maker.

At the outset the decision-maker is at point *A*, but if the decision is unsuccessful he will find himself at point *B* where further losses do not result in large decreases in value. On the other hand, any gains will result in large increases in value, thus, at point *B*, the decision-maker will risk further losses in the hope of making gains. Despite the sunk costs, risky behaviour is much more likely at point *B* than it was at point *A*.

A variation on the theme of entrapment is that of escalation (e.g. see Staw and Ross, 1987a; 1987b). These two phenomena are often related but are analytically separable: entrapment may exist in the absence of escalation. Vivid examples of

Figure 11.1

Prospect theory.

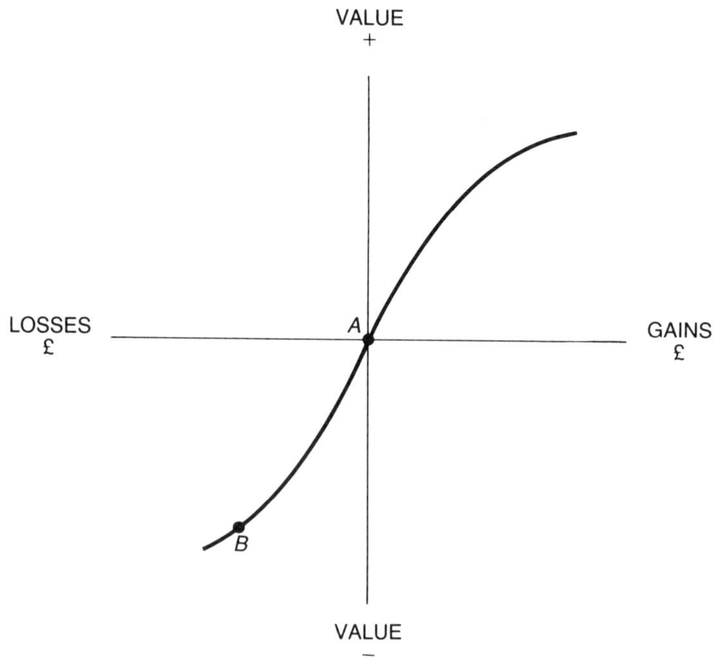

escalation have been experienced in many major projects when the cost outturns prove to be much greater than anticipated: for instance, the Sydney Opera House, Chicago's sewerage system, Concorde, the Channel Tunnel.

This situation highlights one of the major problems faced by accountants in designing performance measurement systems – the partiality of accounting: it is beyond the scope of any accounting system to reflect all the multifaceted aspects of managerial behaviour. Moreover, accounting performance indices may conflict with other performance indices (as when pressures to control costs arise in management development decision-making with the result that the development of staff takes a back seat due to the more conspicuous pressures of reducing costs).

Whatever index of performance is chosen must encompass a variety of factors, but it is extremely difficult to conceive of a single measure that embraces all the key factors, or to identify a measure that only includes factors over which the division manager has control (i.e. influence). An index based on cost is likely to be too narrow since it excludes revenue issues. On the other hand, a profit index accommodates both revenue and cost but excludes such important issues as:

(i) creating customer loyalty;
(ii) establishing good employee relations;
(iii) building a skilled team.

The ability to utilize invested funds efficiently is not captured in a profit index – although it is reflected in a profitability index (to which we will return).

When divisions within a decentralized organization supply one another with goods and services there is the further complication caused by the transfer pricing problem that was discussed in Chapter 9. This arises because divisions are not wholly autonomous: their activities are 'contaminated' by the interaction of one division with another.

While rate of return on investment (ROI) and other financial measures of performance can be useful (to be discussed in Section 11.4 below), as we saw in Chapter 10 there are other measures of a non-financial nature that can also be useful. Indeed, in order to ensure effective control over an organization's performance, it will invariably be necessary to consider a range of measures which includes – but which is not limited to – financial indicators.

If performance was to be assessed against a single indicator (such as ROI or net profit) this might encourage manipulation of the indicator (e.g. by delaying potentially profitable capital expenditure a manager might ensure a higher ROI for the current period, but at the expense of failing to secure higher profit performance over the longer term).

Shillinglaw (1964) has argued that, despite the limitations of profit-based measures of performance, divisional performance must ultimately be measured in financial terms. In so far as profit-based measures are weak, he argues that this is a function of available forms of measurement rather than a conceptual flaw. In so far as profit-based measures are deemed to be incomplete (e.g. for failing to include job satisfaction and so on), he argues that any concern over aspects of organizational activity that are not measured in financial terms stems from:

(i) a belief that good performance in these aspects will contribute to financial performance over a longer period of time;
(ii) our inability to measure the present value of those future benefits.

It is clear from these points that, in Shillinglaw's view, employee welfare activities and so forth must be justified by their anticipated impact on morale (and hence on long-term profits) rather than by increments in short-term profits.

Profit is, of course, a key output measure, and it is necessary to have measures of the outputs from organizational activities and processes in order to:

(i) evaluate efficiency – i.e. outputs/inputs;
(ii) evaluate effectiveness – i.e. actual outputs v. desired outputs.

One benefit of the profit measure is that (with limitations) it can fulfil both these roles, but it inevitably reflects the partiality of any financial measure, and it is not applicable in non-commercial organizations. (In Chapter 10 we considered this question in some detail.)

Designing systems for divisional performance measurement requires the following five steps to be worked through:

(i) a performance indicator (e.g. ROI or residual income (RI) – see Section 11.4) must be selected to represent top management's objective;
(ii) definitions are needed of the terms embodied in the chosen performance indicator, expressed in an operational manner (e.g. 'profit' and 'investment' as the numerator and denominator respectively in ROI);

(iii) a specification is required of the valuation basis that is to be employed in measuring performance (such as historical or replacement cost);
(iv) the establishing of standards of performance that are appropriate for the circumstances facing different divisions must be undertaken; and
(v) the frequency with which performance reports should be produced (e.g. weekly, quarterly) must be determined.

These steps are interdependent rather than sequential, and the design of a viable system must carefully take into account the particular conditions of specific organizations.

For example, the level of environmental uncertainty may play a significant role in the design of an organization's performance measurement system. Govindarajan's 1984 empirical study (undertaken among 58 units within 8 of the largest US corporations) is rooted in contingency theory and supports the following propositions:

(i) that superiors of business units which face higher environmental uncertainty use a more subjective performance appraisal approach whereas superiors of business units facing lower environmental uncertainty use a more formula-based performance evaluation approach;
(ii) that a stronger fit between environmental uncertainty and performance evaluation style is associated with higher business unit performance.

In a perfect world it would be possible to design a performance evaluation system that contained accounting measures that were complete, accurate and neutral. However, since the world is far from being perfect the limitations to a perfect system are often to be found in our limited ability to make accurate predictions. The limitations are:

(i) *Completeness:*
- performance measures are only available for certain quantifiable issues;
- the emphasis of many measures is short-term rather than long-term;
- all measures are surrogates and tend to disguise the variability and interdependence of their component parts.

(ii) *Accuracy:*
- bench-marks may be imposed and fail to reflect a reasonably attainable standard;
- the interpretation of variances is inherently laden with ambiguities;
- conventional accounting rules are inappropriate when applied to internal controls.

(iii) *Neutrality:*
- performance indicators only measure results rather than effort;
- performance indicators are influenced by interdependencies and decisions taken elsewhere within the organization;
- opportunistic behaviour is encouraged by a rigid style of evaluation based on accounting measures.

Several of these limitations may act together to render accounting performance measures highly questionable. But taking cognizance of these limitations – and of the research literature more generally – Emmanuel and Otley (1985) have summarized their view of a potentially viable divisional performance system's characteristics thus:

(i) a flexible, profit-conscious style of evaluation should be used to reduce the tendency of divisional managers to regard the short-term financial performance measure as an end in itself, thereby improving the *completeness* property of the measure;
(ii) separate performance measures should be created for the evaluation of managers on the one hand and divisions on the other, which should improve both *completeness* and *accuracy*;
(iii) performance measures used for managers should not include any cost apportionments, which should improve their *neutrality*;
(iv) controllable RI is likely to provide a less ambiguous target for managers than ROI, although this will depend upon, *inter alia*, the controllable investment base being correctly defined (which will be clearer when you have read through Section 11.4).

We should keep these points in mind as we proceed through the remainder of this chapter.

11.3 Divisionalization

In order that an organization might function effectively it is necessary for top management to delegate various activities (or responsibilities) throughout the managerial hierarchy in such a way that each individual will have some degree of latitude over the execution of those activities. Through responsibility accounting systems (which trace costs, revenues, assets, liabilities and profits to 'responsible individuals') all activities can be planned and controlled in accordance with known organizational responsibilities, as we saw in Chapter 9.

However, it is essential to the success of any control system that an individual is only held responsible for results when the following conditions prevail:

(i) that he knows what he is expected to achieve;
(ii) that he knows what he is actually achieving; and
(iii) that it is within his power to influence what is happening (i.e. that he can bring (i) and (ii) together).

When all these conditions do not occur simultaneously it may be unjust and ineffective to hold an individual responsible, and it will be impossible to achieve the desired level of organizational performance.

From the above comments it will be apparent that targets or results should be compiled in a way that reflects one individual's 'uncontaminated' performance. Thus manager A's budget should contain a clear set of items which are deemed to be controllable at his level of authority, and a further set of items that are either fixed by company policy or are otherwise beyond manager A's influence. These latter items are uncontrollable from A's viewpoint, and his performance should not be assessed in relation to items over which he has no control.

Experience shows that it is not always an easy matter to distinguish between controllable and uncontrollable items. Furthermore, there are shades of influence – some items may be controllable in whole or in part. Time plays a crucial role in control: that which is fixed in the short term (and hence beyond control) may be influenced (i.e. changed) over the longer term. Also, of course, an item that is fixed (and uncontrollable) from the viewpoint of one level in the hierarchy will almost certainly be controllable at a higher level in the hierarchy.

Despite this problem of defining controllability in an absolute sense, responsibility accounting proceeds by identifying the person within the organization who has the greatest influence over the behaviour (i.e. level) of the item in question. This may be the individual who acquires a resource from the environment, or the individual who uses that resource within the enterprise.

In summary, before responsibility accounting can be successfully implemented it is necessary to plan the accountability and authority of those individuals who are to be held responsible for the enterprise's performance. This requires:

(i) a clear definition of the organizational structure;
(ii) a precise specification of individual responsibilities so each person knows his role;
(iii) the full involvement of responsible individuals in the preparation of plans, budgets, etc., by which they are to achieve that which is required of them;
(iv) that those responsible for achieving results are regularly provided with control reports;
(v) that opportunities exist whereby subordinates might report to superiors on significant variances and action taken (or to be taken); and
(vi) that all activities within the organization are made the specific responsibility of named individuals so that everyone knows for what he or she is responsible, and to whom.

The essence of responsibility accounting is control – and performance measurement – at the personalized level of the individual manager (as we have seen in earlier chapters – especially Chapter 9). This presupposes that the responsible manager is able to influence the costs, revenues, profits, etc., for which he is held accountable.

In direct costing, in contrast, the primary interest lies in tracing to a segment those flows that are specifically associated with the existence and activities of that segment. As such, this is an impersonal technique of financial analysis.

Ferrara (1967) raised the question about the apparent conflict between responsibility accounting (with its control orientation) and direct costing (with its decision emphasis). Since both control and decision-making are essential and related it should be possible to find a way of including the interests of both in managerial accounting reports. This is done in Fig. 11.2.

If we restrict our current focus to control rather than to decision-making we know that a *responsibility centre* is made up of the various cost and revenue items, etc., for which a given individual is responsible. It is consequently a personalized concept that may be made up of one or more of the following:

(i) a cost centre;
(ii) a profit centre; or
(iii) an investment centre.

Figure 11.2

Combined performance report.

A. *Responsibility Report*	
Controllable revenues	xxxx
Controllable costs	xxx
Profit contribution	xx

B. *Direct Costing Report*	
Revenue	xxxx
Traceable variable costs	xx
Marginal contribution	xxx
Traceable fixed costs	xx
Profit contribution	xx

C. *Combined Report*	
Revenue	xxxx
Variable costs (under manager's control)	xx
Marginal contribution	xxx
Traceable fixed costs (under manager's control)	xx
Manager's profit contribution	xx
Traceable fixed cost (under control of others)	xx
Profit contribution of activity	xx

Different degrees of delegation and discretion are represented by the use of cost criteria for performance measurement on the one hand and the use of profit or investment centres on the other. The existence of cost centres is indicative of *decentralization* but the existence of profit or investment centres with their greater connotations of managerial discretion are indicative of *divisionalization* (Solomons, 1965). (Ezzamel and Hilton (1980) examined the question of whether or not the discretion of divisional managers – which is the key feature of decentralized management – can be measured. Empirical evidence is reported as being scarce, but Ezzamel and Hilton concluded that a meaningful measure can be found.)

A division is an organizational unit in which the manager is responsible for the costs, revenues and – in some cases – the assets associated with the unit's activities. A divisional manager is therefore responsible not only for *how* operations are performed but also – within the limits of overall corporate policy – for *what* operations are being undertaken. In many respects a division may be treated as a separate entity.

The logic behind the distinction between profit and investment centres is that assets are used to generate profits, and the decentralizing of profit usually requires the decentralization of control over many of a company's assets. The ultimate test, therefore, is the relationship of profit to invested capital within a division, and this measure is specific to investment centres. Much of its appeal lies in the apparent ease with which one can compare a division's ROI with earnings opportunities elsewhere – inside or outside the company. However, ROI is an imperfect measure (as we shall see) which needs to be used with some scepticism and which should be used in conjunction with other performance measurements.

Problems arise in delegating profit responsibility, whether to profit or investment centres:

(i) profit is normally reported on an interim basis, period by period, which means that the results of current decisions are decoupled from the making of those decisions;
(ii) no profit or investment centre is truly independent, and so its performance reflects – to an unknown degree – the impact of other centres or of central services whenever there is the transfer of goods and/or services from one to another.

If there are problems, what is the logic behind the delegation of profit responsibility and the emergence of decentralized, divisionalized organizations?

The expansion of organizations into different markets, new industries and foreign countries, with the accompanying increase in complexity, makes decentralized operations inevitable. Moreover, in the absence of a decentralized structure lines of communication would become impossibly long.

Despite the proliferation of mergers and acquisitions (which provide certain advantages of being large) there is a strong tendency among growing businesses to favour decentralized structures (which offer some of the advantages of being small). This gives an interesting paradox.

Chapter 9 (see pp. 290–2) included a discussion of some key reasons for decentralizing – bounded rationality, labour specialization and managerial motivation – which we can develop a little further.

Among the arguments favouring decentralized profit responsibility are:

(i) a divisional manager is only in a position to make satisfactory trade-offs between revenues and costs when given responsibility for the profit outcome of his decisions (failing which it is necessary for many day-to-day decisions to be centrally regulated);
(ii) managers' performance can be evaluated more precisely if they have complete operating responsibility;
(iii) managers' motivation will be higher if they have greater autonomy;
(iv) the contribution of each division to corporate profit can be seen via divisional profit reports;
(v) divisions resemble miniature businesses and constitute a good training ground for potential general managers;
(vi) divisional managers can be encouraged to act as entrepreneurs and to exercise initiative;
(vii) decisions are likely to be made more quickly, with less bureaucracy, and to be better;
(viii) top management will be free to concentrate on overall policy-making and strategy;
(ix) participation in decision-making is likely to be greater, with important team-building spin-offs;
(x) unprofitable activities are likely to be quickly identified and improved – or eliminated (e.g. where an outside supplier can provide goods at a better price than another division);
(xi) 'functional fixation' will be avoided since managers at the divisional level

will see the impact of their activities on divisional results rather than simply in, say, production or marketing terms;

(xii) managers who might otherwise see their role in the organization at large as being trivial will be able to see the contribution they can make at the divisional level.

On the other side of the coin there are inevitably drawbacks to decentralization, including:

(i) division managers may make mistakes that more experienced corporate managers would avoid (although one certainly learns from making mistakes);

(ii) some actions that may increase one division's profit might only do so at the expense of another division – and of the organization as a whole (which is called *suboptimization*);

(iii) greater staff numbers are likely to be found in divisionalized enterprises due to the need for more decisions to be made at lower managerial levels;

(iv) a concern for profit performance may prompt a short-term focus that underplays non-financial issues and overlooks the longer term;

(v) a divisional structure may create a spirit of competition within an organization that could cause friction rather than cooperation among divisions which may not be in the organization's total interest, or it may cause too much interest in short-term profits at the expense of long-term results as noted in (iv) above;

(vi) more refined (hence expensive) information systems will be required;

(vii) notwithstanding (vi) above, communications among divisions may still be poor;

(viii) transfer prices will need to be established for interdivisional transactions, with attendant behavioural problems.

The main characteristics of divisions, in summary, are to be found in the existence of:

(i) a profit objective, requiring profit-based decision rules;

(ii) divisional managers who have discretion to make decisions affecting the major determinants of profit (including the power to choose markets and sources of supply);

(iii) divisional accountability to corporate management for profit generated.

Characteristic (ii) is invariably constrained by overall organizational policies over financing, capital expenditure and interdivisional dealings.

Within decentralized organizations it is usual for central control to be retained over capital investment decisions (subject to limited delegation to divisions) and the appointment of divisional managers. Pricing policy may also be centralized unless the product range is very wide (as in retailing for example), and purchasing, cash management and public relations activities are all likely to be centralized to ensure efficiency and/or coordination. The main functions that are delegated to divisions are typically operations (manufacturing, materials management, distribution) and selling.

Joel Dean observed some 35 years ago that the details of divisional boundaries and institutional arrangements are important in the effective operation of profit or investment centres. The way in which boundary lines are set will influence the extent to which profit or investment centres are able to operate in the enterprise's interest. A number of tests can be applied in determining suitable boundaries:

(i) if a division is to have adequate scope to reach decisions on a profit-oriented basis, thus achieving a key aim of delegation, it must have *operational independence*;
(ii) if make-or-buy and make-or-sell decisions are to be made correctly the division must have *independent access to sources and markets*;
(iii) if the performance of a division is to be correctly assessed there must be no arbitrary or contentious allocations of costs or revenues – *all* financial flows must be controllable by the divisional manager;
(iv) decisions made by one decentralized unit to improve its own performance must not be at the expense of other units or of the organization as a whole, otherwise the situation would be dysfunctional;
(v) corporate managers (i.e. those at head office) must refrain from interfering in decentralized operations unless emergencies arise.

It has been argued (e.g. Horngren (1982), p. 632) that dysfunctional behaviour is least likely when divisions are wholly independent, and, in these circumstances, decentralization is likely to be most beneficial. A division is only independent if the following conditions prevail:

(i) it does not compete with other divisions for limited resources (e.g. capital funds, managerial talent);
(ii) it does not sell in the same markets or buy from the same sources as other divisions;
(iii) it does not supply goods or services to, or receive goods and services from, other divisions;
(iv) it can make decisions that achieve goal congruence without having to coordinate its behaviour directly with other divisions.

This is asking rather a lot!

The *sine qua non* in managing decentralized operations must be a suitable means of measuring divisional performance. Emmanuel and Otley (1985, pp. 155–6) have summarized the assumptions underlying the conventional view of divisional performance measurement in the following terms:

(i) divisional managers desire certain rewards that top management can give (e.g. esteem, promotion, bonuses);
(ii) divisional managers believe that there is a positive correlation between the performance of their divisions and the receipt of rewards;
(iii) divisional managers attempt to maximize their utility (i.e. self-interest) by meeting the performance indicators set by top management.

In contrast to these assumptions we have those underlying *agency theory*. The emergence of agency theory during the 1970s is worthy of comment. If we view the superior manager as the *principal* and the division manager as the *agent*, we can see that agency theory looks at the design of performance measures/rewards in ways that will encourage division managers (i.e. subordinates) to act in the interests of the whole organization (as represented by their superiors).

Agency theory is built upon certain assumptions about individuals as agents, in particular that:

(i) they behave rationally in seeking to maximize their own utility;
(ii) they seek financial and non-financial rewards;
(iii) they tend to be risk-averse and, hence, reluctant to innovate;
(iv) their individual interests will not always coincide with those of their principals;
(v) they prefer leisure to hard work.

Not surprisingly agents will have greater knowledge about their operating performance and actions than is available to their principals. A significant question is whether or not agents will use this 'private information' in ways that might be against their own best interests – given assumptions (i)–(v) above. If there is a poor relationship between agent and principal one might expect that bias will be present, for instance, in the negotiating of bench-marks for performance evaluation purposes. On the other hand, if a good relationship exists, based on mutual trust and respect, the agent is more likely to reduce bias and act more in line with the organization's interests.

Achieving a commonality of interest between principal and agent, then, is the prime concern of agency theory. A performance evaluation system that is based on the assumptions of agency theory will typically focus on who is to bear risks rather than who is able to exert control (see Puxty, 1985). (See also Chapter 12, pp. 403–4).

11.4 Divisional performance measurement

The principal financial measure of performance for a profit centre is, of course, *profit* itself, whereas the principal performance measure for an investment centre is one that emphasizes *profitability* (i.e. the rate of profit per unit of investment).

We will consider these two in turn, starting with profit measures, following which we will look at alternatives that are applicable in the investment centre setting.

(a) Profit as a performance measure

When it comes to defining profit measures several alternatives are available. An example built up from the data in Fig. 11.3 will help to illustrate some of them.

This data can be analysed in such ways as suggested in Fig. 11.4. One can identify strengths and weaknesses relating to each alternative measure of profit. The *contribution margin* is useful for short-run decision-making since it is not clouded by the inclusion of costs that do not respond to short-run volume changes. From a performance evaluation point of view, however, it is unsatisfactory in that it excludes all non-variable costs.

Controllable profit is a much better measure of the divisional manager's performance because it includes all the costs – whether fixed or variable – that are within his control. When non-controllable fixed costs are taken into account

Figure 11.3

Division A's operating data for July.

Sales revenue generated by Division A	£100,000
Direct costs of Division A:	
Variable operating costs	£ 45,000
Fixed operating costs under control of manager of Division A	£ 25,000
Fixed costs not under the control of manager of Division A	£ 10,000
Indirect costs of Division A:	
Apportioned central costs	£ 15,000

Figure 11.4

Analysis of Division A's operating data.

	Division A contribution margin £	Division A controllable profit £	Division A direct profit £	Division A net profit £
Sales revenue	100,000	100,000	100,000	100,000
Direct costs:				
Variable	45,000	45,000	45,000	45,000
Contribution margin	£ 55,000			
Fixed controllable		25,000	25,000	25,000
Controllable profit		£ 30,000		
Fixed non-controllable			10,000	10,000
Direct profit			£ 20,000	
Indirect costs				15,000
Net profit				£ 5,000

we have the *direct profit* of the division. This is more a measure of the division's performance than it is of the divisional manager's performance, so one needs to consider what it is that one is seeking to assess before one chooses a measure.

Finally, *net profit* (as pointed out in Chapter 4) helps us in assessing a division's performance in full cost terms, but this is not a relevant means of gauging the divisional manager's performance on account of the categories of cost that he is unable to influence either directly or indirectly. It could be argued that divisional managers benefit from seeing the full cost of their division's operations, but if the controllable elements are dwarfed by the uncontrollable (at the divisional level) it may not be highly motivational!

From the above we can reasonably conclude that controllable profit is the best of the specified measures for assessing a divisional manager's performance – at least in principle. In practice it may be found that the manager of a division will act in ways that improve his short-run profit position at the expense of both the division's long-run profit potential and the best interests of the organization as a whole. Examples might include:

(i) eliminating training and management development activities;
(ii) cutting back on advertising, routine maintenance or R & D.

Countering these ways of 'playing the system' must be devised by top management in the form of policy guidelines, etc. But any measure of profit is inevitably suboptimal as an index of divisional performance for a least one of the following reasons:

(i) it typically includes items (such as interest and taxation) that are not under the control of divisional managers;
(ii) it only tells part of the story – something needs to be said about the investment that is needed to generate profit. The next subsection picks up this point.

(b) Profitability as a performance measure

A long-established index of divisional performance that seeks to measure profitability is the *rate of return on investment* (ROI). This is calculated as:

$$\text{ROI} = \frac{\text{Profit margin}}{\text{Invested capital}} \times 100$$

and can be decomposed into its elemental components:

$$\text{ROI} = \frac{\text{Sales revenue}}{\text{Invested capital}} \times \frac{\text{Profit margin}}{\text{Sales revenue}}$$
$$= \text{Capital turnover} \times \text{Margin on sales}$$

The obvious generalizations that can be made about the ROI formula are that any action is beneficial provided that it:

(i) boosts sales;
(ii) reduces invested capital; or
(iii) reduces costs (while holding the other two factors constant).

In other words, an increase in percentage margins or capital turnover without worsening the other will enhance ROI.

Figure 11.5

ROI possibilities (1).

Profit margin	Capital turnover	ROI
2%	12 times	24%
3%	8 times	24%
4%	6 times	24%
6%	4 times	24%
8%	3 times	24%
12%	2 times	24%

There are lots of different combinations of profit margin and capital turnover that can produce a desired ROI. Figure 11.5 illustrates some possibilities.

The data from Fig. 11.5 are plotted graphically in Fig. 11.6 in which the curve shows all the possible combinations that will produce a figure of 24% for the ROI.

Feedforward control can be facilitated by this approach, but so can feedback control. We can illustrate feedback control via Fig. 11.7. This illustrates the performance of three divisions in terms of ROI:

Division A	20%
Division B	35%
Division C	21%

Division A's performance was below the 24% target rate even though the profit margin achieved (10%) was higher than for either of the other divisions. The reason can be found in the low capital turnover (of 2) which suggests that the manager of Division A failed to utilize his assets properly. It may be the case that he had excessive inventories, surplus capacity or idle cash due to inaccurate estimates of demand.

Figure 11.6

ROI possibilities (2).

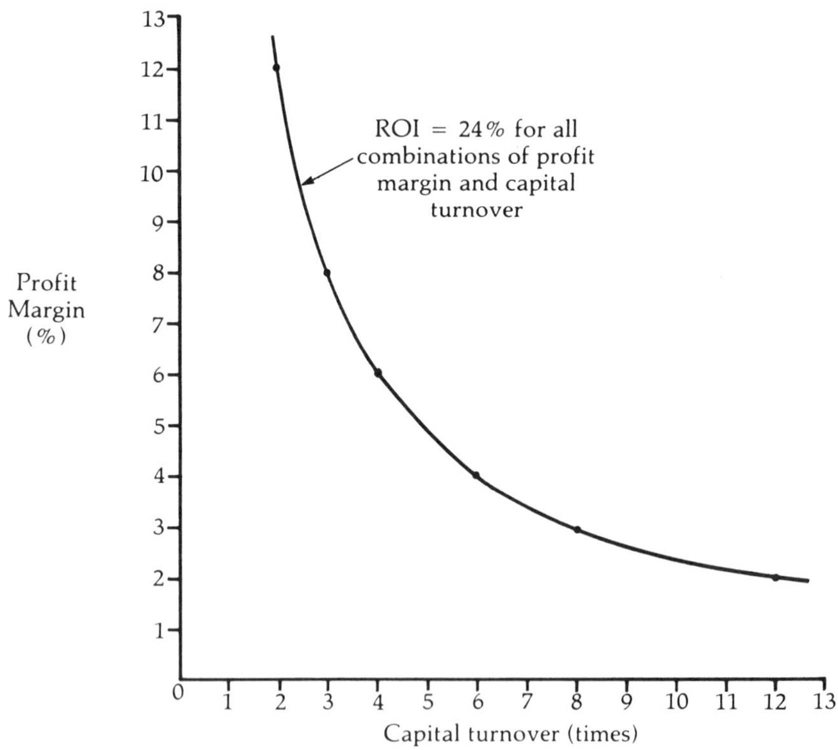

Figure 11.7

ROI assessment.

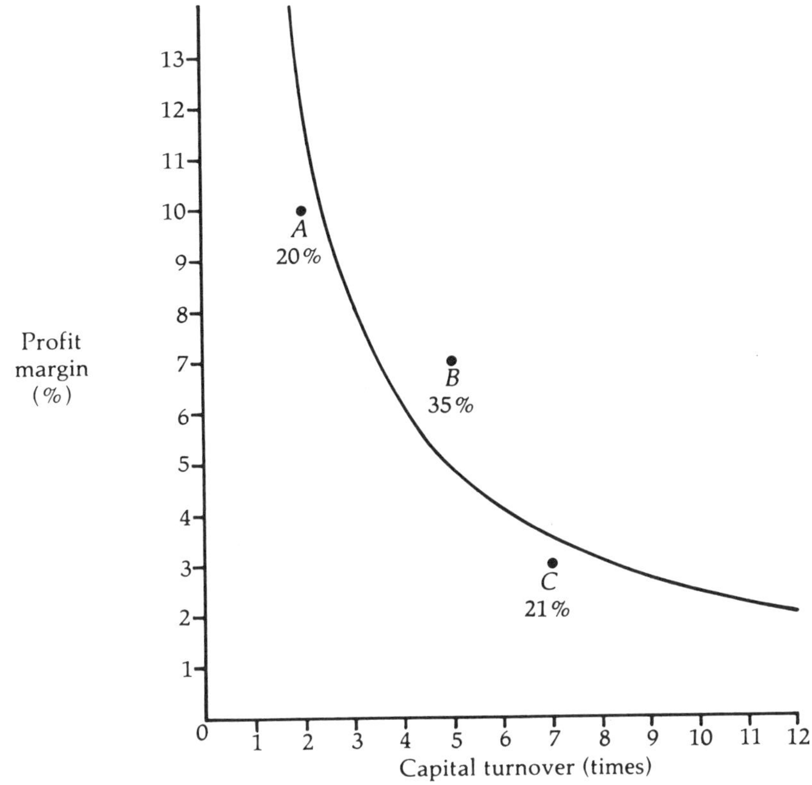

In contrast, Division C has a low margin on sales (3%) but a high capital turnover (of 7). This combination produced a level of performance that was also below the standard of 24%. However, the problems are likely to be in the sphere of cost control: improved cost control should improve the profit margin and hence raise ROI.

Finally, Division B has produced a level of performance that exceeds by a significant margin the target ROI figure by a judicious blending of profit margin (7%) and capital turnover (5 times).

An approach such as this is only a starting point for performance evaluation and diagnosis. It can point to broad areas needing attention but it cannot specify precise causes or cures. The interpretation of profit margins or capital turnover rates must be done in the context of specific industries. Thus a supermarket typically would have a high capital turnover and a low margin on sales whereas a steel mill would be more likely to have a high margin on sales with a low capital turnover. It follows that comparing the performance of divisions operating in different industries must be done with care.

(c) Constituents of ROI

In considering the suitability of ROI for measuring divisional performance we must examine both the numerator and the denominator. Problems exist in defining and then in measuring profit margin and invested capital. Since the denominator – invested capital – is more troublesome than the numerator let us start by examining that.

Alternative definitions of invested capital include:

(i) total assets available, irrespective of their individual purpose;
(ii) total assets employed, excluding idle or excess assets (such as vacant land or construction in progress);
(iii) net working capital plus other assets;
(iv) shareholders' funds;
(v) shareholders' funds plus non-current debt.

It has traditionally seemed reasonable that operating managers should be more concerned with the management of assets than with their long-term sources, so (i)–(iii) have been preferred to (iv) or (v). The use of (ii) is applicable to evaluating a divisional manager's ability to use available assets, but the evaluation of the division in economic terms should focus on (i) on the grounds that *all* assets must be considered. To exclude idle assets would, in the latter context, defeat the object of the exercise. However, goodwill should be excluded from the asset base since it is only a balancing figure in the books of account.

It is possible, and strictly correct, to include what Amey (1969, p. 58) describes as 'concealed investment'. This refers to expenditure that is written off in the period in which it is incurred even though it is expected to bring benefits through a number of periods (which is, as we saw in Chapter 6, the essence of investment). Examples include R & D outlays, advertising expenditure and management development costs.

A problem exists in seeking to associate assets with divisions since some assets will not be employed in a manner that can be directly associated with divisional activities. Even in decentralized organizations some assets are needed for central service functions and it is questionable whether anything is gained by allocating these assets to divisions in an arbitrary manner. For purposes of economic evaluation there is likely to be some benefit in that the central services would presumably have to be performed locally if the division were truly independent, but for managerial evaluation the allocation of centrally administered assets conflicts with the controllability criterion.

Alternative bases for divisional investment allocation are:

(i) traceable assets (i.e. all assets that are specifically identifiable with the division, regardless of their physical location);
(ii) controllable investment (i.e. all assets controlled by division management, net of any current liabilities within its jurisdiction);
(iii) total assets (i.e. all assets of the division – including a portion of corporate cash balances and other centrally administered assets);
(iv) net investment (i.e. the division's share of owners' equity and interest-bearing liabilities – whether long- or short-term);
(v) owners' equity (i.e. the owners' share of the investment in divisional assets).

As ever, a distinction needs to be made between evaluating the manager and evaluating the division. For the former it is essential to use a base that represents the *controllable investment* at the divisional level. In other words, allocated elements of the investment in head office facilities should not form part of the investment base for assessing the performance of divisional managers. On the other hand, a measure of the productivity of the investment in the division itself might usefully include some part of central facilities in the base.

Beyond these questions of determining which investment base to use, and which assets are controllable at the divisional level, there is the major question of deciding how the elements contained within any base should be valued. The main approaches to valuation are as follows:

(i) *Historical cost* – which is only a valuation at one point in time beyond which (at least in most cases) it is economically meaningless. Nevertheless, it might be justified on the grounds that:
   - this prevents the rate of return from artificially increasing as it would when periodic depreciation charges reduce the book value of the investment base;
   - it eliminates the effects of different depreciation methods, thereby facilitating interdivisional comparisons.

(ii) *Book value of the assets* (i.e. historical cost less accumulated depreciation), although this can be potentially misleading. As depreciation charges over time reduce the book value of a division's tangible fixed assets, a given net income will show an increasing ROI due purely to the decreasing investment base. This will be even more distorted during times of changing price levels since:
   - the profit figure will be overstated in so far as depreciation charges are based on historical costs;
   - the investment base will be understated in so far as this is based on historical (rather than replacement) cost.

   A risk therefore exists, if a book value approach is adopted, of divisional managers being reluctant to make new investments since this will reduce a division's profit (due to increased depreciation charges) and increase the investment base, thereby causing ROI to fall.

   Various proposals might be made to overcome these problems associated with the use of book values. For instance:
   - use the *undepreciated* book values of assets, thereby keeping the investment base constant (as in (i) above);
   - use a method of depreciation that makes increasing charges against revenue year by year, thereby reducing both profit and investment;
   - revise the book values – and the associated depreciation charges – by converting from historical to replacement costs (as in (v) below).

(iii) *Net realizable* (or disposal) *value*, which is the opportunity cost of the assets themselves.

(iv) *Net present value*, which is the best method in principle but which has some major drawbacks. Notable amongst these are:
   - it is based on predicted outcomes which are necessarily subject uncertain;
   - more fundamentally, the value of a given asset in use

apart from the whole of which it is a part, and the whole will exhibit *emergent properties* which ensure that it is more than the sum of its separate parts.

(v) *Replacement cost*. A strong case can be made for using an investment base that either:

- Reflects the replacement cost of the assets it represents. Approximations of replacement cost should not be taken to mean the market price of a new asset that would be used to replace an existing asset. For many assets already in use such market prices will not exist since the original physical or technological features will have been superseded. The aim should be to estimate how much it would cost now to obtain similar assets that would generate the same operating cash flows as the existing asset. We can see from this that the key issue is the expected cash flow rather than the asset in a physical sense; or
- Uses an index to increase the original cost to a current equivalent. Adjustments to historic cost that seek to allow for changes in price-levels (whether general or specific) do this by applying index numbers to historical cost data. This is a *restatement* of historical cost which is not the same as *replacement* cost.)

If the assets of different divisions have been acquired at different times it is clearly inappropriate to use the historical costs of those assets when assessing the performance of each division relative to other divisions. Consider, for example, the situation in which Division A's assets were acquired on the dates and at the historical costs shown below:

Buildings	1920	£100,000
Machinery	1960	£50,000
Motor vehicles	1992	£50,000

while those of Division B were acquired as follows:

Buildings	1960	£250,000
Machinery	1975	£100,000
Motor vehicles	1990	£40,000

Since the value of the pound sterling has fallen consistently over the years it is economically meaningless to add the historical costs of each division's as… - depreciated or not – as a basis for comparative performance …n. Instead of dealing in one consistent unit of measurement (i.e. a constant purchasing power) the historical cost approach seeks, in …dd apples to oranges, bananas and pineapples, thereby ending up …ture – a fruit salad. (See Chapter 9 in the companion volume …ccounting: *Method and Meaning* for fuller coverage of the …unting question.)

…e investment denominator to the profit numerator we find …e profit figure may be taken from a financial statement com… …GAAP, e.g. COGS will be based on absorption principles; …utlays on advertising, R & D, etc., will be charged against …fits on interdivisional transfers will have been eliminated. …ch as:

(i) How should inventories be valued?
(ii) How – if at all – should depreciation charges be determined?
(iii) When should revenue be recognized?
(iv) Which costs should be expensed and which capitalized?
(v) How should extraordinary items be handled?
(vi) What treatment should be accorded to interest and tax?

When an organization is independent these problems are significant, and they become even more significant in the context of divisions. This is most conspicuous when central costs are apportioned to divisions. Apart from the inherently arbitrary nature of most apportionments there is a need to reflect upon their impact on divisional managers' motivation. Apportionments do not facilitate control. On the other hand, it is appropriate to use absorption cost-based measures when seeking to evaluate the economic performance of divisions. The choice really boils down to using either:

(i) a direct cost-based (or contribution) measure;
(ii) an absorption cost-based measure.

Whatever figure is taken for the profit numerator should be consistent with the investment base. Thus if an asset base is used interest should not be deducted from earnings since interest is a financing cost rather than an operating cost.

(d) Standards for ROI

The question arises, of course, as to what ROI rate is reasonable. It seems clear that profitability should be adequate:

(i) to give a fair return to shareholders in relation to the level of risk involved;
(ii) to provide for normal replacement of assets;
(iii) to provide, in times of inflation, adequate reserves to maintain the real capital of the business intact;
(iv) to attract new capital when required;
(v) to satisfy creditors and employees of the likelihood of the organization's continued existence.

This list excludes growth, showing that a return above the minimum rate necessary to cover the above points is necessary if growth is to take place. Nevertheless, it does give a basis from which to determine a standard ROI which permits:

(i) the comparison of performance over time;
(ii) the evaluation of alternative investment possibilities.

Establishing standards of performance against which individuals can be held accountable, and which motivate individuals towards goal-striving behaviour, is a difficult problem. In essence it should be solved by specifying what standards should be under prevailing conditions. Suitable bench-marks have been proposed by many writers, and the major ones are of three types:

(i) *Externally derived standards* which are independent of the division's particular operating circumstances. These may be built up on the basis of:
– the ROI achievements of successful competitors within the same industry;

- the ROI of other companies operating under similar risk and skill circumstances;
- the position of the company within its own industry, bearing in mind the degree of competitiveness;
- the level of operating risk faced, with higher risk usually requiring a higher ROI from the investor's point of view;
- the 'expected' ROI as seen by such groups as the financial establishment, creditors, trades unions, etc.

There is nothing to suggest that external ROI results are indicative of real efficiency in operations, so regard must be had to that which is feasible as well as to that which has been achieved in the past.

(ii) *Internally derived standards* based on a divisional plan that embodies expected internal and environmental circumstances and which are considered to be attainable by divisional managers.

(iii) *Ex-post standards* which are established on the basis of environmental circumstances that prevailed in the period in question (e.g. where the inflation rate was actually 5% but only a 3% rate was anticipated, or interest rates were 1% higher than expected).

It is possible, if bench-marks of all three types are available, to evaluate divisional profit performance along the lines of Fig. 11.8. This shows that activity (or economic) appraisal is really an exercise in opportunity costing in that the division's reported profits are compared with the external profit standard (which represents alternative earnings possibilities).

On the other hand, after environmental (i.e. uncontrollable) variances have been removed – which is achieved by comparing actual results with *ex-post* standards – it is possible for self-appraisal and subordinate appraisal to be undertaken.

Otley (1985a) has observed (as other researchers have done) that performance targets are rarely exactly attained, for two major reasons:

(i) the ability of managers to make reliable predictions is imperfect (as we discussed in Chapter 4 and elsewhere);
(ii) organizational reward systems are likely to lead managers to introduce bias into both the setting of performance targets on the one hand and the reporting of actual outcomes on the other.

Measuring the reliability of predictions is one way of attempting to cope with (i), but dealing with (ii) is much more difficult since it will never be clear to what extent a variance is due – at least in part – to bias as opposed to unanticipated (rather than wrongly estimated) environmental circumstances.

(e) ROI summary and evaluation

On the face of it ROI offers a valuable performance measure for a division (or an entity as a whole) since it facilitates comparisons. Its advantages include:

(i) its general acceptance;
(ii) its offer of an index of performance that is readily understood;
(iii) its role in encouraging managers to seek to adopt projects that will improve

Figure 11.8

Appraisal of past profit performance.

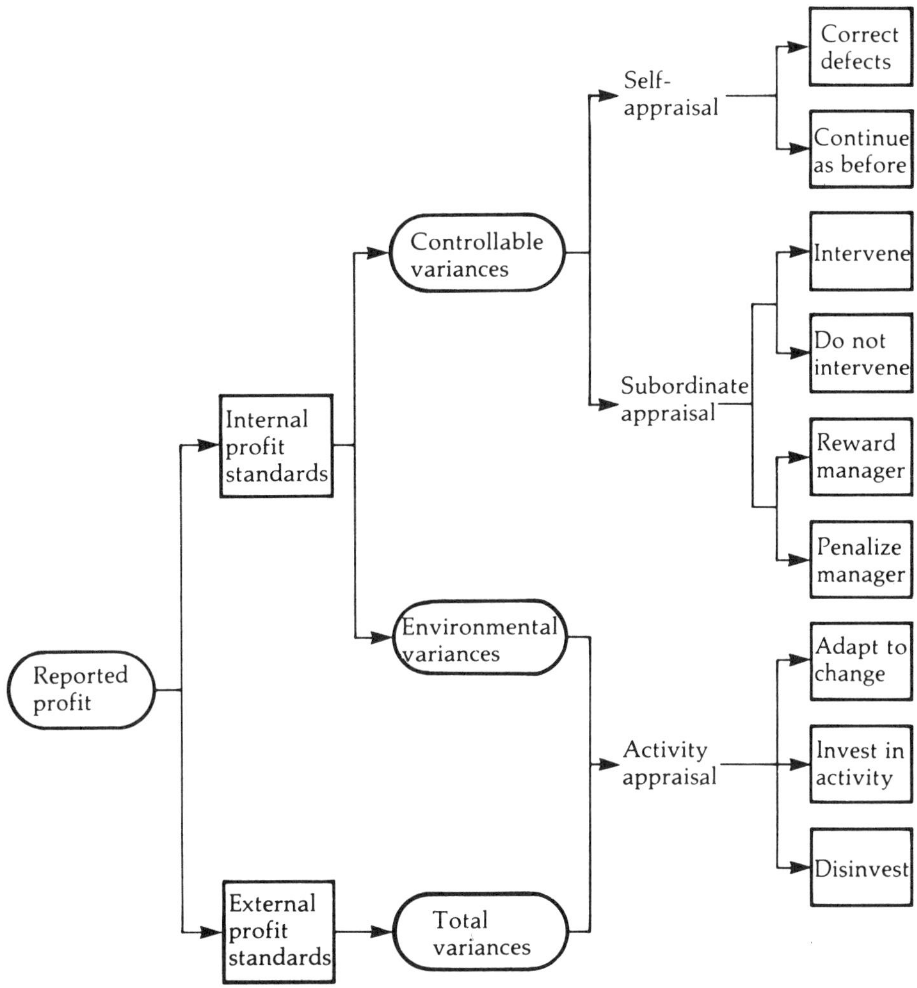

Source: Shillinglaw (1964), p. 158.

their ROI while disposing of or rejecting those activities that do not provide an acceptable ROI;

(iv) as an index ROI can be used by many interested parties (both within and beyond the specific enterprise) to gauge performance and to make comparisons.

As ever, of course, we must weigh the advantages against the limitations of ROI. The latter include:

(i) the lack of consensus on the definition of numerator and denominator;
(ii) the danger that ROI can be manipulated on a period-by-period basis (e.g. by avoiding new capital outlays) which puts long-term prosperity at risk;
(iii) the use of divisional ROI to evaluate performance can distort an enterprise's overall allocation of resources when the manager of one division avoids investing in a project that would improve overall performance for the enterprise but which would reduce that division's ROI, with the result that another division invests the available funds in a project that might improve its ROI but which will not contribute as much to the enterprise as a whole;
(iv) ROI is but one measure and we have emphasized throughout the book the importance of non-financial criteria in evaluating performance: we cannot reduce a multivariate problem to a univariate one.

ROI has established itself as the 'approved' means of assessing divisional performance, but Henderson and Dearden (1966) have challenged this status on the grounds that ROI can be so misleading as to be destructive. They argue their case in the following terms:

- ROI provides information that logically leads to incorrect decisions;
- ROI motivates division managers to take actions contrary to the best interests of the organization;
- ROI provides top management with misleading information about divisional performance.

Underlying these condemnations are Henderson and Dearden's views that ROI fails because it treats as investment centres organizational units which are not truly investment centres; it uses transfer prices that are not really prices at all; and it incorporates irrelevant investment bases.

It is worth considering these points a little more fully. The first is concerned with organizational arrangements. An attempt is made in using ROI (with its investment centres and transfer prices) to control the parts of a complex organization as though they were independent entities. To the extent that there is any interdependence amongst the parts – which there invariably will be – this endeavour cannot succeed. When the freedom of manoeuvre of one division is constrained by the interests of another, or of the organization as a whole, the supposed autonomy of investment centres is seen to be fictional.

Optimal decisions for the organization as a whole can only be made if division managers have information that indicates the impact of their decisions on other parts of the organization, and hence on the organization as a whole. The relevant information is the marginal contribution (i.e. the net change that results from the action following a given decision) which is measured as the difference between the marginal revenue and the marginal cost. As you will know from your study of micro-economics, the optimal point arises when the marginal contribution is at its greatest. However, division managers will typically not know when this point has been reached. In part this is due to faulty transfer prices. If material is transferred from division W to division C its marginal cost will be either:

(i) market price (less selling expenses) where a true market exists, since this is the opportunity cost of not selling the material to an outside party; or
(ii) out-of-pocket costs of the material to W, since this is the sum that must be spent to make the material available to C.

From this it can be appreciated that market prices should be used as transfer prices only when a market actually exists for the quantity of materials in question. Any 'approximate' or 'negotiated' market price cannot truly represent marginal cost: in the absence of a market there is no opportunity cost. And where there is no market it would be inappropriate to base a transfer price on a measure of 'cost' which includes apportioned fixed costs or a profit margin for division W since neither of these items represents out-of-pocket costs either to division W or to the organization as a whole. To the extent that any transfer price is neither based on market price nor on out-of-pocket costs it is not a satisfactory price to include in a system of divisional control.

As a fraction ROI is heavily dependent upon both the numerator and denominator from which it is derived. It is clear that both profit and investment are capable of being measured in many ways so the choice of any particular approach is essentially arbitrary which makes it difficult to justify using it as a basis for divisional control.

With specific reference to the investment denominator:

(i) many items of investment are excluded from the investment base in an arbitrary manner when they are written off against revenue instead of being capitalized (e.g. R & D, patents, training, market research, and promotional costs);
(ii) any relationship between the original cost or replacement cost of an asset and its economic value is coincidental, since economic value is a function of, *inter alia*, technology, markets, and organizational considerations.

The combined effects of the various points raised above give rise to the situation in which division managers will be motivated to manipulate the constituents of ROI so that their performance (as measured by ROI) will be acceptable to top management – i.e. to play the system. But this will often work against the organization's best interests due to the inherent limitations of ROI as a performance measure.

Henderson and Dearden's proposal to overcome the problems of ROI is a system that holds divisional managers accountable only for the things that are within their control. This would operate via a set of budgets for each division for the next year with the budgets being made up of three parts:

- a contribution budget;
- a fixed and managed cost budget;
- a capital budget.

All transfers would be reported at marginal cost, with adjustments being needed to cover activities above and below normal capacity.

One prominent feature of this proposal is that only anticipated cash inflows and outflows are included in the budgets and – subsequently – in the reported actual figures: accruals and interperiod charges for previous investments are excluded. This is easily understood in relation to the contribution budget and the fixed-and-managed cost budget, but perhaps it is not so immediately appreciated in connexion with the capital budget. The logic rests on two main points:

(i) once an investment decision has been made, the initial outlays become sunk costs;

(ii) the operating impacts of investment decisions are to be found in the contribution budgets (via the impacts of the investment on variable cost levels and revenue generation).

Benefits from Henderson and Dearden's proposal are claimed to be:

(i) the provision of an easier basis for determining transfer prices;
(ii) the evaluation of division managers on the actions taken during the period under review (which should discourage attempts to manipulate numerator or denominator – as in ROI – which include arbitrary allocations from earlier investments);
(iii) the tendency towards taking actions to improve short-run performance under ROI will be reduced, since the fixed-and-managed costs budget will seek to balance short and long-term interests (such as R & D, maintenance, and training outlays);
(iv) the monitoring of capital projects will be facilitated by comparing the actual cash flows resulting from them period by period with the anticipated flows when the projects were authorized.

This gives much food for thought.

(f) Residual income

As an alternative to ROI the performance of a division can be measured by means of *residual income* (RI). This can be defined as the operating profit (or income) of a division *less* the imputed interest on the assets used by the division. In other words, interest on the capital invested in the division is treated as a cost (in accordance with long-standing economic tradition) and any surplus is the residual income. This can be contrasted with the usual accounting custom which treats profit – which is itself calculated as a residual resulting from the subtraction of costs from revenue – as the reward to capital.

In the same way that setting a target ROI is problematic so is establishing the rate to impute in measuring residual income. The critical questions are:

(i) What rate should be specified?
(ii) When, and by how much, should it be altered?
(iii) Should the same rate be used in each division?

It seems likely that a uniform imputed rate will cause overall ROI to tend towards that rate – which will probably be lower than is otherwise attainable. A portfolio approach, therefore, which recognizes that returns are a function of risk, is likely to be more satisfactory and is likely to result in different divisions having different desired rates of return depending on the relative investment risks of each. (The companion volume on *Financial Management: Method and Meaning* deals with these issues in detail.)

An example will help demonstrate how RI can be measured and used in a managerial accounting system. Initially, however, we must deal with the allocation of assets to divisions, which was touched upon in Section 11.4(c) above.

It will usually be possible to identify many assets with divisions. This will typically be the case with:

(i) plant and equipment;

Figure 11.9

Allocation of assets and profits.

	Total £	Unallocated £	Division X £	Division Y £	Division Z £
Investment:					
Cash	140,000	30,000	20,000	30,000	60,000
Debtors	230,000		60,000	80,000	90,000
Inventory	520,000		100,000	180,000	240,000
Prepayments	65,000	20,000	10,000	15,000	20,000
Plant and equipment	1,020,000	60,000	200,000	320,000	440,000
Investments	110,000	100,000	10,000	–	–
Total assets	£2,085,000	£210,000	£400,000	£625,000	£850,000
Profit:					
Revenue	1,200,000		100,000	400,000	700,000
Variable costs	650,000		30,000	220,000	400,000
Contribution	550,000		70,000	180,000	300,000
Separable fixed costs	260,000		30,000	90,000	140,000
Division profit	290,000		£40,000	£90,000	£160,000
Common fixed costs	80,000				
Net profit	£210,000				

(ii) inventory;
(iii) receivables.

Cash, on the other hand, will usually be under centralized control, as will:

- headquarters premises;
- investments in securities;
- deferred expenses.

Figure 11.9 illustrates a hypothetical organization in which the assets, revenues and operating costs are allocated (where appropriate) across divisions X, Y and Z. Unallocated items are attributable to the head office, and no performance measure is produced for these items.

From the details of Fig. 11.9 we can compute ROI for the enterprise as a whole and for each division. If the minimum required ROI is known to be 10% it is also possible to calculate RI for the enterprise and its divisions. These figures are given in Fig. 10.10.

In overall terms the enterprise generates slightly more than the minimum ROI target of 10%. Because of the unallocated assets, however, it is necessary for the

Figure 11.10

ROI and RI computations

	Enterprise as a whole	Division X	Division Y	Division Z
ROI:				
Operating profit	£210,000	£40,000	£90,000	£160,000
Investment	£2,085,000	£400,000	£625,000	£850,000
ROI	10.1%	10%	14.4%	18.8%
Residual income:				
Operating profit	£210,000	£40,000	£90,000	£160,000
Required return (10% on investment)	£208,500	£40,000	£62,500	£85,000
Residual income	£ 1,500	–	£27,500	£75,000

divisions to earn in excess of that minimum rate in order that the enterprise as a whole might meet the target. The impact of unallocated assets is seen vividly in the RI section of Fig. 11.10: the overall RI is a mere £1,500 despite the much larger figures generated by divisions Y and Z.

It is argued that the use of ROI as a divisional performance measure will encourage divisional managers to turn down projects that might risk lowering their average ROI even though those projects might promise returns in excess of the organization's minimum rate. A further example will illustrate this situation.

Assume the manager of Division R of WFC Ltd expects her results for this year to be based on an operating profit of £300,000 from an investment amounting to £1 m, thus giving ROI of 30%. WFC Ltd has a minimum required ROI of 20%. If the divisional manager is now presented with a project which promises incremental operating profits of £75,000 during the year in return for an incremental investment (in inventory and debtors' balances) of £300,000, what should she do?

It is clear that the incremental project offers a return of 25% which exceeds WFC's minimum requirement of 20%. On these grounds it would appear to be desirable. However, the manager may reject the project because of its impact on her overall ROI, as Fig. 11.11 illustrates.

If one considers this situation from the viewpoint of WFC Ltd, it is desirable that the profit-generating opportunity be adopted since it offers an ROI in excess of the minimum (both on its own and when viewed as part of the overall picture of Division R). But the manager of that division is bound to consider the measure by which her performance is evaluated, and in this regard an ROI of 30% appears to be better than one of 28.8%.

As a way of dealing with this WFC Ltd could use RI since this highlights the enterprise's policy regarding minimum (rather than maximum) returns. Using the above data Fig. 11.12 shows that it is beneficial both to the division (hence the enterprise) and to its manager to adopt the incremental project since RI increases by £15,000. The logic, of course, is that the RI criterion encourages managers to

Figure 11.11

Relative ROI performance.

Base case:	
Investment	£1,000,000
Operating profit	£300,000
ROI	30%
New case:	
Investment	£1,300,000
Operating profit	£375,000
ROI	28.8%

Figure 11.12

Relative RI performance.

	Base case	New case
	£	£
Investment	1,000,000	1,300,000
Operating profit	300,000	375,000
Minimum ROI at 20%	200,000	260,000
Residual income	£100,000	£115,000

maximize the absolute size of earnings in excess of the minimum required return whereas the ROI criterion focuses on the maximization of profit relative to investment.

(g) ROI v. RI

Both ROI and RI have been subjected to criticisms which include:

(i) overemphasis on short-term results;
(ii) preoccupation with profit rather than qualitative factors;
(iii) inappropriate choice of investment bases;
(iv) unjustifiable comparisons across divisions.

Often there is a real conflict between acting in a way that improves short-run performance at the expense of the longer run, or vice versa. A paradox is that the manager who seeks to produce good short-term results will tend to be valued and gain promotion, so he will be located elsewhere within the organization when the long-term consequences of his short-term actions come home to roost. Conversely, the manager who acts in the enterprise's long-term interests may have such poor short-run results that he loses his job and someone else in due course will inherit the benefits of this departed manager's forethought. We can conclude from this that it is unsatisfactory to evaluate managers and divisions wholly on the basis of measures such as ROI and RI. Qualitative as well as quantitative factors must be taken into account.

In terms of broad principles the above conclusion may be correct, but it fails to help us choose between ROI and RI in a situation in which better measures – whether qualitative or quantitative – are often not available. How might a choice be made?

Solomons (1965) distinguishes two basic cases for which he suggests specific approaches to measuring performance. Between these cases – which are at different ends of a notional continuum – the approach to adopt will hinge upon the degree of control that a division manager exercises over the investment in that division. These two cases are:

(i) If divisional management has little or no control over the level of investment in the division, then ROI is a satisfactory approach to adopt provided interest on capital is not deducted in measuring ROI. (If the focus is on *economic* evaluation the achieved ROI will be compared with a bench-mark figure and to deduct interest would be to invalidate comparisons. If the focus is on *managerial* evaluation the divisional manager will not be able to control the interest charge and so he should not be held accountable for it.)

(ii) In situations in which divisional management has almost total freedom to determine its own investment base it is appropriate to deduct interest and RI becomes the relevant measure of performance.

The controversy over the use of RI as a tool for measuring the performance of managers in a divisional organization – as evidenced by the Amey–Tomkins debate of 1975 in *JBFA* – concerns both its validity and utility. Emmanuel and Otley (1976) sought to identify the practical as well as the theoretical pros and cons of RI as a means of appraising divisional performance in the aftermath of the Amey–Tomkins debate. They concluded, *inter alia*, that RI was a better performance measure than accounting profit in cases in which capital investment decisions are taken at the divisional level. While it was recognized that accounting conventions underlie both measures, the imputed interest charge within the RI measure renders it closer to the notion of economic income (in which interest is viewed as the payment for capital as a factor input). This conforms with Solomons's views.

Emmanuel and Otley found a general agreement in the literature that, when a division's capital base is fixed outside the division, the interest element (hence RI) is irrelevant. The RI controversy, then, is limited to situations in which divisional managers have responsibility for the capital base used in generating their operating profit. Such situations appear to be empirically rather rare: the limited evidence that exists (Reece and Cool (1978) and Tomkins (1973), for instance) suggests that capital investment control is typically centralized, so RI is not an appropriate measure to employ (see Scapens and Sale, 1981).

Given the scarcity of empirical evidence it is worth taking account of one significant empirical study – even though it is now a little dated and relates to the USA. The study by Reece and Cool (1978) among 620 major US corporations was to see how they measured the economic performance of their divisions. As Fig. 11.13 shows, almost one in four corporations had investment centres, and the

Figure 11.13

Incidence of investment centres.

Corporations having:	Number	Percentage
Investment centres	459	74.0
Profit centres	135	21.8
Neither	26	4.2
Total	620	100%

Figure 11.14

Measures of investment centre performance.

Measures used:	Number	Percentage
ROI only	299	65
Residual income only	9	2
ROI and residual income	128	28
Some other measure	17	4
No answer given	6	1
Total	459	100%

use of investment centres tended to be an increasing function of size on the one hand and modern technology on the other.

Among the corporations using the investment centre approach it was found that many (28%) calculate both ROI *and* residual income in recognition that each has its particular strengths as well as weaknesses. Figure 11.14 indicates the measures used by respondent corporations to assess divisional performance.

It is apparent from the details in Fig. 11.14 that ROI was the most popular measure in use and that residual income – despite the strong arguments of those advocating this method's superiority – was only in use on its own in 2% of responding enterprises. Reece and Cool's study also revealed that most corporations using investment centres tended to use definitions of denominator and numerator for calculating ROI that were in line with those used in their published financial statements. This is not very encouraging in terms of giving an economically meaningful measure.

(h) Divisional investment appraisal

A conspicuous paradox has been noted by a number of writers (e.g. Ijiri (1978; 1980), Kaplan (1982)) between the recommended approaches to making investment decisions and the ways in which the outcomes of investment decisions are assessed. As we saw in Chapter 6, and as the companion volume *Financial Management: Method and Meaning* points out, the primary focus in investment decision-making should be on cash flows over the expected duration of the project. In contrast, the usual emphasis for performance evaluation is on some measure of profit (such as ROI or residual income) on a year-by-year basis. There is no direct link between these two approaches: the former relies on economic logic while the latter reflects accounting rationality. (As a vivid indicator of the differences we can take depreciation: this is irrelevant in investment decision-making since it does not entail any cash flows, but it is a deduction from profits in evaluating periodic performance.)

Some congruence could be achieved by either:

(i) basing investment decisions on profit measures, for which there is little economic justification; or
(ii) basing performance assessment on cash flows, for which a better case can be made.

Ijiri's recommendation regarding (ii) is to use the *cash recovery rate* (CRR) which he defines as:

$$\text{CRR} = \frac{\text{Cash flow from operations}^{*}}{\text{Gross assets}^{**}}$$

* Cash flow from operations includes the sale proceeds of long-term assets disposed of during the period, plus changes in working capital.
** Gross assets is the average value of the undepreciated historical cost of all assets in use during the period.

This measure avoids all accounting accruals stemming from the periodicity convention, and Ijiri's studies in the USA have shown that CRR for many enterprises is extremely stable over time, which suggests that the average profitability of projects can be measured by the CRR.

A cautionary point worth noting is that, as with ROI, CRR is a ratio. This could prompt managers whose performance is being evaluated by CRR to turn down project proposals which would lower their average CRR even though those projects might generate positive returns. In this situation an approach that is analogous to the residual income approach might be adopted, i.e. a residual cash flow measure could be devised by deducting from cash flow the product of gross investment and required rate of return.

Capital budgeting control systems have mainly concentrated on the *ex-ante* analysis of investment projects, but distinct advantages can be put forward to support the case for reviews during and at the end of a project's life. Benefits are likely to include the following:

(i) since one learns from evaluating past experience it should be possible to avoid repeating in the future the errors one made in investment decision-making in the past;
(ii) improved estimating should emerge since comparisons of actual outcomes with forecasts raises questions concerning the adequacy of the latter;
(iii) bias reduction may take place – at least to some extent – if those who make investment proposals are aware that the implementation of their proposals will be monitored;
(iv) corrective action can be applied to ensure the project is successful or, if success is improbable, the project can be terminated.

Division managers may resist the evaluation of capital projects (whether on a regular basis or as a post-audit once each project is complete) for a number of reasons. One important reason is political: projects need sponsors, and once a manager has sponsored a particular project which is subsequently implemented he is inevitably associated with it. If the project was found to be less beneficial than initially anticipated – or if the project were to be prematurely terminated – this would be politically threatening to the original sponsor. For this reason sponsors will tend to discourage reviews. (See the comments on *entrapment* in Section 11.2 above.)

Another reason for resisting reviews is the assumption that the review will seek to highlight the errors contained in the basic assumptions underlying the decision to accept the project in the first instance. While one can learn from this (as suggested above) the real benefit from reviews lies not in the analysis of past decisions but more in the projection of experience into the future in order to revise one's expectations (thus linking feedback and feedforward forms of control).

11.5 Transfer pricing

In seeking to treat divisions of an enterprise as profit or investment centres in a way that will allow performance to be assessed it is necessary to establish an appropriate means of dealing with interdivisional transfers. This problem was touched upon in Section 11.4(e) above, and dealt with much more fully in Chapter 9.

It will be apparent that the level of transfer prices will have an impact on the profits of both the selling and buying divisions. If such prices are set at a level that differs from whatever a division would have to pay for a comparable material, product or service in an arm's length transaction in the open market, then the result will be an arbitrary allocation of profits among the divisions. This will inevitably limit the extent to which divisional performance can be adequately assessed. It follows, therefore, that open market prices offer the best basis for setting transfer prices when one wishes to assess a divisional manager's performance. This applies both to the inputs into a 'buying' division and to the outputs from a 'selling' division.

In principle this is easy enough to specify, but in practice there may be serious complications. For instance:

(i) There may be no open market for the intermediate goods or services being transferred, hence no open market prices.
(ii) The goods or services in question may be significantly differentiated from open market offerings, hence the market price may not be wholly appropriate.

One answer to the first of these complications is to seek tenders from outside enterprises to supply the goods or services, and the market price can be inferred from the tender prices. With regard to the second complication, it may be necessary for representatives of the buying and selling divisions to negotiate a price using the nearest market price as a starting point. In the absence of, on the one hand, acceptable open market prices, or, on the other hand, satisfactory ways of handling complications, it will not be possible to use investment centres or profit centres for evaluating managerial performance. Cost control would have to

Figure 11.15

Approaches to transfer pricing.

Use	Recommended method of transfer pricing
Measuring performance	Market price or marginal cost
Decision-making	Marginal cost or differential cost
Profit determination	Full (absorbed) cost (excluding intracompany profit)

Adapted from Bierman and Dyckman (1976), p. 441.

be the basis of assessment in such cases (at least in relation to interdivisional transfers).

In the context of decision-making rather than performance measurement it is worth observing that the best transfer price is that which the enterprise would see if it were not organized into divisions. This is the price that relates to the well-being of the enterprise as a whole and not of a particular division. If an open-market price is available then this should be used. Where no market price exists an approximation of the opportunity cost of the transfer must be determined: standard variable cost is a widely used proxy for the opportunity cost in such a situation.

From this discussion, and that in Chapter 9, we can see that the method of transfer pricing used by a divisionalized enterprise will directly affect the contents of reports used for:

(i) assessing the performance of divisional managers;
(ii) decision-making by divisional managers;
(iii) determining the profit of the divisions and of the organization as a whole.

No single approach to transfer pricing can satisfy all these needs. Figure 11.15 summarizes the approaches that might be adopted for different purposes.

Summary

Performance measurement at the divisional level seeks to monitor the economic behaviour of divisions as well as providing a means of motivating divisional managers. Care must be taken in establishing which of these aims – monitoring or motivating – one has in mind in order that an appropriate system might be designed. Linkages do exist between the two aims. Thus, for example, a divisional manager who is *au fait* with his division's economic performance may be able to learn from this and hence improve his motivation. But targets that are set for managers to achieve must still be differentiated from targets that are set for divisions as economic units.

One critically important distinction that needs drawing out between the evaluation of divisions and managers is that it is the latter who carry responsibility (which can only be made operational when it is personalized), and only the human actors in an evaluative setting have their behaviour influenced by the evaluative process. It is not always the case, of course, that behaviour is influenced for the better! 'Playing the system' is a characteristic of organizational life.

Any accounting performance measure is partial in that it fails to encompass important qualitative and non-financial aspects of organizational activities. Profit may, as Shillinglaw argues, ultimately reflect all these non-financial issues, but other schools of thought argue otherwise – and profit is simply not applicable as a performance criterion in a wide range of non-commercial organizations.

Restricting ourselves to accounting measures, we saw that profit needs to be carefully defined when evaluating the performance of profit centres (with direct or net profit being applicable) or of profit centre managers (with controllable profit being applicable). However, profit measures fail to cater adequately for asset management so we need to consider profitability measures which seek to determine the rate of profit per unit of capital invested.

ROI and RI are competing alternatives, but both require careful attention to be paid to:

(i) definitions of 'profit' and 'investment';
(ii) valuation methods;
(iii) allocation methods;
(iv) the establishing of standards.

The 1975 debate in *JBFA* has been interpreted to suggest that RI is only applicable in situations in which divisions have discretion over the level of capital investment. Since these situations appear to be rather rare the more favoured measure is probably ROI (although empirical evidence on current practices and preferences is also rare).

Finally, we considered the role of transfer pricing in assessing divisional performance. The general rule given in Chapter 9 is confirmed – whether for economic evaluation of divisions or for the evaluation of divisional managers.

Key terms and concepts

Here is a list of the key terms and concepts which have featured in this chapter. You should make sure that you understand and can define each one of them. Page references to definitions in the text appear in bold in the index.

- Agency theory
- Decentralization
- Divisionalization
- Entrapment
- Performance measurement
  - economic
  - managerial
- Performance measures
  - Cash recovery rate (CRR)
  - Rate of return on investment (ROI)
  - Residual income (RI)
- Profit versus profitability
- Valuation
  - book value
  - historical cost
  - net present value (NPV)
  - net realisable (disposal) value
  - replacement cost

Further reading

The classic text on divisional performance is Solomons (1965), but see also the thoughtful articles by Dearden (e.g. 1960; 1961; 1968), Goold and Campbell (1987), and Vancil (1979).

Govindarajan (1984) questions the appropriateness of accounting data in the context of performance evaluation, while various American Accounting Association reports (e.g. 1971b, 1972c) look at measures that are applicable in non-commercial organizations.

On the specific issue of escalation that was raised in this chapter two interesting studies are those by Ross and Staw (1986), and Bowen (1987), but see also Staw and Ross (1987a) (1987b), and Harwood, *et al.* (1991).

The workbook to accompany this chapter begins on p. 595.

PART

4 Overview and the future

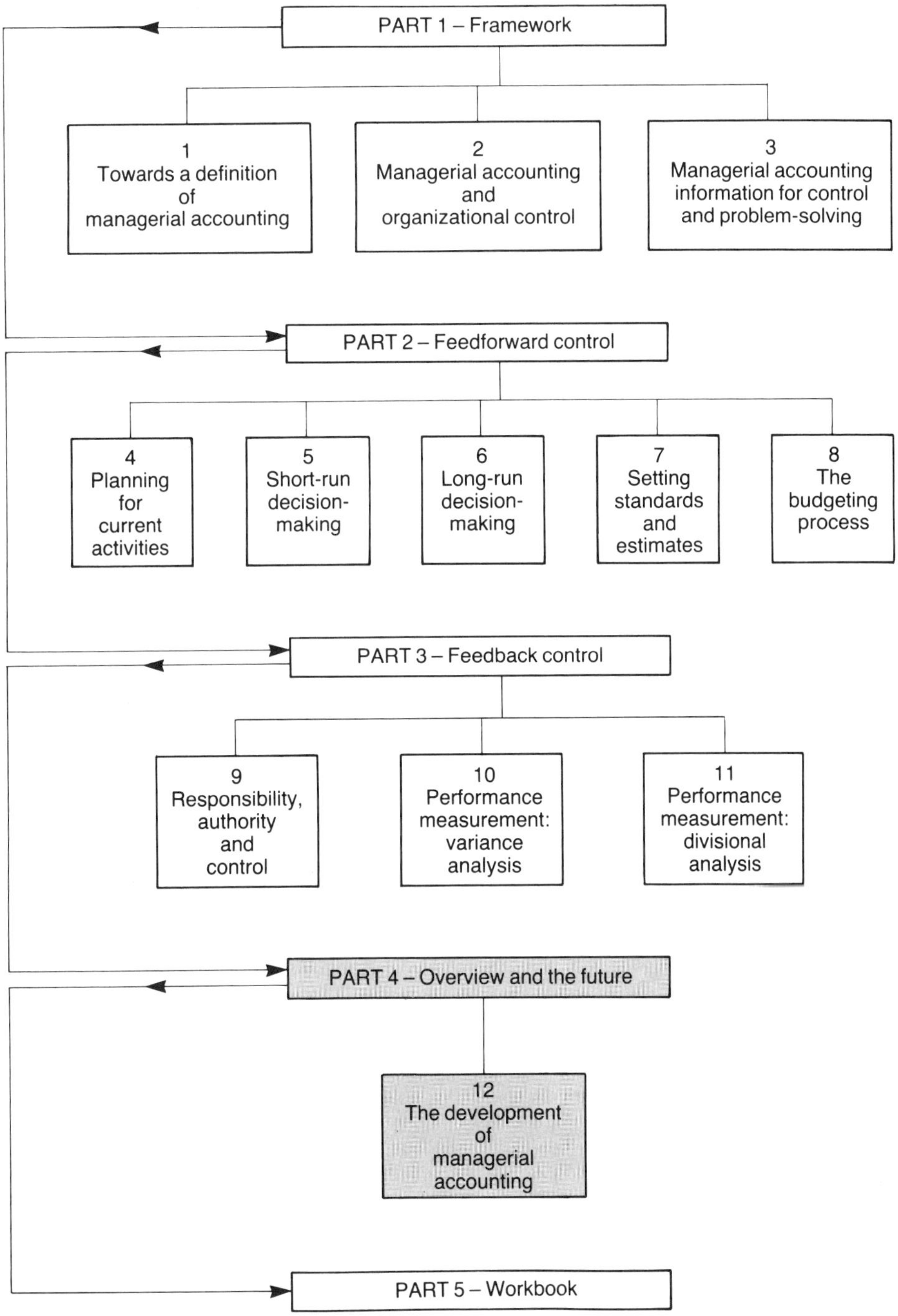

Introduction and overview

Part 4 consists solely of Chapter 12. We have travelled a long route since Chapter 1 and have seen many managerial accounting methods and some of the social meaning of those methods. But how satisfactory is the state of the subject? Does the discipline (if that is what it is) have an adequate theoretical foundation to guide practice, or does practice proceed in virtual isolation of the academic branch of managerial accounting?

Within this chapter we offer an evaluation of the current state of managerial accounting. In many respects this makes for less-than-happy reading, although it offers a challenge to the ambitious among you to work to improve things for the future!

A variety of avenues along which current developments are discernable are reviewed, and prospects for the future are then considered. The future is likely to see increasing interdisciplinary work under the managerial accounting heading, with a stronger behavioural orientation. Managerial accounting systems are but a part of an organization's decision support system, which in turn reflects aspects of the organization and its environment. The partiality of managerial accounting needs to be recognized in this regard since there are some critical elements of organizational control that are beyond the scope of managerial accounting *per se*.

Among the valuable contributions to the literature on the theme of Chapter 12 some from British writers (including those of Otley, Scapens and Hart) are particularly worthy of praise, as are some from American authors (e.g. Johnson, Kaplan and Mattessich).

CHAPTER 12 The development of managerial accounting

Learning objectives

After studying this chapter you should be able to:

- appreciate the main stages in the development of managerial accounting up to the present time;
- assess the current state of managerial accounting;
- project likely (and desirable) directions for the future development of managerial accounting.

12.1 Introduction

In the eleven chapters that precede this one we have sought to explain something of the role of managerial accounting within organizations by discussing a variety of technical elements (the 'methods' of managerial accounting) and their meaning in an organizational setting. Our approach has been neither narrow nor restricted to financial issues, but managerial accounting has not always been seen in such a liberated way.

The historical development of costing and managerial accounting has been admirably covered by Solomons (1952), Parker (1969; 1980), Johnson (1983) and Loft (1986). Two symposia have been organized (1972 and 1979) on the state of the art of managerial accounting by staff in the Department of Accountancy at the University of Illinois (see Dopuch and Revsine (1973) and Holzer (1980) for the proceedings). Various helpful reviews of the subject area have been contributed to the literature by Hart (1981), Kaplan (1981; 1984a), Otley (1980; 1983a; 1983b; 1985b) and Scapens (1980; 1983a; 1983b; 1984; 1985), plus some personal reminiscences (e.g. Anthony (1989), Horngren (1989), and Shillinglaw (1989)). Within these reviews – and within the Illinois proceedings – researchers have made suggestions as to fruitful avenues for the future development of managerial accounting, as have Churchill and Uretsky (1969) and Lowe and Tinker (1977).

These sources will be drawn on in this chapter to reinforce a number of key points made earlier in the text concerning how we got here and where we might go from here.

12.2 The current state of managerial accounting

The current state of managerial accounting is not reflected in a unified theory or in a coherent set of practices. Perhaps the ultimate test of a managerial accounting system – especially in the light of the theme of this book – is whether or not it motivates and assists managers in achieving organizational control. In general, among the various approaches that have guided practitioners and researchers in the design of managerial accounting systems, a concern for organizational control *per se* has not been paramount.

Managerial accounting research had, according to Otley (1983a, 1985b), reached a low point by 1970 in that academics had developed techniques that were largely ignored by practitioners as evidenced by:

(i) techniques having a sound economic pedigree were typically not implemented by practitioners (such as direct costing, methods of transfer pricing and divisional performance measurement that were deemed to be theoretically correct);
(ii) techniques lacking economic validity continued to be widely used (such as cost allocations of all kinds).

In considering this lack of balance between managerial accounting research and practice, it may be true that academic research is simply not relevant to practice (Kaplan, 1981) or that research has moved away from – rather than being ahead of – practice (Otley, 1985b). Alternatively, it may be the case that the data requirements needed to implement and operate approaches to the design of managerial accounting systems recommended by researchers have cost implications that render them non-feasible on cost-benefit grounds. As Scapens has noted (e.g. 1985), academic researchers too often assume that information is freely available.

In response to the question he posed as to why there were so few significant developments (i.e. in terms of the impact of research on practice) in managerial accounting up to 1970, Anthony (1973) offered an array of possible answers (pp. 67–68):

(i) the tendency for academics to investigate 'respectable' topics rather than useful ones;
(ii) the disservice rendered by economic models in focusing attention on the wrong things;
(iii) the absence of a unifying conceptual framework (which also plagues financial accounting but which, with the arrival of the capital asset pricing model, is less of a problem in the domain of financial management);
(iv) the dearth of empirically oriented research (cf. medicine or engineering);
(v) the absence of documented case histories, etc., written by practitioners – with the result that there is limited awareness among practitioners themselves as well as between academics and practitioners as to the state of current practice;
(vi) the limited funding devoted to research means that which is done is fragmentary and done on a part-time basis;
(vii) the existence of dubious assumptions and untested generalizations about

organizational life constitute an inappropriate foundation for valid theories concerning managerial accounting;

(viii) the reluctance of researchers to adapt to changing circumstances.

Several writers (e.g. Kaplan (1983)) have pointed out that the performance of manufacturing organizations in the USA or UK has been much poorer than in Japan or in certain other Western European countries. Production is frequently of higher quality, achieved with fewer workers, and based on lower inventory levels in the latter locations. The role of managerial accounting systems needs to be examined in this regard since a preoccupation with systems that generate simple, aggregate, short-run financial performance measures is hardly conducive to ensuring long-term competitiveness and profitability.

The partiality of managerial accounting systems (in so far as they only include financial information) is at variance with the need to understand more fully the factors that are critical to the effectiveness of, *inter alia*, manufacturing organizations. A broader range of performance indicators needs to be incorporated into managerial accounting systems to cover such matters as:

(i) productivity;
(ii) quality;
(iii) manufacturing flexibility;
(iv) delivery performance.

12.3 Patterns of development

Shillinglaw (1980, pp. 5–8) identified three phases in the evolution of managerial accounting:

(a) The era of scientific management

Phase 1 was *the era of scientific management*, dominated by engineering considerations. The emphasis was on product costing (on an absorption basis) and the control of direct labour and direct material costs (which later developed into standard costing). Innovations were essentially generated by practitioners who built up a common body of knowledge for aspiring management accountants to absorb.

As the first manifestation of a managerial accounting system it is clear that costing emerged to fill a need more closely associated with financial reporting than with the needs of organizational control. Costing initially existed to allocate manufacturing costs between cost of goods sold and inventory, and a belief that 'true' costs could be established was prevalent up until the middle of this century.

Kaplan (1984a) has commented on the way in which, during the earlier years, the major developments in managerial accounting practice emerged *within* organizations, having been stimulated by specific organizational needs. Those engaged in practice did the developing, whereas today's academic managerial accounting literature contains relatively few references to actual organizations, although it is full of references to economic and organizational theorists' writings:

> . . . contemporary researchers' knowledge of managers' behavior is based not on studying decisions and procedures of actual firms, but on the stylized models of managerial and firm behavior that have been articulated by . . . [other] . . . theorists who, themselves, have limited first-hand knowledge of the behavior they have modelled.

(b) The era of managerial control

Phase 2 is described by Shillinglaw as *the era of managerial control* in which the common body of knowledge from phase 1 was added to by using concepts borrowed from academic disciplines (such as economics, mathematics and social psychology). Management accountants were able to move from the factory to the boardroom during this phase.

A change in emphasis was detectable during the 1950s and 1960s: accounting data for internal use was seen to be increasingly necessary – independently of the routines of external financial reporting. Absorption costing, which was very widely used, was recognized as being potentially misleading for decision-making purposes and a relevant costing approach began to gain in acceptance. The era of user-orientation, or the decision-model approach, had arrived, but this was still not synonymous with an organizational control approach.

The less dogmatic and more managerial approach to the development of managerial accounting – as characterized by Shillinglaw's 'era of managerial control' – was a considerable improvement on the 'era of scientific management'. However, it suffered from some fundamental defects, most notable amongst which were:

(i) the failure to take into account the cost of generating accounting information;
(ii) the failure to allow for uncertainty (as an unavoidable characteristic of the future);
(iii) the failure to recognize that the notion of a 'true' cost is illusory in a world inhabited by more than one person since each individual will possess a different set of beliefs about what constitutes 'truth'.

At the end of his excellent paper on the historical development of costing (which covers phases 1 and 2), Solomons (1952, p. 48) made the following significant observation:

> If there is one conclusion to be drawn from the foregoing study, it is that there is remarkably little in modern costing which our fathers did not know about.

This observation preceded the recognition that costing (as an element of managerial accounting) needs to cater for uncertainty, the costs of gathering and analysing information, and the organizational context within which costing is undertaken.

(c) The era of exposure control

Phase 3 is one in which a new accounting response is necessary to cope with management's concern with *exposure control* which has arisen from increasing external intervention in internal managerial processes – whether by government or by pressure groups of various kinds. The focus of this latest phase is on the evaluation of organizations and their activities, and this has considerable relevance to our organizational control perspective.

(d) Contemporary developments

In presenting his analysis in terms of three phases, Shillinglaw fails to pay sufficient attention to strong trends that characterize much of the current literature of managerial accounting. We might term this *contemporary developments*.

Since the 1970s there has been the emergence of approaches that attempt, in their different ways, to provide broader conceptual frameworks for the development of managerial accounting. These include the following

(i) *The contingency theory approach* (which we introduced in Chapter 3 above and to which we will return later).

(ii) *The information-economics approach*, which sees information as a commodity that can be bought and sold. As with other commodities, information has costs associated with it (stemming from its generation) and value to potential users. In principle, it is correct to take cognizance of the cost of producing (or acquiring) information of a specified quality relative to the value of that information to the user. Up to the present time, however, it has not proven possible to develop operationally useful means of incorporating the cost-benefit analysis of information into the design of managerial accounting systems. (See Fig. 6.7 on p. 173).

(iii) *The agency theory approach*, which stems from the recognition that the act of measuring and reporting an individual's actions affects those actions. This, in turn, locates the accounting system within a larger system of accountability in which the manager (or agent) is seen as being accountable to his principal for the effective use of the latter's resources. (See also Section 11.3 in Chapter 11 pp. 373–74.)

The central question posed by agency theory is one that is relevant to the management accountant since it is fundamental to organizational control: how can a superior (principal) who has imperfect information about the running of an organization (or division) motivate his subordinate (agent) to act in the organization's best interests? Otley (1985b) has summarized the agency approach in the following way:

> The agency model considers a principal who hires an agent to perform a task in an uncertain environment. Both principal and agent are assumed to be rational economic individuals, motivated solely by self interest, but who may differ in preferences, information and beliefs. The agent is required to expend effort (which has a disutility to him) in performing his task, but the outcome will depend both upon his effort and upon the realized state-of-the-world. If the principal's information system can accurately report on the agent's effort (and have access to the agent's information) then the problem reduces to one in simple information economics. Agency theory explores the problems that arise from information asymmetry, particularly that arising when the agent's effort cannot be directly observed but only inferred from surrogate measures such as those provided by the management accounting system.
>
> Two problems arise immediately. The first, moral hazard, arises from

the propensity of the agent to shirk because he is aware that his effort is not being accurately monitored. The second, adverse selection, occurs even if accurate information on effort is available, but is due to the principal not knowing the information on which the agent's decisions were based. Agency theory is thus concerned with the role of information in devising contracts that are, in some sense, optimal and, in particular, with the reduction of the problems of moral hazard and adverse selection.

However, the agency model has some severe limitations (Tiessen and Waterhouse, 1983). Firstly, it is essentially a two-person analysis and, although it may be possible to extend it to a whole hierarchical organization, this has yet to be done. Secondly, it is a single period model which neglects the potential impact of a continuing employment relationship (which may well affect the moral hazard problem). Finally, the descriptive validity of the utility maximizing assumptions is open to question.

There is no doubt that the agency model, within its rather severe limitations, provides useful theoretical insights into management accounting. Scapens (1984) notes that management accounting information is used for two distinct purposes within the agency framework. Firstly, it is used to revise beliefs about the expected state of the world. Secondly, it is used to evaluate the outcomes of decisions with a view to ensuring that the agent is motivated to act in the principal's best interests. This distinction between belief revision and performance evaluation corresponds to the management accounting distinction between pre- and post-decision information. The agency model may well provide the basis for a more coherent theory of management accounting, as Scapens suggests:

> 'Nevertheless, the agency framework does offer some new insights into the nature of management accounting. In particular, it has emphasized management accounting's role as a control system, as well as a decision-facilitating system which was the primary concern of earlier research. This new emphasis has led to a recognition of the importance of accounting information in the motivation of organizational participants and of the need to consider the behavioural responses of such participants in designing and choosing accounting systems. Managers within the organization can no longer be considered as machines which respond to signals from information systems. They can be expected to modify their behaviour in response to information according to their personal needs and desires. Thus, behavioural issues are beginning to influence the quantitative, economic-based research in management accounting.'

(iv) *Human information processing (HIP) studies* which focus on the process of individual decision-making and which are based on theories derived from psychology. The main problem has been the trade-off between methodological rigour and the usefulness of the findings: the emphasis on methodological issues has tended to limit the research studies undertaken to the less significant aspects of managerial accounting. In addition, few HIP studies have examined individuals in organizational settings. (See, for example, Driver and Mock (1975) and Ferguson (1988).)

A very recent development from HIP is that of expert systems (see the item by Lin in the Workbook associated with this chapter). Useful models of simple, repetitive decisions have been built to help individuals with their decision-making, so there is a logic in seeking to extend this approach to build models based on more complex decisions requiring expert knowledge. This line of work is a novel aspect of constructing a decision-support system, and it is likely to be a prominent feature of future development in that field.

(v) *Managerial accounting as a social and organizational phenomenon*, involving a shift from the psychological and social psychological approaches underlying human information processing, for example, to approaches representing sociological and anthropological points of view. (See, for example, Roslender (1990).)

In her 1986 paper, Loft vividly contrasts the conventional view that managerial accounting exists as a set of techniques for collecting and processing useful facts about organizational life in a supposedly objective way (i.e. untainted by social values or ideology) with the view that sees managerial accounting as being both social and political *in itself*. Thus the information that is produced by a managerial accounting system is itself a social product:

> . . . . it only has meaning in the context and culture in which it is produced. To the untutored eye of an Azande tribesman an accounting system would have no meaning other than a random pattern upon paper . . .
>
> Loft (1986), p. 138.

Even within industrialized economies the extent to which managerial accounting is used varies across cultures. For instances, there is much less evidence of managerial accounting in Japan than in the USA, and there is a heavier emphasis on financial measures in the UK relative to Germany.

Otley (e.g. 1983) and Scapens (e.g. 1980) have both commented on recent developments in managerial accounting. They have identified two distinct avenues along which work has been done:

- the construction of quantitative decision-making or decision-support techniques;
- the development of behavioural and organizational insights into the functioning of managerial accounting systems.

This distinction has been noted by Gee in the following terms:

> It is a fair generalization to say that scholars in the field of management accounting may broadly be divided into two groups. These groups may be distinguished from each other by their implicit response to this question: from which disciplines should the study of management accounting draw most heavily? To this question, one group would reply 'psychology, sociology and general systems theory' while the other group would say 'statistics, operational research and microeconomics'.
>
> Gee (1986), p. xiii.

The emphasis in the first of these groups has tended to be positive while that of the second has sought to be more normative, yet both have been criticized as being impractical. In the case of quantitative models, this is due to their data requirements and their restrictive assumptions and, in the case of behavioural approaches, it is due to the absence of any prescriptive content. It should also be mentioned that the development of quantitative models in managerial accounting has, in some people's opinion, relied too heavily on economics as a source discipline at the expense of insights from other fields of enquiry.

In a number of papers, Otley (e.g. 1980, 1983a, 1983b, 1985b) has reviewed some key contributions of a behavioural and organizational nature to the development of managerial accounting. In particular, he has looked at contingency theories of managerial accounting which seek to define specific aspects of an accounting system's design that are appropriate to a given set of circumstances. Such theories aim to be both descriptive (in explaining why organizations have the accounting systems that are in operation) *and* prescriptive (in recommending the design of accounting systems that ought to be operated in order that desired ends might be achieved). The critical weakness of work to date lies in the tendency of contingency theorists to overlook the fact that accounting systems design is but one part of the design of an overall organizational control system, and this inhibits the prescriptive potential of contingency theory.

Nevertheless, Otley believes that contingency theories represent one of the most significant developments in managerial accounting – at least in terms of their initial promise – over the last 20 years or so. This promise lies in the provision of a theoretical framework that might help explain practice, although the central tenets of a contingency theory of managerial accounting (i.e. that there should be a matching of an organization's accounting system with its context and that there is no single, universally applicable design for an accounting system) are likely to be a statement of the obvious to the average practitioner who devotes much of his effort to ensuring that this is so.

In a complementary manner to Otley, Scapens (e.g. 1980, 1983b, 1984, 1985) has reviewed selective developments in managerial accounting without dealing in detail with those of a behavioural or organizational nature. His chosen perspective was an economic rather than a behavioural one, although his more recent work embodies a major shift towards the behavioural and organizational.

Once again, there is a clear recognition in Scapens' reviews that there is a worrying gap between theory and practice (see his short 1983 article on this theme). The necessary change in emphasis in managerial accounting research is for researchers to approach the gap by investigating the nature of managerial accounting practice rather than by further abstract – and empirically empty – theorizing.

> '[This] . . . should lead to a better understanding of the situations and contexts in which particular theoretical techniques may be appropriate in practice' (Scapens (1985), p. 186).

12.4 Prospects for the future

In a chronological sequence we can review the proposals that a number of writers have put forward for the future development of managerial accounting.

Taking Churchill and Uretsky's 1969 paper as our starting point, they offered the view that:

> In looking at the present [1969] state of management accounting and the directions it is likely to take, the field of information processing must be considered along with the developments taking place in the management and behavioral sciences. Of equal, if not greater, importance is the careful examination of emerging patterns of information use.

These directions continue to be of significance more than 20 years on.

A decade later, in his synthesis session at the 1979 Illinois Symposium (see Holzer (1980), pp. 248–9), Schoenfeld concluded that three distinct directions could be envisaged for the future development of managerial accounting:

(i) additional quantitative methodology;
(ii) integration with findings of systems theory;
(iii) the development of new qualitative tools.

(Readers can relate these terse recommendations with the more elaborate explanation Schoenfeld offers of the likely future development of managerial accounting which is included in the Workbook pp. 619–23.)

If we now turn to consider the views of British researchers we find that some basic questions that still need answering have been posed by Scapens (1980, pp. 291–2):

(i) What costs should be used by a rational decision-maker acting under conditions of uncertainty?
(ii) What costs are used by decision-makers in practice?
(iii) What are the effects on resource allocation of basing decisions on various measures of cost?
(iv) Are the academically accepted costing methods appropriate in the organizational context of managerial accounting?

While this listing is not exhaustive, it indicates quite clearly that there is a long way to go in building up a rigorous body of knowledge concerning managerial accounting.

Scapens has also suggested (1980) that future research in managerial accounting needs to encompass:

(i) the problems of implementing the quantitative techniques that have been proposed by academic researchers. In particular, more attention needs to be given to:
   - estimating the necessary information in a world characterized by uncertainty;
   - the costs of data collection and analysis;
(ii) the organizational context of managerial accounting including, for example, a clarification of the purposes that managerial accounting might serve and the characteristics of the techniques that are likely to be adopted in practice;
(iii) individual decision-making and information-processing – with a view to producing less naive models then those derived from neoclassical economics.

Following from his technique-oriented review of major recent developments in managerial accounting, Hart (1981, p. 114) was also able to suggest some specific directions for future developments. These were:

(i) a concentration on fundamental analysis (taking note of social, environmental, and interdisciplinary implications) rather than 'technically correct solutions' in designing more flexible managerial accounting systems;
(ii) an increasing emphasis on viewing managerial accounting in the context of organization theory (which is implicit in (i) above, but worthy of special mention);
(iii) the giving of greater attention to systems technology in implementing the essential informational role of managerial accounting;
(iv) the accordance of more emphasis to the behavioural implications of control systems and on the provision of essential non-financial information;
(v) the wider use of corporate modelling (and, in particular, greater use of scenario writing in the planning field – which accords with the view of Mattessich (1980, p. 217)).

Finally, Otley (1983, 1985b) has argued that developments on the interface of behavioural science and accounting have set the scene for the 'rise' of managerial accounting research. (By this, he means the emergence of a basis for work that interprets the provision and use of managerial accounting information in its organizational context, thereby helping to re-establish the link between research and practice.) The developments that Otley had in mind were:

(i) the increasing recognition that managerial accounting is but one part of organizational life which has reciprocal interdependencies with other parts. Thus, accounting controls are merely a subset of an organization's range of controls and must be studied in context;
(ii) the perceived importance of theories *of* managerial accounting rather than just theories *in* managerial accounting. The latter (the antecedents) are concerned with what causes accounting systems to develop as they do, while the former (the consequences) concern themselves with the results of those systems and hence locate managerial accounting within an organizational context;
(iii) the increasing acceptance of research methods that emphasize exploratory contextual understanding (e.g. using interpretative methods which tap the perceptions of those who are involved in the situations being studied) rather than the testing of hypotheses derived from previous research literature. Not least of all, this will involve practitioners more fully *and* get researchers into organizations in order to observe and document what is happening;
(iv) the increasing impact of computer technology on managerial accounting practice (such as the use of spreadsheet packages by which budgets can be developed in an iterative manner), including the emergence of expert systems. This should ensure that 'different costs' can be supplied for 'different purposes';
(v) the establishing of linkages between the behavioural and quantitative branches of managerial accounting research since this best reflects the organizational context within which managerial accounting must be practised;
(vi) the setting of managerial accounting in a wider theoretical context, such as

that of organizational control (or, possibly, contingency theory or agency theory) which has interdisciplinary characteristics and which will facilitate empirical research.

As one might expect, several key themes emerge from those experts' sets of proposals. In summary, they cover the development of:

(i) further empirical awareness of how managerial accounting systems work;
(ii) the organizational context of managerial accounting;
(iii) non-financial measures;
(iv) managerial accounting as a sub-set of organizational control;
(v) implementation issues;
(vi) our understanding of information use;
(vii) linkages between qualitative and quantitative factors.

In considering the future role and functions of managerial accounting, Churchill and Uretsky (1969) highlighted various forces that would, in their view, influence the outcome. These were:

(i) The tendency towards the integrating of activities that were previously distinct (and possibly functionally separate) in organizations that have become extensively computerized. (One example is the domain of physical distribution.)
(ii) The combination of circumstances that produces changes in the environment and, consequently, in management's need to respond. (Accounting for social costs – such as pollution – is an obvious example.)
(iii) The 'technical' developments that were then in their early stages, such as systems simulation or human resource accounting, but which have the potential to bring about considerable change in the practice of managerial accounting.
(iv) Factors reflecting increases in organizational size and in the complexity of organizational activities which will bring increasing demands for information.

One can add to these factors (almost as a catch-all):

(v) Changes in manufacturing technology, the increase in service industries, and the adoption of a stronger managerial (and value for money) philosophy within government and other non-commercial enterprises all need to be reflected in the nature of managerial accounting, which will have to adapt to ensure that it is relevant to managers' information needs.

Perhaps we should reflect on the principal criterion against which any development might be gauged. Anthony (1973) and Shillinglaw (1980) both argue that managerial accounting is a practical subject, so the test of research in managerial accounting should be the help it gives in satisfying the present and future needs of managers who use information from managerial accounting systems. We would extend this criterion a little by linking the needs of managers for managerial accounting information to the definition of managerial accounting we put forward in Chapter 1: the provision of information to facilitate better decision-making in order to achieve organizational control and enhance organizational effectiveness.

Otley has expressed surprise (e.g. 1983, p. 149) that managerial accounting is so lacking in its theoretical foundations, and he sees an organizational control framework as one that offers perhaps the greatest scope for the future development of managerial accounting. (See Lowe and Machin (1983) and Chua, *et al.* (1989) for a full discussion of the relevant issues.) This would give scope for the construction of theories of, and theories about, managerial accounting which, in turn, could help in answering such important questions as:

(i) What roles does managerial accounting serve within different organizations?
(ii) How have organizations arrived at the design of the accounting systems that they now operate?
(iii) How is accounting information modified to serve particular purposes?
(iv) What function do accounting numbers serve in various kinds of decisions?

By seeing managerial accounting as a control device the development of relevant theory should relate it to the context of organizational control (i.e. as part of the more general study of organizational functioning). En route to this desirable end, it will be necessary for much more descriptive work to be undertaken (such as that in progress at the Universities of Aston and Birmingham – see the proposal by Coates, Rickwood and Stacey in the Workbook associated with this chapter). There is very little empirical awareness of the actual operation of managerial accounting systems within organizations. As a consequence, theoretical developments are often (if not usually) unrelated to actual practice, so the need exists to bring these two aspects of managerial accounting closer together as a priority. A behavioural orientation in accounting research gives scope for the emergence of what Mattessich (1980, p. 214) terms '. . . a truly empirical science . . .'.

Summary

As we have tried to argue throughout the book, managerial accounting must serve the control needs of the organization, which requires a focus on strategic issues and the all-important question of effectiveness. Managerial accounting . . . cannot exist as a separate discipline, developing its own set of procedures and measurement systems and applying these universally to all firms without regard to the underlying values, goals and strategies of particular firms' (Kaplan, 1984a). Thus some organizations (as suggested in Chapter 2) will have primary strategies that emphasize cost reduction while others will have strategies emphasizing product innovation, quality, customer service or employee morale. If management accountants maintain a preoccupation with financial – or even economic – information, this may render their contribution to the control effort less and less relevant as managers increasingly recognize that the critical success factors for their organization include, but are certainly not limited to, financial indicators.

In their early phases, cost and managerial accounting were strongly empirical and technically narrow. As academic researchers have devoted attention to the study of managerial accounting a gap between textbook prescriptions and actual practice has grown which highlights, *inter alia*, the need for more empirically based research studies:

> Until the determinants of existing management accounting practice are better understood it will be extremely hazardous to make generalized prescriptive statements about such accounting concepts and techniques as, for example, cost-volume-profit analysis, cost allocations and even marginal costing.
>
> Scapens (1985), pp. 186–7.

The absence of a unifying framework for the study of managerial accounting has also proved problematic:

> It is . . . obvious that the continuation of randomly adding pieces of knowledge to our field without examining their position in an overall framework is not likely to accelerate the development of managerial accounting.
>
> Schoenfeld, in Holzer (1980), p. 249.

A strongly held view of the best framework for the development of managerial accounting is offered by Mattessich:

> Management accounting is an applied and purpose-oriented discipline; as such, the most appropriate frame of analysis seems to be that of systems theory and its underlying instrumental methodology and philosophy.
>
> Mattessich (1980), p. 212.

This view is one to which the authors of this text also subscribe, but a great deal more work needs to be carried out before there is a coherent body of managerial accounting knowledge within an appropriate framework.

There was a view held some years ago by many people – including some eminent researchers in the field (e.g. Anthony (1972; 1973)) – that the major problems in managerial accounting had been solved and that little research was left to be done. It has become increasingly apparent that the surface has hardly been scratched!

Key terms and concepts

Here is a list of the key terms and concepts which have featured in this chapter. You should make sure that you understand and can define each one of them. Page references to definitions in the text appear in bold in the index.

- Agency theory
- Contingency theory
- Expert systems
- Human information processing (HIP)
- Information economics
  - cost-benefit analysis of information

Further reading

Among some of Otley's excellent contributions to the literature you will find his 1985 paper in the *British Accounting Review* particularly helpful, along with his

1987 text which offers coverage of many points discussed within this book, as does Siegel and Ramanauskas-Marconi (1989).

While Otley focuses on behavioural issues see Scapens' 1985 review of more technical matters, and an American perspective is provided by Johnson and Kaplan's 1987 book (which is the subject of their 1987 article). Some intriguing personal perspectives linking the past, present and future of managerial accounting are to be found in Anthony (1989), Horngren (1989), and Shillinglaw (1989).

Helpful reviews of the interface of managerial accounting and psychology on the one hand and sociology on the other are given by Ferguson (1988) and Roslender (1990) respectively. An authoritative overview of behavioural research in accounting is offered by Hopwood (1989). Finally, the domain of expert systems is comprehensively reviewed by Connell (1987), but see also Boer (1989) and the item by Lin in Workbook Chapter 12.

The workbook to accompany this chapter begins on p. 610.

PART 5 Workbook

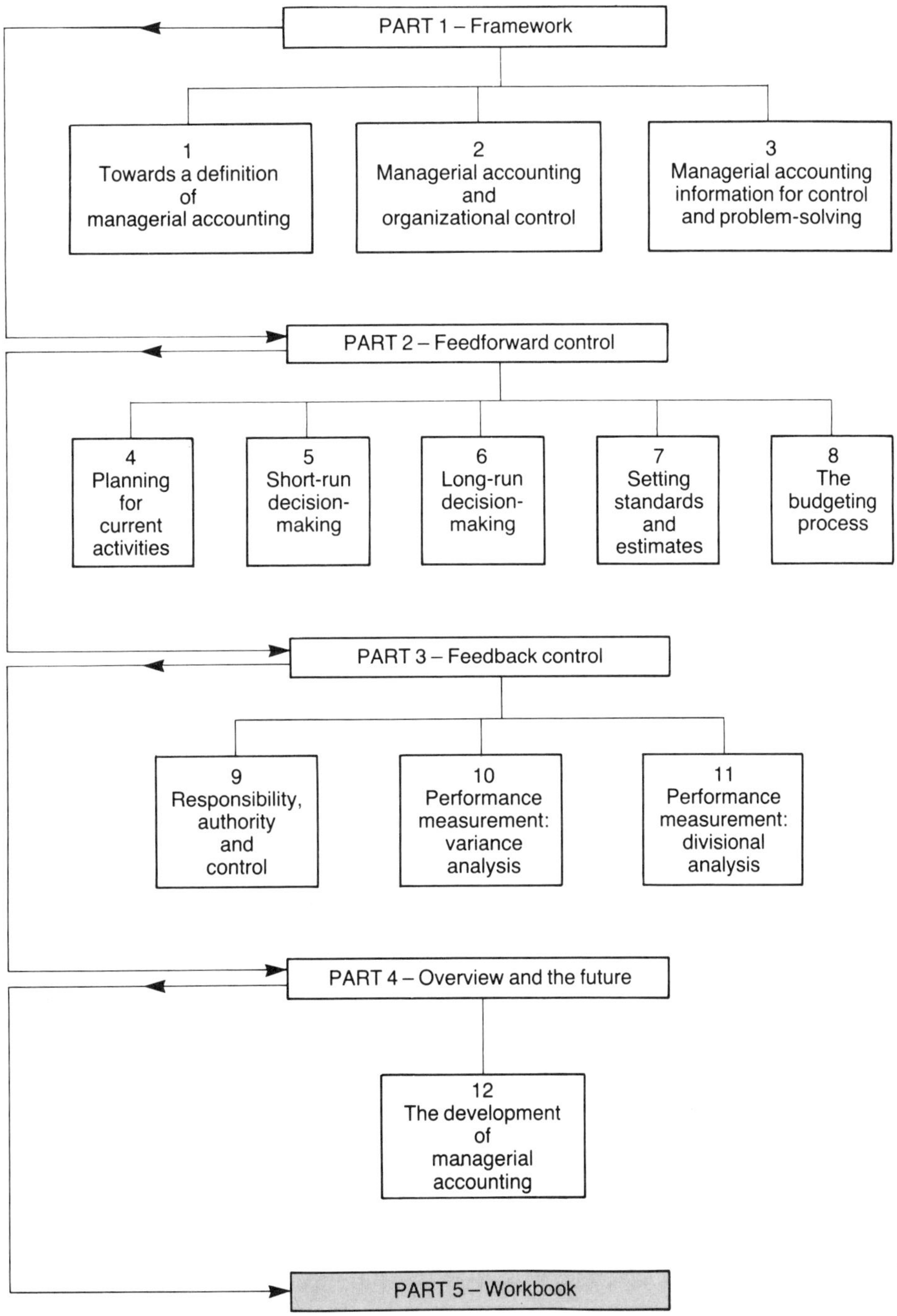

CHAPTER

1 Towards a definition of managerial accounting

WORKBOOK

W1.1 Introduction

In Chapter 1 of the text we argued that attempting to define managerial accounting by looking at what it is at present and what it was in the past was unsatisfactory. There was much diversity in the field of managerial accounting practice, research and education in terms of the origins of practice, the type of tasks performed by management accountants, and the roles played by managerial accounting information in organizations. We then proposed a normative definition of managerial accounting that draws a link between the production of accounting information and the satisfaction of people's needs for information in order to achieve organizational control and enhance organizational effectiveness.

In this Workbook chapter we shall attempt to explore in more detail the diversity of the 'craft' of managerial accounting.

W1.2 Revision topics

Question 1.1
Why is it unsatisfactory to define managerial accounting by listing the various technologies that have come to be perceived as being within the ambit of managerial accounting?

Answer
This approach to definition seems attractive as we could follow broad textbook classifications and list technologies such as costing, budgeting, transfer pricing, performance evaluation, etc. However, such an approach ignores the 'fact' that costing as a practice varies significantly in detail and significance among organizations. There is much diversity in the practice of managerial accounting. In addition, such an approach fails to highlight the social and organizational dynamics involved in the use of information in organizations. Accounting information may become involved in individual battles for career advancement, territorial struggles, empire-building, all of which require an understanding of when, where and how to present and use information. Finally, linkages are not made between the provision of managerial accounting information and overall organizational control and effectiveness.

Question 1.2
What are some of the diverse factors suggested by authors to explain the rise of managerial accounting practice?

Answer
Some authors have proposed an evolutionary account of managerial accounting and suggested that it changes in response to changing environments and organizational structures. Still other authors have pointed to the role of governments and professional bodies in the shaping of managerial accounting practice. Finally, the field has also been influenced by more general debates in society and in other knowledge areas about the need for individual and organizational efficiency.

Question 1.3
What role(s) is (are) a managerial accounting information system intended to play in an organization?

Answer
A managerial accounting information system is intended to provide financial and non-financial information to people within an organization in order that they might make better decisions and thereby achieve organizational control and enhance organizational effectiveness.

It is important to remember that this is an aim, an ideal. In practice, managerial accounting information may play quite diverse roles.

Question 1.4
What are some of the roles that might be played by managerial accounting information systems in practice?

Answer
Three main roles were identified in the text: technical, political and symbolic. A technical role is performed when an accounting technology is used to perform calculations – of costs, transfer prices, and measures of performance, for example. In practice such calculations may reflect political considerations and trade-offs among the conflicting interests of different stakeholder groups in an organization. In addition, calculations may be performed in particular ways in order to represent the beliefs and values of dominant groups within an organization. For instance, in Company A the budget may be prepared only by top management because it is believed that they know the business best. In Company B, there might be a more participatory style of budgeting where lower-level managers are involved because there is an organizational emphasis on equitable, democratic styles of management. (See Chapter 8 for a fuller discussion of budgeting.)

Question 1.5
Why do managerial accountants increasingly have to provide non-financial information?

Answer
Partly because service and government-related organizations now form a significant proportion of the organizational world. For such organizations, non-

financial information might be easier to obtain and be more useful. For instance, it is helpful for a health care manager to know how many days a patient stayed in hospital, how long the elective surgery waiting list is, or how many patients are readmitted within 20 days with the same illness. In addition, community expectations have changed and organizations are now held accountable for their impact upon the natural and social environment. In some countries, therefore, companies are required to monitor and report on the amount of waste discharged or the levels of pollution produced.

Question 1.6
What is missing in current descriptions of the role of managerial accounting in organizations?

Answer
See Fig. 1.3 in Chapter 1 of the text. Essentially, the issues that are neglected in current descriptions of the role of managerial accounting are:

(i) the provision of non-financial information that is necessary for the maintenance of organizational control;
(ii) individual and social processes that give meaning and sense to managerial accounting information. Some of these processes, which include people's values and personalities, interests and power considerations, indicate that managerial accounting information may be used to shape perceptions in certain ways for political purposes. Thus, through social interaction, the outcome of a managerial accounting system may differ from that predicted by traditional views of managerial accounting information as an unambiguous entity;
(iii) the relationship between managerial accounting information and organizational control.

W1.3 Discussion topics

Question 1.1
'An accountant is like one of the blind men with the elephant except he/she only sees pennies and pounds. All problems are reduced to those terms.' This statement suggests that managerial accounting information actively shapes people's perceptions of problems. Do you agree that managerial accountants always reduce all problems to 'pennies and pounds'?

Question 1.2
Give two examples of decisions or choices in:

(a) a non-commercial organization; and
(b) a commercial organization

that cannot be easily evaluated in financial terms.

Would managerial accounting information be of use in making such decisions? If so, what kind of information would be useful?

Question 1.3
Cost accounting emerged in different industries in different countries at different times. Attempt some research by going to the library and seeking out one or two historical papers that discuss the emergence of cost accounting in your country or region.

Question 1.4
Obtain an annual report from both a commercial organization and a non-commercial organization. Can you identify some of the differences in the content and style of these reports?

Question 1.5
UNIVERSITY ACCOUNTANT: 'Don't bother looking at the budgets of this university. Like all other universities, resource allocation depends only on who you are and who you know.'

What are some characteristics of universities that might help account for this statement?

Question 1.6
Obtain definitions of management accounting and the role of the management accountant from major professional associations in your country. Compare these with those cited in the text.

W1.4 Illustrative material

Introduction
The agreement between the Department of Employment – Training, Enterprise and Education Directorate (TEED) and the Chartered Institute of Management Accountants (CIMA) sets out its aims as follows:

'3.1 The contractor (CIMA) shall:

(1) delineate the occupational area and core territory of the Management Accountancy profession;
(2) develop and systematically test, with a substantial number of employers and CIMA members, nationally agreed occupational standards for the management accountancy profession.'

A detailed analysis of the occupational area and core territory has been undertaken. This analysis describes the activities actually carried out by management accountants. The work has been confirmed by job descriptions for newly qualified management accountants.

Account has been taken of:

- views expressed at a workshop on the future of the management accounting profession;
- commentaries received from members of the Advisory and Steering groups for the project.

This report is a summary of the main conclusions contained as a result of that analysis. It includes the following:

(i) the occupational territory of the management accountant;
(ii) the core territory of the management accountant;
(iii) overlaps with other professions;
(iv) the key purposes of the professional management accountant;
(v) next steps.

(i) The occupational territory of the management accountant

The following Key Results Areas (KRAs) define the occupational territory of the management accountant (see Fig W1.1):

– strategic financial management services; (KRA 1)
– management information services for developmental activities; (KRA 2)
– management information services for organizational effectiveness; (KRA 3)
– management information services for operational efficiency and economy; (KRA 4)
– finance management and the provision of funds; (KRA 5)
– taxation computation and administration; (KRA 6)
– corporate reporting to management; (KRA 7)
– coordination and management of the organization's management information and accountancy services function. (KRA 8)

Key Results Areas 1 to 7 are management accountancy services. KRA 8 is concerned with the management of the function and is subdivided into the following:

– provide strategic direction to the function; (KRA 8A)
– market and sell the professional service; (KRA 8B)
– manage information and communication systems technology; (KRA 8C)
– organize and structure networks of relationships and develop staff within the function. (KRA 8D)

The information contained in the analysis of KRAs will be used to define the range of situations in which a particular competence should be displayed and for defining underpinning knowledge and understanding.

The occupational territory of the management accountant will further evolve in response to changing demands.

(ii) The core territory of the management accountant

The core territory illustrated in the Venn diagram (Fig W1.2) consists of five Key Results Areas (KRAs 1, 2, 3, 4, and 8). These KRAs are central to the management accountancy profession.

Key Results Areas 5, 6 and 7 are related to the core territory, but as defined are not wholly part of that core:

Most management accountants have responsibilities which fall within one or all of KRAs 5, 6 and 7, notably in finance management and corporate reporting to management. Often the management accountant will focus on a particular aspect of the area (e.g.the impact of taxation on decision analyses). In any event a competent management accountant will need skills within the core of these areas and at least a wide underpinning knowledge and understanding of the rest of them.

Figure W1.1

The occupational territory of the management accountant.

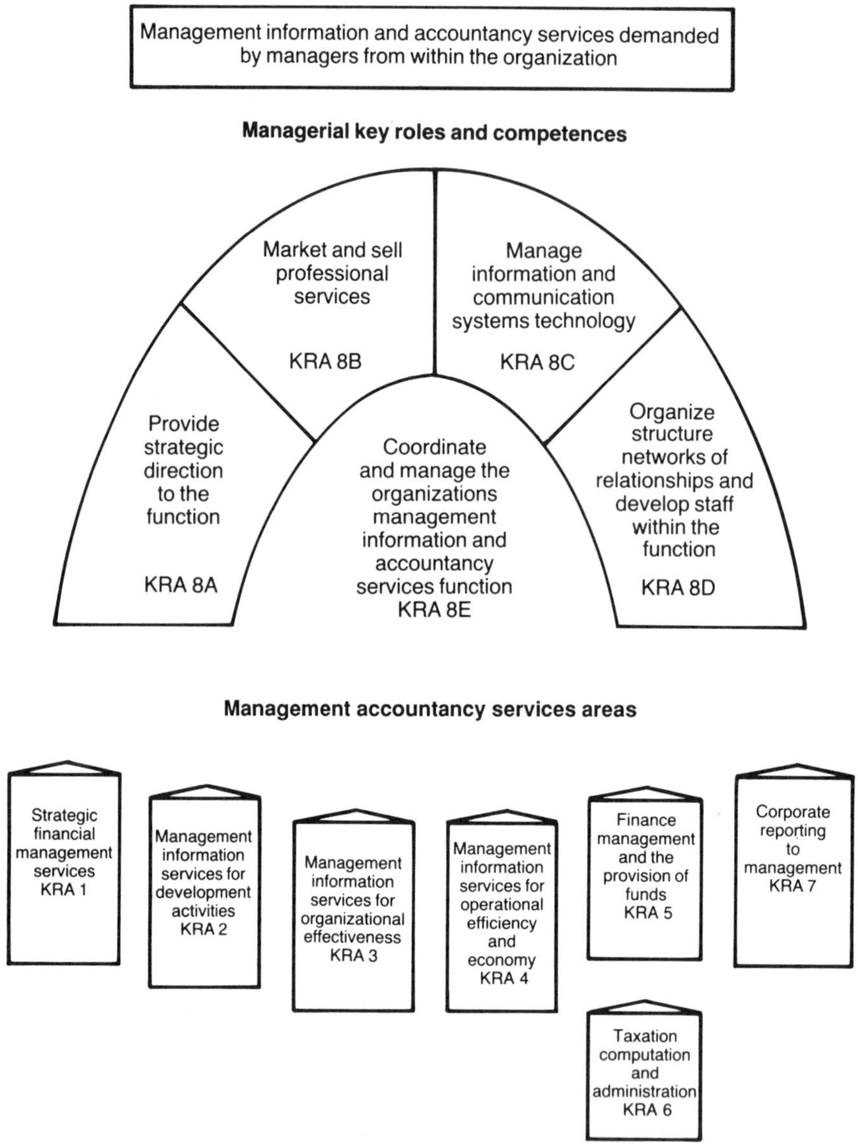

(iii) Overlaps with other professions

There is overlap between management accountancy and other occupations, notably those illustrated in Fig W1.2. The following occupations are related:

– management who serve administrators, shareholder/investors and directors in organizations;
– financial accountants who provide historic and current corporate reports to shareholders/investors and administrators; act as stewards of the properties of the organization and maintain financial accounts;
– treasurers who, as specialist experts employed by management, raise, allocate, provide and control the finances of organizations;
– taxation specialists employed by management to plan, compute, negotiate and resolve taxation obligations;
– strategic planners;
– business economists and financial analysts;
– statisticians and operations researchers;
– information and communication systems technologists and applications managers;
– cost engineers.

The detailed report carefully differentiates the role of the professional management accountant.

(iv) The key purposes of the professional management accountant

The map of the occupational territory is the foundation for a functional analysis* of the occupation. This is currently being developed. The first stage in functional analysis is to determine the key purpose of the occupation in outcome terms. The following definition is based on the description of the Key Results Areas.

The key purposes of the professional management accountant are:

> 'To design, operate and manage financial and economic information and other systems to enhance value, effectiveness and efficiency and to enable managers to achieve controlled change within organizations, and thereby realize stakeholder objectives.'

Notes on key purposes

(a) As a 'professional' member of the management team the management accountant should continuously improve services and systems, meet recognized ethical standards of behaviour and comply with legal and fiscal constraints.
(b) 'Information' is provided and communicated through systems. It is derived from both external and internal sources, relates to future projections, plans and targets as well as past experience and includes the translation of competitive and non-economic data into financial terms.
(c) 'Organizations' may be of any type, size or purpose. The definition includes the constituent parts of an organization, public service, non-profit as well as profit-making enterprises.
(d) The management accountant employs information, communication, planning, resourcing, decision support, finance and reporting 'systems'.

* Functional analysis is the examination and specification of competence according to functions. The focus is on the purpose and outcome of work activity and differs from 'task analysis' approaches which focus on tasks and procedures.

Figure W1.2

The core territory of the management accountant.

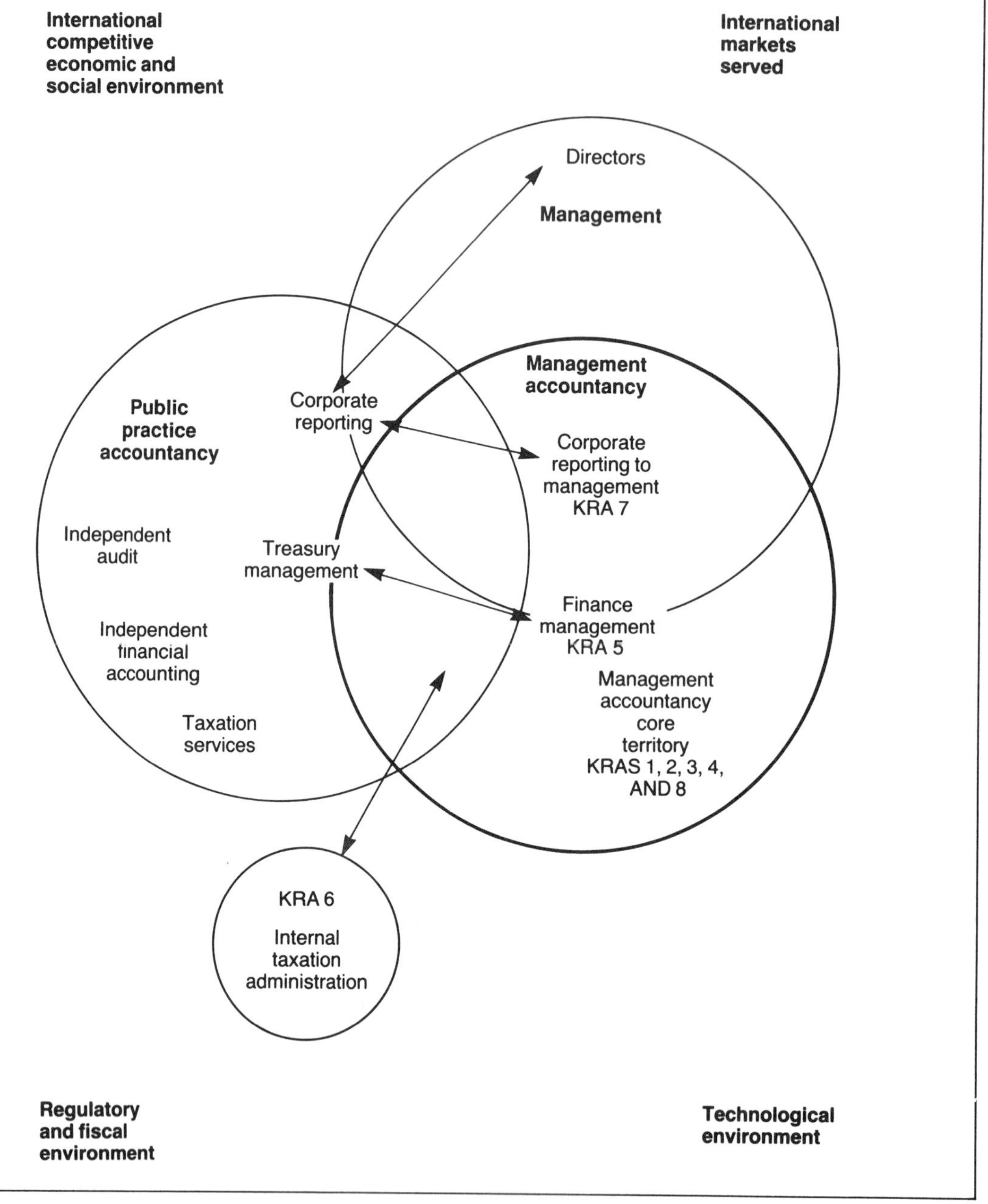

(v) Next steps

Standards of competence

The next stage of the functional analysis is to define standards of competence for each function expressed in outcome terms.

The map of the occupational territory of the management accountant is being used to identify those activities which employers would expect a newly qualified Associate member to undertake.

Standards of competence have so far been developed for the management accountancy services areas and tested in a series of review workshops conducted during March 1991. They are presented in draft in a separate report. These standards require further development and refinement.

Subsequent development will differentiate managerial standards of competence for the management accountant.

The assessment and verification of competence

When the standards of competence have been established and widely tested with employers the most appropriate means for assessing the competences of a management accountant for qualification as an Associate member will be developed. A further review will then be undertaken of the verification arrangements needed to ensure the quality of the assessment system.

CHAPTER 2 Managerial accounting and organizational control

WORKBOOK

W2.1 Introduction

In Chapter 2 of the text we developed a definition of organizational goals and of managerial accounting that drew the links between the production of accounting information and the satisfaction of people's needs for information in order to maintain organizational control and achieve organizational effectiveness. This is illustrated in Fig. W2.1.

We pointed out that this was an aspiration, an ideal picture of the role of managerial accounting. In practice, the actual roles that managerial accounting plays in organizations depend upon complex human interactive processes and the contexts surrounding interaction. Different people make sense of the 'same' information differently and to different ends.

In this Workbook chapter we shall attempt to clarify our definition of organizational control and emphasize the role of human sense-making processes in understanding how managerial accounting systems function in organizations.

Figure W2.1

The intended role of managerial accounting information.

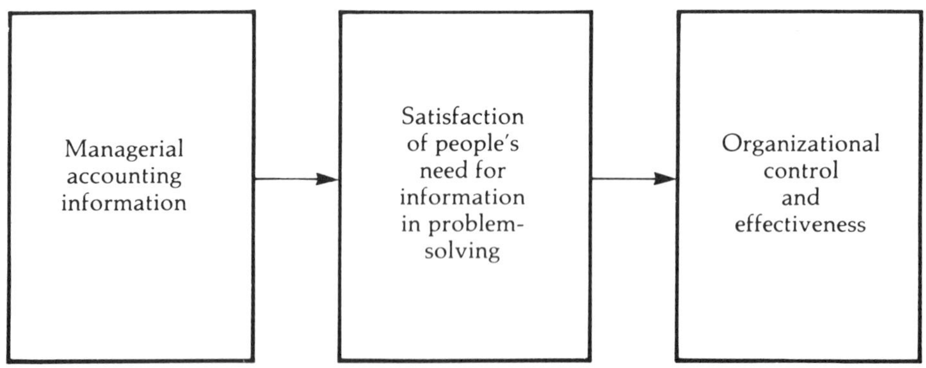

W2.2 Revision topics

Question 2.1
What do you understand by the term 'organizational control'?

Answer
Organizational control is the process of ensuring that an organization is pursuing courses of action that will enable it to achieve its purpose(s). If an organization is not adopting strategies that are 'on course' in terms of its organizational goal, it may be said to be out of control.

For instance, if a short-term goal of BHP is to be one of the leading computer software houses in the United Kingdom within five years, and the company does not invest in competent and high-calibre staff, it might be said to be out of control.

Question 2.2
How is the notion of organizational goal defined in this book?

Answer
The goal of an organization is defined by the feasible set of inducements and contributions that are minimally necessary to satisfy all interest groups in the long-run. The interest groups that should be satisfied are all those that are necessary and sufficient for the organization to exist.

For instance, the goal of a profit-making organization such as Harrods should be the feasible set of all inducements and contributions from relevant interest groups such as management, workers, shareholders, customers, suppliers and creditors. Similarly the goal of a non-commercial organization such as the Salvation Army should be the feasible set of all inducements and contributions from the hierarchy of the Army, ordinary members and the community.

Question 2.3
What is the difference between organizational efficiency and effectiveness?

Answer
Efficiency measures the ratio of output to inputs. Effectiveness measures the extent to which goals are achieved. An organization may be efficient but ineffective. That is, it produces a high level of outputs for a given level of inputs but these are not the outputs desired by the dominant coalition of the organization.

Question 2.4
What is 'sense-making'? Why is it important for accountants to recognize sense-making processes?

Answer
Sense-making is the process whereby people interpret data and attribute particular meanings to that data. At times, people may attach private, specific meanings to a piece of information. For instance, a lower pay rise to a particular individual may be interpreted by that individual as an outcome of a previous argument with the boss. At other times, people may draw upon public, intersubjective meanings. For instance, a lower profit figure is usually understood as an undesirable event.

It is important for accountants to recognize sense-making processes because accountants are in the business of producing, interpreting and receiving information. They need to know how to interpret the signals given by others and to anticipate how the information which they provide to stakeholders will be interpreted and acted upon.

W2.3 Discussion topics

Question 2.1
Identify some important stakeholders in (a) a private organization, and (b) a public sector organization. (Examples of stakeholders or interest groups in an organization include shareholders, the community at large, creditors, competitors, government agencies, etc.) For each stakeholder or interest group, list their objectives for the organization.

Question 2.2
'Universities never teach the most important requirement of being a good management accountant – the ability to relate to all kinds of people and to understand their different needs, values and beliefs.'

Why is it important for management accountants to understand and communicate well with people? How do individual differences play a part in the effective reporting and use of management accounting information for organizational control?

Question 2.3
The same piece of information may be presented differently depending upon the objective of the sender of that information. Suppose you had a mark of 53% as your final accounting mark. How would you present that piece of information to a close friend, your parents, a prospective employer and your tutor?

Question 2.4
What do you think are the goal(s) of your university, polytechnic, or college? How would you measure its (their) efficiency and effectiveness?

Question 2.5
Trade unions and management are often said to have conflicting goals. How could accounting information be used by either stakeholder group to advance its particular goals?

W2.4 Case studies

Case study 2.1
Companies A and B have different organizational cultures. In Company A, employees have to report by 8.30 a.m. If they do not, the managing director personally sends a memo to remind the staff member that it is company policy to report for work by 8.30 a.m. The granting of sick leave, holidays and maternity leave is also strictly monitored. So is the use of stationery, the number of private

telephone calls made by staff and the length of lunch and tea breaks. The company views 'time-wasting' as an unacceptable form of behaviour. The managing director feels that time is money and because all costs have to be minimized, so too does 'wasted time'.

Company B, by contrast, operates a flexi-time schedule. Employees are allowed to arrive between 7.30 a.m. and 9.30 a.m. and leave at the appropriate time after eight hours of work. The scheme is, however, carefully arranged such that the office is always adequately manned. The managing director, who is a firm believer in certain aspects of Japanese management styles, also seeks to motivate his staff to consider the company as an extension of their families. Several social outings are arranged through the year for the staff and their families. The granting of leave and the use of company resources is not monitored in detail. However, members of staff are encouraged not to waste company resources, in the same way as they are encouraged to make efficient use of their family resources.

Required:

(a) How do you think the managerial accounting system is structured in Company A and Company B? Consider the structure of authority (who reports to whom, who has access to management information) and the emphasis placed on meeting budget targets.

(b) What do you think this case illustrates about the design and operation of managerial accounting information systems in organizations?

Case study 2.2

MEDICAL SUPERINTENDENT: 'These accountants do not understand our problems. We have patients' lives to save and all they can talk about are cash limits and budget targets. The trouble with the National Health Service is insufficient funds and too many accountants. If we continue to meet these cash limits, we shall have patients in the corridors.'

HOSPITAL ACCOUNTANT: 'Look, you are ten years behind! The days when you did not have to worry about cash limits are well and truly over. We are here to try and help you plan your services better so that you can optimize your allocation of resources as efficiently as possible given current constraints. There is no point wishing for more money, because it is not going to materialize!'

Required:

(a) Evaluate the accountant's response to the medical superintendent. Do you think that was a successful attempt at communicating the role of the management accountant?

(b) How does this case illustrate Dearborn and Simon's (1958) research that different professionals have different definitions of 'the problem'? How can these different perceptions be reconciled?

(c) Managerial accounting has come to play a more prominent role in the management of non-commercial organizations. What factors may have contributed to its emerging importance? What contributions could managerial accounting make to decision-making and organizational control in non-commercial organizations?

Case study 2.3

BMC plc has proposed the construction of a large office and retailing centre in one of the northern suburbs of Edinburgh. A financial feasibility study shows that the project is viable if the company builds twin tower blocks 35 storeys high and builds linking passages to existing large retail stores in the vicinity.

However, the company did not include in its study the effect which the shadow of these tower blocks would have on the suburb's prized remembrance rose garden, or the impact of the centre on the traffic of the suburb and on nearby residential properties.

As the management accountant of BMC plc:

(a) submit a report justifying the omission of these social costs and benefits; and
(b) act as a devil's advocate and argue against the omission of these social costs and benefits.

CHAPTER

3 Managerial accounting information for control and problem-solving

WORKBOOK

W3.1 Introduction

In Chapter 2 of the text we discussed in detail the relationship between managerial accounting information systems and the achievement of organizational control and effectiveness. In Chapter 3 we focused our attention on specific forms or types of control that help in the attainment of overall organizational control. The main types of control discussed were both examples of closed-loop control: feedforward control and feedback control. We also pointed out that this categorization of types of control, although in common use, is not the only one in existence. Hofstede (1981), for instance, developed a different typology of forms of control, that ranges from routine control to political control.

We should expect such differences in categorization. Typologies are developed in order to help us understand and explain the phenomena that we are studying. There is nothing fixed or sacrosanct about theoretical categories. The main test of their usefulness is the extent to which they clarify the problem(s) being investigated.

We next highlighted the manner in which a managerial accounting information system acts as a control system (that is, enables a situation to be controlled). In Chapter 2 we had glossed over these details in order that we might arrive at satisfactory definitions of managerial accounting, organizational control, organizational goals and the achievement of organizational effectiveness. In Chapter 3 we were able to discuss how managerial accounting could help in:

- the clarification of objectives;
- the development of a predictive model of input-output relationships;
- the measurement of outputs;
- the specification of alternative courses of action.

We also reiterated the intrinsic ambiguity associated with the actual roles played by managerial accounting information. The above discussion of the role of managerial accounting information for control is again an aspiration, an intention. The practice of managerial accounting in complex organizations may differ from that ideal.

Finally, we saw how managerial accounting for control essentially means helping managers to solve problems effectively. To solve a problem effectively is to achieve control. Compare the four conditions necessary for control:

- objective(s);
- a predictive model of the relationship between inputs and outputs;
- choice of alternative actions or strategies;
- measurement of results,

with the steps in solving a problem:

- problem definition;
- generation of alternative solutions;
- choice of a particular strategy;
- implementation of strategy;
- monitoring and reviewing the strategy implemented.

As can be seen, achieving control is identical to solving a problem effectively. Yet it is strange that while some authors write of problem-solving in isolation, others write of control in isolation. In fact, the two concepts describe processes that are identical.

In this Workbook chapter we will explore the issues of types of control, control systems and problem-solving for organizational control in more detail.

W3.2 Revision topics

Question 3.1
What is open-loop control?

Answer
It is a form of control in which no adjustments are made to actions that are initiated. No attempt is made to continually monitor the activities of the system/organization and its environment. Neither are the outputs of the system measured and compared with expected output.

Question 3.2
What is closed-loop control?

Answer
The direct opposite of open-loop control. Adjustments are made to the system/organization once actions or strategies have been implemented.

Question 3.3
What is feedforward control?

Answer
A type of closed-loop control in which an organization and its environment are continually scanned in order to ensure that the organizational goal may be realized. A feedforward control system may be defined as a 'measurement and prediction system which assesses the system and predicts the output of the system at some future date' (Bhaskar and Housden (1985)).

Question 3.4
What is feedback control?

Answer
a form of closed-loop control in which outputs are measured, compared with expected outputs and corrective action taken if a deviation exists.

A feedforward system differs from a feedback system in that it seeks to anticipate, and thereby avoid, deviations between actual and desired outcomes.

Question 3.5
What are the requirements for a situation to be controlled?

Answer
According to the Tocher control model discussed by Otley and Berry (1980), there are four requirements:

(i) an objective for the system being controlled;
(ii) a means of measuring desired outputs;
(iii) a predictive model of input–output relationships;
(iv) a choice of relevant alternative courses of action.

Question 3.6
What are the steps depicted in a rational process of problem-solving?

Answer
See Fig. 3.7 (p. 61).

The six steps involved are:

* problem definition, identification or diagnosis;
* solution generation;
* solution evaluation;
* solution choice;
* solution implementation;
* solution monitoring.

W3.3 Discussion topics

Question 3.1
For each of the following activities within an organization, identify whether the main type of control being exercised is feedforward or feedback control:

(a) preparing a schedule of the expected capital investments for the organization for the next ten years;
(b) recording the amounts spent on a special project that was authorized in the previous financial year;
(c) estimating the amounts of raw materials and labour time that would be needed to produce a new line of product;
(d) analysing the deviations from the budget for sales;

(e) making investment decisions that hedge against adverse changes in the exchange rate;
(f) comparing the organization's sales growth with that of a rival organization.

Question 3.2
What are the implications of feedforward control for the design of managerial accounting systems?

Question 3.3
Briefly describe Hofstede's (1981) typology of controls. Which form of control was argued to be most effective in which type of situation?

Question 3.4
Draw a plan of the Tocher control model. Briefly describe how managerial accounting information may play a role in achieving control within this model.

Question 3.5

(a) As a student, your learning and performance in this subject is being controlled. What do you think is the control system being used? (Identify the four elements of the control system that is in operation.)
(b) Identify the four elements of control in a thermostat.
(c) Compare the two control systems in (a) and (b). What are some of the salient differences?

Question 3.6
How did you decide to:

(a) attend this college, polytechnic or university;
(b) study accounting;
(c) wear the clothes you are wearing now;
(d) brush your teeth this morning?

In each of the decisions described above, comment on the range of alternatives available to you, and whether you adopted all the six steps of problem-solving described by Huber (1980).

Question 3.7

(a) Question 3.6 highlights the point that problem-solving is not a strictly analytical, rational process. What other personal and/or social factors influence the solving of problems?
(b) What implications do these personal and/or social factors have upon the design of managerial accounting systems?

Question 3.8
It can be argued that accounting reports only reflect what has happened in the past, whereas management's interests really lie in the future. In what ways is managerial accounting information of a historical nature helpful (if at all) to management?

Question 3.9
Discuss why the time dimension is important in the provision of managerial accounting information.

3.4 Case study

Mr Ahmed migrated to the United Kingdom 15 years ago and recently opened a clothing factory in London. His company is essentially a subcontractor to large stores such as C & A, Woolworth and British Home Stores. The business receives cut garments from other suppliers to these stores and is responsible for sewing them according to strict specifications. Recently, Mr Ahmed has been disappointed with his company's performance. He has called in an accountant to help and explain his difficulties:

'I always have lots of business but am always short of cash. Because I don't get paid until a few weeks after delivery and have to pay my suppliers quite quickly, I frequently use my overdraft facility. Sometimes, I don't even have money to pay my employees on time. It is all rather hit and miss at the moment. Actually, we have a problem right now. I did £3,000's worth of work for Iris Fashions but I got this letter from some accounting firm that tells me that Iris is now bankrupt. I will not get even one penny for all the work that I've done. That really is criminal.

'Also, I need new machines but I don't know how many exactly and whether the bank will lend me more money for them.

'Finally, it has become difficult to know on a regular basis how well the company is doing. I have a simple accounting system that has worked for me so far. I keep all my receipts in one box and record all my payments in one book. At the end of the financial year, I hand over both items to the accountant who helps me with my tax return. But this simple system appears to be insufficient now. I would really like to know more frequently how well my company is doing. Have you any suggestions for change?'

Required:
As the management accountant called in to help, what kinds of information for feedforward and feedback control could you provide that would help Mr Ahmed manage his company better?

CHAPTER 4 Planning for current activities

WORKBOOK

W4.1 Introduction

From the organizational control framework of the previous chapters we now move on to deal with some computational issues that seek to raise questions about the enterprise's current allocation of effort and the productivity of that allocation. This gives a basis for control via the reallocation of effort to reach a preferred future position.

Before proceeding to the computations themselves it will help if we spend a little more time on the apportionment and absorption of indirect (or overhead) costs.

(This discussion is taken, with permission, from Wilson, R.M.S. (1985) *Cost Control Handbook*, Gower).

The apportionment and absorption of indirect manufacturing costs (overheads)

On pp. 91–100 of the text we looked at the steps to follow in determining the full (or absorbed) cost of manufactured outputs. It may be helpful to deal a little more fully with steps (iii) and (iv), and readers will find it useful to refer back to Fig. 4.9 (p. 93) to place the following discussion in context.

(a) Apportionment of indirect manufacturing costs

The whole question of apportioning service department costs to production departments is complicated by the fact that some service departments render services in a reciprocal manner to each other – the boiler house supplies heating to the stores which in turn supply stores to the boiler house, and the canteen supplies meals for personnel department employees who in turn help in administering the canteen. This problem can be dealt with in various ways:

(i) It may be thought best to disregard the cost of any service rendered by one service department to another, and to apportion the total expenses of each service department directly to the manufacturing departments.

(ii) It may be felt to be most appropriate to apportion first the expenses of that service department that renders services to the greatest number of other service departments but which receives in return the least service from these other departments. The expenses of the next most important provider of services can then by apportioned over the remaining service departments, and so on until all the expenses have been distributed to manufacturing departments.

(iii) Perhaps the most accurate – and also the most complex – method is to proceed as in (ii) above, but with the difference that when the expenses of the second service department are apportioned, some of these expenses may be carried back to the first department, provided that it has benefited from the services rendered by the second department. The whole cycle of apportioning service department expenses in this way will have to be repeated on account of the re-apportionments until the remaining balances are so small that they can be charged directly to manufacturing cost of sales.

In addition to resolving the problem of reciprocal service department costs management must specify the *cost centres* that are to be used – the company itself as one all-embracing cost centre; major service and production departments; sub-departments; responsibility centres; or some variation of these.

Costs that are directly attributable to the selected centres should be allocated to them. Once this has been done, the objective is to apportion service centre costs to production cost centres on a 'reasonable' basis, which means some basis that seems to reflect the benefits received by each production centre (and service centre if the approach suggested in (iii) above is adopted), or which is seen to represent a 'fair share' of service centre costs.

Possible bases for apportioning service department costs are generally related to physical identification (e.g. (ix), (x) and (xi) below), facilities provided (e.g. in (iv), (v) and (vi) below), or the ease of apportionment itself (e.g. in (iii) below). Before apportioning costs it will usually be necessary to make a survey of the factory to ascertain the floor space per department, the number of employees and their distribution throughout the organization, the investment in plant and equipment per department, the horsepower hours worked by each department, and similar matters. Suggested bases of apportionment for service department costs are:

(i) *Direct wages* paid to production employees.
(ii) *Direct material costs* incurred by production departments.
(iii) *Number of employees per department*. This is especially useful for apportioning personnel, canteen, welfare, supervision and costing office costs. But its efficacy is affected by differences in the skilled/unskilled ratio, the rate of labour turnover and the variations in attention given by different services to different production departments irrespective of the number of employees – as when the people using a subsidized factory canteen do not represent a proportional cross section of employees.
(iv) *Floor area occupied* (in square feet). This is frequently used for apportioning rent, rates, building costs, insurances and depreciation. However, it presupposes that each square foot of space is of equal value to the organization, and it is complicated by having to find ways of dealing with corridors, stairways, washrooms, etc.
(v) *Cubic space occupied*. This modification of (iv) can be used for the same purposes, but is more useful for heating costs.
(vi) *Capital employed*. Maintenance, depreciation, rates and insurance costs can all be apportioned on this basis. Care must be taken in deciding on the values to be put on capital assets: replacement value may be more appropriate than written-down book value.
(vii) *Direct labour hours worked*. As a measure of productive activity this can

be useful for apportioning personnel, medical and production planning/control costs.

(viii) *Machine hours worked.* As with (vii), this can be a good basis for production planning and similar costs, and it is particularly suitable for dealing with maintenance costs.

(ix) *Actual measurement/technical estimates.* Electricity, gas, water, oil, compressed air and steam can either be metered so that the actual consumption per department will be given, or technical estimates can be made with reasonable accuracy.

(x) *Units of output.* Materials handling, production control, stores, maintenance, depreciation, etc., can be spread on the basis of physical output.

(xi) *Number of requisitions received.* Purchasing, stores, tool-room activity revolve around the processing of requisitions which make the number of requisitions processed a sensible basis for making apportionments. However, it must be borne in mind that differing degrees of attention must be paid to different requisitions – some materials are easy to obtain while suppliers must be sought for others; some items can be issued simply from stores while others must be cut before being issued.

(b) Absorption of indirect manufacturing costs

The absorption or recovery of indirect costs entails computing and applying indirect cost rates for each production department to products passing through those departments. The absorbed costs of each job or process can be derived by adding the indirect cost element (calculated on the basis of one of the methods shown below) to the *prime cost* (which is the sum of the direct costs) of the job/process. A more accurate absorbed cost will tend to result from indirect cost rates developed for each cost centre through which a product passes as opposed to the absorbed cost that results from one company-wide indirect cost absorption rate. The essential rationale is to consider why one unit of product or a particular job should bear more indirect cost than another, and then to select a suitable basis from the seven given below to reflect the answer. The bases on which indirect production costs (including apportioned service department costs) may be absorbed are:

(i) *As a percentage of prime cost.* This is given by:

$$\frac{\text{Expected indirect costs}}{\text{Estimated prime cost}} \times 100$$

Its major failing is in not considering the time factor since many indirect costs tend to be incurred over time. Unless a standard product is being manufactured that requires constant material and labour inputs per unit the absorbed cost computed on this basis will be inaccurate (see (ii) and (iii) below).

(ii) *As a percentage of direct labour cost*, given by the formula:

$$\frac{\text{Expected indirect costs}}{\text{Estimated direct labour costs}} \times 100$$

This basis gives some consideration to the factor of time since, for a given grade of labour, the higher the cost the greater the time spent. It has the advantage of simplicity and is economical in that it can be developed directly from payroll data, but it fails to allow for different mixes of labour or for overtime or for payments by results.

(iii) *As a percentage of direct material costs*, given by:

$$\frac{\text{Expected indirect costs}}{\text{Estimated direct material cost}} \times 100$$

Only when output is uniform (i.e. when only one kind of product is manufactured, involving a constant material input for each unit of output) is this method fair. Fluctuations in material prices render it unstable, and because an expensive material may be used on one product in a multiproduct company, this does not mean that that product should be expected to recover a proportionately higher amount of indirect cost.

(i)–(iii) will only be acceptable if indirect costs vary in proportion to the cost base selected – prime cost, direct labour cost or direct material cost. Any variations in wage rates or material prices will require a change in the absorption rate.

(iv) *As a rate per unit of productive output*. This method is appropriate for flow production (i.e. process costing) and separate rates can be developed for each process. The rate is derived by applying the formula:

$$\frac{\text{Expected indirect costs}}{\text{Estimated output (in units)}} \times 100$$

and is only suitable when the units being produced are homogeneous and receive identical (or nearly identical) attention.

(v) *As a rate per direct labour hour*, computed as:

$$\frac{\text{Expected indirect costs}}{\text{Estimated direct labour hours}} \times 100$$

This base depends for its accuracy on proper records being kept of the direct labour time being spent on each activity. It is best suited to labour-intensive operations and may not give very satisfactory results when one group of operatives uses machines and another group does not.

(vi) *As a rate per machine hour*, given by:

$$\frac{\text{Expected indirect costs}}{\text{Estimated machine hours}} \times 100$$

This complements (v) above in being suitable for capital intensive situations.

(vii) *As a rate per production hour* for situations which are neither suitable for method (v) nor for method (vi). The formula is:

$$\frac{\text{Expected indirect costs}}{\text{Estimated production hours}} \times 100$$

Since fixed indirect costs are related to time it is often suggested that time (i.e. methods (v), (vi) and (vii)) is the most important dimension for indirect costs absorption. There seems to be a very general acceptance that rates based on time or output (i.e. methods (iv)–(viii) above) are to be preferred to those based on value (i.e. methods (i)–(iii) above). But whether they are developed in relation to time or output, indirect cost absorption rates should be based on a consideration of such factors as:

(i) the nature of the manufacturing processes – manual versus mechanical;
(ii) the nature of the materials used;
(iii) the constancy (or otherwise) of material prices and quality;
(iv) the differentials in pay rates;
(v) the seasonality (if any) of production;
(vi) the extent to which available capacity is utilized.

Some worked examples are provided in Section W4.4 below.

W4.2 Revision topics

Question 4.1
What do you understand by the term 'cost'? Is it desirable in a managerial context to use the term without a qualifying adjective?

Answer
In conceptual terms cost is synonymous with *sacrifice*. This arises because we live in a world of scarcities, so the cost of using scarce resources for one purpose is the sacrifice due to not being able to use those same resources for some other purpose.

When seeking to measure the cost of something one must initially define that something. In doing this one needs to qualify the noun with a suitable adjective, thus:

(i) *the full* cost of running a car;
(ii) the *direct* cost of producing a suit;
(iii) the *average* cost per unit of output;
(iv) the *comparative* cost of graduates from polytechnics as opposed to universities.

In operational terms cost is meaningless without a qualifying adjective, so it is *essential* to be precise in defining the category of cost in which you are interested.

Question 4.2
What essential characteristic distinguishes a direct cost from an indirect cost?

Answer
A direct cost is one that can be specifically related (or traced) to a given cost object. When this specific link is absent the cost must be indirect relative to the cost object.

Question 4.3
Discuss the criteria you feel should be used for assigning indirect costs to cost objects.

Answer
Some suggestions were given in Section W4.1 above:

(i) reasonableness;
(ii) benefits received;
(iii) fair shares;
(iv) physical identification;
(v) facilities provided;
(vi) ease;
(vii) causal relationships.

Each has its strengths and weaknesses, with 'reasonableness' being a highly subjective criterion and causality being difficult to establish (to take but two examples).

Question 4.4
What are the relative advantages and disadvantages of departmental versus company-wide indirect cost absorption rates?

Answer
To a large extent the answer will depend on what is being produced: if large numbers of like items are being manufactured it may be satisfactory to use company-wide rates, whereas departmental rates would be more appropriate when lots of different items are being produced. Since it is expensive to operate (as well as to develop and install) costing systems, there is no point in having a system that generates more detailed information than one can sensibly use – which could happen when departmental rates are used with standardized products. Conversely, when one does need detailed information (i.e. via departmental rates), this should be available.

The cost characteristics of different production departments within a factory are likely to differ (e.g. some will be labour-intensive and some capital-intensive). There will be different patterns of cost accumulation whenever particular jobs spend different amounts of time, or receive more or less attention, in one department rather than another. In this situation departmental rates are helpful.

In order to have as sound a base as one reasonably can for determining the allocation of effort to the range of an enterprise's activities – since subsequent decisions will tend to stem from this – the appropriate system should be chosen in accordance with the operating characteristics of the enterprise.

Question 4.5
Why have management accountants traditionally devoted less attention to the study of marketing costs than to manufacturing costs?

Answer
The essence of this matter is to be found in the origins of cost accounting – which were in the factory, focusing on the costs of processes and products. Manufacturing activities have tended to be more repetitive and identifiable than marketing activities, and have therefore received more attention from management accountants over the years. Apart from the intangible nature of many marketing phenomena, and limited knowledge concerning causal relationships as a basis for reliable measurement, the need for costing with a manufacturing focus to produce inventory valuations and cost of sales data to meet the needs of financial accounting has reinforced the rather introspective stance of 'traditional'

managerial accounting systems. From a control point of view this is not very helpful.

W4.3 Discussion topics

Question 4.1
Are financial costs more important to managers than non-financial costs?

Question 4.2
Identify the main cost objects that relate to your academic and extra-curricular pursuits.

Question 4.3
In relation to a manufactured product of your choice give examples of:

(i) a direct material cost;
(ii) a direct labour cost;
(iii) an indirect material cost;
(iv) an indirect labour cost;
(v) a direct cost other than material or labour;
(vi) an indirect cost other than material or labour.

Question 4.4
Would you agree that cost allocations are arbitrary?

Question 4.5
Discuss the uses and limitations of full (or absorption) costing from a managerial viewpoint.

Question 4.6
Explain why LIFO and FIFO produce different measures of profit.

Question 4.7
'Consider the cost of manufacturing a pair of shoes. The rent of the factory in which the shoes are made and the depreciation of the machinery used in their manufacture are costs of producing the shoes, just as much as the costs of labour and materials. Equally, if the firm borrows in order to buy a factory, the interest on that borrowing is as much a cost of manufacture as if the firm were paying rent. Before the firm can make a profit *all* these costs must be covered: to ignore any of them in calculating the cost of producing a pair of shoes would be misleading.'

Amey and Egginton (1973), p. 439.

Examine the validity and implications of this argument.

Question 4.8
For some years the British government has discriminated between UK/EEC-based students and students from other countries by requiring higher education institutions to charge the latter full cost fees. How would you go about determining the full cost of tuition in your college/polytechnic/university?

W4.4 Worked examples

Question 4.1 Stevens & Sons – calculating full cost
Stevens & Sons manufacture a particular type of picnic table. The costs for a typical month are:

	£
Rent of premises	225
Utilities	150
Insurance	75
Office expenses	450
Depreciation	300
Supervision	600
	£1,800

The direct costs per table are:

	£
Materials	25
Labour	15
	£40

Geoff Stevens, the manager of the firm, expects that 200 tables will be made in a normal month, and views the individual table as the most important cost object.

(i) What is the full cost of each table?
(ii) If another firm asked Stevens & Sons to supply finished tables at cost, would you expect any difference of opinion to exist over the figure to use?

Answer

(i) The full cost per table in this simple example will consist of direct costs (as given) plus a portion of the indirect costs reflecting normal activity (i.e. 1,800/200 = £9). Full cost per table is therefore:

	£
Direct costs	40
Indirect costs	9
	£49

(ii) From Stevens' point of view the preferred figure would probably be £49 per table, but the other firm would probably challenge the indirect cost element on two grounds:
- it covers costs that will be incurred whether Stevens gets the order or not;
- if the order is given to Stevens it will change the denominator from 200 to something bigger, which will reduce unit cost.

Question 4.2 Lambda Ltd – the treatment of indirect manufacturing costs
The following information relating to the month of June is extracted from the cost records of Lambda Ltd, which makes mechanical toys, the parts of which are made in Department A and assembled in Department B.

	Total	Dept A	Dept B
Direct materials consumed (£)	6,500	5,000	1,500
Direct labour (£)	9,000	4,000	5,000
Direct labour hours worked	80,000	30,000	50,000
Machine-hours worked	30,000	25,000	5,000
Factory rent, heat, light (£)	1,500		
Supervision wages (£)	600	250	350
Depreciation of machinery (£)	500		
Power (£)	400		
Repairs to machinery (£)	200	160	40
Indirect labour (£)	400	200	200
Machine horse-power (hp)	400	300	100
Book-value of plant (£)	5,000	4,000	1,000
Floor space (ft^2)	20,000	10,000	10,000
Number of machines – ratio between depts		2	1
The costs of batch X252 have been booked as follows:			
Materials (£)	320	270	50
Labour (£)	750	300	450

Direct labour hours worked on batch X252 were 2,500 in Department A, and 5,000 in Department B. Machine-hours worked on this batch were 1,250 in Department A and 600 in Department B.

You are asked:

(a) to advise how indirect manufacturing costs might be allocated to batch X252;
(b) to consider objections which might be raised against the bases and methods of allocation used;
(c) to calculate the cost of each unit in batch X252, assuming there are 1,000 units in the batch.

Answer

(a) The most likely procedure would be to allocate indirect manufacturing costs first to departments on 'appropriate' bases, separating machine costs from others, thus:

Departmental Allocation

Expense	Basis	Total £	Dept A £	Dept B £
Depreciation	Plant values	500	400	100
Power	Horse-power hours*	400	375	25
Repairs to machinery	Actual	200	160	40
Machine costs		£1,100	£935	£165

Calculated thus:
* Machine hours × horse power A = 7,500,000
Machine hours × horse power B = 500,000
8,000,000

7,500,000/8,000,000 × 400 = 375; 500,000/8,000,000 × 400 = 25.

Expense	Basis	Total £	Dept A £	Dept B £
Rent, etc.	Floor space	1,500	750	750
Supervision	Actual	600	250	350
Indirect labour	Actual	400	200	200
Non-machine costs		£2,500	£1,200	£1,300

In each department, machine costs might now be allocated on the basis of a machine-hour rate, and other costs on the basis of a direct labour rate. These rates would be:

	Dept A	Dept B
Machine-hour rate:	$\frac{£935}{25{,}000} = 3.74p$	$\frac{165}{5{,}000} = 3.30p$
Labour-hour rate:	$\frac{£1{,}200}{30{,}000} = 4.0p$	$\frac{1{,}300}{50{,}000} = 2.6p$

This would give an on-cost allocation to batch X252 as follows:

			£	£
Dept A:	Machine costs	1,250 hrs at 3.74p	47	
	Other costs	2,500 hrs at 4.0p	100	147
Dept B:	Machine costs	600 hrs at 3.30p	20	
	Other costs	5,000 hrs at 2.6p	130	150
Total indirect cost allocation				£297

(b) The allocation of indirect manufacturing costs which has been made above on the basis of the information given is open to considerable objection on the grounds of the inappropriateness of the bases in detail and of the whole procedure in general. As regards the bases of allocation adopted:

(i) A floor-space basis for rent, etc., assumes that every square foot of space gives service of the same value as every other.

(ii) Spreading supervision evenly over labour hours assumes that all labour needs the same amount of supervision. This is not often true.
(iii) The allocation of depreciation on the basis of plant values disregards differences in the extent to which different pieces of plant are subjected to wear and tear.
(iv) A flat machine-hour rate for power costs within each department assumes that all machines in the department consume equal quantities of power per hour.
(v) Similarly, all machines do not need equal amounts of maintenance per hour run.

Some of these objections could be met by breaking the departments down into cost centres, with a separate machine rate for each centre. All machine hours would then not be treated as being equally costly.

Objections on other grounds are:

(i) No distinction is made between fixed and variable expenses (see Chapter 5). Avoidable costs will therefore be obscured by the type of calculation shown.
(ii) A fall in production would result in a rise in the absorption rate. This, if passed on to customers, might cause the fall in business to become cumulative.

(c)

	Department A		Department B		Total	
	Total	Unit	Total	Unit	Total	Unit
	£	£	£	£	£	£
Direct materials costs	270	0.270	50	0.050	320	0.320
Direct labour costs	300	0.300	450	0.450	750	0.750
Indirect costs	147	0.147	150	0.150	297	0.297
Cost per component	£717	£0.717	£650	£0.650	£1,367	£1.367

Question 4.3

Kappa Ltd – the allocation of indirect manufacturing costs between jobs on an absorption basis

The estimated total figures of a factory for a year are budgeted as follows:

	£
Materials	40,000
Labour	60,000
Prime cost	100,000
Indirect costs	80,000
Total cost	180,000
Profit (10% of total cost)	18,000
Sales	£198,000

The total indirect costs are £80,000, the total hours of direct labour are 400,000, and the total number of machine-hours are 320,000, so average indirect costs per man-hour are £0.20 and per machine-hour are £0.25. Similarly, the total indirect cost is twice the material cost, giving an indirect cost rate of twice the job's material cost (800/400), and on a labour basis the relationship becomes 133 per cent of the labour cost (with total labour being £60,000 and the indirect costs £80,000).

What is the full cost of a given job needing £800 of materials and £200 of labour (requiring 1,100 man-hours and 1,000 machine-hours) estimated by the following methods:

(a) Non-departmental indirect cost rates?
(b) Departmental indirect cost rates?

Answer

(a)

Non-departmental rates

	(1) Material £	(2) Direct labour £	(3) Prime cost £	(4) Man-hour £	(5) Machine-hour £
Material	800	800	800	800	800
Labour	200	200	200	200	200
Prime cost	1,000	1,000	1,000	1,000	1,000
Indirect costs					
(2 × £800) =	1,600	($\frac{4}{3}$ × £200) = 267	($\frac{4}{5}$ × £1,000) = 800	(1,100 × £0.2) = 220	(1,000 × £0.25) = 250
Total cost	2,600	1,267	1,800	1,220	1,250
Profit	260	127	180	122	125
Sales	£2,860	£1,394	£1,980	£1,342	£1,375

(b)

Departmental rates

KAPPA LTD might have been organized in two departments, with departmental budgets as follows:

	Department A		Department B
	£		£
Materials	30,000		10,000
Labour	40,000		20,000
Prime cost	70,000		30,000
Indirect costs	60,000		20,000
Total cost	130,000		50,000
Profit	13,000		5,000
Sales	143,000		55,000
Man-hours	200,000		200,000
Man-hour rate (60,000 ÷ 200,000) =	£0.30	(20,000 ÷ 200,000) =	£0.10
Machine hours	200,000		120,000
Machine-hour rate (60,000 ÷ 200,000) =	£0.30	(20,000 ÷ 120,000) =	£0.16

Then the cost of the contract, requiring 750 man-hours and 750 machine-hours in Department A, and 350 man-hours and 250 machine-hours in Department B, would, under methods (4) and (5), be as follows:

	Man-hour method		Machine-hour method	
	Dept A	Dept B	Dept A	Dept B
	£	£	£	£
Materials	600	200	600	200
Labour	120	80	120	40
Prime cost	720	280	720	280
Indirect costs	(750 × £0.3) = 225	(350 × £0.1) = 35	(750 × £0.3) = 225	(250 × £0.16) = 40
Total cost	945	315	945	320
Profit	95	31	95	32
Sales	1,040	346	1,040	352

Note: It should be appreciated that the purpose of this illustration is to show the attempts commonly made in practice to allocate indirect costs. For the following reasons these attempts, on the bases used, may not be useful:

(i) there is an assumption that the particular method of allocation is relevant to all management purposes;
(ii) hence it may ignore the characteristics of the particular purpose in mind;
(iii) allocations are usually made on an absorption basis rather than an incremental basis, and therefore ignore the problems relating to fixed costs, common costs, etc;
(v) it proceeds by way of 'equitable' or 'reasonable' apportionments, rather than those based upon economic realities.

W4.5 Computational problems

Question 4.1
Woodhouse & Co. manufacture a range of kitchen utensils. The firm's approach to setting prices is to add a profit mark-up to the full cost of each product line, and data relating to the year just finishing is given below for item X (which sells at a steady rate of 5,000 units p.a.):

	Unit cost
	£
Direct materials cost	1.50
Direct labour cost	3.00
Indirect manufacturing cost	2.50
Marketing and administrative cost	1.50
Full cost	8.50
Profit mark-up (10% of full cost)	0.85
Selling price	£9.35

It is estimated that the direct costs will increase next year by 10% for materials and 5% for labour, while indirect manufacturing costs are likely to increase by £4,000 in total. Marketing and administrative costs are not expected to change, and the level of demand for item X is expected to remain at 5,000 units.

Using the same approach to pricing as shown above, what will be the price of item X next year?

Question 4.2

Douglas Beaumont recently left the large accounting firm through which he had qualified to set up his own practice. His anticipated monthly costs are:

	£
Secretary's salary	500
Rent of office	250
Other services, etc.	450
Total costs	£1,200

In addition, Mr Beaumont aims to earn £2,000 per month for himself through the practice for which he anticipates having to bill clients for 160 hours of his time each month.

(i) Calculate the hourly charge out rate that Mr Beaumont must use to bill his clients.

(ii) If, in a given month, he is only able to charge clients for 100 hours of his time, what will he earn in that month? (Assume all costs are non-variable.)

Question 4.3

Strines & Co. is engaged in marketing three products, X, Y and Z. During May 1992 the sales volume, unit selling price and gross margin of each product was as follows:

	X	Y	Z
Sales (units)	10,000	15,000	25,000
Selling price (£)	50	20	10
Gross margin (%)	45	50	55

Order-getting and order-filling costs for the month were:

	£
Personal selling	180,000
Advertising	70,000
Transportation	90,000
Warehousing and handling	60,000
General	37,500

Certain additional information is available:

	X	Y	Z
Kilos shipped	90,000	50,000	60,000
Salesmen's time	20%	45%	35%
Advertising effort	40%	25%	35%

Required:
Prepare a profit statement showing the relative profit performance of each product line. Make whatever assumptions you feel to be necessary, but state all the assumptions you have made.

Question 4.4
While management of RST Company realize that additional marketing/distribution cost studies are needed, the company lacks the personnel and funds at present to establish accurate cost standards. They do, however, believe that they may be accepting too small an order. As a result, they analyse the order sizes received last year and break their orders down by the simple categories of small (1–20 items), medium (21–100 items) and large (over 100 items).

The actual marketing and distribution costs incurred last year were as follows:

Cost	Amount (£)	Basis for distribution
Marketing personnel salaries	27,000	Number of personnel
Marketing manager's salary	20,000	Time spent
Salespeople's commissions	3,000	Amount of sales
Advertising and direct selling	37,500	Amount of sales
Packaging and shipping	26,250	Weight shipped
Delivery	19,000	Weight shipped
Credit and collection	15,000	Number of orders

An analysis of their records produced the following statistics:

	Order sizes			
	Small	Medium	Large	Total
Number of personnel	5	3	1	9
Time spent by marketing manager	60%	10%	30%	100%
Amount of sales (£)	250,000	300,000	200,000	750,000
Weight (kg)	6,090	2,940	1,470	10,500
Number of orders	612	170	68	850

Required:

(a) Prepare a detailed schedule showing the marketing cost per order size and marketing cost as a percentage of total sales for each order size.
(b) What recommendations would you make to management regarding the size of order they should accept?

Question 4.5 Indirect cost rate – non-manufacturing firm
Franklin Associates is a management consulting firm. Each consulting engagement is covered by a contract. The contract price is negotiated in advance, sometimes as a fixed fee, sometimes as professional staff time plus traceable expenses. The billing rates for the various members of the professional staff are always fixed in advance and are expected, in the aggregate, to cover non-traceable (indirect) costs and provide a margin of profit.

The company uses a job costing system to measure the costs of each contract.

All costs not directly traceable to specific contracts are recorded as indirect costs; a single predetermined indirect cost rate is used to assign indirect costs to contracts, based on the number of professional staff hours.

Budgeted time and costs for the year and actual time and costs for February were as follows:

	Annual budget		February	
	Hours	Cost	Hours	Cost
Direct costs:				
Professional staff	25,000	£300,000	1,800	£25,000
Secretarial staff	6,000	36,000	550	3,300
Artwork and printing		7,000		800
Copying		2,000		200
Travel		35,000		2,700
Total		£380,000		£32,000
Indirect costs:				
Professional staff	5,000	£60,000	600	£7,400
Secretarial staff	12,000	72,000	800	3,300
Artwork and printing		3,000		300
Copying		1,000		100
Travel		8,000		400
Other		56,000		4,700
Total		£200,000		£16,200

Required:

(a) Prepare a predetermined hourly rate for indirect costs.

(b) The following direct cost data were recorded during February for one of the company's contracts. How much cost was assigned to this contract during February?

	£
Professional staff (70 hours)	910
Secretarial staff (10 hours)	65
Artwork and printing	60
Copying	10
Travel	280

(c) Would this contract have been more profitable or less profitable if the indirect cost rate had been based on the company's actual cost experience in February?

Question 4.6 Determining functional cost

The personnel department of Mansdowne Manufacturing Company has the following costs in one month:

	£
Salaries	£17,000
Advertising	1,200
Rent	1,000
Postage and supplies	400
Telephone	200
Depreciation	100
Computer services	300
Total	£20,200

Five personnel functions have been identified:

- personnel records;
- recruiting;
- management development;
- labour relations;
- wage and salary administration.

You have the following additional information:

(i) The salaries of the department's ten employees are classified as follows:

	No of employees	Total salaries
Director	1	2,800
Assistant director	1	2,200
Recruiting	2	3,600
Labour relations	1	2,400
Personnel records	2	2,000
General clerical	3	4,000
Total	10	£17,000

(ii) The director has made the following estimates for five employees who work on more than one function:

	Director	Assistant	Clerical
Personnel records	–	10%	20%
Recruiting	10%	40	30
Management development	50	30	20
Labour relations	10	10	10
Wage and salary administration	30	10	20

(iii) All advertising costs relate to the recruiting function.

(iv) The department is charged rent for the space it occupies in the company's headquarters building. The rental charge is based on the average cost of owning and operating the building. Comparable space in the building is now being rented to other tenants at £1,500 a month, but a considerable amount of rentable space is now vacant. The amount of work space occupied by individual employees varies only slightly from employee to employee.

(v) The director estimates that half of the postage and supplies and half of the telephone charges relate to recruiting; another 20% relates to management development; the rest is unidentified.
(vi) Computer services are 90% for personnel records, 10% for wage and salary administration.
(vii) Depreciation is for office furniture and equipment and is approximately equal to average replacement expenditures.

Required:

(a) Prepare estimates of the costs of each of the five functions. Explain each of your allocations in a word or a phrase. You should allocate only those costs that seem relevant to managerial decisions relating to individual functions.
(b) What are the most likely uses of this functional cost information?
(c) Which of these functions should be allocated to segments for purposes of product-line analysis?

Question 4.7 Sullivan Company

Sullivan Company does custom information retrieval and report preparation for a variety of clients. There are two production cost centres: Information Retrieval and Report Writing. Supporting service cost centres are Data Processing and Library Services. Sullivan Company does not attempt to charge costs for Data Processing and Library Services to projects according to actual use of these services, but rather at month-end allocates these costs to Information Retrieval and Report Writing according to the number of direct labour hours spent on projects in those two production centres. Then each project is charged an amount per direct labour hour for each production cost centre's overhead.

Indirect costs are primarily rent, utilities and labour. Rent and utilities are allocated to the four cost centres according to square footage of office space; indirect labour is assigned to each department as incurred. Information Retrieval and Report Writing each occupy 5,000 square feet. Data Processing occupies 1,250 square feet and Library Services occupies 10,000 square feet.

The following transactions took place in November:

(i) £560 (80 hours) of direct information retrieval labour were incurred for Project A.
(ii) £175 (25 hours) of direct information retrieval labour were incurred for Project B.
(iii) £1,120 (160 hours) of direct information retrieval labour were incurred for Project C.
(iv) £140 (20 hours) of direct report preparation labour were incurred for Project A.
(v) £70 (10 hours) of direct report preparation labour were incurred for Project B.
(vi) £350 (50 hours) of direct report preparation labour were incurred for Project C.
(vii) £2,000 rent expense.
(viii) £3,200 indirect Data Processing labour expense.
(ix) £1,380 indirect Library labour expense.

(x) £350 indirect Information Retrieval labour expense.
(xi) £400 utilities expense.
(xii) £1,000 other Data Processing expense.
(xiii) £100 other Library expense.

Required:

(a) Determine the amount of direct costs for each project during November.
(b) Calculate indirect costs for each of the production and service departments for November.
(c) Calculate the rates at which indirect costs should be allocated to each project for each of the two production departments.
(d) Determine the full costs of each of the three projects carried out in November.

Question 4.8

The profit and loss account for last month's operations of ABC Ltd is given in Fig. W4.1, showing a net profit of £14,070.

Derek Needham, ABC's chief executive, is interested in knowing the profitability of the company's three customers. Since this cannot be ascertained from Fig. W4.1 as it stands he asks his management accountant, Philip Randall, to carry out the necessary analysis.

In addition to the five *natural* accounts shown in the profit and loss account Mr Randall has identified four *functional* accounts:

- Personal selling
- Packaging and despatch
- Advertising
- Invoicing and collection.

His investigations have revealed that:

Figure W4.1

ABC Ltd profit and loss account.

ABC LTD
Profit and Loss Account

	£	£
Sales revenue		255,000
Cost of goods sold		178,500
Gross profit		76,500
Expenses		
Salaries	37,500	
Rent	7,500	
Packaging materials	15,180	
Postage and stationery	750	
Hire of office equipment	1,500	62,430
Net profit		£14,070

Figure W4.2

ABC Ltd basic product data.

Product	Manufactured cost per unit £	Selling price per unit £	Number of units sold last month	Sales revenue £	Relative bulk per unit
A	105	150	1,000	150,000	1
B	525	750	100	75,000	3
C	2,100	3,000	10	30,000	6
			1,110	£255,000	

(i) Salaries are attributable as follows:

Sales personnel	£15,000
Packaging labour	£13,500
Office staff	£9,000

Salesmen seldom visit the office. Office staff time is divided equally between promotional activities on the one hand and invoicing/collecting on the other.

(ii) The rent charge relates to the whole building, of which 20% is occupied by offices and the remainder by packing/despatch.

(iii) All the advertising expenditure relates to product C.

(iv) ABC Ltd markets three products, as shown in Fig. W4.2. These products vary in their manufactured cost (worked out on absorption lines), selling price and volume sold during the month. Moreover, their relative bulk varies: product A is much smaller than product B, which in turn is only half the size of product C. Details are given in Fig. W4.2.

(v) ABC's three customers each requires different product combinations, places a different number of orders, and requires a different amount of sales effort.

Figure W4.3

ABC Ltd basic customer data.

Customer	Number of sales calls in period	Number of orders placed in period	Number of units of each product ordered in period		
			A	B	C
Charles	30	30	900	30	0
James	40	3	90	30	3
Hugh	30	1	10	40	7
Totals	100	34	1,000	100	10

As Fig. W4.3 shows, James received more sales calls, Charles placed more orders, and Hugh made up most of the demand for product C.

Required:

(a) Using the data that has been presented, and making any assumptions you feel to be appropriate (which must be stated and justified), you are required to apply absorption costing principles in order to determine the net profit or loss attributable to each of ABC's customers.
(b) On the basis of your answer to (a), what course of action would you propose? Give your reasons.

W4.6 Case studies

The following case study is included in Wilson R.M.S.(1981), Vol. 1, pp. 240–2.

NUTS
A Tragedy in One Act

The Scene: A small store deep in the jungle of accounting logic.
The Time: Today – and tomorrow, if you are not careful.
The Cast: Joe, owner and operator of a small store-restaurant in the jungle; an accounting efficiency expert.

As the curtain rises we find Joe dusting his counter and casting admiring glances at a shiny new rack holding brightly coloured bags of peanuts. The rack is at the end of the counter. The store itself is like all small store-restaurants in the jungle of accounting logic. As Joe dusts and admires his new peanut rack, he listens almost uncomprehendingly to the earnest speeches of the accounting efficiency expert.

EFF. EX.: Joe, you said you put in these peanuts because some people ask for them, but do you realize what this rack of peanuts is costing you?

JOE: It isn't going to cost anything. Indeed it will make a profit. Sure, I had to pay £20 for a fancy rack to hold the bags, but the peanuts cost only 6 pence a bag and I sell them for 10 pence. I reckon I will sell 50 bags a week at first. It will take 10 weeks to cover the cost of the rack. After that I've got a clear profit of 4 pence a bag. The more I sell, the more I make.

EFF. EX.: That is an anticipated and completely unrealistic approach, Joe. Fortunately, modern accounting procedures permit a more accurate picture which reveals the complexities involved.

JOE: Huh?

EFF. EX.: To be precise, those peanuts must be integrated into your entire operation and be allocated their appropriate share of business overhead. They must share a proportionate part of your expenditures for rent, heat, light, equipment, depreciation, decorating, salaries for waitresses, cook . . .

JOE: The cook? What has he to do with peanuts? He does not even know I've got them.

EFF. EX.: Look, Joe, the cook is in the kitchen, the kitchen prepares the food, the food brings people in, and while they're in, they ask to buy peanuts. That is why you must charge a portion of the cook's wages, as well as a part of your own salary to peanut sales. This sheet contains a carefully calculated cost analysis which indicates the peanut operation should pay exactly £1,278 per year towards these general overhead costs.

JOE: The peanuts? £1,278 a year for overhead? That's NUTS!

EFF. EX.: It's really a little more than that. You also spend money each week to have the windows washed, to have the place swept in the mornings, and keep soap in the washroom. That raises the total to £1,313 per year.

JOE: But the peanut salesman said I'd make money. Put them at the end of the counter, he said, and get 4 pence a bag profit.

EFF. EX.: (*With a sniff*) He's not an accountant. Do you actually know what the portion of the counter occupied by the peanut rack is worth to you?

JOE: It is not worth anything. There is no stool there. It is just a dead spot at the end.

EFF. EX.: The modern cost picture permits no dead spots. Your counter contains 60 square feet and your counter business grosses £15,000 a year. Consequently, the square foot of space occupied by the peanut rack is worth £250 per year. Since you have taken that area away from the general counter use, you must charge the value of the space to the occupant.

JOE: You mean I've got to add £250 a year more to the peanuts?

EFF. EX.: Right. That raises their share of the general operating costs to a grand total of £1,563 per year. Now then, if you sell 50 bags of peanuts per week, these allocated costs will amount to 60 pence per bag.

JOE: (*Incredulously*) What?

EFF. EX.: Obviously, to that must be added your purchase price of 6 pence per bag, which brings the total to 66 pence. So you see, by selling peanuts at 10 pence a bag, you are losing 56 pence on every sale.

JOE: Something's crazy!

EFF. EX.: Not at all! Here are the figures. They prove your peanut operation cannot stand on its own feet.

JOE: (*Brightening*) Suppose I sell a lot of peanuts – a thousand bags a week instead of 50?

EFF. EX.: (*Tolerantly*) Joe, you don't understand the problem. If the volume of peanut sales increased, your operating costs will go up – you will have to handle more bags, with more time, more general overhead, more everything. The basic principle of accounting is firm on that subject: 'The bigger the operation the more general overhead costs must be allocated.' No, increasing the volume of sales won't help.

JOE: Okay. You are so smart. You tell me what I have to do.

EFF. EX.: (*Condescendingly*) Well – you could first reduce operating expenses.

JOE: How?

EFF. EX.: Take smaller space in an older building with cheaper rent. Cut salaries. Wash the windows fortnightly. Have the floor swept only on Thursday. Remove the soap from the washroom. This will also help you decrease the square foot value of your counter. For example, if you can cut your expenses by 50%, that will reduce the amount allocated to peanuts from £1,563 down to £781.50 per year, reducing the cost to 36 pence per bag.

JOE: (*Slowly*) That's better?

EFF. EX.: Much, much better. However, even then you would lose 26 pence per bag if you charge only 10 pence. Therefore, you must also raise your selling price. If you want a net profit of 4 pence per bag, you would have to charge 40 pence.

JOE: (*Flabbergasted*) You mean even after I cut operating costs 50% I still have to charge 40 pence for a 10 pence bag of peanuts? Nobody's that nuts about nuts! Who'd buy them?

EFF. EX.: That's a secondary consideration. The point is at 40 pence you'd be selling at a price based upon a true and proper evaluation of your then reduced costs.

JOE: (*Eagerly*) Look! I've got a better idea. Why don't I just throw the nuts out – put them in the ash can?

EFF. EX.: Can you afford it?

JOE: Sure, all I've got is about 50 bags of peanuts. I am going to lose 20 on the rack, but I will be better off out of this nutty business, and no more grief.

EFF. EX.: (*Shaking head*) Joe, it isn't quite that simple. You are IN THE PEANUT BUSINESS. The minute you throw those peanuts out, you are adding £1,563 of annual overhead to the rest of your operation. Joe – be realistic – can you afford to do that?

JOE: (*Completely crushed*) It's unbelievable! Last week I was making money. Now I'm in trouble – just because I thought peanuts on my counter would bring me some extra profit – just because I thought it would be easy to sell 50 bags of peanuts a week.

EFF. EX.: (*With raised eyebrow*) That is the reason for modern cost studies, Joe – to dispel those false illusions.

Required:
Discuss this case.

AJAX MANUFACTURING*

This short case deals with a company which manufactures three product lines directed at industrial markets. Whilst the case is highly simplified it is still a realistic representation of the situation faced by a large number of companies. The basic issues can be readily identified.

It is generally expected that individual products within a company's product range should both cover their costs and provide an adequate return on invested capital. If cross-subsidization is to exist this should be undertaken in the full knowledge of the underlying cost patterns.

Whenever there are multiple products in a product range that are manufactured by the use of common facilities, the problem of accuracy in product costing arises. This presumes, of course, that an absorption approach is adopted and that it is seen as being useful to generate cost data that includes apportioned indirect costs. Such an approach facilitates the determination of profit by product line and hence segmental productivity analysis. It can also help in pricing decisions. If the approach to absorbing indirect costs is inappropriate then it follows that the value of the resulting information will also be suspect.

Three approaches to absorption costing will be considered via this case: a traditional approach, a 'modern' approach, and an activity-based approach.

* This case has been adapted from Shank and Govindarajan (1988) and is used here with permission.

The traditional approach

Figure W4.4 gives details of the basic information relating to Ajax Manufacturing and its three products. In addition to sales price and sales volume data Figure W4.4 also shows production and standard cost details. The target sales prices reflect the need to achieve a budgeted gross margin of 35%. Product costs are arrived at as follows:

- standard raw material cost for each product is given by:
  sum of purchased components x standard cost per component;
- standard direct labour cost for each product is give by:
  standard labour hours per unit x standard labour cost per hour;
- indirect manufacturing costs are assigned by means of a two-stage approach:

  Stage 1 involves the assigning of indirect costs to production departments, based on relevant measures of activity (such as number of employees for personnel department costs, square feet occupied for occupancy costs, etc.). In this

Figure W4.4

Basic information

	A	B	C	
Production	10,000 units in 1 run	15,000 units in 3 runs	5,000 units in 10 runs	
Shipments	10,000 units in 1 shipment	15,000 units in 5 shipments	5,000 units in 20 shipments	
Selling prices:				
Target	£162.61	£134.09	£ 81.31	
Actual	£162.61	£125.96	£105.70	
Manufacturing costs:				
Raw material	5 components @ £4.00=£20	6 components @ £5.00=£30	10 components @ £1.00=£10	
Labour usage (labour=£20/hour including fringe benefits)				*Total*
Set-up labour	10 hours per production run	10 hours per production run	11 hours per production run	150 hours
Run labour	½ hour per part	⅓ hour per part	¼ hour per part	11,250 hours
Machine usage (Machine cost = £70/hour)	¼ hour per part	⅓ hour per part	½ hour per part	10,000 hours

There is only one production department – 'machines' – and it takes a little more than one labour hour for each machine hour (11,250/10,000) with the current product mix.

Other indirect costs:

Receiving Department	£300,000
Engineering Department	500,000
Packing Department	200,000

Figure W4.5

Indirect costs.

Apportioned indirect costs		
Set-up	£ 3,000	
Receiving	£300,000	
Engineering	£500,000	
Packing	£200,000	
		£1,003,000
Production indirect costs		
Machines costs (10,000 hours × £70/hr)		£ 700,000
Total indirect costs		£1,703,000

simple case it is assumed that there is only one production department, so all the indirect costs must be attributable to this one department.

Stage 2 involves the assigning of indirect costs to units of product based on some measure of throughput or output volume. This is typically direct labour hours or direct labour cost.

If we include set-up labour the total indirect cost of the machines department is as shown in Figure W4.5.

An indirect cost absorption rate can be derived by dividing the total indirect costs by the direct labour cost:

$$\frac{\pounds 1{,}703{,}000}{11{,}250 \text{ hrs.} \times \pounds 20/\text{hr.}} \times 100 = \frac{\pounds 1{,}703{,}000}{\pounds 225{,}000} \times 100$$

$$= 757\%$$

This traditional approach gives the unit full cost figures for product lines A, B and C shown in Figure W4.6.

Building up from Figure W4.6 allows us to compile a product line profit report (Figure W4.7) which compares actual figures with target figures – assuming that there were no cost variances.

Figure W4.7 shows us that A was achieving the budgeted margin. Product B, however, has come under heavy price pressure from foreign competitors and has only achieved a margin of 31%. The sales director of Ajax suspects foreign competitors of 'dumping' (i.e. selling below cost to gain market entry in this country)

Figure W4.6

Unit full costs — 1.

	A	B	C
Raw material	£ 20.00	£30.00	£10.00
Direct labour	10.00	6.67	5.00
Indirect cost	75.70	50.49	37.85
Total	£105.70	£87.16	£52.85

Figure W4.7

Product line profit report — 1.

	A	B	C
Target selling price	£162.61	£134.09	£ 81.31
Standard cost	105.70	87.16	52.85
Gross margin	£ 56.91	£ 46.93	£ 28.46
Target gross margin (%)	35%	35%	35%
Actual selling price	£162.61	£125.96	£105.70
Standard cost	105.70	87.16	52.85
Gross margin	£ 56.91	£ 38.80	£ 52.85
Actual gross margin (%)	35%	31%	50%

and has reacted to this by cutting price. Even though B has the highest volume of all the Ajax lines its volume is well below budget, but the management of Ajax are reluctant to let the price fall further.

In contrast to B the margin on C is higher than target at 50%, due to Ajax's ability to raise its price. Despite the price increase there has been little challenge from competitors, so Ajax appears to have a very profitable, low-volume niche with little competition.

A modern approach

Concern over the position of B has led the finance manager of Ajax to adopt a few refinements to the company's costing system. These refinements are:

- To charge set-up labour directly to each product line based on the formula:

  $$\frac{\text{Set-up time per production run}}{\text{Number of units in production run}}$$

  Thus, for product A, we are aware from Exhibit 1 that one set-up involves 10 labour hours at £20 per hour, and one production run generates 10,000 units. The set-up cost per unit is, for each line:

  $$\text{A} \quad \frac{10 \times £20}{10{,}000} = £0.02$$

  $$\text{B} \quad \frac{10 \times £20}{5{,}000} = £0.04$$

  $$\text{C} \quad \frac{11 \times £20}{500} = £0.44$$

  When set-up times differ by product, or when the length of production run varies by product, or when the number of production set-ups varies by product, this refinement can be important.
- To charge indirect costs that are related to material cost (e.g. receiving, inbound inspection) to product lines based on material cost rather than labour cost.

For the product lines in question the total of indirect costs related to materials is £300,000 from the Receiving Department. The total material costs are:

A	10,000 units ×	5 components × £4 =	£200,000
B	15,000 units ×	6 components × £5 =	£450,000
C	5,000 units ×	10 components × £1 =	£50,000
			£700,000

Taking these together gives an on-cost of

$$\frac{£300,000}{£700,000} \times 100 = 43\%$$

This refinement is potentially significant when product lines differ in their raw material content.

- To substitute machine hours for labour cost (or labour hours) as the key measure of production volume. This reflects the tendency towards machine-paced manufacturing – which is highlighted by the absorption rate of 75% based on direct labour cost, showing that the latter is far from being a dominant component of cost. In fact, direct labour cost at Ajax is only 8% of total cost:

Raw material costs	£ 700,000	27%
Direct labour costs	£ 225,000	8%
Indirect costs	£1,703,000	65%
Total costs	£2,628,000	100%

This suggests it is not a primary determinant of other costs. Since machine-related costs (at 10,000 hours × £70 per hour = £700,000) are almost three times the direct labour cost it is likely that machine hours represent a better base for apportioning indirect costs.

A machine hours basis for apportioning indirect costs gives a rate of £140 per hour derived as follows:

Machines	£ 700,000
Engineering	£ 500,000
Packing	£ 200,000
Total costs	£1,400,000

$$\text{Rate} = \frac{\text{Costs}}{\text{Machine Hours}} = \frac{£1,400,000}{10,000} = £140$$

On the basis of these three refinements Figure W4.8 has been compiled to show absorbed unit cost by product line.

This can be developed a little further (see Figure W4.9) to show a product line profit report, again assuming there are no cost variances. Figure W4.9 paints a very different figure from Figure W4.7: far from offering a gross margin of 35% across all product lines the targets have now been shown to range from 55% for A to −10% for C. Product B promised only 28% but actually achieved less at 24%, so this reinforces the argument against lowering prices further.

Figure W4.8

Unit full costs — 2.

	A	B	C
Raw material	£20.00	£30.00	£10.00
Materials-related (43%)	8.60	12.90	4.30
Set-up labour	0.02	0.04	0.44
Direct labour	10.00	6.67	5.00
Other indirect costs:			
(Machine hours basis)			
¼ hour × £140	35.00		
⅓ hour × £140		46.67	
½ hour × £140			70.00
Total	£73.62	£96.28	£89.74

Figure W4.9

Product line profit report — 2.

	A	B	C
Target selling price	£162.61	£134.09	£81.31
Standard cost	73.62	96.28	89.74
Gross margin	£ 88.99	£ 37.81	£(8.43)
Target gross margin (%)	55%	28%	(10%)
Actual selling price	£162.61	£125.96	£105.70
Standard cost	73.62	96.28	89.74
Gross margin	£ 88.99	£ 29.68	£ 15.96
Actual gross margin (%)	55%	24%	15%

Product A is much more profitable than had been previously thought, but C is clearly a problem. It is surprising that C was previously thought to be profitable, when the revised target margin comes out at −10%. Even with an increase in price from £81.31 to £105.70 (i.e. a 30% increase) the demand for C has continued at budgeted volume, and there seems to be scope for increasing prices further.

Regardless of the improvements from the 'traditional' to the 'modern' approach there is still a fundamental flaw which results in the misallocation of indirect costs to product lines. We need to recognize that each category of indirect cost is caused by some activity (i.e. cost driver) and it follows that products should be charged according to the proportion of that activity which they cause. For example, the costs of production scheduling are caused by the number of production runs to be scheduled, hence these costs should be apportioned according to the number of production runs each product generates. This will mean that a product generating lots of production runs will bear a proportionate share of scheduling costs under an activity-based system, whereas it will always bear a less than proportionate share under any volume-based system. Scheduling costs are *not* a function of volume, so neither a labour hours nor a machine hours output measure is appropriate for apportioning them. The same logic applies to shipping costs and receiving costs (which are much more likely to be a function of shipping orders and receiving orders respectively).

Given the increasing proportion of indirect costs in most businesses the imperative to apportion these costs according to the transactions which generate them is increasingly difficult to ignore. This leads us to the third approach to product costing.

An activity-based approach to costing

A summary of cost-causing activities within the indirect cost areas of Ajax is shown in Figure W4.10.

The logic is essentially straightforward, even if the calculations may often be complex. For instance, receiving cost is caused by the bulk of receipts, the weight of receipts, other characteristics of receipts – such as fragility, and the number of shipments received. In other words, receiving cost is a function of receiving workload rather than, say, production volume. In Figure W4.10 this is reflected in the weights: for A, which requires five components per unit and one production run, the weight is 5 × 1 = 5; for B it is 6 × 3 = 18; and for C it is 10 × 10 = 100. (This implies a JIT inventory policy.) The total receiving cost (as given in Figure W4.4) is £300,000 which means that A generates 5 ÷ (5 + 18 + 100) × 100 = 4% of this, or £12,000, and so a unit of A should carry a cost of £(12,000 ÷ 10,000) = £1.20. Using the same approach for B and C the unit cost figures are £3.00 and £48.60 respectively.

Turning to shipping costs their cause is shipping orders, so the packing costs of £200,000 (as given in Figure W4.4) can be apportioned to produce a unit cost for A of £(200,000 ÷ 10,000) × (1 ÷(1 + 5 + 20)) = £0.80. The relevant figures for B and C are £2.53 and £30.80 respectively.

Finally, for engineering costs, the apportionment of costs will be determined by the number of engineering works orders generated by each product line. Figure W4.10 shows A to be a standard, smooth-running product line whereas C is a complex product that has special problems.

An activity-based approach to costing gives the unit costs shown in Figure W4.11.

The machine costs have been reduced from £140 per hour (Figure W4.8) to £70 per hour (as in Figures W4.4 and W4.11), due to the separate treatment of engineering and packing costs.

Figure W4.10

Indirect activities.

	A	B	C
Receiving orders	5(4%)	18(15%)	100(81%)
Packing orders	1(4%)	5(19%)	20(77%)
Engineering workload	25%	35%	40%

Figure W4.11

Unit full costs — 3.

	A	B	C
Raw material	£20.00	£30.00	£10.00
Direct labour	10.00	6.67	5.00
Set-up labour	0.02	0.04	0.44
Machine costs:			
¼ hour × £70	17.50		
⅓ hour × £70		23.33	
½ hour × £70			35.00
Receiving	1.20	3.00	48.60
Shipping	0.80	2.53	30.80
Engineering	12.50	11.67	40.00
Total	£62.02	£77.24	£169.84

Figure W4.12

Product line profit report — 3.

	A	B	C
Target selling price	£162.61	£134.09	£81.31
Standard cost	62.02	77.24	169.84
Gross margin	£100.59	£ 56.85	£(88.53)
Target gross margin (%)	62%	42%	(109%)
Actual selling price	£162.61	£125.96	£105.70
Standard cost	62.02	77.24	169.84
Gross margin	£100.59	£ 48.72	£(64.14)
Actual gross margin (%)	62%	39%	(61%)

By using the unit cost data from Figure W4.11 in a product line profit report we get Figure W4.12.

A summary of Figs. W4.7, W4.9, and W4.12 is given in Fig. W4.13, from which it is abundantly clear that both the traditional and modern approaches have over-costed products A and B, whilst dramatically undercosting product C.

It is evident that the high-volume product will be overcosted relative to the low-volume product by any system that apportions indirect costs on the basis of volume. Since many indirect costs are due to the complexity of product line variety on the one hand, and the specific requirements of low-volume items on the other, rather than by the volume of output, it follows that high-volume products in a volume-based costing system will either be overpriced or show a low apparent margin, and vice versa for low-volume products. In this situation the high-volume products are providing a hidden subsidy for the low-volume products.

The above argument suggests that a company adopting an activity-based approach in an industry where other enterprises are using a volume-based approach will be able to adopt a strategy of attacking high-volume segments with

Figure W4.13

Summary of different results.

	A	B	C
Selling price	£162.61	£125.96	£105.70
Unit cost:			
Traditional approach	£105.70	£ 87.16	£ 52.85
Modern approach	73.62	96.28	89.74
Activity-based approach	62.02	77.24	169.84
Gross margin:			
Traditional approach	£ 56.91	£ 38.80	£ 52.85
Modern approach	88.99	29.68	15.96
Activity-based approach	100.59	48.72	(64.14)
Actual gross margin (%):			
Traditional approach	35%	31%	50%
Modern approach	55%	24%	15%
Activity-based approach	62%	39%	(61%)

aggressively low prices. This is probably the explanation for the performance of B: competitors may simply have a better understanding of product costs and be unwilling to subsidize low-volume lines (such as C).

Conclusions

Some of the signs of a flawed costing system are:

- gross margins that are not as expected, and which are hard to explain (e.g. high margins on C and low margins on B under volume-based systems);
- lack of objections from customers when prices are increased (e.g. in the case of C, which is absurdly under-priced due to faulty cost information);
- products appearing to have high margins are not attacked by competitors (e.g. product C, which Ajax is selling at a price well below cost):
- overall profitability is declining even though the emphasis is moving from apparently low margin products to apparently high margin products (e.g. from B to C).

It is not possible for Ajax to develop an effective strategy to allow it to respond to its competitive problems if it continues to use flawed cost information.

Figure W4.14 shows the overall situation for Ajax under the alternative approaches.

W4.7 Illustrative material

The debate on ABC is reflected in the following short articles, reprinted with permission from *Management Accounting* (CIMA).

TESTING ABC LOGIC

J.A. Piper and P. Walley of Loughborough Management Centre question the fundamental assumption on which activity-based costing is based, i.e. that activity causes cost.

Figure W4.14

Overall summary.

	A	B	C	Total
Base case (Budget)				
Revenue	£1,626,100	£2,011,350	£ 406,550	£4,044,000
Costs:				
Material				700,000
Direct labour				225,000
Set-up labour				3,000
Machines				700,000
Receiving				300,000
Engineering				500,000
Shipping				200,000
				£2,628,000
Gross margin				£1,416,000
Traditional approach				
Revenue	£1,626,100	£1,889,400	£ 528,500	£4,044,000
Costs	1,057,000	1,307,400	264,250	2,628,000
Gross margin	£ 569,100	£ 582,000	£ 264,250	£1,416,000
	35%	31%	50%	35%
'Modern' approach				
Revenue	£1,626,100	£1,889,400	£ 528,500	£4,044,000
Costs	736,200	1,444,200	448,700	2,628,000
Gross margin	£ 889,900	£ 445,200	£ 79,800	£1,416,000
	55%	24%	15%	35%
Activity-based approach				
Revenue	£1,626,100	£1,889,400	£ 528,500	£4,044,000
Costs	620,200	1,158,600	849,200	2,628,000
Gross margin	£1,005,900	£ 730,800	£ (320,700)	£1,416,000
	62%	39%	(61%)	35%

There have been numerous articles recently in all the popular accounting publications, explaining and justifying the concept of Activity Based Costing (ABC). Many advocates of ABC have reached an almost evangelical state in their mission to establish it as the new manufacturing costing system. However, the frequency with which an argument is repeated does nothing to enhance its logic. This article suggests that these advocates have not looked critically enough at their base arguments. We question the fundamental assumption on which ABC is based i.e. that *activity causes cost,* and the logic that has been applied to arrive at that assumption.

There is now much vested interest in ABC and this justifies a more critical appraisal of the concept. A recent article by Jeans and Morrow (*Management*

Accounting, November 1989) is used as the basis of our critique. Their article is considered typical of ABC expositions.

In the introduction to their article, they make four empirical statements which would not be contentious to the majority of the journal's readers:

- 'management accounting practice has become distorted by the needs of financial reporting'
- 'direct labour has shrunk as a percentage of total cost for the majority of manufacturing companies . . .'
- 'complexity has increased . . .'
- 'the market is more competitive . . .'

Along with these readily acceptable statements go two assertions:

- 'overhead costs are no longer a mere burden to be minimised . . . (they) . . . are as important to the customer as are the physical processes on the shop floor';
- 'Quite simply, the essence of ABC is to appreciate that it is *activities which cause cost*, not products, and it is products which consume activities'.

There is not a logical link between the two assertions and the preceding empirical statements, although there is an implication that these generally acceptable empirical statements support the assertions. The first assertion is difficult to analyse into its component parts, but presumably it is about the need for elements of the overhead cost to add value to the company's offerings. This would appear to be a reasonable and acceptable assertion.

On what basis can the second assertion that activity causes cost be founded? There are competing assertions on the causality of cost, for example that decisions cause cost or that the passage of time causes cost. Alternatively one could question the validity of such a deterministic perspective that there is a clear causality of cost.

Perhaps all of these assertions about the cause of cost can be useful in different contexts, but it is dangerous to believe that only one is correct or true. It can be argued that the proposition *that decisions cause cost is superior to the argument that activity causes cost as decisions precede activity*.

If the argument was to be resolved by the application of decision logic, it would be necessary to raise the question of why one would want to know the causality of cost. In managerial terms the answer would be in terms of making decisions. In order to make decisions it is desirable that the decision-making problem is thoroughly analysed, and in performing this analysis it is likely that activity and changes in activity should be studied. And to this extent the concept of cost drivers may not useful, but the relevant costs will be the differential costs between alternative courses of action. A change in activity cannot be inferred to necessarily result in a change in differential costs.

Consider, for example, that a reduction in production volume may not result in a reduction of costs in many indirect production areas, yet there may be a reduction in activity. This straightforward example would appear to demonstrate that activity does not have a clear causal relationship with cost, yet that is what ABC is founded upon.

The proposition that ABC-based product costs are superior to more conventional product costs will now be reviewed. Jeans and Morrow use a 'straw man' argument to make their case for the superiority of ABC-based product costs.

A straw man argument consists of establishing a weak or non-viable option and then demonstrating the superiority of the proposed option to this straw man. Jeans and Morrow argue that: 'For the growing majority of companies, the traditional approach to costing simply fails to be relevant in the face of the above factors' (referring to the empirical statements made previously). It has long been established that product costs calculated using financial accounting principles, particularly the prudence, objectivity and accrual principles, produce information which is not particularly relevant for many decision-making situations. What Jeans and Morrow set out to do is propose that ABC is better than this straw man alternative which is already discredited. This is an easy task, but the superiority of ABC to viable alternatives such as the contribution approach is seldom, if ever, argued publicly.

We are told that, 'the use of multiple cost drivers attributes the resulting costs to the products and customers which cause it'. In addition we are informed that 'ABC provides *meaningful* product cost. . . .' The first argument is clear tautology, as the assertion that activities cause costs is used to justify ABC. If one does not accept the assertion the argument is a *non sequitur*.

The second argument is even more interesting, for it depends upon what *meaningful* means. One potential interpretation is that ABC produces a more accurate product cost, but that would infer moving towards a true or real product cost. However, to use an absolute truth philosophy of cost is very limiting. If meaningful means more relevant to decision-making then the case needs to be made more explicitly.

So far it has been argued that the assertion that activity causes cost is limited, and that other factors such as decisions or time are potential candidates for causality. All of this is limited from a philosophical position. John Stuart Mill (p. 142) refers to the idea that an event or outcome has one specific cause as a logical fiction that people use in everyday conversation. For example, if a person falls down a ladder and dies, what caused his death – was it the faulty ladder, his poor balance or that his heart stopped beating? As Mill points out, cause is related to a series of concomitant events. In the case of costing the concomitant events are decisions, activity, time and volume and possibly other factors. To choose one factor, as is done with ABC, is to create a logical fiction.

This last criticism should be borne in mind as the case studies used by Jeans and Morrow to support their case for ABC are now reviewed.

The evidence

SIEMENS ELECTRIC MOTOR (EMW)

In this case study the company faced competitors with a cost advantage. The management decided to respond by producing high quality customised motors resulting in smaller batch sizes. This strategy was supported with capital investment in production facilities. The costing system had not changed since the 1930s. The authors advocate ABC so that, 'In this way, motors were penalised for the overhead costs they incurred'. Did the new costing system produce better quality information in terms of decision-making? Better than what? Better than the old system or better than contribution costing?

The fundamental point is that it can be argued that it was the strategic decision that changed the cost structure not the activity which resulted from the decision.

JOHN DEERE COMPUTER WORKS

In this case study the company faced a decline in demand, the management redesigned capacity and introduced modern manufacturing methods. A new internal profit centre was created. Overhead was absorbed on a combination of direct labour cost, machine hours and material cost. The profit centre used the costing system to price their quotations. They ended up with spare capacity and tended to be successful in securing low volume orders. It was concluded that the costing system did not provide good information for pricing decisions. By using ABC and seven cost drivers they were able to arrive at suitable allocation rates. What does 'suitable' mean? Once again perhaps ABC produced better information for decision-making than previously existed, but the information was not necessarily better than other costing approaches. Once again the case does not demonstrate how activity causes cost, nor is there any evidence to suggest that the seven overhead allocation bases reflect how the costs are incurred.

TEKTRONIX PORTABLE INSTRUMENTS DIVISION

In this case study, a division of Tektronix suddenly became aware of strong overseas competition. The company management responded by changing manufacturing methods and rearranging production in an attempt to improve their competitiveness. As part of this restructuring the existing old and widely distrusted accounting system was replaced by an activity-based cost system and a new innovative set of departmental performance measures was also introduced.

The first point that must be made is that the change of the accounting system was only a small part of a major organizational change. Factors such as the plan and location, the level of investment, the management ability and culture, the climate of crisis in the organization, the replacement of older members of staff with younger MBAs and the influence of measures of performance are mentioned but they have rarely been given as much credit as ABC in regard to the improvement to the organization. This would appear to be an example of logical fiction.

The second point is that in this case there appears to be some confusion about whether the system was a behavioural accounting system, i.e. that it did not intended to model the financial dynamics of the business, instead it influenced behaviour by exaggerating certain costs and by directing attention to certain operational areas that needed improvement. Thus the statement that the system was 'accurate' (p. 44) is not demonstrated.

The cost-driver approach may be useful to direct attention to problem areas, or to assist in the analysis of problems, but the assertion that 'activity causes cost' has not been empirically established and therefore the usefulness of it for overhead absorption has to be questioned. An alternative hypothesis would be that 'decisions cause cost' and we would argue that this is a logically superior proposition although this argument also is in danger of the logical fiction.

Summary

ABC is frequently being advocated as a solution to the perceived deficiencies of traditional product costing systems. ABC is on the surface appealing and logical, but it does not stand up to close scrutiny. Whilst the cost driver concept may be useful to help analyse problems, to use the concept as a basis for overhead allocation founded upon the logic that 'activity causes costs' is not empirically or logically established.

One method used to 'prove' the superiority of ABC is to compare it to the straw man of traditional costing. Another approach is to provide examples of successful applications of ABC. However these cases do not demonstrate the logic of ABC. Perhaps ABC does provide more relevant information than traditional product costing, but does it provide more decision-relevant information than a contribution approach?□

M. JEANS and M. MORROW: 'The Practicalities of Using Activity Based Costing', *Management Accounting*, November 1989.

J.S. MILL: 'The nature of a cause', in I. Hospers' *Readings in Introductory Philosophical Analysis*. Routledge and Kegan Paul, 1977.

Management Accounting, **68**(8) September 1990, 37–42

EXPLICATING THE LOGIC OF ABC

Robin Cooper, Associate Professor of Business Administration at Harvard Business School, responds to a recent article which, he believes, draws conclusions based on several serious but commonly held misconceptions about activity-based costing and its objectives.

Piper and Walle in their September 1990 article 'Testing ABC Logic,' conclude, 'ABC is on the surface appealing and logical, but it does not stand up to close scrutiny.' P & W arrive at their conclusions based on several serious but commonly held misconceptions about ABC. These misconceptions, which indicate a lack of practical experience with ABC, centre on the primary objective of the cost information reported by cost systems.

P & W adopt a decision-relevant, short-term, spending orientation. This orientation has emerged to solve the types of problems found in textbooks by specifying the incremental costs (and revenues) related to the decision. These problems assume that the cashflow consequences of decisions are instantaneous and independent of other decisions. In the typical problem, fixed costs remain fixed and relevant costs equal unit variable cost × the change in the number of units produced. This approach, however appealing for classroom exposition, is too simplistic for most complex real world decisions.

In contrast, ABC adopts an attention focusing, longer-term, resource consumption orientation. This orientation has evolved to support decisions in environments where the number of products is large, costs are influenced by many factors other than the volume of production,[1] and decisions are not independent. In such settings, the consequence of a series of decisions taken independently can be quite different from the sum of the predicted effects of those individual decisions.

For example, the decision to drop one product will typically not change 'fixed' overhead spending. In contrast, dropping 50 products might allow considerable savings. Stated somewhat tritely, the sum of the parts (the decisions to drop individual products) is not equal to the sum of the whole (the realisable savings from having dropped 50 products). To help them make effective decisions, managers require cost systems that provide insights into the whole, not just isolated individual parts.

Cost systems designers recognize that when decisions are interdependent, it is impractical to design cost systems that report costs which are useful for individual decisions. Instead, they design cost systems to focus managerial attention. For this purpose, a reasource-consumption orientation appears to be superior to a spending one because it captures the lag between changes in resource consumption and the subsequent changes in the level of spending on resources.

For example, a resource-consumption orientation captures the drop in demand for 'fixed' overhead when a single product is dropped, even though this drop might not result in an immediate reduction in spending. The acknowledgment of a drop in resource consumption allows managers to understand the potential savings from dropping 50 products. To capture this potential, the ABC orientation recognizes the long-term cashflow consequences from decisions, not their short-term impact.

ABC system design and hence its logic reflects trade-offs between simple theoretical models and practical realities. It is appropriate for academics to use a simplistic contribution approach to demonstrate the important concept of relevant costs. It is inappropriate for them to argue without evidence that those simplistic approaches function in complex real-world settings. The simplistic approach adopted in the classroom leads to misconceptions about the real world. This article identifies and dispels six commonly held misconceptions about ABC.

Misunderstanding 1: Cost systems report decision relevant costs

P & W begin their article by discussing whether activities cause cost. They argue that the proposition *'that decisions cause cost is superior to the argument that activity causes cost as decisions precede activities'* (emphasis original). While decisions clearly precede activities, the number of decisions that can be made in a practical setting is so large that it is not possible to report decision-relevant costs economically for even a few of the potential decisions managers face. As my colleague Robert S. Kaplan is fond of pointing out, a company with only one hundred products has a potential of 2^{100} product mix decisions to evaluate. Even if each alternative could be dismissed in a second, the task of exploring each alternative would take longer than the universe has been in existence.

Recognizing this reality, the designers of ABC (or any cost system for that matter) have wisely chosen a more realistic objective, namely to help managers know where best to focus their attention. ABC focuses attention by reporting the costs of activities. This focus allows managers to ask if they can perform an activity more efficiently by changing the production process or by acquiring new technologies. Or if they can perform an activity less frequently by changing product design or customer or product mix. Furthermore, relating activities to products and customers helps managers determine if price changes are appropriate.

Misunderstanding 2: ABC cost systems predict spending

P & W illustrate a second common misconception about activity-based costing when they state, 'a change in activity cannot be inferred to necessarily result in a change in differential costs'.[2] This misconception emerges because the differential cost of a decision has typically been interpreted to measure the change in level of spending on resources; i.e. cashflow. In contrast, ABC systems measure changes in the level of consumption of resources. Put more formally, ABC is a model of resource consumption, not a model of spending.

What is the difference between these two types of models? A resource consumption model looks at the demand for activities, while a spending model looks at the capacity provided to perform those activities. The authors' simple example provides a perfect illustration of the differences between the two types of model. Their illustration goes: 'Consider for example, that a reduction in production volume may not result in a reduction of costs in many indirect production areas, yet there may be a reduction in activity'.

P & W use this straightforward example to prove that activity does not have a clear causal relationship with cost. The validity of this assertion depends on the definition of 'cost'. If cost is defined in terms of spending, then frequently no instantaneous relationship between activities and costs will be observed. In contrast, if cost is defined in terms of resource consumption, then an instantaneous relationship will be observed.

A difference arises between spending and consumption because management must take actions to bring spending in line with resource consumption. For example, the level of spending on inspection will vary with the number of inspectors. Spending levels will only reflect changes in the level of demand when management adjusts the number of inspectors to match demand.

The lag between changes in the level of spending and consumption varies depending on the resource. For some resources, changes in the level of consumption are almost immediately reflected in the level of spending. Examples of such resources include direct materials and the power required to run the production machines.[3] For other resources, the lag can be extensive. For example, this is typically the case for equipment. In P & W's example, many resources, such as direct labour, and most indirect production costs will at least temporarily shift into a position of excess capacity. The emergence of excess capacity is seen as a failure of costs (spending definition) to reflect changes in the level of activity. ABC, however, distinguishes between spending on resources that are currently being used productively and spending on resources that are currently in excess supply.

Misunderstanding 3: Traditional cost systems are a straw man

P & W now discuss the question of whether ABC product costs are 'superior' to more conventional product costs. They argue that such a comparison is irrelevant because traditional costs are a 'straw man'. As they state, 'It has long been established that product costs calculated using financial accounting principles, particularly the prudence, objectivity, and accrual principles, produce information which is not particularly relevant for decision making purposes'.

P & W apparently fail to realise that, while the inappropriateness of traditional product costs for decision-making purposes has long been known,[4] managers in companies are still using those costs as a basis for making decisions. Having observed more than 150 cost systems in the last seven years, it is clear to me that traditional costs are not a straw man. In every firm I have visited, the traditional cost systems report individual product costs. These costs help focus managers' attention and often act as a basis for decisions. If traditional product costs were a straw man, traditional cost systems would report only the total cost of goods sold and ending inventory valuations. They would not report the individual unit product costs required by those calculations.

The emergence of ABC is testimony to the importance to managers of the individual product costs reported by cost systems. As the cost structures of firms have changed and competition has become more intense, managers have become increasingly concerned about the adequacy of their cost systems. ABC has attracted attention because managers perceive it as having superior ability to focus managerial attention and thereby help them make better decisions about product and customer mix, product design, and process improvements.

Misunderstanding 4: ABC logic contains a tautology

At the core of ABC are the twin assertions that 'activities cause costs' and that 'products and customers consume activities.' To capture the economics of production or customer service typically requires the use of multiple cost drivers to attribute costs to the products and customers that cause the activities. P & W argue that ABC logic is based upon a 'clear tautology, as the assertion that activities cause costs is used to justify ABC'.

ABC systems are designed using the two-stage procedure that underlies most modern cost systems. In an ABC system, the first stage determines the cost of activities (this stage relies on the assertion that activities cause costs). The second stage determines the cost of products, customers or any other cost object for that matter (this stage relies on the assertion that products or customers consume activities). The second stage plays a totally separate role from the first stage.

P & W apparently do not understand the clearly different roles played by each stage in the two-stage resource costing procedure. The role of the second stage in reporting product costs can be illustrated using the following simple example.

A firm introduces two new products. Each requires five engineering changes. The first product's changes are very complex and take a long time to complete. The second product's changes are very simple and can be completed quickly.

If the costs of the engineering changes (EC) are assigned to the products using the basis EC hours, then the first product will have more cost traced to it than the second. In contrast, if we use the driver number of ECs, both products will have the same EC costs assigned to them. Thus the simple example demonstrates the lack of tautology. While the total reported costs of the EC activity remain unchanged, the reported costs of the products vary depending upon the choice of cost driver. ABC systems, by expanding the complexity of the second stage, provide superior cost information to their traditional counterparts.

Misunderstanding 5: Accuracy suggests truth

P & W state: 'One potential interpretation is that ABC produces more accurate product cost, but that would infer moving towards a true or real product cost'. P & W and the academic community in general discredit the concept of a true product cost because they have adopted a conditional-truth cost perspective. They ask 'how can a product have a true cost when its cost is decision-relevant?'. The ABC version of accuracy does not relate to the short-term spending consequences from long-term product commitments and decisions. Instead, ABC relates to the consumption of resources by products. The ABC perspective argues that it is theoretically possible to approximate the cost of the resources consumed in the production of a given product.

When it is possible to measure the consumption of a resource by products, the superiority of ABC over traditional cost systems can be easily demonstrated.[5] For example, in a traditional system the cost of the resources consumed in performing engineering changes (EC) will be assigned to products in proportion to the number of units produced.

This assignment procedure, dictated by traditional systems' sole reliance on bases that capture characteristics of the product unit, will report distorted product costs. A well designed ABC avoids this distortion by using a basis such as the number of ECs performed to assign EC costs to products. This basis captures a characteristic of the product, not the product unit. Consequently, it does not assign costs in proportion to the number of units produced but rather in proportion to the number of ECs the product consumes. ABC systems by adopting a resource consumption orientation avoid the conditional-truth perspective engendered by a spending orientation.

Misunderstanding 6: ABC contains a logical fiction

According to P & W, 'In the case of costing, the concomitant events are decisions, activity, time, and volume and possibly other factors. To choose one factor, as is done with ABC (i.e. activities cause costs) is to create a logical fiction'. This observation draws on the work of the philosopher John Stuart Mill. Mill pointed out that the idea that an event or outcome has one specific cause is a logical fiction that people use in everyday conversation. In reality, as Mill points out, causes are related to a series of concomitant events.

If ABC were a decision tool, P & W's perspective would identify a serious flaw in ABC logic. But as an attention-focussing device, no such flaw in the logic exists. The message that ABC sends (e.g. this is a very unprofitable product – take a closer look to see what you can do about it) acknowledges that causality is due to a series of concomitant events. Thus ABC instead of trying to select a single cause such as a decision, leaves it to the manager to identify causality, a philosophically more appealing perspective.

Summary

Towards the end of their article, P & W state, 'The cost driver approach may be useful to direct attention to problem areas or to assist the analysis of problems, but the assertion that activities cause cost has not been empirically established and therefore the usefulness of it for overhead absorption has to be questioned'. The assertion that activities cause cost is not an empirically testable statement. It is the theoretical construct used to design activity based cost systems. The 'usefulness' of the construct for overhead absorption is an empirically testable assertion that is evidenced (but not proven) by the three case studies discussed by P & W. The ultimate empirical test for ABC logic lies is how many firms adopt it and derive benefits from so doing. To date, the favourable evidence is accumulating rapidly.

There is no flaw in the logic of ABC. It is based on two important premises: first, ABC is a model of resource consumption, not spending and, second, ABC systems are designed to focus managerial attention not to provide decision relevant costs. The Harvard Business School cases on ABC systems and the work of practitioners such as Jeans and Morrow (on whose article P & W base their critique),[6] provide a significant body of empirical support for the usefulness of the assertion that activities cause costs as the basis for the design of cost systems. The answer to P & W's last question, 'does ABC provide more decision-relevant information than a contribution approach?' is moot until they can provide an equivalent amount of empirical support for the practical value of their contribution approach. □

1 See Cooper: 'Cost classification in unit-based and activity-based manufacturing cost systems', *Journal of Cost Management in the Manufacturing Industry*, Fall.
2 As far as I can tell, P & W use the terms relevant costs, differential costs, and contribution interchangeably.
3 The observation that, for material, consumption and spending levels automatically match is embedded in the theory of throughput accounting. See Waldron and Galloway: 'Throughput accounting', *Management Accounting*, November 1988 – February 1989.
4 The inherent flaws in traditional product costs are documented in *Relevance Lost*, Johnson and Kaplan, Harvard Business School Press, 1987.
5 It is not always possible to observe a relationship between the consumption of resources and the manufacture of products. For example, the cause of machine breakdowns can rarely be identified with products.
6 Jeans and Morrow: 'The practicalities of using activity-based costing', *Management Accounting*, November 1989.

Management Accounting, **68**(10) November 1990, 58–60

ABC relevance not found

J.A. Piper and P. Walley respond to Professor Cooper's recent criticism of their September article and remain unconvinced . . .

Professor Cooper in his November 1990 article, 'Explicating ABC logic' criticises our article 'Testing ABC logic' (September 1990 which questioned the logical basis of ABC and the case for its application which was made in an article by Jeans and Morrow, 'The practicalities of using activity-based costing' (November 1989). Cooper's article provides explication of the ABC model, but our position remains that ABC is logically flawed and the case for its application is both questionable and unproven.

Jeans and Morrow advocated ABC as a 'more accurate' approach to product costing and thereby a better costing system. In our September 1990 article we disputed the logic that they used and the benefits of using ABC. They also attempted to justify the benefits of ABC by the use of several case examples. We argued that these cases did not prove or even demonstrate the benefits of ABC, as there were many other changes taking place in the case companies.

In his November article, Cooper, besides defending ABC, also attacks our preferred decision-relevant approach and its pedigree, and accuses us, and by inference others, of several misconceptions about the rationale and logic of ABC. In this article we argue that we do not have the misconceptions he infers and continue the critique of ABC.

Before continuing the debate on the logic and desirability of ABC we will deal with Cooper's attack on a decision-relevant approach. In addition to his attack Cooper weakens his case by attacking ourselves and our experience, which he under-estimates, instead of concentrating on arguing the issues concerning ABC.

The decision-relevant approach

Cooper attacks both the decision-relevant approach and its proponents:

- We, as advocates of a decision-relevant approach, are accused of a simplistic, textbook approach. Certainly, the decision-relevant approach is extolled in textbooks, but so is ABC and other more conventional absorption approaches. One might also criticise ABC as a simplistic approach since it treats the relationship between activity and resource consumption as being linear, absolute and certain
- Cooper asserts that our preference for a 'conditional truth' rather than an absolute truth philosophy' is simplistic. On economic grounds, conditional truth is defensible. The absolute-truth approach when applied to product costing, whether ABC or not, requires the subjective classification of costs as revenue or capital, product or period, direct or indirect, the selection of absorption criteria, the criteria for cost allocation and a volume assumption. All of these subjective judgments combined produce a complicated product costing system, but not necessarily an accurate or useful one. Conditional truth claims relevance not accuracy.

The time assumption — a misconception

Cooper wrongly assumes that we use a short-term planning horizon, since we wish to adopt a decision-relevant approach. This is not the case; we do not propose a short-term orientation. A decision-relevant approach adopts whichever planning horizon the decision-maker considers appropriate for a given situation. A long-term planning horizon may mean less precision in forecasting, radical changes internally or in the environment, and that the time value of money would all be included in the analysis, if appropriate. In contrast, the ABC approach uses a small sample of historical information and simply extrapolates this to a long-term situation. This is a serious deficiency of ABC, especially in a rapidly changing environment.

Cooper also assumes that a decision-relevant approach is the same as a contribution approach; this is not the case. The current interest in strategic financial management (SFM)[1] and shareholder value analysis (SVA)[2] are both examples of using a long-term decision-relevant approach. Therefore Cooper's claim that ABC takes a long-term perspective, and a decision-relevant approach does not, is ill-founded, not logically argued and the contrary may be the case.

The role of activity

We clearly agree that the analysis of activity is important. What we cannot agree is that it is necessary to attribute a very arbitrary cost to it. The analysis of activity is concerned with that activity which can be avoided or which does not add adequate value. The decision-relevant approach clearly addresses the value issue, because it takes account of the differential cashflow including both inflows and outflows.

The analysis of management activity has a long pedigree, at least back to Fredrick Taylor, and has a contemporary focus within the just-in-time and total-quality philosophy, but neither of these approaches requires the apportionment of an arbitrary cost for the consumption of activity. We would be curious to know whether Japanese management would use ABC costing. There is evidence that they use labour-based overhead absorption systems as a behavioural costing system which encourages operational staff to reduce costs by reducing the labour element. This does not require an 'accurate' cost but an information system which motivates employees to reduce unnecessary activity.[3]

What do and should cost systems report?

ABC is an absorption costing system and as we have previously argued suffers from the inherent deficiencies of the absorption costing model. These deficiencies basically have two sources — the underlying model of absorption and the quality of the information provided.

As already stated, absorption costing systems are built on a series of subjective and dubious cost allocations, a choice of absorption base and volume assumptions. ABC deals with only one of these elements, the choice of absorption base. The other limitations remain, i.e. the distribution between revenue and capital, product and period costs, direct and indirect costs, etc. With such an arbitrary series of classifications and multiple time horizons how can Cooper assert that: 'ABC focuses attention by reporting *the* cost of activities' (our emphasis)?

ABC reports a cost of an activity; whether this cost is useful depends on whether it provides useful information, whether for attention-directing, scorekeeping or problem solving.

Our further critique of absorption costing and thereby ABC is that it does not provide useful information. Cooper states that: 'Relating activities to products and customers helps managers determine if price changes are appropriate'.

We would contend that in the majority of cases, especially as markets increase in sophistication, and with the increasing application of marketing and competitive strategies, the linkage between price and cost is far too complex to capture by means of an absorption costing system, ABC or otherwise. As regards cost control and reduction, just-in-time and total-quality philosophies are concerned with the reduction of waste in all its forms, but whilst both of these emphasize activity they do not require the computation of a cost for an activity, especially an arbitrary cost. They are concerned with actions which add value.

Resource consumption versus cashflow

In his article Cooper also appears to be making the case that ABC is different to other absorption costing systems because it is a system concerned with resource consumption, and the cost of the consumption of resources. We have already stated that it is concerned with *a* cost not *the* cost. Cooper refers to the decision-relevant approach as a 'spending' approach; we prefer to call it a cashflow approach.

Cooper states: 'If cost is defined in terms of spending, then frequently no instantaneous relationship between activities and costs will be observed. In contrast, if cost is defined in terms of resource consumption, then an instantaneous relationship will be observed'. This assertion is based upon a tautology; if cost is defined and calculated in relation to activity then of course a change in activity will cause a change in the computed cost!

Cooper argues that there is a relationship between consumption and cashflow, but that this is lagged and differs depending on the type of resource. Our concern is that ABC assumes that changes in resource usage will result, in due course, in a change in cashflow. Cashflow is fundamentally important to organizations and the decision-relevant approach emphasises the prediction of future cashflows and the monitoring of cashflows, thereby reviewing previous decisions.

The decision-relevant cashflow approach can be used for all of the fundamental management control tasks of forecasting, deciding, monitoring and accountability. Cooper argues that ABC is solely for attention-directing. This is a major limitation, especially when the attention directing is based on a spurious cost of an activity.

Traditional costing system — a straw man?

Cooper appears to misunderstand the point we were making in our article when we suggested that traditional cost systems are used as a 'straw man' aganst which ABC can be justified. We agree totally with him that management are using traditional product costs and that this practice does not produce high-quality decision-relevant information. The arguments for this are well documented and we agree with these sentiments. Our concern is that management make the mistake that Cooper wrongly accuses us of making, i.e. they treat ABC-based product costs as a realistic and accurate measurement of organization cashflow behaviour, in whichever time horizon the user chooses.

Our experience has been that management do not always make the distinction between changes in product costs and organizational cashflow. Our 'straw man' analogy was used to highlight the selling techniques used by ABC advocates and thereby reveal the limitations of what is being said.

The contribution approach which is based on the conditional-truth cashflow philosophy is often perceived as a product-costing system. The contribution per unit is a representation of the incremental or decremental cashflow behaviour of the organization. The costs which are not directly or linearly related to volume changes do behave in a complex way and need to be understood and controlled by management. This can be achieved by understanding what adds cost and value to an organization within a given time assumption, but this can be achieved without a subjective and spurious model of product costing that has an unknown and tenuous relationship to cashflow behaviour, includes irrelevant past cost and ignores opportunity costs.

ABC and other conventional product-costing systems should be compared to a decision-relevant cashflow approach and not other product-costing systems. Only then are two fundamentally different approaches being considered.

ABC contains a tautology

In his refutation of our argument that ABC contains the tautology that activities cause costs and that products and customers cause activities, and thereby links activity to product costs, he provides an interesting simple example: 'A firm introduces two new products. Each requires five engineering changes. The first product's changes are very complex and take a long time to complete. The second product's changes are very simple and can be completed quickly'.

Cooper refers to the two-stage procedure of computing a cost for a product, the first stage involving the calculation of the cost for the activities and then the second stage of absorbing these costs to the products or customers. We have already referred to the limitations and arbitrary assumptions of computing a cost for an activity, thereby producing a dubious base for the second stage. Referring to the above example Cooper notes that if engineering changes are used as the absorption basis then both products receive the same cost, whereas if the time taken for engineering changes is used the first product absorbs more cost. So, clearly, ABC costs vary significantly according to the choice of 'drivers'. Our point remains that product costs will reflect whatever definition(s) of activity is used to absorb the costs because activity has been assumed to cause cost.

Cooper concludes his argument by stating: 'ABC systems by expanding the complexity of the second stage, provide *superior* cost information to their traditional counterparts' (our emphasis). We assume 'superior' means 'more accurate' – or does it mean more useful? If so, once again this is defined in relation to the 'straw man' of 'their traditional counterparts'.

The value of ABC?

Cooper asserts: 'The ultimate empirical test for ABC logic lies in how many firms adopt it and derive benefit from so doing'. This assertion has two elements – the adoption of ABC and the benefit derived. As regards adoption we would make the following points:

(a) Some very large and powerful consulting organizations have devoted substantial resources into the promotion of ABC; we would therefore expect an increase in adoption. It will be interesting to see the retention rate that occurs with ABC. Is testing the approach also being defined as adoption? Our experience is that firms are experimenting with the approach, but have not yet decided whether to adopt it.
(b) There may be other benefits from the adoption of ABC than attention-directing or decision-making, for example the justification of prices by companies, especially those involved in defence contracting. We should therefore observe the types of organization that adopt ABC. With regard to the benefits of ABC, Bromwich and Bhimani[4] in a recent CIMA report stated, 'there is no real evidence that . . . profitability can be increased if this new technique is used in firms'. The same report also questions the validity of the case examples in ABC implementation. We repeat our assertion that ABC is only one of a number of factors which *may* have resulted in the performance improvement in these instances. Were Cooper to show that companies which adopt ABC are more profitable in the long term than companies which adopt alternative decision relevant approaches, otherwise we will remain unconvinced.

ABC and the level of decision making

A major concern about the use of ABC is the decision level at which it is being used, operational or strategic. Whilst ABC may be used at an operational level to highlight to managers the need to pay attention to activity alongside other factors, it is sometimes used by proponents to justify major strategic decisions, such as the deletion of tails in product ranges. It is at the strategic level where the cashflow approach is most appropriate because it take account of cashflow both into and out of the organization, thereby forcing management to consider the organization's relationship with its environment; it also forces the management to be explicit about their time horizon, a critical strategic factor. ABC cannot be linked to SFM or SVA because they are based on fundamentally different cost philosophies.

Our position is that ABC is inappropriate at the strategic level, and that at the operational level management can be motivated by physical measures, e.g. delivery speed, delivery reliability, number of engineering changes etc, without a dubious cost being ascribed to them, or if a cost is ascribed its behavioural and operational role is clearly delineated.

In conclusion

We remain unconvinced of the basis for the internal logic of ABC and, more importantly, the extent to which, over either a short or long timescale, it provides useful information for management decision-making. The underlying reason is that there is no evidence that it in any way models actual or potential organizations cashflows, and that it is changes in these cashflows which are ultimately of interest to corporate management.

Not only is the underlying philosophy of ABC unconvincing, the empirical justification is also spurious. The fact that some organizations are using ABC does not necessarily mean that they will achieve superior profits by so doing. In our previous paper (September 1990) we made this point in relation to several case studies that supposedly prove the benefits of ABC. The advocacy of ABC has had, most likely, millions of pounds put behind it by some well established consultants and practitioners. So have PPBS, ZBB, DCF etc. Is ABC an in vogue management technique or is it a profound development in our understanding of cost behaviour? We strongly suspect the former. Analysis of activity is clearly a worthwhile activity, but ABC may not be. □

1 ALLEN, D.: *Strategic Financial Management*. Financial Times Business Information, 1988.
2 RAPPAPORT, A.: *Creating Shareholder Value*. The Free Press, 1986.
3 HIROMOTO, T.: 'Another Hidden Edge – Japanese Management Accounting', *Harvard Business Review*, July–August 1988, pp. 22–26.
4 BROMWICH, M. and BHIMANI, A.: *Management Accounting – Evolution not revolution*. CIMA, 1989.

Management Accounting, **69**(3) March 1991, pp. 42, 44, 54

CHAPTER

5 Short-run decision-making

WORKBOOK

W5.1 Introduction

While Chapter 4 emphasized an approach that helped in raising questions, Chapter 5 has decision-making (i.e. the generating of answers) as its theme. Our interest is limited to the short-run (but this will be extended to the long-run in Chapter 6).

W5.2 Revision topics

Question 5.1
Are direct costs necessarily variable costs?

Answer
The answer is no: direct costs may be fixed, mixed or variable.

In Chapter 4 the key characteristic of a direct cost was identified: this is traceability to a given cost object. In contrast, a variable cost is one that responds to changes in the level of activity (however defined). You will see, therefore, that these categories are not identical. If the cost object is an academic department, the salaries of staff will be both direct *and* fixed costs, whereas the cost of handouts for that department's courses will be direct *and* variable (i.e. a function of the number of courses and of the number of students). On the other hand, the salary of the head of the academic institution will be fixed and indirect relative to the cost object stated above, while the cost of stationery for the administration's computer will be variable and indirect.

Question 5.2
Prepare profit reports relating to each of the following situations using a contribution approach:

Case	Sales revenue £	Variable costs as % of sales revenue	Fixed costs £
1	300,000	60	80,000
2	700,000	55	220,000
3	50,000	30	41,000
4	100,000	75	22,000

Answer

Starting from the basic equation we have SR = VC + FC + P which can be rearranged thus:

$$(SR - VC) - FC = P$$

Now (SR − VC) is the *contribution* which, in percentage terms, can be calculated from the given data:

Case	Contribution (%)
1	(100 − 60) = 40
2	(100 − 55) = 45
3	(100 − 30) = 70
4	(100 − 75) = 25

From this we can readily compute the profit outcomes from each case:

Case	(SR × Contribution) − FC = Profit
1	(300,000 × 0.40) − 80,000 = £40,000
2	(700,000 × 0.45) − 220,000 = £95,000
3	(50,000 × 0.70) − 41,000 = (£6,000)
4	(100,000 × 0.25) − 22,000 = £3,000

Question 5.3

(a) What distinguishes full costs from differential costs?
(b) Are full costs more useful for decision-making than differential costs?

Answer

(a) Their purpose differs, so this is a major distinction: full cost data aims to help in raising questions whereas differential cost data helps in producing answers. Full cost is an approximation to an unknown (and unknowable) figure made up of direct plus apportioned indirect costs. This classification of costs requires the specification of a cost object, but it fails to reflect the behaviour of those costs as the level of activity varies – or if an activity is terminated or newly begun. For this purpose one needs the differential definition which refers to future costs that differ between one course of action and another.
(b) Since their purposes differ it is not helpful to condemn one or the other. Their roles are complementary but not substitutional.

Question 5.4

From a decision-making point of view, what is the distinction between the short-run and the long-run?

Answer

In essence this is given by the *scale* of an enterprise, which has capacity (hence fixed cost) connotations. The short-run is that period during which the scale of the enterprise (e.g. its productive capacity) is essentially given. Some scope will exist to increase output from a given scale by working overtime, putting on additional shifts, introducing productivity bonus schemes, streamlining work-flow or improving administration, but the physical plant, etc., will remain unchanged.

W5.3 Discussion topics

Question 5.1
Define what is meant by the term 'opportunity cost' and give some illustrations from your own experience.

Question 5.2
Explain the relationship between the scarcity of resources and the difficulty of decision-making.

Question 5.3
What is meant by the 'relevant range' in the context of decision-making? Why is this significant?

Question 5.4
Contrast the behaviour patterns of fixed and variable costs. In what circumstances are fixed costs variable and variable costs fixed?

Question 5.5
Specify the concept of cost that is most useful in a decision-making context. What are its key characteristics?

Question 5.6
How many alternative 'views of the future' can you propose? In what ways do they differ?

Question 5.7
Are sunk costs ever relevant to decision-making?

Question 5.8
Distinguish between absorption costing and variable costing, indicating the benefits and drawbacks of each.

W5.4 Worked examples

Question 5.1
You are Derek Drive, manager responsible for motor transport at Aberdeen Airport. The Airport Director has asked for guidance on a number of points based on the cost information provided in Fig. W5.1 below.

(a) There are five cars under your control. What are their total annual costs assuming that the annual mileage is 75,000 (15,000 miles for each car)?
(b) If one of the cars under your control was driven 10,000 miles per year, what would be its average unit cost per mile? And if it was driven 20,000 miles per year?
(c) If one of your cars was used to take a manager from Aberdeen and a manager from Edinburgh on a 200 mile business trip, with your Edinburgh colleague agreeing to share the costs of the journey, how much should he pay?
(d) You receive a request from Glasgow Airport to provide a car and driver for 3 months. The car is expected to travel 2,500 miles during that period. The driver's employment costs for the period are estimated at £3,000. The motor transport manager at Glasgow offers you £1,500 as a hire charge to cover

Figure W5.1

Car running costs.

Assume the following are the costs of running a car for 15,000 miles a year:

	£
Petrol: 750 gallons at £2.00	1,500
Oil changes: 6 at £10	60
Tyre wear (based on life of 20,000 miles; a new set of 4 costs £160)	120
Regular maintenance and repair	330
Insurance	250
RAC subscription	25
Road fund	100
Garage rent	300
Depreciation (£8,000 ÷ 4 year life)	2,000
Interest on capital	500
Total	£5,185

employment, standing and running costs. Is it adequate? How much should Derek seek to negotiate?

(e) It has been suggested that you might consider doubling the number of cars that are available, even though the total annual mileage will remain at 75,000. What will be the additional annual costs of this course of action? What will be the average cost per mile of the enlarged fleet?

(f) A well known car leasing company offers you £25,000 for the 5 cars on a sale and leaseback arrangement. The leasing charge would be £250 per month for each car (to include insurance, road fund, and RAC subscription). In addition, your department would incur the running costs based on 15,000 miles p.a. for each car. The written down value of the car fleet is £30,000. Taxation considerations should be ignored. Should Derek accept the offer?

Answer

(a) The total annual cost of running one car is £5,185.
For five vehicles the cost is £5,185 × 5 = £25,925.

(b) The first step is to consider the behaviour patterns of the costs involved. We can classify costs in the following way:

Variable:	*Fixed*:
Petrol	Interest
Oil	Insurance
Maintenance	Road fund
Tyres	Depreciation
	Garage rent
	RAC subscription

From this base we can calculate the average cost per mile for any given annual mileage. Thus, as Fig. W5.2 shows, the total annual cost of running one car

Figure W5.2

Cost behaviour patterns (1).

	10,000 miles p.a.		15,000 miles p.a.		20,000 miles p.a.	
		£		£		£
Petrol	500 gal at £2.00	1,000	750 gal at £2.00	1,500	1,000 gal at £2.00	2,000
Oil	4 at £10.00	40	6 at £10.00	60	8 at £10.00	80
Maintenance		220		330		440
Tyre wear		80		120		160
Total variable costs		£1,340		£2,010		£2,680
Variable cost per mile		13.4p		13.4p		13.4p
Interest		500		500		500
Insurance		250		250		250
Road fund		100		100		100
Depreciation		2,000		2,000		2,000
Garage rent		300		300		300
RAC subscription		25		25		25
Total fixed costs		£3,175		£3,175		£3,175
Total costs p.a.		£4,515		£5,185		£5,855
Average cost per mile		45.1p		34.6p		29.3p

Figure W5.3

Cost behaviour patterns (2).

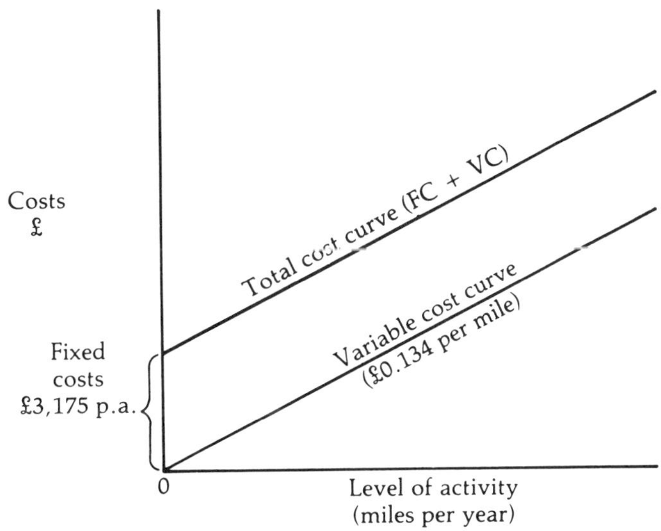

is [£3,175 + (annual mileage × £0.134)]. The higher the annual mileage, therefore, the lower is the average cost per mile since the fixed costs are being spread over a larger level of activity.

These details can be expressed in algebraic terms:

$$TC = FC + VC$$

and also graphically, as in Fig. W5.3.

This gives a basis for calculating the average cost per mile over a year, which is 45.2p when the annual mileage is 10,000 and 29.3p when the mileage is 20,000. In fact, the variable cost per mile is 13.4p which is the same irrespective of annual mileage. In total the fixed costs are the same (£3,175), but their impact on average unit cost depends upon the annual mileage.

(c) The decision concerning the amount a colleague should pay for a 200 mile journey is not as straightforward as it might initially appear. As a *minimum* it might reasonably be set at 50% of the variable costs: (200 × 13.4p)/2 = £13.40, or even as low as 50% of the petrol costs: $\frac{1}{2}$[(£1,500/15,000) × 200] = £10.00. On the other hand, unless the fixed costs are incurred it is impossible to use the car, so a portion of these costs might reasonably be included. As a *maximum* the figure would be:

$$\frac{\left(\frac{200}{15{,}000} \times £3{,}175\right) + (200 \times £0.134)}{2} = £34.53$$

This gives a range from £10.00 to £34.53 within which a choice must be made. If the trip would be undertaken with or without the colleague it may be appropriate to go for the lower end of the range; but if it is being made at his instigation, perhaps the contribution should be towards the upper end.

If the Edinburgh colleague was willing to pay, say, 20p per mile towards the cost of the trip, it is apparent that this more than covers the variable costs and makes a contribution of (20p − 13.4p) = 6.6p per mile towards the car's fixed costs. Should sufficient miles be paid for on this basis over a year the picture given in Fig. W5.4 might emerge. The shaded area shows the contribution (i.e. SR − VC) at different levels of activity, and the hatched area shows the losses that will be incurred (due to SR < TC). Break-even would be achieved when £3,175/£(0.20 − 0.134) = 48,106 miles p.a. were paid for.

(d) The costs to be borne by Aberdeen during the three month hire period are:

	£
Employment costs of driver	3,000.00
Standing costs of car (1/4 × £3,175)	793.75
Running costs 2,500 miles at 13.4p	335.00
	£4,128.75

Some managers would argue that the hire charge to Glasgow should be at least £4,128.75 to ensure that *all* the costs of the car are covered during the 3 month period. They would also argue that a profit element should be included (of say, 25% on cost) to give a hire charge of £5,160.

Figure W5.4

Cost and revenue aspects.

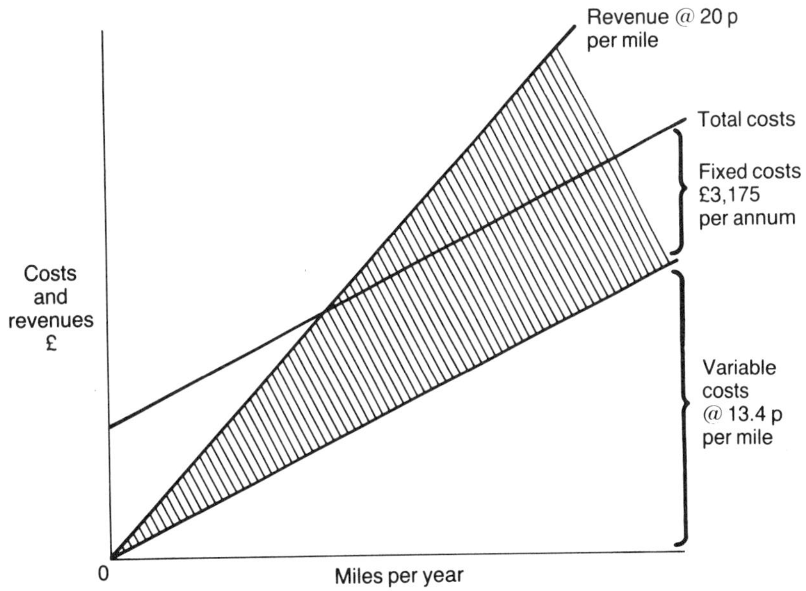

However, the economic point of view needs to be considered. The employment costs of the driver and the standing costs of the car may remain regardless of whether the car is hired to Glasgow. Therefore, from the short-term (3 month) point of view, the objective should be to ensure that at least the variable costs of the car are covered since these are the differential costs which are *relevant* in this situation. If a hire charge of, say, £2,000 is finally agreed with Glasgow, then the economic and financial situation will be as follows:

	£
Hire charge	2,000
Less Running costs	335
Balance towards standing charges and employment charges	£1,665

On this economic analysis, the hire charge to be negotiated will be at least £1,500 (since this is Glasgow's *initial* offer) but it need not be as high as £4,129. This is subject to considerations of *opportunity cost*. For example:

(i) Can the car be hired elsewhere for a charge higher than Glasgow are prepared to pay?
(ii) Is the car surplus to requirements at Aberdeen? (In other words would it be idle if not hired out?) Clearly, it would be a mistake to hire the car to Glasgow if it was required for use at Aberdeen!

(e) We can see from the tables in the answer to part (b) above that variable costs are *not* relevant to this question. Annual running costs for any number of cars which, in total, travel 75,000 miles will be:

75,000 × 13.4p = £10,050

However, for every car there will be fixed costs of £3,175.
In summary, therefore, we have:

	5 cars	10 cars	Differential
Annual mileage	75,000	75,000	0
Fixed costs	£15,875	£31,750	£15,875
Variable costs	£10,050	£10,050	0
Total costs	£25,925	£41,800	£15,875
Average cost per mile	34.6p	55.7p	21.2p

All the additional costs are fixed costs, totalling (£31,750 – £15,875) = £15,875, and this causes a much higher average cost per mile of (34.6p + 21.2p) = 55.7p.

(f) (i) If leasing arrangements proceed the annual costs will be:

	£	£
Car rental: 5 cars at £3,000 per year		15,000
Car running costs:		
5 cars at £2,010	10,050	
Garage rent: 5 at £300	1,500	11,550
		26,550
Less Interest at, say, 8% net of tax on the cash proceeds of £25,000		(2,000)
Net annual cost		£24,550

(ii) If the leasing arrangement does *not* proceed the annual costs will be:

	£
5 cars at total annual cost of £5,185	£25,925

Accountants would argue that a loss on the disposal of the car fleet of £5,000 would arise (£30,000 written down value of the five cars less the proceeds from sale of £25,000). Notwithstanding this loss on disposal the leasing option is the (marginally) more cost-effective. However, some thought must be given to cash flow considerations and the replacement policy concerning company cars.

Question 5.2

The profit and loss account for Delaney's Department Store's most recent operating period is shown below. The approach adopted is one that shows departmental performance on a full cost basis.

		Department 1		Department 2		Department 3		Total
	£	£	£	£	£	£	£	£
Sales revenue		200,000		300,000		500,000		1,000,000
Cost of sales		100,000		250,000		450,000		800,000
Gross profit		100,000		50,000		50,000		200,000
Expenses:								
Selling	10,000		15,000		25,000		50,000	
Administration	12,000	22,000	18,000	33,000	30,000	55,000	60,000	110,000
Net profit/loss		£78,000		£17,000		£(5,000)		£90,000

Administrative expenses, which represent the only fixed cost, have been assigned to departments on the basis of their relative sales volumes.

Required:
A reasoned recommendation as to whether or not Department 3 should be closed.

Answer
The fixed administration costs, and their apportionment, give the focus of this exercise. In the short-run these costs will not change, so they are unavoidable and any full cost computation will provide an unsatisfactory basis for making a rational decision concerning the future of Department 3.

We can reallocate administration costs to Departments 1 and 2 (as below) using the same basis as specified in the question:

		Department 1		Department 2		Total
	£	£	£	£	£	£
Sales revenue		200,000		300,000		500,000
Cost of sales		100,000		250,000		350,000
Gross profit		100,000		50,000		150,000
Expenses:						
Selling	10,000		15,000		25,000	
Administration	24,000	34.000	36,000	51.000	60,000	85,000
Net profit/loss		£66,000		£(1,000)		£65,000

This shows that the overall profit (both gross and net) falls if Department 3 is closed, but it also suggests that Department 2 is unprofitable. The reason, of course, is the arbitrary reallocation of fixed costs.

A contribution approach avoids the ambiguity and confusion that full cost data can create when decisions need to be made. The following statement offers a clear-cut view of the relative profit performance of all three departments:

		Department 1		Department 2		Department 3		Total
	£	£	£	£	£	£	£	£
Sales revenue		200,000		300,000		500,000		1,000,000
Variable costs:								
Cost of sales	100,000		250,000		450,000		800,000	
Selling expenses	10,000	110,000	15,000	265,000	25,000	475,000	50,000	850,000
Contribution		90,000		35,000		25,000		150,000
Fixed costs:								
Administration expenses								60,000
Net profit								£90,000

From this we can see that each department makes a positive contribution, and this is the amount by which overall profit would be reduced if a department was closed. Thus, in the case of Department 3:

Overall profit *with* Department 3 =	£90,000
Overall profit *without* Department 3 =	£65,000
Reduction in profit	£25,000

This figure of £25,000 is the contribution made by Department 3, so it should not be closed down on the basis of the data given in the question. On the other hand, if a better use for the space was put forward this might favour an alternative course of action.

Question 5.3

The Wing Manufacturing Corporation produces a chemical compound, product X, which deteriorates and must be discarded if it is not sold by the end of the month during which it is produced. The total variable cost of the manufactured compound, product X, is £50 per unit, and its selling price is £80 per unit. Wing can purchase the same compound from a competing company at £80 per unit plus £10 freight per unit. Management has estimated that failure to fill orders would result in the loss of 80% of customers placing orders for the compound. Wing has manufactured and sold product X for the past 20 months. Demand for the product has been irregular, and at present there is no consistent sales trend. During this period monthly sales have been as follows:

Units sold per month	Number of months
8,000	5
9,000	12
10,000	3

Required:

(i) Compute the probability of sales of product X of 8,000, 9,000 or 10,000 units in any month.

(ii) Compute what the contribution margin would be if 9,000 units of product X were ordered and either 8,000, 9,000 or 10,000 units were manufactured in that same month (with additional units, if necessary, being purchased).

(iii) Compute the average monthly contribution margin that Wing can expect if 9,000 units of product X are manufactured every month and all sales orders are filled.

(AICPA adapted)

Answer

(i) The probability of sales being at any of the specified levels in a given month can be determined from the frequencies given in the question:

Units (1)	Frequency (2)	Probability (3)	Expected value (1) × (3) = (4)
8,000	5/20	0.25	2,000
9,000	12/20	0.60	5,400
10,000	3/20	0.15	1,500
			8,900

Thus sales of 8,000 units occurred in 5 out of the 20 months, giving a probability of 1 in 4 or 0.25, and so on for the other levels of sales. From these we can compute *expected values*, with 8,900 units being the best sales estimate for any month.

(ii) If 9,000 units are ordered at £80 per unit the sales revenue will be £720,000. In order to calculate the contribution we need to know the variable costs, which are as follows:

Case 1	Manufactured:	8,000 at £50 =	£400,000
	Bought out:	1,000 at £90 =	£90,000
			£490,000
Case 2	Manufactured:	9,000 at £50 =	£450,000
Case 3	Manufactured:	10,000 at £50 =	£500,000

The contributions are:

Case 1	£720,000 − £490,000 =	£230,000
Case 2	£720,000 − £450,000 =	£270,000
Case 3	£720,000 − £500,000 =	£220,000

This highlights the costs of inaccurate forecasting: the underestimate of 8,000 units (Case 1) has a cost associated with it of (9,000 − 8,000) × (£90 − £50) = £40,000, while the overestimate of 10,000 units (Case 3) has a penalty cost of 1,000 × £50 = £50,000.

(iii) The average monthly contribution can be calculated by relating the various levels of demand, at a given price per unit, to the relevant costs, and weighting the outcomes by their probability of occurrence. Thus:

Case 1: Demand = 8,000 units

Sales revenue	8,000 × £80	=	£640,000	
Variable costs	9,000 × £50	=	£450,000	
Contribution			£190,000	
Probability			0.25	
Expected value				£47,500

Case 2: Demand = 9,000 units

Sales revenue	9,000 × £80	=	£720,000	
Variable costs	9,000 × £50	=	£450,000	
Contribution			£270,000	
Probability			0.60	
Expected value				£162,000

Case 3: Demand = 10,000 units

Sales revenue	10,000 × £80	=	£800,000	
Variable costs	9,000 × £50 1,000 × £90	=	£540,000	
Contribution			£260,000	
Probability			0.15	
Expected value				£39,000
Average monthly contribution				£248,500

Question 5.4

The Modern Manufacturing Company currently manufacturers Part 601K in the Precision Machinery Department for assembly into one of its major products. Management has for some time been considering closing down the parts-making operation, which is the only activity of the Precision Machinery Department, and purchasing the parts from an outside supplier.

After some careful scrutiny of the prices charged by available suppliers, Watson Tool Company was selected as a prospective source. The company is able to supply all the parts required – a rate of 6,000 a year at present – for £120,000 per year.

The Chairman compared Watson's figure with the cost figures prepared by the accountant for the manufacture of 6,000 such parts over a period of one year, which were as follows:

	£
Direct materials	56,000
Direct labour	40,000
Departmental manager's salary	3,000
Indirect labour	6,400
Rent	6,800

	£
Depreciation of machinery (straight-line basis)	12,000
Maintenance of machinery	2,880
Power, light and heat	12,600
Share of general administrative overhead	15,000
	£154,680

The Chairman's immediate reaction was that the Precision Machinery Department should be closed down and negotiations be completed with Watson's. He wished, however, to discuss the proposal with the departmental manager before action was taken. The manager of the Precision Machinery Department was informed that his position was not in jeopardy since another managerial position would soon be available at equal pay and opportunity should his department be closed. This offer involved the creation of a new post which appeared to be simply an excuse not to make him redundant.

A few days later the following conversation occurred:

DEPARTMENTAL MANAGER: What will become of the machinery? It cost £96,000 five years ago, but probably would only fetch £16,000 on the market now, even though it's good for another three years. Also, there's the stock of metal castings and rings (a special stock) we bought a year ago. It cost us £80,000 and at the rate we're using it, it will last us for another four years or so. We used about one-fifth of it last year. The accountant's figure of £56,000 for materials probably included about £16,000 for this special stock. Although we purchased it for £400 a ton, you could not buy it today for less than £480 a ton. If we sold it, after covering handling expenses, we would be left with no more than £320 a ton.

ACCOUNTANT: I think my figures are conclusive. Besides, we are paying £6,800 a year in rent for a warehouse two miles away. If we closed the department, we would not need all the warehouse space, and I estimate this saving to be £3,200 a year.

CHAIRMAN: Another problem is that of labour if the department was closed. The other departments are already over-staffed, so we would not be able to redeploy any men. However, two of the men have been with the company over 40 years and I suggest that they receive a small pension – £200 a year each. Redundancy costs would be £67,200.

DEPARTMENTAL MANAGER: What about the £15,000 for the general administrative overhead?

ACCOUNTANT: That cost will still remain if the department is closed.

Required:

(a) A calculation showing whether the Precision Machinery Department should be closed.

(b) What other factors in addition to those dealt with in your calculations would you bring to the attention of management in assisting them to arrive at a decision whether to make or buy Part 601K?

Answer

(a) This is a reasonably straightforward make-or-buy decision which requires you to identify the avoidable and unavoidable costs associated with each alternative.

Most costs are expressed on a per annum basis, but some are of a one-off nature. Taking these first:

If the buy option is chosen, the equipment can be sold for £16,000 (generating a cash inflow), although this will involve a book loss of £20,000:

	£
Cost	96,000
Depreciation (5 × £12,000)	60,000
WDV	36,000
Proceeds	16,000
Loss on disposal	£20,000

Similarly, the inventory of castings, etc., can be sold for £51,200 (generating a further cash inflow), but this will involve a stock write-off of £12,800:

	£
Cost of inventory (4/5 × £80,000)	64,000
Sale proceeds (320/400 × £64,000)	51,200
Stock loss	£12,800

Note that the sum of the cash inflows from these items (£16,000 + £51,200) equals the redundancy costs of £67,200 (as a matter of contrived convenience!).

The loss on disposal/stock write-off will affect reported profit on a once-only basis, but the economic basis of the make-or-buy choice does not reflect this aspect.

A classification of the costs into avoidable/unavoidable (relative to the make-or-buy choice) gives the following:

If Part 601K is bought out, annual costs will be:

Avoidable		*Unavoidable*	
DM	56,000	Manager's salary	3,000
DL	40,000	Rent (part)	3,600
Rent (part)	3,200	General o/h	15,000
M/c mtce	2,880	Pensions	400
Dep'n	12,000	Indirect labour	6,400
Power, etc.	12,600		28,400
	£126,680		
		Quoted price	120,000
		Total	£148,400

This gives a saving of £(154,680 – 148,400) = £6,280 p.a. in favour of buying out. Given the increase in price of the castings, etc., the inventory will cost more to replace than its original cost of £400 per ton, with the annual cost four years hence rising from £16,000 to £19,200 (ie £16,000 × 480/400). At face value this will favour buying-out even more, but this presumes that Watson Tool's price does not increase proportionately.

Conclusion
Using the data in the way suggested above, it is better to close the Precision Machinery Department and buy Part 601K from Watson Tool Company. However, the economic advantage of this course of action is marginal (£6,280 = 4% of £154,680) which may not warrant closure – especially in light of the points in (b) below.

(b) Several points require consideration, including:

- danger of single-period analysis;
- continuity of supply;
- quality control;
- stock-out risk;
- likely pattern of future demand;
- set-up costs if Watson Tool ceases to supply;
- variability of costs with volume changes;
- alternative uses of freed resources;
- impact of closure on morale;
- and so on.

Question 5.5
Omicron Ltd consists of three departments – grinding, turning, and milling – all of which have the same productive capacity. The overheads budget for the next cost period of 1,000 machine-hours' capacity for each department is as follows:

	Fixed costs £	Directly variable costs (per machine-hour) £
Grinding	2,000	0.25
Turning	1,000	0.20
Milling	750	0.375

A tender by the company is invited in respect of each of three contracts, X, Y, and Z, and it appears to the management that no other work is likely to become available during the cost period in question.

The Works Manager has studied the specifications relating to these three contracts and makes the following calculations with regard to costs and production times:

	Contract X £	Contract Y £	Contract Z £
Direct materials costs	1,800	1,610	1,240
Direct labour costs (rate per hour) which differ due to the varying skills involved:			
Grinding	0.30	0.25	0.45
Turning	0.20	0.25	0.40
Milling	0.15	0.20	0.225
Use of capacity (in machine-hours):			
Grinding	660	400	400
Turning	760	500	420
Milling	864	400	320

It will be necessary to employ three men in each department for the number of hours during which machine facilities are used on the work in respect of each of the three contracts.

Required:

(a) A comparative statement showing the minimum amount at which the firm could afford to accept each of these contracts.
(b) Would it make any difference to your calculations if you were informed that it was necessary to employ at least one person (included under direct labour) in each department regardless of the level of activity? If so, indicate the necessary amendments to your computations under (a) above.
(c) Assuming that each of the three tenders would be accepted by the customer concerned if the manufacturer quoted the following prices: contract X £4,100, Y £3,200, Z £2,650, advise the manufacturer what he should do concerning contracts to be accepted, if any, if the circumstances are (i) as in (a) above, and (ii) as in (b) above.

Answer

(a) Avoidable costs of the jobs

		Contract X £		Contract Y £		Contract Z £
Materials		1,800		1,610		1,240
Labour:						
Grinding	198		100		180	
Turning	152		125		168	
Milling	130		80		72	
	480 × 3 =	1,440	305 × 3 =	915	420 × 3 =	1,260

		Contract X £		Contract Y £		Contract Z £
Directly variable costs:						
Grinding	165		100		100	
Turning	152		100		84	
Milling	324		150		120	
		641		350		304
Minimum amount on avoidable cost basis		£3,881		£2,875		£2,804
(b) The wages for one worker would now be a fixed cost and should therefore be deducted from the avoidable costs		3,881 480		2,875 305		2,804 420
Revised avoidable cost		£3,401		£2,570		£2,384
(c) (i)						
Contract prices		4,100		3,200		2,650
Avoidable costs as in (a) above		3,881		2,875		2,804
Net revenue (or loss)		£ 219		£ 325		£ (154)

Capacity is sufficient to undertake each of the three contracts separately, or contracts Y and Z combined. It will pay the manufacturers to accept contract Y only on the basis of the above calculations.

	Contract X £	Contract Y £	Contract Z £
(ii)			
Contract prices	4,100	3,200	2,650
Avoidable costs as in (b) above	3,401	2,570	2,384
Net revenues	£ 699	£ 630	£ 266

combined profit (Y and Z)
£896

In these circumstances it would be preferable to accept contracts Y and Z combined, since capacity is sufficient and the total net revenue exceeds that from contract X.

Question 5.6

Heskett (1976, pp. 410–18) gives the example of a marketing proposal from the Safety Razor Division of the Gillette Company for a line of blank audio cassettes. The market penetration of the SRD's razors and blades was such that no further increase was likely, thus growth would have to come via diversification. Estimates of the size and rate of growth of the market for blank audio cassettes made it particularly attractive.

In the USA the most popular tape was the 60 minute one, available as follows:

Type	*Price*
Budget quality	$1.00
Standard quality	$1.75–$2.00
Professional quality	$2.98

Competition was fierce and price-oriented: some 50% (by value) of tape sales were of budget quality, typically unbranded, with well-known companies supplying standard and professional quality tapes under such brand names as Sony, 3M, and Memorex.

If SRD used 10% of its existing sales force's effort to sell cassettes via existing outlets with the 50% discount off retail price that was customary for cassettes, and if an advertising budget for year 1 was set at $2 m (and $1.2 m per annum thereafter), and if unit costs were as follows:

Cassette case (bought out)	$0.159
Standard quality tape (60 mins.)	$0.214
Professional quality tape (60 mins.)	$0.322
Assembly labour	$0.200

and if the fixed annual costs of an assembly plant with capacity to handle 1 million cassettes per month were $500,000, there is the basis for an economic appraisal of alternative marketing programmes.

Figure W5.5

Economic appraisal of marketing strategy — standard quality at budget prices.

Item		*Computation*
Price to final consumer		$1.30 per tape
Price to retailer or wholesaler (50% of list price)		$0.650
Variable costs per tape:		
Cassette case	$0.159	
Standard quality tape	$0.214	
Assembly labour	$0.200	
Total		$0.573
Contribution		$0.077
Fixed costs per annum:		
Assembly plant	$500,000	
Sales force costs (10%)	$550,000	
Advertising	$2,000,000	
Total		$3,050,000

Break-even sales volume: $\dfrac{\$3{,}050{,}000}{\$0.077} = 39{,}600{,}000$ tapes

39,600,000 × $1.30 = $51.5 m retail value

Figure W5.5 shows an outline programme offering standard quality cassettes at a price that is a little higher than that applicable to budget cassettes. The break-even volume is almost 40 million units per annum, which is greatly in excess of the capacity of the assembly plant. It also represents 85% of the total retail market of budget-priced cassettes (totalling $65 m). On grounds of feasibility this does not appear to be a viable proposition.

Alternative marketing programmes to allow SRD to enter the cassette market might entail:

- raising list price (with or without an increase in quality);
- reducing trade margins;
- using a small sales team and only selling via wholesalers;
- reducing the proposed advertising budget;
- investing in manufacturing facilities (rather than just assembly).

These alternatives might be considered individually (on a *ceteris paribus* basis) or interactively (on a *mutatis mutandis* basis) and there would be knock-on effects for other elements of the marketing mix also.

Significant effort would need to be applied (via market research) to define the market, its segments, growth rates, etc., in order to determine the viability of alternative marketing programmes. Relevant factors would include:

- the quality of forecasts;
- the rate at which market conditions favourable to entry might change;
- alternatives to blank cassette tapes as vehicles for SRD's growth;
- assumed buyer behaviour patterns within the cassette market;
- assumptions about other elements of the marketing mix.

Three alternative marketing programmes have been developed by SRD, and the evaluated alternatives are shown in Fig. W5.6.

These alternatives are the marketing of budget cassettes, the marketing of standard cassettes at a low price, and the marketing of professional cassettes. Only the latter two would use the Gillette brand name, although all three would have to generate an equivalent profit to Gillette's overall level (at 20% of sales revenue). It is clear from Fig. W5.6 that Alternative 3 is non-viable, and that Alternative 1, whilst viable, is more challenging than Alternative 2.

W5.5 Computational problems

Question 5.1

Baldwin Enterprises Ltd is a small manufacturing company that makes a standard product widely available from alternative sources, and other products to customer specification. The company's management accountant, John Ellis, prepared the following income statement for last year:

	Standard product	Customer specified products	Total
Sales revenue	£250,000	£500,000	£750,000
Material	80,000	100,000	180,000
Labour	90,000	200,000	290,000
Depreciation	36,000	63,000	99,000
Power	4,000	7,000	11,000
Rent	10,000	60,000	70,000
Heat and light	1,000	6,000	7,000
Other	9,000	4,000	13,000
Total expenses	230,000	440,000	670,000
Net profit	£20,000	£60,000	£80,000

The depreciation charges relate to equipment used currently only for standard products or customer specified products in separate departments.

Power costs are apportioned in accordance with estimates of power consumed. Rent, heat and light costs are apportioned according to floor space occupied by

Figure W5.6

An economic analysis of three alternative strategies for designing and marketing SRD cassettes.

	Alternative 1	Alternative 2	Alternative 3
Determination of Product characteristics	Budget cassette, sold under a name other than Gillette	Standard cassette, sold under Gillette name	Professional cassette, sold under Gillette name
Elements of marketing program			
Price (list) to ultimate buyer	$1.20/cassette	$1.50/cassette	$2.50/cassette
Channels	Current Gillette retail outlets, wholesalers: total margin = 25%	Current Gillette retail outlets, wholesalers: total margin = 30%	Audio shops, wholesalers: total margin = 60%
Promotion	Advertising = $2.0 million per year: personal selling = $.5 million per year	Advertising = $2.0 million per year: personal selling = $.5 million per year	Advertising = $1.0 million per year: personal selling = $.2 million per year
Relevant target market	Teenagers for pop music: 50% of total dollar value	Young adults, business people for dictation, letter writing: 40% of total dollar value	Serious audiophiles for convenient high-fidelity recording of music: 10% of total dollar value

Calculation of			
Price to ultimate buyer	$1.20/cassette	$1.50/cassette	$2.50/cassette
Price to SRD	$ .90	$1.05	$1.00
Variable costs and profit per tape			
Unloaded cassette	$ .159	$ .159	$ .159
Tape of each quality	.214	.214	.322
Assembly	.200	.200	.200
Profit (20% of sales)	.180	.210	.200
Total	$ .753	$ .783	$ .881
Contribution to fixed costs	$ .147/cassette	$ .267/cassette	$ .119/cassette
Fixed costs for			
Assembly plant (per year)	$ 500,000	$ 500,000	$ 500,000
Sales force salaries	500,000	500,000	200,000
Advertising	2,000,000	2,000,000	1,000,000
Total	$3,000,000	$3,000,000	$1,700,000
Target sales level (units)	$3,000,000/.147 = 20,408,163	$3,000,000/.267 = 11,235,955	$1,700,000/.119 = 14,300,000
Value to ultimate customers of target sales level	$24,489,795	$16,853,932	$35,800,000
Estimated 1970 target market size ($ and % of $130 million)	$65,000,000 (50%)	$52,000,000 (40%)	$13,000,000 (10%)
Appraisal of			
Likelihood of success (share of target market), including potential for competitive response, channel, and market acceptance of strategy	38% share of target market required to break even	32% share of target market required to break even	275% share of target market required to break even
Potential risk	High fixed investment	High fixed investment	Moderate fixed investment
Potential return on investment at capacity operations	Would require expanded investment in manufacturing facilities	Would require expanded investment in manufacturing facilities	Would require expanded investment in manufacturing facilities

No Go

(Source: Adapted from Heskett (1976), pp. 416–17).

the departments manufacturing standard products on the one hand and customer specified products on the other.

The building has been leased for 10 years at an annual rental charge of £70,000. All other costs are direct costs of the product line to which they have been charged.

Stephen Cook, who is a regular customer of the company, has asked if 5,000 units of a special item can be produced for him with some urgency. Baldwin Enterprises is currently operating at full capacity and it is clear that some other business would have to be given up to meet Mr Cook's request. However, the company's sales director is unwilling to renege on other orders for customer specified products that have already been accepted.

One way of accommodating Mr Cook's order would be to cut back on the production of the company's standard product by about 50% for a year and devote the capacity thus freed to Mr Cook's order. The unit costs are estimated to be:

Direct material	£20.00
Direct labour	£36.00

A special piece of plant will be needed to help make the product and this will cost £20,000 with no likely value at the end of the year.

Mr Cook is willing to pay £70.00 per unit.

Required:

(a) Calculate the following figures:
- (i) the incremental cost of Mr Cook's order;
- (ii) the full cost of the order;
- (iii) the opportunity cost to Baldwin Enterprises of accepting the order;
- (iv) the sunk costs relating to the order.

(b) If you were John Ellis would you recommend that the order be accepted? Justify your answer.

Question 5.2

Briar Ltd manufacture high quality, handmade pipes, and have experienced a steady growth in sales over the past five years. However, increased competition has led the managing director, Mr Bruno Condor, to believe that an aggressive advertising campaign will be necessary in order to maintain Briar's present growth rate into next year – 19X4.

To prepare for next year's advertising campaign, the company's accountant has prepared the following data for Mr Condor relating to 19X3. (Briar Ltd operates on a calendar year basis.)

Cost Schedule

Variable costs:	£	
Direct labour	8.00	per pipe
Direct materials	3.25	per pipe
Variable indirect	2.50	per pipe
Total variable costs	£13.75	per pipe

	£	
Fixed costs:		
Manufacturing	25,000	
Selling	40,000	
Administrative	70,000	
Total fixed costs	£135,000	
Selling price	£25.00	per pipe
Expected sales (19X3) 20,000 units	£500,000	
	Tax rate: 40%	

Bruno Condor has set the sales target for 19X4 at a level of £550,000 (i.e. 22,000 pipes at £25.00).

Required:

(i) What is the projected after-tax net income of Briar Ltd for each of 19X3 and 19X4?
(ii) What is the break-even point (in units) for each of 19X3 and 19X4?
(iii) Mr Condor believes that an additional outlay of £11,250 for advertising in 19X4 (with other costs remaining constant) will be needed to achieve the sales target set for that year. What will be the after-tax net income for 19X4 if this additional £11,250 is spent?
(iv) What will be the break-even point (in £s) for 19X4 if the additional £11,250 is spent?
(v) Assuming the advertising campaign is undertaken, what is the required 19X4 sales level (in £s) to equal 19X3's after-tax net income?
(vi) At a sales level of 22,000 units, what is the maximum amount that can be spent on advertising if an after-tax net income of £60,000 is desired?
(vii) What are the major weaknesses in the approaches you have adopted in answering (i)–(vi) above?

Question 5.3

The Capital Motor Co. Ltd recently suffered a strike that lasted for two weeks. During that time no motor cars were produced. The company issued a press statement to the effect that the cost of the strike was £5,000,000. This figure was estimated on the basis of lost production of 1,000 vehicles, each of which could have been sold for £5,000, a total loss of turnover of £5,000,000.

The company's accountant, Martin Bennett, feels that this figure overstates the cost of the strike and produced the following statement to support his view:

	£
Expenses avoided:	
Materials (£1,000 per car)	1,000,000
Production labour (£500 per car)	500,000
Depreciation of machinery	1,750,000
Indirect costs: 200% on production labour	1,000,000
	4,250,000
Loss of sales revenue	5,000,000
Cost of strike	£750,000

The following additional information is available:

(a) Depreciation of machinery is based on the straight-line method of calculation. However, the plant manager estimates that the machinery will fall in value by £200,000 each week regardless of the level of production. He feels that, in addition, its value will fall by £150,000 for each 100 cars that are produced.
(b) Indirect manufacturing costs are recovered at the rate of 200% on production labour. Most of these expenses are unaffected by the level of production (for example, rent, rates, maintenance and staff wages) but some (such as power and lighting) vary directly with production. The general manager estimates that the latter type of indirect cost amounts to £10,000 for every 100 cars produced.
(c) During the period of the strike the maintenance staff, whose wages are included in the fixed indirect costs, carried out a major overhaul on one of the company's machines using materials costing £10,000. This overhaul would normally have been performed by an outside contractor at a price, including materials, of £100,000.
(d) The sales manager feels that about one half of the production lost could be made up and sold in the next month by the production labour working overtime. Labour is paid at the rate of time and one half for overtime working.

Does the press statement or the accountant's revised statement properly reflect the cost of the strike to Capital Motor Co. Ltd?

Question 5.4

Stanbridge & Partners manufacture rotary clothes driers. Last July the firm made a batch of 10,000 units that turned out to be defective. The total cost of the batch was £50,000.

Two options seem to be available:

either (i) sell the batch in its present state for £2.50 per unit;
or (ii) correct the defects at an estimated unit cost of £3.00 and then sell the batch at the normal price of £7.50 per unit.

Required:

(a) State (with reasons) which option the firm should choose.
(b) If the correcting of defective units meant forgoing the manufacture of a further batch of 20,000 units, which option would you then favour?

Question 5.5

Production and other operating data for Kay (Chronometers) Ltd last year was as follows:

Sales (units)	100,000
Selling price per unit	£16
Production (units)	120,000
Opening inventory	0
Manufacturing cost per unit:	
Direct material	£4

Direct labour	£6
Variable indirect	£1
Fixed indirect	£3
Marketing and administrative costs:	
Variable	£50,000
Fixed	£80,000

Required:

(a) Calculate the company's profit under:

(i) absorption costing;
(ii) variable costing;

and explain the difference.

(b) Determine the company's:

(i) break-even point;
(ii) margin of safety.

Question 5.6

Commercial Products Corporation, an audit client, requested your assistance in determining the potential loss on a binding purchase contract that will be in effect at the end of the corporation's fiscal year. The corporation produces a chemical compound that deteriorates and must be discarded if it is not sold by the end of the month during which it is produced.

The total variable cost of the manufactured compound is £25 per unit, and it is sold for £40 per unit. The compound can be purchased from a vertically integrated competitor at £40 per unit plus £5 freight per unit. It is estimated that failure to fill orders would result in the complete loss of 8 out of 10 customers placing orders for the compound.

The corporation has sold the compound for the past 30 months. Demand has been irregular, and there is no sales trend. During this period, sales per month have been:

Units sold per month	Number of months*
4,000	6
5,000	15
6,000	9

* Occurred in random sequence.

(a) For each of the following prepare a schedule (with supporting computations in good form) of the:

(i) probability of sales of 4,000, 5,000 or 6,000 units in any month;
(ii) contribution to income if sales of 4,000, 5,000 or 6,000 units are made in one month and 4,000, 5,000 or 6,000 units are manufactured for sale in the same month. Assume all sales orders are fulfilled;
(iii) average monthly contribution to income the corporation should expect over the long run if 5,000 units are manufactured every month and all sales orders are filled.

(b) The cost of the primary ingredient used to manufacture the compound is £12 per unit of compound. It is estimated that there is a 60% chance that the primary ingredient supplier's plant may be shut down by a strike for an indefinite period. A substitute ingredient is available at £18 per unit of compound, but the corporation must contract immediately to purchase the substitute, or it will be unavailable when needed. A firm purchase contract for either the primary or the substitute ingredient must now be made with one of the suppliers for production next month. If an order were placed for the primary ingredient and a strike should occur, the corporation would be released from the contract and management would purchase the compound from the competitor.

Assume that 5,000 units are to be manufactured, and all sales orders are to be filled.

(i) Compute the monthly contribution to income from sales of 4,000, 5,000 and 6,000 units if the substitute ingredient is ordered.

(ii) Prepare a schedule computing the average monthly contribution to income the corporation should expect if the primary ingredient is ordered with the existing probability of a strike at the supplier's plant. Assume that the expected average contribution to income from manufacturing will be £65,000 using the primary ingredient or £35,000 using the substitute, and the expected average monthly loss from purchasing from the competitor will be £25,000.

(iii) Should management order the primary or substitute ingredient during the anticipated strike period (under the assumptions stated in (b) (ii) above)? Why or why not?

(iv) Should management purchase the compound from the competitor to fill sales orders when the orders cannot be otherwise filled? Why or why not?

(AICPA adapted)

*Question 5.7**

The Amsweet Corporation has diversified since it was founded by Chairman Alan Sweet from the manufacture of domestic electronic goods to being a major supplier of computers and peripherals.

Initial success in the highly competitive computer market was based on the production of a low-priced personal computer, the design of which allowed an economical use of cheap imported computer chips. The target market was the hobbyist or small business user for whom price was a primary consideration. The range has since expanded and grown in sophistication, but still depends heavily on buying chips and other imported components at an advantageous price from overseas. Corporate plans now include further expansion into the more limited but highly lucrative business computer market with a good quality product. Alan Sweet hopes that success will allow the company to continue to fight off takeover attempts by competitors.

Now, near the end of the financial year, there have been problems of quality control of chips, a labour shortage in the overseas country of origin of the chips, and finally pressure exerted on the company via government agencies to 'buy

---

*Used by permission of Dr Alicia M. Gazely.

British'. These problems are forcing the company to consider cancelling its overseas contracts and converting an existing facility to chip production. (This facility, situated in Wales, has recently been set up for hi-fi unit assembly and has just started production.) If the conversion decision is taken then it will be with immediate effect.

Some financial information is available as follows:

Targets and estimated costs for the coming financial year

Production target – hi-fi units	500,000 units
Production target – computers	300,000 units
Average number of chips, per computer	20 chips
Average variable costs:	
Hi-fi (assembly, per unit)	£0.95
Chips (manufacture, each)	£0.89
Average cost, bought-in:	
Hi-fi (assembly contracted out, per unit)	£1.90
Chips (overseas contract, each)	£0.93
Purchasing and administrative costs:	
Chip import operation	£120,000 p.a.

Costs associated with the Welsh facility	£
Accommodation costs	135,000 p.a.
Administrative costs (in Wales)	75,000 p.a.
Administrative costs (allocated from Head Office)	110,000 p.a.
Costs in preparing facility for hi-fi assembly	200,000
Estimated cost of preparing facility for sterile chip production	150,000
Hi-fi assembly:	
Quality control and supervisory costs	55,000 p.a.
Chip production:	
Research, development and quality control	240,000 p.a.
Other:	
Estimated legal and compensation costs in connection with cancellation of overseas chip contracts	160,000

Required:

(a) Prepare a concise financial statement showing the consequences of cancelling the import contracts and commencing chip production, up to the end of the coming financial year.

(b) Discuss briefly the assumptions underlying the statement you have prepared in (a).

W5.6 Case study

The Rothwell Valve Company

The Rothwell Valve Company supplies valves for use in industrial heating systems. It has three products:

First, the high pressure safety valve with which the company started in the 1960s and which, over the years, had attained such a good reputation.

Secondly, the radiator valve which it manufactured specifically for Disborough Heating Limited, a company in a nearby location which had developed its own, highly successful range of radiators. Disborough and Rothwell also had a joint marketing arrangement whereby Rothwell provided the selling capability for the radiators and recovered the cost via an increased margin on the radiator valves supplied to Disborough. This arrangement worked well and the radiator valves were showing a net profit of 17.3% on sales, very respectable in this type of industry.

Thirdly, there was the automatic pump valve which had recently been introduced after a long development period.

Rothwell was under pressure financially because of the development costs of the new valve. Three years ago there was no such valve. The company had designed, tested and produced the valve from scratch, writing off the development costs as it went along. This present policy of writing off had, however, two major effects: it had been a drain in the company's cash and had led to a reduced distributable profit which had not pleased the shareholders who had shown their displeasure by selling enough shares to cause the market price to fall to such an extent that a takeover bid was only a matter of time. In fact the Managing Director of Disborough had hinted that he might be interested in acquiring Rothwells as part of a rationalization scheme. Jim Evans, Rothwell's Managing Director, had taken this hint and he knew that Disborough had plenty of cash after a recent sale of surplus land. Evans felt that Disborough could soon make an offer that the Rothwell shareholders might find very tempting.

Evans had another problem; the new valve which was his 'brainchild' was not the success that had been hoped. Indeed, despite having no development costs to bear, the valve was making a loss.

Evans called his fellow directors together to discuss what could be done to try and resolve Rothwell's problems. At the meeting, Rod Selby, the Marketing Director, Frank Knott, the Production Director, and Colin Peters, the Finance Director, all placed the blame for the company's position at the door of the new valve.

SELBY: It is quite hopeless trying to sell these new valves, we just don't have the name in that field. The safety valves sell themselves, the radiator valves are relatively easy because of the package that we can put together with Disborough's. But these new ones are not easy. I'm sorry Jim.

EVANS: I know that it isn't easy Rod, and that you have done very well with those that you have already sold. I also know that the new valve is felt to be my albatross but I am convinced that without the diversity that it provides we would be an even riper fruit for the picking.

KNOTT: My problem is that the plant and processes aren't interchangeable. Even if I stop making the new valve I cannot switch resources over to the other two.

EVANS: We deliberately tooled up for the new valve knowing that it was different to our normal products. What you are saying, Frank, is what we agreed three years ago and that is we were going to give ourselves a whole bundle of fixed costs which we could not eliminate even if we failed. But of course, we didn't expect to fail.

PETERS: You asked for some figures, Jim, comparing the costs and sales figures of the valves. I've had our costing people draw up this statement so that we can have some solid evidence to talk about. (*The four men study the statement given in Figure W5.7 closely.*)

SELBY: If we scrap the pump valve we will be able to increase net profits by 3% at a stroke. It doesn't make sense to continue wasting our time on a product that could ultimately ruin the company.

Figure W5.7

Statement of costs of products.

	Total £	Radiator valve £	Pump valve £	Safety valve £
Sales	500,000	75,000	50,000	375,000
Costs	450,000	62,000	51,500	336,500
Net profit	51,500	13,000	–	38,500
Net loss	1,500	–	1,500	–
	£50,000			

Figure W5.8

Breakdown of costs.

	Total £	Radiator valve £	Pump valve £	Safety valve £
Production costs:				
Payroll	75,000	3,000	12,000	60,000
Rent and rates	15,000	2,000	1,000	12,000
Other	10,000	–	2,000	8,000
Materials	250,000	35,000	15,000	200,000
Other supplies	50,000	5,000	5,000	40,000
Selling costs:				
Payroll	10,000	3,500	3,500	3,000
Cars	5,000	1,690	1,620	1,690
Advertising	20,000	6,760	6,480	6,760
Distribution costs:	15,000	5,050	4,900	5,050
		62,000	51,500	336,500

KNOTT: I agree, I have always felt that we put too many resources into the new pump and despite not being able to switch them back I say that we should not continue to throw good money after bad.

EVANS: Have you got a breakdown of the figures, Colin?

PETERS: I've brought along a note of the costs broken down among production, selling and distribution. (*The four men study the breakdown given in Figure W5.8.*)

PETERS: Of course 'Materials' and 'Other supplies' vary with levels of production and we regard payroll as a fixed expense.

The meeting continued, after considering these figures, with Jim Evans setting out the pros and cons of continuing production of the pump valve.

EVANS: I believe that it is quite simple: we continue to produce an (at present) loss-making product in the hope that it will, eventually, make a profit. Against that we have professional marketing advice to forget it and financial evidence that if we discontinue production we will immediately increase net profits by 3%. Despite my emotion saying continue my head says stop.

SELBY: We can easily meet outstanding orders from stock even if we stop production today.

The meeting decided in favour of discontinuing production. Were they right?

CHAPTER 6 WORKBOOK

Long-run decision-making

W6.1 Introduction

The longer term perspective, coupled with a greater concern for the notion of competitive position, are emphasized in this Workbook chapter. Through the reprinted article in Section W6.6 you will see that these ideas are important in practice.

W6.2 Revision topics

Question 6.1
What major differences exist in considering the provision of managerial accounting information over the short run as opposed to the long run?

Answer
A variety of factors differ between the short run (SR) and long run (LR). The former is much more constrained than the latter, which means that managerial accounting information is more likely to be systematized and routine in the short run. Over the long run there is greater uncertainty and more scope for change.

Particular points to note include:

(i) scale/capacity are given in SR but not in LR;
(ii) inflation cannot be ignored in LR;
(iii) the time value of money is of LR significance;
(iv) differential costs and revenues in SR tend to be *marginal* whereas in LR they are *incremental* (which has connotations of increased magnitude);
(v) there is greater scope for relaxing constraints over LR;
(vi) complexity tends to increase over time;
(vii) uncertainty also typically increases as the time horizon is extended.

Question 6.2
Draft an explanatory note on the concept of present value addressed to someone with limited business experience.

Answer
Perhaps the easiest way of explaining this is by reference to compound interest: one would expect any investment in, say, a building society to earn interest as a reward both for postponed consumption and risk. It follows that £1 today is worth

more than £1 in a year's time because one could invest the money to earn interest in the intervening period. Thus, at an annual rate of interest of 10% one would have £1.10 in a year's time if one invested £1 today. In two years' time this would increase to £1.21 (i.e. £1.00 × 1.1 × 1.1), and so on. The formula for compound interest is contained in the following:

$$A = P(1 + r)^n$$

where A = sum to be received in the future
P = initial sum invested
r = interest rate
n = number of periods.

In effect this formula takes a present sum, P, and *compounds* it to a future sum, A. The converse process would be to take a future sum, A, and *discount* it to its present value, P, by means of the formula:

$$P = \frac{A}{(1 + r)^n}$$

This answers questions such as what is the value today of the sum of £121 that we expect to receive in two years' time, with a prevailing interest rate of 10%? (The answer, of course, is £100!)

Question 6.3
If you had £600 to invest on 1 January 1993, what interest rate compounded annually would you have to obtain to ensure that you had £1,800 on 31 December 1998?

Answer
This can be tackled in one of three ways: by using a calculator, logarithms, or compound interest tables. By adopting the first of these and using the formula:

$$A = P(1 + r)^n$$

we solve for r:

$$\begin{aligned} £1{,}800 &= £600\,(1 + r)^6 \\ 3 &= (1 + r)^6 \\ 1 + r &= 3^{1/6} \\ 1 + r &= 1.20 \\ r &= 20\% \end{aligned}$$

W6.3 Discussion topics

Question 6.1
Suggest ways in which decisions of a strategic nature might be categorized, making clear the benefits of categorization.

Question 6.2
What factors might limit the role of the management accountant in the context of strategic decision-making?

Question 6.3
What does it mean if the net present value of an investment project is exactly equal to zero?

Question 6.4
Discuss the significance of the time dimension in managerial accounting. How important do you consider the past to be relative to the future?

Question 6.5
Specify the ways in which inflation might have an impact on the design and operation of managerial accounting systems.

Question 6.6
To what extent can managerial accounting systems be designed to accommodate the array of environment factors that influence organizational performance?

Question 6.7
Explain how sensitivity analysis can contribute towards better decision-making.

Question 6.8
Identify the key characteristics of strategic management accounting.

W6.4 Worked examples

Question 6.1
Dave Seeberger, president of Olympic Instruments Ltd, feels that the time has come for a price increase on the company's most important product. 'Our costs on this line have gone up 32% since our last price increase,' he said, 'and I think that justifies a price hike now. We're almost down to the break-even level and for the first time in 20 years we can't pay a dividend to the shareholders. It's a good thing that we have a higher margin on most of our other products. Without those we'd really be in the soup!'

The product is sold directly to industrial users at a price of £160. The factory cost estimates at the time of the last price increase and at present are shown in the following table:

	Then	Now
	£	£
Direct material costs	17.50	20.40
Direct labour costs	32.50	40.00
Indirect manufacturing costs	65.00	91.60
Total factory cost per unit	£115.00	£152.00

The product specifications have not been changed since the previous price increase. Wage rates have gone up by 30%, but some labour has been saved as a result of method changes that have been effected during this period.

Indirect manufacturing costs are assigned to products on the basis of a plant-wide absorption rate, reflecting estimated costs at current volume. The rate is brought up to date once a year. The indirect cost files at the time of the increase and at present show the following:

	Then	Now
Indirect cost absorption rate (per direct labour pound)	£ 2.00	£ 2.29
Estimated monthly volume (direct labour cost)	£120,000	£110,000
Variable indirect cost	£ 36,000	£ 31,900

All of the company's salespeople are on salary and all selling and administrative costs are regarded as fixed. Even so, they have gone up in total from £70,000 a month to £75,000 a month. Sales have dropped from about £700,000 a month to £550,000, despite price increases on some other products.

Brad Pierce, Olympic's sales manager, is against any price increase. 'We have a tough enough time now,' he said. 'Our competitors' list prices are about the same as ours, but my guess is that they're doing a little unofficial price cutting. Everybody in the industry has cut back, but we've been hit harder than most. Our market share on this product has fallen from about 50% to maybe 40%. If anything, we should be offering a few deals of our own, not raising prices.'

(a) Calculate this product's contribution margin, then and now.
(b) Which elements have had the greatest impact on unit cost in this period?
(c) Which kinds of cost increases is the company most likely to be able to pass on to its customers? Should the price be increased at this time? If not, what should Mr Seeberger do?

Answer

(a) Calculation of contribution margin:

	Then	Now
	£	£
Direct material costs	17.50	20.40
Direct labour costs	32.50	40.00
Variable indirect costs	9.75*	11.60†
Total variable cost	59.75	72.00
Selling price	160.00	160.00
Contribution margin	£100.25	£88.00

$$^{*}\ \frac{£120,000}{£32.50} = 3,692$$

$$\frac{£36,000}{3,692} = £9.75$$

$$^{\dagger}\ \frac{£110,000}{£40.00} = 2,750$$

$$\frac{£31,000}{2,750} = £11.60$$

(b) Students who have not been through Chapter 4 may have some difficulty in analysing the cost change in quantitative terms. For this reason we have phrased the instruction in very general terms, permitting a very partial analysis of the situation. The minimum breakdown would be:

	£
Increase in variable cost (from (a))	12.25
Increase in fixed cost[†]	24.75[‡]
Total increase	£37.00

[‡] $\frac{£110,000}{£40.00} = 2,750$

$\frac{£220,000}{2,750} = £80.00$

$\frac{£204,000}{3,692} = £55.25$

£24.75

Both of these can be subdivided further, and the following analysis is intended to show how much can be done with the data.

Calculation of the indirect cost changes:

	Old figures	Current figures
Statistics:		
Volume (direct labour cost)	£120,000	£110,000
Indirect cost absorption rate	£2.00	£2.29
Total indirect manufacturing cost	£240,000	£251,900
Variable indirect cost	£36,000	£31,900
Fixed indirect cost	£204,000	£220,000

Effect of change in factory volume on fixed cost component of the indirect cost absorption rate:

$$\left(\frac{£220,000}{£110,000} - \frac{220,000}{120,000}\right) \times £40.00 \qquad £\ (6.67)$$

Effect of increase in total fixed indirect cost on the absorption rate (indirect cost 'spending'):

$$\left(\frac{£220,000}{£120,000} - \frac{£204,000}{£120,000}\right) \times £40.00 \qquad £\ (5.33)$$

Effect of change in labour cost per unit on absorption of fixed cost:

$£(32.50 - £40.00) \times \dfrac{£204,000}{£120,000}$	£(12.75)
Total change in fixed cost absorbed	£(24.75)

Effect of change in variable cost per direct labour pound:

$\left(\dfrac{£31,900}{£110,000} - \dfrac{£36,000}{120,000}\right) \times £40.00$	£ 0.40

Effect on variable indirect cost of change in labour cost per unit:*

$£(40.00 - 32.50) \times \dfrac{£36,000}{£120,000}$	£ (2.25)
Total change in unit indirect cost	£(26.60)†

* This assumes that variable indirect costs do in fact vary with direct labour cost. This difference could be separated into a rate change effect and a methods change effect.

† Fixed:
£(6.67) + (5.33) + (12.75) = £(24.75)
Variable:
£(2.25) + 0.40 = £(1.85)

£(26.60)

Summary of changes in unit cost:

	£
Material price increase	(2.90)
Labour:	
Rate increase (£32.50 × 30%)	(9.75)
Methods reduction	2.25
Indirect manufacturing costs:	
Increase in total fixed indirect cost	(5.33)
Increase in absorption of fixed indirect costs due to change in overall factory volume and change in product labour cost	(19.42)
Decrease in variable cost per direct labour pound	0.40
Effect on variable indirect costs of increase in labour cost	2.25
Total	£(37.00)

Changes in selling and administrative costs cannot be analysed from the data supplied, and in any event are unlikely to be related to the activity in this product.

(c) The changes in labour and material costs come from causes that presumably might permit passing them on to customers. The changes in variable cost and the £5.33 increase in average fixed cost might also be passed on if other conditions warrant. More than half of the total increase, however, is due to low aggregate volume and the increased share of total volume represented by one unit of this product. Raising prices to offset these effects is likely to be self-defeating. Market share has been falling, idle capacity is widespread, and competitors' list prices are no higher than Olympic's. Olympic might try to be a price leader, but such an effect is likely to fail if competitors have in fact been shading prices.

It would seem that a new marketing plan, product redesign, cost reduction, a search for new products or markets, or some combination of these would be in order rather than a price increase.

Question 6.2

XYZ plc is considering a proposal to invest £100,000 in product improvement and promotion to bring these into line with its major competitor, ABC plc, in order to increase its market share from 25% to 35%.

ABC plc has 20% of the market and has been gradually gaining on XYZ plc. If XYZ plc takes no action it is expected that ABC will gain market share at XYZ's expense at the rate of 1% per annum.

By carrying out its proposed improvements XYZ expects to obtain 4% market share from ABC and 6% from the smaller competitors.

The price of market offerings of XYZ and ABC currently stands at £10 per unit, with XYZ making 5% margin on sales and ABC making 3%. An 80% experience curve applies: cumulative experience to date amounts to 200,000 and 150,000 units respectively for XYZ and ABC.

Cost of capital can be taken as 15%.

Anticipated market demand over the next six years is:

Year	*Units*
1	100,000
2	100,000
3	120,000
4	150,000
5	180,000
6	180,000

Prices have tended to decline by about 3% per annum in real terms, and each of the major competitors would expect the other to match reductions. The management accountant in XYZ sees no reason for this pattern to change in the light of relative cost structures.

Required:
Evaluate the proposal put forward by XYZ plc and offer a justified recommendation.

Answer

Figures W6.1 and W6.2 show that the investment is wholly justifiable. Note how much clearer the evaluation is when competitor data is included to test the validity of the calculations.

As Fig. W6.1 shows, if XYZ plc does not go ahead with the investment it is almost certain to lose competitive position relative to ABC plc. Not only does ABC's market share look set to rise, but also its cumulative experience will bring greater cost reductions than XYZ can achieve, hence improving profit figures.

Figure W6.1

Base case (no action).

Year	1	2	3	4	5	6
Market size (000 units)	100	100	120	150	180	180
Market price (£)	9.70	9.41	9.13	8.85	8.59	8.33
XYZ plc						
Market share (%)	25	24	23	22	21	20
Sales (000 units)	25.0	24.0	27.6	33.0	37.8	36.0
Accumulated sales (000 units)	225.0	249.0	276.6	309.6	347.4	383.4
Increase in accum. sales (%)	12.5	10.7	11.2	11.9	11.9	10.4
Experience effect –						
Reduction in cost per unit*	0.34	0.28	0.30	0.33	0.30	0.28
Cost per unit (current = £9.50)	9.16	8.88	8.58	8.25	7.95	7.67
Profit per unit	0.54	0.53	0.55	0.60	0.64	0.66
Total profit (£000)	13.5	12.7	15.2	19.8	24.2	23.8
Present value deflator (15%)†	1.0	0.870	0.756	0.658	0.572	0.497
PV of profits (£000)	13.5	11.0	11.5	13.0	13.8	11.8
ABC plc						
Market share (%)	20	21	22	23	24	25
Sales (000 units)	20.0	21.0	26.4	34.5	43.2	45.0
Accumulated sales (000 units)	170.0	191.0	217.4	251.9	295.1	340.1
Increase in accum. sales (%)	13.3	12.4	13.6	16.1	17.1	15.3
Experience effect –						
Reduction in cost per unit*	0.36	0.34	0.37	0.42	0.45	0.40
Cost per unit (current = £9.70)	9.34	9.00	8.63	8.21	7.76	7.36
Profit per unit	0.36	0.41	0.50	0.64	0.83	0.97
Total profit (£000)	7.2	8.6	13.2	22.1	35.9	43.7
Present value deflator (15%)†	1.0	0.870	0.756	0.658	0.572	0.497
PV of profits (£000)	7.2	7.5	9.8	14.5	20.5	21.7

* The reduction in costs per unit can be determined by either graphical (using log/log paper) or algebraic methods. See Chapter 7.

† See discount tables on p. 650.

Figure W6.2 shows the expected consequences of XYZ proceeding with the investment. In this alternative to the base case XYZ looks set to gain market share and, through this, to secure cost reductions and enhanced profit performance. Its competitive position relative to ABC is likely to be greatly improved.

Figure W6.2

Investment alternative.

Year	1	2	3	4	5	6
Market size (000 units)	100	100	120	150	180	180
Market price (£)	9.70	9.41	9.13	8.85	8.59	8.33
XYZ plc						
Market share (%)	35	35	35	35	35	35
Sales (000 units)	35.0	35.0	42.0	52.5	63.0	63.0
Accumulated sales (000 units)	235.0	270.0	312.0	364.5	427.5	490.5
Increase in accum. sales (%)	17.5	14.9	15.6	17.0	17.3	14.8
Experience effect – Reduction in cost per unit*	0.46	0.40	0.42	0.44	0.46	0.40
Cost per unit (current = £9.50)	9.04	8.64	8.22	7.78	7.32	6.92
Profit per unit	0.66	0.77	0.91	1.07	1.27	1.41
Total profit (£000)	23.1	27.0	38.2	56.2	80.0	88.8
Present value deflator (15%)†	1.0	0.870	0.756	0.658	0.572	0.497
PV of profits (£000)	23.1	23.5	28.9	37.0	45.8	44.1
ABC plc						
Market share (%)	16	16	16	16	16	16
Sales (000 units)	16.0	16.0	19.2	24.0	28.8	28.8
Accumulated sales (000 units)	166.0	182.0	201.2	225.2	254.0	282.8
Increase in accum. sales (%)	10.7	9.6	10.4	11.9	12.9	11.3
Experience effect – Reduction in cost per unit*	0.28	0.26	0.27	0.32	0.34	0.31
Cost per unit (current = £9.70)	9.42	9.16	8.89	8.57	8.23	7.92
Profit per unit	0.28	0.25	0.24	0.28	0.36	0.41
Total profit (£000)	4.5	4.0	4.6	6.7	10.4	11.8
Present value deflator (15%)†	1.0	0.870	0.756	0.658	0.572	0.497
PV of profits (£000)	4.5	3.5	3.5	4.4	5.9	5.9

* The reduction in costs per unit can be determined by either graphical (using log/log paper) or algebraic methods.

† See discount tables on p. 650.

Question 6.3

The management of Chi Ltd has before it three mutually exclusive investment projects. Each project will require an initial investment of £50,000 and will have no residual value.

It is expected that the revenues less the outlays, receivable at the end of each year, will be as follows:

Project X £35,000 p.a. for 2 years.
Project Y £20,000 p.a. for 5 years.
Project Z £12,000 p.a. for 10 years.

The minimum acceptable rate of return to Chi Ltd is 15%.

(a) Calculate for each of the three projects:
   (i) the payback period;
   (ii) the accounting rate of return (based on the initial investment);
   (iii) the net present value (to the nearest £);
   and rank the projects under each method.
(b) Advise management which of the projects should be accepted.

Extracts from discount tables:

The present value of 1 per annum

Years	15%
1	0.869565
2	1.62571
3	2.28323
4	2.85498
5	3.35216
6	3.78448
7	4.16042
8	4.48732
9	4.77158
10	5.01877

Answer

(a) (i) Payback:

			Rank
X	$\frac{50,000}{35,000} = 1.43$	years	1
Y	$\frac{50,000}{20,000} = 2.5$	years	2
Z	$\frac{50,000}{12,000} = 4.2$	years	3

(ii) Accounting rate of return:

X	$\frac{35,000 - 25,000}{50,000} \times 100 = 20\%$	1
Y	$\frac{20,000 - 10,000}{50,000} \times 100 = 20\%$	1
Z	$\frac{12,000 - 5,000}{50,000} \times 100 = 14\%$	3

(iii) NPV:

		Rank
X	(35,000 × 1.62571) − 50,000 = 56,899 − 50,000 = £6,899	3
Y	(20,000 × 3.35216) − 50,000 = 67,043 − 50,000 = £17,043	1
Z	(12,000 × 5.01877) − 50,000 = 60,225 − 50,000 = £10,225	2

The NPV calculations are performed with the help of discount tables. Thus, for project X, the sum of £35,000 is expected each year for two years, with a minimum required rate of 15%. The relevant discount factor (relating 2 years and 15%) is 1.62571 which, when multiplied by £35,000, gives the present value for the inflows of £56,899. By deducting the initial investment of £50,000 we arrive at the NPV of £6,899 for the project. And similarly for projects Y and Z.

(b) There are conflicts over the rankings given by the various techniques to the three projects: X is ranked first and first equal by payback and the accounting rate of return respectively, whereas Y is ranked first and first equal by NPV and the accounting rate of return. No technique ranks Z higher than second, with two of them ranking it third.

NPV is a more rigorous approach that, *inter alia*, allows for the time value of money which might cause one to recommend the acceptance of project Y. On the other hand, if Chi's liquidity is a problem, project X might be preferred because it has a shorter payback period.

Consider also risk factors: how might the expected returns be affected by changes in patterns of demand, for example? The characteristics of the projects, as well as the circumstances of Chi Ltd, need to be considered in arriving at a suitable recommendation.

W6.5 Computational problems

Question 6.1

The Lundstrom Company's factory consists of three production departments and two service departments, with the following normal monthly indirect costs:

	Production Departments			Service Departments	
	A	B	C	M	N
	£	£	£	£	£
Variable	5,200	16,000	10,500	7,500	–
Fixed – divisible	6,000	4,500	2,000	–	–
Fixed – indivisible	800	1,500	3,000	2,000	10,000
Allocated (full cost basis):					
General factory	2,000	2,000	2,000	–	–
Department M	1,000	4,000	5,000	–	–
Department N	5,000	2,000	2,500	500	–
Total	£20,000	£30,000	£25,000	£10,000	£10,000
Normal volume	20,000 direct labour hours	10,000 direct labour hours	12,500 machine-hours	2,000 service-hours	100,000 sq. ft.

Consumption of service department M's services is regarded as a divisible fixed cost in department A and as proportionately variable with volume in departments B and C. General indirect manufacturing costs are entirely fixed and largely indivisible.

Product X has just been developed by the Lundstrom Company and is now ready for commercialization. It will be listed in the company's next product catalogue, and orders will be taken for immediate or deferred delivery at list price.

Product X will compete with more than 100 products offered by 36 competing companies in the Lundstrom market area. Its biggest competition will come from the Deane Company's product P, which now sells 5,000 units a month, about 35% of the potential market for product X, at a unit price of £59. Lundstrom's market share in other product lines in its own region ranges from 5 to 35%, with most products between 10 and 15%. Prices in this market have been relatively stable for several years.

Product X has a number of significant advantages over product P and other competing products already on the market, and competitors will not be able to match these distinctive features for at least a year. The Lundstrom sales department is enthusiastic about the new product and feels that at a competitive price product X could achieve a good share of the market, perhaps as much as 15%, during the first year. Whether it could keep or increase its market share in subsequent years would depend in part on customers' experience with the product and in part on competitors' responses to product X.

The company's development engineers estimate that after an initial six month learning period, production inputs for a unit of product X will be: direct materials, £5; direct labour, £25; department A, three direct labour hours; department B, one and a half direct labour hours; and department C, two machine-hours. Errors in the engineers' estimates at this stage of product development have generally been within 10% of actual costs in the past, and underestimates have been just as frequent as overestimates.

Mark-ups over factory cost on the company's other regular products average about 40% of full factory cost and generally range between 25 and 45%.

Most selling and administrative expenses will be the same no matter what price is set on product X. Selling costs attributable to this product are expected to amount to about £5,000 a month, not counting any special price deals that might be made to stimulate sales during the introductory period.

(a) Prepare a unit cost estimate or estimates that you feel would help management arrive at a price for product X. Discuss your reasoning.

(b) Recommend a selling price for product X. Support your recommendation, using figures from the problem to whatever extent you deem appropriate.

(c) How, if at all, would your answer to (a) differ if the decision were whether to accept a single order for 100 units of product X to be shipped to a customer outside Lundstrom's ordinary sales area at a time when factory capacity in each department was only 75% utilized?

(d) Assuming that product X is now in the line, selling 500 units a month, and that factory production capacity is not fully utilized, what unit cost figure would you use in a rough test of the desirability of discontinuing production and sale of product X? Explain.

Question 6.2

The Maryland Dairy has a machine which cost £40,000 four years ago. Its net book value is now £24,000 and it could be sold for £15,000. The company plans to purchase a new machine costing £55,000 which will have an estimated useful life of 10 years. Shipping and installation costs are expected to be approximately £1,500. The new machinery is expected to produce additional annual profits of £8,000 p.a. over its expected life, before charging depreciation on a straight line basis. However, an additional investment in working capital will also be required of £3,500. The enterprise's cost of capital is estimated at 12%. (Ignore taxation.)

Evaluate the proposed investment in the new machinery.

Question 6.3

The marketing director of Beauchief Co. Ltd (which manufactures and markets small electrical domestic appliances) is proposing to add a new product to its line. Market studies suggest a likely annual sales volume of 10,000 units at a selling price of £40 per unit.

The necessary production/distribution facilities can be provided at an estimated capital cost of £750,000. These would be financed by a bank loan at 12% and have an expected life of 10 years with no scrap value.

Variable costs per unit are anticipated at £14 and additional specific fixed costs of £40,000 p.a. are to be budgeted if the project goes ahead.

Required:

(a) Present a report to justify the decision you would recommend concerning the adoption of this proposal.

(b) Comment on the impact of a reduced selling price (£30 per unit) and an increased level of sales (10,750 units p.a.) on your recommendation in (a).

(c) Would your recommendation in (b) be changed if the rate of interest was 10% rather than 12%? Explain.

Note: Extracts from the table of present value of 1 per annum:

	10%	12%
10 years	6.144	5.650

Question 6.4

The following table gives details of the market performance of all firms offering product X over the last three years within a given industry.

On the basis of an analysis of the given data you are required to advise the management of Firm A on its future strategy relating to product X.

Product X	Volume (000 units)	Sales revenue (£000)	Market share (%)	Profit (£000)
Firm A				
19 × 1	200	700	20	90
19 × 2	312	1,000	21	130
19 × 3	384	1,200	17	171
Firm B				
19 × 1	400	1,400	40	200
19 × 2	700	2,200	47	400
19 × 3	1,200	3,600	51	792
Firm C				
19 × 1	280	1,000	29	118
19 × 2	380	1,200	26	170
19 × 3	660	2,000	29	258
Firm D				
19 × 1	112	400	11	40
19 × 2	90	300	6	20
19 × 3	64	200	3	5
Total market				
19 × 1	992	3,500	100	448
19 × 2	1,482	4,700	100	720
19 × 3	2,308	7,000	100	1,226

W6.6 Illustrative material

A NOTE ON THE PRODUCT LIFE CYCLE

Reprinted with permission from Wilson, R.M.S. (1983), pp. 454–8

A product life cycle is a way of portraying (either before or after the event) the cash flow/profitability/sales level of a product. In Figure W6.3 a product's life cycle is represented in terms of funds flows: prior to its launch all funds flows are negative due to R & D and related activities. Even after the launch it takes some time for positive funds flows to counteract the heavy initial promotional and other launch outlays. When the product is deleted, funds cease flowing altogether.

Figure W6.4 looks at the product life cycle in a slightly different way: it not only separates revenue and profit, but it also identifies different phases of the life cycle. The development phase may last about six years on average, and the post-launch period will last for a similar length of time. Within the development phase, of course, are the various screening stages from concept testing to test marketing, and these exist in parallel with laboratory work, pilot plant activity, and main-line production planning (including methods and materials).

In the introduction phase costs will be high, sales revenue low, and profits probably negative. The skill that is exhibited in testing and launching the product will rank high in this phase as a critical factor in securing success and initial market acceptance.

Following a successful launch is the growth phase, during which the product's market penetration – hence sales – will increase. Since costs will be lower than

Figure W6.3

Product life cycle – 1.

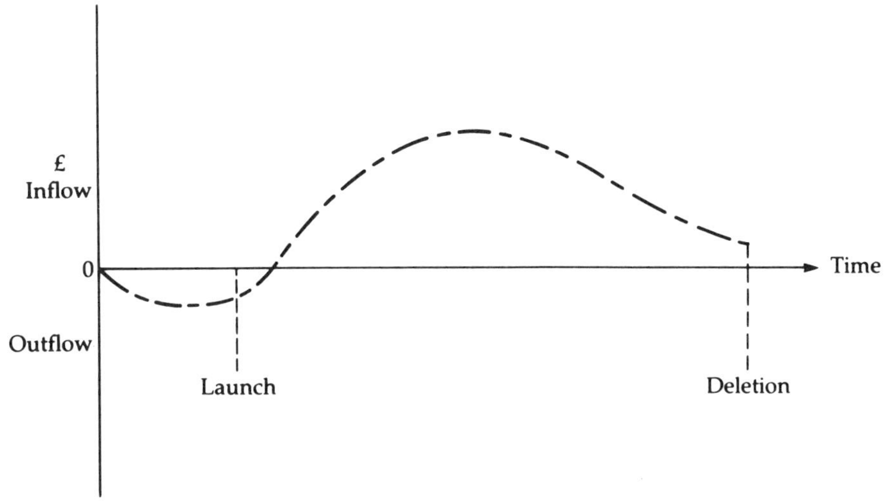

Figure W6.4

Product life cycle – 2.

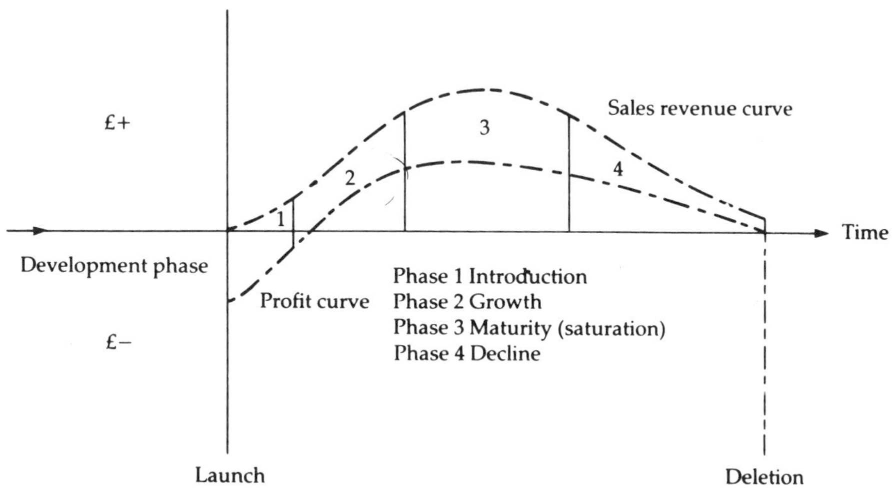

in the earlier phases the product will start to make a profit contribution. Following the consumer acceptance in the launch phase it now becomes vital to secure wholesaler/retailer support.

As growth levels out we reach the phase of maturity. This is characterized by stable prices and profits and the emergence of competitors. However, as the market becomes saturated pressure is exerted for a new product, and sales (along with profit) begin to fall. Intensified marketing effort may prolong the period of maturity – but only by increasing costs disproportionately. (Saturation and decline stem from a range of very similar competitive offerings that do not offer the consumer a differentiated choice in terms of value or technological superiority.)

Growing price competition as sales decline will reduce profitability until it reaches zero, at which point the product's life is commercially complete. Cost control is especially important in the period of decline in order that the product may be deleted before it begins to incur losses.

An appreciation of the concept of the product life cycle is useful in any cost control exercise relating to R & D, marketing, manufacturing, distribution, or finance in that it brings out some general guidelines. These are:

1. That products have finite lives and pass through the cycle of development, introduction, growth, maturity, decline, and deletion at varying speeds.
2. Product cost, revenue, and profit patterns tend to follow predictable courses through the life cycle: profits first appear during the growth phase and, after stabilizing during the maturity phase, decline thereafter to the point of deletion.
3. Products require different functional emphases in each phase – such as an R & D emphasis in the development phase and a cost control emphasis in the decline phase.

These general guidelines can be used to help in controlling the development of both new and existing products. They indicate that the introduction of a new product so that it reaches its earnings peak as other products decline is helpful in maintaining at least a constant level of profits. Alternatively, as a product reaches its peak, a major modification may help to prolong this phase; or it may be promoted to new markets, or for new uses, or for more frequent use. Figure W6.5 shows the way in which product B can be introduced to take over from the declining product A, and so on. The other case is shown in Figure W6.6 in which a single product

Figure W6.5

Life cycle phasing.

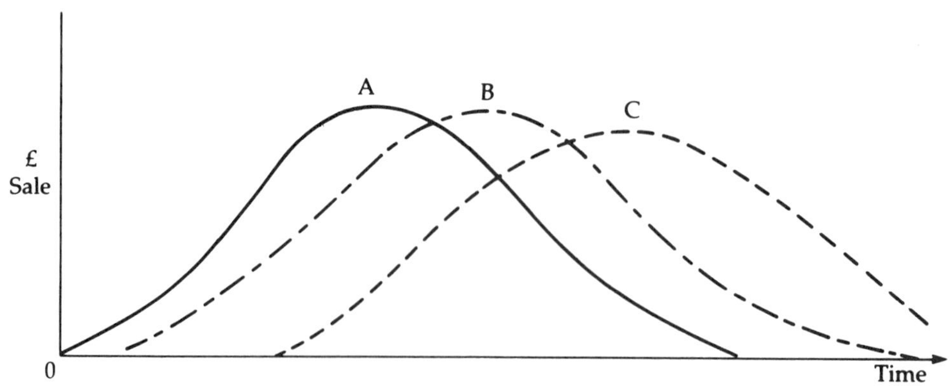

Figure W6.6

Life cycle extensions.

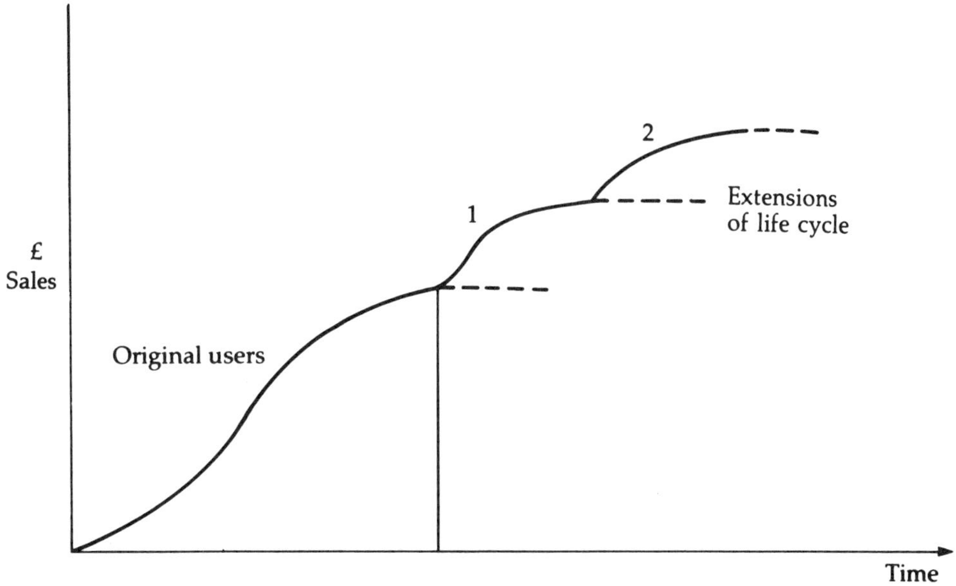

has its life prolonged – and performance improved – by being promoted to new market segments.

The short article on p. 528 was written by the erstwhile finance director of Cadbury's, David Allen, and vividly highlights the interface of the short- and long-run. It is reprinted with permission from *AA*, November, 1986.

STRATEGIC COST ANALYSIS
by
Richard M.S. Wilson
Adapted from *Management Accounting* (CIMA), **68** (9), October, 1990, pp. 42–3.

Strategic focus

Strategic cost analysis is an approach to management accounting that explicitly highlights strategic issues and concerns. It sets cost analysis in a broader context in which cost information is used to develop superior strategies.

The idea of strategy can be considered at various levels, but the main focus in the context of strategic cost analysis is that of *business strategy* which exists at the level of a particular business or division, dealing primarily with the question of competitive position. We can define strategy as:

> **An integrated set of actions aimed at securing a sustainable competitive advantage.**

The notion of *competitive advantage* requires that a given business be viewed relative to its competitors, and continuing success requires that a competitive

BLOW THOSE CLOUDS AWAY

David Allen suggests that success at the tactical and operational level of management can cloud strategic vision

The concept of strategy is one of the most popular topics today: in discussion among managers, in business literature and in consultancy assignments. But like many other management subjects, it lacks any authoritative terminology or structure.

Some of the most useful language is borrowed from military parlance. There it is quite clear that tactics are all about how to proceed in a particular battle, while strategy is about making sure that whatever battles are waged are at the time and place most conducive to victory.

So business tactics are about managing the resources and markets which characterise the particular enterprise, while strategy is about choosing which resources and markets to identify with. These are quite different functions and, as with the military, very few good tacticians are also good strategists.

It is very easy to oversimplify. A few years ago, for instance, 'market orientation' was being propagated as a fundamental principle of good strategic management. Choose and define your market carefully, the advice ran, and realign your resources to attack that market most effectively. But many businesses which followed that seductive advice found (too late in some cases) that the cost, effort and time involved in the realignment was prohibitive. They also found themselves competing fiercely with other businesses which had chosen to attack the same market.

The hostile economic environment of the late 1970s and the 1980s has pushed virtually every business into much shorter planning horizons. In these conditions a 'resource orientation' stance is more appropriate: success – perhaps even survival – is seen to depend on maximising the value of the output from the resources which are currently available.

This latter stance is a very natural one. As individuals we look to exploit the skills we have, rather than seek to replace them. It is also more innovative, in terms of the development of new materials, products, applications and

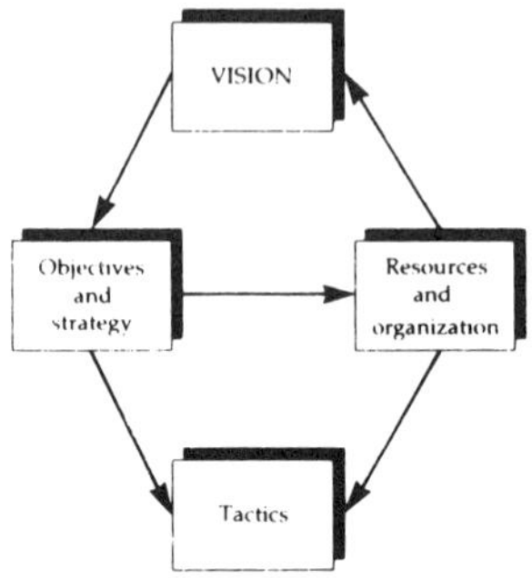

The management strategy diamond

markets. Most of the world's major inventions have resulted from the urge to apply knowledge rather than the urge to satisfy an anticipated demand.

Which orientation prevails in a particular enterprise at any one time is usually clear from its organisation structure and its management accounting system. The jobs of the people reporting directly to the chief executive of a market-oriented enterprise will be defined in terms of the markets for which they are responsible.

In turn their respective management accounting systems will concentrate on measuring the relative profitability of the products and markets served. The sales manager of such a business will not be thanked for identifying markets for which existing resources are not suitable.

The last sentence in each of the two preceding paragraphs emphasise the narrowing of focus which is implied by either orientation. Activities outside the mainstream are seen as a distraction – a negative factor. In terms of pursuing a chosen objective, this is undoubtedly valid and effective. It is, in other words, as eminently suitable approach to the tactical level of management. Strategy, however, is something quite different.

The fact is that defining a business in terms of either *a* market or *a* resource is a clearly static concept, whereas the environment is undoubtedly dynamic. Market requirements and technologies are changing very rapidly: failing to respond will inevitably drive a business into ever-decreasing circles. The evidence of this is overwhelming, as more and more enterprises spin off peripheral businesses in order to concentrate on core activities and take pride in the pace of reduction of numbers.

Two layers down from the chief executive of an enterprise – be it market or resource oriented – the organisation becomes functionalist. Reporting to a general manager we have people with titles like purchasing manager, manufacturing manager, sales manager, finance manager. Again, the benefits of this in terms of operational efficiency are clear.

The British engineering industry's experience over the last five years or so provides numerous examples. Companies in that industry, almost without exception, have been oriented to particular markets, or even sub-sectors like motor cars. The engineering strike, the ensuing settlement and then the massive strengthening of the pound left many of them grossly over-resourced. In particular, they found themselves with too many factories.

In circumstances such as these, a functionalist - structure is an essential feature of implementing the desired rationalisation strategy. If all factory activities report through to one manufacturing director, then local jealousies can be subordinated to the overall best interests of the business. Unit costs will be driven down, and if all goes well the business will emerge much smaller, but viable – until the enviroment changes again.

Again the price paid for this operational efficiency is a deadening of the strategic nerves. The manufacturing function is not likely to embrace enthusiastically any 'opportunities' to increase unit costs. That is unfortunate if, as most observers see, we are in an era in which the provision of a greater variety and a higher service level are key to competitive success. Likewise, if they are being judged by their performance against volume budgets, sales/marketing managers are most unlikely to risk venturing into new areas of activity.

It has to be said that traditional management accounting systems, being essentially analytical, often encourage the ever-decreasing-circle syndrome. If overall performance is inadequate, the accountant can pinpoint which plant, product or market sector is to blame: adverse variances get the lion's share of attention. Plants are closed down, products withdrawn or prices increased until equilibrium (in this case budgeted performance) is restored.

To sum up, we can be proud of the organisational and accounting practices we have in place for the implementation of chosen strategies and their subsequent management at the tactical level: the bottom half of the diamond in the chart.

What needs to be recognised is that the success achieved at the lower level can, and evidently does, cloud the vision required to manage the top half. Dispersing this cloud is the essence of strategic management. Financial managers have a crucial role to play in this task, but to do so they need to replace analysis with synthesis. ■

advantage (e.g. in superior product quality, lower costs, or more efficient distribution) be sought and maintained.

It needs to be emphasized that 'strategy' is not synonymous with 'long-term plan', but rather consists of a business's attempts to reach some preferred future state by adapting its competitive position as circumstances change. Whilst a series of strategic moves may be planned, competitors' actions and reactions will typically mean that the actual moves taken will have to be modified to accommodate those actions and reactions.

Strategic thinking has distinguished between *strategic missions* (such as building, holding, and harvesting) on the one hand, and *generic strategies* on the other. On the latter theme the work of Michael Porter has been particularly influential. He has argued that sustainable competitive advantage can be achieved by means of one or other of the following generic strategies:

(i) *cost leadership*, through which the business seeks to be the lowest cost producer within its industry;
(ii) differentiation, through which the business seeks to offer some unique dimension in its product/service that is valued by consumers and which can thereby command a premium price.

If we take the strategy of cost leadership it is intuitively the case that a business having a cost advantage (i.e. a lower unit cost for a market offering of given specification that is comparable with the market offerings of competitors) is likely to be strong, whilst those having a cost disadvantage are likely to be weak. By relating this to the logic underlying the *experience curve* (i.e. that real costs decline as cumulative experience increases), it will be appreciated that the enterprise that has the greatest experience should have the lowest unit costs. This position of cost leadership should give rise to higher profits.

A comparison of approaches

Significant differences can be readily identified between conventional approaches to cost analysis and a strategic approach. To some extent these differences reflect the training that management accountants have received. In addition, they reflect the tendency to think in financial terms that are associated with existing activities. For example, a conventional approach to cost analysis might give attention to controlling working capital, decreasing work-in-progress, reducing wastage rates, or negotiating modest wage increases as means to improve a business's performance. But if the business is suffering from intense competitive pressures, is in a declining industry, or is lagging behind in the adoption of current technology, no amount of marginal adjustments to insignificant details will improve its fortunes.

The contrast between conventional and strategic approaches to cost categorization is highlighted in Fig. W6.7. This suggests that the traditional focus in the top right-hand quadrant is inadequate if a more comprehensive strategic approach is required.

It is characteristic of traditional management accounting systems to be reactive and to deal in a programmed way with one-off decisions. By contrast, a strategic approach needs to be proactive and designed to deal in an unprogrammed way with each phase of strategic decision-making; but, most significantly, it needs

Figure W6.7

A total view of cost categories.

	Strategic	Operational
Tangible	• Debt charges • New plants • Product development • Market development	• Labour • Materials • Energy • Supplies • Contract services
Intangible	• Poor product positioning • Technological obsolescence • Poor location of facilities	• Poor quality • Absenteeism • Labour turnover • Low morale • Lost output • Late delivery

(Adapted from Richardson (1988), p. 30)

to be capable of dealing with one business's position (in terms of costs - plus prices, revenues, market shares, volumes, and profits) relative to the positions of competing businesses. The key notion here is that of relative competitive position. This has largely been overlooked by management accountants – despite the long-standing encouragement of Ken Simmonds through his pioneering work on strategic management accounting.

Insofar as competitive advantage is cost-based, we need to recall that conventional cost analysis:

- concentrates on manufacturing activities;
- ignores the impact of other activities;
- overlooks linkages among activities by analysing each activity in a discrete way;

Figure W6.8

Conventional vs. strategic cost analysis.

Conventional characteristics	*Strategic characteristics*
Historical	Prospective
Single entity	Relative position
Single period	Multiple periods
Single decision	Sequences, patterns
Introspective	Outward looking
Manufacturing focus	Competitive focus
Existing activities	Possibilities
Reactive	Proactive
Programmed	Unprogrammed
Overlooks linkages	Embraces linkages
Data orientation	Information orientation
Based on existing systems	Unconstrained by existing systems
Built on conventions	Ignores conventions

- fails to assess the cost positions of competitors in relative terms;
- relies too heavily on existing accounting systems.

In contrast, strategic cost analysis focuses on:

- the determinants of relative cost position;
- the ways in which a firm might secure a sustainable cost advantage;
- the costs of differentiation.

A summary of differences is given in Fig. W6.8.

Undertaking strategic cost analysis
Porter identified the *value chain* as a means of breaking down an enterprise's strategically-relevant activities in order to understand the behaviour of costs. Competitive advantage comes from carrying out these activities in a more cost-effective way than one's competitors.

A value chain consists of nine interrelated activities. They are, in part, primary activities (inbound logistics, operations, outbound logistics, marketing – including sales, and service), and, in part, support activities (infrastructure, human resource management, technology development, and procurement). The latter exist to facilitate the former, with the particular configuration reflecting any given enterprise's history, strategy, and the underlying economics of its situation.

The value aspect is to be found in the price that customers are willing to pay, hence the margin to be made depends upon the cost-effectiveness of primary and support activities on the one hand, and the market's perception of the firm's offering on the other. This is shown in Fig. W6.9 (based on Brock).

Any enterprise's cost position (relative to its competitors) is derived from the cost behaviour patterns associated with its value chain. These in turn depend upon *cost drivers* (which are the structural determinants of activities' costs). Some cost drivers are within the enterprise's control, but some are not, and a given activity's cost may be due to several cost drivers acting together. It will be apparent that a

Figure W6.9

The strategic triangle.

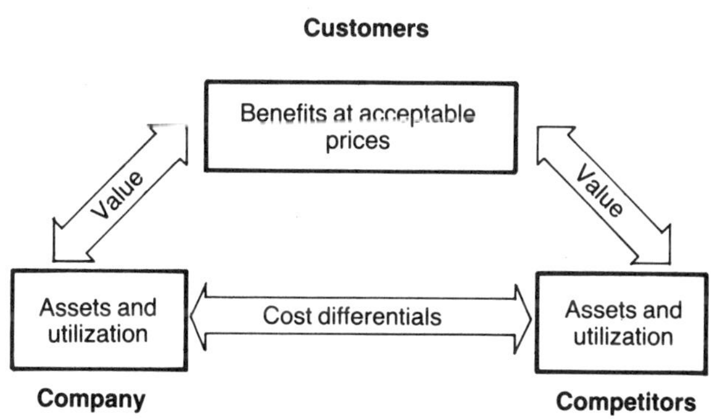

particular enterprise's cost position on any activity within the value chain will depend on whichever cost drivers are at play. The impact of different cost drivers will vary from enterprise to enterprise – even within the same industry. If an enterprise can understand which of these cost drivers affect its relative cost position it should be in a good position to achieve cost advantages over its competitors.

In order to gain real benefits from this type of analysis, attempts should be made to quantify the impact of each cost driver influencing the cost of a value or activity. Having done this for one's own enterprise the next step is to do it for one's competitors. In this way relative cost advantages can be identified and exploited. However, a cost advantage needs to be maintained once it has been established, and this requires continuous effort.

References

Brock, J.J. (1984). Competitor analysis: some practical approaches. *Industrial Marketing Management* **13**, pp. 225–31.

Porter, M.E. (1985). *Competitive advantage: creating and sustaining superior performance*. Free Press, New York.

Simmonds, K. (1981). Strategic management accounting. *Management Accounting* **59** (4) April, pp. 26–9. Reprinted in R. Cowe (ed.) (1988) *Handbook of Management Accounting* (Second edn). Gower, Aldershot.

Wilson, R.M.S. (1990). Strategic management accounting, Chapter 5 (pp. 82–105) in Ashton, D.J., T.M. Hopper and R.W. Scapens (eds) *Issues in Management Accounting*. Prentice-Hall, London.

CHAPTER

7 Setting standards and estimates

WORKBOOK

W7.1 Introduction

In Chapter 3 we identified two forms of control – feedforward and feedback. The former was seen to relate more to the future than the latter. Feedforward control is essentially concerned with determining the future, while feedback control is concerned with evaluating the past. However, in this chapter we illustrate how a strict dichotomy between feedforward and feedback control cannot always be maintained. Indeed, there is no theoretical necessity to separate feedforward precisely from feedback control in everyday managerial accounting practice.

The discussion on estimates, standards and budgets highlights that while these managerial accounting tools are essentially ways of controlling the future, they also form the basis for feedback control. Thus, individual managers and departments may be evaluated through a comparison of their current level of performance with their budgeted or estimated level of performance. Hence the same set of information may be used both to control the future and to evaluate the quantity and quality of output.

Chapter 7 of the text discusses a number of accounting and statistical techniques that may be used to derive estimates and standards. It also outlines the effects of learning and experience on the development of such estimates. Because of the computational nature of these techniques it was decided to provide reasonably detailed revision notes in this Workbook chapter.

In addition we have sought to discuss the operation of estimates and standards in non-manufacturing contexts. Theoretically there is little difference between the development of such estimates and standards. In practice the information required to develop non-manufacturing estimates and standards may be much harder to obtain than that required for manufacturing estimates and standards. In particular, standards relating to the quality of output/service are extremely difficult to develop. For instance, it is debatable how one might set a standard for the quality of customer service or the degree of rapport between a health professional and his/her client. In general, non-manufacturing estimates and standards are input-related and these are often used as surrogate output measures. For example, standards might be set for the number of customer complaints that are satisfactorily dealt with, the number of trains that are punctual, the length of time taken to correct after-sale faults, etc. Such measures attempt to approximate a measure of output quality. However, their success depends on the extent to which they map or tap the underlying output phenomenon.

W7.2 Revision topics

Question 7.1
Explain how estimates act as elements of feedforward control.

Answer
In order to act as a feedforward regulator the managerial accounting system should supply information that is:

(i) future-oriented;
(ii) predictive;
(iii) performance-centred; and
(iv) which acts as a basis for control.

These characteristics are necessary because information for feedforward control is intended to enable the organization to know and to predict its future performance. In addition, feedforward information may be used to provide feedback control, that is, information on how well the organization has performed when compared to its initial expectations.

Predictions of the following are required:

(i) output or activity levels expected;
(ii) inputs and their availability; and
(iii) the relationship between levels of output and required inputs.

The predictive input-output model should also be able to anticipate changes, whether emanating from the environment or from the organization itself, and to predict their impact on the organization.

Predicting the future implies being able to manipulate existing organizational structures and strategies efficiently and effectively given prior predictions of the future. For instance, a management accountant may predict that the exchange rate between the Japanese yen and sterling would move against sterling and therefore he could potentially increase the Japanese loan interest payments which the organization needs to make each quarter. In order to manage the future the accountant may decide to enter into certain contracting arrangements (the technical term is 'forward cover') which ensure that the organization's liability to its Japanese creditors is as low as possible.

Feedforward information usually consist of three types:

(i) estimates;
(ii) standards; and
(iii) budgets

All three types of feedforward information are needed in public sector as well as in private sector organizations.

Among the most important items that are estimated in organizations are costs. In times of high inflation or stagflation cost control becomes one of the means by which an organization may maintain and expand its competitive edge. In estimating costs three questions are important:

(i) Which costs are fixed, variable or mixed?
(ii) Which variables are related to or influence the costs under investigation?

(iii) What is the functional relationship that best describes the observed cost pattern?

In attempting to answer these questions, a variety of estimation methods may be used. These include:

(i) the industrial engineering approach;
(ii) the account inspection method;
(iii) the visual fit method;
(iv) the high-low method;
(v) regression analysis.

Coverage of these methods will be found in Chapter 7 of the text.

Question 7.2
In what ways do standards act as elements of control?

Answer
A standard is a preset estimate of input or output which is used as a benchmark or yardstick for the comparison of expected with actual performance. A standard serves as a norm, an example, a criterion of acceptable performance or behaviour.

A standard may be set in monetary terms, in physical units or in qualitative terms. It may also be set for any aspect of an organization's activity, irrespective of whether the organization is a commercial or non-commercial enterprise.

Standards setting and standard costing systems are said to have the following control functions:

(i) to act as a form of feedforward control by planning for future inputs and outputs;
(ii) to act as a basis for feedback control and as a means of performance evaluation;
(iii) to motivate employees by communicating clear, challenging goals;
(iv) to determine the cost of products and services for income determination, establishing pricing policies and inventory valuation.

Standards should not be set at too tight or high a level or they may lead to low employee morale and dissatisfaction. They should be set such that an attainable level of satisfactory performance is achieved.

Question 7.3
How can the learning curve help in the standard setting process?

Answer
A learning curve is a cost function that shows how the average labour cost per unit of output declines as cumulative production rises. As employees become more familiar with a task the time taken to perform that task declines.

The basic formula for a learning curve is

$$Y = aX^b$$

where Y = cumulative average time (or cost) per unit (or per lot)
a = time (cost) for the first unit or batch

X = cumulative number of units (or lots produced)
b = the learning exponent, which is log learning rate/log 2.

This equation may be put into the logarithm form by taking logarithms of both sides of the equation. This results in:

$$\log Y = \log a + (b \times \log X)$$

Let us illustrate the use of this formula with an example: Killara plc produces widgets in batches of 10 units and the firm experiences an 80% learning curve. One hundred minutes are required for the first lot each time the product is manufactured. The relationship between the number of units produced and the time taken is shown below:

Cumulative number of units	Cumulative average time per unit	Cumulative total time
10	100/10 = 10.000	10 × 10.000 = 100
20	10 × 80% = 8.000	20 × 8.000 = 160
40	8 × 80% = 6.400	40 × 6.400 = 256
80	6.4 × 80% = 5.120	80 × 5.120 = 409.6
160	5.12 × 80% = 4.096	160 × 4.096 = 655.36

With the help of the formula above we can now work out the cumulative average time for batches or units other than those shown above. Assume that we wish to find out what the cumulative average time per batch is for the first 45 batches. For an 80% learning curve the value of b is approximately −0.3219. Using the formula we obtain:

$$\begin{aligned} \ln Y &= \ln a + b \ln X \\ &= \ln 100 + (-0.3219) \ln 45 \\ &= 4.605 + (-0.3219)(3.8067) \\ &= 3.3796 \end{aligned}$$

The antilog of 3.3796 is approximately 29.36.

Therefore the average cumulative time taken per batch for the first 45 batches is 29.36 min. The total time would have been 29.36 × 45 = 1,321 min.

Note that in the example we have used natural logarithms. This was purely a matter of convenience. You could have used logarithms taken to any base.

The learning effect is not always found in all manufacturing operations. In general, the greater the amount of labour required for production, the greater the opportunity for learning effects to occur. Highly mechanized and automated production processes offer little opportunity for learning to occur. (But perhaps even robots or their designers learn!)

Learning usually tapers off and ceases altogether at certain levels of activity. At times, learning may not stop but there may be externally imposed constraints on the amount of improvement that could be made. For instance, although learning effects could further reduce the amount of time taken to attain a certain level of activity, union regulations may prohibit such an occurrence.

Question 7.4
Comment on the use of standards in non-commercial organizations.

Answer
Standards in non-commercial organizations may be more difficult to set and quantify than in commercial organizations. This is largely because the input-output relationships are often unclear.

At times input standards are used as surrogates of output. For instance, in judging the quality of care delivered by a hospital, we may use standards such as the ratio of medical staff to patients or the number of nursing staff per patient. Essentially, these are input standards but there is an implicit assumption that the greater the availability of inputs, the higher would be the quality of output.

W7.3 Discussion topics

Question 7.1
What do estimates, standards and budgets have in common?

Question 7.2
Why is it important to develop estimates, standards and budgets for an organization?

Question 7.3
How is feedforward information useful for feedback purposes?

Question 7.4
What are the limitations of the account inspection method and the high-low method?

Question 7.5
What is a scattergram? A management accountant analysed a variable cost by plotting recorded accounting data for a 10-year period on a scattergram and fitting a line by inspection. How valid is the advice of the accountant based on this result?

Question 7.6
'Regression analysis is the only foolproof method of estimating costs. I would recommend it without hesitation for all organizations.'

To what extent would you agree with this statement?

Question 7.7
'The highest possible standards should be set in order that employees might be motivated to achieve their best.'

Discuss this statement and its implications for the setting of standards.

Question 7.8
'We are a hospital here. Standard-setting has little application when we are interested in saving lives. How would you set a standard for the quality of care or for how many X-ray machines ought to be purchased? We use resources as and when necessary. We are naturally efficient because it is a matter of life and death!' Discuss the applicability of a standard cost system in a non-commercial organization like a hospital. What kinds of standards may be set for such organizations?

W7.4 Worked examples

Question 7.1

Gladstone plc requires information on the cost of electricity used in its factory. This cost is estimated to have both a fixed and a variable component. The following data on the cost of electricity used and machine hours worked are available for the last six months of the previous financial year:

Month	Cost of electricity	Machine hours
January	£16,600	3,000
February	£14,800	2,700
March	£13,400	2,500
April	£21,500	5,200
May	£19,500	4,650
June	£17,450	3,900

Assuming that Gladstone plc uses the high-low method of analysis, what is the estimated cost of electricity per machine hour?

Answer

Under the high-low method, the estimated variable cost of electricity is calculated as follows:

$$\begin{aligned}\text{Cost of electricity} &= £[21{,}500 - 13{,}400]/[5{,}200 - 2{,}500]\\ &= £8{,}100/2{,}700\\ &= £3.00\end{aligned}$$

It is also possible to use the high-low method to separate the fixed and variable elements of a mixed cost. This is illustrated in Fig. W7.1, in which the high and low observations are plotted. The slope of the line joining these points reflects the variable cost per machine hour, and the intercept on the y axis represents the fixed cost element. This is £5,900, which can be proved as follows:

$$TC = FC + VC$$

At the high level $TC = £21{,}500$
$VC = £3.00$ per machine hour

$$\begin{aligned}\therefore £21{,}500 &= FC + £(3 \times 5{,}200)\\ \therefore FC &= £21{,}500 - £15{,}600\\ FC &= £5{,}900\end{aligned}$$

You can confirm this figure by substituting FC = £5,900 and VC = £3.00 per machine hour in the low level observations: £13,400 = £5,900 + £(3 × 2,500).

Question 7.2

Newbridge is a construction company. It has just completed a bridge over the Derwent River. This was the first bridge the company had ever built and it required 100 weeks to complete. Now, having hired a bridge construction crew with some experience, the company would like to continue building bridges. Because of the investment in heavy machinery needed continuously by this crew, the company believes it would have to bring the average construction time down to less than one year (52 weeks) per bridge in order to earn a sufficient return. The

Figure W7.1

Separating fixed from variable costs.

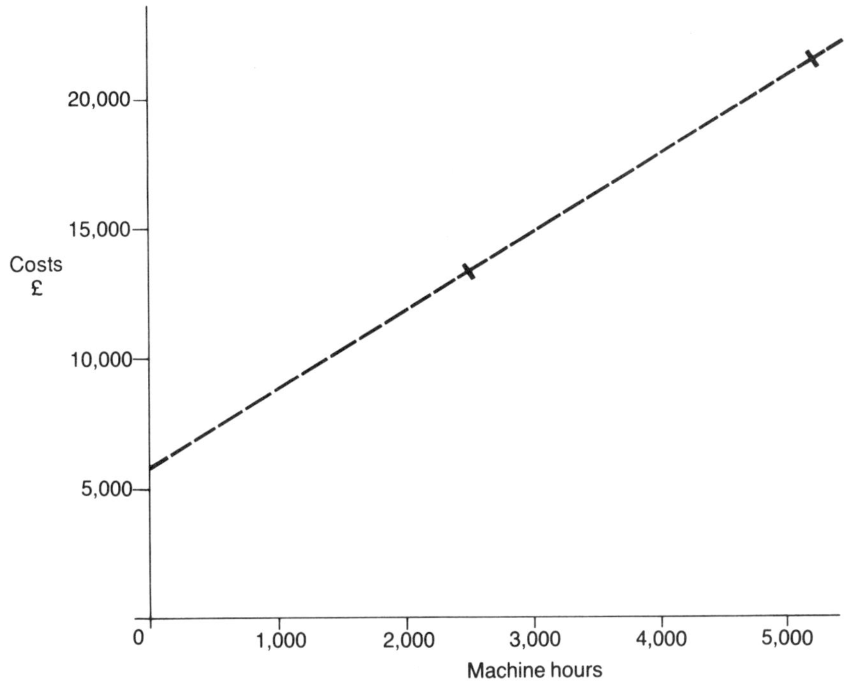

average construction time is expected to follow an 80% learning curve. In order to bring the average construction time (over all bridges constructed) below one year per bridge, what is the minimum number of bridges that the crew will need to build? (Assume all bridges are identical.)

(CMA adapted)

Answer

In order to answer this question we need to construct an average-time learning curve table. This is shown below:

Cumulative number of bridges	Cumulative average weeks per bridge
1	100.0
2	100 × 80% = 80.0
4	80 × 80% = 64.0
8	64 × 80% = 51.2

In order to reduce the the average construction time (over all bridges constructed) to below 52 weeks per bridge the company needs to build seven additional bridges.

Question 7.3

The Flower Factory manufactures and sells perfumes distilled from flowers and herbs. Sales appear to be heavily dependent upon the level of advertising. In order to obtain more precise information upon this belief the management accountant has been asked to analyse the relationship between the annual advertising expense for several well-known brands and their annual sales. The following information was obtained:

Brand	*Annual advertising expense* (£ m.)	*Annual sales* (£ m.)
Jasmine	2	5
Rose	4	7
Honeysuckle	3	6
Lavender	1	2

The management accountant has decided to fit a regression line to this information using the least squares method. It has been decided that sales is the dependent variable (y) and advertising expenditure is the independent variable (x).

Required:

(a) Calculate the values of a and b, and thereby complete the predicted regression equation.

(b) Based on the regression equation, an advertising expenditure of £2.5 m. should produce what amount of sales on average?

Answer

(a) Using the normal equations (given on pp. 217–18 of Chapter 7):

$$b = \frac{4(58) - 10(20)}{4(30) - (10)^2} \qquad a = 20/4 - 1.6(10/4)$$

$$= 5 - 4$$

$$= 32/40 \qquad = 1$$

$$= 1.6$$

Therefore the predicted regression equation is:

$$y^p = a + bx \text{ (in £m.)}$$
$$= 1 + 1.6x$$

(b) If £2.5 m. were spent on advertising expenditure the regression equation predicts that sales would on average be:

$$y^p = 1 + 1.6(2.5)$$
$$= 1 + 4$$
$$= \text{£}5\text{ m.}$$

W7.5 Computational problems

Question 7.1

Paine Corporation wishes to determine the fixed portion of its electricity expense (a mixed expense) as measured against direct labour hours for the first three months of 1993. Information for the first three months of 1993 is as follows:

	Direct labour hours	Electricity expenses (£)
January	34,000	610
February	31,000	585
March	34,000	610

Required:
What is the fixed portion of Paine's electricity expense, rounded to the nearest pound?

(AICPA adapted)

Question 7.2
The maintenance expenses of Rastus Enterprises are being analysed for the purpose of constructing a budget. Examination of past records disclosed the following costs and volume measures:

	Highest	*Lowest*
Cost per month	£39,200	£32,000
Machine hours	24,000	15,000

Required:

(a) Using the high-low method of analysis calculate the estimated variable cost per machine hour.
(b) Using the high-low technique estimate the annual fixed cost for maintenance expenditures.

(AICPA adapted)

Question 7.3
ABC Company is seeking more accurate cost information. The management accountant has undertaken an analysis of heating costs in one of the company's offices. The data for this analysis is presented below:

Week	Heating costs (£)	Hours of supply
1	110	11.0
2	120	15.2
3	235	15.0
4	315	14.5
5	250	20.0
6	400	18.5
7	510	20.4
8	450	26.0

Required:

(a) Using regression analysis, calculate the values of (i) intercept and (ii) slope.
(b) Write a short explanation that interprets the results of the regression analysis to management.

Question 7.4

Kenzo Manufacturing Corporation produces plastic rings in lots of 100 units and 8 hours are required for the first lot. The firm experiences an 80% learning curve. What is the total time required to produce 400 rings?

(CMA adapted)

Question 7.5

Hampden Park Company manufactures and sells trivets. Production is subject to an 80% learning curve. The trivets are produced in lots of 300 units and 60 minutes of labour are required to assemble the first lot. Using the formula for a 80% learning curve, calculate the cumulative average minutes required per lot to complete four lots of trivets.

(CPA adapted)

Question 7.6

The accountant of the EEC Electronics Company believes that identifying the variable and fixed components of the firm's costs will enable its managers to make better planning and control decisions. Among the costs she is concerned about is the behaviour of indirect supplies expense. She believes there is some correlation between the machine hours worked and the amount of indirect supplies used.

A member of the accountant's staff has suggested that a simple linear regression model be used to determine the cost behaviour of the indirect supplies. The regression equation shown below was developed from 40 pairs of observations using the least-squares method of regression. The regression equation and related measures are as follows:

$$S = £200 + £4H$$

where S = total monthly costs of indirect supplies
H = machine hours per month

Required:

(a) Explain the meaning of 200 and 4 in the regression equation S = £200 + £4H.
(b) Calculate the estimated cost of indirect supplies if 900 machine hours are to be used during a month.

W7.6 Case study

Unique Engineering Ltd

Unique Engineering Ltd has a sound reputation for its ability to design and manufacture, or make to customer specifications, highly specialized products. These include pressure vessels, tanks and complete plants for the food and beverage processing and paint and chemicals manufacturing industries.

The cutting, forming and welding of the materials for many of the products requires special knowledge and innovative techniques. The company has attracted well motivated, highly skilled tradesmen who find the work interesting and challenging.

The firm is organised into four service departments, responsible only to, and reporting directly to, the general manager, and two functional line departments, marketing and production. Within the production department there are two major sections, each under the control of a section head. The organization chart is shown in Fig. W7.2.

Overall results have been quite satisfactory but very frequently there are wide discrepancies between estimates and actual costs for jobs. Favourable and unfavourable variances have tended to offset one another and the general manager is concerned that this has been partly due to luck. He is anxious to improve control of estimating and operations.

Meetings have been held and investigations carried out in an effort to improve matters. In particular a customer order for three specialized, stainless steel, steam-jacketed, lagged and sheathed road tankers has been subjected to special study.

The cost estimates on which the price quoted to the customer was based is given

Figure W7.2

Unique Engineering Ltd.

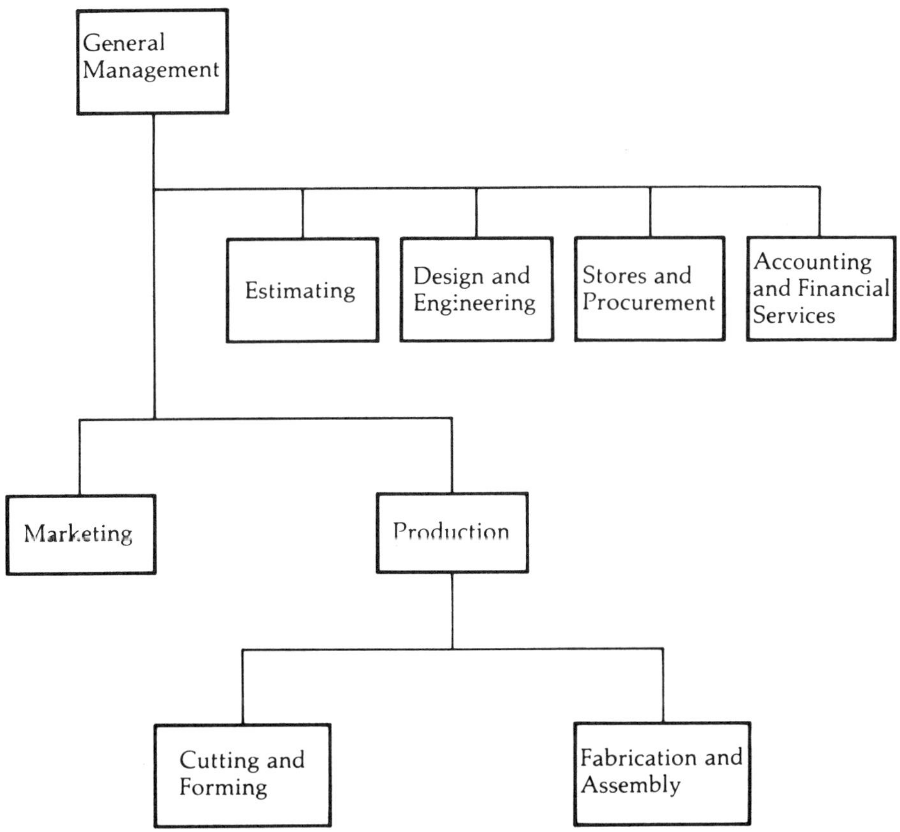

Figure W7.3

Cost estimate 1 road tankeı — design type 228.

	£000
Direct materials	30
Direct labour: 5,000 hours at £10 per hour	50
Design and engineering expenses	5
Direct expenses	15
Indirect manufacturing costs: calculated at £12 per direct labour hour	60
	160

Price quoted: £200,000 per unit (for each of 3 units)

Figure W7.4

Cost information on 3 tankers.

Job number:	1018	1019	1020
Direct labour hours recorded	5,200	5,800	4,500
	£000	£000	£000
Direct materials issued	28	38	30
Design and engineering expenses	11	14	2
Direct expenses	14	17	17

in Fig. W7.3. The three tankers were built under job numbers 1018, 1019 and 1020. Information about the completed jobs is given in Fig. W7.4.

Required:

(a) Calculate the completed cost for each job and for the total customer order.
(b) Calculate the gross margin on each job and for the total customer order.
(c) Calculate the gross margin percentage (on sales) for each job and for the total customer order.
(d) In respect of job 1019 stainless steel of incorrect specification was issued from the store. This was cut, formed and welded into the job before the error was discovered. It was then cut out and scrapped. More materials were requisitioned to complete the job. Cost of the wasted materials charged to the job was £9,000.

A total of 600 normal direct labour hours charged against the job were wasted working with and cutting out the incorrect material. Also, because of the delay, the delivery date could not be met so the production manager authorized 200 hours overtime paid for at normal rate plus 50%. Although it was normal procedure to treat any overtime premiums as factory overhead, in this particular case the time was recorded and charged to the job as though 300 normal hours had been worked.

The customer became aware of the problems with job 1019 and did not want to accept a cut and patched tanker. This resulted in several conferences with the customer, some of which took place in the fabrication and assembly shop. As a consequence work was held up and 200 hours of idle labour time resulted. These also were charged against job 1019.

Finally, design and engineering staff were heavily involved in the rectification work and conferences with the customer. This inflated the internal charge from the design and engineering department for job 1019 by £10,000.

Calculate what the actual cost for job 1019 would have been if the error with the steel had not occurred and recalculate the gross margin and gross margin percentage (on sales) for the job on the revised total cost.

(e) The chief estimator said that in estimating an order of this kind, account was taken of the learning effect that would occur during the manufacture of three unusual but identical jobs in sequence. A detailed estimate was then prepared for each job, to which was added all components of cost from the three estimates, and which was averaged to produce a unit cost estimate of the kind reported in this case. The chief estimator said this was done because both the marketing department and the accounting department preferred it this way.

Discuss this in relation to discrepancies between estimated and actual costs for jobs, and for control and performance evaluation purposes. Suggest an improvement in company procedures.

(f) The chief estimator also pointed out that there was no great concern about cost variances (i.e. differences between actual and estimated costs) on particular jobs, claiming that it was due to expertise in the estimating department that the overall results of the firm were satisfactory. Some jobs were very costly to produce because of the time required in the cutting and forming section where labour hours were low but where a great deal of power was used in operating automatic cutting, bending and rolling machines for which depreciation costs were very high. To take account of this the staff just inflated the estimated number of direct labour hours for jobs requiring a lot of work in the cutting and forming section and reduced the estimate of direct labour hours for jobs that involved mainly fabrication and assembly.

Discuss this information and recommend changes to cost accounting procedures that should improve control and help to eliminate one cause of variances between estimated and actual costs.

(This case study was prepared by Mr Terry Vagg and is published here with his permission).

CHAPTER

8 The budgeting process: technical and social aspects

WORKBOOK

W8.1 Introduction

Budgets and budgetary processes constitute one of the most important organizational control mechanisms. Most organizations operate a budgetary system, however rudimentary. Indeed, most sole proprietorships and even families find it necessary to construct budgets that help them to know and control their futures. For these reasons budgets and the human processes that surround them have long generated considerable research interest. With each new research perspective, budgets, like actors on a stage, have been cast into different roles.

One of the earlier lines of research focused on budgets as elements of feed-forward control – as a means to plan and thereby control the future. Budgets have also been seen as instruments for performance evaluation and feedback control which generate certain behavioural outcomes. More recently research interest has focused on the social and political processes which pervade the construction of budgets. In addition, budgets have been seen as constructive instruments (that is, as mechanisms that shape and interpret organizational events).

In Chapter 8 of the text we briefly discussed each of these roles of budgeting. In this Workbook chapter we shall reinforce this discussion in addition to helping you to construct simple master budgets.

W8.2 Revision topics

Question 8.1
Why do organizations budget?

Answer
Budgets play a number of roles and help achieve a variety of organizational, group and individual purposes. These diverse roles include:

(i) the communication and stabilization of organizational objectives – often, managerial objectives are set in broad terms and these need to be operationalized and made concrete via specific budget targets for key programmes and activities;
(ii) the identification of alternative courses of action and the financial consequences of a particular course of action;

(iii) the expression of input–output relationships;
(iv) the provision of a basis for performance evaluation and feedback control;
(v) the making sense of organizational processes, events and facts – budgets help us to interpret processes, numbers and facts in certain ways. They help to shape *patterns of visibility* in organizations. That is, like spotlights, they focus on matters that are considered important by key decision-makers and direct attention away from other (less important?) matters. In addition, they are a means of expressing power and dominant values and beliefs within organizations. Finally, budgets give a sense of order and of rational behaviour within an organization. This sense of order may be genuine in certain circumstances but deceptive in other situations where budget targets are determined primarily through political processes instead of through the application of neutral (?) decision rules.

Question 8.2
How might budgeting be undertaken in non-commercial organizations?

Answer
Budgeting for non-commercial operations is essentially similar in principle to budgeting for commercial operations. In both cases, the level of desired output is first predicted and this then determines the relevant costs and revenues. For instance, a local authority council would first need to estimate the amount of rates and government grants that could be collected and this would determine the amount that could be spent on the council's activities. The main differences in budgeting for non-manufacturing operations are:

(i) input-output relationships are often unclear;
(ii) due to uncertainty about input-output relationships, budgetary changes are often incremental;
(iii) there is greater emphasis on control of measurable inputs, that is, on the control of expenditure;
(iv) performance evaluation based on a budget is difficult as it is often difficult to measure outputs such as the quality of medical care, the effective delivery of social services, etc.

Question 8.3
What are the links between budgeting and, on the one hand, motivation and, on the other, participation?

Answer

(a) Budgets and motivation. Much research has been conducted on the role of budgets in motivating and encouraging employees to perform at high levels. A summary of these research results indicates that:

(i) budgets have no motivation effect unless they are accepted by the individuals responsible for achieving budget targets;
(ii) in general, given acceptance, the more difficult the target the higher the level of performance achieved;

(iii) specific, difficult budget targets are perceived as being of greater relevance to organizational decision-making than loose budgets. This finding is supported by much evidence from a body of psychological literature called goal-setting theory;
(iv) budgets are more likely to be accepted where good upward communication exists; and
(v) cultural and organizational climate factors all influence the individual's reaction to a budget target.

(b) **Budgets and participation.** The literature on budgeting and participation owes much to the work of writers like Maslow, Herzberg and McGregor. These are essentially writers who propound a content theory of motivation. Basically, they argue that, in general, people have already satisfied their lower-order needs, hence these do not act as motivators. Only higher-order needs (such as self-actualization and self-esteem needs which are relatively unsatisfied) act as motivating forces on people. Participation in decision-making and in budgeting is seen as a means of satisfying higher-order needs and, therefore, acts as a motivator.

Participation also accords well with process theories of motivation which suggest that motivation is a function of the valence of outcomes, the E-P and the P-O probability estimates.

(i) Valence refers to the degree of desirability or utility of an outcome.
(ii) The E-P probability estimate is also called *expectancy* and refers to the probability that (more) effort will lead to (better) performance.
(iii) The P-O probability estimate is also called *instrumentality* and refers to the probability that performance will lead to second-order outcomes such as increased salary, promotion, etc.

Participative budgeting should lead to higher levels of motivation by providing budgetees with greater knowledge of the E-P and P-O probability estimates. In addition, participative budgeting is said to have the following advantages:

(i) it promotes acceptance of budget targets;
(ii) through participative budgeting, an employee's job is enriched and this leads to greater job satisfaction;
(iii) it encourages more positive attitudes towards the organization as a whole and higher levels of morale;
(iv) participation should help to decrease the distortion of information.

Does participation work? Research shows that:

(i) participation leads to more positive attitudes towards the budget, the organization and to higher levels of employee satisfaction; but
(ii) participation does not always lead to higher levels of performance. Cultural and personality factors appear to confound this relationship.

Question 8.4
Do budgets have a feedback control role?

Answer

Not only are budgets feedforward control tools; they may also be used as a means of performance evaluation and of providing feedback information. There is relatively little research on the effects of budgets as a form of feedback. Psychological research, however, indicates that the following relationships could also apply to budget feedback:

(i) feedback is less relevant the longer the delay between receipt of feedback and performance of the activity;

(ii) the more frequent the feedback the better is an individual's performance;

(iii) negative feedback needs to be relayed with care as it tends to be less well-received by recipients;

(iv) to be accepted, budget feedback must originate from a source that is regarded as credible and trustworthy by the recipient;

(v) feedback should be provided primarily on those financial factors that are within the control and responsibility of the recipient; and

(vi) because individual personality traits influence the perception of feedback, there is a need to tailor feedback to the person who is receiving it.

W8.3 Discussion topics

Question 8.1

What are the top-down and bottom-up approaches to budgeting?

Question 8.2

What is the difference between a comprehensive or master budget and a flexible budget?

Question 8.3

What is a PPBS? Describe some of the advantages and disadvantages of operating a PPBS.

Question 8.4

Briefly outline Maslow's hierarchy of needs and the expectancy theory of motivation. How have these theories been used to explain the effects of participative budgeting in organizations?

Question 8.5

Think of the ways in which your examination results may be communicated to you. What effects do different forms of feedback have upon your future behaviour?

Question 8.6

Imagine that you are a member of a group involved in a business game. As part of this game your group has to produce a budget for your organization. How can knowledge about the working of groups help you in this exercise?

Question 8.7
If you were asked to forecast your performance in the final examination for your course why might you not provide estimates that give an accurate picture of your expected performance?

Question 8.8
Many organizations, especially government agencies, follow the practice of incremental budgeting. What this practice effectively means is that senior management approves next year's budget on the basis of the current year's spending. For example, if a government department spent £300,000 out of its £320,000 budget this year, and the budget is to be subjected to a 10% increase, the department's budget in the following year would be 110% × £300,000 = £330,000. It will not be £352,000 (320,000 × 110%).

Comment on the potential benefits and disadvantages of this method of budgeting.

(Adapted from Hirsch and Louderback (1986).)

Question 8.9
Tim Failes, a young, ambitious manager has the following opinion of budgets: 'Budgeting is really a game. There are winners and losers. Numbers are just tools to be "fixed" so that they tell the story that you want senior management to hear. Those guys are not stupid, they know budgets are games. And like any game, there are rules of the game. As long as you play by the rules, for instance, don't be too greedy and don't tell too many obvious lies, it's OK.'

Discuss Failes' interpretation of what budgeting 'really' is. How will this attitude influence the budget estimates that he submits to other managers?

Question 8.10
Below is B. Waller's budget of his car expenses for the 1993 financial year. Waller always constructs an expenses budget but never a revenue budget as he does not obtain any financial gains from his car. How does this budget act as a sense-making instrument?

Budgeted Motor Expenses for 1993

	£
Motor insurance	467
Road fund	120
Petrol	1,000
Repairs and service	500
RAC membership	23
Total	£2,110

W8.4 Computational problems

Question 8.1
The management of BHP Company has just decided that it would be useful to

prepare budgets on a regular basis. The following data is available for the first four months of the year:

Month	Budgeted sales in units	Budgeted production in units
January	6,000	10,000
February	6,000	10,000
March	6,000	12,000
April	15,000	12,000

(i) Direct materials cost = £8 per unit of production.
(ii) Desired closing inventory at month end is equal to $\frac{1}{2}$ of next month's production requirements. There were no opening inventories in January.
(iii) Usual payment policy is to pay for 75% of all material purchases in the month of purchase and the remainder in the month after.

Required:

(a) Prepare a materials purchase budget for the period January–March.
(b) Prepare a cash disbursements budget for materials purchase for the period January–March.

Question 8.2

ANU Company manufactures a single product called Nurdle. The manufacturing costs for the product are shown below:

Direct material costs	£4.00	per unit
Direct labour costs	£2.00	per unit
Variable indirect manufacturing costs	£0.40	per unit
Fixed indirect costs (includes depreciation of £2,000)	£10,000	per month

In addition, budgeted sales and production for the period June–August are as follows:

Month	Unit sales budgeted	Unit production budgeted
June	6,000	10,000
July	6,000	10,000
August	9,000	12,000

Other information is as follows:

(i) There are no opening inventories and no debtor balances.
(ii) Selling and administrative expenses are all fixed and equal £3,000 per month.
(iii) Office depreciation = £600 (included in (ii) above).
(iv) The selling price of a unit of Nurdle is £12.00.
(v) Collections are: 80% in the month of sale; 18% in the month following sale; 2% uncollectable.
(vi) Closing inventories of direct materials will be $\frac{1}{2}$ of next month's production requirements.

(vii) Payments for direct labour, indirect manufacturing costs, and selling and administrative expenses will be made in the month in which the expenses are incurred.

(viii) Payments for direct materials are made monthly; 75% of each month's purchases will be paid for in the month of purchase, and the remainder will be paid for in the following month. At the end of May all purchases of direct materials had been paid for.

Required:
Prepare a budget of the cash receipts and disbursements for the period June–July.

Question 8.3

Kelly Company is a retail sporting goods store that uses accrual accounting for its records. Facts regarding Kelly's operations are as follows:

(i) Sales are budgeted at £220,000 for December 1993 and £200,000 for January 1994.

(ii) Collections are expected to be 60% in the month of sale and 38% in the month following the month of sale, while 2% of sales are expected to be uncollectable.

(iii) Gross margin on sales is 25%.

(iv) 80% of the merchandise for resale is purchased in the month prior to the month of sale and 20% is purchased in the month of sale. Payment for merchandise is made in the month following the purchase.

(v) Other expected monthly cash expenses are £22,600.

(vi) Annual depreciation is £216,000.

Answer the following questions:

(a) What is the budgeted operating income for the month of December 1993?

(b) What is the projected balance on the accounts payable account as at 31 December 1993?

(CMA adapted)

Question 8.4

Loretto College is a private Catholic college for girls. It has asked for your assistance in developing its budget for the coming academic year. You are supplied with the following data for the current year:

	Lower forms (Years 1–3)	*Upper forms (Years 4–6)*
Average number of students per class	25	20
Average salary of teaching staff	£10,000	£10,000
Average number of teaching hours allocated each year per student	33	30
Enrolment including scholarship students	2,500	1,700
Average teaching load per member of teaching staff per year (ten classes of three teaching hours)	30	30

For the coming year, lower-form enrolment is expected to increase by 10% and upper-form enrolment is expected to remain stable. Salaries of members of the teaching staff will be increased by a standard 5%, and additional merit increases to be awarded to individual staff members will total £90,750 for the lower forms and £85,000 for the upper forms.

The current budget is £210,000 for operation and maintenance of plant and equipment; this includes £90,000 for salaries and wages. Experience of the past three months suggests that the current budget is realistic but that expected increases for the coming year are 5% in salaries and wages and £9,000 in other expenditures for maintenance and equipment.

The budget for the remaining expenditures for the coming year is as follows:

Administrative and general	£240,000
Library	160,000
Health and recreation	75,000
Athletics	120,000
Insurance and retirement	265,000
Interest	48,000
Capital outlay	300,000

The college expects to award 25 tuition-free scholarships to lower-form students and 15 to upper-form students. Tuition is £22 per teaching hour and no other fees are charged.

Budgeted revenues for the coming year include the following:

Endowments	£114,000
Net income from auxiliary services	235,000
Athletics	180,000

The college's remaining source of revenue is an annual support compaign held during the spring.

Required:

(a) Prepare a schedule for the coming year, computing for each division (i.e. lower and upper):
   (i) the expected enrolment;
   (ii) the total teaching hours to be allocated;
   (iii) the number of staff members needed.

(b) Prepare a schedule computing the budget for staff salaries by forms for the coming year.

(c) Prepare a schedule computing the tuition revenue budget by forms for the coming year.

(d) Assuming that the staff salaries budget computed in part (b) was £2,400,000 and that the tuition revenue budget computed in part (c) was £3,000,000, prepare a schedule computing the amount that must be raised during the annual support campaign in order to cover the coming year's expenditures budget.

(CPA adapted)

W8.5 Case study

CARTER PLC

Joe Reagan and Neil Mitchell strolled back to their plant from the administrative offices of Carter plc. Joe was manager of the machine shop in the company's factory; Neil was manager of the equipment maintenance department.

The men had just attended the monthly performance evaluation meeting for plant department heads. These meetings had been held on the third Tuesday of each month since Ruby, the chairman's daughter, had become plant manager a year earlier.

As they were walking Joe Reagan spoke. 'Boy, I hate those meetings! I never know whether my department's accounting reports will show good or bad performance. I'm beginning to expect the worst. If the accountants say I saved the company a pound, I'm called "Sir", but if I spend even a little too much – boy, do I get in trouble. I don't know if I can hold on until I retire.'

Joe had just received the worst evaluation he had ever received in his long career with the company. He was the most respected of the experienced machinists in the company. He had been with Carter plc for many years and was promoted to supervisor of the machine shop when the company expanded and moved to its present location. The chairman (Maxwell Carter) had often stated that the company's success was due to the high quality of the work of machinists like Reagan. As supervisor, Joe stressed the importance of craftsmanship and told his workers that he wanted no sloppy work coming from his department.

When Ruby Carter became the plant manager she directed that monthly performance comparisons be made between actual and budgeted costs for each department. The departmental budgets were intended to encourage the supervisors to reduce inefficiencies and to seek cost reduction opportunities. The company controller was instructed to have his staff 'tighten' the budget slightly whenever a department attained its budget in a given month; this was done to reinforce the plant supervisor's desire to reduce costs. The young plant manager often stressed the importance of continued progress toward attaining the budget; she also made it known that she kept a file of these performance reports for future reference when she succeeded her father.

Joe Reagan's conversation with Neil Mitchell continued as follows:

'I really don't understand, Neil. We've worked so hard to get up to budget and the minute we make it they tighten the budget on us. We can't work any faster and still maintain quality. I think my men are ready to quit trying. Besides, those reports don't tell the whole story. We always seem to be interrupting the big jobs for all those small rush orders. All that set-up and machine adjustment time is killing us. And quite frankly, Neil, you were no help. When our hydraulic press broke down last month your people were nowhere to be found. We had to take it apart ourselves and got stuck with all that idle time.'

'I'm sorry about that, Joe, but you know my department has had trouble making budget, too. We were running well beyond at the time of that problem, and if we'd spent a day on that old machine we would never have made it up. Instead we made the scheduled inspections of the forklift trucks because we knew we could do those in less than the budgeted time.'

'Well, Neil, at least you have some options. I'm locked into what the scheduling department assigns to me and you know they're being harassed by sales for those special orders. Incidentally, why didn't your report show all the supplies you guys wasted last month when you were working in Bill's department?'

'We're not out of the woods on that deal yet. We charged the maximum we could to our other work and haven't even reported some of it yet.'

'Well, I'm glad you have a way of getting out of the pressure. The accountants seem to know everything that's happening in my department, sometimes even before I do. I thought all that budget and accounting stuff was supposed to help, but it just gets me into trouble. It's all a big pain. I'm trying to put out quality work; they're trying to save pennies.'

Reagan's performance report for the month in question is reproduced below. Actual production volume for the month was at the budgeted level.

Machine Shop – October 19x9
J. Reagan, Supervisor

	Budget £	Actual £	Variances £
Direct labour	39,600	39,850	250 (U)
Direct materials	231,000	231,075	75 (U)
Depreciation – equipment	3,000	3,000	–
Depreciation – buildings	6,000	6,000	–
Power	900	860	40 (F)
Maintenance	400	410	10 (U)
Supervision	1,500	1,500	–
Idle time	–	1,800	1,800 (U)
Set-up labour	680	2,432	1,752 (U)
Miscellaneous	2,900	3,300	400 (U)
	£285,980	£290,227	£4,247 (U)

Required:

(a) Identify the problems that appear to exist in Carter plc's budgetary control system and explain how the problems are likely to reduce the effectiveness of the system.

(b) Explain how Carter plc's budgetary control system could be revised to improve its effectiveness.

(CMA adapted)

W8.6 Illustrative material

The following article is reprinted with permission from the *Pittsburgh Business Review*.

BUDGETING AND INTERGROUP CONFLICT IN ORGANIZATIONS

Louis R. Pondy

This paper was stimulated by field studies made by the author of capital budgeting practices in large manufacturing corporations. Capital budgeting is the process by which funds for plant and equipment are allocated to the various investment projects proposed by operating divisions or by functional departments (e.g., marketing, engineering). Budgeting is necessary because demands for capital funds invariably outrun the resources available. The budget provides a way of choosing among these competing claims for resources.

The engineering economics literature and the accounting literature usually treat the budgeting and resource allocation problem solely as a problem in economics, e.g., to choose those projects which will maximize the present value of invested capital. To understand and explain the practices observed during the field studies, however, it became necessary to use additional concepts from the behavioral sciences. In brief, it proved helpful to interpret capital budgeting for resource allocation as a process of resolving intergroup conflict.

The organization as a conflict system

The classical bureaucratic way of describing an organization is as a hierarchy with each person responsible to the person directly above him in the authority structure. Through the pyramiding of this authority structure, each participant in the organization has eventual responsibility and loyalty to the organization's prime goal (presumably profit in the case of a business organization).

Development of subgroup loyalties

But each participant is a member not only of "the corporation," but also of the Marketing Department or of Division X, as well as of various professional organizations. In fact, because the Marketing Department is smaller and more congenial than "the corporation," there is a good chance that he has a closer identification with its immediate goals than with the long range goals of "the corporation."[1] This insight into the multiple membership and subgroup identifications of each organizational participant suggests the following alternative to the classical description: The organization is a collection of interest groups who have goals which may be only partially consistent with those of other interest

[1]There are both motivational and cognitive processes producing subgroup identification. Examples of motivational factors are conformity of group goals and the self-image and affective ties with other group members. Examples of cognitive factors are the selective exposure to environmental cues (marketing personnel talk most to customers and therefore are most sensitive to marketing and commercial goals), reinforcement of group attitudes by ingroup communication, and uniform professional training and its effects on perception. See J.G. March and H.A. Simon, *Organizations* (New York: Wiley, 1958), pp. 93–106, 150–54.

groups and with the superordinate goal of the organization.[2]

Subgroup loyalties develop not only because of a common professional background of the subgroup members, not only because of a selective exposure of the business environment, not only because in-group communication supports and reinforces subgroup goals, but also because each subgroup engages in competition with every other subgroup for an adequate share of the available resources.[3]

Effect of subgroup loyalties

The existence of subgroup loyalties has an important effect on the budgeting process. Characteristically each functional department either originates or participates actively in the organization and development of investment projects. It is natural that the production department will be most energetic in the development of projects which improve production facilities, the marketing department in projects which improve product quality or customer service, and so on. Thus each functional department has a vested interest in each of its projects considered for the budget, and will find it very hard to be objective in judging the entire set of projects or in genuinely accepting the budgeting decisions of an impartial budget committee.[4]

Not only do subgroup loyalties distort the perceptions of the investment projects, but they lead subgroups to adopt "political strategies" for more nearly assuring approval of its projects. What strategies are adopted depend on the particular loopholes available in the budgeting system of the parent company.[5] For example, in companies which have long-range facilities plans, it is advantageous for an operating division or functional department to place a project in the long-range plan on a presumably tentative basis, only to have it gradually assume a more certain status. Or, if the budget committee requests the division to *rank* all of its proposed projects, the division will rank last those projects the budget committee is known to favor and is likely to approve regardless of the ranking, and rank first those projects the division favors most but which have the least chance of approval otherwise. Or again, if the budget committee sets up a minimum acceptable rate of return, the division is likely to "doctor" the economic analysis of marginal projects so that the target rate is met. In one case the division accounting department has been blocking a project for several years because the division manager could not prove rigorously that anticipated savings from

[2]See, J.G. March, The Business Firm as a Political Coalition, *Journal of Politics*, December 1962.

[3]See Muzafer Sherif *et al.*, *Intergroup Cooperation and Conflict: The Robbers Cave Experiment* (Norman, Okla.: Institute of Intergroup Relations, University of Oklahoma, 1961) for a description of the effect of intergroup competition on in-group loyalties in a boys' summer camp.

[4]See Jane S. Morton and Robert R. Blake. The Influence of Competitively Vested Interests on Judgement. *Journal of Conflict Resolution* 6, no. 2 (June 1962): pp. 149–53, for experimental documentation of the effects of subgroup loyalties on perception and satisfaction in a judgment situation.

[5]Aaron Wildavsky has studied the use of subgroup strategies in the formation of the federal budget. In particular these include the cultivation of the "confidence" of the Budget Bureau and congressional committees, where confidence refers to affective ties and mutual rapport between the agency and the official group (private communication). See also his Political Implication of Budgetary Reform. *Public Administration Review* 21, no. 4 (Autumn 1961): pp. 183–90.

a renovation would be assured. Eventually the division manager overrode the accounting department and made a rough guess of the savings so that the target rate of return would be exceeded by about three percentage points. The assistant to the division manager was quite candid in reporting the handling of this project.

The budget committee and conflict resolution

In order to mediate this intense intergroup competition for funds most companies have set up budget committees, composed of functional representatives, to review the proposals made by the operating divisions or by the central staff. Representatives of the operating divisions are not usually members of the committee. That there is considerable conflict among the committee members is almost certain. To demonstrate the divergence of judgments and evaluations of projects in a large primary metal processing firm, the author asked two comparable members of the marketing and engineering-planning departments to make independent rankings from project summaries of nine projects from the company's previous budget. Though each man was familiar with all nine projects, the degree of agreement between their rankings was not statistically significant. These differences of course provide the basis for interfunctional conflict on the budget committee. Though no direct evidence is available on how these conflicts of project preference are settled, it is likely that bargaining and compromise take precedence over analytical efforts. This is true partially because group loyalties affect evaluation criteria as well as specific project preferences.

Project classifications as bargaining residues

The loyalties to evaluation criteria are reflected in the project classification system. Characteristically the accounting and finance representatives on the budget committee insist that all projects satisfy economic criteria, such as rate of return or payback. The legal representative of course will insist that compliance with government regulations (e.g. regarding smoke control or stream pollution) obviously is consistent with the firm's financial well-being and needs no economic justification. Similarly the marketing representative will insist that market share is really a more appropriate measure of the worth of a project than is rate of return. The production representative will push for operating efficiency criteria to supplement the financial criteria, all the time arguing of course that his criteria, while superficially different, are really related to the financial criteria and, in fact, are more operational.[6] To avoid resurrecting the criterion conflict anew each time, the committee legitimizes the use of different criteria by defining different investment categories. A typical classification system comprises cost reduction, replacement, commercial, legal, and employee welfare categories. I choose to interpret these investment categories as "residues" from past conflict and bargaining among the functional departments over the issue of appropriate investment criteria.

[6]March and Simon (*Organizations*, pp. 156–7) assert that bargaining behavior will take precedence over analytic behavior in the absence of shared, operational goals. My own observations suggest that long-run profit maximization is *not* an operational goal when it comes to ranking complex capital investment projects.

Once formed, these investment categories provide an institutional framework for resolving the interfunctional conflict since each category requires a different set of criteria, so that the criterion conflict is repressed.[7] The project preference conflict is alleviated as follows: A rough, and more or less unintentional, balance is maintained among the various categories. There is no conscious attempt to allocate X percent of the budget to cost reduction projects, for example, but it does appear that, by unwritten rule, the share of the budget spent on cost reduction projects may legitimately range *only* between certain percentages of the total budget or between certain dollar amounts.

Other devices for conflict resolution

Two other miscellaneous devices for resolving conflict may be more accurately described as defense mechanisms for the budget committee. A complete ranking of the projects is not attempted, so that some unresolved conflict remains latent. A practice adopted by one company is to break the budget up into four priority increments to be authorized for expenditures in increments (if at all) by the board of directors.

The use of long-range plans is in some sense a defense mechanism. Suppose that only $10 million can be spent in each of the next three years, and each of these divisions has a prime project which will require the entire $10 million. Engineering economics or financial analysis may indicate which of the three projects to approve, but will provide no answer on how to handle the disappointment of the other two divisions. It is small consolation to the "losers" to know that they came out a close second. On the other hand, if the division knows that its project has been placed in a long-range plan for the next year hence, its feelings will at least be partially mollified, and the budget committee will experience less pressure from the divisional management.

Conclusion

We have argued that two factors are sufficient for intergroup conflict to exist: subgroup loyalties and intergroup competition. Both these factors were shown to be present in the budgeting-resource allocation process in the modern, large corporation. Budgeting can therefore be viewed as a process of resolving intergroup conflicts. This finding has crucial implications for the design of budgeting systems. Not only must the system provide procedures for the rational, economic analysis of budget proposals, but it must also provide procedures for the resolution of intergroup conflict over scarce resources that will inevitably arise.

[7]One of the other strategies commonly employed by subgroups is to classify, with appropriate justifications, a marginal project in a category which is currently favored by the central staff on the firm. Once a project is placed in a certain category, it tends to be compared only with the other projects in that category.

CHAPTER

9 Responsibility, authority and control

WORKBOOK

W9.1 Introduction

In the Tocher control model that was adapted by Otley and Berry (see Chapter 3 of the text) it was pointed out that one of the essential components for control was the comparison of the output of a system with the objectives of that system. In Chapter 9 we realized that it is equally important that somebody be made responsible for any variances that occur in order that effective corrective action may be implemented. It is extremely difficult to rectify a problem when people do not know whose responsibility it is to do so. Hence the need exists to devise a responsibility system even in the smallest of organizations.

A responsibility accounting system assigns the responsibility for particular financial items to specific individuals or departments. As will be illustrated later on, this division of responsibilities may be extremely difficult to achieve where there is much interdependence among different departments in an organization. Interdependence among different divisions in a decentralized organization brings additional problems – the negotiation of transfer prices that simultaneously achieve two conflicting aims: the granting of autonomy for decision-making to divisional managers on the one hand and the achievement of overall organizational effectiveness on the other. We shall look in detail at each of these areas of difficulty in the next section.

W9.2 Revision topics

Question 9.1
What principles underlie the design and operation of a responsibility accounting system?

Answer
Responsibility accounting is a system of allocating responsibility for the control of costs, revenues and profit outcomes to specific individuals who incur those costs and generate those revenues and profits. Financial elements do not control themselves. And control in organizations is not effected until people take actions that help to achieve agreed goals. It is people who spend an organization's resources, and it is people who must be held accountable for spending and for achieving desired results.

Responsibility accounting does not introduce any new accounting technique. Instead, available data is organized differently. Thus, instead of collecting cost information for the purpose of, say, product costing, cost information is collected so as to place responsibility for cost control on the employees who incur those costs. The important question is not 'what were the costs?' but rather 'who incurred which costs?'.

A responsibility accounting system operates by providing feedback information and functions as an error-controlled regulator in the sense that any disturbance from the environment would have already affected the performance of the organization before its effect is monitored and reported by the responsibility accounting system.

The effective operation of a responsibility accounting system rests on two assumptions:

(i) All costs, revenues and profits are controllable by somebody at some time;
(ii) An individual should only be held responsible for those costs, revenues and profits which are within his/her control.

Question 9.2

How might a responsibility accounting system be designed for a decentralized organization?

Answer

Decentralization means that decision-making authority is delegated to employees within the authority hierarchy. Authority is not centralized in a handful of corporate headquarters staff but allocated to responsibility centre (also division) managers. There are several types of responsibility centres, the chief ones being:

(i) cost centres;
(ii) profit centres; and
(iii) investment centres.

Question 9.3

Outline the nature of the transfer pricing problem along with possible solutions.

Answer

One of the major difficulties with divisionalization is the appropriate pricing of interdivisional transfers. A transfer price is the price at which goods and services are transferred between divisions. Transfer pricing is a complex issue because a transfer price usually needs to play a number of roles. First, it should encourage divisional managers to maximize divisional profitability subject to the constraint of overall organizational profitability. Second, a transfer price should encourage divisional autonomy and discretion in decision-making. Often these roles conflict and a transfer price may be appropriate for one role but not for the other.

If a competitive market exists for the intermediate product transfers should be priced at market prices. A competitive market is one in which the selling division can sell any quantity internally or externally and the buying division can buy any quantity internally or externally without influencing the market price. In such competitive market conditions each division will act as though it were an independent organization. There will be no economies associated with dealings between divisions.

However, the market price rule cannot always be followed. Where competitive market conditions cannot be established the theoretically ideal transfer price is equal to the marginal cost (or incremental or variable cost) of the selling division plus the opportunity cost to the organization as a whole of having an internal transfer. The opportunity cost to the organization as a whole depends on whether the selling division is operating at maximum capacity and whether alternative uses can be made of any spare capacity. If the selling division is not operating at maximum capacity and alternative uses for any spare capacity cannot be found, the opportunity costs are zero.

In practice a number of methods for calculating transfer prices are in operation. Most of these are cost-based transfer prices, although prices may also be obtained through linear programming models and through negotiation. Of the cost-based transfer prices it is important to use standard as opposed to actual costs to avoid the passing on of cost inefficiencies. In certain circumstances a dual pricing system may be considered but this can give rise to confusion.

Question 9.4

How do social and individual controls impact upon organizational control?

Answer

Social controls include the use of particular leadership styles, team and group development techniques and the successful management of the dynamic processes of a working group. Much human relations research suggests that a democratic and participative style of management could lead to both high levels of productive activity and employee satisfaction. However, the field has not been thoroughly researched and could represent more an ideological plea than a well-grounded empirical theory.

Individual controls emphasize the building of an individual's motivation and commitment to the objectives of the organization as a whole. Again, conflicting research results have been generated. Thus, although we know that motivation is an important form of self-control, we are unclear about the precise factors which motivate individuals across a wide range of work settings and personalities.

W9.3 Discussion topics

Question 9.1

What are some of the potential difficulties with a responsibility accounting system?

Question 9.2

What are the advantages and disadvantages associated with decentralization?

Question 9.3

'The question for the organization as a whole is whether the transfer between divisions should occur, not the price at which the transfer should take place.' Is this a correct statement? If so, why?

Question 9.4

Susan Marrick is one of several purchasing officers with Engineering Components Ltd, a major retail outlet for engineering parts. She is responsible for purchasing 100 different components. Each month she is given a performance report which shows the budgeted price for each of the 100 components and the price at which she purchased them. She is particularly upset with last month's performance report which shows that she bought 20,000 units of Item 131 at 20% above the budgeted price, thus showing an adverse variance from budget of £250,000.

Ms Marrick had received an urgent order from the sales department early last month for 40,000 units of Item 131. She did not have sufficient items in stock and required an additional 20,000 units. None of her regular suppliers could provide the amount required. In order to satisfy the sales department she spent a good deal of time contacting other suppliers who might possess stocks of Item 131. Eventually, after much hard work, she managed to buy the additional 20,000 units but at a much higher price than budgeted. She had sent a memo to the senior purchasing officer and to the finance and administration department last month explaining the situation. That explanation appears to have been ignored in the compilation of the monthly performance report.

Discuss the following:

(a) Was Ms Marrick responsible for the adverse variance from budget?
(b) If not, to which department should the excess of £250,000 be assigned?
(c) Should the finance and administration department have ignored Ms Marrick's explanation?

Question 9.5

Beaver Brothers is a multinational organization that produces and markets a range of household products ranging from soap powder, fabric softener, toothpaste and soap to margarine and cooking oil. It runs an extensive training programme for all newly recruited university graduates. Each graduate spends 6–12 months in each of the company's six major divisions, that are segregated according to product line.

In the past, the salaries of the trainees were charged to a corporate personnel account. It is now proposed that each division should be charged individually with the salaries of trainees who work in those divisions. A trainee would now be counted as any other ordinary employee of a division.

Bill Copeland, one of the divisional managers, is unhappy and makes the following comments:

> 'It is unfair to charge a trainee's salary to our division. I have no control over the hiring and firing of these people. I simply have trainees allocated to my division by the central personnel department. How can I be held responsible for their salaries? In addition, we manufacture Beaver Brothers' major product. Hence we tend to be allocated more trainees than other divisions because it is likely that those trainees will eventually end up working here. Look at Division C! It is allocated only half our number of trainees because they do not need many graduate staff.'

Discuss Bill Copeland's point of view. How would you treat the trainees' salaries?

Question 9.6

Unique Engineering requires specialized steels in order to fabricate road tankers. The corporate management accountant is at present reviewing the control procedures within the organization. She has identified a number of weaknesses:

(a) The purchasing manager tends to delay purchase of special grade steel until stocks are very low. When he does purchase, he buys large lots at extremely favourable prices. Unfortunately the stores department sometimes cannot handle these large purchases efficiently. On numerous occasions steel of a wrong quality and diameter has been stored for some weeks before the errors were discovered. In addition, due to a lack of warehouse space, some of the steel had to be left in the open for long periods. In the winter months this practice produces a thick layer of rust on the surface of the steel which then requires extra cleaning in the cleaning department. The purchasing manager feels that his actions are justified because he is being evaluated upon his ability to purchase materials at standard price.

(b) The production manager complains constantly about the actions of the purchasing department. He is responsible for the cost and output of the production, stores and cleaning departments. He feels strongly that cost overruns in his area of responsibility are due directly to the selfish policies of the purchasing department. Production, he claims, seldom receives special steel of the right quality, in the right quantity at the right time.

Discuss the weaknesses identified by the corporate management accountant. How would you correct these problems?

W9.4 Worked examples

Question 9.1

Consider the following example, where Division A sells an intermediate product to Division B.

Sales of Division A to Division B

Sales: 10,000 units @£4	£40,000
Variable costs: 10,000 units @£3	£30,000
Contribution margin	£10,000
Fixed costs	£ 6,000
Gross margin	£ 4,000

Sales of Division A to outside customers

Sales: 5,000 units @£7	£35,000
Variable costs: 5,000 units @£4	£20,000
Contribution margin	£15,000
Fixed costs	£ 3,000
Gross margin	£12,000

Note that the outside price of the product is £7, while the internal transfer price is only £4. At this internal price Division A is making a margin of £1 on variable costs and only 40 p on variable and fixed costs. The transfer price to Division B appears to be based on some version of cost – a cost plus mark-up transfer price.

If a competitive market exists for this intermediate product there is a case for Division A charging Division B the market price of £7. With a competitive market, Division B would have to pay £7 if it bought from an outside supplier. Changing the transfer price from £4 to £7 will not affect the organization as such; it merely alters the divisional gross margin. If the transfer price were £7, Division A would show a higher margin than at present, while Division B's margin would be reduced by a corresponding amount.

Assume that the manager of Division B has received a special offer from an outside company to supply 10,000 units at £3.80. If Division B took up this offer the division would be better off, but Division A would be worse off, and indeed the organization as a whole would be worse off, as shown below:

Division B's purchase of 10,000 units @£3.80	£38,000
Less Division A's variable cost savings: 10,000 × £3	(£30,000)
Overall organizational loss: 10,000 × £.80	£8,000

Clearly, the organization as a whole would be better off if the transaction were to be conducted internally. Other things being equal, the organization as a whole would gain by Division B's purchasing from outside only when the outside price (at present £3.80) is less than the variable costs of Division A (£3 per unit). In addition, this special offer by an outside supplier may only be a one-off offer that cannot be repeated in the future.

Thus, from the point of view of the organization as a whole, Division B needs to be persuaded to buy internally. Central management could dictate that the transaction should occur, but this would violate the autonomy of divisional managers. A second option is to persuade Division A to lower its price. If Division A has no alternative use for its resources, and its fixed costs would continue to be incurred irrespective of this transaction, the division could consider transferring at a price between £3 and £3.80.

However, if Division A did have some alternative use for its resources, were it not to produce the 10,000 units of the intermediate product for Division B, this would influence the transfer price set. Assume that the alternative use of Division A's resources could yield a contribution margin of £15,000. Should Division A decide to carry on production of the intermediate product and transact with Division B, this £15,000 would be forgone profit. Applying the general marginal cost rule, Division A should include this opportunity forgone in negotiating a transfer price. It would therefore seem reasonable that a transfer price of at least £3 (variable cost) plus £1.50 (15,000/10,000) per unit be set. If Division B is not prepared to pay this price of £4.50 it should seek an alternative supplier. Note that in these circumstances, with all other things remaining equal, it would be more profitable to the organization as a whole for Division B to buy from the outside supplier at £3.80 and for Division A to devote its resources to the alternative use.

Question 9.2

A multi-divisional company with a long-established transistor division has just acquired a radio division. The company's chief executive takes the view that the radio division should buy transistors from the transistor division, since the latter has excess capacity.

The transistor division has an established selling price of £3.50 per unit and its costs per unit are:

Direct material	£1.00
Direct labour	1.15
Variable indirect	0.50
Fixed indirect*	0.30
Total cost	£2.95

* Based on a current activity level of 1,000,000 units.

The radio division has hitherto purchased transistors at £3.50 less a 10% discount from an established supplier.

A range of possible transfer prices has been discussed by both top and divisional managers. These include:

(i) *Prime cost*: £2.15
This is inappropriate, since it fails to cover all the variable costs of the transistor division.

(ii) *Variable cost*: £2.65
This approximates the marginal cost to both the transistor division and the company as a whole. In the face of under-utilized capacity, the market price is not a measure of opportunity cost but the variable cost is. The variable cost is less than the external price of £3.15 and so benefits would accrue both to the radio division and to the company as a whole if this basis for transfer pricing were adopted.

(iii) *Full cost*: £2.95
This is not an approximation of marginal cost, due to the apportioned fixed overhead element. If it were to be adopted, all the benefits would be to the radio division.

(iv) *Market price*: £3.15
If both the radio and transistor divisions are to be treated as wholly autonomous, this price would be appropriate since it represents what is, to the radio division, the market price.

(v) *Full cost plus mark-up*: £3.50
This is the market price at which the transistor division sells, but it is not appropriate as a transfer price since it is not a measure of the opportunity cost to the transistor division (which has excess capacity) or to the company as a whole. In addition, of course, it exceeds the price at which the radio division can buy from its existing supplier, so it would be unacceptable on all grounds.

(vi) *Negotiated price*: £2.90
This proposed transfer price splits the difference between the radio division's existing buying price of £3.15 and the transistor division's variable costs of

£2.65 in a way that gives half the benefit to the company to each participating division.

W9.5 Computational problems

Question 9.1

The Mar Company operates two decentralized divisions, X and Y. Division X has been buying a particular component from Division Y at a price of £75 per unit. Because Division Y plans to increase the price to £100, Division X has looked for and found an outside supplier who will furnish the component at £75 per unit. Division Y incurs the following costs:

Variable cost per unit of component	£70
Annual fixed costs	£15,000
Annual production of component	1,000 units

If Division X does buy from an outside supplier the facilities that Division Y devotes to producing the component would be idle.

Required:

Select the best answer to the following question: What would be the effect if Mar Company forces Division X to buy from Division Y at a transfer price of £100?

(a) It would be suboptimization for the enterprise as a whole because X should buy from an outside supplier at £75 per unit.
(b) It would provide lower overall company profit than a transfer price of £75.
(c) It would provide higher overall company profit than a transfer price of £75.
(d) It would be more profitable for the company than allowing Division X to buy from an outside supplier at £75 per unit.

(CPA adapted)

Question 9.2

The blade division of Dana Company produces hardened steel blades. One-third of the division's output is sold to the Lawn products division of Dana, and the remainder is sold to outside customers. The blade division's budgeted results for the coming year appear below.

	Lawn products £	Outsiders £
Sales	15,000	40,000
Variable costs	(10,000)	(20,000)
Fixed costs	(3,000)	(6,000)
Profit	£2,000	£14,000
Unit sales	10,000	20,000

The fixed costs are allocated on a per unit basis and are all unavoidable. The Lawn products division has the opportunity to buy 10,000 blades of identical quality at £1.25 per unit. The blade division cannot increase its outside sales.

Required:
Determine whether it is in Dana Company's best interest for the Lawn products division to buy blades outside.

(CPA adapted)

Question 9.3

The manager of the Frigidwind division of National Industries, plc, believes that he can increase sales of his air conditioners if he reduces the selling price by £20. A budgeted income statement for the coming year, without considering the proposed reduction, is given below:

	£
Sales 4,000 units at £400	1,600,000
Variables costs at £200 per unit	800,000
Contribution margin	800,000
Fixed costs	420,000
Profit before taxes	£380,000

The proposed price reduction would increase volume by 500 units according to a market research study in which the manager has a great deal of confidence. Part of the variable cost of the product is a compressor that the division now buys for £70 from an outsider supplier. The manager approaches the manager of the compressor division of National Industries and offers to pay £50 per unit for a compressor that the division currently makes and sells exclusively to outside firms. The manager of Frigidwind will not accept fewer than 4,500 units.

Data for the compressor division are given below:

	£	£
Budgeted sales 17,000 units at £100		1,700,000
Variable costs:		
Production	510,000	
Selling	102,000	612,000
Contribution margin		£1,088,000

The compressor division has the capacity to produce 20,000 units per year. The division would not incur the variable selling costs on units sold to Frigidwind.

Required:

(a) Should the compressor division supply the 4,500 units to Frigidwind? The managers of divisions are evaluated on the basis of profit earned.
(b) Is it in the best interests of the enterprise as a whole for the compressor division to supply the units to Frigidwind division?
(c) What is the lowest price that the compressor division could accept for the units without reducing profits below what they would be if none were sold to Frigidwind?

(CMA adapted)

W9.6 Case studies

ARGON DISTRICT HOSPITAL

The Argon District Hospital is located in a well-known summer resort area. The population of the district doubles during the vacation months (June–September) and hospital activity more than doubles during these months. The hospital is organized into several departments. Although it is a relatively small hospital, its pleasant surroundings have attracted a well-trained and competent medical staff.

An administrator was hired in July 19X2 to improve the business activities of the hospital. Among the new ideas he has introduced is responsibility accounting. This programme was announced along with quarterly cost reports supplied to department managers. Previously, cost data were presented to department managers infrequently. Excerpts from the announcement are presented below as is the report received by the laundry department manager.

> The hospital has adopted a *responsibility accounting system*. From now on you will receive quarterly reports comparing the costs of operating your department with budgeted costs. The reports will highlight the differences (variations) so that you can zero in on the departures from budget costs. Responsibility accounting means you are accountable for keeping the costs in your department within the budget. The variations from the budget will help you identify what costs are out of line and the size of the variation will indicate which ones are most important. Your first such report accompanies this announcement.

The annual budget for 19X3 was constructed by the new administrator. Quarterly budgets were computed as one fourth of the annual budget. The administrator compiled the budget from analysis of the prior three years' costs. The analysis showed that all costs increased each year, with more rapid increases between the second and third years. He considered establishing the budget at an average of the prior three years' costs hoping that the installation of the system would reduce costs to this level. However, in view of the rapidly increasing prices, he finally choose 19X2 costs less 3% for the 19X3 budget. The activity level measured by patient days and kilograms of laundry processed was set at 19X2 volume, which was approximately equal to the volume of each of the past three years.

Argon District Hospital
Performance Report – Laundry Department
For 1st Quarter, 1 June to 31 August 19X3

	Budget	Actual	(Over) Under budget	(Over) Under budget
Patient days	9,500	11,900	(2,400)	(25)
Kilograms processed (laundry)	125,000	162,500	(37,500)	(30)
Costs:	£	£	£	%
Laundry labour	9,000	12,500	(3,500)	(39)
Supplies	1,100	1,875	(775)	(70)
Water, water heating and softening	1,700	2,500	(800)	(47)

	Budget	Actual	(Over) Under budget (£)	(Over) Under budget (%)
Maintenance	1,400	2,200	(800)	(57)
Supervisor's salary	3,150	3,750	(600)	(19)
Allocated administrative costs	4,000	5,000	(1,000)	(25)
Equipment depreciation	1,200	1,250	(50)	(4)
	£21,550	£29,075	£(7,525)	(35)%

Administrator's comments: Costs are significantly above budget for the quarter. Particular attention needs to be paid to labour, supplies and maintenance.

Required:

(a) State the essential principles on which a responsibility accounting system should be based.
(b) Critically evaluate the way in which the quarterly budget has been prepared and the variations from budget reported for the laundry department.

(CMA adapted)

ARROW WORKS PRODUCTS COMPANY

Edwin Hall, chairman of the board and managing director of Arrow Works Products Company, founded the company in the early 1970s. He is a talented and creative engineer. Arrow Works was started with one of his inventions, an intricate die-cast item that required a minimum of finished work. The item was manufactured for Arrow Works by a Barnsley, Yorkshire, foundry. The product sold well in a wide market.

The company issued ordinary shares in 1972 to finance the purchase of the Barnsley foundry. Additional shares were issued in 1975 when Arrow purchased a fabricating plant in Coventry to meet the capacity requirement of a defence contract.

The company now consists of five divisions. Each division is headed by a manager who reports to Hall. The Basingstoke division contains the product development and engineering department and the finishing (assembly) operation for the basic products. The Barnsley plant and Coventry plant are the other two divisions engaged in manufacturing operations. All products manufactured are sold through two selling divisions. The southern sales division is located in Birmingham and covers the English and Welsh markets. The northern sales division, which covers the Scottish and Northern Irish markets, is located in Glasgow. The northern sales division is the newest operation and was established just eight months ago.

Hall, who still owns 53% of the issued shares, actively participates in the management of the company. He travels frequently and regularly to all of the company's plants and offices. He says, 'Having a business with locations in five different cities spread over half the United Kingdom requires all my time.' Despite his regular and frequent visits he believes the company is decentralized, with the managers having complete autonomy. They make all the decisions and run their own shops. Of course they don't understand the total business as I do, so I have to straighten them out once in a while. My managers are all good men, but they can't be expected to handle everything alone. I try to help all I can.'

The last two months have been a period of considerable stress for Hall. During this period John Staple, manager of the fabricating plant, was advised by his physician to request six-months' sick leave to relieve the work pressures that had made him nervous and tense. This request was followed three days later by a telephone call in which Hall had directly and bluntly blamed Staple for the lagging production output and increased rework and scrap of the fabricating plant. Hall made no allowances for the pressure created by the operation of the plant at volumes in excess of normal and close to its maximum rated capacity for the previous nine months.

Hall thought he and Staple had had a long and good relationship prior to this event. Hall attributed his loss of temper in this case to his frustration with several other management problems that had arisen in the past two months. The sales manager of the Glasgow office had resigned shortly after a visit from Hall. The letter of resignation stated he was seeking a position with greater responsibility. The sales manager in Birmingham asked to be reassigned to a sales position in the field; he did not feel that he could cope with the pressure of management.

Required:

(a) Explain how centralized management should differ from decentralized management.
(b) Analyse whether Arrow Works Products Company is as decentralized as Edwin Hall believes.
(c) What suggestions do you have for alleviating some of the problems at Arrow Works?

(CMA adapted)

MERRIMAN COMPANY

Thomas Dauton is manager of reports in the office of senior regional manager Frank Lee of Merriman Company. Until five months ago Lee was a regional manager in charge of manufacturing operations for Region 8 of the company and Dauton was his assistant. Then Lee was promoted to senior regional manager and given responsibility for all of Merriman's manufacturing operations. Twelve regional manufacturing managers report to him.

Lee has visited each region since taking over his new job, and Dauton has accompanied him on most of these trips. Relations with each regional manager, as Dauton observes them, range from fairly cool and correct to informal and enthusiastic cooperation. Lee's replacement in Region 8 had been one of Lee's stronger assistants; each of the other 11 regional managers had been in his job for at least six months (and as long as ten years) before Lee's promotion. The least enthusiastic greeting came from the regional manager who was the other most likely candidate for senior regional manager. Dauton also noted that one other regional manager appeared uninterested in the visit and did not seem enthusiastic about the new organizational arrangement; this regional manager has been in his present position for eight years and is due to retire within the next 18 months.

Each regional manufacturing manager is required to file a monthly report that contains detailed comparisons of budgeted and actual costs and production for the previous month and an explanation of the differences from budget. Prior to Lee's appointment as senior regional manager of manufacturing these reports had been sent by the tenth day of the following month to the general manager's office. The reports are still due in the general manager's office by the tenth of the month, but Lee now receives the reports first. The 12 regional reports are then submitted by Lee, along with his own summary and narrative, to the general manager's office.

The new reporting arrangement was Lee's idea and he insists that the summary be carefully prepared before it is submitted to the general manager's office. The company policy guide, as yet unchanged, requires the regional managers to submit their reports by the tenth day. Lee has asked the regional managers to submit the reports by the seventh of the month. This will allow Dauton adequate time to prepare the analysis for Lee's review before it is submitted to the general manager's office. The request is not unreasonable as the company recently installed an efficient computer-based information system that can get the necessary information to the regional managers by the fourth day of each month.

The regional managers have acknowledged the request and have agreed to try to meet the schedule requested by Lee. Two regions, however, have not met the schedule for the past three months even though Dauton is sure they could with a little effort. He believes one region is not cooperating because its manager is still irked at not being promoted to the senior regional manager position. The office for this region has called each of the last three months on the seventh day to say the report was not ready but would be ready on the tenth day. The other report, from the region headed by the manager near retirement, has arrived on the tenth day each month, but no notice or explanation of the delay has been given.

This past month Lee made it clear to Dauton that he wanted the report he would submit to the general manager's office ready for his review by noon on the ninth day, rather than late on the tenth day. The reports from all but the two regions mentioned arrived early on the seventh day. Dauton waited until the eighth day before drafting the report, hoping that the two recalcitrant division reports would arrive. When the reports did not arrive Dauton called his counterparts in the divisions to get what information he could so that he could complete the draft of the report. From these informal sources plus the regular reports of the other divisions he was able to complete the draft on time. The final report, more carefully prepared than in prior months, was ready for the general manager's office by noon on the tenth day. The details that had been acquired by telephone for the two divisions were verified when their reports were received. The report was delivered by mid-afternoon to the general manager's office.

Required:

(a) Identify and discuss the organizational and behavioural factors that cause the difficulties Frank Lee and Thomas Dauton are experiencing in preparing a complete and timely summary report for the general manager's office every month.

(b) How should Lee and Dauton proceed to improve the reporting process?

(CMA adapted)

W9.7 Illustrative material

The following item (reprinted with permission from *The Times*) shows responsibility accounting in practice in BR.

BR TO SPLIT NATIONAL NETWORK INTO LOCAL AREAS
By Michael Dynes, Transport Correspondent

British Rail is to embark on one of the most far-reaching changes in the organisation of the rail network since nationalisation in 1948, John Welsby, British Rail's chief executive, said yesterday.

From the end of April, the five regions, inherited from the days of private ownership, London Midland, Eastern, Western, Southern, and Scottish, will be progressively abolished and replaced by about 20 smaller units, or profit centres.

The Railways Board will retain responsibility for strategic matters, such as investment programmes, financial targets and railway safety, but most aspects of the day-to-day running of the railway will be devolved to the profit centres.

British Rail's three passenger sectors, InterCity, Network SouthEast, and Regional Railways, will be sub-divided into several profit centres, run by a director, who will effectively own all the rolling stock, track and signalling equipment needed.

Malcolm Rifkind, the transport secretary, has pledged to introduce a bill to privatise British Rail after the next general election. Transport officials are still examining the options, which include privatisation of BR as a single unit, the creation of a track authority and its break up into regional companies.

Under the reorganisation, Network SouthEast, which provides rail services in London and the South East region, will be divided into nine semi-autonomous divisions. Some of these divisions will be substantial businesses. South West, for example, which embraces all services from Waterloo, has an income of £252 million a year, employs about 8,000 staff and covers 500 route-miles. Others, such as the London Tilbury and Southend division, with an income of £65 million, employs about 1,500 and covers 70 route-miles, will be considerably smaller.

InterCity will be divided into five route divisions. Regional Railways, which provides commuter, passenger and cross-country services, will also be split into five sub-divisions.

In an effort to make each profit centre more cost conscious, charges will be levied on trains from one profit centre using the tracks of another. Directors will know exactly what they are responsible for and accountability for shortcomings will be instant. "There will be no more alibis," Mr Welsby said.

The division of the national rail network into what is effectively 20 semi-autonomous railways, is the final phase of the radical reorganisation of the rail network introduced in the early 1980s by Sir Robert Reid, the former British Rail chairman.

By reorganising British Rail's passenger sectors around the markets rather than the regions they serve, Mr Welsby is determined to bring about a substantial improvement in the quality of services. "I'm not changing the organisation for the fun of it," he said. "The changes are vital to improve the quality of service to passengers."

The move is being watched closely by continental rail organisations, particularly those in France and Germany, which are already following the example set by British Rail with the introduction of the five sectors in the 1980s.

The reorganisation is expected to take about a year to complete, and is likely to cost in the region of £50 million. Mr Welsby said that British Rail was not trying to facilitate or impede government plans to privatise the railways.

(The Times, 11 April, 1991, p. 24)

CHAPTER 10 Performance measurement: variance analysis

WORKBOOK

W10.1 Introduction

In seeking to achieve desired goals it is necessary to know not only what those goals are but also to have a means of achieving them. The budget, along with standards, provides an important part of the means.

However, control requires that managers know from time to time how well they are performing relative to budgets and goals. In the absence of this knowledge it will not be possible to adapt one's behaviour in order to make appropriate decisions if actual performance has departed from the desired level of performance. Within this Workbook chapter we look at departures from budgets and standards.

W10.2 Revision topics

Question 10.1
Does the isolation of variances ensure that organizational control is achieved?

Answer
The essence of control is adaptive behaviour in relation to some desired goal. Given this, the isolation of variances is clearly not in itself sufficient to ensure that organizational control will be achieved. For instance, variances are often isolated for activities that constitute relatively minor parts of an organization, and it should not be assumed that applying variance analysis to its parts will necessarily bring about control of the organization as a whole. Moreover, the isolation of variances is not control: it is the action that stems from the analysis and explanation of variances that constitutes control.

Question 10.2
Favourable variances are good news and thus require no investigation, whereas unfavourable variances are bad news and do require investigation. Do you agree?

Answer
We hope you do not agree! The lack of symmetry suggested by this question is a striking feature of budgeting in practice. Our view is that *any* significant variance – whether favourable or unfavourable – warrants investigation. If a

manager is doing something wrong (leading to an unfavourable variance) it is important to find out the cause and cease doing it. Equally, if a manager is doing something right it is worth finding out what, why, etc., in order to continue doing things right. This is the basis of learning.

A budget seeks to provide a coordinated means to desired ends, and any variance can upset the intended coordination. Thus over-achieving on revenue or under-achieving on costs can have knock-on effects in the same ways that under-achieving on revenues or over-achieving on costs can. The figures represent underlying activities, and the existence of any significant variance suggests that these activities have not been carried out as intended. This warrants investigation whether the variances are 'good' or 'bad'.

Question 10.3
How might a manager determine whether or not a variance should be investigated?

Answer
Only *significant* variances warrant investigation. In its strict statistical sense 'significant' was discussed in the text (see pp. 344–9): a significant variance is one that did not arise due to chance.

If a less pure approach than that of statistical quality control is being taken (as is usually the case), a manager may investigate any variance that is:

(i) above a given *relative* size (e.g. 10% or more of the standard or budget figure);
(ii) above a given *absolute* size (e.g. in excess of £100).

On the other hand, of course, he may feel he knows the reason for the variance and decide not to do anything more formal by way of an investigation.

Question 10.4
In what ways does inflation affect the usefulness of information contained in managerial accounting reports?

Answer
One might approach this question by thinking of what stems from a failure to allow for the impacts of inflation when compiling managerial accounting reports. For instance:

(i) asset values are understated;
(ii) costs (e.g. depreciation) are understated;
(iii) profit is overstated;
(iv) profitability is overstated;
(v) comparisons between actual and standard are invalid if the latter failed to include an inflation factor;
(vi) comparisons over time are invalid;
(vii) resource allocations are inefficient when based on invalid data;
(viii) pricing decisions will be inappropriate when based on invalid data.

Planning, decision-making and control will all be impeded. Since inflation is a key variable in our economic environment, and since it distorts the unit of measure (£) used by management accountants, it inevitably reduces the usefulness of financial reports unless its impacts are acknowledged and allowed for.

W10.3 Discussion topics

Question 10.1
Any manager worth his salt can find a good excuse for a variance.' Discuss.

Question 10.2
Explain what is meant by 'management by exception'.

Question 10.3
What does variance analysis seek to achieve?

Question 10.4
It could be argued that a manager's performance can only be measured after the event, at which time there is nothing that can be done to change what has happened. Evaluate this view with reference to the role of variance analysis.

Question 10.5
For a variance to be worth investigating it must be presumed that the standard in question was valid. Would you agree?

Question 10.6
Why are total material and total labour variances typically decomposed into quantity and price variances?

Question 10.7
Explain how the following variances arise:

(i) yield variance;
(ii) calendar variance;
(iii) sales mix variance.

Question 10.8
Would you agree that random variances are attributable to management's implementation decisions and hence require no corrective action?

W10.4 Worked examples

There are three examples in this section:

(i) Post Electric Corporation (adapted from the Kinkead Equipment Ltd case in Shank (1981)), which deals with the analysis of variances from a marketing viewpoint;
(ii) Pi Ltd, which deals with variance analysis from a manufacturing viewpoint;
(iii) Ram Jam Ltd, which looks at the variance investigation decision.

Question 10.1
John Swann, managing director of Post Electric Corporation, glanced at the summary profit and loss statement for 1992 which he was holding (see Fig. W10.1) and tossed it to Sandy Cunningham. Swann looked out of the window of his office and declared, somewhat smugly, 'As you can see, Sandy, we exceeded our sales goal for the year, improved our margin, and earned more profit than we had planned. Although some of our expenses seemed to grow a little faster than sales, 1992 was a pretty good year for us, don't you think?'

Figure W10.1

Post Electric Corporation 1992 operating results.

	Budget £000	Actual £000
Sales	5,400	5,710
Manufacturing costs	2,000	2,090
	3,400	3,620
G & A expenses	1,500	1,650
Net income before taxes	£1,900	£1,970

Sandy Cunningham, a recent graduate of a highly regarded business school, was serving a training period as executive assistant to Swann. He looked over the figures and nodded his agreement. Swann continued: 'Sandy, I'd like you to prepare a short report for the board meeting next week summarizing the key factors that account for the favourable overall profit variance of £70,000. I think you're about ready to make a presentation to the board if you can pull together a good report. Check with the controller's office for any additional data you may want. Remember, the board doesn't want a long complex presentation. See what you can come up with.'

Sandy Cunningham agreed to the assignment and gathered the data shown in Fig. W10.2. How can he present an analysis of 1992 operating results to the board?

Answer

Part of the profit variance of £70,000 is due to General and Administrative expenses being £150,000 over budget for the year. There is no basis for gaining

Figure W10.2

Post Electric Corporation: additional data. Post's products are grouped into two main lines of business for internal reporting purposes. Each line includes many separate products which are averaged together for the purposes of the question.

	Meters		Generators	
	Budget £000	Actual £000	Budget £000	Actual £000
Price	30	29	150	153
Manufacturing cost	15	16	40	42
Margin	£15	£13	£110	£111
Units sold	80,000	65,000	20,000	25,000
Industry sales (units)	800,000	700,000	200,000	250,000

explanatory insights into this variance since many items within the total will be fixed costs, so the variance must be due to the non-fixed items – whatever they may be. This £150,000 adverse variance on G & A is much greater than the increase in the volume of activity, e.g.

$$\frac{\text{Actual revenue}}{\text{Budgeted revenue}} = \frac{5,710,000}{5,400,000} = 1.06$$

$$\text{G \& A expenses (budget)} \times 1.06 = £1,590,000$$

which is a long way short of the G & A expenses (actual) of £1,650,000.

In total, the profit variance from the two product groups must be the sum of the overall profit variance and the G & A expenses variance: £70,000 + £150,000 = £220,000. It is possible to carry out analyses to gain insights into this variance.

Let us begin our analysis by recasting the given data (from Figs W10.1 and W10.2 in the question) in a way that highlights the performance of each product group. This is done below for meters (Fig. W10.3). We will look at meters in some detail, and then apply the same approach to generators prior to summarizing the overall position.

It is clear that there is an adverse outcome in terms of the margin on meters. Instead of achieving £1,200,000 the result was £845,000. This is partly due to:

(i) an unfavourable variance relating to sales volume; and
(ii) an unfavourable variance relating to the margin on each unit sold.

In turn, the variance due to sales volume shortfall can be attributed to differences between:

(iii) actual and anticipated total market size; and
(iv) actual and anticipated market share.

Figure W10.3

Data relating to meters.

	Budget	Actual	Variance
Revenue			
Sales (units)	80,000	65,000	(15,000)
Price per unit (£)	30	29	(1)
Total revenue (£)	2,400,000	1,885,000	(515,000)
Market			
Total size (units)	800,000	700,000	(100,000)
Share of market (%)	10	9.3	(0.7)
Costs			
Manufacturing cost per unit (£)	15	16	(1)
Total manufacturing costs (£)	1,200,000	1,040,000	160,000
Margin			
Per unit (£)	15	13	(2)
Total margin (£)	1,200,000	845,000	(355,000)

(Adverse variances in brackets)

We can see, therefore, that a variation between the budgeted and actual margin for meters can be due to variations in price per unit, cost per unit, total market size and market penetration. This can be expressed in quantitative terms as follows:

(a) *Profit variance*:

$(C_a - C_p) \times Q_a = £(13 - 15) \times 65{,}000 = £(130{,}000)$

(b) *Volume variance*:

$(Q_a - Q_p) \times C_p = (65{,}000 - 80{,}00) \times £15 = £(225{,}000)$

(c) *Net variance*:

	£
Profit variance	(130,000)
Volume variance	(225,000)
	£(355,000)

where: C_a = actual margin per unit
C_p = planned margin per unit
Q_a = actual quantity sold in units
Q_p = planned quantity of sales in units.

However, (b) can be analysed further to take into account the impact of market size and penetration variations:

(d) *Market size variance*:

$(M_a - M_p) \times S_p \times C_p = (700{,}000 - 800{,}000) \times 0.10 \times £15 = £(150{,}000)$

(e) *Market share variance*:

$(S_a - S_p) \times M_a \times C_p = (0.093 - 0.10) \times 700{,}000 \times £15 = £(75{,}000)$

(f) *Volume variance*:

	£
Market size variance	(150,000)
Market share variance	(75,000)
	£(225,000)

where: M_a = actual total market in units
M_p = anticipated total market in units
S_a = actual market share
S_p = planned market share.

In summary we have:

	£	£
Budgeted profit margin		1,200,000
Volume variance:		
Market size variance	(150,000)	
Market share variance	(75,000)	(225,000)
Profit variance		(130,000)
Actual profit margin		£845,000

Figure W10.4

Data relating to generators.

	Budget	Actual	Variance
Revenue			
Sales (units)	20,000	25,000	5,000
Price per unit (£)	150	153	3
Total revenue (£)	3,000,000	3,825,000	825,000
Market			
Total size (units)	200,000	250,000	50,000
Share of market (%)	10	10	–
Costs			
Manufacturing cost per unit (£)	40	42	(2)
Total manufacturing costs (£)	800,000	1,050,000	(250,000)
Margin			
Per unit (£)	110	111	1
Total margin (£)	2,200,000	2,775,000	575,000

(Adverse variances in brackets)

It can be seen that the unfavourable profit margin from meters in 1992 was due to a combination of unfavourable constituent variances. What was the picture regarding generator sales? (Data is given in Fig. W10.4.)

Through the application of the above formulae we get the following:

(a) *Profit variance*:

£(111 − 110) × 25,000 = £25,000

(b) *Volume variance*:

(25,000 − 20,000) × 110 × £550,000

(c) *Net variance*:

	£
Profit variance	25,000
Volume variance	550,000
	£575,000

(d) *Market size variance*:

(250,000 − 200,000) × 0.10 × £110 = £550,000

(e) *Market share variance*:

(0.10 − 0.10) × 250,000 × £110 = £0

(f) *Volume variance*:

	£
Market size variance	550,000
Market share variance	0
	£550,000

In summary this gives:

	£	£
Budgeted profit margin		2,220,000
Volume variance:		
Market size variance	550,000	
Market share variance	0	
		550,000
Profit variance		25,000
Actual profit margin		£2,775,000

Thus generators produced a favourable profit variance due, principally, to maintaining their share in a growing market. A modest gain was also produced because the unit price increased by marginally more than the increase in manufacturing costs over the year.

Finally, let us put all these pieces together:

	£
Total variance – meters	(355,000)
Total variance – generators	575,000
Total variance – G & A expenses	(150,000)
Net total profit variance	£70,000

The favourable profit variance of £70,000 is attributable to the excellent performance of generators which outpaced the poor performance of meters and the overrun on G & A expenses.

Sandy Cunningham's report should summarize the above analysis.

Question 10.2

Pi Ltd operates a system of standard costs. For a given four-week period, budgeted for sales of 10,000 units at £5 per unit, actual sales were 9,000 units at £5.125 per unit. Costs relating to that period were as follows:

	Standard £	Actual £
Materials	25,000	25,740
Wages	7,500	7,087
Fixed overhead	2,000	1,881
Variable overhead	1,000	925
Semi-variable overhead	270	243
Standard hours	50,000	–
Actual hours	–	40,500

Notes:

(i) The standard material input is 25 kg per unit at 10p per kg. The actual material content of each unit was 26 kg at 11p per kg.

(ii) The standard wages per unit are 5 hours at 15p per hour; actual wages were 4.5 hours at 17.5p per hour.

(iii) Mixed indirect costs consist of five-ninths fixed expense and four-ninths variable expense.

(iv) There were no opening stocks and the whole production for the period was sold.
(v) The four-week period was a normal period.

You are required to draft a statement reconciling the standard net profit for the period with the net profit actually realized.

Figure W10.5

Pi Ltd: statement reconciling standard net profit with realized net profit.

	Unfavourable	Favourable	
			£
Budgeted sales (10,000 units at £5 per unit)			50,000
Standard cost of sales (£25,000 + 7,500 + 2,000 + 1,000 + 270)			35,770
Standard Net Profit (£1.423 per unit)			14,230
Variances:	Unfavourable	Favourable	
	£	£	
1. Sales volume:			
(10,000 − 9,000) × 1.4230	1,423		
Sales price:			
9,000 × £ 0.125		1,125	
2. Materials price:			
26 × 9,000 × 1p	2,340		
Materials usage (or efficiency):			
1 × 9,000 × 10p	900		
3. Labour rate (or price):			
4.5 × 9,000 × 0.25	1,012		
Labour efficiency:			
(45,000 − 40,500) × 15p		675	
4. Variable overhead expenditure (or budget):			
£1,033 − (9,000 × £0.112) or £1,033 − (45,000 × £0.0224)	25		
5. Fixed overhead budget (or expenditure):			
£2,016 − £2,150		134	
Fixed overhead efficiency:			
£0.043 (40,500 − 45,000)		193	
Fixed overhead volume:			
£0.043 (50,000 − 40,500)	408		
	£6,108	£2,127	3,981 U
Realized net profit (9,000 × £5.125) − £35,876 =			£10,249

Answer

The statement reconciling standard net profit with realized net profit is given in Fig. W10.5.

Notes

(i) Budgeted hours 10,000 units × 5 hours = 50,000 std. hours.
Actual hours 9,000 " × 4.5 " = 40,500 hours.
Actual output 9,000 " × 5 " = 45,000 std. hours.

(ii) $$\text{Variable indirect cost rate} = \frac{\text{Budgeted variable indirect costs}}{\text{Budgeted hours}} = \frac{1{,}000 + (4/9 \times 270)}{50{,}000} = 0.0224$$

(iii) $$\text{Fixed indirect cost rate} = \frac{\text{Budgeted fixed indirect costs}}{\text{Budgeted hours}} = \frac{2{,}000 + (5/9 \times 270)}{50{,}000} = 0.043$$

Figure W10.6

Pi Ltd. variance analysis.

	Actual	Flexible budget variance	Flexible budget	Sales volume variance	Fixed budget
Units	9,000	–	9,000	1,000	10,000
	£	£	£	£	£
SR	46,125	1,125 F	45,000	5,000 U	50,000
VC	33,860	3,602 U	30,258	3,362 F	33,620
Contribution	12,265	2,477 U	14,742	1,638 U	16,380
FC	2,016	134 F	2,150	–	2,150
NP	£10,249	£2,343 U	£12,592	£1,638 U	£14,230

Flexible budget variance   Sales volume variance

£3,981 U
Profit variance

F = favourable
U = unfavourable

Some of the main causes of indirect cost variances are:

(a) *Volume variances*:
  (i) decreases in consumer demand;
  (ii) excess plant capacity;
  (iii) plant stoppages due to poor scheduling or input bottlenecks;
  (iv) calendar fluctuations that have not been allowed for.
(b) *Efficiency variances*:
  (i) waste of materials;
  (ii) poor labour performance;
  (iii) employees not being properly supplied with work;
  (iv) machine breakdowns;
  (v) lack of inputs (e.g. operatives, tools, materials, instructions);
  (vi) use of wrong grades of material and labour.
(c) *Budget variances*:
  (i) unforeseen market price changes;
  (ii) an inability to obtain the most favourable prices.

It is evident, therefore, that standard costing variance analysis provides a basis from which to investigate changes in costs but is not sufficiently subtle to analyse variances by detailed causes.

A simple analysis of the variances of Pi Ltd, highlighting flexible budget and sales volume variances, is given in Figure W10.6 (which also emphasizes contribution as well as net profit variances).

Reconciliation:

	£
Expected profit	14,230
Actual profit	10,249
Variance	£3,981 U

Pi Ltd can be solved by following a series of steps, as shown below:

Step 1: Determine total variance. This is given by (Budgeted sales less Standard costs) minus (Actual sales less Actual costs):

		£
£50,000 – £35,770	=	14,230
£46,125 – £35,876	=	10,249
Total Variance		£3,981 U

Step 2: Determine direct material variances – See Fig. W10.7.

Step 3: Determine direct labour variances – see Fig. W10.8.

Figure W10.7

Pi Ltd: direct materials variances.

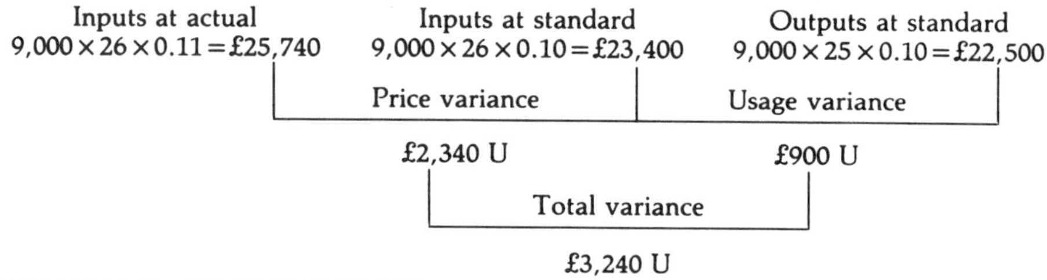

Figure W10.8

Pi Ltd: direct labour variances.

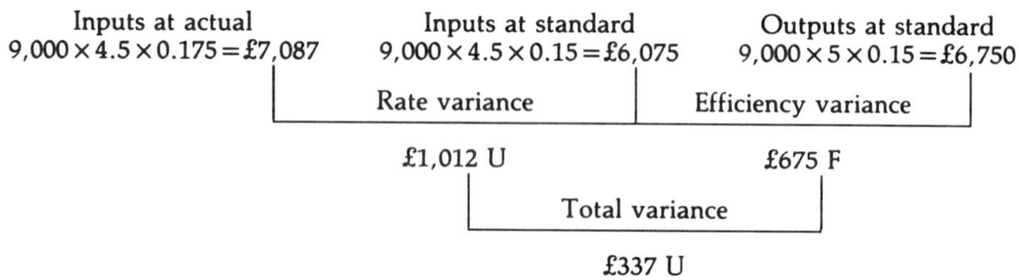

Step 4: Determine indirect cost variances. Initially we must establish separate recovery rates for both fixed and variable indirect costs. The analysis of fixed and variable indirect cost variances is shown in Fig. W10.9.

Step 5: Determine sales variance:

Sales price variance: 9,000 × 0.125 = £1,125 F
Sales volume variance: (50,000 − 35,770) − (9,000 × 1.423) = £1,423 U

Step 6: Put all the bits together – see Fig. W10.10.

Question 10.3

Assume the management of Ram Jam Ltd is trying to determine whether or not to inspect an automatic production process. There is an 80% probability that the process is in adjustment and a 20% probability that it is out of adjustment. Relevant costs are as follows:

Inspection will cost	£200
Adjustment, if necessary, will cost	£300
Excess operating costs if out of adjustment	£2,000

Should the process be inspected?

Answer

Managers responsible for certain types of processes must often decide whether or not to shut down the process for inspection and adjustment, if necessary. In general, management wants to shut down the process only when it is out of

Figure W10.9

Pi Ltd: variable indirect cost variances; (b) fixed indirect cost variances.

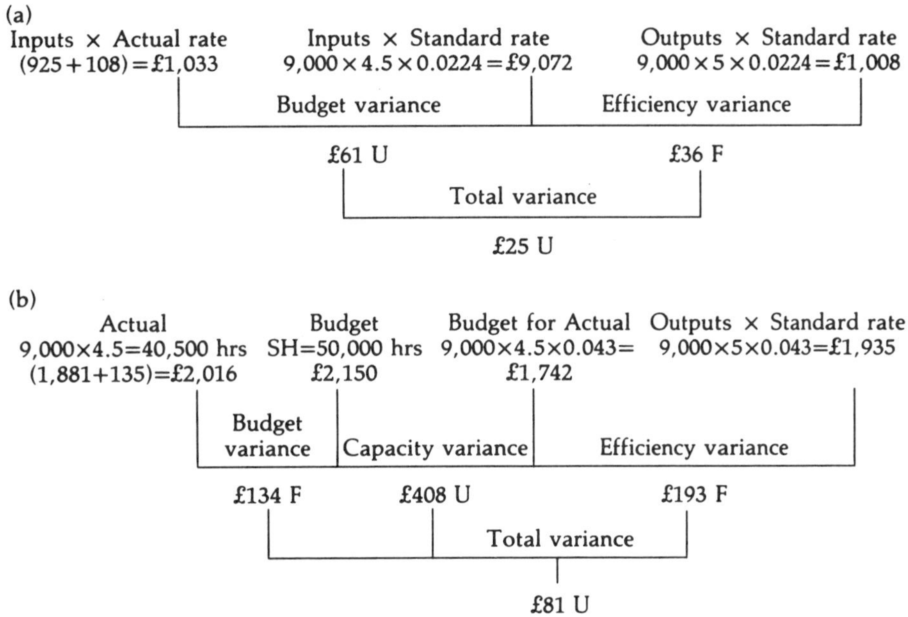

Figure W10.10

Pi Ltd: total variances.

	£	£	£
Total variance			3,981 U
DMPV	2,340 U		
DMUV	900 U		
DLRV	1,012 U		
DLEV		675 F	
VIBV	61 U		
VIEV		36 F	
FIBV		134 F	
FICV	408 U		
FIEV		193 F	
SPV		1,125 F	
SVV	1,423 U		
Total variance	£6,144 U	£2,163 F	£3,981 U

adjustment. However, there is no way of knowing for certain whether the process is in adjustment or out of adjustment except by shutting it down and performing an inspection. Obviously if the process is in adjustment no further action is necessary, and if the process is out of adjustment it will be necessary to adjust it.

If the managers do not shut the process down for inspection they may incur excess operating costs if the process is, in fact, out of adjustment. Conversely, there will be no excess operating costs if it is in adjustment.

In summary, there are two possible actions:

(i) inspect and adjust if necessary; and
(ii) do not inspect.

There are also two possible events (or states):

(i) the process is in adjustment; and
(ii) the process is out of adjustment.

Pay-off tables are often used to summarize the outcomes of these alternative actions and events. The pay-off table for this decision is presented in Fig. W10.11. Since the assumed objective is to minimize expected costs, the best action here is to inspect and adjust if necessary.

Figure W10.11

Pay-off tables for variance investigations.

Action	Event (probability)		Expected cost of action
	In adjustment (0.80)	Out of adjustment (0.20)	
Inspect and adjust if necessary	£200	£500*	£260**
Do not inspect	£0	£2,000	£400***

* Inspection costs of £200 + Adjustment costs of £300
** (£200) (0.80) + (£500) (0.20)
*** (£0) (0.80) + (£2,000) (0.20)

W10.5 Computational problems

Question 10.1

The following data relates to product X for last month:

	Budget	Actual	Variance
Sales	£990,000	£800,000	£190,000
Units sold	110,000	100,000	
Unit price	£9.00	£8.00	

Explain the variance of £190,000.

Question 10.2

The following data relates to the most recent quarter's results of Hallam Enterprises:

	Actual	Budget
Sales (units)	90,000	100,000
Selling price/unit (£)	25	30
Sales (£)	2,250,000	3,000,000

Calculate and explain:

(i) sales price variance;
(ii) sales volume variance; and
(iii) total sales variance for the period.

Question 10.3

The following standards have been established for the LMN Company for each detailed activity within the transportation function:

	Product line A		Product line B	
	Unit cost (£)	Estimated units of variability	Unit cost (£)	Estimated units of variability
Handling claims (per shipment)	1.00	180	1.10	200
Loading and unloading (per pound loaded)	0.60	1,000	0.50	800
Drivers' and helpers' wages (per truck-mile)	0.70	700	0.40	680

The following actual units of variability and actual costs were incurred for the company's two product lines:

	Product line A		Product line B	
	Unit cost (£)	Actual units of variability	Unit cost (£)	Actual units of variability
Handling claims	1.20	160	1.15	220
Loading and unloading	0.70	1,100	0.65	900
Drivers' and helpers' wages	0.74	710	0.48	710

Required:
Prepare variance analysis statements for each product line.

Question 10.4

The ABC Company provides you with information concerning the standards established for the detailed transportation function. Actual data is also included in the following:

Function	Budgeted cost £	Standard cost per unit £	Actual cost £	Actual cost per unit £
Clerical work (per shipment)	1,000	2.00	1,350	2.25
Planning and supervision (per unit shipped)	8,000	0.50 + £4,000 per period	8,880	0.60 + £4,020 per period
Loading and unloading (per pound loaded)	975	0.65	1,131	0.78
Drivers' and helpers' wages (per truck-mile)	2,400	0.80	2,646	0.84

Required:
Calculate variances for each of the functions detailed.

Question 10.5

Peter Price is the finance manager of the Rook Company which operates in an inflationary economy: the rate of inflation has recently been running between 10% and 12% per month. This high rate has been accompanied by wide variations in relative price changes (i.e. some prices have been going up at a much faster rate, while others have been lagging behind).

There is a major difficulty in these circumstances when it comes to preparing short-run budgets and evaluating performance against those budgets. Peter Price has collected the following data as at the end of the current month (April, 19X1):

Anticipated sales during June, 19X1: 1,000 units
Inputs per unit of output: 10 kilos material M
5 hours labour L
Current costs of inputs are: M 6 shekels/kilo
L 20 shekels/hr
Current selling price of output: 250 shekels/unit

In developing a budget for the month of June 19X1, Peter Price is considering three alternative approaches:

A1 A budget based on April 19X1 price levels.
A2 A budget based on a general increase in prices during May of 10%, with no change in relative prices.
A3 A budget based on:
(i) an increase in output prices of 10%;
(ii) an increase in labour rates of 8%;
(iii) an increase in material costs of 15%.

You are required to produce the following:

(a) Budgets for June 19X1 based on each of the approaches outlined above.

(b) If actual results for June 19X1 were:

(i) 900 units sold at an average price of 277 shekels/unit;

(ii) 9,100 kilos of M used at a cost of 60,970 skekels;
(iii) 4,450 hours of L consumed at a cost of 103,240 shekels,
prepare a flexible budget for June 19X1 under each of the three approaches A1, A2, A3.

(c) For each flexible budget, using the formulae given below, compute the following variances:

(i) selling price variance (SPV);
(ii) material price variance (MPV);
(iii) material quantity variance (MQV);
(iv) labour rate variance (LRV);
(v) labour quantity variance (LQV).

Be sure to reconcile the total of these individual variances with the overall variance.

$$\begin{aligned} SPV &= (AP - SP) \times AQ \\ SVV &= (AQ - SQ) \times SP \\ MPV &= (AP - SP) \times AQ \\ MQV &= (AQ - SQ) \times SP \\ LRV &= (AR - SR) \times AH \\ LQV &= (AH - SH) \times SR \end{aligned}$$

where: AP = actual price per unit
SP = standard price per unit
AQ = actual quantity (total)
SQ = standard quantity (total)
AH = actual hours (total)
SH = standard hours (total)
AR = actual rate per hour
SR = standard rate per hour
SVV = sales volume variance.

Label favourable variances F
unfavourable variances U

(d) Government statistics were released in July 19X1 which showed the following increases in prices over the period from 1 May 19X1 to 30 June 19X1:

Item	% increase
General Price Index	12%
Products similar to Rook's output	12%
Material similar to M	10%
Labour similar to L	14%

Using this data, revise your analysis of variances in part (c) under the A3 approach to produce:

(i) relative price variances (showing the difference between the actual prices faced by Rook and those that would have been predicted using the government's statistics);
(ii) forecast variances (showing the difference between the A3 assumptions

and the predictions that would have been made using the government's statistics).

(e) Comment on the value of this exercise in explaining variances during times of changing price levels. Which set of budget assumptions and variance analyses would seem most (or least) helpful?

(Adapted from problem 9–6, pp. 315–17, in Kaplan (1982).)

Question 10.6
Armor Company use various statistical models in their system of quality control. They have established that the probability of their process being in control is 0.90 and the probability of an out-of-control situation is 0.10. Costs of investigation average about £4,000 and the cost of making corrections tends to approximate £6,000. The present value of benefits are expected to be about £12,000. Management wants to know whether or not to investigate out-of-control situations.
Advise management.

W10.6 Case study

The following case study is reprinted with permission from J.K. Shank (1981).

KINKEAD EQUIPMENT, LTD.

Andrew MacGregor, managing director of Kinkead Equipment, Ltd., glanced at the summary profit and loss statement for 1992 which he was holding (Fig. W10.12), then tossed it to Douglas McCosh and looked out the window of his office overlooking the industrial centre of Glasgow.

Figure W10.12

Kinkead Equipment Ltd, preliminary operating results 15 January 1992 (£000).

		Budget 1992	Percent of Turnover		Actual 1992	Percent of Turnover
Turnover		£6,215	(100)		£6,319	(100)
Trading margin		2,590	(41.7)		2,660	(42.1)
Less other expenses						
Selling	£706		(11.4)	£740		(11.7)
Administrative	320		(5.1)	325		(5.1)
Research	318	1,344	(5.1)	325	1,390	(5.1)
Profit before taxes		£1,246	(20.05)		£1,270	(20.10)

Summary for 1991

	Budget	Actual	Variance
Turnover	£6,215	£6,319	104 F
Expenses	4,969	5,049	80 U
Profit before taxes	£1,246	£1,270	24 F

'As you can see Douglas, we beat our turnover goal for the year, improved our trading margin a bit, and earned more profit than we had planned. Although our selling costs did seem to grow faster than our turnover, all things considered, I would say 1992 was a good year for the firm.'

Douglas McCosh, a recent graduate of a well-known European business school, was serving a training period as executive assistant to Mr MacGregor. He looked over the figures and nodded his agreement.

'Douglas, I'd like you to prepare a short report for the management committee meeting next week summarizing the key factors which account for the favourable overall profit variance of £24,000. That might not be much for a firm like ours, but it would still pay your salary for quite a while, wouldn't it?' he laughed. 'I think you're about ready to make a presentation to the committee if you can pull together a good report.

'Check with the financial director's staff for any additional data you may

Figure W10.13

*Additional information.**

	Electric Meters	Electronic Instruments
Selling prices per unit		
Average standard price	£30.00	£150.00
Average actual prices, 1992	29.00	153.00
Product costs per unit		
Average standard manufacturing cost	15.00	40.00
Average actual manufacturing cost	16.00	42.00
Average standard selling commission	1.00	15.00
Average actual selling commission	.98	14.90
Volume information		
Units produced and sold – actual	65,369	28,910
Units produced and sold – planned	82,867	24,860
Total industry turnover, 1992	£24,860,000	£37,290,000
Kinkead's share of the market – planned	10%	10%
Kinkead's share of the market – actual	10%	8%

Firm-wide expenses
(Thousands of Pounds)

	Planned	Actual
Fixed manufacturing expenses	£1,388	£1,399
Fixed selling expenses	250	245
Fixed administrative expenses	320	325
Fixed research expenses	318	325

* Kinkead's products are grouped into two main lines of business for internal reporting purposes. Each line includes many separate products, which are averaged together for purposes of this case.

need or want. Just remember to keep it on a commonsense level – no high-powered financial double-talk. How about giving me a draft to look at in a day or so?'

Douglas McCosh smiled somewhat meekly as he rose to return to his office. 'I'll give it a try, sir,' he said. His first step was to gather the additional information shown in Fig. W10.13.

Required:
Prepare the report which you feel Douglas McCosh should present to Mr MacGregor.

This case was prepared by Professor John Shank based on materials originally collected by Professor Frank Aguilar. It is designed for class discussion rather than to reflect either effective or ineffective handling of an administrative situation. All rights reserved.

CHAPTER

11 Performance measurement: divisional analysis

WORKBOOK

W11.1 Introduction

The measurement of performance – whether at the level of the enterprise, the division, the department or the individual – may seem to be a wholly technical matter. However, the human factor is of central importance and it is too short-sighted to ignore the impact of performance measures on the motivation of individual managers. In working through this Workbook chapter you should consider the behavioural implications of the issues you deal with.

W11.2 Revision topics

Question 11.1
If an enterprise's rate of return on investment is low and management wishes to improve it, discuss the immediate strategies for investigating and identifying the problem areas.

Answer
If an enterprise's return on investment is low management's first task should be to identify the possible problem areas. As a first step, the components of the ROI ratio should give some indication as to the source of the problem.

A common ROI measure is given as:

$$\frac{\text{Net profit after taxation and before interest}}{\text{Investment in net total assets}}$$

If this ratio is falling over time or below expectations at a point in time the reasons will be found in one or both of the components of the ratio – either the net profit or the level of investment. The manager should examine the two secondary ratios: the net profit margin and the capital turnover ratios. If the net profit margin is found to be declining then further analysis of revenue and cost behaviour to locate the source of the decrease is required. If the capital turnover ratio is declining (indicating that there is an insufficient level of sales being generated per £ of invested capital) then further analysis of the revenues and asset utilization will be necessary.

Question 11.2
How would you define and measure residual income?

Answer

Residual income was defined on p. 385 as '. . . the operating profit (or income) of a division *less* the imputed interest on the assets used by the division'. This involves treating the (imputed) interest on the capital invested in the division as a cost, with any surplus after the sum of *all* costs have been deducted from revenue being the residual income. Thus, for a hypothetical division for last month:

	£
Revenue	25,000
Less: Operating costs	15,000
Operating profit	10,000
Imputed interest (15% on, say, investment of £50,000)	7,500
Residual income	£2,500

Question 11.3

Profit margins can vary substantially from industry to industry. Discuss the reasons why this is so, giving relevant examples.

Answer

Profit margins vary significantly from industry to industry. In examining the reasons for this it is best to consider profit margins at two levels: the gross level and the net level.

Gross profit measures the difference between sales and the cost (material, labour and an element of indirect manufacturing cost) of those sales. Net profit measures the residual remaining to shareholders after all other expenses but usually before taxation. It is also the pre-tax return on the assets employed by the enterprise.

The enterprise's main concern is to ensure that the return on the assets employed is sufficient and this is a function of the level of investment in assets as well as the net profit margin. However, it should become clear that two companies with significantly different net and gross profit margins could be earning sufficient return on assets as the following example indicates:

	Enterprise A		Enterprise B	
	£	%	£	%
Turnover	10,000	100	10,000	100
Cost of sales	8,000	80	5,000	50
Gross margin	2,000	20	5,000	50
Expenses	1,200	12	1,800	18
Net margin	800	8	3,200	32
Net asset investment	5,000		22,000	
Return on assets	16%		14.5%	

Profit margins can vary between industries for a variety of reasons. Our discussion in Chapter 11 (pp. 374–85) should enable you to consider how you might begin investigating the causes of such variations. For example, where the investment in assets is relatively low (as in Enterprise A above) it may be possible to operate with low profit margins provided the overall return on assets is acceptable. Travel agencies are a good example of enterprises which earn low margins but which can generate a sufficient volume of transactions at low margin to earn a good return on assets. Supermarket stores operate on a low gross profit margin but earn substantial interest revenue on cash deposits which ensures that a sufficient rate of net profit is earned to generate an acceptable return on assets. Conversely, manufacturing industry often has to earn high gross and net profit margins in order to earn a satisfactory return on assets.

For class discussion the example of the pharmaceutical industry can be used to help to generate controversy about the issues involved.

W11.3 Discussion topics

Question 11.1
Identify the relative benefits and drawbacks of centralized versus decentralized organizational structures.

Question 11.2
Should divisional managers be expected to make decisions that enhance the well-being of their divisions or of the organization as a whole?

Question 11.3
If you were a senior manager in a divisionalized organization would you prefer to have product line reports that included or excluded allocations of joint distribution and manufacturing costs that are beyond the control of individual product line managers?

Question 11.4
Define 'controllability'. What is its relevance to the design of divisional performance measurement systems?

Question 11.5
What problems need to be overcome in devising a performance index for a division?

Question 11.6
Assuming that it is possible to trace assets and profits to the divisions of a decentralized enterprise, would you recommend the use of gross asset values or net asset values in ROI calculations?

Question 11.7
Given that accountants use different methods to calculate profit, how will this affect any attempt to assess the relative performance of different enterprises?

Question 11.8
If changes in the general level of prices are beyond management's control, why might information on price level changes be of interest to managers?

Question 11.9
The confectionery division of Multi-Division Ltd is in the process of planning a major plant extension, in the expectation that there will be increasing demand for its products over the next ten years.

Bertie Bassett is the manager of the confectionery division and he is trying to decide whether the plant should be built on a scale that will enable it to be operated at full capacity on completion (thus showing a large ROI) or whether some excess capacity should be built into the system. If the latter alternative is adopted it will have the effect of lowering the immediate ROI, although there will be benefits over the longer term.

Recognizing that it is both difficult and expensive to build on to the plant in a piecemeal manner, the planning group has recommended that the plant be built with 50% excess capacity. Mr Bassett expects to be in charge of his current division for about two more years, before being transferred to the paints division.

If you were Mr Bassett, what course of action would you propose?

W11.4 Worked examples

Question 11.1

For XYZ Ltd relevant data for 19X9 are follows:

Operating profit	£20,000,000
Sales turnover	£300,000,000
Investment	£100,000,000

Calculate:

(a) Investment turnover;
(b) margin on sales;
(c) return on investment; and
(d) show how (a), (b) and (c) interrelate.

Answer

(a) Investment turnover is given by:

$$\frac{\text{Sales turnover}}{\text{Investment}} = \frac{\pounds300{,}000{,}000}{\pounds100{,}000{,}000}$$
$$= 3 \text{ times}$$

(b) Margin on sales is given by:

$$\frac{\text{Operating profit}}{\text{Sales turnover}} \times 100 = \frac{\pounds20{,}000{,}000}{\pounds300{,}000{,}000} \times 100$$
$$= 6.7\%$$

(c) Return on investment is given by:

$$\frac{\text{Operating profit}}{\text{Investment}} \times 100 = \frac{\pounds20{,}000{,}000}{\pounds100{,}000{,}000} \times 100$$
$$= 20\%$$

(d) The interrelationship is given by:

$$\text{Investment turnover} \times \text{Margin on sales} = \text{ROI}$$
$$3 \times 6.7\% = 20\%$$

Question 11.2
The following data are available for four medium sized private enterprises in the printing industry:

	W £000	X £000	Y £000	Z £000
Sales	2,000	1,000	1,500	2,500
Net profit after tax	300	50	225	300
Total assets	1,500	750	1,500	2,400
Shareholders' funds	1,000	5,000	1,400	1,000

(a) Calculate the asset turnover ratio, the net profit margin and the return on shareholders' funds for each enterprise.
(b) Evaluate each enterprise's performance by comparing it with the industry averages given below:

Asset turnover	1.4
Net profit margin	0.12
Return on shareholders' funds	0.25

Answer
(a)

Ratio	W	X	Y	Z	Industry average
Asset turnover ratio:					
$\frac{\text{Sales}}{\text{Total assets}}$	1.33	1.33	1.00	1.04	1.40
Net profit margin:					
$\frac{\text{Net profit after tax}}{\text{Sales}} \times 100$	15%	5%	15%	12%	12%
Return on shareholders' funds:					
$\frac{\text{Net profit after tax}}{\text{Shareholders' funds}} \times 100$	30%	1%	16.07%	30%	25%

(b) This question is designed to underline for you how important it is for users of accounting ratios to be extremely cautious. There are a number of instances in the above example which help to bring out this point.

The asset/turnover ratio indicates that each of the companies is generating sales below the industry average. Two difficulties should be highlighted: first, the problem of comparing results to an average (i.e. forgetting that on average 50% of the industry will be below 1.4); secondly, that you should beware of concluding on the ratio evidence until further analysis has been carried out of the composition of the asset base in each of the companies. For example, it may be that in the period under review enterprise Y made a substantial investment in fixed assets which could temporarily depress the asset turnover ratio.

Enterprise X is generating close to the average turnover per £ of assets invested but earns a relatively low net margin on sales and an extremely low return on shareholders' funds. In the first instance, therefore, we should direct our attention to the analysis of the cost structure of this enterprise.

Enterprise Z is a more interesting case. Here we find the enterprise earning a high return on shareholders' funds, a satisfactory net profit margin but a low turnover per £ of assets employed. This profile can occur where an enterprise, despite its low market penetration, manages to utilize its assets extremely efficiently.

Question 11.3

West Side plc is a large diversified company with headquarters in London. West Side is the holding company for four subsidiaries, each operating in different markets. The segments are domestic audio and visual equipment, toiletries and cosmetics, stationery and writing materials, and scientific instruments. The following information was obtained from the most recent published annual report:

Subsidiary	Turnover	Operating profit	Total net assets
	£m.	£m.	£m.
Audio-visual	754.5	243.0	458.8
Toiletries and cosmetics	687.0	60.6	321.5
Stationery and writing materials	252.7	4.0	255.6
Scientific instruments	380.2	38.0	298.9

(a) Relate the annual profit to sales to assess which subsidiary was most successful in generating profit for a given £ of sales.
(b) Relate the annual profit to investment to assess which subsidiary was most successful in generating profit for a given £ of assets invested.
(c) Discuss the relationship one might expect to find between turnover and assets invested in each of these subsidiaries.

Answer

(a), (b)

	$\frac{\text{Operating profit}}{\text{Turnover}}$	$\frac{\text{Operating profit}}{\text{Net assets}}$	$\frac{\text{Turnover}}{\text{Net assets}}$
Subsidiary			
Audio-visual	32.20%	51.83%	1.61
Toiletries and cosmetics	8.82%	18.84%	2.13
Stationery and writing materials	1.58%	1.56%	1.00
Scientific instruments	10.00%	12.71%	1.27

(c) As far as possible, enterprises attempt to optimize sales turnover per £ of assets invested; it is a measure of the efficiency with which assets are utilized. It is difficult to generalize about the relationship which should exist between asset investment and sales turnover because it is in large part a function of the trading success of the particular enterprise. Nonetheless, other things being equal, there are some broad trends evident in different types of industry. The above examples of asset turnover do fit reasonably closely with one's expectations for the particular industries and hence are helpful illustrations.

The stationery and writing materials industry is labour and capital intensive and it is competitive. Moreover, it is presently suffering a cut in its profit margins because of the high costs of processing timber. The figures presented in the question also suggest that the particular firm chosen is one which may be in serious financial difficulty and hence it is not surprising to find it generating low turnover per £ of assets invested. By contrast, the cosmetics industry, while heavily competitive (see moderate margin on sales) is not as capital intensive as any of the other industries and shows a high turnover per £ of assets invested. The audio-visual industry and the scientific instruments industry are similar in many respects – production technology is advanced, but because of the huge consumer demand in the audio-visual market this industry is able to generate higher profit margins and asset turnover than the scientific instruments industry.

W11.5 Computational problems

Question 11.1

The Doddery Company has two divisions, Lorst and Gawn, and evaluates its managers on the ROI criterion.

Budgets for next year are as follows:

	Lorst	Gawn	Total
	£	£	£
Investment	1,200,000	1,000,000	2,200,000
Revenue	600,000	300,000	900,000
Operating expenses	300,000	200,000	500,000
Profit	£300,000	£100,000	£400,000

A new investment opportunity has arisen and could be adopted by either division. It requires an investment of £200,000 and promises annual operating profits of £40,000.

Required:

(a) Which (if either) of the divisional managers would accept the new project? Why?

(b) If an RI criterion (with minimum ROI of 18%) were in use, which manager (if either) would accept the new project? Why?

(c) With minimum ROI of 18%, should the new project be accepted from the viewpoint of the Doddery Company as a whole? Justify your answer.

Question 11.2

The following schedule of investment possibilities has been drawn up by the manager of the Marsupial Division of the Marsfield Company to show the required investment and anticipated annual operating profit from each potential project:

Project	Required investment £	Anticipated operating profit £
A	500,000	90,000
B	700,000	200,000
C	1,000,000	230,000
D	1,100,000	300,000
E	1,200,000	280,000

At present the total investment in the Marsupial Division amounts to £5,000,000 and the annual operating profit for the current year is expected to be £1,250,000.

Required:

(a) If the manager of the Marsupial Division wishes to maximize his ROI:
  (i) Which projects should be selected?
  (ii) What ROI will be earned?

(b) If the manager of the Marsupial Division wishes to maximize RI for that division with a minimum ROI requirement of 15%:
  (i) Which projects should be selected?
  (ii) What RI will be earned?
  (iii) Will your answer to (i) and (ii) differ if the minimum ROI requirement was 20%?

Question 11.3

The Jolly Jelly Company employs four sales representatives, each covering a large territory. A basic salary of £800 per month is paid, plus a commission at the rate of 1% of sales revenue. All the salesmen have expense accounts to cover travelling and entertaining.

Additional data relating to October 1992 is given below:

	Sales Representatives			
	Colin	Rob	Tony	Sue
Days on the road	22	22	22	22
Miles travelled	2,200	3,000	2,800	4,000
Calls made	88	110	66	72
Sales revenue	£200,000	£160,000	£180,000	£240,000
Travelling expenses	£330	£440	£390	£510
Entertaining expenses	£200	£300	£400	£600

Required:

Assume the role of the company's sales manager. Write a report to the marketing director evaluating the performance of each sales representative for the month of October 1992.

Question 11.4

Along with four business colleagues you set up Busybee Shoes Ltd to operate a chain of retail shoe stores. You appoint Patricia McHugh, a bright young graduate, to manage the operation and it is agreed that in addition to her salary she is to be paid an annual bonus of 2% of the net cash flow into the business. Ms McHugh had a very successful first year in 1992: five stores were opened and two further outlets are planned. The following is a summary of the events for the first year:

(i) Purchased five leasehold properties for five stores for a total of £120,000. Each lease has a 25 year life.
(ii) Alterations to existing properties to make them suitable as shoe stores – total cost £68,000. The alterations are expected to last for ten years.
(iii) Ms McHugh employed one manager and four sales assistants for each store. Managers are paid £7,500 p.a. and assistants are paid £4,000 p.a.
(iv) The cost of goods sold was £73,000. Trade creditors at the end of the year were £5,000.
(v) Sales during the first year amounted to £218,000. Debtors at the end of the year were £8,000.
(vi) Other operating expenses paid in cash amounted to £28,000.
(vii) On 30 November 1992 Busybee signed leasehold agreements for two new premises.

Required:

(a) Prepare a cash flow statement for the first year of operations and calculate Ms McHugh's bonus.
(b) Discuss the measure for evaluating performance on which Ms McHugh's bonus is based.

Question 11.5

Podmore Products is proposing to launch a new product to which the following data applies:

Estimated annual sales volume	100,000 units at £25.00
Estimated annual fixed costs:	
Marketing	£300,000
Administration	£50,000
Production	£250,000
Estimated variable costs:	
Selling, etc.	£2.00 per unit
Manufacturing	£8.00 per unit
Estimated average investment in the product	£3,600,000
Target return	25% ROI

Assume that the product has been launched and, eight months following the launch, it seems likely that annual sales will be 80,000 units for the next few years. However, a major mail-order firm has offered to buy 20,000 units per annum over the next three years at £15.00 per unit.

Required:
As the sales manager of Podmore Products, would you accept this order? Justify your decision.

Question 11.6

GB Oil operates through a number of divisions, and the following report relates to the activities of its Retail Division for the first quarter of 19X7:

The GB Oil Company: Retail Division
Profit statement for January-March, 19X7

Sales (5,000,000 litres)		£1,800,000
Costs:		
Cost of product sold*	1,080,000	
Local delivery	60,000	
Storage & handling	24,000	
Selling costs	12,000	
Accounting & finance costs	10,800	
Administration	15,000	
Advertising & sales promotion	36,000	
Management fee	90,000	
Total		£1,327,800
Profit for quarter		£ 472,200

*At transfer price from Refining Division.

Required:

(a) Discuss the nature of each cost category. Which costs are direct and which are allocated? What allocation bases are likely to have been used for the latter?
(b) If you were evaluating the performance of the manager of the Retail Division, would you use the figure of £472,200?
(c) If the cost of product to the Retail Division was £1,620,000 instead of £1,080,000, should the sale of the product to retail outlets be terminated?
(d) If you were considering the building of an additional petrol station, what factors would you take into account in making your decision? Which costs would be relevant?

Question 11.7

The Yellow Division of the Rainbow Corporation is operating at full capacity and has been asked by the Green Division to supply it with component 321. This component is sold by the Yellow Division to its regular customers at £15.00 each, and the Green Division has offered to pay £10.00 per unit. Green is proposing to use component 321 in an assembly it is manufacturing for a major customer on the basis of cost plus a fixed fee. At the present time the Green Division is operating at 50% of its available capacity.

Yellow's variable cost per unit for component 321 is £8.50, and Green's costs for the assembly in question are:

Purchased components (from external sources)	£45.00
Component 321	10.00
Other variable costs	28.00
Fixed overheads	16.00
	£99.00

Green's manager believes that he will lose the customer for the assembly if he has to pay more than £10.00 per unit for component 321.

Bearing in mind that the top management of Rainbow Corporation assess divisional performance via ROI:

(a) If you were the manager of Yellow Division would you be willing to supply component 321 to Green Division at £10.00 per unit?
(b) Would your answer to (a) be to the short-run economic advantage of the Rainbow Corporation?
(c) What behavioural issues are involved in this situation, and how might the chief executive of Rainbow Corporation act to avoid disharmony?

W11.6 Case study

The following case, Ackroyd plc by B.D. Styles, was first published in the *Business Case File in Accountancy* (edited by C. Hutchinson and published by Van Nostrand Reinhold (UK) in 1986). It is reprinted here with the author's permission.

Aykroyd plc: Divisionalized performance measurement

B D Styles *Bristol Polytechnic*

Brian Styles was Head of Accountancy and Dean of the Faculty of Business and Management at Sheffield City Polytechnic before moving to Bristol Polytechnic as Assistant Director (Resources). He has been extensively involved in consultancy as well as case study teaching at graduate and postgraduate levels.

Case summary The case concentrates on the relationship between transfer pricing systems and their impact on assessing divisional performance.

INTRODUCTION

The Aykroyd Group of Companies was established nearly one hundred years ago and has developed into a diverse, multi-divisional organization with sales in excess of £1,000m per annum. One of its divisions runs five quarries in Derbyshire, England. The quarries are spread over the county and provide dry stone (crushed limestone graded by size), road stone (a limestone-based road building material composed of bitumen and graded dry stone) and asphalt (a sand-based road and path topping made by mixing sand, bitumen and fine graded stone). In addition, the Division runs a transport fleet of forty lorries for deliveries and offers a laying service through its eight road laying gangs.

Currently, the Division's sales are £110m and their capital employed, based on net book values, is £50m. The capital employed is mainly made up of lorries, earth-moving equipment, buildings, quarry land and stocks of stone. Given that the Division's pre-tax profits have fluctuated around the £2m mark for the last three years, the management of the company are very unhappy about both the return on capital and the profit to sales ratio of the Quarry Division. This unhappiness was reflected recently in the replacement of the Managing Director by an experienced manager, Barry Smith, who has a reputation for 'turning round' poorly performing Divisions.

THE INDUSTRY

The Quarry Division is located in the Roadstone Industry with the majority of its sales being made in the areas of road building, resurfacing and related ancillary projects, e.g. farm roads, car parks, etc. Competition in the industry falls into two main categories: the specialists and the vertically integrated groups like Aykroyd. The specialists only offer part of the service, i.e. dry/coated stone or a laying service, but not both. Another important feature of the market is the existence of geographical supplying areas. This arises because of the high cost of transport, which means that the material can only be sold profitably over a relatively small area, and the short 'shelf-life' of the coated products. These products must be laid within four to six hours of production. Aykroyd's sales profile is made up, by value, of 35% to its own laying gangs and the remainder to specialist laying organizations. They do not supply any material to the two major vertically integrated groups operating in their geographical area.

In general, the vertically integrated groups are of two types; firstly, large national organizations of which there are currently four and secondly, smaller regionally-based companies, like Aykroyd's, which have no national presence but a significant market share in one geographical area. In comparison with the four national organizations the specialist laying organizations are small but they do often have a significant market share in one geographical area. The specialists tend to have one favoured supplier within their geographical area. In Aykroyd's geographical area, two national companies operate, one large specialist laying company and a number of small specialist laying and quarrying companies. This competitive structure is not a typical of most parts of commercial/industrial England.

Currently, competition within the industry is strong because of overcapacity caused by the substantial fall in new road building. As a result of the overcapacity, margins have been kept very tight for at least the last three years. However, recognition of the low margins has recently led to a development of a policy of 'orderly pricing' among suppliers which had improved margins, slightly.

SECTIONS WITHIN THE QUARRY DIVISION

(1) **Dry stone quarrying.** The dry stone is produced by crushing large pieces of rock which have previously been blasted from the quarry's rock face. After being transferred from the quarry to the crusher, the output from the crusher is then graded according to size using a series of screens which filter out stones above a certain size and allow all smaller stones to 'pass through' to be further graded. The plant requirements for this are diggers and lorries to move the rock to the crusher, the crusher, conveyor belts, screens and hoppers. A major technical difficulty occurs as the crusher cannot be set to produce particular proportions of various sizes, therefore it delivers relatively fixed proportions of each size. This means that if a quarry was to receive an order for a substantial quantity of one size, it would have to produce large quantities of other sizes as an unavoidable by-product.

(2) **Coating plant.** The coating plants are attached to the quarries and produce two major types of coated material; road stone (graded stone and bitumen) and asphalt (sand, bitumen and a small amount of fine stone). In essence the process is very simple: it involves the mixing of hot bitumen with stones and/or sand. However, to produce material of an acceptable quality and at the lowest production cost, careful control of ingredient proportions and temperature is required. The coated materials are all made to the relevant British Standards and the objective of the plant manager is to ensure the least cost mix which is within the band set by the Standard. Once produced the coated material must, in normal circumstances, be laid within four to six hours. This means that material cannot be produced in advance and stored. The major costs of the coating process are the bitumen and the energy required to heat the materials. In comparison the labour and plant costs are insignificant.

(3) **Laying operation.** The laying operation buys all its materials from Aykroyd's quarries and coating plants. The key factors for successful operation were defined by the manager in charge as:

(a) Accurate estimation of the labour and material content of a prospective job to allow for a reasonable tender to be submitted.
(b) Ensuring that deliveries of materials arrive exactly when they are required to avoid having men standing idle.
(c) Supervision of the quality of the material as it arrives on the site and the thickness and compactness of the lay. If the quality in any of these respects falls below that specified in the contract, the client can either insist that it is relaid or receive a substantial discount on the price.

(d) Scheduling of work and the supervision of labour to ensure that overtime and weekend working is kept to a minimum.

(4) **Transport.** The transport section is responsible for organizing the delivery of all materials not carried by the customers' vehicles. The core demand is met from its own fleet of lorries and additional demands are met by hiring outside transport. The other sections are charged for transport in two ways. If internal vehicles are used the charge is the average cost per mile (this is calculated every six months, in arrears, by taking the total cost of internal transport and dividing by the miles covered during that period) plus 5% profit for the Transport section. When external vehicles are hired, the cross-charge is the invoiced cost of the hire plus a handling charge of 5%.

CURRENT MANAGEMENT CONTROL SYSTEM

The current control system identifies a monthly profit against each of the four sections (Dry Stone, Coated Stone, Laying and Transport). In the past these sectional profit figures have been treated as part of the information system and no great stress was attached to them. Barry Smith feels that the performances of the sections should be highlighted and the individual delegation of responsibility for return on capital employed is the key to improved profitability. This pressure on sectional profitability has focused a great deal of attention upon the prices at which materials and services are transferred between sections.

TRANSFER PRICING SYSTEM

The dry stone used by the coating plants and the laying operation is presently charged at £1.80 per tonne. This figure was calculated on the basis of the long-run average production cost per tonne produced (i.e. fixed and variable production costs).

In the case of the laying operation, the road stone is transferred at a fixed price of £1.80 a tonne and the asphalt at £26 a tonne. In addition the haulage costs of delivery to the site are charged as outlined earlier. Currently these prices are slightly (50p and 90p respectively) below the rates charged to large independent layers, but the relationship between these two markets does fluctuate. In general, if market prices are firm then the transfer price is below that charged to the large independent layers, and if they are soft then it is above.

VIEWS OF THE CURRENT TRANSFER PRICES

Norman Jones, the manager in charge of dry stone quarrying, feels very strongly that his credit of £1.80 a tonne is far too low and gives the division little chance of making a profit. Firstly he explains that the per tonne figure is well below the average ex-works price to other customers (currently £2.60 a tonne) and that secondly, he is expected to ensure that sufficient stocks of graded stone are held so that the coating plants never run out. Their unpredictable demand, in terms of both quantity and grade, means that high stone stocks must be held. He adds that the new management's use of return on capital employed had highlighted the cost of carrying these high stocks. He suggested that a reasonable transfer price should be £2.60 a tonne plus a yearly stocking charge based on agreed levels.

Sidney Pointer, the manager responsible for the Coating Plants, felt that the only major problem was the fact that he had to supply the laying operation with materials at a fixed price. He felt that this represented a fair price when general demand was low, but when demand was high he could sell all he could make at higher prices. He therefore suggested that the current transfer prices should remain with the addition of a 'high season premium' which would come into effect during peak times.

Patrick O'Connor, who is in charge of the Laying Operation, saw the current system as militating against his ability to make a profit. He highlighted a number of factors which he felt made his performance inevitably poor.

(1) He had to tender for contracts on the basis of fixed material prices from the Coating Plant. Competitors, he stated, were in a position either to 'shop round' for supplies, or

if vertically integrated, obtain preferential prices from their respective Coating Plants. Having to pay more for the basic materials, which often accounted for over 80% of the total contract price, put him in a very uncompetitive position making profitable volume difficult to achieve.

(2) In busy times his jobs were always the last to be serviced if lorries or coated material were in short supply. This meant that he often had men standing idle in the mornings but had to pay them overtime in the evenings in order to keep jobs on schedule.

(3) The quality of the material, always near the British Standards minimum, was difficult to lay and often had to be put on thicker than planned to ensure that the contract specification was met and penalties not incurred.

He summed up by saying that in terms of making a profit he felt his hands were tied and, until he was allowed to buy materials from wherever he wished, profitability would always be low or negative.

Sidney Pointer, confronted with these comments, remarked that there was some truth in them but that their impact over a year was small and that the major reason for the laying operation problems was inefficiency. He added that if they were supplied at low prices in order to increase volume, it would lead to competitive action by other companies and result in the collapse of the current orderly marketing scheme.

QUESTIONS

(1) Barry Smith is interested in improving the system of sectional performance reporting and feels that it may be necessary to make some changes to the current transfer pricing system to ensure that they give a true picture of each section's ROCE. Comment on the current system and evaluate possible changes.

(2) While Barry Smith was considering the whole question of the transfer prices, news reached him that Aykroyd's had failed to secure a major motorway contract. He knew this contract was an essential part of next year's budgeted sales. He pondered what to do as he read O'Connor's comment on the bottom of the letter which simply read, 'We could not absorb the additional £1 a tonne for materials compared with competitors'.

Should this additional information influence his consideration of the transfer prices and the management control system?

CHAPTER 12 The development of managerial accounting

WORKBOOK

W12.1 Introduction

This chapter differs from the previous Workbook chapters in that there are no discussion questions or exercises. The contents consist entirely of illustrative material reflecting the development of managerial accounting.

W12.2 Growth of accountability knowledge 1775–1975

The illustration given in Fig. W12.1 is reproduced from *The GAO Review*, Fall 1972, p. 31. Its author is Leo Herbert, Director of the Office of Personnel Management, US General Accounting Office, Washington DC.

W12.3 Expert systems and management accounting research

The following extract is reprinted with permission from *Management Accounting: News and Views* **4** (1), Spring 1986, pp. 11–13. The author is Thomas W. Lin of the University of Southern California.

A current topic of interest in accounting is the subject of expert systems. Expert systems are one area of research related to the subject of artificial intelligence. Artificial intelligence and expert systems have been identified by the AICPA (1985) Future Issues Committee as one of the major issues significant to the accounting profession with rapidly emerging implications for the future. Recently, several articles have shown the use of expert systems in accounting and auditing, e.g. Dugan and Chandler (1985), Elliott and Kielich (1985), Hansen and Messier (1982), and Messier and Hansen (1984). The USC Symposium on Expert Systems and Audit Judgment, held in February 1986, had more than 200 accounting researchers and practitioners attend. These events are indicative of the growing degree of interest in expert systems research in accounting.

This article first presents an overview of expert systems in terms of definitions and components of expert systems. It then describes the implications for management accounting research by providing potential management accoun-

Figure W12.1

Growth of accountability knowledge 1775–1975.

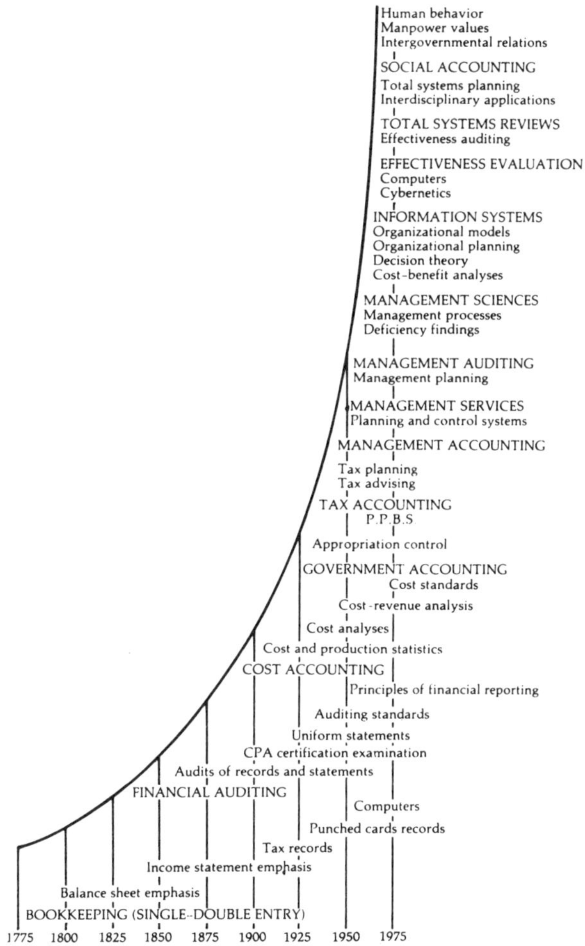

Source: Herbert (1972), p. 31.

ting application areas, research issues/opportunities, and difficulties encountered in expert systems research.

Expert systems: what are they?

Artificial intelligence and expert systems

Artificial Intelligence (AI) is a subfield of computer science which is concerned with developing intelligent computer systems to simulate human reasoning. AI has focused on research areas of robotics, natural language understanding, voice recognition, image processing, and expert systems.

Expert systems (ES) are problem solving computer programs that use expert knowledge and inference procedures to perform functions similar to those normally performed by a human expert in some specialized problem areas.

The major benefits of ES are saving money, sharing knowledge, better quality decisions, and providing training tools. The major limitations of ES are difficulties in extracting expertise from humans, and long development times to build ES and in developing ES that are creative, adaptive, and have common sense.

Components of expert systems

There are five major components of an ES: (1) the knowledge base, (2) the inference engine, (3) the knowledge acquisition module, (4) the explanation module, and (5) the language interface.

A knowledge base contains facts, decision making rules, and hypotheses. Barr and Feigenbaum (1982) described several techniques of knowledge representation. The most common techniques are production rules, frames, and semantic nets. Under production rules, knowledge is represented by a set of rules; it is a formal way of specifying a recommendation or strategy expressed in the IF CONDITION (premise), THEN ACTION (conclusion) statements. In the frames method, knowledge is represented by a cluster of statements that associate features with nodes representing concepts or objects. Semantic nets consist of a network of nodes standing for concepts, events or objects connected by areas describing the relation between nodes.

The brain of the ES is the inference engine with reasoning capabilities. It controls the search through the knowledge base. Goodall (1985) described various ways of reasoning about rules. The most common reasoning procedures are forward chaining and backward chaining. Forward chaining involves reasoning from data to hypotheses; that is, rules are matched against facts to establish new facts. Backward chaining starts with a goal or hypothesis, and then attempts to find data or evidence that support the goal or hypothesis. There are three common ways of representing uncertain information in an ES: Bayesian inference, certainty factor, and fuzzy logic approaches. (See Goodall [1985] for details.)

The knowledge acquisition module requires a knowledge engineer to accumulate, transfer, and transform expertise from some knowledge source, e.g., an expert, to a computer program for constructing or modifying the knowledge. The common knowledge acquisition techniques are interviewing, protocol analysis, and simulation methods.

The explanation module can explain why the system reached a particular decision or why it is requesting a particular piece of information.

The language interface provides English-like query language or graphics for the user to interact with the ES.

Implications for management accounting research

Potential management accounting applications

Expert systems have been used for diagnosis, design, planning, control, prediction, monitoring and training purposes. Management accountants can use ES to solve the complex problems of capital budgeting, transfer pricing, variance analysis and investigation, performance evaluation, incentives and compensation systems, corporate planning and budgeting, product pricing, and information systems selection. An ES can also be used to train management accountants.

Research issue/opportunities

Expert systems provide new research opportunities for management accounting professors. The following is a list of potential research issues/opportunities:

1. Research on psychological characteristics of expert decision makers. For example, see Shanteau (1986).
2. Research on how experts formulate and solve complicated, semi-structured management accounting problems.
3. Evaluate different knowledge representation techniques such as rules vs. frames in representing various management accounting problems.
4. Evaluate different reasoning procedures such as forward chaining vs. backward chaining for various management accounting tasks.
5. Evaluate different ways of representing uncertain information such as Bayesian inference vs. the certainty factor approach for various management accounting problems.
6. Evaluate the effectiveness of different knowledge acquisition techniques such as protocol analysis vs. simulation methods on various management accounting problems.
7. Evaluate the effectiveness of a management accounting ES vs. other decision aids or models.
8. Develop a normative framework on how knowledge should be elicited and represented in the knowledge base.
9. Research on memory organization and structure as well as the strategy for memory retrieval.
10. Research on how to effectively validate an ES and compare the effectiveness of different validation techniques. See O'Leary (1986) and Hayes-Roth et al. (1983) on various validation techniques.

Potential difficulties in ES research

Prospects for expert systems research in management accounting can be summarized as typical good news/bad news. The good news is that there is a demand for research in ES as shown in the above management accounting application areas. The bad news is that this type of research is time-consuming, costly, and difficult. The development of most expert systems usually takes four to 15 man-years.

Several companies have developed expert systems programs called 'shells.' A shell has a specific set of inference engine approaches, an explanation module, and an empty knowledge base. Shells shorten the ES development time and cost. But these packages have drawbacks of providing only one reasoning mechanism and one knowledge representation technique as well as poor documentation and maintenance. The researcher has to justify the selection of a particular shell before conducting ES research or an application. Another shortcoming of most shells is that they lack traditional computer capabilities, such as database management and sophisticated computations that many management accounting applications require.

Most of the existing ES research focuses on 'system development' instead of scientific research.' Management accounting researchers should undertake a systematic research approach to making contributions to accounting knowledge, and let management accountants take an engineering approach to developing management accounting expert systems.

References

AICPA, 'The Future Issues Committee – First Annual Report to the Board of Directors,' June 1985.

Barr, A. and E. Feigenbaum, *The Handbook of Artificial Intelligence* (Vol. 2, Kaufmann Publications, 1982).

Dugan, Chris W. and John S. Chandler, 'Auditor: A Microcomputer-Based Expert System to Support Auditors in the Field,' *Expert Systems* (October 1985), pp. 210–221.

Elliott, Robert K. and John A. Kielich, 'Expert Systems for Accountants,' *Journal of Accountancy* (September 1985) pp. 125–134.

Goodall, Alex, *The Guide to Expert Systems, Learned Information* (Medford, New Jersey, 1985).

Hansen, James V. and William F. Messier, Jr., 'Expert Systems for Decision Support in EDP Auditing,' *International Journal of Computer and Information Sciences* (1982). pp. 357–379.

Hayes-Roth, F., D.A. Waterman, and D.B. Lenat (eds.), *Building Expert Systems* (Reading, Mass.: Addison-Wesley, 1983).

Messier, William F., Jr. and James V. Hansen, 'Expert Systems in Accounting and Auditing: A Framework and Review,' In E. Joyce and S. Moriarity (eds.), *Decision Making and Accounting: Current Research*, (University of Oklahoma, 1984).

O'Leary, Daniel E., Validation of Business Expert Systems,' Paper presented at the University of Southern California Symposium on Expert Systems and Audit Judgment, February 17–18, 1986.

Shanteau, James, 'Psychological Characteristics of Expert Decision Makers,' Paper presented at the University of Southern California Symposium on Expert Systems and Audit Judgment, February 17–18, 1986.

W12.4 A research proposal

The following paper is a research proposal for an investigation into the causes and reasons for differences in the theory and practice of management accounting. Its authors are J.B. Coates and R.J. Stacey of the University of Aston, and C.P. Rickwood of the University of Birmingham.

Proposal

1. To investigate differences between the management accounting techniques and approaches as recommended in academic research publications and textbooks and those found in practice in industrial organizations. These differences have been observed extensively in the course of consultancy

assignments and other visits to firms and, more formally, through a pilot survey of firms[1] as a precedent to the current research.

2. To present case studies as evidence of current managerial accounting practices, highlighting (i) applications of, and (ii) any divergences from, practice as advocated by standard texts. It is also intended that wherever possible, these studies would put the practical applications into a context which explains why information was originated and how it was used.

Given that a substantial gap exists between theory and textbooks on the one hand, and practice on the other, the consequences are numerous: for example, academic teaching and research in so far as they are vocationally directed could be seriously misdirected while it could also be that poor transfer of knowledge has left industry employing greatly inferior accounting methods. An example is marginal costing and marginal cost analysis: for many years widely recommended in academic writing, but *much less* in evidence as accepted industrial practice. There are many instances where what one has been led to expect to find as established, accepted operating practice is simply missing or is actually being carried out on an alternative basis.

As a result of the pilot survey a number of areas where further detailed investigation was considered valuable were identified; the two regarded as central to the entire research programme, are outlined below. The areas are:

(a) Cost behaviour analysis;
(b) Transfer pricing.

(a) Cost behaviour analysis

Texts on this subject tend to imply a simple breakdown of cost into two elements: fixed costs and variable costs. They further suggest that methods are available which make identification and separation a relatively straightforward matter. On this basis, many situations are analysed purporting to assist management decision-making; in important aspects of running the business, such as determining product profitability, in particular, it is suggested that short-term variable costs are to be uniquely identified.

In contrast, many of the companies where interviews were carried out had little or no knowledge of the behaviour of their costs and revenues with changes in the volume and mix of production. Various comments were made on this issue such as, 'It is too expensive and time consuming to analyse cost behaviour and keep an analysis up to date', or 'It is not necessary to do this kind of analysis.'

It is clear that in many, perhaps most, practical situations, such a separation is far from simple, even if relevant, many costs being semi-variable by nature or even inversely variable. It is difficult, however, to visualize how basic management decisions and techniques can be meaningfully applied without a fair understanding of cost behaviour in the business. Among major areas greatly influenced are:

(i) How can budgetary control be satisfactorily employed without flexed budgets based upon appropriate understanding of cost behaviour?
(ii) How adequate is the understanding of product profitabilities within the business?
(iii) How 'valid' are pricing and transfer pricing decisions?

(iv) How many product lines, departments, factories, etc., have been shut down without consideration of or through failing to understand cost behaviour?
(v) What would a cost behaviour study within a business entail and how could it be accomplished?
(vi) How significant are the alternative treatments of costs (i.e. as fixed or variable) on the decisions of companies? For example, BRS treat depreciation and labour as fixed costs while a competitor, United Carriers, treat both as variable.

And perhaps most importantly:

(vii) Are the important decisions of businesses with and without a knowledge of cost behaviour significantly different?

(b) Transfer pricing

The accounting and economics literature contains a considerable number of articles concerned with transfer pricing problems. The earliest (e.g. Hirshleifer[2], Dean[3] and Cook[4]) all produce suggested solutions which relate the transfer pricing problem to the determination of an equilibrium market price by the use of neoclassical economics. Many later articles (e.g. Gould[5]) develop these models to recognize some of the imperfections that are recognized in the neoclassical models. Another major group of articles represent suggestions for the implementation of the rules provided by the earlier articles (e.g. Ronen and McKinney,[6] Piper[7]). Yet another significant type of article in this area utilizes the powerful tools associated with mathematical programming (Baumol and Fabian,[8] Onsi,[9] Hass,[10] Whinston,[11] Dopuch and Drake[12]). Despite the mathematical elegance of these solutions, they do not seem to have found the general acceptance which might be implied by the source articles.

In the pilot survey the lack of adherence to any of these models and the variability between practices among firms was more apparent than the adoption of any method. Some organizations adopted a mixture of methods for setting transfer prices and a significant number used negotiation between divisions to set the transfer prices despite the strong criticism for this approach that is found in all the articles adopting a neoclassical basis. Indeed, many of the organizations surveyed apparently did not appreciate the potential impact of their transfer price system on their decisions. On the other hand, despite the ease with which the articles considered are able to criticize the methods found in business, it is hard to accept their validity if we accept that human action and the decisions of businessmen are purposeful. It may be easier to be critical of the underlying assumptions of the neoclassical approach: i.e. examples of the possible purposes of transfer pricing systems include the following processes: the coordination of decentralized organizations; the adaptation of divisional operations to changes in the environment identified at the local divisional level only; the communication of information relating to economic conditions identified at the divisional level. These purposes may not be fulfilled by setting transfer prices which may be optimal under conditions of static equilibrium, perfect coordination of firms and perfect knowledge. In particular, concentration on an optimal *position* gives little regard to processes at all. Study of extant processes may be a particularly fruitful approach in this area.

Transfer pricing is found in organizations which have decentralized. Watson and Baumler[13] consider that there are two main problems associated with decentralization, namely, (i) integration of the parts and (ii) differentiation of the activities of the parts to enable semi-autonomous operation. Transfer pricing can be seen as both an integrating and differentiating mechanism. Under these conditions the central direction which is needed to implement the neoclassical approaches may be entirely inappropriate.

Major points of interest for the research are:

(i) What purposes is transfer pricing considered by users to fulfil?
(ii) What use do transfer prices have in evaluation – as part of a local profit performance measure or by comparison of transfer price and external prices?
(iii) What decisions are likely to include transfer prices and at what level in the organization?
(iv) What policy is currently laid down for setting transfer prices, and how consistently is that adhered to in particular cases throughout the firm?
(v) How regularly is the policy reviewed/revised; how regularly are transfer prices revised?
(vi) What are the sources of information used in setting transfer prices; where and by whom are they determined?

Research procedure

In-depth field studies are the principal means of furthering the research. This means that we adopt the same procedure as in the pilot survey, i.e. personal interviewing, based on a questionnaire, but not rigidly tied to it.

Interviews are carried out in teams of two and conducted where possible at different levels within an organization.

To establish any valid observations of business practice requires a great deal of personal involvement with the particular organization. We consider achievement of such involvement to be likely to produce markedly better results than the use of the mailed questionnaire: it greatly enhances the reliability and scope of information which can be obtained. It is admittedly a time consuming approach and would permit only a relatively small sample of companies to be covered; these in turn would be selected by direct choice rather than statistically. Further, no attempt is being made to test any preconceived hypothesis unless it be confirmation or rejection of the supposed differences between theory and practice. We are looking for an elucidation of practice in order to compare, contrast and explain it against the precepts of theory. There is no presupposition that either theory or practice is wrong in any sense either totally or in part. With a limited sample, we are not aiming to provide total substantiation of findings, but to point to consequences in allowing situations to remain unclarified and to generate new thinking.

Research conducted in this manner could be dismissed as statistically unsupported empiricism. We repeat, the intention is not to substitute new, statistically clean, generalizations for already existing ones, but to concentrate on discovering reasons for observed variations between theory and practice.

Validity of research method

Our approach represents a departure from classical research procedures. However, it is one which is becoming more widely seen as acceptable and indeed necessary in the field of accounting research. Groves and Tomkins[14] state for example: '. . . Academics in accounting, or at least a significant proportion of them . . . need to place less emphasis on "detached" mathematical analyses, surveys and laboratory tests and move into detailed *field work* [their emphasis] where they can focus upon studying how *practitioners* [their emphasis] perceive the world of accounting . . .' This is precisely our intention. Otley[15] gives further support to this approach.

With respect to the need for this kind of work to be done Groves and Tomkins[24] also say: 'In fact a recent examination of all leading accounting journals over the period 1976–79 revealed that only 7 out of more than 650 articles could be described as case/field studies . . . .' This finding naturally accords with the results of our own literature survey.

An example of accepted accounting publications which adopt an approach similar to our own is Briston and Tomkins,[16] and Briston,[17] though it has been more widely employed in the field of industrial sociology, e.g. Woodward,[18] Watson,[19] Jaques and Brown,[20] and Argyris.[21]

More recently Kaplan[22] and Mohr[23] provide further support for the case study approach.

References

1. ICMA Management Accounting Research and Practice (August 1983). Part II, Paper 7.
2. Hirshleifer, J. (1956). On the economics of transfer pricing. *Journal of Business*, July.
3. Dean, J. (1955). Decentralisation and intra company prices. *Harvard Business Review*, July/August.
4. Cook, P.M. (1955). Decentralisation and the transfer price problem. *Journal of Business*, April.
5. Gould, J.R. (1964). Internal pricing in firms when there are costs of using an outside market. *Journal of Business*, January.
6. Ronen, J. and McKinney, G. (1970). Transfer pricing for divisional autonomy *Journal of Accounting Research*, Spring.
7. Piper, A.G. (1977). Guidance on how to avoid the pitfalls of transfer pricing. *Accountants Weekly*, April.
8. Baumol, W. and Fabian, T. (1964). Decomposition, pricing for decentralisation and external economies. *Management Science*, September.
9. Onsi, M. (1970). A transfer pricing system based on opportunity cost. *Accounting Review*, July.
10. Hass, J.E. (1968). Transfer pricing in a decentralised firm. *Management Science*, February.
11. Whinston, A. (1964). Price guides in decentralised organisations. In Cooper, W., Leavitt, H. and Shelly, M. (eds) *New Perspectives in Organization Research*. Wiley.
12. Dopuch, N. and Drake, D. (1964). Accounting implications of a mathe-

matical programming approach to the transfer pricing problem. *Journal of Accounting Research*, Spring.
13. Watson, D. and Baumler, J. (1975). Transfer pricing – a behavioral context. *Accounting Review*, July.
14. Groves, R. and Tomkins, C.R. (1981). The everyday accountant and researching his reality. Paper presented to the Management Accounting Research Conference: University of Aston, September.
15. Otley, D.T. (1980). Behavioural and organisational research in management accounting. Paper presented to Management Accounting Research Conference: University of Manchester, December.
16. Briston, R.J. and Tomkins, C.R. (1970). The impact of the introduction of corporation tax upon the dividend policies of the UK companies. *Economic Journal*, September.
17. Briston, R.J. (1970). The Fison stockholder survey: an experiment in company–shareholder relations. *Journal of Business Policy*, Autumn.
18. Woodward, J. (1965). *Industrial Organisation: Theory and Practice*. Oxford University Press.
19. Watson, T.J. (1977). *The Personnel Managers*. Routledge & Kegan Paul.
20. Jaques, E. and Brown, W. (1965) *The Glacier Project Papers*. Heinemann, London.
21. Argyris, C. (1952) *The Impact of Budgets on People*. Cornell.
22. Kaplan, R.J. (1984). The case for case studies in management accounting research. Paper prepared for Symposium on the Role of Accounting in Organisations and Society: The University of Wisconsin-Madison. July.
23. Mohr, L.B. (1982). The reliability of the case study as a source of information. Unpublished paper. September.
24. Groves, R. and Tomkins, C.R. (1981). A review of research writings and methods in accounting, Working paper. University of Wales Institute of Science and Technology.

W12.5 Management accounting: discernible future directions

The following extract is taken from H.M. Schoenfeld's paper 'Management accounting: discernable future directions', and is reproduced with permission from Holzer, H.P. (ed.) *Management Accounting 1980*, Proceedings of the University of Illinois Management Accounting Symposium, Department of Accountancy, University of Illinois at Urbana-Champaign, pp. 243–8. In this extract Schoenfeld endeavours to identify lines for development by means of the diagram given in Fig. W12.2.

> If the space of required information to be filled by managerial accounting data and models is visualized as three dimensional (for simplicity's sake, although it appears to be n-dimensional), then some cells representing techniques of analysis have already been filled in the past, while others are still open. The whole space, however, should be regarded as unbounded for the time being, since its boundaries cannot be perceived with today's knowledge.
>
> 1. Past developments have occurred largely along the A-axis, adding quan-

Figure W12.2

Conceptual model for development of management accounting.

Exhibit 1: Conceptual Model for Development of Management Accounting

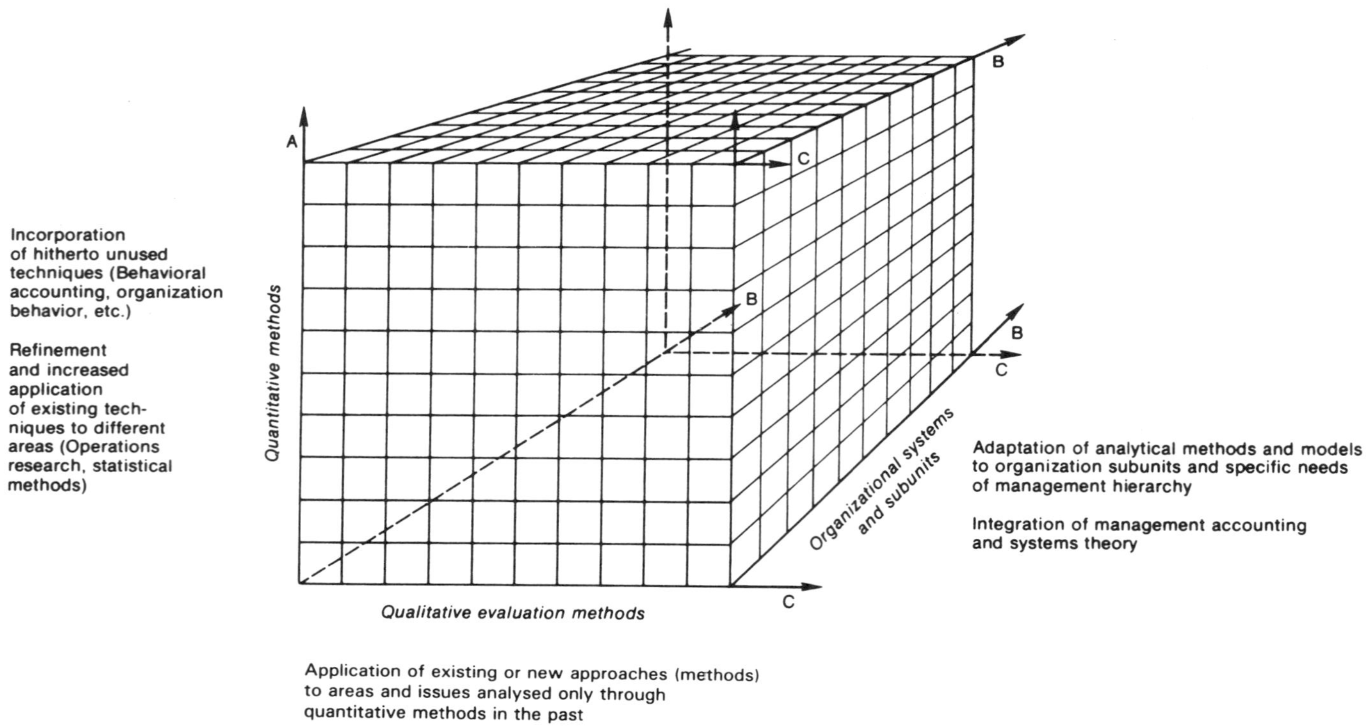

Source: Schoenfeld (1980).

titative techniques to managerial accounting. As Shillinglaw[1] has already noted, these applications were limited by and large to manufacturing industries. Additional developments utilizing similar quantitative techniques are needed for all other sectors of the economy (service industries, public sector) and will emerge as a response to society's increasing accountability demands and real or artificial scarcity of certain resources. This represents a linear development of managerial accounting; in addition, certain ideas from behavioral and organizational theory will assist in introducing a higher degree of sophistication into traditional analysis by adding new insights to address issues such as changes in productivity, individual, and group responses to budgets and evaluation measures. However, none of these inputs is likely to change the basic analytical process which is dominated by cost-benefit (however defined) comparisons.

This entire development will be accelerated through the availability of less expensive computer technology, because many techniques hitherto regarded as too costly will become economically feasible. Since these techniques will be applied increasingly to questions raised by the need to deal with social accounting issues, quantitative analyses will be extended to new areas. As a result of this, an extension of managerial accounting into measurements using other than monetary data seems to be unavoidable. This will introduce the additional problem of noncomparable measurements for decision-making purposes.

2. The second dimension (B-axis) of development within reach of our present capabilities is the adaptation of existing analytical methods to specific needs of the underlying operating system. The improved in-depth understanding of such systems, as for example, the need to use loose couplings for survival,[2] the ability to define specific information requirements for subunits, understandability requirements for data, avoidance of overloads, information loss through aggregation, required speed of feedback or feedforward, and so forth, will facilitate the adjustment of existing more general applications to specific organizations, their subunits, and activities. At the same time, enhanced knowledge about the behavioral impact of data will permit the assessment of the efficiency of such subsystems. As a result, more widespread application of certain operations research models can be expected since the known limitations inherent in such models will allow appropriate model selection for specific limited purposes. The previously mentioned availability of computational facilities will encourage widespread routine use. The utilization of quantitative models at various organizational levels will definitely have an impact on the size and content of data banks.

As an inevitable result of this development, the field of managerial accounting may appear to become even more fractionalized, because decision-adequate model adaptation for organization subunits will result in a proliferation of models with limited applicability. Since not all organizational subunits will require the utilization of all these models, the theoretically possible array resulting from the combination of techniques (methods) and decision needs of organizational subunits in our conceptual model is likely to contain a large number of empty cells. Nevertheless, this approach should at least permit an applicability classification of quantitative management accounting techniques and will permit research concerning the modification of existing models for identifiable information needs of other organizational subunits.

3. The third dimension (C-axis) of our model represents the development of different approaches to managerial accounting which are relatively new to this field, although not entirely new to accounting. Churchman[3] has already explored the 'intuitive' part of management decision making, which undeniably exists; without it, the differences in performance of otherwise similar companies having the same measurement, analysis, and decision techniques available could not be explained. This dimension has its counterpart in managerial accounting. Obviously so-called 'intuition-based decisions' are not without reasoning, even if this type of reasoning is not strictly formalized and thus not routine. Usually it results in qualitative performance improvements. Consequently, the yardsticks employed to assess and evaluate changes and their impact must also be qualitative to fit the problem. Existing quantitative models do not permit the evaluation of such qualitative dimensions; in fact, they mostly make the implicit assumption that quality is held constant. This leads to the question of whether there are ways to provide such qualitative assessments – and to provide them in a formalized (not necessarily quantifiable) manner. If the answer to this question is negative, then this dimension of the management accounting systems will always remain empty and must be left to managerial intuition.

In examining this need for qualitative assessment, it is immediately apparent that it involves quality of overall and partial performance; the latter also includes the quality of the managerial accounting system itself. Quality measurements – or evaluation even if they remain judgmental – imply the idea of targets, the existence of a scale of measuring (or at least ranking), and the existence of alternatives to attain an objective; without these characteristics, a comparison could not be operationalized. Managerial accountants can no longer bypass the quality issue, since quality of performance has provided the competitive advantage for many companies. Evidence for this can be found when, for example, the reasons for the success of major multinational companies are examined (even if such superior quality does not always exist in all activities).

The evaluation of effectiveness, that is, the qualitative adequacy of performance for a given objective, suggests the utilization of systematic comparative analysis, which can be accomplished in management accounting by using ranking techniques for outcomes. Such methods have been employed successfully in other areas. Operational auditing, for example, has used comparative qualitative dimensions to arrive at its assessments even in cases where no absolute measures exist. Zünd strongly suggests this approach as a major solution in multinational environments, which do not allow meaningful quantitative measurements in the conventional sense.[4] This approach has also been tried in inter- and intra-company comparisons to investigate causes of quantitative differences; however, it is not yet integrated into managerial accounting. Other useful inputs for this approach can be gained from value analysis which today represents an accepted tool in engineering. None of these attempts have so far been systematically investigated by managerial accountants.

This idea is reinforced by the recognition of qualitative performance variations which are generally recognized in the form of organizational and budgetary slack.[5] Such slack – aside from being apparently impossible to control – has defied measurement. Since it can be brought about by deliberately adjusting performance quality, even in the context of a well-defined quantitative framework, it has provided managers with a higher degree of freedom to take 'uncontrollable actions' than usually assumed. Even if this is desirable under certain circumstances, it nevertheless points to an out-of-control situation, as long as it cannot be measured. Whether this problem is related to inadequate performance quality or may — as has been suggested — indicate an unnecessarily high level of quality is almost beside the point. From its mere existence emerges a managerial accounting need for systematic performance quality assessment methods.

The introduction of qualitative measures is required to complete the management accounting system if it is to fulfil its function as a comprehensive internal evaluation and control system for management. As a first step, this suggests the systematic integration of operational auditing techniques in order to (1) control the qualitative dimension of management performance and (2) evaluate managerial accounting; auditing has been a long-accepted supplementary analysis in financial accounting. Other methods, such as attempts for qualitative evaluation of marketing channels or the goal-oriented performance measurement of branch banks,[6] as well as attempts by individual companies to assess required qualitative performance levels of specific activities, suggest that first steps are taken everywhere to develop such evaluation measures. Profile analysis, as developed in psychology, seems to provide a promising set of methods which might fill this gap in management accounting or at least serve as a starting point for the development of new methods.

References

1. G. Shillinglaw, 'Old Horizons and New Frontiers: The Future of Managerial Accounting,' p. 3 of this publication (i.e. Holzer (1980).)
2. H.A. Simon, 'The Organization of Complex Systems,' in A.A. Pattee, *Hierarchy Theory* (New York: George Braziller, 1973), pp. 3–27.
3. W. Churchman 'Intuition and Information,' p. 167 of this publication (i.e. Holzer (1980).)
4. A. Zünd, *Kontrolle und Revision in der Multinationalen Unternehmung* (Bern and Stuttgart: Paul Haupt Verlag, 1973).
5. R.M. Cyert and J.G. March, *A Behavioral Theory of the Firm*, (New York: Prentice Hall, 1963).
6. B. Bellinger, 'Multidimensionale Bewertung und Bestgestaltung von Bankfilialen,' *Oesterreichisches Bankarchiv*, vol. 27, no. 4 (1979): 138–54: this approach is based on a method described in detail in Charles E. Osgood, Charles E. Suci and P.H. Tannenbaum, *The Measurement of Meaning*, 5th ed. (Urbana, 1957).

W12.6 Management accounting: evolution not revolution

The Executive Summary of a CIMA-sponsored study undertaken by M. Bromwich and A. Bhimani is reprinted here with permission.

The manufacturing environment in many countries is undergoing rapid changes. Technological advances in flexible manufacturing, robotics, automated production and computerised engineering and planning are affecting markets and raising quality and services levels whilst lowering costs. Competition between manufacturers is intensifying with the ability to provide product diversity, price advantages, via lower costs, better delivery and service performance coupled with increased quality and an ability to respond swiftly to changes in demand. Similar changes are taking place in the service sector.

The report was sponsored by the Chartered Institute of Management Accountants in October 1988 to identify *'the criticisms being made, the way in which management accounting techniques already exist to meet them, and the findings of research in this field and any gaps that might initiate further research'*.

The report therefore examines the relationship between changes in the manufacturing environment and management accounting in order to aid practitioners in adapting to these changes. The service sector is not emphasised because reforms to accounting have not yet been studied to the same degree.

This report reviews the many challenges and opportunities facing management accounting. This Executive Summary outlines some of the findings in the report and offers some possible actions management accountants might consider to meet these challenges and opportunities. Fuller details can be obtained from the relevant chapter in the report.

The report indicates that for a growing but still small number of companies the technological environment is one of rapid change. However, almost all companies are feeling some of the effects of these changes and can expect to be affected at an increasing rate. The changes in the service sector are believed to be as great and to be affecting a larger number of companies.

A number of commentators and accounting bodies, mainly in the USA, have argued that these changes make much of extant management accounting redundant.

Some of the problems perceived as not yet satisfactorily dealt with in management accounting include:

1 the alleged subservience of management accounting to external financial accounting requirements;
2 the lack of strategic considerations in management accounting and project appraisal;
3 the reliance of management accounting on redundant assumptions concerning manufacturing processes. This is reflected in an over-concern with direct labour and components produced within the firm, rather than overheads and bought-in components. This is to be dealt with by the adoption of activity costing, where overheads are recovered on the basis of the activities believed to cause them rather than using some more general base such as machine hours and by different approaches to material costing;
4 the maintenance of traditional assumptions in performance evaluation and the continued short-term orientation of this process.

Both the National Association of Accountants (now the Institute of Management Accountants) in the USA and the Society of Management Accountants of Canada, especially the latter, have strongly endorsed some of these criticisms. Both seem to officially subscribe to activity costing and, indeed, SMAC seems to have gone much further and to believe that *'much of what is currently taught in management/cost accounting courses is unlikely to be of much use in managing contemporary operations or in guiding strategy*' (article in the *CMA: The Management Accounting Magazine*, June 1988, co-authored by the executive director of the Society).

This amounts to the most heavily publicised challenge ever faced by management accounting. *However, the report counsels caution in responding to this challenge* (Chapters 4 and 6) but does suggest that experiments be encouraged. The report is cautious because:

> *'The evidence and arguments advanced by advocates of wholesale changes in management accounting are not yet sufficient to justify the wholesale revision of management accounting. Evidence of the benefits of new accounting techniques and the continued benefits of some conventional techniques is only beginning to emerge. No general crisis has been identified within the management accounting profession vis-à-vis a changing manufacturing environment and therefore no radical reforms are recommended at this stage'.*

There is a need for the management accountant to become more expert in these new approaches, including activity costing, accounting for quality and for Just-in-Time and other work flow methods (see Chapter 4). However, there is yet little to support the acceptance of activity-based costing, at least in the UK, and considerable evidence that firms do not change their accounting systems easily. The strong evidence for this suggests that existing accounting systems encompass other objectives not considered by those who favour such changes. It is known that activity costing changes product costs substantially. There is as yet little to suggest that it enhances profits. Finally, some of the reasons adduced for introducing activity costing seem to be, in fact, examples of deficient management practices as much as poor accounting. For example, some of the US firms which have been surveyed produced an impossibly wide range of products and seemed to rely on cost plus pricing of a very conventional type.

The number of opportunities for the profession offered by these current concerns about management accounting are very wide and need to encompass the results of these American and more recently consultant-backed challenges but this should not divert attention from other opportunities, solutions to which will help in giving an even more solid foundation to financial management in the twenty-first century.

Included in these opportunities are:

1 the accounting and control of materials and subcomponents and the evaluation of sub-contractors. This is a very important element of the new manufacturing environment which seems to have been neglected;
2 management accounting in the new environment facing the service sector generally and especially the financial sector;
3 the development of strategic management accounting and strategic investment appraisal.

Other challenges which will continue to need attention include:

1 The accounting and control of *decision driven* overheads costs which do not vary with either the volume or the diversity of output, an area untouched by activity costing but for which other solutions are becoming available, including strategic management accounting.
2 Developing more market orientated management accounting. Some solutions,

such as customer profitability analysis, are becoming available in both these areas.

3 Integrating the vast resource of non-financial data provided by advanced manufacturing technology and its equivalents in the service sector into management accounting systems.
4 Recognising the roles which management accounting systems can play which were not anticipated by their designers and, more importantly, understanding the true reasons for their existence.
5 Positioning management accounting so that it can play a more important role in informally managed organisations and in chains of organisations, such as the sub-contractor chain, where the boundaries of individual entities are becoming blurred.

Below we briefly summarise the contents of each chapter of the report, highlighting the most important findings.

Chapter 1 briefly considers the contribution of the manufacturing industry to the growth of the national economy in recent years identifying some implications for management accounting. Criticisms of traditional accounting systems are reviewed in the light of changes in the manufacturing environment. Investment appraisal, changes in the manufacturing cost mix and performance evaluation are identified as representing areas of management accounting which have received a great deal of attention in recent years as companies adopt advanced manufacturing technologies.

Chapter 2 describes the types of technological advances and work organisation techniques which are changing the manufacturing environment and which are viewed to be of importance for management accounting processes.

Chapter 3 examines Japanese management and accounting practices based on a limited set of organisations, for which information is available. Following a consideration of characteristics of Japanese management style, cost accounting and cost control in the Japanese context are discussed. Some observations about links between management accounting and corporate goals are also made.

Chapter 4 explores the challenges raised above which US commentators see as facing management accountants in US firms. An examination is made of the ways in which the adoption of advanced manufacturing technology affects the whole area of cost management. Central to this discussion is a consideration of activity-based accounting. The chapter also reviews findings of US company surveys on changing accounting practices. Among the findings are:

1 that the use of cost drivers to apply costs which vary with product diversity and complexity of production is becoming an overwhelming cry. Cost drivers attempt to link costs with scope of output rather than scale of output thereby generating less arbitrary product costs for decision-making. Such approaches have drawbacks and are not yet supported by empirical work confirming the accrual of increased profits from these methods;
2 there is no doubt that where activity caused costs can be measured in a meaningful way, activity-based costing can be expected to yield substantial benefits but the cost of the process needs to be considered.

Chapter 5 reports on empirical studies in the UK, the bulk of which have been sponsored by CIMA, of firms' reactions to fast changing products markets and manufacturing environments. Particular emphasis is placed on implications for management accounting practitioners. Here the findings include:

1 Management accountants need to alter what some managers perceive of as their often self-assumed role as watchdogs rather than as suppliers of information and as parties to decision-making which is the role that managers and many management accountants expect management accountants to fulfil.

   The overwhelming influence of financial controls and the emphasis on short-term monetary returns by UK managers is seen as inhibiting the implementation of advanced manufacturing technology.

2 Management accountants need to adopt a more outward-looking and strategic perspective both for investment justifications and for broader decision-making, following those sectors of British manufacturing industry where some firms have already adopted such a stance.

Chapter 6 brings together the many findings, approaches, perspectives and calls for change which have been examined in the report. In this light, broader social and technical as well as management issues are discussed in considering the future of management accounting. The question of how far reforms in management accounting should be undertaken at this stage is discussed with particular reference to the role of the management accounting practitioner. Although the report is aimed at exploring the challenges and opportunities facing management accounting and does not therefore attempt to solve all the problems identified, a number of findings emerge including:

1 Responsibility accounting systems, information flows and organisational control measures may be affected by the new production methods. Management accounting can hinder or can enhance new attitudes to manufacture.

2 Non-financial accounting information has been found to become increasingly important in many different manufacturing environments even where the use of advanced manufacturing technology varies substantially in various industrialised countries. Qualitative and non-financial quantitative information will have a high and growing level of significance in enterprise management and its incorporation into management accounting systems provides important challenges for management accountants.

3 Strategic investment appraisal techniques and strategic management accounting both also seem to be becoming increasingly important as means of processing relevant management accounting information and need to become more important. Enterprise accounting systems would seem to need to be geared more to the market where demand has to be retained and competition overcome.

   The cost of achieving the value added of the firm's products relative to competitors needs to be determined and continually monitored.

4 Evidence of the benefits of new accounting techniques and the continued benefits of some conventional techniques is only beginning to emerge.

   No general crisis has been identified within the management accounting profession in the UK *vis-à-vis* the changing manufacturing environment and therefore no radical reforms are recommended at this stage. The evidence and arguments advanced by advocates of wholesale changes in management accounting are not yet sufficient to justify the wholesale revision of management accounting in the UK.

5 There is urgent need for management accountants to experiment, to seek out new ways of using their existing expertise, and to enlarge their competence by seeing management accounting as a much broader function.

6 It is recommended that techniques, such as activity costing and target pricing as used by some Japanese firms, where price is determined by the price required to win a desired market share rather than to cover '*full cost*', discussed in this report as well as others originating within the context of British manufacturing organisation, be used and further developed.

7 Concerns with the problems identified here should not reduce the emphasis placed on other challenges and opportunities in management accounting. Included in these opportunities are:
   (a) Management accounting in the new environment facing the service sector generally and particularly the financial sector.
   (b) The accounting and control of materials and subcomponents and the evaluation of sub-contractors. This is a very important element of the new manufacturing environment which seems to have been neglected.

8 The other challenges which will continue to need attention include:
Integrating non-financial data provided by advanced manufacturing technology and its equivalents in the service sector into the management accounting system and positioning management accounting so that it can play a more important role in informally managed organisations and in chains of organisations, such as the sub-contractor chain, where the boundaries of individual entities are becoming blurred.

A number of challenges to and opportunities for management accounting have been identified in this report. All are only beginning to develop. Management accountants must lead in the further growth of successful innovations if they wish to play a major role in the twenty-first century financial management.

Source: Michael Bromwich and Al Bhimani,
Management Accounting: Evolution not Revolution. CIMA, London.

Bibliography

Abdel-Khalik, A. and Lusk, E.J. (1974). Transfer pricing – a synthesis. *The Accounting Review* **49** (1), January, pp. 8–23.

Abernathy, W.J. and Wayne, K. (1974). Limits of the learning curve. *Harvard Business Review* **52** (5), Sep.-Oct., pp. 109–119.

Ackoff, R.L. (1970). *A Concept of Corporate Planning*. Wiley, New York.

Ackoff, R.L. (1978). *The Art of Problem-Solving*. Wiley, New York.

Akers, M.D., Porter, G.L., Blocker, E.J. and Mister W.G. (1986). Expert systems for management accountants. *Management Accounting*, (NAA), **67** (9), March, pp. 30–34.

American Accounting Association (1956). Tentative statement of cost concepts underlying reports for management purposes. *The Accounting Review* **31**, April, pp. 182–193.

American Accounting Association (1971a). Report of the committee on accounting practices of not-for-profit organizations. In *Supplement to Vol. 46 of The Accounting Review*, pp. 80–163.

American Accounting Association (1971b). Report of the committee on non-financial measures of effectiveness. In *Supplement to Vol. 46 of The Accounting Review*, pp. 164–211.

American Accounting Association (1972a). Report of the committee on courses in management accounting. In *Supplement to Vol. 47 of The Accounting Review*, pp. 1–14.

American Accounting Association (1972b). Report of the committee on concepts of accounting applicable to the public sector. In *Supplement to Vol. 47 of The Accounting Review*, pp. 77–108.

American Accounting Association (1972c). Report of the committee on measures of effectiveness of social programs. In *Supplement to Vol. 47 of The Accounting Review*, pp. 336–396.

American Accounting Association (1974). Report of the committee on not-for-profit organizations. In *Supplement to Vol. 49 of The Accounting Review*, pp. 224–249.

American Accounting Association (1975). Report of the committee on nonprofit organizations. In *Supplement to Vol. 50 of The Accounting Review*, pp. 1–39.

Ames, B.C., and Hlavacek, J.D. (1990). Vital truths about managing your costs. *Harvard Business Review* **68** (1), Jan–Feb., pp. 140–7.

Amey, L.R. (1969). *The Efficiency of Business Enterprises*. Allen & Unwin, London.

Amey, L.R. (1975). Tomkins on 'residual income'. *Journal of Business Finance and Accounting* **2** (1), pp. 55–68.

Amey, L.R. and D. Egginton (1973). *Management Accounting: A Conceptual Approach*. Longmans, London.

Ansari, S.L. and Tsuji, M. (1981). A behavioral extension to the cost variances investigation decision. *Journal of Business Finance and Accounting* **8** (4), Winter, pp. 573–591.

Ansoff, H.I. (1965). *Corporate Strategy*. McGraw-Hill, New York.

Anthony, R.N. (1972). Management accounting for the future. *Sloan Management Review*, Spring, pp. 17–34.

Anthony, R.N. (1973). Some fruitful directions for research in management accounting. In Dopuch N. and Revsine L. (eds). *Accounting Research 1960–1970: A Critical Evaluation*, pp. 37–68. Monograph No. 7, Center for International Education and Research in Accounting, University of Illinois.

Anthony, R.N. (1974). The case method in accounting. In Edwards J.D. (ed.). *Accounting Education: Problems & Prospects*, Chapter 36, pp. 329–340. AAA, Sarasota, Florida.

Anthony, R.N. (1988). *The Management Control Function*. Harvard Business School Press, Boston, Mass.

Anthony, R.N. (1989). Reminiscences about management accounting. *Journal of Management Accounting Research* **1**, Fall, pp. 1–20.

Anthony, R.N. and Dearden, J. (1980). *Management Control Systems* 4th edn. Irwin, Homewood, Illinois.

Anthony, R.N. and Herzlinger, R. (1980). *Management Control in Non-Profit Organizations* (revised edn.). Irwin, Homewood, Illinois.

Anthony, R.N. and Reece, J.S. (1983). *Accounting: Text & Cases* 7th edn. Irwin, Homewood, Illinois.

Antle, R., and Demski, J.S. (1988). The controllability principle in responsibility accounting, *The Accounting Review* **63** (4), October, pp. 700–18.

Argyris, C. (1952). *The Impact of Budgets on People*. Controllership Foundation, New York.

Armstrong, P. (1989). Variance reporting and the delegation of blame: a case study. *Accounting, Auditing and Accountability Journal* **2** (2), pp. 29–46.

Arnold, J.A., Carsberg, B.V. and Scapens, R.W. (eds) (1980) *Topics in Management Accounting*. Philip Allan, Deddington.

Arnold, J.A. and Hope, A.J.B. (1990). *Accounting for Management Decisions*. Prentice Hall, London. 2nd. ed.

Asch, S.E. (1951). Effects of group pressure upon the modification and distortion of judgements. In Guetzkow, H. (ed.) (1951). *Groups, Leadership and Men*. Carnegie Press, Pittsburg.

Ashby, W.R. (1956). *An Introduction to Cybernetics*. Chapman & Hall, London.

Ashton, R.H. (1976). Deviation-amplifying feedback and unintended consequences of management accounting systems. *Accounting, Organizations & Society* **1** (4), pp. 289–300.

Australian Society of Accountants (1983). *Statement of Auditing Practice No. 12*.

Bailey, A.D. and Boe, W.J. (1976). Goal and resource transfers in the multi-goal organization. *The Accounting Review* **51** (3), July, pp. 559–573.

Bancroft, A.L. and Wilson, R.M.S. (1979). Management accounting in marketing. *Management Accounting* (ICMA) **57** (11), December, pp. 25–30.

Barnard, C.I. (1938). *The Functions of the Executive*. Harvard UP, Cambridge, Mass.

Baron, R.M., Cowan, G., Ganz, R.L. and McDonald M. (1974). Interaction of locus of control and type of performance feedback: consideration of external validity. *Journal of Personality and Social Psychology* **30** (2), pp. 285–292.

Barrett, M.E. and Bruns, W.J. (1982). *Case Problems in Management Accounting*. Irwin Homewood, Illinois.

Barwise, P., Marsh, P. Thomas, K. and Wensley, J.R.C. (1986). Research on strategic investment decisions. Chapter 1.2 in J. McGee and H. Thomas (eds) *Strategic Management Research*. Wiley, Chichester.

Bass, B.M. and Leavitt, H.J. (1963). Some experiments in planning and operating. *Management Science* **9**, July, pp. 574–585.

Bastable, C.W. and Bao, D.H. (1988). The fiction of sales-mix and sales quantity variances. *Accounting Horizons* **2** (2), June, pp. 10–17.

Becker, S. and Green, D. (1962). Budgeting and employee behavior. *Journal of Business* **35**, October, pp. 392–402.

Bedford, N.M. (1980). The basis of the evolution of management accounting. In Holzer, H.P. (ed.) (1980). *Management Accounting 1980*, pp. vii–ix. Proceedings of the Illinois Management Accounting Symposium, University of Illinois at Urbana-Champaign.

Belkaoui, A. (1980). *Conceptual Foundations of Management Accounting*. Addison-Wesley, Reading, Mass.

Belkaoui, A. (1983). *Cost Accounting: A Multidimensional Emphasis*. Dryden Press, Chicago.

Benke, R.L. and Edwards J.D. (1980). *Transfer Pricing: Techniques and Uses*. National Association of Accountants, New York.

Benston, G.J. (1966). Multiple regression analysis of cost behavior. *The Accounting Review* **41** (4), October, pp. 657–672.

Berle, A.A. and Means, G.C. (1932). *The Modern Corporation and Private Property*. Macmillan, New York.

Berliner, C., and Brimson, J.A. (eds) (1988). *Cost Management for Today's Advanced Manufacturing: The CAM-I Conceptual Design*. Harvard Business School Press, Boston, Mass.

Berry, A.J. (1984). The control of capital investment. *Journal of Management Studies* **21** (1), pp. 61–81.

Berry, A.J., Capps, T., Cooper, D., Ferguson, P., Hopper, T. and Lowe, E.A. (1985). Management control in an area of the NCB: rationales of accounting practices in a public enterprise. *Accounting, Organizations & Society* **10** (1), pp. 3–28.

Bhaskar, K.N. and Housden, R.J.W. (1985). *Accounting Information Systems & Data Processing*. Heinemann, London.

Bierman, H. Jnr. and Dyckman, T.R. (1976). *Managerial Cost Accounting* 2nd edn. Macmillan, New York.

Birnberg, J.G. and Gandhi, N.M. (1976). Toward defining the accountant's role in the evaluation of social programs. *Accounting, Organizations & Society* **1** (1), June, pp. 5–10.

Birnberg, J.G. and Nath, R. (1967). Implications of bel managerial accounting. *The Accounting Review* **42** (3), J

Boer, G. (1989). *Use of expert systems in management accounting*. National Association of Accountants, Montvale, N.J.
Boland, R.J. (1979). Control, causality and information system requirements. *Accounting, Organizations & Society* **4** (4), pp. 259–272.
Boland, R.J. and Pondy, L.R. (1983). Accounting in organisations: a union of natural and rationale perspectives. *Accounting, Organizations & Society* **8** (2/3), pp. 223–234.
Boland, R.J. and Pondy, L. (1986). The micro-dynamics of a budget-cutting process: modes, models and structure. *Accounting Organizations & Society* **11** (4/5), pp. 403–422.
Boston Consulting Group (1970). The product portfolio. *Perspectives*. August.
Boulding, K.E. (1956). General systems theory: the skeleton of science. In *General Systems Yearbook of the Society for the Advancement of General System Theory*, pp. 11–17.
Bowen, M.G. (1987). The escalation phenomenon reconsidered: decision dilemmas or decision errors? *Academy of Management Review* **12** (1), January, pp. 52–66.
Brock, J.J. (1984). Competitor analysis: some practical approaches. *Industrial Marketing Management* **13**, pp. 225–31.
Brockner, J. *et al.* (1986). Escalation of commitment to an ineffective course of action. *Administrative Science Quarterly* **31** (1), March, pp. 109–126.
Bromwich, M., and Bhimani, A. (1989). *Management Accounting: Evolution not Revolution*. CIMA, London.
Brown, C. (1985). Causal reasoning in performance assessment: effects of cause and effect temporal order & covariation. *Accounting, Organizations & Society* **10** (3), pp. 255–266.
Brownell, P. (1981). Participation in budgeting, locus of control and organisational effectiveness. *The Accounting Review* **56** (4), October, pp. 844–860.
Brownell, P. (1982). The role of accounting data in performance evaluation, budgetary participation, and organizational effectiveness. *Journal of Accounting Research* **20** (1), Spring, pp. 12–27.
Brownell, P. (1986). Budgetary participation, motivation, and managerial performance. *The Accounting Review* **61** (4), October, pp. 587–600.
Brownell, P., and Dunk, A.S. (1991). Task uncertainty and its interaction with budgetary participation and budget emphasis: some methodological issues and empirical investigation. *Accounting, Organizations and Society* **16** (8), pp. 693–703.
Brownell, P. and Hirst, M. (1986). Reliance on accounting information, budgetary participation and task uncertainty: test of a three-way interaction. *Journal of Accounting Research* **24** (2), Autumn, pp. 241–249.
Bruns, W.J. and Waterhouse, J.H. (1975). Budgetary control and organisation structure. *Journal of Accounting Research* **13** (2), Autumn, pp. 177–203.
Bryan, J.F. and Locke, E.A. (1967). Goal setting as a means of increasing motivation. *Journal of Applied Psychology*, June, pp. 274–277.
Burchell, S., Clubb, C, Hopwood, A., Hughes, J. and Nahapiet, J. (1980). The roles of accounting in organisations and society. *Accounting, Organizations & Society* **5** (1), pp. 5–28.
Burrell, G. and Morgan, G. (1979). *Sociological Paradigms and Organisational Analysis*. Heinemann, London.

CAM-I (1988). *Management Accounting in Advanced Manufacturing Environments – A Survey*. CAM-I, Arlington, Texas.

Cameron, K.S. and Whetten, D.A. (1983). *Organizational Effectiveness: A Comparison of Multiple Models*. Academic Press, New York.

Capettini, R., and Clancy, D.K. (eds) (1987). *Cost Accounting, Robotics, and the New Manufacturing Environment*. American Accounting Association, Sarasota, Florida.

Caplan, E.H. (1966). Behavioral assumptions of management accounting. *The Accounting Review* **41** (3), July, pp. 496–509.

Carsberg, B.V. (1969). *An Introduction to Linear Programming for Accountants*. Allen & Unwin, London.

Casey, C.J. and Sandretto, M.J. (1981). Internal uses of accounting for inflation. *Harvard Business Review* **59** (6), Nov.-Dec., pp. 149–156.

Chartered Institute of Public Finance and Accountancy (1974). *Output Measurement Discussion Papers 4–6*. CIPFA, London (See also IMTA (1972).)

Chenhall, R.H. (1986). Authoritarianism and participative budgeting – a dyadic analysis. *The Accounting Review* **61** (2), April, pp. 263–272.

Chenhall, R.H., Harrison, G.L. and Watson, D.J.H. (eds) (1981). *The Organizational Context of Management Accounting*. Pitman, Boston, Mass.

Cherrington, D.J. and Cherrington, J.O. (1973). Appropriate reinforcement contingencies in the budgeting process. *Empirical Research in Accounting: Selected Studies, Supplement to Vol. 11 of the Journal of Accounting Research*, pp. 225–253.

Choudhury, N. (1986). Responsibility accounting and controllability. *Accounting and Business Research* **16** (63), Summer, pp. 189–98.

Chua, W.F. (1986). Radical developments in accounting thought. *The Accounting Review* **61** (4), October, pp. 601–32.

Chua, W.F., Lowe, E.A. and Puxty, A.G. (eds) (1989). *Critical Perspectives in Management Control*. Macmillan, Basingstoke.

Churchill, N.C. & Uretsky, M. (1969). Management accounting tomorrow. *Management Accounting* (NAA), June, pp. 46–53.

Churchman, C.W. (1961). *Prediction & Optimal Decisions*. Prentice-Hall, Englewood Cliffs, NJ.

Churchman, C.W. (1968). *The Systems Approach*. Delacorte Press, New York.

Churchman, C.W. (1971). *The Design of Inquiring Systems*. Basic Books, New York.

Churchman, C.W. (1972). In Klir, G.J. (ed.) (1972). *Trends in General Systems Theory*. Wiley, New York.

Clark, J.M. (1923). *Studies in the Economics of Overhead Costs*. Chicago UP, Chicago.

Clegg, S. and Dunkerley, D. (1980). *Organization, Class and Control*. RKP, London.

Clinton, G.S. (1984). *Case Exercises in Costing*. DP Publications, Eastleigh.

Collins, F. (1978). The interaction of budget characteristics and personality variables with budgetary response attitudes. *The Accounting Review* **53** (2), April, pp. 324–335.

Collins, F. *et al.* (1987). The budgeting games people play. *The Accounting Review* **62** (1), January, pp. 29–49.

Committee of Inquiry on Industrial Democracy (1977). *Report of the Committee*

of Inquiry on Industrial Democracy (Bullock Report). Cmd. 6706, HMSO.
Connell, N.A.D. (1987). Expert systems in accountancy: a review of some recent applications. *Accounting and Business Research* **17** (67), Summer, pp. 221–233.
Connolly, T., Conlen, E.J. and Deutsch, S.J. (1980). Organisational effectiveness: a multiple constituency approach. *Academy of Management Review* **5** (2), April, pp. 211–217.
Cook, D. (1968). The effect of frequency of feedback on attitudes and performance. *Empirical Research in Accounting: Selected Studies, Supplement to Vol. 6 of the Journal of Accounting Research*, pp. 213–224.
Cooper, D.J. (1980). A social and organizational view of management accounting. In Bromwich, M. and Hopwood, A.G. (eds) (1980). *Essays in British Accounting Research*, pp. 178–205. Pitman, London.
Cooper, D.J., Hayes, D. and Wolf, F. (1981). Accounting in organised anarchies: understanding and designing accounting systems in ambiguous situations. *Accounting, Organizations & Society* **6** (3), pp. 175–191.
Cooper, D.J., Scapens, R.W. and Arnold, J.A. (eds) (1983). *Management Accounting Research and Practice*. ICMA, London.
Cooper, R. (1989a). How many cost drivers do you need and how do you select them? *Journal of Cost Management for the Manufacturing Industry* **2** (4), Winter, pp. 34–46.
Cooper, R. (1989b). What do activity-based costing systems look like? *Journal of Cost Management for the Manufacturing Industry* **3** (1), Spring, pp. 38–49.
Cooper, R. (1989c). You need a new cost system when. . . . *Harvard Business Review* **67** (1), Jan–Feb., pp. 77–82.
Cooper, R. (1990). Explicating the Logic of ABC. *Management Accounting* (CIMA) **68** (10), November, pp. 58–60.
Cooper, R., and Kaplan, R.S. (1988). Measure costs right: make the right decisions. *Harvard Business Review* **66** (5), Sept–Oct., pp. 96–103.
Coulthurst, N. and Piper, J.A. (1986). The terminology and conceptual basis of information for decision-making. *Management Accounting* (ICMA) **64** (5), May, pp. 34–38.
Covaleski, M.A. and Dirsmith, M. (1983). Budgeting as a means for control and loose coupling. *Accounting, Organizations & Society* **8** (4), pp. 323–340.
Covaleski, M.A. and Dirsmith, M. (1986). The budgetary process of power and politics. *Accounting, Organizations and Society* **11** (3), pp. 193–214.
Covaleski, M.A., Dirsmith, M.W. and Jablonsky, S.F. (1985). Traditional and emergent theories of budgeting: an empirical analysis. *Journal of Accounting and Public Policy*, Winter, pp. 277–300.
Cravens, D.W., and Lamb C.W. (1986). *Strategic Marketing Cases and Applications* (Second edn.). Irwin, Homewood, Illinois.
Crozier, M. (1964). *The Bureaucratic Phenomenon*. Tavistock, London.
Cummings, L.L. (1977). Emergence of the instrumental organisation. In Goodman, P.S. and Pennings, J.M. (eds) (1977). *New Perspectives in Organisational Effectiveness*, pp. 56–62. Jossey-Bass, San Francisco.
Cushing, B.E. (1982). *Accounting Information Systems & Business Organizations*. Addison-Wesley, Reading, Mass.
Cyert, R.M. and March, J.G. (1963). *A Behavioral Theory of the Firm*. Prentice Hall Englewood Cliffs. NJ.

Dale, E. and Michelon, L.C. (1969). *Modern Management Methods*. Penguin, Harmondsworth.

Dalton, M. (1959). *Men Who Manage*. John Wiley & Sons, New York.

Dean, J. (1957). Profit performance measurement of division managers. *The Controller* **25**, September, pp. 423–4, 426, 449.

Dearborn, D.C. and Simon, H.A. (1958). Selective perception: a note on the departmental identifications of executives, *Sociometry* **21**, pp. 140–144.

Dearden, J. (1960). Problem in decentralized profit responsibility. *Harvard Business Review* **38** (3), May–June, pp. 79–86.

Dearden, J. (1961). Problem in decentralized financial control. *Harvard Business Review* **39** (3), May–June, pp. 72–80.

Dearden, J. (1968a). Appraising profit center managers. *Harvard Business Review* **46** (3), May–June, pp. 80–87.

Dearden, J. (1968b). 'Time-span' in management control. *Financial Executive* **36** (8), August, pp. 23–4, 26–8, 30.

Demski, J.S. (1980). *Information Analysis* 2nd edn. Addison-Wesley, Reading, Mass.

Dent, J.F. (1990). Strategy, organization and control: some possibilities for accounting research. *Accounting, Organizations and Society* **15** (1/2), pp. 3–26.

Dent, J.F. (1991). Accounting and organizational cultures: a field study of the emergence of a new organizational reality. *Accounting, Organizations and Society* **16** (8), pp. 705–32.

Dery, D. (1982). Erring and learning: an organizational analysis. *Accounting, Organizations & Society* **7** (3), pp. 217–223.

Dev, S.F.D. (1980). Linear programming & production planning. In Arnold, J.A., Carsber, B.V. and Scapens, R.W. (eds) (1980). *Topics in Management Accounting*, Chapter 7, pp. 121–147. Philip Allan. Deddington.

Dominiak, G.F. and Louderback, J.G. (1985). *Managerial Accounting* 4th edn. Kent, Boston, Mass.

Dopuch, N., and Drake, D. (1964) Accounting implications of a mathematical programming approach to the transfer pricing problem. *Journal of Accounting Research*, **2** (1), Spring, 10–24.

Dopuch, N. and Revsine, L. (1973). *Accounting research 1960–1970: A critical evaluation*. Champaign Illinois: Center for International Education and Research in Accounting, University of Illinois.

Dopuch, N., Birnberg, J.G. and Demski, J.S. (1982). *Cost Accounting* 3rd edn. Harcourt, Brace, Jovanovich, New York.

Drebin, A.R. and Bierman, H. (1978). *Managerial Accounting: An Introduction* 3rd edn. W.B. Saunders, Philadelphia.

Driver, M.J., and Mock T.J. (1975). Human information processing, decision style theory, and accounting information systems. *The Accounting Review* **50** (3), July, pp. 490–508.

Drucker, P.F. (1954). *The Practice of Management*. Harper and Brothers, New York.

Drury, J.C. (1992). *Management & Cost Accounting* 3rd edn. Chapman & Hall, London.

Dugdale, D. (1990a). Costing systems in transition: a review of recent developments. *Management Accounting* (CIMA) **68** (1), January, pp. 38–41.

Dugdale, D. (1990b). The uses of activity-based costing. *Management Accounting* (CIMA) **68** (9), October, pp. 36–8.

Emmanuel, C.R. and Gee, K.P. (1982). Transfer pricing: a fair and neutral approach. *Accounting and Business Research* **12** (48), Autumn, pp. 273–278.

Emmanuel, C.R. and Otley, D.T. (1976). The usefulness of residual income. *Journal of Business Finance & Accounting* **3** (4), pp. 43–51.

Emmanuel, C.R. and Otley, D.T. (1985). *Accounting for Management Control*. Van Nostrand Reinhold, Workingham.

Emmanuel, C.R., Otley, D.T. and Merchant, K. (1990). *Accounting for Management Control*. (Second edn.). Chapman & Hall, London.

Emore, J.R., and Ness, J.A. (1991). The slow pace of meaningful change in cost systems. *Journal of Cost Management for the Manufacturing Industry* **4** (4), pp. 36–45.

Ezzamel, M.A. and Hilton, K. (1980). Can divisional discretion be measured? *Journal of Business Finance & Accounting* **7** (2), pp. 311–329.

Ferguson, P. (1988). The contribution of cognitive psychology to the design of accounting information systems. *British Accounting Review* **20** (1), April, pp. 5–20.

Ferrara, W.L. (1967). Responsibility reporting vs. direct costing — is there a conflict? *Management Accounting* (NAA), June, pp. 43–54.

Foster, G., and Gupta, M. (1990). Manufacturing overhead cost driver analysis. *Journal of Accounting and Economics* **12**, pp. 309–37.

French, J.R.P., Israel, J. and As, D. (1960). An experiment on participation in a Norwegian factory: interpersonal dimensions of decision-making. *Human Relations*, February, pp. 3–19.

Friedlander, F. and Pickle, H. (1968). Components of effectiveness in small organizations. *Administrative Science Quarterly* **13**, pp. 289–304.

Gabor, D. (1964). *Inventing the Future*. Penguin, Harmondsworth.

Garcke, E. and Fells, J.M. (1887). *Factory Accounts*. Crosby Lockwood, London.

Gee, K.P. (1979). A note on cost escalation clauses. *Journal of Business Finance & Accounting* **6** (3), pp. 339–346.

Gee, K.P. (1986). *Advanced Management Accounting Problems*. Macmillan, London.

Gibson, J.L., Ivancevich, J.M. and Donnelly, J.H. (1979). *Organizations, Behavior, Structure, Processes*. Business Publications, Dallas, Texas.

Gibson, B. (1990). Determining meaningful sales relational (mix) variances. *Accounting and Business Research* **21** (81), Winter, pp. 35–40.

Gietzmann, M. (1991). Implementation issues associated with the construction of an activity-based costing system in an engineering components manufacturer. *Management Accounting Research* **2** (3), September, pp. 189–99.

Goldthorpe, J.H., Lockwood, D., Bechhofers, F. and Platt, J. (1970). *The Affluent Worker: Industrial Attitudes and Behaviour*. Cambridge University Press, Cambridge.

Goodman, P.S. and Pennings, J.M. (1977). *New Perspectives on Organizational Effectiveness*. Jossey-Bass, San Francisco.

Goold, M. (1986). Accounting and Strategy. Chapter 10 (pp. 181–91) in M. Bromwich and A.G. Hopwood (eds) (1986). *Research and Current Issues in Management Accounting*. Pitman, London.

Goold, M., and Campbell, A. (1987). *Strategies and Styles: The Role of the Centre in Managing Diversified Corporations*. Basil Blackwell, Oxford.

Goold, M., and Quinn, J.J. (1990). *Strategic Control: Milestones for Long-Term Performance*. Hutchinson/The Economist, London.

Gordon, L.A., Larcker, D.F. and Tuggle, F.D. (1978). Strategic decision processes and the design of accounting information systems: conceptual linkages. *Accounting, Organizations & Society* **3** (3/4), pp. 203–213.

Gordon, L.A., and Myers, M.D. (1991). Post-auditing capital projects: are you in step with the competition? *Management Accounting* (NAA) **72** (7), January, pp. 39–42.

Govindarajan, V. (1984). Appropriateness of accounting data in performance evaluation. *Accounting, Organizations & Society* **9** (2), pp. 125–135.

Greenwood, R.G. (1974). *Managerial Decentralization: A Study of the General Electric Philosophy*. D.C. Heath, Lexington, Mass.

Harrell, A.M. (1977). The decision-making behavior of Air Force officers and the management control process. *The Accounting Review* **52** (4), October, pp. 833–41.

Harrison, G.L. (1991). The F-scale as a measure of authoritarianism in accounting research. *Behavioral Research in Accounting* **3**, pp. 13–24.

Hart, H. (1981). A review of some major recent developments in the management accounting field. *Accounting & Business Research* **11** (42), Spring, pp. 99–115.

Harwood, G.B., Pate, J.L. and Schneider, A. (1991). Budgeting decisions as a function of framing: an application of prospect theory's reflection effect. *Management Accounting Research* **2** (3), September, pp. 161–70.

Hayes, D.C. (1977). The contingency theory of managerial accounting. *The Accounting Review* **52** (1), January, pp. 22–39.

Hayes, D.C. (1983). Accounting for accounting: a story about managerial accounting. *Accounting, Organizations & Society* **8** (2/3), pp. 241–250.

Heitger, L.E. and Matulich, S. (1980). *Managerial Accounting*. McGraw-Hill, New York.

Henderson, B.D. and Dearden, J. (1966). New system for divisional control. *Harvard Business Review* **44** (5), September–October, pp. 144–160.

Henley, Sir D. *et al.* (1983). *Public Sector Accounting and Financial Control*. Van Nostrand Reinhold, Wokingham.

Herbert, L. (1972). Growth of accountability knowledge 1775–1975. *The GAO Review*, Fall, p. 31.

Hermans, E.S. (1981). *Corporate Control, Corporate Power*. Cambridge University Press, New York.

Herzberg, F., Mausner, B. and Synderman, B.B. (1959). *The Motivation to Work*. John Wiley & Sons, New York.

Heskett, J.L. (1976). *Marketing*. Macmillan, New York.

Higgins, J.A. (1960). Responsibility accounting. In Thomas, W.E. (ed.) (1960). *Readings in Cost Accounting, Budgeting and Control* 2nd edn. South-Western Publishing Company, Cincinnati, Ohio.

Hills, F.S. and Mahoney, T.A. (1978). University budgets and organisational decision making. *Administrative Science Quarterly* **23** (3), September, pp. 454–465.

Hirsch, M.L. and Louderback, J.G. (1992) *Cost Accounting*. South-Western, Cincinatti, 3rd ed.

Hirschmann, W.B. (1964). Profit from the learning curve. *Harvard Business Review* **42** (1), Jan.-Feb., pp. 125–139.

Hirst, M.K. (1981). Accounting information and the evaluation of subordinate performance: a situational approach. *The Accounting Review* **56** (4), October, pp. 771–784.

Hofer, C.W. and Schendel, D. (1978). *Strategy Formulation: Analytical Concepts*. West Publishing Co. St Paul, Minn.

Hofstede, G. (1967). *The Game of Budget Control*. Tavistock, London.

Hofstede, G. (1981). Management control of public and not-for-profit activities. *Accounting, Organizations & Society* **6** (3), pp. 193–211.

Holzer, H.P. (ed.) (1980). *Management Accounting 1980*. Proceedings of the University of Illinois Management Accounting Symposium, Department of Accountancy, University of Illinois at Urbana-Champaign.

Hopper, T.M. and Powell, A. (1982). Making sense of behavioural research into management accounting: a review of its underlying paradigms. Paper presented to ICMA/SSRC Management Accounting Research Conference, University of Aston in Birmingham, 21–22 September.

Hopwood, A.G. (1972). An empirical study of the role of accounting data in performance evaluation. In *Empirical Research in Accounting: Selected Studies, Supplement to Journal of Accounting Research* **10** (1), pp. 156–182.

Hopwood, A.G. (1973). *An Accounting System and Managerial Behaviour*. Saxon House, Farnborough.

Hopwood, A.G. (1974a). *Accounting and Human Behaviour*. Haymarket, London.

Hopwood, A.G. (1974b). Leadership climate and the use of accounting data in performance evaluation. *The Accounting Review* **49** (3), July, pp. 485–495.

Hopwood, A.G. (1987). The archaeology of accounting systems. *Accounting, Organizations and Society* **12** (3), pp. 207–34.

Hopwood, A.G. (1988). Accounting and organizational action. *Accounting from the Outside, The Collected Papers of Anthony G. Hopwood*, Garland, New York, pp. 212–25.

Hopwood, A.G. (1989). Behavioral accounting in retrospect and prospect. *Behavioral Research in Accounting* **1**, pp. 1–22.

Horngren, C.T. (1982). *Cost Accounting: A Managerial Emphasis* 5th. edn. Prentice-Hall, Englewood Cliffs, N.J.

Horngren, C.T. (1989). Cost and management accounting: yesterday and today. *Journal of Management Accounting Research* **1**, Fall, pp. 21–32.

Horngren, C.T. and Foster, G. (1987). *Cost Accounting: A Managerial Emphasis* 6th edn. Prentice-Hall, Englewood Cliffs, NJ.

Howell, R.A. (1987). World class manufacturing controls: management accounting for the factory of the future. Session Two, pp. 2.1–2.22 in Capettini, R., and D.K. Clancy (eds).

Huber, G.P. (1980). *Managerial Decision-Making*. Scott, Foresman, Glenview.

Ijiri, Y. (1978). Cash flow accounting and its structure. *Journal of Accounting, Auditing & Finance* **1**, Summer, pp. 331–348.

Ijiri, Y. (1980). Recovery rate and cash flow accounting. *Financial Executive* **47**, March, pp. 54–60.

Ijiri, Y., Kinard, J.C. and Putney, F.B. (1968). An integrated evaluation system for budget forecasting and operating performance with a classified budgeting bibliography. *Journal of Accounting Research* **6** (1), pp. 1–28.

Ilgen, D., Fisher, C.D. and Taylor, M.S. (1979). Consequence of feedback on behavior in organisations. *Journal of Applied Psychology* **64** (4), pp. 349–371.

Innes, J., and Mitchell, F. (1990a). *Activity-based Costing: A Review with Case Studies*. CIMA, London.

Innes, J., and Mitchell, F. (1990b). Activity-based costing research. *Management Accounting* (CIMA) **68** (5), May, pp. 28–9.

Innes, J. and Mitchell, F. (1991). Presentation made to Management Accounting Research Group Conference. London School of Economics, 19 April.

Institute of Municipal Treasurers & Accountants (1972). *Output Measurement Discussion Papers 1–3*. IMTA, London. (See also CIPFA (1974).)

Jaques, E. (1966). *Time-Span Handbook*. Heinemann, London.

Jevons, S. (1871). *The Theory of Political Economy*. Macmillan, London.

Johnson, G. and Scholes, K. (1988). *Exploring Corporate Strategy*. Prentice-Hall, London. 2nd. edn.

Johnson, H.G. (1967). Key item control. *Management Services*, Vol. 4, No. 1, pp. 21–6. January–February.

Johnson, H.T. (1980). Markets, hierarchies, and the history of management accounting. Paper prepared for the Third International Congress of Accounting Historians, London Business School, London, August 16–18.

Johnson, H.T. (1983). The search for gain in markets and firms: a review of the historical emergence of management accounting systems. *Accounting, Organizations & Society* **8** (2/3), pp. 139–146.

Johnson, H.T. and Kaplan, R.S. (1987a). *Relevance Lost: The Rise and Fall of Management Accounting*. Harvard Business School Press, Boston, Mass.

Johnson, H.T. and Kaplan, R.S. (1987b). The rise and fall of management accounting *Management Accounting* (NAA), **68** (7), January, pp. 22–30.

Johnston, J. (1972). *Statistical Cost Analysis*. McGraw-Hill, London.

Jones, C.S. (1985). An empirical study of the evidence for contingency theories of management accounting systems in conditions of rapid change. *Accounting, Organizations & Society* **10** (3), pp. 303–328.

Kahneman, D., and Tversky, A. (1984). Choices, values and frames. *American Psychologist* **39**, pp. 341–50.

Kaplan, R.S. (1981). The impact of management accounting research on policy and practice. In Buckley, J.W. (ed.) (1981). *The Impact of Accounting Research on Policy and Practice* (Proceedings of the Arthur Young Professors' 1981 Roundtable), pp. 57–76. Arthur Young, Reston, Virginia.

Kaplan, R.S. (1982). *Advanced Management Accounting*. Prentice-Hall, Englewood Cliffs, NJ.

Kaplan, R.S. (1983). Measuring manufacturing performance: a new challenge for managerial accounting research. *The Accounting Review* **58** (4), October, pp. 686–705.

Kaplan, R.S. (1984a). The evolution of management accounting. *The Accounting Review* **59** (3), July, pp. 390–418.

Kaplan, R.S. (1984b). Yesterday's accounting undermines production. *Harvard Business Review* **62** (4), July–August, pp. 95–101.

Kaplan, R.S. (1988). One cost system isn't enough. *Harvard Business Review* **68** (1), Jan–Feb., pp. 61–6.

Kaplan, R.S., and Atkinson, A.A. (1989). *Advanced Management Accounting* (Second edn.). Prentice-Hall, Englewood Cliffs, N.J.

Katz, D. and Kahn, R.L. (1966). *The Social Psychology of Organisations*. John Wiley & Sons, New York.

Keeley, M. (1978). A social justice approach to organisational evaluation. *Administrative Science Quarterly* **23** (2), June, pp. 272–290.

Kenis, I. (1979). Effects of budgetary goal characteristics on managerial attitudes and performance. *The Accounting Review* **54** (4), October, pp. 707–721.

Khandwalla, P.N. (1972). The effect of different types of competition on the use of management controls. *Journal of Accounting Research* **10** (2), Autumn, pp. 275–285.

Koontz, H. (1962). Making sense of management theory. *Harvard Business Review* **40** (4), July–August, pp. 24–46.

Koontz, H. and Bradspies, R.W. (1972). Managing through feedforward control. *Business Horizons*, June.

Laughlin, R.C. and Gray, R.H. (1988). *Financial Accounting: Method and Meaning*. Van Nostrand Reinhold, Wokingham.

Lawler, E.E. and Rhode, J.G. (1976). *Information & Control in Organizations*. Goodyear, Pacific Palisades, California.

Lehman, C., and Tinker, A.M. (1987). The 'real' cultural significance of accounts. *Accounting, Organizations and Society* **12** (5), pp. 503–22.

Likert, R. and Seashore, S.E. (1963). Making cost control work. *Harvard Business Review* **41** (6), Nov.–Dec. pp. 96–108.

Lin, T.W. (1986). Expert systems and management accounting research. *Management Accounting – News and Views* **4** (1), Spring, pp. 11–13.

Lindblom, C.E. (1959). The science of muddling through. *Public Administration Review* **19**, Spring, pp. 79–88.

Livingstone, J.L. (ed.) (1975). *Managerial Accounting: The Behavioral Foundations*. Grid, Columbus, Ohio.

Locke, E.A., Sarri, L.M., Shaw, K.N. and Lathan, G.P. (1981). Goal setting and task performance: 1969–1980. *Psychological Bulletin* **90** (1), pp. 125–152.

Loft, A. (1986). Towards a critical understanding of accounting: the case of cost accounting in the UK, 1914–1925. *Accounting, Organizations & Society* **11** (2), pp. 137–169.

Lowe, E.A. (1970). The information content of financial statements, financial planning, and management control: towards an integration. *Journal of Business Finance* **2** (2), Summer, pp. 3–11.

Lowe, E.A. (1971). On the definition of 'systems' in systems engineering. *Journal of Systems Engineering* **2** (1), Summer, pp. 95–98.

Lowe, E.A. and Chua, W.F. (1983). Organisational effectiveness and management control, pp. 271–287 in Lowe, E.A. and Machin, J.L.J. (eds) (1983).

Lowe, E.A. and Machin, J.L.J. (eds) (1983). *New Perspectives in Management Control*. Macmillan, London.

Lowe, E.A. and Shaw, R.W. (1968). An analysis of managerial biasing: evidence from a company's budgeting process. *Journal of Management Studies* **5** (3), October, pp. 304–315.

Lowe, E.A. and Soo, W.F. (1980). Organisational effectiveness – a critique and proposal. *Managerial Finance* **6** (1), pp. 63–77.

Lowe, E.A. and Tinker, A.M. (1977). New directions for management accounting. *Omega* **5** (2), pp. 173–183.

Luckett, P.F., and Eggleton, I.R.C. (1991). Feedback and management accounting: a review of research into behavioural consequences. *Accounting, Organizations and Society* **16** (4), pp. 371–94.

Lumijärvi, O.P. (1991). Selling of capital investments to top management. *Management Accounting Research 2* (3), September, pp. 171–88.

Lupton, T. (1963). *On the Shopfloor*. Pergamon, London.

McGregor, D. (1960). *The Human Side of Enterprise*. McGraw-Hill, New York.

Macintosh, N.B. (1985). *The Social Software of Accounting & Information Systems*. Wiley, Chichester.

Magee, R.P. (1986). *Advanced Managerial Accounting*. Harper & Row, New York.

Malcom, R.E. (1978). The effect of product aggregation in determining sales variances. *The Accounting Review* **53** (1), January, pp. 162–9.

Mann, N.R. (1989). *The Keys to Excellence: the Deming Philosophy*. Mercury, London.

March, J.G. and Olsen, J.P. (1976). *Ambiguity and Choice in Organisations*. Universitetsforlaget, Bergen, Norway.

March, J.G. and Simon, H.A. (1958). *Organizations*. Wiley, New York.

Marsh, P., Barwise, P., Thomas, K., and Wensley, J.R.C. (1988). Managing strategic investment decisions. Ch. 4 (pp. 86–136) in A.M. Pettigrew (ed.). *Competitiveness and the Management Process*. Blackwell, Oxford.

Maslow, A.E. (1954). *Motivation and Personality*. Harper and Row, New York.

Mason, R.O. and Mitroff, I.I. (1973). A program for research on management information systems. *Management Science* **19** (5), January, pp. 474–487.

Mattessich, R.V. (1980). Management accounting: past, present, & future. In Holzer, H.P. (ed.) (1980). *Management Accounting 1980*, pp. 209–240. University of Illinois at Urbana-Champaign.

Mayston, D.J. (1985). Non-profit performance indicators in the public sector. *Financial Accountability and Management* **1** (1), Summer, pp. 51–74.

Mento, A.J., Cartledge, N.D. and Locke, E.A. (1980). Maryland vs. Michigan vs. Minnesota: another look at the relationship of expectancy and goal difficulty to task performance. *Organisational Behavior and Human Performance*, June, pp. 419–440.

Merchant, K.A. (1981). The design of the corporate budgeting system. *The Accounting Review* **56** (4), October, pp. 813–829.

Merchant, K.A. (1985). Organizational controls and discretionary program decision-making: a field study. *Accounting, Organizations & Society* **10** (1), pp. 67–85.

Meyer, H.H. and Walker, W.B. (1961). A study of factors relating to the effectiveness of a performance appraisal program. *Personnel Psychology*, Autumn, pp. 291–298.

Milani, K. (1975). The relationship of participation in budget-setting to industrial supervision performance and attitudes: a field study. *The Accounting Review* **50** (1), April, pp. 274–284.

Miles, R.E. and Vergin, R.C. (1966). Behavioral properties of variance controls. *California Management Review* **9** (3), Spring.

Miller, P. (1990). On the interrelationships between accounting and the state. *Accounting, Organizations and Society* **15** (4), pp. 315–38.

Miller, P., and T. O'Leary (1987). Accounting and the construction of the governable person. *Accounting, Organizations and Society* **12** (3), pp. 235–66.

Moore, P.G. and Thomas, H. (1976). *The Anatomy of Decisions*. Penguin, Harmondsworth.

Morgan, G. (1988). Accounting as reality construction: towards a new epistemology for accounting practice. *Accounting, Organizations and Society* **13** (5), pp. 477–85.

Moritarity, S. (ed.) (1985). *Cases From Management Accounting Practice* NAA, Montvale, NJ.

Morse, N.C. and Reimer, E. (1956). The experimental change of a major organisational variable. *Journal of Abnormal and Social Psychology*, January, pp. 120–129.

Morse, W.J., Davis, J.R. and Hartgraves, A.L. (1984). *Management Accounting*. Addison-Wesley, Reading, Mass.

Mundell, M. (1967). *A Conceptual Framework for the Management Sciences*. McGraw-Hill, New York.

Myers, R.E. (1966). Performance review of capital expenditures. *Management Accounting* (NAA) **48** (4), December, pp. 21–26.

Nadler, D.A. and Lawler, E.E. (1977). Motivation: a diagnostic approach. In Hackman, J.R., Lawler, E.E. and Porter, L.W. (eds) (1977). *Perspectives on Behavior in Organizations*. McGraw-Hill, New York.

Nahapiet, J. (1988). The rhetoric and reality of an accounting change: a study of resource allocation. *Accounting, Organizations and Society* **13** (4), pp. 333–58.

National Association of Accountants (1981). Management Accounting Practices Committee promulgates definition of management accounting. *Management Accounting* (NAA), January, pp. 58–59.

National Association of Accountants (1991a). *Cost Management Update* **1**, January.

National Association of Accountants (1991b). *Cost Management Update* **2**, April.

Neale, C.W. (1989). Post-auditing practices by UK firms: aims, benefits and shortcomings. *British Accounting Review* **21** (4), December, pp. 309-28.

Neimark, M. and Tinker, A.M. (1986). The social construction of management control systems. *Accounting, Organization and Society* **11** (4/5), pp. 369–95.

Newton, R. (1991). Why ABC may never leave the classroom. *Management Consultancy*, March, pp. 30, 33.

Novick, D. (1973). *Current Practice in Program Budgeting (PPBS) Analysis and Case Studies covering Government and Business*. Heinemann, London.

Nurnberg, H. (1986). The ambiguous high-low method. *Issues in Accounting Education* **1** (1), Spring, pp. 143–147.

Oakland, J.S. (1989). *Total Quality Management*. Heinemann, Oxford.

Odiorne, G. (1965). *Management of Objectives*. Pitman, New York.

Otley, D.T. (1978). Budget use and managerial performance. *Journal of Accounting Research* **16** (1), Spring, pp. 122–149.

Otley, D.T. (1980). The contingency theory of management accounting: achievement and progress. *Accounting, Organizations & Society* 5 (4), pp. 413–428.

Otley, D.T. (1983a). The fall & rise of management accounting. The inaugural Tom Robertson Memorial Lecture, Department of Accounting and Business Method, University of Edinburgh.

Otley, D.T. (1983b). Behavioural and organisational research in management accounting. In Cooper, D.J., Scapens, R.W. and Arnold, J.A. (eds) (1983). *Management Accounting: Research & Practice*, pp. 136–58. ICMA, London.

Otley, D.T. (1985a). The accuracy of budgetary estimates: some statistical evidence. *Journal of Business Finance & Accounting* **12** (3), pp. 415–428.

Otley, D.T. (1985b). Developments in management accounting research. *The British Accounting Review* 17 (2), Autumn, pp. 3–23.

Otley, D.T. (1987). *Accounting Control and Organizational Behaviour*. Heinemann, London.

Otley, D.T. and Berry, A.J. (1980). Control, organisation and accounting. *Accounting, Organizations & Society* 5 (2), pp. 231–244.

Parker, R.H. (1969). *Management accounting: an historical perspective*. Macmillan, London.

Parker, R.H. (1980). History of accounting for decisions. In Arnold, J.A., Carsberg, B.V. and Scapens, R.W. (eds) (1980). *Topics in Management Accounting*, Chapter 13, pp. 262–276. Philip Allan, Deddington.

Pennings, J.M. and Goodman, P.S. (1977). Toward a workable framework. In Goodman, P.S. and Pennings, J.M. (eds) (1977). *New Perspectives in Organisational Effectiveness*, pp. 146–184. Jossey-Bass, San Francisco.

Perrow, C. (1961). The analysis of goals in complex organisations. *American Sociological Review*. December, pp. 854–866.

Perrow, C. (1986). Economic theories of organisation. *Theory and Society* **15** (1/2), pp. 11–45.

Peters, T.J. and Waterman, R.H. (1982). *In Search of Excellence: Lessons from America's Best-Run Companies*. Harper & Row, New York.

Pfeffer, J. and Salancik, G.R. (1978). *The External Control of Organizations. A Resource Dependence Perspective*. Harper & Row, New York.

Pfeffer, J. and Moore, W.L. (1980). Power in university budgeting: a replication and extension. *Administrative Science Quarterly* **25** (4), December, pp. 637–653.

Piper, J.A. (1983). Classfiying capital projects for top management decision making. In Thomas, W.E. (ed.) (1983). *Readings in Cost Accounting, Budgeting & Control* 6th edn. pp. 189–207. South-Western, Cincinnati.

Piper, J.A., and Walley, P. (1990). Testing ABC logic. *Management Accounting* (CIMA) **68** (8), September, pp. 37, 42.

Piper, J.A., and Walley, P. (1991). ABC relevance not found. *Management Accounting* (CIMA) **69** (3), March, pp. 42, 44, 54.

Pirie, R.C. (1986). Managing strategic information. *CMA Magazine* **60** (5), Sep.–Oct., pp. 41–44.

Plossl, G.W. (1990). Cost accounting in manufacturing: dawn of a new era. *Production Planning and Control* **1** (1), pp. 61–8.

Pollard, W.B. (1986). Teaching standard costs: a look at textbook differences in overhead variance analysis. *Journal of Accounting Education* **4** (1), Spring, pp. 21–220.

Porter, L.M. and Roberts, K.H. (eds) (1977). *Communication in Organizations*. Penguin, Hardmondsworth.

Porter, M.E. (1985). *Competitive Advantage: Creating and Sustaining Superior Performance*. The Free Press, New York.

Poulet, R. (1986). How businesses bust themselves. *Management Today*, July, pp. 68–71.

Preston, A. (1986). Interactions and arrangements in the process of informing. *Accounting, Organizations & Soceity* **11** (6), pp. 521–540.

Price Waterhouse (1987). *Survey of Cost Management Systems in the North-West Manufacturing Sector*. Mimeograph.

Puxty, A.G. (ed.) (1985). *Critiques of Agency Theory in Accountancy*, Issues in Accountability. No. 12. Strathclyde Convergencies, Glasgow.

Puxty, A.G. and Dodds, J.C. (1991). *Financial Management: Method & Meaning*. 2nd. ed. Chapman & Hall, London.

Ramanathan, K.V. (1985). A proposed framework for designing management control systems in not-for-profit organizations. *Financial Accountability & Management* **1** (1), Summer, pp. 75–92.

Rappaport, A. (1967). Sensitivity analysis in decision-making. *The Accounting Review* **42** (3), July, pp. 441–456.

Rathe, A.W. (1960). Management control in business. In Malcolm, D.G. and Rowe, A.J. (eds) (1960). *Management Control Systems*. Wiley, New York.

Rawls, J. (1971). *A Theory of Justice*. Harvard UP, Cambridge, Mass.

Rayburn, L.G. (1986). *Principles of Cost Accounting: Managerial Applications* 3rd edn. Irwin, Homewood, Illinois.

Read, W.H. (1962). Upward communication in industrial hierarchies. *Human Relations*, February, pp. 3–16.

Reece, J.S. and Cool, W.R. (1978). Measuring investment center performance. *Harvard Business Review* **56** (3), May–June, pp. 28–46, 174, 178.

Reider, B., and Saunders, G. (1988). Management accounting education: A defense of criticisms. *Accounting Horizons* **2** (4), December, pp. 58–62.

Richardson, A.J. (1988). Accounting knowledge and professional privileges. *Accounting, Organizations and Society* **13** (4), pp. 381–96.

Richardson, P.R. (1988). *Cost Containment*. The Free Press, New York.

Ridgway, V.F. (1956). Dysfunctional consequences of performance measurement. *Administrative Science Quarterly* **1** (2), September, pp. 240–247.

Rockart, J.F. (1979). Chief executives define their own data needs. *Harvard Business Review* **57** (2), March–April, pp. 81–93.

Roethlisberger, F.J. and Dixon, W.J. (1939). *Management and the Worker*. Harvard UP, Cambridge, Mass.

Ronen, J. and Livingstone, J.L. (1975). An expectancy theory approach to the motivational impacts of budgets. *The Accounting Review* **50** (4), pp. 671–685.

Roslender, R. (1990). Sociology and management accounting research. *British Accounting Review* **22** (4), December, pp. 351–72.

Ross, J. and Staw, B.M. (1986). Expo 86: An escalation prototype. *Administrative Science Quarterly* **31** (2), June, pp. 274–97.

Rotch, W., Allen, B.R. and Smith, C.R. (1982). *Cases in Management Accounting & Control Systems*. Reston Publishing Company, Virginia.

Ryan, R.J. and Hobson, J.B. (1985). *Management Accounting: A Contemporary Approach*. Pitman, London.

Sassenrath, J.M. (1975). Theory and results on feedback and retention. *Journal of Educational Psychology* **67** (4), pp. 894–899.

Scapens, R.W. (1979). Profit measurement in divisionalised companies. *Journal of Business Finance & Accounting* **6** (3), pp. 281–305.

Scapens, R.W. (1980). Overview of current trends and directions for the future, pp. 277–295 in Arnold, J.A., Carsberg, B.V. and Scapens, R.W. (eds) (1980).

Scapens, R.W. (1983a). Closing the gap between theory and practice. *Management Accounting* (CIMA) **61** (1), January, pp. 34–36.

Scapens, R.W. (1983b). Management accounting – a change of emphasis, pp. 5–21 in Cooper, D.J., Scapens, R.W., and Arnold, J.A. (eds) (1983).

Scapens, R.W. (1985). *Management Accounting: A Review of Recent Developments*. Macmillan, London.

Scapens, R.W., Otley, D.T. and Lister, R.J. (eds) (1984). *Management Accounting, Organizational Theory, & Capital Budgeting: Three Surveys*. Macmillan/ESRC, London.

Scapens, R.W. and Sale, J.T. (1981). Performance measurement & formal capital expenditure controls in divisionalised companies. *Journal of Business Finance & Accounting* **8** (3), pp. 389–419.

Schiff, M. and Lewin, A.Y. (1970). The impact of people on budgets. *The Accounting Review* **45** (2), April, pp. 259–268.

Schiff, M. and Lewin, A.Y. (eds) (1974). *Behavioral Aspects of Accounting*. Prentice-Hall, Englewood Cliffs, NJ.

Schmenner, R.W. (1988). Escaping the black holes of cost accounting. *Business Horizons* **31** (1), pp. 66–72.

Schoenfeld, H.M.W. (1980) Management accounting: discernable future directions, in H.P. Holzer (ed.).

Schreyögg, G. and Steinmann, H. (1987). Strategic control: a new perspective. *Academy of Management Review* **12** (1), January, pp. 91–103.

Seibert, J.C. (1973). *Concepts of Marketing Management*. Harper & Row, New York.

Sevin, C.H. (1965). *Marketing Productivity Analysis*. McGraw-Hill, New York.

Shank, J.K. (1981). *Contemporary Managerial Accounting: A Casebook*. Prentice-Hall, Englewood Cliffs, NJ.

Shank, J.K. (1989). Strategic cost management: new wine, or just new bottles? *Journal of Management Accounting Research* **1**, Fall, pp. 47–65.

Shank, J.K. and Churchill, N.C. (1977). Variance analysis: a management oriented approach. *The Accounting Review* **52** (4), October, pp. 950–957.

Shank, J.K. and Govindarajan (1988). The perils of cost allocation based on production volumes. *Accounting Horizons* **2** (4) December, pp. 71–9.

Shillinglaw, G. (1964). Divisional performance review: an extension of budgetary control. In Bonini, C.P., Jaedicke, R.K. and Wagner, H.M. (eds) (1964). *Management Controls: New Directions in Basic Research*. McGraw-Hill, New York.

Shillinglaw, G. (1980). Old horizons & new frontiers: the future of managerial accounting. In Holzer, H.P. (ed.) (1980). *Management Accounting 1980*, pp. 3–16. University of Illinois at Urbana-Champaign.

Shillinglaw, G. (1982). *Managerial Cost Accounting* 5th edn. Irwin, Homewood, Illinois.

Shillinglaw, G. (1987). Look back from the future. Session Nine, pp. 9.1–9.14 in Capettini, R., and Clancy, D.K. (eds).

Shillinglaw, G. (1989). Managerial cost accounting: present and future. *Journal of Management Accounting Research* **1**, Fall, pp. 33–46.

Siegel, G., and Ramanauskas-Marconi, H. (1989). *Behavioral Accounting*. South-Western, Cincinnati, Ohio.

Simmonds, K. (1972). From data-oriented to information-oriented accounting. *Journal of Business Finance* **4** (1), pp. 17–23.

Simmonds, K. (1980). Strategic management accounting. Paper given to ICMA Technical Symposium, Oxford, December.

Simmonds, K. (1981). Strategic management accounting. *Management Accounting* (ICMA) **59** (4), April, pp. 26–29.

Simmonds, K. (1982). Strategic management accounting for pricing: a case example. *Accounting & Business research* **12** (47), Summer, pp. 206–214.

Simmonds, K. (1985). How to compete. *Management Today*, August, pp. 39–43, 84.

Simmonds, K. (1986). The accounting assessment of competitive position. *European Journal of Marketing* **20** (1), pp. 16–31.

Simon, H.A. (1959). Theories of decision making in economics and behavioral science. *American Economic Review* **49**, June, pp. 253–283.

Simon, H.A. (1960). *The New Science of Management Decision*. Harper & Row, New York.

Simon, H.A., Guetzkow, H., Kozmetsky, G. and Tyndall, G. (1954). *Centralisation v. Decentralisation in Organising the Controller's Department*. Controllership Foundation, New York.

Simons, R. (1987). Accounting control systems and business strategy: an empirical analysis. *Accounting, Organizations & Society* **12** (4), pp. 357–374.

Sizer, J. (1981). Performance assessment in institutions of higher education under conditions of financial stringency, contraction & changing needs: a management accounting perspective. *Accounting & Business Research* **11** (43), Summer, pp. 227–242.

Sizer, J. and Coulthurst, N. (eds). *A Casebook of British Management Accounting*, Volume 1 (1984), Volume 2 (1985). ICAEW, London.

Solomons, D. (1952). The historical development of costing. In Solomons, D. (ed.) (1968). *Studies in Cost Analysis* 2nd edn., pp. 3–49. Sweet & Maxwell, London.

Solomons, D. (1965). *Divisional Performance: Measurement & Control*. Irwin, Homewood, Illinois.

Sorensen, J.E. and Grove, H.D. (1977). Cost-outcome and cost-effectiveness analysis: emerging non-profit performance evaluation techniques. *The Accounting Review* **52** (3), July, pp. 658–675.

Spicer, B.H. and Ballew, V. (1983). Management accounting systems and the economics of internal organisation. *Accounting, Organizations & Society* **8** (1), pp. 73–95.

Spybey, T. (1984). Traditional and professional frames of meaning in management. *Sociology* **18** (4), pp. 550–62.

Stallman, J.C. (1974). Inquiry in the accounting classroom. In Edwards, J.D. (ed.) (1974). *Accounting Education: Problems & Prospects*, Chapter 25, pp. 203–211. AAA, Sarasota, Florida.

Stanton, W.J. and Buskirk, R.H. (1969). *Management of the Sales Force* Homewood, Illinois.

Starr, M.K. (1971). *Management: A Modern Approach*. Harcourt, Brace, Jovanovich, New York.

Staubus, G.J. (1971). *Activity Costing and Input-Output Accounting*: Irwin, Homewood, Illinois.

Staubus, G.J. (1990). Activity costing: twenty years on. *Management Accounting Research* 1 (4), December, pp. 249-64.

Staw, B.M., and Ross, J. (1987a). Behavior in escalation situations: antecedents, prototypes and solutions. *Research in Organizational Behavior* **9**, pp. 39–78.

Staw, B.M., and Ross, J. (1987b). Knowing when to pull the plug. *Harvard Business Review* **65** (2), March–April, pp. 68–74.

Stedry, A.C. (1960). *Budget Control & Cost Behavior*. Prentice-Hall, Englewood Cliffs, NJ.

Steers, R.M. (1977). *Organisational Effectiveness: A Behavioral View*. Goodyear, Pacific Palisades, California.

Tanzola, F.J. (1975). Performance rating for divisional control. *Financial Executive* **43** (3), March, pp. 20–24.

Terleckyj, N.E. (1970). Measuring progress towards social goals: some possibilities at national & local levels. *Management Science* **16** (12), August, pp. 765–777.

Thomas, M.F. (1989). An application of socio-technical systems analysis to accounting variance control theory. *Journal of Management Accounting Research* **1**, Fall, pp. 149–56.

Tiessen, P. and Waterhouse, J.P. (1983) Towards a descriptive theory of management accounting. *Accounting Organizations and Society*, **8** (2/3), 251–68.

Tinker, A.M. (1975). An accounting organisation for organisational problem solving. Unpublished PhD thesis, University of Manchester.

Tinker, A.M., Merino, B. and Neimark, M. (1982). The normative origins of positive theories: ideology and accounting thought. *Accounting, Organizations and Society* **7** (2), pp. 167–200.

Tocher, K. (1970). Control. *Operational Research Quarterly*, Vol. 21, No. 2, June, pp. 159–180.

Tocher, K. (1976). Notes for discussion on 'Control'. *Operational Research Quarterly* Vol. 27, No. 2, June, pp. 231–239.

Tomkins, C.R. (1973). *Financial Planning in Divisionalised Companies*. Haymarket, London.

Tomkins, C.R. (1975a). Another look at residual income. *Journal of Business Finance & Accounting* **2** (1), pp. 39–53.

Tomkins, C.R. (1975b). Residual income – a rebuttal of Professor Amey's arguments. *Journal of Business Finance & Accounting* **2** (2), pp. 161–168.

Tomkins, C.R. and Groves, R.E.V. (1983). The everyday accountant and researching his reality. *Accounting, Organizations & Society* **8** (4), pp. 361–374.

Trist, E.L. and Bamforth, K.W. (1951). Some social and psychological consequences of the longwall method of coal getting. *Human Relations*, February, pp. 3–38.

Turney, P.B.B. (1991). How activity-based costing helps reduce cost. *Journal of Cost Management for the Manufacturing Industry* **4** (4), Winter, pp. 29–35.

Urban, G.L. and Hauser, J.R. (1980). *Design and Marketing of New Products*. Prentice-Hall, Englewood Cliffs, NJ.

Vancil, R.F. (1979). *Decentralization: Managerial Ambiguity by Design*. FERF, New York.

Van Gigch, J.P. (1978). *Applied General Systems Theory* 2nd edn. Harper & Row, New York.

Vickers, Sir G. (1965). *The Art of Judgement*. Chapman & Hall, London.

Vickers, Sir G. (1968). *Value Systems and Social Process*. Tavistock, London.

Vickers, Sir G. (1972). *Freedom in a Rocking Boat: Changing Values in an Unstable Society*. Penguin, Harmondsworth.

von Bertalanffy, L. (1956). General system theory. *General Systems Yearbook of the Society for the Advancement of General System Theory*, Society for General Systems Research, Louisville, Kentucky. pp. 1–10.

Vroom, V.H. (1960). *Some Personality Determinants of the Effects of Participation*, The Ford Foundation Doctoral Dissertation Series. Prentice-Hall, Englewood Cliffs, NJ.

Vroom, V.H. (1964). *Work and Motivation*. John Wiley & Sons, New York.

Walters, D.W. (1972). Planning the distribution system: an operational approach. *International Journal of Physical Distribution* 3 (2), pp. 109–150.

Ward, T., and Patel, K. (1990). ABC — a framework for improving shareholder value. *Management Accounting* (CIMA) **68** (7), July–August, pp. 34–6.

Watson, D.J.H. (1975). Contingency formulations of organizational structure: implications for managerial accounting. In Livingston, J.L. (ed.) (1975). *Managerial Accounting: The Behavioral Foundations*, Chapter 4, pp. 65–80. Grid, Columbus, Ohio.

Watson, D.J.H. and Baumler, J.V. (1975). Transfer pricing: a behavioral context. *The Accounting Review* **50** (3), July, pp. 466–474.

Weinshall, T.D. (ed.) (1977). *Culture & Management*. Penguin, Harmondsworth.

Welsch, L.A. and Cyert, R.M. (eds) (1971). *Management Decision-Making*. Penguin, Harmondsworth.

Westwick, C.A. (1987). *How to use management ratios*, Gower, Aldershot. 2nd. ed.

Wiener, N. (1948). *Cybernetics*. MIT Press, Cambridge, Mass.

Wildavsky, A. (1968). Budgeting as a political process. In Sills, D.L. (ed.) (1968). *The International Encyclopedia of the Social Sciences*, *2*, pp. 192–199. Crowell, Collier and Macmillan, New York.

Wildavsky, A. (1979). *The Politics of the Budgeting Process* 3rd edn. Little, Brown, Boston.

Williams, K. (1989). CAM-I: on the leading edge. *Management Accounting* (NAA), June, pp. 18–21.

Williamson, O.E. (1964). *The Economics of Discretionary Behavior: Managerial Objectives in a Theory of the Firm*. Prentice-Hall, Englewood Cliffs, NJ.

Wills, G.S.C., Wilson, R.M.S., Manning, N. and Hildebrandt, R. (1972). *Technological Forecasting*. Penguin, Harmondsworth.

Wilson, R.M.S. (1970). Perspectives in accounting for control. *Management Accounting* (ICMA) **48** (8), August, pp. 285–294.

Wilson, R.M.S. (1972). Financial control of physical distribution: some basic considerations. *International Journal of Physical Distribution* **3** (1), pp. 7–20.

Wilson, R.M.S. (1973). *Management Controls in Marketing*. Heinemann, London.

Wilson, R.M.S. (1974). *Financial Control: A Systems Approach*. McGraw-Hill, London.

Wilson, R.M.S. (1978). Management control of non-profit organizations: the problem of specifying outputs. *AUTA Review* **10** (1), pp. 6–21.

Wilson, R.M.S. (1979). *Management Controls and Marketing Planning* (revised edn.). Heinemann, London.

Wilson, R.M.S. (compiler) (1981). *Financial Dimensions of Marketing: A Source Book* (2 volumes). Macmillan, London.

Wilson, R.M.S. (1983). *Cost Control Handbook* 2nd edn. Gower, Aldershot.

Wilson, R.M.S. (1984). Financial control of the marketing function. In Hart, N.A. (ed.) (1984). *The Marketing of Industrial Products* 2nd edn., Chapter 12. McGraw-Hill, London.

Wilson, R.M.S. (1986). Accounting for marketing assets. *European Journal of Marketing* **20** (1), pp. 51–74.

Wilson, R.M.S. (1988). Marketing & the management accountant. In Cowe, R. (ed.) (1988). *Handbook of Management Accounting* 2nd edn. Chapter 13. Gower, Aldershot.

Wilson, R.M.S. (1988). Cost analysis. In Lock, D. (ed.) (1988). *The Gower Handbook of Management* 2nd edn., Chapter 11. Gower, Aldershot.

Wilson, R.M.S. (1990). Strategic cost analysis. *Management Accounting* (CIMA) **68** (9), October, pp. 42–3.

Wilson, R.M.S. (1991a). Strategic management accounting. Chapter 5 (pp. 82–105) in Ashton, D.J., Hopper, T.M. and Scapens, R.W. (eds) *Issues in Management Accounting*. Prentice-Hall, London.

Wilson, R.M.S. (1991b). Corporate strategy and management control. Chapter 4 (pp. 115–65) in Hussey, D.E. (ed.). *International Review of Strategic Management*. John Wiley, Chichester.

Wilson, R.M.S. (1983). *Accounting for Marketing*. Academic Press, London.

Wilson, R.M.S. and Bancroft, A.L. (1983). *The Application of Management Accounting Techniques to the Planning & Control of Marketing Consumer Non-Durables*. ICMA, London.

Wilson, R.M.S. and Gilligan, C.T. with Pearson, D.J. (1992). *Strategic Marketing Management*. Butterworth-Heinemann, Oxford.

Wilson, R.M.S. and McHugh, G.J.P. (1987). *Financial Analysis: A Managerial Introduction*. Cassell, London.

Winer, L. (1966). A profit-orientated decision system. *Journal of Marketing* **30** (2), April, pp. 38–44.

Woodward, J. (1965). *Industrial Organisation: Theory and Practice*. Oxford University Press, London.

Zammuto, R.F. (1982). *Assessing Organizational Effectiveness: Systems Change, Adaption, and Strategy*. State University of New York Press, Albany.

Appendix

Present value of £1 received *n* years hence, at a discount rate of *x*% per year

Years (*n*)	1%	2%	3%	4%	5%	6%	7%	8%	10%	12%	14%	15%	16%	18%	20%	22%	25%	28%	30%	35%	40%	50%
1	0.990	0.980	0.971	0.962	0.952	0.943	0.935	0.926	0.909	0.893	0.877	0.870	0.862	0.847	0.833	0.820	0.800	0.781	0.769	0.741	0.714	0.667
2	0.980	0.961	0.943	0.925	0.907	0.890	0.873	0.857	0.826	0.797	0.769	0.756	0.743	0.718	0.694	0.672	0.640	0.610	0.592	0.549	0.510	0.444
3	0.971	0.942	0.915	0.889	0.864	0.840	0.816	0.794	0.751	0.712	0.675	0.658	0.641	0.609	0.579	0.551	0.512	0.477	0.455	0.406	0.364	0.296
4	0.961	0.924	0.888	0.855	0.823	0.792	0.763	0.735	0.683	0.636	0.592	0.572	0.552	0.516	0.482	0.451	0.410	0.373	0.350	0.301	0.260	0.198
5	0.951	0.906	0.863	0.822	0.784	0.747	0.713	0.681	0.621	0.567	0.519	0.497	0.476	0.437	0.402	0.370	0.328	0.291	0.269	0.223	0.186	0.132
6	0.942	0.888	0.837	0.790	0.746	0.705	0.666	0.630	0.564	0.507	0.456	0.432	0.410	0.370	0.335	0.303	0.262	0.227	0.207	0.165	0.133	0.088
7	0.933	0.871	0.813	0.760	0.711	0.665	0.623	0.583	0.513	0.452	0.400	0.376	0.354	0.314	0.279	0.249	0.210	0.178	0.159	0.122	0.095	0.059
8	0.923	0.853	0.789	0.731	0.677	0.627	0.582	0.540	0.467	0.404	0.351	0.327	0.305	0.266	0.233	0.204	0.168	0.139	0.123	0.091	0.068	0.039
9	0.914	0.837	0.766	0.703	0.645	0.592	0.544	0.500	0.424	0.361	0.308	0.284	0.263	0.225	0.194	0.167	0.134	0.108	0.094	0.067	0.048	0.026
10	0.905	0.820	0.744	0.676	0.614	0.558	0.508	0.463	0.386	0.322	0.270	0.247	0.227	0.191	0.162	0.137	0.107	0.085	0.073	0.050	0.035	0.017
11	0.896	0.804	0.722	0.650	0.585	0.527	0.475	0.429	0.350	0.287	0.237	0.215	0.195	0.162	0.135	0.112	0.086	0.066	0.056	0.037	0.025	0.012
12	0.887	0.788	0.701	0.625	0.577	0.497	0.444	0.397	0.319	0.257	0.208	0.187	0.168	0.137	0.112	0.092	0.069	0.052	0.043	0.027	0.018	0.008
13	0.879	0.773	0.681	0.601	0.530	0.469	0.415	0.368	0.290	0.229	0.182	0.163	0.145	0.116	0.093	0.075	0.055	0.040	0.033	0.020	0.013	0.005
14	0.870	0.758	0.661	0.577	0.505	0.442	0.388	0.340	0.263	0.205	0.160	0.141	0.125	0.099	0.078	0.062	0.044	0.032	0.025	0.015	0.009	0.003
15	0.861	0.743	0.642	0.555	0.481	0.417	0.362	0.315	0.239	0.183	0.140	0.123	0.108	0.084	0.065	0.051	0.035	0.025	0.020	0.011	0.006	0.002
16	0.853	0.728	0.623	0.534	0.458	0.394	0.339	0.292	0.218	0.163	0.123	0.107	0.093	0.071	0.054	0.042	0.028	0.019	0.015	0.008	0.005	0.002
17	0.844	0.714	0.605	0.513	0.436	0.371	0.317	0.270	0.198	0.146	0.108	0.093	0.080	0.060	0.045	0.034	0.023	0.015	0.012	0.006	0.003	0.001
18	0.836	0.700	0.587	0.494	0.416	0.350	0.296	0.250	0.180	0.130	0.095	0.081	0.069	0.051	0.038	0.028	0.018	0.012	0.009	0.005	0.002	0.001
19	0.828	0.686	0.570	0.475	0.396	0.331	0.277	0.232	0.164	0.116	0.083	0.070	0.060	0.043	0.031	0.023	0.014	0.009	0.007	0.003	0.002	
20	0.820	0.673	0.554	0.456	0.377	0.312	0.258	0.215	0.149	0.104	0.073	0.061	0.051	0.037	0.026	0.019	0.012	0.007	0.005	0.002	0.001	
21	0.811	0.660	0.538	0.439	0.359	0.294	0.242	0.199	0.135	0.093	0.064	0.053	0.044	0.031	0.022	0.015	0.009	0.006	0.004	0.002	0.001	
22	0.803	0.647	0.522	0.422	0.342	0.278	0.226	0.184	0.123	0.083	0.056	0.046	0.038	0.026	0.018	0.013	0.007	0.004	0.003	0.001	0.001	
23	0.795	0.634	0.507	0.406	0.326	0.262	0.211	0.170	0.112	0.074	0.049	0.040	0.033	0.022	0.015	0.010	0.006	0.003	0.002	0.001		
24	0.788	0.622	0.492	0.390	0.310	0.247	0.197	0.158	0.102	0.066	0.043	0.035	0.028	0.019	0.013	0.008	0.005	0.003	0.002	0.001		
25	0.780	0.610	0.478	0.375	0.295	0.233	0.184	0.146	0.092	0.059	0.038	0.030	0.024	0.016	0.010	0.007	0.004	0.002	0.001	0.001		
26	0.772	0.598	0.464	0.361	0.281	0.220	0.172	0.135	0.084	0.053	0.033	0.026	0.021	0.014	0.009	0.006	0.003	0.002	0.001			
27	0.764	0.586	0.450	0.347	0.268	0.207	0.161	0.125	0.076	0.047	0.029	0.023	0.018	0.011	0.007	0.005	0.002	0.001	0.001			
28	0.757	0.574	0.437	0.333	0.255	0.196	0.150	0.116	0.069	0.042	0.026	0.020	0.016	0.010	0.006	0.004	0.002	0.001	0.001			
29	0.749	0.563	0.424	0.321	0.243	0.185	0.141	0.107	0.063	0.037	0.022	0.017	0.014	0.008	0.005	0.003	0.002	0.001	0.001			
30	0.742	0.552	0.412	0.308	0.231	0.174	0.131	0.099	0.057	0.033	0.020	0.015	0.012	0.007	0.004	0.003	0.001	0.001				
40	0.672	0.453	0.307	0.208	0.142	0.097	0.067	0.046	0.022	0.011	0.005	0.004	0.003	0.001	0.001							
50	0.608	0.372	0.228	0.141	0.087	0.054	0.034	0.021	0.009	0.003	0.001	0.001	0.001									

Present value of £1 received each year for *n* years

Years (n)	*1%*	*2%*	*3%*	*4%*	*5%*	*6%*	*7%*	*8%*	*10%*	*12%*	*14%*	*15%*	*16%*	*18%*	*20%*	*22%*	*25%*	*28%*	*30%*	*35%*	*40%*	*50%*
1	0.990	0.980	0.971	0.962	0.952	0.943	0.935	0.926	0.909	0.893	0.877	0.870	0.862	0.847	0.833	0.820	0.800	0.781	0.769	0.741	0.714	0.667
2	1.970	1.942	1.914	1.886	1.859	1.833	1.808	1.783	1.736	1.690	1.647	1.626	1.605	1.566	1.528	1.492	1.440	1.392	1.361	1.289	1.224	1.111
3	2.941	2.884	2.829	2.775	2.723	2.673	2.624	2.577	2.487	2.402	2.322	2.283	2.246	2.174	2.106	2.043	1.952	1.868	1.816	1.696	1.589	1.407
4	3.902	3.808	3.717	3.630	3.546	3.465	3.387	3.312	3.170	3.037	2.914	2.855	2.798	2.690	2.589	2.494	2.362	2.241	2.166	1.997	1.849	1.605
5	4.853	4.713	4.580	4.452	4.329	4.212	4.100	3.993	3.791	3.605	3.433	3.352	3.274	3.127	2.991	2.864	2.689	2.532	2.436	2.220	2.035	1.737
6	5.795	5.601	5.417	5.242	5.076	4.917	4.767	4.623	4.355	4.111	3.889	3.784	3.685	3.498	3.326	3.167	2.951	2.759	2.643	2.385	2.168	1.824
7	6.728	6.472	6.230	6.002	5.786	5.582	5.389	5.206	4.868	4.564	4.288	4.160	4.039	3.812	3.605	3.416	3.161	2.937	2.802	2.508	2.263	1.883
8	7.652	7.325	7.020	6.733	6.463	6.210	5.971	5.747	5.335	4.968	4.639	4.487	4.344	4.078	3.837	3.619	3.329	3.076	2.925	2.598	2.331	1.922
9	8.566	8.162	7.786	7.435	7.108	6.802	6.515	6.247	5.759	5.328	4.946	4.772	4.607	4.303	4.031	3.786	3.463	3.184	3.019	2.665	2.379	1.948
10	9.471	8.983	8.530	8.111	7.722	7.360	7.023	6.710	6.145	5.650	5.216	5.019	4.833	4.494	4.192	3.923	3.571	3.269	3.092	2.715	2.414	1.965
11	10.368	9.787	9.253	8.760	8.306	7.887	7.499	7.139	6.495	5.938	5.453	5.234	5.029	4.656	4.327	4.035	3.656	3.335	3.147	2.757	2.438	1.977
12	11.255	10.575	9.954	9.385	8.863	8.384	7.943	7.536	6.814	6.194	5.660	5.421	5.197	4.793	4.439	4.127	3.725	3.387	3.190	2.779	2.456	1.985
13	12.134	11.348	10.635	9.986	9.393	8.853	8.358	7.904	7.103	6.424	5.842	5.583	5.342	4.910	4.533	4.203	3.780	3.427	3.223	2.799	2.469	1.990
14	13.004	12.106	11.296	10.563	9.899	9.295	8.745	8.244	7.367	6.628	6.002	5.724	5.468	5.008	4.611	4.265	3.824	3.459	3.249	2.814	2.478	1.993
15	13.865	12.849	11.938	11.118	10.380	9.712	9.108	8.559	7.606	6.811	6.142	5.847	5.575	5.092	4.675	4.315	3.859	3.483	3.268	2.825	2.484	1.995
16	14.718	13.578	12.561	11.652	10.838	10.106	9.446	8.851	7.824	6.974	6.265	5.954	5.669	5.162	4.730	4.357	3.887	3.503	3.283	2.834	2.489	1.997
17	15.562	14.292	13.166	12.166	11.274	10.477	9.763	9.122	8.022	7.120	6.373	6.047	5.749	5.222	4.775	4.391	3.910	3.518	3.295	2.840	2.492	1.998
18	16.398	14.992	13.754	12.659	11.689	10.828	10.059	9.372	8.201	7.250	6.467	6.128	5.818	5.273	4.812	4.419	3.928	3.529	3.304	2.844	2.494	1.999
19	17.226	15.678	14.324	13.134	12.085	11.158	10.335	9.604	8.365	7.366	6.550	6.198	5.877	5.316	4.843	4.442	3.942	3.539	3.311	2.848	2.496	1.999
20	18.046	16.351	14.878	13.590	12.462	11.470	10.594	9.818	8.514	7.469	6.623	6.259	5.929	5.353	4.870	4.460	3.954	3.546	3.316	2.850	2.497	1.999
21	18.857	17.011	15.415	14.029	12.821	11.764	10.835	10.017	8.649	7.562	6.687	6.312	5.973	5.384	4.891	4.476	3.963	3.551	3.320	2.852	2.498	2.000
22	19.660	17.658	15.937	14.451	13.163	12.042	11.061	10.201	8.772	7.645	6.743	6.359	6.011	5.410	4.909	4.488	3.970	3.556	3.323	2.853	2.498	2.000
23	20.456	18.292	16.444	14.857	13.488	12.303	11.272	10.371	8.883	7.718	6.792	6.399	6.044	5.432	4.925	4.499	3.976	3.559	3.325	2.854	2.499	2.000
24	21.243	18.914	16.936	15.247	13.798	12.550	11.469	10.529	8.985	7.784	6.835	6.434	6.073	5.451	4.937	4.507	3.981	3.562	3.327	2.855	2.499	2.000
25	22.023	19.523	17.413	15.622	14.094	12.783	11.653	10.675	9.077	7.843	6.873	6.464	6.097	5.467	4.948	4.514	3.985	3.564	3.329	2.856	2.499	2.000
26	22.795	20.121	17.877	15.983	14.375	13.003	11.825	10.810	9.161	7.896	6.906	6.491	6.118	5.480	4.956	4.520	3.988	3.566	3.330	2.856	2.500	2.000
27	23.560	20.707	18.327	16.330	14.643	13.211	11.986	10.935	9.237	7.943	6.935	6.514	6.136	5.492	4.964	4.524	3.990	3.567	3.331	2.856	2.500	2.000
28	24.316	21.281	18.764	16.663	14.898	13.406	12.137	11.051	9.307	7.984	6.961	6.534	6.152	5.502	4.970	4.528	3.992	3.568	3.331	2.857	2.500	2.000
29	25.066	21.844	19.188	16.984	15.141	13.591	12.277	11.158	9.370	8.022	6.983	6.551	6.166	5.510	4.975	4.531	3.994	3.569	3.332	2.857	2.500	2.000
30	25.808	22.396	19.600	17.292	15.372	13.765	12.409	11.258	9.427	8.055	7.003	6.566	6.177	5.517	4.979	4.534	3.995	3.569	3.332	2.857	2.500	2.000
40	32.835	27.355	23.115	19.793	17.159	15.046	13.331	11.925	9.779	8.244	7.105	6.642	6.233	5.548	4.997	4.544	3.999	3.571	3.333	2.857	2.500	2.000
50	39.196	31.424	25.730	21.482	18.256	15.762	13.800	12.233	9.915	8.304	7.133	6.661	6.246	5.554	4.999	4.545	4.000	3.571	3.333	2.857	2.500	2.000

Author index

Subject index

Entries in **bold** refer to definitions.